D0583924

Weimar Thought

Weimar Thought

A Contested Legacy

Edited by **Peter E. Gordon and John P. McCormick**

PRINCETON UNIVERSITY PRESS

Princeton and Oxford

Copyright © 2013 by Princeton University Press
Published by Princeton University Press, 41 William Street,
Princeton, New Jersey 08540
In the United Kingdom: Princeton University Press, 6 Oxford Street,
Woodstock, Oxfordshire OX20 1TW

press.princeton.edu

Jacket art: Raoul Hausmann (1886–1971), *The Spirit of Our Age (Mechanical Head)*, 1919.
Wooden head with various objects attached to it. 32.5 x 21 x 20 cm. AM 1974-6.
Photo Credit: CNAC/MNAM/Dist. RMN-Grand Palais / Art Resource, NY.
© 2013 Artists Rights Society (ARS), New York / ADAGP, Paris

All Rights Reserved

Library of Congress Cataloging-in-Publication Data

Weimar thought : a contested legacy / Edited by Peter E. Gordon and John P. McCormick.
     pages   cm
  Includes bibliographical references and index.
   ISBN 978-0-691-13510-6 (alk. paper)   1. Germany—Intellectual life—20th century.
2. Germany—History—1918–1933.   3. Social sciences—Germany—History—20th century.
4. Humanities—Germany—History—20th century.   5. Political culture—Germany—History—
20th century.   I. Gordon, Peter Eli, editor of compilation   II. McCormick, John P., 1966–
editor of compilation
DD239.W365 2013
943.085–dc23   2012038154

British Library Cataloging-in-Publication Data is available

This book has been composed in Minion Pro and Ideal Sans

Printed on acid-free paper. ∞

Printed in the United States of America

10 9 8 7 6 5 4 3 2 1

Contents

Part IV: Themes of an Epoch

Weimar Thought

Introduction

Weimar Thought: Continuities and Crisis

Peter E. Gordon and John P. McCormick

This volume brings together a broad range of papers on diverse themes pertaining to the intellectual and cultural history of the Weimar Republic. It includes a great variety of contributions by scholars affiliated with manifold disciplines, including, but not limited to, history, political theory, philosophy, sociology, the history of science, film theory, art history, and literary criticism. Our aim has been to provide a critical companion for specialized research that, while adding to current scholarship, would nonetheless remain accessible to the more general reader. Few if any single-volume works have succeeded at offering a unified portrait of the rich developments of Weimar thought, and we believe the time is right to offer a guidebook to the German interwar era, a compendium focused primarily on the major intellectual trends of the time.

What was "Weimar thought"? To a remarkable degree, much of the literature we now regard as foundational for modern thought derives from a single historical moment: the astonishing cultural and intellectual ferment of interwar Germany circa 1919–33. The era of the Weimar Republic was arguably the foremost crucible of intellectual innovation in political theory and sociology, cultural criticism and film theory, psychology and legal theory, physics and biology, and modernism in all of its diverse forms. Its brief lifespan saw the emergence of intellectuals, scholars, and critics who rank amongst the foremost thinkers of the twentieth century. A representative list would no doubt include philosophical radicals such as Walter Benjamin, Martin Heidegger, and Max Scheler; theorists of political crisis such as Carl Schmitt, Ernst Jünger, Hannah Arendt, Hans Kelsen, and Oswald Spengler; innovators in theology such as Karl Barth, Franz Rosenzweig, Gershom Scholem, and Ernst Bloch; and exponents of aesthetic rebellion in literature, film, drama, music, and the fine arts, including Alfred Döblin and Siegfried Kracauer, Bertolt Brecht and Ernst Krenek, Hannah Höch and Kurt Schwitters. No doubt the list could well be expanded to far greater length.

Intellectual labors of the era were noteworthy, too, for the way in which they exemplifed a boldness of inquiry that would, in current jargon, be characterized as "interdisciplinary." Scholars, critics, and artists frequently cut across the customary boundaries separating philosophy, history, and artistic criticism, political theory and theology, not to mention science and metaphysics. In this respect it might be argued that the leading figures in Weimar thought not only anticipated, but actually helped to found and inspire the ongoing interdisciplinarity of our own day. This is especially obvious when one considers the contemporary actuality of these theorists, whose ideas, even today, continue to enrich academic and cultural discourse within and beyond the university. An intellectual-historical survey of Weimar thought in all its many facets is thus in no small measure a pre-history of our own intellectual present.

On some of these topics much has been written already. Yet the increased specialization of research has all-too-frequently been achieved at the expense of contextual and historical understanding. Scholars have often failed to recognize just how much the leading intellectuals of that time worked within a shared intellectual horizon. Especially in the past twenty years, we have witnessed a terrific burst of dehistoricized "theory," a mode of inquiry that plundered the past for its insights but often neglected its historical character and effaced the salient (though by no means insurmountable) differences between past and present.

But the largely ahistorical character of modern theory is now fading, thanks in part to recent innovations in historical and philosophical method, and, perhaps most especially, to the renaissance of intellectual history, a discipline which only twenty years ago seemed in decline. The great efflorescence of intellectual history in the last two decades has helped to break down many of the previously-enforced boundary lines between the humanities and the social sciences. Under the auspices of a new generation of philosophers, political theorists, historians, and literary-cultural critics, scholars have begun to appreciate the fruitful tension between hermeneutic contextualism and transcendental claims to truth. The time is therefore ripe to bring these insights to bear on the theoretical heritage of the Weimar era. A major advantage of this interdisciplinary volume of essays is that it demonstrates both the unity and diversity of this inheritance, and it identifies anew those characteristics that helped to make Weimar a veritable birthplace of European intellectual modernity.

The Unity and Diversity of Weimar Thought

In his synthetic history of the Weimar Republic published over twenty years ago, the German historian Detlev Peukert observed that our present image of Weimar is marked by an irresolvable paradox: it combines "the hopeful picture of avant-garde cultural achievement" with "the bleak picture of political breakdown and social misery."[1] For Peukert this paradox was not only resistant to resolution, it was in point of fact emblematic of "classical modernity" as such: The tensions of the age were taken to represent the conflicts and crises of the modern era itself. But the governing theme of a "classical" phase in modern history merely names without wholly explaining the paradox Peukert sought to diagnose. The historian's impulse to unify divergent features of a political-cultural epoch is unlikely to prove genuinely satisfying since it derives from the naïve and ultimately *un*historical expectation that every age must somehow subscribe to a common theme. The paradoxical character of the Weimar Republic no longer strikes us as paradoxical once we abandon the retroactive search for a governing logic and open ourselves to the diversity and disunity of narratives within any given historical epoch.

Even the idea of a unique chronology can mislead. In political terms the definitive events that mark Weimar's beginning and end will remain open to debate: Did it begin with the sailors' mutiny at Kiel in October 1918, with the signing of the Versailles Treaty in June 1919, with the signing of the Weimar Constitution in August 1919, or perhaps only with the final stabilization of currency in 1924? In cultural and intellectual terms, the definitive events are even less certain. Many of the cultural movements associated with Weimar began well before the outbreak of the Great War: German Expressionism was born with the Dresden artistic circle of *die Brücke* in 1905; the literary careers of the Mann brothers, Thomas and Heinrich, antedate the Weimar Republic by many years and continued well after its collapse. The great founder of German sociology, Max Weber, died in June 1920, although his memory exerted a singular influence over the intellectual history of the twenties. Georg Simmel, that other and inimitable theorist of modernity, died in September 1918, several months before the official founding of the Republic. Both the political-legal theory developed by Carl Schmitt and the social philosophy associated with the leading thinkers of the Institute for Social Research (the so-called "Frankfurt School") continued to develop and transform well into the later 1930s, after the Republic had collapsed and even after the Second World War. Persistent interest in both theoretical traditions over the past half century is an encouraging sign that "Weimar thought" has not yet come to an end. But thinking always exceeds its moment of origin. Indeed, possibilities of continued inspiration and reappropriation may serve to remind us that the most consequential forces of cultural and intellectual history are not easily confined within given boundaries of chronological time.

One of the persistent difficulties that has confronted the intellectual history of the Weimar years is that of a political meta-narrative: It is all too easy to assume that culture must somehow track, reflect, or otherwise serve as an allegory for politics. This premise was arguably at work even in Peter Gay's masterpiece of cultural history, *Weimar Culture* (originally published in 1968): An exceptionally powerful work of interpretative synthesis, Gay's book sought to embrace the major cultural and intellectual movements of the time within what we might call a "psychoanalytic frame." The story of Weimar culture ultimately gained its intelligibility and unity only insofar as it could be narrated according to the larger psycho-political drama of the Republic itself: the failure of the one implied the failure of the other. Just as the birth of functional democracy in Germany was concomitant with cultural and political emancipation from the forces of paternal authority, so too the tragedy of Weimar culture was ascribed to a youth rebellion that, ironically, confirmed rather than undermined paternal authority: the rightward turn of the sons thus served the "revenge of the fathers." Weimar culture was in this sense essentially a tragedy of perverted Oedipal rebellion. Even today (more than forty years since its original publication) the tremendous appeal of Gay's narrative remains undiminished. But its dramatic unity is also its chief liability: By projecting the psychodrama of Oedipal development upon an entire epoch, a narrative that was chiefly concerned with intellectual and cultural events risked obscuring the diversity of culture, its conflictual tempo, and the contested meanings that resist containment within a single politico-psychoanalytic frame.

But a certain awareness of the political narrative cannot be avoided. It would be naïve to believe that one could write the intellectual and cultural history of the Weimar Republic without taking cognizance of the tragedy that followed its collapse. The continuities between culture and politics are too thick to permit such compartmentalization, and one can hardly deny the patterns of thought and cultural sensibility, long incubating during the 1920s, that prepared the way for, or otherwise nourished the ideological tendencies commonly associated with the Third Reich. All the same, even if most scholars have long ago abandoned the crude logic of linear causation that conflates continuity with teleology, it is worth repeating the methodological desideratum that preparation is not determination: Although National Socialism is surely traceable to patterns of intellectual and cultural history that long antedated the Nazi seizure of power in 1933, intellectual and cultural historians of the Weimar years have not always resisted the impulse to narrate the events of the 1920s with a single-minded anticipation of the Republic's political denouement. The political and social historian Hans Mommsen made this point quite well: "Just as it would be misleading to imagine National Socialism was a unique phenomenon that destroyed the foundations of the Weimar Republic from the outside, so it would be a mistake to interpret Weimar's external and internal development as a mere prelude to the history of the Third Reich."[2] Continuity is a permissible instrument of historical understanding; teleology is not.

The very diversity of disciplines and themes that characterized the Weimar years may also counsel against any imposition of strong narratives organized around the primacy of political experience. Once we recognize that politics cannot determine the tempo for all divergent modes of inquiry, we may better appreciate the way that each domain of intellectual and cultural life—in the arts, literature, poetry, and architecture, in natural sciences and religion, in philosophy and law as well as sociology—tends to follow principles that are properly its own. The historicist dogma of a unified time or *Zeitgeist* suits Weimar thought no better than it suits the spirit of any other age. In our current day, facile talk of interdisciplinarity may strike more cautious scholars as an invitation to mere eclecticism. But we should not lose sight of the multidisciplinary character of intellectual labor, especially in a milieu that exemplified its many strengths. It is more helpful to sustain even within the confines of a single volume a strong appreciation for the diversity and multiple temporalities of Weimar thought, and we should resist the thought that painting and literature, legal theory and sociology, architecture and cultural criticism all subscribe to or instantiate a singular rule: the very notion of "Weimar thought" or "Weimar culture" in this respect may invite skepticism. Yet even while we want to insist in a nominalist spirit that the intellectual history of the 1920s cannot be subsumed under a single narrative, it is nevertheless striking how various thinkers in different domains identified their age as one of dissension and disorientation. Indeed, if there is one theme that seems to appear across the entire range of Weimar intellectual history it is the very awareness of anxiety signified by the prevalence of the term *crisis*.

Crisis was and can be defined in many ways. The term derives from the Greek word for separation—and in the 1920s and early '30s German intellectuals were seized by the question of historical discontinuity. Crisis should not be construed as indicating a fully-achieved separation from the past. Notwithstanding its much deserved reputation for novelty and innovation, Weimar thought was in some ways still quite traditional. Patterns of ideology and ideas inherited from the *Kaiserreich* would persist well after the Wilhelmine Empire's demise, but individuals and movements engaged in rapid and radical experimentation within traditional university or disciplinary forms. Crisis may serve as a unifying theme in most intellectual engagements with the Weimar Republic. But we should nonetheless keep in mind that "crisis" is only intelligible given the strength of preceding and persisting tradition.

Among political historians it is often claimed that excessive continuity with the *Kaiserreich* was a major weakness of the Weimar Republic. Theorists of a German *Sonderweg* once argued that Germany tracked a peculiar path to modernity and that the absence of a strong bourgeois revolution in the nineteenth century permitted traces of an unbourgeois socio-political past to survive well into the twentieth century: The presence of a national civil and military bureaucracy, trained and acculturated in the authoritarian atmosphere of the Wilhelmine *Reich*, exercised a tremendous counterforce against Germany's post-war experiment with democracy, and ultimately undermined the Weimar Republic from within. But the *Sonderweg* theory assumes without sufficient documentation that the professionals who came of age in the Reich were fundamentally disloyal to the Republic; on the contrary, prominent members of the bureaucracy and military openly expressed disillusionment with liberal democracy only rather late in the republic's history, when, arguably, successive crises had shaken the commitments to the status quo of many other social actors. Even the holdover conservative judges who comprised a majority of the Weimar judiciary consistently upheld the Republic's laws throughout the twenties and early thirties. More accurately, one might say that the legal-administrative bureaucracy reliably implemented the Republic's principles and policies and that the military rank and file (who, after all, had initiated the overthrow of the monarchy) were at best fully loyal to, or at worst merely wary supporters of the Republic for as long as the latter seemed a viable socio-political form.

Other lines of continuity between pre– and post–Great War Germany served not to impede but actually to advance patterns of democracy within the Republic. The statute positivism developed by public lawyers under the Wilhelmine regime thrived within the republic. Once the Kaiser was removed as the ultimate authority above the statutory system of legal norms and the German citizenry was established as the unassailable legitimating foundation below it, Weimar's social forces began to experiment with the idea of popular sovereignty through law, facilitating unprecedented and ingenious efforts at democratic self-rule. Moreover, the radical innovations in art and literature associated with Weimar culture had deep roots within the *Kaiserreich*. Expressionism, Cubism, and abstractionism were already well-established movements before the war and laid the groundwork for extension and revision by both Dadaism and *Neue Sachlichkeit* in the twenties and early thirties.[3]

The German universities themselves exhibited both continuity and innovation. On the one hand the universities sustained throughout the Weimar years many of the forms and rituals that belonged to the nineteenth-century legacy. The high status of a full professorship (*Ordinarius*) still conferred upon its bearer the social prestige of inclusion in a quasi-archaic caste. To gain this membership was and remained the animating goal of most scholars. The low status and uncertain remuneration of the mere *Dozent* typically had to be endured for many years, and one's livelihood depended upon fees paid by the students who attended one's lectures. As Max Weber observed in his lecture, "Science as a Vocation," the typical *Dozent* in the German system taught and therefore earned much less than he wished. But the structure of the university remained plutocratic: to survive in this condition without external support (typically from one's family) was quite rare and the assistant's position was "often as precarious as . . . that of any quasi-proletarian existence." The process of professional advancement in the university remained vulnerable to prejudice and corruption. "I know of hardly any other career on earth," Weber observed, "where chance plays such a role."[4] To fail or to find one's path obstructed because of inadequacies either real or perceived condemned the young scholar to an uncertain life at the margins of society. Many relished this marginal status: Walter Benjamin's "flâneur" and Karl Mannheim's "free-floating intelligentsia" were terms that captured the mobility and modernity of a new type of critic who wrote for newspapers and journals and did not feel the inhibitions of academic custom.

There were clear signs of innovation. With the founding of the Republic new institutions were born where those who had previously suffered delay and discrimination found new opportunities for professional recognition. The University of Hamburg, for example, was founded only in 1919 and served as a major site for new developments in the philosophy of culture spearheaded by Ernst Cassirer. Even more striking was the development in the 1920s of para-academic institutions, often privately funded, where talented outsiders and intellectual mavericks could gain a foothold. The Institute for Social Research (*Die Gesellschaft für Sozialforschung*) originated in Frankfurt in 1923 and grew into the creative center of Western Marxism. The Warburg Library (*Kulturwissenschaftliche Bibliothek Warburg*) was founded in 1921 by Aby Warburg with funds inherited from his father, the banker Moritz Warburg, and in the 1920s became a flourishing center for art history and comparative ethnography. But this was also the age of esoteric societies, amongst which the most celebrated was the George-Kreis, founded well before the war (in 1892 in association with the journal *Blätter für die Kunst*) by the charismatic poet Stefan George and later frequented by notables such as Friedrich Gundolf and Ludwig Klages. The constrained forms and mores of university life were further broadened and enriched by intellectual discussion groups, for example, the famous "Sunday society" that convened at the Heidelberg home of Marianne and Max Weber.

It is therefore important that we discern in the history of Weimar thought a balance between innovation and tradition, between continuity and crisis. Although we recognize the substantial continuities between pre-war and Weimar culture, the enduring hegemony of Wilhelmine cultural and intellectual patterns within the Republic should not be exaggerated. For even while much of Weimar intellectual life remained indebted to the past it is nonetheless striking to note how intellectuals both progressive and conservative conceived of tradition itself in new ways. As Eric Weitz has observed, none of the great contributors to Weimar thought and culture advocated a facile retreat into the styles of the pre-1914 world. They were united by "the restless questioning of what it means to live in modern times, the search for new forms of expression suitable to the cacophony of modern life, and the belief in the possibilities of the future."[5]

It may be helpful to recall that the diverse forms of intellectual and cultural crisis in the 1920s took shape in an era of unprecedented political unrest. The crises that erupted intermittently throughout Europe and North America throughout the interwar period were experienced more profoundly in Germany than in any contemporary industrial society. Abject material deprivation during the era of hyper-inflation, occupation by foreign forces, and psychological burdens associated with war guilt, all conspired to intensify the perception of a broad-scale crisis of culture and civilization. However, it would be incorrect to attribute the intensity of these crises more to indigenous rather than to extraneous factors. The strength of the Republic's political right, for instance, was arguably fostered and certainly sustained by the war guilt and penalties imposed on Germany; and the depth of Germany's economic crisis is largely traceable to the fact that the Republic was more financially dependent on the U.S. economy than was any other industrialized nation of the era. When the American stock market crashed in 1929, virtually all of Germany's socio-economic institutions followed suit, something that was not true elsewhere in Europe.

But dramatic crises may also have afforded Germany's political leaders a unique set of opportunities for improvisation and innovation. In the realm of international affairs, an astute statesman like Gustav Stresemann could pursue a new course for Germany. Had events not intervened so adversely, Stresemann's strategy of rapprochement with France, increased economic and political ties with England and America, and unilateral conciliation with the Soviet Union contained the potential of strengthening Germany's geo-political situation, placing the Republic in a more favorable position internationally than the Reich enjoyed before the war.

Moreover, the adverse circumstances that brought together disparate parties like the SPD, the Center, the DVP, and the DDP, into the Grand Coalition portended a chance for the social integration of constituencies like workers, Catholics, and progressive business groups into a long-term and workable political coalition. The success of the coalition structure during the Weimar Republic represents a successful model that was arguably more progressive than that found in any other capitalist democracy before the onset of the Second World War. Indeed, it is a model that remains more appealing than a great many of those that survived into or emerged from the post-war world.

Even the use of emergency powers afforded the *Reichspräsident* by Article 48, commonly assumed to be the fatal flaw of the Weimar constitution—and directly associated with the demise of Weimar liberal democracy and the rise of authoritarian dictatorship—was first used in the Republic by Friedrich Ebert, with widespread popular support, to suppress far-left and far-right enemies of constitutionalism. The Weimar constitutions could have specified greater oversight by the Reichstag over the president's emergency powers, or encouraged greater cooperation between those two institutions during crises. But political history suggests that "crisis" did not always undermine the Republic but, in important moments and circumstances, may have actually helped to strengthen it.

Nevertheless it would be inappropriate to paint too rosy a picture of Weimar's socio-political predicament. As Heinrich August Winkler observed in his monumental history of the Weimar Republic, the collapse of Germany's first experiment with democracy is also the first chapter in the catastrophe of world history; no treatment of the period 1918–33 can entirely ignore our knowledge of its aftermath. Although the Weimar era should not be seen as a mere antechamber to the violent age that followed, the historical study of the Weimar era is itself, inevitably "a work of mourning."[6] We have tried in this book to recognize this tragic dimension even while we also want to resist the teleological impulse that would emphasize only those aspects of Weimar thought that seem to forecast the rise of National Socialism.

The essays included in this volume are presented in four parts.

The essays comprising Part I focus on law, politics, and society in the Weimar Republic, or, more specifically, on intellectual engagements with these topics during the interwar era. David Kettler and Colin Loader examine the status of the fledgling but burgeoning field of sociology from the waning days of the *Kaiserreich* through the last moments of the Republic. Two intellectual giants who did not live very long into the Republic's founding, Max Weber and Georg Simmel, set the agenda for the study of society in Weimar. Indeed, as Kettler and Loader suggest, it was the early demise of Weber and Simmel that permitted their heirs, most prominently Karl Mannheim, to render their writings canonical and to pursue the questions of modernity, rationalization, capitalism and the relationship of ideas and ideology to those phenomena with something like a common language—if not a language that facilitated intellectual consensus on any of these themes. Mitchell Ash describes the indeterminate place of professional psychology between the natural sciences and the humanities in the epoch, and the manner in which members of the discipline, especially the *Gestalt* theorists of the "Berlin School," revealed a preoccupation with "holism" and the "immediately given" characteristic of other fields of thought in the contemporary moment of crisis.

The fraught but not necessarily hopeless relationship of law and the *Sozial-staat* is the focus of John P. McCormick's piece on Weimar jurisprudence. Mc-Cormick traces the way in which liberal and social democratic lawyers like Richard Thoma and Hermann Heller attempted to constitutionally legitimize novel efforts at political regulation, economic redistribution and social integra-tion while avoiding the intellectual either/or's insisted upon by the dominant legal theorists of the epoch, Hans Kelsen and Carl Schmitt. Confronting still too frequently leveled charges of intellectual and even political excess directed at the later writings of Max Weber, Dana R. Villa dissociates Weber's thought not only from a radical "student" of Weber's like Schmitt, who would eventually embrace Hitler, but also from his much more intimate protégé, Georg Lukács, who would become almost equally notorious for endorsing Stalin. Because the contribu-tions to Part I deal with intellectual giants such as Simmel, Weber, Mannheim, Kelsen, and Schmitt, each of whom cast such a disproportionately enormous shadow over the intellectual life of the Republic, other important figures in so-ciology (such as Ferdinand Tönnies and his followers, Werner Sombart, Hans Freyer, et al.) and law (most notably Gustav Radbruch), unfortunately receive little mention, and less notable figures who are discussed within the essays (e.g., Heller and Thoma) are given less emphasis.

Part II addresses developments in philosophy, theology, and science. John Michael Krois offers an excursus on the philosophy of culture, a discipline pio-neered by the sociologist Georg Simmel and perfected by the philosopher Ernst Cassirer especially in his monumental, three-volume masterpiece, *The Philoso-phy of Symbolic Forms*. Frederick Beiser offers a provocative challenge to the prevailing image of neo-Kantianism: in a polemically revisionist account of this major intellectual movement, he casts neo-Kantians as somewhat less than benevolent purveyors of pacifism and cosmopolitanism, explaining how long-simmering cultural and philosophical traditions of pessimism and nihilism ul-timately displaced the authoritative role of genuinely Kantian themes in their writings. Peter E. Gordon provides a critical survey of general patterns and de-bates in Weimar theology from liberal Protestants (Adolf von Harnack) to crisis-theologians (Karl Barth, Emil Brunner, Friedrich Gogarten) alongside Jewish philosophers (Cohen, Rosenzweig, Buber) and partisans of political theology on both the right and the left (Schmitt, Benjamin, Bloch). Charles Bambach ad-dresses the philosophy of history and the so-called crisis of historicism as un-derstood by a diverse array of scholars such as Oswald Spengler, Ernst Troeltsch, Heinrich Rickert, and Martin Heidegger. Cathryn Carson offers a powerful and accessible survey of developments across the wide terrain of the natural sciences, from physics (Planck, Einstein, Bohr, Heisenberg, Schrödinger) to biology (Plessner, Driesch, von Uexküll) to the philosophy of mathematics and scientific method (Reichenbach, Cassirer, Carnap).

Part III is devoted to themes in aesthetics, literature, and film. Michael Jen-nings offers a careful exposition of themes and debates in Weimar *Kulturkritik*, or cultural criticism, focusing on its two greatest exemplars, Walter Benjamin and Siegfried Kracauer. Karin Gunnemann provides a literary and historical glimpse into the political fortunes of the great writers and novelists of the Weimar era, focusing on Kurt Tucholsky, Alfred Döblin, and the brothers Thomas and Heinrich Mann. Martin Ruehl takes us on a historical journey into the *George-Kreis*, the mysterious circle that surrounded the poet and political visionary Stefan George, whose many acolytes included Karl Wolfskehl, Ernst Bertram, and the historian Ernst Kantorowicz. In her essay, Sabine Hake provides a careful reconstruction of major themes and points of critical tension amongst Béla Balázs, Siegfried Kracauer, and Rudolf Arnheim, the three greatest theorists of film during the Weimar period. John V. Maciuika contributes a wide-ranging survey of the politics and aesthetics of developments in interwar German architecture, with special attention to the key institution of Weimar architectural modernism, the Bauhaus. Last but not least, Michael Steinberg draws our attention to the anthropological imagination of Aby Warburg, the great student of world culture and comparative mythology whose "Warburg Library," founded in Hamburg, served as the meeting place for Weimar philosophers, historians, and cultural critics.

General cultural, social and political themes running through the entire interwar period occupy the contributors to Part IV of the volume. Susanne Marchand examines Weimar-era fascination with "the East" typified by Hermann Graf Keyserling's *Schule der Weisheit*. Despite exhibiting the expected primitivizing, essentializing, and romanticizing characteristic of any form of "orientalism" this movement nevertheless opened German religious, historical, literary, and philosophical circles to a greater appreciation for Chinese, Indian, Egyptian, and Islamic traditions, among others. Tracie Matysik weighs the gains and losses experienced by the economically mobilized and politically enfranchised women of the Great War and Weimar eras. Women within Wilhelmine intellectual circles had already explored at length and with great sophistication the aspirations for social advancement held by moral subjects who understood themselves to be fundamentally different from their male counterparts. Matysik demonstrates the reaction of a representative group of such women (Helene Stöcker, Marianne Weber, and Lou Andreas-Salomé) to, firstly, the mass mobilization of women in the war effort, and then formal enfranchisement within the Republic, both of which represented forms of "participation" that were thrust upon German womanhood without its consultation and that closed off the realization of many of its pre-war aspirations for an alternative form of citizenship. Martin Jay challenges long-perpetuated and exaggerated narratives concerning the mistakes and missed opportunities of the German Left during the Republic: neither the brutal repression of radical socialists at the Republic's birth nor recurrent fissures between the Social Democrats and Communists throughout its history guaranteed either the collapse of the Republic or a diminishing influence of the SPD within it. Ultimately, however uninevitable were the disastrous outcomes that befell the Republic and especially members of the Left. Jay insists that a fresh engagement with Weimar political history might serve as lessons for future socialist movements within liberal and social democracies.

While much of the volume has focused on continuities between the *Kaisser-reich* and the Republic, Anson Rabinbach's piece concludes the book with some chilling reflections that highlight certain continuities between the Republic and the Third Reich. We, the editors, earlier in this introduction pledged ourselves to avoid any repetition of the tiresome teleology of earlier works on Weimar that conveyed a sense of inevitable tragedy. But we also wish to register the Republic's Nazi future in a way that will not leave the reader with an illusory image of Weimar as an island in time. In this spirit, Rabinbach demonstrates how fluid and flexible Nazi ideology was in practice—so amenable to multiple interpretations and accommodations, in fact, that the majority of elites and masses could demonstrate fealty to the regime in multiple ways and thereby maintain a continued and even increased level of "normalcy" after the Nazi *Gleichschaltung*, notwithstanding the tragic fates suffered by too many of those who had once been citizens of the Republic.

Acknowledgments

In the several years it took to shepherd this volume into print the editors have incurred a great many debts. We are especially grateful to Ian Malcolm, formerly of Princeton University Press, for his dedication to the project proposal during its initial phases. We are equally indebted to Brigitta van Rheinberg at Princeton University Press for her guidance and unflagging enthusiasm for bringing the book to completion. We would also like to thank Alex Traub (Harvard College) for his work in preparing the chronology, and Martin L. White for his superb work in creating the index. Finally, we wish to express our gratitude to our copyeditor, Catja Pafort, and our production editor, Kathleen Cioffi at Princeton University Press. Most of all we are grateful to each of the contributors for their patience and their professionalism in committing themselves to the complexities of a multi-authored volume.

Notes

1. Detlev Peukert, *The Weimar Republic: The Crisis of Classical Modernity*, trans. Richard Deveson (New York: Hill and Wang, 1992), xiii.
2. Hans Mommsen, *The Rise and Fall of Weimar Democracy*, trans. Elborg Forster and Larry Eugene Jones (Chapel Hill: University of North Carolina Press, 1996), ix.
3. Peukert, *The Weimar Republic*, 164–67.
4. Max Weber, "Science as a Vocation," in *From Max Weber: Essays in Sociology*, trans. and eds. H. H. Gerth and C. Wright Mills (Oxford: Oxford University Press, 1958), 131.
5. Eric Weitz, *Weimar Germany: Promise and Tragedy* (Princeton: Princeton University Press, 2007), 253.
6. Heinrich August Winkler, *Weimar 1918–1933: Die Geschichte der ersten deutschen Demokratie* (Munich: C. H. Beck, 1993), 11.

Part I

Law, Politics, Society

1

Weimar Sociology

David Kettler and Colin Loader

Although it would take an ironist with the genius of Georg Simmel to do justice to the complex of competing teachings and practices that comprised Weimar sociology, it was nonetheless a bounded field, and even a distinctive discipline in formation. Simmel himself could not have written such an account of the discipline, since he had died before the end of the Great War. But he is nevertheless a significant presence in the story that follows here. Like his contemporary Max Weber, who also did not survive beyond the initial months of the Weimar Republic, Simmel helped to set an agenda for the generation that followed. In the embattled condition of sociology in the universities, moreover, their reputations among a wider public also provided an internal password and external legitimation for a largely self-selected and widely distrusted circle of young outsider aspirants to university careers. Together Simmel and Weber bequeathed to Weimar sociologists a legacy to be both explored and contested as they sought to realize Nietzsche's well-known injunction to become what they were.

We speak of irony, because most contemporaries questioned whether sociology was more than a label and because the books by sociologists that were admired were more likely to be taken as exercises in high journalism than scholarly works, let alone sociological "classics." Although institutionalization of the discipline had in fact begun, its struggle for widespread acceptance was difficult, partly because of its identification with republican constitutional institutions. This overlapping of theoretical, institutional and political competition is an important part of our story. For these reasons, after examining the legacy of Simmel and Weber, we turn to Karl Mannheim, the thinker who wrote perhaps the most discussed of such books, but who also most significantly engaged the work of the earlier masters and thereby played a noteworthy role in the emerging institutionalization of Weimar sociology and its relationship to political citizenship.

To understand Mannheim's significance for Weimar sociology, one must locate the field within both its academic and political contexts. The strong identification of the German university establishment with the imperial state before the war has been well documented.[1] There was little challenge within academia to the belief that the state provided a spiritual unity for the nation, and thus was hierarchically above the fragmented, interest-oriented sphere of civil society. The first generation of authors whose work became canonical for German sociology challenged the elevated standing of the state without great success, and they could not displace the image of society—and sociology—as a dangerously disruptive realm. This perception was heightened by the very important circumstance that Simmel, Weber, and the others seriously engaged the new, sophisticated, university-trained generation of intellectual Marxists, some of whom even received their patronage. Their academic opponents maintained that sociology fostered narrowly limited standpoints—such as mechanistic positivism or radical socialism—divorced from the higher unity of traditional disciplines.[2] Sociology was accordingly never recognized as a university discipline before the war, and the imperial "sociologists" who found university positions held appointments in disciplines such as political economy or philosophy. Even then, their "sociological" writings, although they were in fact neither positivistic nor socialistic, received only marginal scientific recognition within the universities.

The demise of the imperial political establishment in the trauma of the war and the subsequent declaration of the republic were disorienting for many citizens of the new republic, including its most prominent academic voices. In the chaos of the first post-war years, they looked back on the empire as a more stable time, when the disruptive forces now on the loose had been subjected to the harness of "tradition" and authority. While the changes brought by the Weimar Republic were exhilarating to some, they aroused only feelings of disorientation and even anger among the predominant mandarins.[3] Their disillusionment was reflected in the prevalence of the term "crisis" during these years. Many in the imperial generation within the university joined in Friedrich Meinecke's 1923 pseudo-classical lament: "everything is relative, everything is flux—give me a place where I can stand."[4] Writing at the very end of the Weimar epoch—in a brief journalistic essay for two liberal newspapers published after the disastrous election of November 1932—Karl Mannheim, in contrast, deprecated those who portrayed the widely-discussed "spiritual crisis" as "nothing but an evil that must somehow be eliminated" or as something that can be understood by "grandiose surveys based on intellectual history." What are called "spiritual crises," he observed, may be "worthily worked through" and they can, in any case, be understood only by close examination of the concrete displacements of individuals and groups, the obsolescing of their orientations, and of their "readjustment efforts." They are by no means merely "spiritual." To give weight to these reflections, Mannheim reports on an exercise in survey research that he evidently conducted earlier in that year. The individuals who report experiencing such a crisis also indicate on their questionnaires that they experienced a major change in circumstances—and there is evidence that some at least treated the crisis as a dramatic opening to a new realism and autonomy.[5]

Mannheim's protest can serve here as a helpful reminder that Weimar society, like the republic itself, was hardly doomed from the start. Many of the academic intellectuals in the social sciences worked to build and retain a civil and productive process, even across the lines that would soon prove cruelly impassable: the labor lawyer, Franz Neumann, eagerly accepted the hospitality of Carl Schmitt's seminar in 1932 to present his argument for exempting the collective bargaining guarantees of the Weimar Constitution from Schmitt's cherished presidential emergency powers;[6] and Karl Mannheim allied with Hans Freyer in 1932 to defend "contemporary studies" as a legitimate part of the sociological curriculum (even if he openly disdained Freyer's proto-fascist idealization of arbitrary will). Such collaborations were integral to the work of building the plural social constitutions that proved so vital to the fabric of Weimar. Mannheim remains the best known of the scholars dedicated to the constitution of sociology in that setting, and he is often recognized as a representative figure, whose career offers a special insight into the course and prospects of sociological development.[7]

For young intellectuals like Mannheim, born twenty to thirty years later than Meinecke's generation, despairing cries of "crisis" seemed like surrender. The younger generation looked instead to the legacy of the two thinkers whose heroic detachment promised an orientation to both the actuality and the promise of the alleged "crisis of culture"—and whose early deaths made it easier to accord their work an iconic status. Although both Simmel and Weber gained a posthumous prestige for the rich detail of their principal "sociological" writings, their chief legacy to the post-war sociological generation concerned their final, more didactic statements, first delivered as public lectures at historically acute moments. In November 1917, Weber spoke to students in Munich on "Science as a Calling," and in January 1919, during the first tumultuous months of the republic, he spoke in the same venue on "Politics as a Calling." Between Weber's two speeches, Georg Simmel, speaking in the last months of the war, lectured on "The Conflict in Modern Culture," rather soberly completing a cycle of public offerings on this topic, several of the earlier of which were marred by uncharacteristic bursts of wartime enthusiasm. By the middle of 1920, both Weber and Simmel were dead.

Simmel was born in 1858 into an assimilated Jewish commercial family in Berlin, the metropolis in which he spent most of his life and which provided the inspiration for much of his work. The learning and wit of his lectures at the University of Berlin attracted large audiences, composed mostly of enthusiastic students and the larger cultivated public. Mannheim and his mentor Georg Lukács, Siegfried Kracauer and Walter Benjamin were among the many young intellectuals who attended these lectures. Despite Simmel's popularity, his eclectic modernism, his association with left-wing circles, the petty jealousies of less innovative thinkers, and—above all—the anti-Semitism prevalent in the German academy, denied him a professorial chair in Berlin. Only by accepting a move to a provincial university in 1914 could he receive the academic rank he had long been denied.

While Simmel's family background was in the "disruptive" socio-economic sphere, Weber, who was six years Simmel's junior, grew up within the "unified" political establishment. He was exposed not only to his father's liberal political associates, but also to the many prominent academics visiting the Weber household. Hailed as a rising star in both history and political economy, as well as a promising political figure, he was called to a chair in political economy at the University of Heidelberg in 1896. There he presided over one of the most dynamic intellectual circles in Germany, which was frequented by many of those who attended Simmel's lectures. However, within two years his academic career was disrupted by a severe mental breakdown. Although he emerged from his illness in 1904, produced an amazing series of seminal works, and challenged the elders of political economy in institutions such Association for Social Policy, he was not able to return to the academy until the last years of his life, remote from his core constituency in Heidelberg. Like Simmel, although for different reasons, he remained at the margins of the imperial university.

The common starting point of what became their testamentary lectures was a decisive break with the expectation that it might somehow be possible to realize the harmonistic, unpolitical liberalism derived from Wilhelm von Humboldt, whose central slogan of *"Bildung"* embodied the notion that a conjunction of individual self-cultivation, collective cultural achievement, and a public order both prosperous and ethical belonged to the natural course of social development. Although both Simmel and Weber had served on the editorial board of *Logos*, the pre-war journal that in many ways embodied Fichte's faith in cultural and ethical progress, neither of them could see a way to resurrect that model, which in their eyes seemed to have been decisively undermined by anti-bourgeois theorists such as Nietzsche, Schopenhauer, and even Marx. While they did not reject the elements of the earlier cultural-liberal complex, they discerned paradoxes in their interrelations. Weimar sociology took its brief from their newly ironic orientation. Weber and Simmel were of course quite dissimilar: Weber remained interested in historical development, while Simmel's method was largely ahistorical; Weber appealed to causality whereas Simmel made impressionistic use of analogy; Weber examined larger social structures based on individual orientation and conduct, whereas Simmel studied smaller social and cultural forms as interactions.[8] But their lectures, delivered at a moment of fundamental transition, articulated a constellation of themes that challenged the fledgling discipline of sociology. Mannheim would later claim Max Weber as his principal model while defending his *Ideologie und Utopie* against a prominent cultural conservative on the eve of his brief career as professor.[9] And he would draw on Simmel (whose courses he had attended for a semester during his student years and whose diagnosis of cultural crisis he had made the starting point for an ambitious philosophical lecture he had delivered in Budapest in 1918)[10] when in 1930 he laid out the rationale of his first sociology course in Frankfurt.[11] In both cases Mannheim demonstrated the importance of the thematic legacies of these two masters to the emerging sociological field. Ironically, he would also claim that his own generation was distinguished by a certain hopefulness, in contrast to the "disillusioned realism" he found in Max Weber, whose clear-sightedness nevertheless remained his ideal.[12]

Georg Simmel: Sociology and Cultural Fragmentation

Simmel's 1918 lecture was his final statement on the "tragedy" of culture, a conception he expressed in a distinctive essayistic language combining elements of Kantian philosophy with the *Lebensphilosophie* of the pre-war decades.[13] The lecture, a social and cultural diagnosis with great resonance, presented cumulative human achievements as a mounting threat to the human capacity for achieving. Defining culture as an actualization of humanity's vital and spiritual forces, Simmel acknowledges the catalogue of Kantian antinomies as limitations on rational self-command but concentrates on a single fundamental polarity—the relation between life and form. "Life," resistant to precise definition or delimitation, is flux, formless vitality, creativity, will, the dynamic force of the individual.[14] It can, however, "become [cultural] reality only in the guise of its opposite," which is "form," constituting human creations and interactions and, ultimately, both culture and society. Moreover, culture is the locus where the individual psyche (or soul) crystallizes out of the flux of life and develops an internal unity through its interaction with the creations of other psyches. This constituted agent may be creative in turn, and its creations figure in new creations in turn. It is form that makes creations accessible to others. Forms, then, comprise the "objective culture," which is the precondition for the "subjective cultures" of creative agents. Yet this cultural promise has a tragic dimension, since those forms, as a condition of communicability, gain an identity, logic, and validity of their own, which tend to become remote from the vitality that created them and to being experienced as a reified entity alienated from both the vitality of life and the individual soul.

Simmel had rendered richly concrete the dark side of this general analysis in his earlier masterpiece, *The Philosophy of Money* (1900), where he argued that modern capitalism must be understood as the highest development of a culture centered upon money. Money is a means of leveling: it brings both the equalization and freedom liberalism extols, but also a diminishing heterogeneity, individualism, personality, and qualitative distinction, insofar as it reduces things to their lowest common denominator; in so doing it transgresses against the ideals celebrated by liberal theorists such as John Stuart Mill and Wilhelm von Humboldt. In the money economy, the qualitative relationships that bind one personality to another are replaced by technical economic relationships facilitated by an increasing division of labor, such that one is tied to many more individuals than had previously been the case; but these ties are impersonal and devoid of the capacity to germinate subjective culture.[15] A culture of things takes the place of a culture of personalities, giving rise to intellectual and cultural practices that find value only in the objective world.

During the early years of the war, Simmel's characteristic disinterestedness gave way to a sense of duty when he was grudgingly appointed professor in Strasbourg, the most problematic location in the Reich at war. But for the most part his subtle writings avoided theorizing solutions and remained concentrated on the signs of the condition he diagnosed; indeed, he sought to identify the factors and actions that permitted a productive temporizing with these ineluctable circumstances. Before 1917, he had dramatized the war experience, especially at the front, as a moment of contact with vital forces, and at times he had hinted that the war might permit a breakthrough beyond the "crisis" of objectification in culture, a belief echoed in the early Marxist writings of Georg Lukács, where it is "revolution" rather than "war" that dissolves reification. But in the last of the wartime lectures Simmel returned to his view of the tensions between objective and subjective culture as an inherent "conflict" whose continual management is the stuff of social existence. From this standpoint, efforts of abrupt deformalization, such as expressionist art or the vogue for mysticism, seemed to him merely to express a denial of culture.

Simmel saw sociology as an intellectual practice distanced from the crisis of culture. Yet this distance, without showing how liberal harmony can be restored, itself enacts a mode of being in the world that precludes despair. For the sociologist, Simmel wrote, society is not a concrete thing or substance, but a happening (*Geschehen*). These dynamics must be studied, for they bring the realization that individuals are richly differentiated by their interactions with other individuals. Sociology's task is the examination, and illumination, of the forms of these interactions. He preferred the term "sociation" (*Vergesellschaftung*) to "society" (*Gesellschaft*) so as to emphasize that what the study investigates is not a thing in itself but only one aspect of a variety of interactions. Simmel's kind of cultural sociology, as Mannheim wrote in one of his first sociological exercises, itself enacts a conditionally creative encounter with experience.[16] Simmel comprehended the issues posed by the fashionable cultural pessimism of the pre-war decades, but he balanced this diagnosis with an appreciation for the human elaboration of its limited—and perhaps shrinking—possibilities. One could even argue that Simmel's sociological writings bequeathed to the next generation a practice little affected by his forebodings about the crisis of culture, but rather shaped by the aesthetically charged relativism that such gifted cultural commentators as Siegfried Kracauer viewed as Simmel's most basic impulse.[17] Notwithstanding the wide range of human interactions that Simmel brought forth for sensitive sociological analysis, the political dimension of power and resistance remained largely neglected.

Max Weber: Sociology and Power

Power was, in contrast, the central motif in Max Weber's work. And it was especially evident in a series of influential and expressly political, wartime periodical and newspaper articles, culminating in his well-known January 1919 lecture on "Politics as a Vocation." Weber had been invited by an association of students whose basic opposition to the domination of university life by reactionary fraternities made them a congenial audience, precisely because of rightist protests outside the hall. Although the state of political affairs in early 1919 Munich remained threatening, there had just been an orderly local election with a moderate outcome, seemingly normalizing the situation after the revolutionary "circus" that Weber had detested. He could in effect anticipate the political frame of the eventual Weimar coalition in his address, a circumstance that facilitated its reception as a minor classic when it was published nine months later—and then again more prominently by Marianne Weber in October 1920, a few months after his death. During the next decade and long after that, it served as both a summary statement of Weber's political legacy and a classical rendering of political liberalism under harsh conditions.

The central figure of Weber's address is the politician who is described as capable of subjecting himself to an "ethic of responsibility." This figure is an "ideal type" (a heuristic construct according to Weber's scientific method), by reference to which historical appearances are to be understood. But he is also a model to be emulated, since the talk is itself political. To be a politician in this sense is, first, to be engaged in the struggle for power within the dominant political unit of the modern age—the territorial state—with its effective claim to a monopoly of legitimate violence. Weber ingeniously draws on his typology of differently legitimated modes of domination to specify, second, the kind of engagement he has in mind for his politician. Domination, he maintains, should be understood by reference to one of three types of authority: first, a traditional form, usually patriarchal in design, second, a form structured by legal-bureaucratic relations, and third, a charismatic form, defined by special personal qualities claimed by and imputed to a leadership figure lacking both traditional and legal grounding. The pure form of the latter is illustrated at the instance of supra-institutional religious, military, or revolutionary figures of extraordinary uniqueness and control, but Weber's modulation of the model for his own time, where he implicitly situates it within an institutional—or constitutional—setting, applies it above all to strong-willed and dedicated party leaders with a sense of mission (with the English Liberal, Gladstone, as a prime example) who are able to motivate subordinates by the force of their will and to sustain a mass following, above all by their demagogic-oratorical skills and their command of organization.[18]

Somewhat surprisingly in view of the unconditionality that marks the actions of many of his pre-modern paradigm cases, but understandably in the context of a political address, Weber qualifies the charismatic politician's self-constitutive project by an "ethic of responsibility," which he defines, first of all, by contrast to an absolute "ethic of conviction." In Weber's explication of the latter, he sounds chords reminiscent of Kantian doctrines of pure duty, their Pietistic religious counterparts, and—most pointedly—utopian standards of perfect actions, where the exemplification of the principle is the sole and final standard, regardless of practical efficacy or consequence. To be sure, the ethic of responsibility that is the mark of the political "calling" cannot itself dispense with convictions, lest it become a mere excuse for opportunism. But it requires a cool assessment of probable consequences, as accurate as possible, as well as a willingness to own both the harms and benefits of a course chosen, and above all, the cost in violence and disruption of quotidian life.[19]

Weber's advocacy of the political vocation thus understood is directed against three contrasting models. First, it offers an alternative to the ideal of politics as a mode of personal spiritual, moral, or aesthetic self-expression, however dedicated and high-minded, a conception of political engagement Weber attributed to the more revolutionary among his listeners, as well as to admired personalities like the romantic anarchist Gustav Landauer or Weber's own former protégés, Ernst Bloch and Georg Lukács. Second, it contrasts with the figure of the unprincipled "professional politician," which Weber saw epitomized in the purely materialistic "party bosses" familiar to him from American muckraking literature of the Progressive era. Third, and by far the most important, it is directed against the pervasive regime of officials and bureaucrats, a favorite target of Weber's criticism during the preceding decades and especially during the war.[20]

Weber saw the barely resistible rise of bureaucratic power as the source of grave and eventually fatal flaws in German society. But he also viewed it as the political dimension of the larger societal process that elevated the institutions of calculative means above the human possibilities of chosen ends—a portrait comparable in certain respects to the devitalization Simmel described in his "crisis of culture." Simmel's aesthetic and meditative account of this process bears some resemblance to Weber's approach several years earlier, in the gloomy conclusion of his *Protestant Ethic and the Spirit of Capitalism* (1904–5), which offers a famous denunciation of capitalist humanity as "specialists without spirit, sensualists without heart." But in the 1919 lecture Weber now credits the genuinely "professional" exercise of political power with the capacity to manage the encounter with these events, if not to shape them to human wishes. This power is housed in the motives and institutionalized relations of society, not embodied in some transcendent Hegelian sphere. Because responsible political judgment requires as precise a weighing as possible of the practicality, costs, and consequences of actions in society, it cannot deny the knowledge attainable through the limited rationality of sociological method.

The best-known and most-debated statement on these questions by Weber was his lecture on "Science as a Vocation" delivered in the same brilliant essayistic mode as his lecture on politics before the same university student group, though a year earlier, while the war was still in its last phases. Unlike his intramural and philosophically complex articles on method in the social sciences, this lecture expressly addressed his student audience, offering counsel and touching repeatedly on presumptions he thought prevalent among "the youth." No elaborate philosophical reasoning is offered in this lecture to support the central thesis: that scientific study of the physical and mental universes, whatever methods are used, cannot furnish answers to question of choice among alternatives in any of the diverse value spheres. In all of the latter, reflective individual actors are always ultimately confronted with conflicts that cannot be resolved by reason. It is treated as logically self-evident that statements of fact cannot resolve questions of value: "is" can never determine "ought." Weber's prime targets are professors who pose as prophets, as well as the students, whose confused yearning for "experience" leads them to crave such misuse of the professor's position in the lecture hall. Science is a matter of ascetic dedication to the constitutive norms of the respective disciplines (and specialization of fields is integral to scientific development), which may differ in method but which uniformly preclude the attempt to answer Tolstoy's great question, "What shall we do and how shall we live?"[21]

Science nevertheless affects the world in which choices have to be made, inasmuch as it is an integral part of the ongoing progress of intellectualization

and rationalization that disenchants the world and renders previously established grounds of judgment insecure. In turn, as reiterated at the end of Weber's
"politics" lecture, science need not remain irrelevant to the sphere of choices.
The sciences can provide, first, techniques for managing the calculable aspects
of things; second, the methods of thought for devising such techniques; and
third, the clarity gained from knowing the costs and consequences of available
alternatives—the likely effects of a choice on other valued ends—and indeed
the logical interconnections among complexes of preferences. In language that
seems paradoxical in a world deprived of enchantment, Weber suggests that gods
are ultimately in conflict in every sphere, and that scientific understanding can
at most help one to recognize the gods and to make one's decision efficacious.[22]
To speak of Weber's position as relativistic, while technically correct in the accepted language of intellectual history, understates the weight he attaches to the
idea of responsibility in preparing the way for the choices that must be made,
and renders incomprehensible his disdain for those whose choices he judges to
be harmful to the spheres in which they act—those who lack the requisite sense
of "calling" (or vocation) for the tasks at hand.

Karl Mannheim (1893–1947): Sociology and Politics

Weber developed his theory of scientific rationality in a series of papers that
served as a programmatic statement for the *Archiv für Sozalwissenschaft und
Sozialpolitik* on behalf of the new collective editorship that in 1904 initiated the
journal's development into the primary forum for both disciplinary differentiation and interdisciplinarity in the social sciences. Karl Mannheim's career
in Heidelberg, beginning in the early 1920s, was punctuated by a series of five
publications in this very same journal between 1923 and 1930, tracking his own
course from philosopher to a sociologist of the guild. The high standing of Emil
Lederer, the responsible editor during those years, with key cultural officials
contributed to Mannheim's securing his professorship in Frankfurt. It is not too
much to say that the *Archiv* was a part of Max Weber's legacy to Weimar sociology. Mannheim's own steadfast involvement with the periodical serves as a measure of his immersion in Weber's legacy even during the years when he found
much in it to criticize.

Karl Mannheim was born in Budapest, Hungary in 1893 and died in London,
England in 1947. His early training in his native Budapest was in philosophy,
culminating with his doctoral dissertation on "The Structural Analysis of Epistemology." Like many of the Jewish intelligentsia, he was a member of several
intellectual circles, most notably that of his informal mentor, Georg Lukács. Although he did not join Lukács in his conversion to Communism, Mannheim
was also forced to flee when the short-lived Soviet regime in Hungary was over-
thrown in 1919, and the new rulers persecuted anyone they distrusted. Between
1919 and 1933, he lived in Germany. Mannheim's German academic career did
not begin in sociology, then, although the field's organization became his most

pressing concern in its latter years. His first German stop in 1919 was Freiburg, where he attended lectures by Edmund Husserl and Martin Heidegger. Moving to Heidelberg, he sought to habilitate with either Karl Jaspers or Heinrich Rickert, but eventually, when neither of the philosophers supported the project, he brought his proposal concerning the philosophical foundations of cultural sociology to Max Weber's brother Alfred. Mannheim's German periodical publications between 1921 and 1930 document his shift from, on the one hand, a relationship to sociology very much like that of Simmel—one that made philosophers aware of the interest and relevance of sociological findings and questions to their own self-reflective inquiries into a culture in crisis—toward, on the other, a greater investment in sociology as a distinct discipline, in conjunction with a steadily increasing appreciation of Max Weber's sociological practices, whatever philosophical differences may have remained. The latter development was over-determined, it should be said, since its high point coincided with Mannheim's appointment in 1930 as the professor of sociology in Frankfurt, thanks not only to the public and professional success of his *Ideologie und Utopie*, but also to the patronage of a key Prussian official, Carl H. Becker, a friend of Max Weber who was determined to install sociology in German universities as a resource for republican political education and as a counterbalance to the conservative bias of most faculties elsewhere in Germany.[23] In the Spring of 1933, soon after Hitler became Chancellor, Mannheim was excluded from his university professorship and forced into exile by the Nazis because he was a foreigner, a Jew, and reputedly a friend of their enemies. As a refugee in England, Mannheim secured a teaching position at the London School of Economics from 1933 to 1943 and a professorship in the sociology of education at the University of London for the last years of his life.

Mannheim's very first publication in German, a review of Lukács's last book before his turn to communism, appeared in 1920 in *Logos*, a journal dedicated to "Philosophy of Culture," which Weber himself had chosen three years earlier as the venue for the last of his academic articles on "ethical neutrality in the social sciences."[24] Interestingly, *Logos* was also a primary reference point when Mannheim outlined the frame of reference of the Georg Lukács group in Budapest, on whose behalf he initiated a lecture series in 1918. In view of the closeness between Lukács and Weber at this time—Weber even cites him as authority for a scientific framing of aesthetics—it is unlikely that Mannheim's reference would have been made in ignorance of Weber's seminal article. Two years later, in any case, writing in a Hungarian exile publication, Mannheim had already made it clear that he had to choose the side of Max Weber in any contest between Weber's intellectual heirs and the devotees of Stefan George, who criticized Weber's theoretical stance concerning the limits of demonstrable knowledge.

In 1934, from his asylum at the London School of Economics, Mannheim offered a valedictory address for German sociology, in which he defined his field as riven between two generations, his own generation and that of his older competitors, notably Leopold von Wiese and Hans Freyer. He acknowledged the contributions of the others (treating them cursorily as familiar to his audience), but strik-

ay distinguish two stages in the process by which Mannheim came to
t a sociology at home in the university and yet congruent with Becker's
r its political effects: the first centers on *Ideologie und Utopie* (1929) and his
rs in Heidelberg, and the other focuses on his brief career in Frankfurt and
fied by his 1932 constitutional proposal for sociology as a university subject.
background are not only Mannheim's deep familiarity with Simmel, but also
nheim's preoccupation, first, with the Hegelian Marxism of Lukács, and, sec-
, with Weber's writings, both of which were subjects of seminars Mannheim
ght as *Privatdozent* in Heidelberg. Weber was also to have been the subject of a
ok for which Mannheim received a contract as well as a leave of absence during
is last Heidelberg semesters. Both phases will be characterized in relation to the
hemes of crisis and vocation inherited from Simmel and Weber.

In the light of Mannheim's well-known emphasis on "intellectuals" as uniquely
qualified for reflective social and political knowledge, it is important, first, to establish that Mannheim cared about the university as a focal point for organizing, transmitting, and advancing such knowledge. After all, "intellectual" refers
above all to the loose-knit social formation comprising journalists, literary figures, students, artists, and the like, with academics taking part, like the others,
only in their "amateur" capacities. Like his systematic monograph on Max Weber,
Mannheim's book-length study on intellectuals remained incomplete, although
in this case there are many pages collected in his papers, a trail of distinctions
and classifications reminiscent as much of Simmel's subtle explorations of social
locations in the processes of sociation as they are of Weberian typologies. Yet it
is clear that Mannheim thought that intellectuals require university discipline in
order to move beyond the realm of public opinion and to give effective voice to
the knowledge that their location opens to them.

Mannheim spoke to the subject before he committed to sociology in 1922,
in a newspaper article decrying the failure of university faculties to enter into
effective exchanges with the young people who arrived with new kinds of valuable artistic, religious, communitarian, and literary experiences and intuitions,
where he nevertheless left no doubt that these impulses must be appropriated
and constrained by scientific disciplines and not treated as spontaneous prophe-
cies and authoritative revelations, whatever the students and their extra-mural
mentors wished to believe. Writing in 1921 in one of Max Weber's favorite forums, the higher education section of the influential *Frankfurter Zeitung*, he
tweaks Weber's position on the students' enthusiasm for their experiences, but
he uses it not to supersede university disciplines and their critical ways, but to
broaden them, in the manner of Simmel's concern to infuse "life" into forms.[29]

A similar recognition of university discipline appeared in Mannheim's treatment of Ernst Troeltsch, whom he otherwise recognized, alongside Max Scheler,
to be Max Weber's peer as a classic forebearer of the sociology he envisions. He
writes about a "spiritual divide" within German thought,

> between a brilliant, often very profound world of independent scholarship
> and aestheticism, which often loses itself in untestable vagaries, however,

ingly affirms: "The man on whose work the y\
most safely is Max Weber, whose formulation o₁\
empirical investigation have become representati\
not cite either of the lectures that were earlier so im⌐\
what he considered to be Weber's transcendence of th\
alists" and "idealists" in the aftermath of Marx, notably .\
lished *Wirtschaft und Gesellschaft*. Weber's work, accord\
as a whole and without undue emphasis on *The Protesta*\
of Capitalism, showed that "we cannot separate spheres of \
change on the one hand from the sphere of a change in ment\
the other. The greater art of the sociologist consists in his attem⌐\
changes in mental attitudes to changes in social situations."[26]

With this homage to his great predecessor, Mannheim introd\
sociology of knowledge, as "the most surprising event in the rece\
ment of sociology," because it had shown that differences in "styles o\
grounded in different social locations and situations "penetrate into th\
of philosophy, and the different scientific disciplines."[27] The recognition\
"embarrassing" circumstance, Mannheim declared, led to "an attempt a\
criticism" designed to "ostracize . . . the influence of our *Weltanschauung* h\
all social sciences"—a "purge," he conceded, that was especially needed in G\
many. This awareness also required an acknowledgment, however, that the ef-\
fects of differences in socially derived perspectives could never be wholly ex-\
purgated from social thought, and that the criteria and procedures of scientific\
work in this domain will have its own distinct norms of "asceticism" and rigor.\
These norms would derive no less from the interpretive achievements of cultural\
commentators like Simmel than from the anti-ideological ideals of explanatory\
scientific trends. While Mannheim remarks Max Weber's empirically rigorous\
comparisons across wide historical and cultural divides, when citing him as a\
model for his own generation, he also notes that his attention to "the rise and\
development of capitalism" aimed at a "diagnosis of the contemporary situation"\
and that questions about "our place in the present crisis" are "latent in Weber's\
empirical investigations":

> He was one of the first to see the dangers inherent in our social tendencies
> and in the *Kulturkrise* or "crisis of culture." He realized that the destiny of
> any society depends upon the texture of its organization and on the trans-
> formation and adaptation of the human mind.[28]

Mannheim's retrospective account in the London School of Economics's *Politica*
is naturally oriented to his negotiations with the English academic establishment
upon which he was now dependent. What is most interesting is the consistent way
in which Mannheim in effect offers himself as leader in a kind of constitution-
making process—an eminently political role—both in his recollection of the
Weimar era and in his project in exile. His efforts were concentrated above all on
the "texture of [the] organizations" that mattered most, while his hopes rested
on the consequent "transformation and adaptation of the human mind."

because it lacks inner or outer constraining bonds, on the one side, and, on the other, a scholarly world constrained by its academic positions and mastering its materials, but distant from the living centre of contemporary life.[30]

At the time of his arrival in Heidelberg in 1921, finally, he expressly associates a slightly more localized version of this distinction with Max Weber:

> Heidelberg's spiritual life may be calibrated by two polar opposites. One pole consists of the sociologists and the other, the Georgians. The ideal-typical representative of the one is the already deceased Max Weber, and that of the other is the poet, Stefan George. On the one side, the university, and on the other, the unbounded extramural world of the literati.[31]

There is no doubt where Mannheim took his stand.

Interestingly, Mannheim also linked Weber, in the same article, with a political role. Weber "had at his disposal everything that would have fitted him for political leadership," Mannheim says, but he was thwarted by his absence from the capital city. "He could only play a guest role in politics." Mannheim's list of the attributes requisite for leadership was reminiscent of Weber's comparable criteria: "unbounded (!) sociological and economic knowledge, a feeling for political realism, an animated temperament." Yet that common formula also hides difference in the conception of the political vocation, which was related above all to a different reading of the "crisis of modernity." If the decisive manifestation of crisis for Weber was the hyper-rationalization of social and political life, whose symptom was the rise to power of bureaucracies, Mannheim saw the critical and cumulative defect rather in the failure of comprehensive practical political knowledge, capable of orienting the democratic organizations and public constituencies which have become the prime actors in political life.

Mannheim introduces *Ideologie und Utopie*, the brilliant work on which his subsequent reputation has mostly rested, by noting that its chapters represented thought experiments, in which certain problems were viewed from a number of viewpoints that resisted premature reconciliation. This applied specifically to the contrast between his article on "politics as a science" and his exploration of the critical structural weakness in political thinking. In his essay on utopia, Mannheim depicts a crisis of devitalization, very much in the manner of Simmel. The pure model of utopian thinking, according to Mannheim, is exemplified by chiliastic movements like the Anabaptists. From their standpoint, the existing state of things is a worthless confusion. The displacement of the present state of things by a perfect state was not conditioned in any way by considerations of cost, timeliness, or realism; and knowledge pertains only to the end. While this paradigm was also reminiscent of Weber's ethics of conviction, Mannheim related it to a way of knowing the world and not simply to a mode of conduct. Having defined the pure chiliastic ideal type, Mannheim attempted to identify the "utopian" element in a wider array of political ideologies, even conservatism, treating some measure of denial of the present reality and aspiration for something altogether different as a vital, energizing force—Simmel would have said "life"—in those political outlooks. His narrative, however, presumed a progressive decline in the utopian element: Critical encounters with ideologies and utopias fostered a kind of static realism that paradoxically destroyed the meaningfulness of all political endeavor, since it lacks an active design for anything new, the pursuit of which is central to his basic conception of the political, as distinct from the sphere of bureaucratic routine.[32]

This rather bleak study of utopia was not prominent in Mannheim's larger sociological approach to political knowledge in its various modes. He constructed his "sociology of knowledge" from the study of ideologies, seeing it as a way of intervening in a "crisis" that contains promise as well as danger. The sociology of knowledge strategy involves two steps. First, the variety of ideas in the modern world is classified according to a scheme of historical ideological types, few in number, in keeping with Mannheim's thesis that the ideological field has moved from a period of atomistic diversity and competition to a period of concentration. Liberalism, conservatism, and socialism are the principal types. Second, each of these ideologies is interpreted as a function of some specific way of being in the social world, as defined by location within the historically changing patterns of class and generational stratification. Liberalism is thus referred to the capitalist bourgeoisie in general, and various stages in its development are referred to generational changes. Similar analyses connect conservatism to social classes harmed by the rise to power of the bourgeoisie, and socialism to the new industrial working class. Approaches in the human sciences (*Geisteswissenschaften*)— and notably the social sciences among them (*Sozialwissenschaften*)—have their own ideological lineages, albeit in more sublimated form.

Each of the ideologies is said to manifest a characteristic "style" of thinking, a distinctive complex of responses to the basic issues that systematic philosophy has identified as constitutive of human consciousness, such as conceptions of time and space, the structure of reality, human agency, and knowledge itself. The political judgments and recommendations on the surface of purely ideological texts must be taken in that larger structural context. Not every ideology elaborates such a philosophy, and the elaborated philosophies associated with an ideology may not provide an adequate account of the underlying ideological structures. Such philosophical statements are ideological texts like others, and require structural analysis and sociological interpretation to be fully comprehended. The style of thinking is most apparent in the way concepts are formed, according to Mannheim, and in the logic by which they are interlinked. These are the features that must be uncovered to identify the distinctive style.

Each of the styles, in turn, expresses some distinctive design upon the world vitally bound up with the situation of one of the social strata present in the historical setting. He derived the ideology concept proximately from Marxism, but Mannheim is emphatic in his original German texts (if not in the revised English translation), that this design cannot be simply equated to a group "interest," not least because he disavows the theory of motivation and the indifference to social psychological group processes associated with the stress on interest. The sociologist of knowledge has no direct authoritative information about the formative will he postulates as the principle of integration and immanent development in ideological wholes. The self-explanations offered by groups in their ideologies and utopias are the starting points for knowledge about underlying styles and principles; these may indicate the logic of the social location of such groups, including accounts of their interests. It is the view of the "totality" that is Mannheim's objective. Sociology of knowledge seeks to give an account of the whole ideological field, in its historical interaction and change, together with an account of the historically changing class and generational situations that the ideologies interpret to the groups involved. To have a method for seeing all this, according to Mannheim, means to be able to see in a unified and integrated way what each of the ideologically oriented viewers can only see in part. It is to have the capacity for viewing the situation at a distance and as a whole, without it losing the quality of being a situation in which actions matter. Choice gains in importance as a central feature of the experimental life, which is the epitome of the sociological attitude.

Mannheim draws on Marxism for a conception of politics as a process of dialectical interplay among factors more "real" than the competing opinions of liberal theory. But neither the proletariat nor any other socio-political force is bearer of a transcendent rationality, historically destined to reintegrate all the struggling irrationalities in a higher, pacified order. The contesting social forces and their projects in the world are complementary and in need of a synthesis that will incorporate elements of their diverse social wills and visions. Syntheses in political vision and *Sozialwissenschaften* are interdependent. Sociology of knowledge presages and fosters both.

In sum, while Mannheim derived the ideology concept from the Hegelianized Marxism developed by Lukács, he grounded it in the relationships between diverse and in their own terms irreconcilable structurings of knowledge, and the perspectives and designs arising from different locations in social space and historical time. Here the economic determinants of class are of great importance, but they are not the sole criteria of a relevant social perspective, and here no perspective has an inherently valid view of reality or unique title to rule. The crisis was intensified, according to Mannheim, by the fact that the parties in conflict—each constituted and integrated by a distinct ideology—are also all informed by a vulgar version of the insight into ideology as deemed grounded in social group interests. As a result they mutually seek to discredit one another by an exposé of the ideological character of all their ideas, a maneuver that purports to show that their respective claims about political and social life are nothing but weapons in a struggle among competing interests. Under these conditions, there cannot be any movement towards the synthetic view that Mannheim had elsewhere credited to the operations of competition among ideologies during the nineteenth century. Political agents—and under conditions of democratization this encompasses everyone—were now trapped within an array of collective solipsisms, each in their all encompassing partisan posture.[33]

Revolution cannot be counted on to provide a definitive breakthrough, as Lukács argued, but neither can a decisive political leader, however charismatic.

Mannheim proposed instead that a mode of political knowledge grounded in the peculiar interstitial situation of the intellectuals—whose individual cultivation and experiences detached them from their native milieus and perspectives—could generate and transmit a common orientation to the historical realities and possibilities sufficient to permit the parties to escape from their mutual isolation and to engage in politics with one another. The work on this synthetic interpretation of historical configurations and trends, according to Mannheim, is "political sociology." Mannheim was clear that the political role of the political sociologist is as researcher and teacher, although he does not preclude a mode of this work in conjunction with one or another "party school." In the latter case, the intellectuals, by virtue of their links to one another, would loosen the dogmatic forms of party ideologies and enhance the likelihood that the parties could find some common language. Where political sociology constituted itself as a field of study, the work of comprehending the changing reality would still eventuate, as Weber himself claimed, in acts of choice.[34]

Mannheim expressly invited the comparison with Weber. After registering, in agreement with Weber, that the synthetic, trans-ideological political knowledge he thinks attainable does not presume to teach the political decisions that individuals must make in their capacities as political persons, he distinguishes his position from Weber. He notes that both aim at a "common platform for investigation of the political field," but he claims that Weber conceives of this platform in terms of the liberal ideal of an intellectual domain, where pure rationality might reign free, remaining categorically distinct from the dynamics of practice, while Mannheim himself, in contrast, envisions a platform that is achievable only from moment to moment, as elements derived from the ideological conflict are provisionally balanced against one another and made into the organon of studies that moderates and orients the ongoing political competition. Mannheim in effect applies the classical Marxist formulation of the unity of theory and practice, except that he insists on the dependence of the unified practical view on the partial and partisan insights of the ideologists: No ideology is fully valid, if only because it expresses a merely partial and perspectival view of the social world. But no ideology is worthless in Mannheim's version of perspectivism, because of the genuine insights that each perspective yields. Because the sociologist must work with and upon political-ideological matter, and because the work of the sociologist is inherently an intervention in political life, there can be no bright line between the political and scientific vocations. In this sense, Mannheim concluded, there can indeed be a politics as *science*.

Ideology and Utopia stands in a complex relationship to Mannheim's effort to create a recognized "platform" for sociology. While the success of the book beyond the university, documented by a unique and extended dispute in a wide range of media,[35] helped to boost the standing of the field with the relevant public (and certainly advanced his own career), its controversial claims and essayistic manner did not lend Mannheim any special authority or power within the profession. He remained an outsider. While some looked askance at Mannheim's abstruse interests and complex manner of expression, Carl Becker, as Prussian cultural minister, sought to promote sociology as locus of a political education congruent with the values of the democratic republic, and he hoped that Mannheim would build on *Ideologie und Utopie* to effectuate some such program. While Mannheim doubtless shared Becker's interest and gave themes relevant to political education a prominent place in his lecture courses, after *Ideologie und Utopie*—and especially after his establishment as professor—he devoted the greater share of his work to laying out a curricular and research program together with his students that would accommodate the work of other academics associated with sociology in German universities.

Mannheim's attempt to shift from the periphery to the center of the emerging profession was already evident in his newspaper report on the 1928 conference of the German Sociological Society. Notwithstanding his own serious challenge to the institutional leadership (notably Leopold von Wiese and Alfred Weber) he identified mutual acceptance and corporate unification as the dominant motifs of the meetings.[36]

Mannheim's willingness to bracket the most controversial elements in his sociology of knowledge—and indeed, to treat this study as a rather modest subfield within an academic design that expressly gave room to the methods and aims of von Wiese's "formal" sociology as well as Hans Freyer's version of sociology as a study of present reality (*Wirklichkeitswissenschaft*)—is formalized in a constitutional proposal on "the current tasks of sociology" that he offered in 1932. Three aspects of this text are of special interest. First, Mannheim proposed a threefold introduction to sociology, although he put weight on only the first two as comprising the pedagogical (and organizational) core of the discipline: formal sociology, initiated by Georg Simmel and continued by Leopold von Wiese, and empirical, comparative sociology associated with Max Weber. Mannheim also acknowledged a historicist approach, which he now treated as a method of radical individualization and relegated to an auxiliary status. In an extraordinary diminution of *Ideology and Utopia,* he put sociology of knowledge together with other applications of sociological reasoning in cognate disciplines, while also depoliticizing it, so that its focus became nothing but the investigation of perspectival constraints on other studies. Third, he put the large questions of cultural crisis into a distinct compartment, designated "cultural sociology," which he linked to the sociological core by loose and unsystematic ties. In this sphere, the sociologist functions almost extramurally, since his method is speculative; although he is bound to subject any factual claims these global interpretations offer to empirical tests.

One understands the significance of Mannheim's constitutional proposal more clearly when one contrasts it to his earlier attempts at reviewing the organization of sociology in an unpublished study written before he actually chose the field.[37] In this treatise, Mannheim expressed only qualified respect for the types of sociology derived from Simmel and Weber; he criticizes their failure to ascend to the level of the third type, which he then characterized in terms very close to his presentation ten years later of "cultural sociology." This drastic reorganization did not mean that Mannheim was less dedicated to the latter type of inquiry at that time: he believed in any case that sociological researchers would be driven to questions that belong there if they work conscientiously in whatever mode they choose. The broadest questions of historical meaning and the human condition—philosophical in that sense—represent a qualitatively different species from the work that must proceed within far more limited boundaries, and it is this constrained work that constitutes sociology as an academic discipline. Mannheim's own research in Frankfurt as well as the work of his students and other associates took as their principle model the sociology of Max Weber. The research program developed there shows that this conception offered a practical way forward for Weimar sociology as a cooperative if not collaborative enterprise.[38] But with Weimar's end these plans went unrealized.

There is a structural similarity between Mannheim's two-stage constitutional project for sociology and the Weimar constitution itself, at least as the latter was understood by many in the Social Democratic Party. While the constitutional order itself was designed to provide a reflexive legal context for a good deal of self-management and pluralistic bargaining, there was also an expectation that this dynamic regime would eventuate, if implemented in good faith, in a collective Rousseauist democracy able to effectuate its emergent socialist will. The one was a result of the other, but it could not be its express aim.[39] Similarly, a diagnosis of social and cultural crisis as well as a therapeutic strategy—a comprehensive inquiry that yielded an adequate reading of the meaning of social development in a given historical setting—was a consistent hope in Mannheim's work, but its attainment presupposed a far more ascetic mode of inquiry within the realm of sociology as such. From this standpoint, Mannheim's program was far more than a bundle of compromises. It was a genuine constitution of sociological work, and it might have accomplished much. That it was swamped by events whose signs it failed to give sufficient weight does not say everything about the things to be learned from Mannheim and the enterprise he represented—as may be said more generally about the experiments of Weimar.

Notes

1. Fritz K. Ringer, *Decline of the German Mandarins: The German Academic Community, 1890–1933* (Cambridge, MA: Harvard University Press, 1969).
2. Most outspoken was Georg von Below, "Soziologie als Lehrfach. Ein kritischer Beitrag zur Hochschulreform," *Jahrbuch für Gesetzgebung, Verwaltung und Volkswirtschaft im Deutschen Reich* 43 (1919), 59–110.
3. See Ringer, *Decline of the German Mandarins.*
4. Friedrich Meinecke, *Schaffender Spiegel*: Studien zur deutschen Geschichtschreibung und Geschichtsauffassung (Stuttgart: K. F. Koehler, 1948), 214, 224
5. Karl Mannheim, "The Spiritual Crisis in the Light of Sociology," in Mannheim, *Sociology as Political Education*, trans. and eds. David Kettler and Colin Loader (New Brunswick, NJ: Transaction, 2001), 169–73; Reinhard Laube, *Karl Mannheim und die Krise des Historismus* (Göttingen: Vandenhoeck & Ruprecht, 2004), 609; David Kettler et al., *Karl Mannheim and the Legacy of Max Weber* (Aldershot: Ashgate, 2008), 159.

6. Franz L. Neumann, *Koalitionsfreiheit und Reichsverfassung* (Berlin: Heymanns, 1932); Kettler, *Domestic Regimes, the Rule of Law, and Democratic Social Change* (Berlin: Galda & Wilch Glienecke, 2001).

7. René König, *Soziologie in Deutschland* (Munich: Carl Hanser, 1987); Kettler, "The Secrets of Mannheim's Success," in *Soziologie, Politik und Kultur*, ed. Eberhard Demm (Frankfurt: Peter Lang, 2003), 141–53.

8. Cf. Lawrence A. Scaff, *Fleeing the Iron Cage* (Berkeley: University of California Press, 1989), 121–151, 193–201.

9. Mannheim, "Problems of Sociology in Germany," in Mannheim, *From Karl Mannheim* (New Brunswick, NJ: Transaction, [1929] 1993), 399–437.

10. Mannheim, "Seele und Kultur," in Mannheim, *Wissensoziologie*, ed. Kurt H. Wolff (Neuwied: Luchterhand, [1918] 1970), 66–84.

11. Mannheim, "An Introduction to Sociology" [1930], in Mannheim, *Sociology as Political Education*, 3–78.

12. Mannheim, *Conservatism* (London: Routledge, [1925] 1986), 176.

13. Simmel, *Simmel on Culture*, eds. David Frisby and Mike Featherstone (London: Sage, 1997), 55–107.

14. Simmel, *Simmel on Culture*, 107.

15. Simmel, *Simmel on Culture*, 244–47; Simmel, *The Philosophy of Money* (London: Routledge & Kegan Paul, 1978), 121–23, 175, 279–80, 336.

16. Mannheim, *Structures of Thinking*, eds. David Kettler et al. (London: Routledge & Kegan Paul, [1922] 1982), 120-122.

17. Kracauer, *The Mass Ornament*, trans. and ed. Thomas Y. Levin (Cambridge, MA: Harvard University Press, 1995), 225–27.

18. Weber, *From Max Weber*, eds. H. H. Gerth and C. Wright Mills (New York: Oxford University Press, 1946), 78–79, 113.

19. Weber, *From Max Weber*, 120–21.

20. Weber, *From Max Weber*, 108–9, 116–17, 95.

21. Weber, *From Max Weber*, 143.

22. Weber, *From Max Weber*, 150–55.

23. Becker, *Gedanken zur Hochschulreform* (Leipzig: Quelle & Meyer, 1919).

24. Mannheim, "A Review of Georg Lukács' *Theory of the Novel* [1920]," in *From Karl Mannheim*, ed. Kurt H. Wolff (New Brunswick, NJ: Transaction, 1993), 131–35.

25. Mannheim, "German Sociology (1918–1933)," in *Essays on Sociology and Social Psychology* (London: Routledge & Kegan Paul, 1953), 218.

26. Mannheim, "German Sociology," 219.

27. Mannheim, "German Sociology," 220–21.

28. Mannheim, "German Sociology," 218.

29. Mannheim, "Science and Youth," in *Sociology as Political Education*, 99–104; Loader and Kettler, *Karl Mannheim's Sociology as Political Education* (New Brunswick, NJ: Transaction, 2002), 39–40.

30. Mannheim, "Historicism" [1925], in Mannheim, *Essays on the Sociology of Knowledge*, 84–133, quotation on 98.

31. Mannheim, "Heidelberg Letters," in *Sociology as Political Education*, 91.

32. Mannheim, *Ideology and Utopia* (New York: Harcourt, Brace, 1968), 190–97, 222–36; Loader, *The Intellectual Development of Karl Mannheim* (Cambridge: Cambridge University Press, 1985), 101–11.

33. Mannheim, *Ideology and Utopia*, 67–87, 238–56.

34. Mannheim, *Ideology and Utopia*, 97–104, 136–71.

35. Volker Meja and Nico Stehr, eds., *Knowledge and Politics. The Sociology of Knowledge Dispute* (London: Routledge, 1990).

36. Mannheim, "Der sechste deutsche Soziologentag in Zürich," *Frankfurter Zeitung* (October 5, 1928), 1–2.

37. Karl Mannheim, "The Distinctive Character of Cultural Sociological Knowledge," in *Structures of Thinking* (New Brunswick, NJ: Transaction, 1982), 98–118.

38. Kettler, Loader, and Meja, *Karl Mannheim and the Legacy of Max Weber: Retrieving a Research Programme* (Aldershot: Ashgate, 2008).

39. See discussions of Franz L. Neumann in Kettler, *Domestic Regimes, passim.*

2

Weimar Psychology

Holistic Visions and Trained Intuition

Mitchell G. Ash

In recent discussions of Weimar culture, increasing attention is being paid to ambivalences of modernist thought, particularly in the human sciences.[1] Historians of natural sciences, technology, and medicine have also shown that previous distinctions between modernism and anti-modernism in Weimar science are too inflexible. Holistic positions could be advocated by scientists on the left as well as the right;[2] popular fascination with technologies such as rocketry and technocratic social projects like eugenics was as constitutive of Weimar modernity as was anxious opposition to "machine thinking."[3]

Psychology is an appropriate site for closer examination of these issues, and their interactions. One reason for this is psychology's problematic institutional location: to the extent that it was institutionalized at all in Weimar-era Germany, the discipline called psychology straddled the divide between the natural sciences and the humanities that had given structure to German academic culture since the late nineteenth century. Another reason has to do with psychology's strategic societal and cultural location: Weimar-era psychological thought and practice straddled the divide between the articulation of empirically supported world views and the generation of social practices in industrial, labor management and personnel selection.

To the extent that psychological practices achieved societal anchorage in German-speaking culture in the 1920s, they participated in a long-term trend that Lutz Raphael has called the "scientific penetration of the social sphere" (*Verwissenschaftlichung des Sozialen*)—a development that was central to the emergence of a knowledge-based society founded on the increasing employment of scientifically trained experts in the twentieth century.[4] Given the importance of this process, it seems altogether appropriate to include the thinking implicit or embodied in such psychological practices in a historical discussion of Weimar thought. At the very least it must be clear that conventional approaches in intellectual and cultural history that focus on highly abstract statements by academic elites, or on avant-garde movements like psychoanalysis, are insufficient to grasp fully what was actually going on in Weimar-era psychology.

A complete survey of psychological discourse and practices in the Weimar era cannot be presented here. The following discussion focuses on three topics: (1) definitions and institutional locations of Weimar-era psychology; (2) natural scientific and humanistic approaches to psychology in Weimar-era crisis talk; (3) trained intuition, psychological practice, and the cultural grounding of expertise. Unifying the discussions in parts two and three is the centrality of holistic thought—and the effort to establish alternative forms of scientific objectivity and expert practice compatible with holism.

Weimar-Era Psychology: Definitions and Locations

The term "psychology" has multiple meanings in contemporary culture, and this was also the case in the first third of the twentieth century. A partial list of psychologically oriented fields and practices that achieved visibility in the Weimar era might include the following: the medical specialty called psychiatry; medical and non-medical psychotherapy, including psychoanalysis; academic psychology, both natural scientific and philosophical; and the many writings ostensibly dedicated to psychological topics like sexuality and male-female relationships or to self-improvement published by journalists, literary people, or visionaries of various stripes. These discursive and practical realms were never fully differentiated, nor did they form a wholly unified field; indeed, their representatives were avidly engaged in ignoring or excluding one another. But in German-speaking Europe, very little of this vast array of theoretical or research approaches—and psycho-babble—was institutionalized in the academic discipline called psychology.[5] Most strongly represented academically, then as now, was psychiatry. Psychoanalysis in this period completed its breakthrough into the cultural avant-garde that had begun before 1914, but psychoanalytic research and practice took place in settings entirely separate from those in which other kinds of psychological thinking and practice were propagated.

For this reason, the following remarks break with conventional approaches by not referring to psychoanalysis at all, and mention psychiatry only briefly, where developments in that field were taken up in psychological thought outside psychiatry. The focus here will be on the approaches to general psychology represented by members of the discipline called by that name, as well as explicitly psychological writings of some philosophers. In the latter case the treatment is necessarily selective; thus, there will be no discussion of phenomenological psychology. Cultural uses of psychological categories and interpretive frameworks, e.g., in the study of art or music, by writers who were not psychologists, must also be excluded for reasons of space.[6]

Given this demarcation of the topic, a brief remark on the institutional status of the discipline called psychology is needed. In German-speaking countries, psychology, in particular experimental psychology, had already acquired many of the accoutrements of discipline formation, such as independent scientific journals, by 1900; a "Society for Experimental Psychology" was founded in 1904. Nonetheless, in the German-speaking universities of the Weimar era, psychology did not yet have the status of an autonomous discipline with its own professorships. Insofar as it was institutionalized at all, academic psychology was still

treated as a subfield of philosophy.[7] Its leading representatives generally held chairs of philosophy, for philosophy and psychology, or even philosophy, psychology, and education (*Pädagogik*), and led research laboratories called psychological institutes or seminars that were linked to these chairs. This dual or hybrid institutional identity based on institutionalization within philosophy had developed logically within the German university system. An examination in psychology had been part of the state examination in philosophy required of secondary school teachers since the nineteenth century.[8] Since the middle of the nineteenth century the content and methods of the discipline had become increasingly natural scientific, but whether psychology should be a natural or a human science (*Geisteswissenschaft*) was a hotly disputed issue in the late nineteenth century and in the Weimar era as well.

The institutional status of the discipline had a direct impact on its content, including the topics addressed and the methods employed to study them. Experimental psychology had emerged in the nineteenth century as a bold attempt to re-establish philosophy, especially the theory of knowledge, on an empirical basis. The subject had therefore been defined from the start as the study of the normal, adult, conscious mind focusing mainly, though not entirely, on sensation, perception, and cognition. In the 1920s the leading representatives of psychology continued to regard their field as an empirical science and a foundational discipline for the human sciences, whether or not they remained as committed to natural scientific methods as their predecessors had been. But this does not mean that they engaged only in abstract speculation. Alongside empirical research in fields such as perception and cognition, advocates of child and youth psychology like William Stern and Martha Muchow in Hamburg, Wilhelm Peters in Jena and Charlotte Bühler in Vienna placed their work in the service of school reform and other social projects in the 1920s. In this way they helped to give Weimar and Vienna modernity a technocratic aspect. To realize this project Peters and Stern used quantitative and statistical studies of individual differences, while in Vienna Charlotte Bühler and her (mainly female) collaborators tried to establish empirical norms for psychical development on the basis of so called "infant tests" (*Kleinkindertests*) based on systematic observation of behavior, but also including humanistic methods such as the comparative interpretation of diary entries.[9]

The predominance of the laboratory experiment as the privileged path to scientific psychological knowledge remained in place in the Weimar era. However, at the eleventh congress of the "Society for Experimental Psychology" in Vienna in 1929, psychologists showed that they had begun to move with the times. In that year the name of the society was changed to "German Psychological Society" (*Deutsche Gesellschaft für Psychologie*). In a statement justifying this move published as a preface to the congress proceedings, the Society's board explicitly stated that the field had begun to loosen its all too "rigid" fixation on natural scientific methods.[10] The change was not immediately or universally accepted. Proponents of psychology as a natural science considered leaving the Society, and a new professional society for practical psychologists was founded in 1930 under the leadership of professors Walter Moede (Technical Academy Charlottenburg), Walther Poppelreuter (University of Bonn), Narziß Ach (University of Göttingen), the head of the psychological department of the Reichswehr, Johann Baptist Rieffert, and others. The organization failed, but the effort revealed the tensions pulling the discipline apart in an era of social and cultural fragmentation.[11]

To summarize: Weimar psychology was a hybrid entity in three respects. The discipline was torn between science and philosophy, divided between natural science and humanistic approaches, and divided again between commitments to basic science for its own sake and to bringing science into the social sphere. In other words, Weimar psychology reflected the tensions and ambivalences of modern scientific culture, as the discipline continues to do to this day.

In this context, two trends of the period stand out: the many and varied revivals and new formulations of holistic thought in psychology; and equally varied efforts to give psychological expertise an intellectual foundation consistent with German cultural assumptions as articulated at the time. Each of these trends will be considered in turn in the following two parts.

Psychology in Weimar-Era Crisis Talk

In German-speaking Europe, both the "crisis of psychology" announced by Vienna professor Karl Bühler in 1926[12] and ideological battles over holism in psychology reflected the hothouse atmosphere of the interwar years.[13] When Bühler claimed that psychology was in crisis, he did not refer to the cultural crisis pervasively diagnosed at that time, but rather to the apparent inability of psychologists to agree on the subject matter, methods, and goals of their young science. The roots of this crisis reached back to the turn of the twentieth century and even earlier; in 1900 William Stern had written that there were "many psychologies, but no one new psychology."[14] The controversy returned to public attention in the early 1920s, as a number of books appeared with titles such as "The Unique Characteristic of the Mental" (*Die Eigenart des Geistigen*).[15] Common to these critiques was the demand for a psychology that included the peculiar German entity called *Seele*, rather than the "positivistic" psychology supposedly lacking "soul." The broader context for such assertions was clearly the reassertion of German cultural traditions in the face of defeat in the First World War; seen in this light, Weimar-era psychological debates directly reflected the identity politics of the educated middle classes.

Both to articulate and to respond to this challenge, psychologists, philosophers, and others made increasing use of terms such as "wholeness" (*Ganzheit*), "Gestalt," "immediate experience" (*Erlebnis*), "organic" thought, or intrinsic "meaning" (*Sinn*)—terms which, for critics of natural scientific psychology, signaled a persistant allegiance to humanism. Because the language of holism was a key theme in the identity crisis of German *Bildungsbürger*, their writings have often been taken to be signs of anti-modernist sentiment. However, most of the leading academic psychologists in this period organized their discourse around the same key words, even though they had been trained as natural scientists and would thus be classified as "modernists" in conventional dualistic interpretations. They, like their philosophical critics, were members of the *Bildungsbürgertum*, and they fully shared the wish for renewed, secure identity that Peter Gay once described as a "hunger for wholeness."[16]

In German-speaking psychology there were many efforts to still that hunger, and also to show that the goal was not the "materialization of mind," as the critics had claimed.[17] The most widely received view internationally was that of the so called "Berlin school" of Gestalt psychology. Actually developed in Frankfurt before 1914 by Max Wertheimer, Wolfgang Köhler, and Kurt Koffka, Gestalt theory was an attempt to give concepts like "wholeness" (*Ganzheit*), Gestalt and intrinsic meaningfulness (*Sinn*) natural scientific content. In the 1920s, the intellectual epicenter of the group shifted to Berlin, after Wertheimer transferred there during the First World War and Köhler was appointed professor of philosophy and director of the psychological institute in 1922; hence the term "Berlin school." The Gestalt theorists claimed, among other things, that immediately perceived wholes (*Gestalten*) and relationships rather than punctiform, atomistic sensations were the fundamental units of conscious experience. As Max Wertheimer formulated it, the goal was to show that natural scientific methods of studying conscious experience need not lead inevitably to an atomizing "cutting up" (*Zerstückelung*) of consciousness. Wertheimer vehemently opposed the view that consciousness could be grasped "piecewise" (*Stückhaft*) or that it emerged from merely accidental associative connections of sense data, which he eloquently termed "and-sums" (*Und-Summen*) or "and-connections" (*Und-Verbindungen*). Instead, he proposed that psychologists begin with the phenomenally given, "natural" units and relations present in human experience, develop explanations for their appearance in consciousness as structured wholes or systems of relations, and construct a natural scientific world view on this foundation.[18] The Gestalt psychologists did not claim only that so-called "Gestalt qualities" could be found in immediate experience alongside other sensory qualities. Rather, and more radically, they asserted that Gestalten—meaning both perceived wholes and the structured relationships among them—were immanent qualities of conscious experience itself. This meant that immediate experience in itself is self-organizing, and that the quality of wholeness is present *in the phenomena themselves*, not imposed upon essentially meaningless "sensory qualities" by a consciousness that somehow lay behind and operated upon sensations.[19]

Going still further, Wertheimer, Köhler, and Koffka claimed that dynamic self-organizing principles were at work in human and animal perception and behavior, in the development of higher organisms and even in the physical world. In studies with animals carried out on the island of Tenerife during the First World War, for example, Köhler demonstrated that various species of animals, including chickens, can perceive relationships (e.g., that one shade is darker than another) and that anthropoid apes are capable of employing immediate "insight" in intelligent problem solving (e.g., by discovering with their eyes, so to speak, that an object such as a stick on the ground could be used to pull in a banana located too far away to reach with their hands).[20] In his monograph on "physical Gestalten," published in 1920 and reissued in 1924, Köhler argued that even non-living nature could have Gestalt characteristics.[21] The distribution of current on a conductor, for example, becomes chaotic if current flow is disturbed, but re-establishes itself spontaneously when current flow is restored. Going still further, Köhler suggested that such figurative flow patterns might be present in the optical sector of the human brain, and proposed that such patterns could be the physical basis for the perception of form and relations. With their rejection of what they termed "atomism" and "elementistic" thinking and their attempt to prove the existence of self-organizing processes in both the mental and the physical worlds, the Gestalt theorists attempted to combine holism and natural science, and thus to overcome the gap between the humanities and the natural sciences by establishing a new, unified science of structural and Gestalt principles.

To readers today this may sound like a reversion to German Romanticism, but the ideas of the "Berlin school" were quickly translated into solid laboratory research and were recognized internationally as innovative. One interesting example of this work was Karl Duncker's Berlin dissertation on what he called "induced motion" - what happens when we sit in a train, see another train moving, and then have the impression that the train we are sitting in, too, is moving, or when we watch automobile or bicycle wheels move and see, not the rotary motion of the wheels *or* the forward motion of the vehicle, but both kinds of motion at once, though we often also have the impression that the wheel is rolling backward. To explain such phenomena, he made use of the concept of "frame of reference" (*Bezugsystem*), taken from Einstein's special theory of relativity. The issue in this study thus became not so much why people have illusions of motion, but how they act as participants engaged in perceptual situations and use particular portions of the phenomenal field as reference points to orient their gaze.[22] The Gestalt theorists also acted on their commitment to combine philosophy and natural science by participating actively in discussions of the Berlin "Society for Scientific Philosophy" organized by Hans Reichenbach and publishing in the journal *Erkenntnis*, the organ of logical empiricist, "scientific" philosophy.[23]

Decades ago Fritz Ringer termed the Gestalt psychologists modernizers because theirs was one of many attempts in the Weimar era to overcome traditionally accepted dualisms and work out what contemporaries called a "third way" between positivism and idealism.[24] Seen in the context of the present discussion, Wertheimer and his colleagues attempted to rework in modern form traditional discursive elements usually thought to be signs of anti-modernity. The academic enemies of the Weimar Republic frequently employed, for example, the topos of the Beethoven symphony in support of their evocations of holism, an "organic" view of society and the state, and against democracy and individualism. In opposition to such tendencies, Wertheimer employed the same topos at the end of a public lecture in 1924 by arguing that the voluntary cooperation of free individuals in the work place as well as in politics is more natural than authoritarian structures. Asking his listeners to imagine a plateau, on which musicians are seated and playing, Wertheimer suggested there were in principle three possibilities: each could play anything in particular, creating accidental effects; or whenever someone played a "c," another would play "f" a certain number of seconds later, thus creating a structure, but one with no intrinsic meaning; or we could imagine the musicians playing a Beethoven symphony, which would give us the possibility of grasping the principle of the whole from any given part of that whole.[25] Interestingly enough, Wertheimer mentions no conductor in this passage, instead leaving the impression that the players achieved harmony among themselves. Wertheimer clearly opposed the predominant technocratic view of natural knowledge as the domination of nature, without automatically subscribing to an authoritarian alternative. Given views like these, it is not surprising that many, though not all, of the Gestalt psychologists located themselves to the left of center politically.

Nearly all participants in these debates agreed on the central importance of key words like *Ganzheit* and *Gestalt*, but the actual content of these terms differed across the political spectrum. Hamburg professor William Stern's "personalism" doctrine focused on the individual as a "psychophysical whole" in a manner congruent with liberal individualism: "As much as the person is co-determined by all the transpersonal fields to which he belongs," Stern observed, "he does not derive his individual wholeness from them, but asserts in opposition to them something autonomous, and enriches their influences by incorporating them into his own being."[26] In contrast, Felix Krueger, Wilhelm Wundt's successor as professor in Leipzig and head of the so-called Leipzig school of "holistic psychology" (*Ganzheitspsychologie*), emphasized the role of feeling and will in the constitution of experience, to which he added the dimension of time, in order to build a bridge to historically developed "cultural wholes."[27] As he claimed, the Gestalt theorists ignored the dimension of feeling in favour of an "objectification" of consciousness; yet emotion is prior to cognition in human development, and it is feeling that gives "depth" to experienced totality. He and his associate Friedrich Sander criticized Gestalt theory for ignoring the emergence, or "microgenesis" of Gestalten in perception, studies of which allegedly revealed so-called "pre-Gestalt" phenomena that indicated the impact of feelings alongside that of cognitive processes.[28] Krueger made his Neo-Romantic, culturally conservative political agenda clear when he recommended reading romantic German nationalists such as Friedrich Ludwig Jahn, Ernst Moritz Arndt, and Wilhelm Riehl: "These deep thinkers, because they were also whole men and understood their *Volk*, knew about the growth laws of true community and the core structure of the soul."[29]

Such controversies were inseparable from the parlous situation of psychology as a discipline in Germany, described above in part one. The challenge of advocates of a humanistic (*geiteswissenschaftliche*) psychology strengthened the hand of culturally conservative holists and raised the pressure to develop modern research instruments congruent with German cultural traditions.[30]

Important for this discussion is that advocates of a humanistic (*geisteswis-senschaftliche*) psychology also tried to structure their positions as scientific, albeit not natural scientific arguments. For example, in his *Psychology of World Views*, first published in 1919, psychiatrist and philosopher Karl Jaspers distinguished between active, contemplative, mystical, and „enthusiastic" attitudes toward the world (*Welteinstellungen*), and between sensory-spatial, spiritual-cultural (*seelisch-kulturellen*), and metaphysical world pictures (*Weltbildern*).[31] All of these entities he understood to be ideal types, in the manner of his close friend and former Heidelberg colleague Max Weber. Thus, no single such entity or combination of entities need be present in pure form in any single person— description or classification depended on the relative dominance of any type in a given individual.

The most prominent position of this kind in the Weimar era was that of the Berlin philosopher and educationist Eduard Spranger. Though little known today, Spranger was astoundingly popular and influential in his time. His books routinely went into multiple editions, and in his correspondence he reported that over 1,000 people attended his lectures, which had to be held in the university's largest auditorium. It was Spranger who created the term "humanistic psychology" (*geisteswissenschaftliche Psychologie*).[32] He saw himself in this and in other respects as the intellectual successor to Wilhelm Dilthey, the grey eminence of Berlin philosophy in the Wilhelmian period. His approach was typological, like Jaspers's, but his was a system of personality rather than world view types. Spranger's theory of personality (or "character" as he and his contemporaries called it) was based on a system of six types—theoretical, economic, aesthetic, social, religious, and power—to each of which he linked specific "forms of life" (*Lebensformen*). Dilthey had emphasized the historical development of personality over time, and Spranger's approach also had a historical dimension; in his view, some of these "life forms" were more dominant in certain historical periods than in others. His use of ideal types was not so schematic and stereotypical as it might appear. Individuals could be mixtures of types, with one being dominant over the others. Important to Spranger was the centrality of such "mental totalities" (*geistige Totalstrukturen*), rather than the "primitive perceptual and behavioral structures" studied by the experimental psychologists.[33] As early as 1894, Dilthey had argued that only a psychology capable of grasping persons in their entirety and in historical context would be useful to philosophers, historians, and political theorists.[34] Spranger argued that only on the basis of such a system of "totalities" could a pedagogical theory be developed that would enable German youth to return to the idealistic world view of their forefathers.

The common foundation of these and other attempts to construct a "humanistic" psychology in the Weimar period was the claim that immediate intuitive insight was superior to the supposedly mechanical application of experimental methods, because it allowed its users to penetrate to the depths and see through to the essential core of (mental) reality, whereas the natural scientists remained on the merely empirical surface of things. In contrast to the allegedly deterministic and causal thinking of the experimentalists, Jaspers, for example, emphasized that the truth content of his typology of world views could only be assessed by its "intuitive self-evidence" (*Evidenz*). He meant by this neither rational argument, historical documentation, nor the careful, rule-governed interpretation of texts, but conceptual clarity and above all the ability of his readers to grasp his meaning immediately and intuitively.[35] This emphasis on the immediacy of intuition connected approaches like that of Jaspers or Spranger with other, explicitly racist typological schemas which also came out of the humanities, even though neither Jaspers nor the "race psychologists" of his time wished to have anything to do with one another.

Ludwig Ferdinand Clauß, the creator of what he called a "racial soul doctrine" (*Rassenseelenlehre*), explicitly presented his approach as *geisteswissenschaftlich*. A student of Freiburg professor Edmund Husserl, the founder of phenomenological philosophy, Clauß called his method "phenomenological" in the 1920s and claimed to strive for an "essential gaze" (*Wesenschau*)—that is, an immediate, intuitive view capable of grasping the essential nature of a given "racial soul."[36] What may seem mystical to readers today was for Clauß a method analogous to that employed by art historians, who may still imagine that they can read off the characteristic style of an epoch directly from its works of art or architecture (as in: "these are characteristic features of Gothic style"). In a similar manner, Clauß asserted, it is possible to read off or directly see the "essence" of "Nordic," "desert people" (*wüstenmenschlichen*) or "pure semitic" (*ursemitischen*) styles from gazes or body postures as displayed in photographs. To make this claim, Clauß had merely to translate the category of "truth to style" (*Stilechtheit*) then commonly in use in art history and the history of literature into "truth to the race" (*Artgemäßheit*). His approach aimed from the beginning toward the clearest possible distinction of the characteristic "physiognomy" of his own (supposedly Nordic) people from those of others, but the construction of distinction was dual: the Nordic type differed essentially from the "desert people," but both of these were to be distinguished from the Jews, which he conceived to be an essentially mixed type (or, as the Nazis would later say, "mongrelized"). However, Clauß emphasized that although he was speaking of essential differences, these were not to be interpreted as differences in the value or worth of racial groupings.[37]

Clauß's books appeared in multiple editions in the Weimar period, but the "racial studies" (*Rassenkunde*) of Hans F. K. Günther circulated far more widely.[38] Günther claimed to identify and systematically classify different sub-groups of the German people, which he gave grandiloquent sounding, actually banal geographical names like "Nordic," "eastern" (*ostisch*), or "western" (*westisch*), with the aid of certain typological features allegedly characteristic of each. Günther had been trained as a German teacher and not as a physical anthropologist or psychologist, but the psychological dimension of his "method" is hard to miss. Here, too, a kind of trained intuition is being advocated; as in the work of Clauß, Günther employed photographs to demonstrate the defining, essential expressive physical features in question, which were supposed to be recognizable intuitively. Though it may seem easy in retrospect to dismiss all this as pseudoscience, recent work on the history of scientific objectivity suggests that intuitive expert judgments of this kind were widely used and accepted as legitimate procedure in the natural as well as the human sciences in this period.[39]

Toward the end of the Weimar period, in 1932, Gerhard Pfahler, then professor of education and psychology in Tübingen, published a book entitled "Heredity as Destiny," in which he developed what he called a "hereditary characterology" (*Erbcharakterologie*) that combined basic categories and standard methods of experimental psychology with an interpretive framework that exhibited some affinities to Günther's racial studies.[40] On the basis of quantitative measurements of subjects' more directly focused or diffuse attention span, Pfahler assigned people to character types in a manner analogous to the way race anthropologists—and Günther—assigned people to racial types on the basis of cephalic indices measuring long or broad skulls. In the year this book appeared, Pfahler became one of only two full professors in psychology who joined the Nazi party before 1933.

As early as 1931, Günther himself was appointed professor of "social anthropology" at the University of Jena, through the intervention of the National Socialist Wilhelm Frick, then Minister of Culture in Thuringia. There he joined the psychologist Wilhelm Peters (mentioned above), a pioneer of intelligence testing and differential psychology in Germany, who had been professor since 1923 and had headed the psychological laboratory since its founding in 1925. Peters's chair was located in the Faculty of Mathematics and Natural Sciences, while Günther's was located in the Philosophical (Humanities) Faculty. Although the presence of representatives of such fundamentally different approaches alongside one another in the same university lasted only two years, the fact is symbolic of the hybrid situation of psychological thought in the Weimar era.

Trained Intuition and Technocratic Expertise

As stated in the introduction, psychological practices, to the extent that they achieved societal anchorage in the 1920s, participated in what Lutz Raphael has termed the "scientific penetration of the social sphere" (*Verwissenchaftlichung des Sozialen*). In order to grasp the processes at work in such settings, it is necessary to focus on centers of practical activity outside the university, as well as the active involvement of academic psychologists in such locations. Calling work done in such settings "applied science" distorts, and may sometimes reverse the processes involved. Indeed, there was often as yet no scientific knowledge available to be "applied" in such contexts. Rather than being sites of knowledge transfered from academic laboratories to social or economic settings, such centers of practical activity often became locations for the generation of new science in response to societal demand. It is therefore appropriate to speak of psychology in contexts of application or use, rather than of applied psychology.[41]

Recent literature has expanded our knowledge of psychological thought and practice in industry and in labor administration in Weimar Germany.[42] In this section the focus will be on three different sites for (and styles of) practical thinking in the Weimar era: industrial "psychotechnics" and the psychology of work; employee assessment in office work settings; and officer selection in the military. In the first setting, technologies of labor optimization drawn from psychophysics and experimental psychology were challenged by the modernistic, holistic alternative presented by Berlin psychologist Kurt Lewin. In employee selection and military psychology, in contrast, approaches employing trained intuition and systematic typology began to take hold in the later Weimar years. Thus, in the practical sphere as well as in intellectual discourse natural scientific and humanistic styles of psychological thinking and practice lived uneasily alongside, and often in competition with one another.

The term "psychotechnics," invented by Hugo Münsterberg in 1912, refers to methods developed from the turn of the twentieth century onward to optimize the productivity of individuals and factory units in industry and elsewhere by paying more attention to the "human factor," either by choosing workers according to their suitability for a given task, or by restructuring the production site itself.[43] In so called "industrial psychotechnics," the aim was to derive objective norms for intentional action—such as the handling of machine tools or railway switches—and to use these as standards for the testing of workers in factories, post offices, railroad yards, and the like. The technocratic, utopian aim as well as the selectionistic practices involved are nicely expressed in the often-used phrase, "the right man in the right job"—a phrase designed to align these practices with Weimar-era strategies for rationalizing production.[44] After its successful debut during the First World War in the selection of drivers, aircraft observers, and the like, "psychotechnics" enjoyed a second high point in the mid-1920s. Its techniques were actually used and constantly refined, most extensively in the Psychotechnical Laboratory of the Reichsbahn and in the Reichspost, but also in the selection and psychological conditioning of athletes and sports trainers.[45]

It is important to note that the majority of participants in this activity were engineers, not psychologists. Training programs for them were developed by Walter Moede and Fritz Giese, who worked at technical academies (*Technische Hochschulen*) in Berlin-Charlottenburg and Stuttgart, respectively, rather than at universities. Associated research in the field of "labor science" (*Arbeitswissenschaft*) was carried out by Georg Schlesinger at the Technical Academy in Berlin-Charlottenburg.[46] Fritz Giese in particular explicitly characterized "psychotechnics" as a form of social engineering.[47] Seen from the perspective of social and cultural history, such uses of psychological knowledge in practical contexts belong to the history of what British historian Harold Perkin has called the expert society.[48] Nikolas Rose suggests that such work contributed not only to the formation of psychological thought, but also to the construction of the rationalized and reliable "selves" who were the objects of such thinking.[49] However, even before the German economy slipped into crisis in the late 1920s, managers expressed disappointment about the lack of actual proof of productivity gains, and protests against psychotechnics also grew within the labor movement, which had previously endorsed rationalization. Even before the Depression there was much talk of a "crisis of psychotechnics."[50]

An important component of the intellectual style of "psychotechnics" is the concept of psychical work or labor. Soon after scientists and engineers applied the idea of energy conservation to human labor in order to create a science of work intended to make the "human motor" run more efficiently, Emil Kraepelin and others extended the effort to "mental work"; the Münster psychologist Ernst Meumann developed the idea further.[51] Such approaches were challenged during the Weimar period in the writings of Max Wertheimer's and Wolfgang Köhler's younger Berlin colleague Kurt Lewin, who worked in the Department of Applied Psychology of the Berlin Psychological Institute. Lewin is often described as an adherent of Gestalt psychology, and he expressed clear affinity to the "Berlin school" in his writings in the mid-1920s. In central respects, however, his approach differed from that of the Gestalt theorists. His work was directed from the beginning toward a new theoretical foundation of psychology that would make possible a productive connection of science and practice, in particular a humanization of the labor process. By recreating real life situations in the laboratory and studying their general structure and dynamics, he hoped to refute the most common criticism of humanists against natural scientific psychology, the claim that its methods were far removed from actual human existence.

This program also served a practical goal, which he articulated as early as 1920 in an essay entitled "The Socialization of Taylorism."[52] The essay appeared shortly after the abortive German revolution in a monograph series published by the independent Marxist theoretician Karl Korsch—an acquaintance of Lewin's from the socialist youth movement. Here Lewin argued that a thorough collaborative study of the psychodynamics of the labor process by psychologists, managers and workers could make possible both the rationalization and humanization of industrial work. He and his Berlin students tried to carry out this program in the 1920s in a series of studies on topics such as the "satiation effects" of repetitive tasks, the retention of completed and uncompleted tasks, and the effects of success and failure on the motivational level of children and adults.[53] Lewin thus belonged to the socialistically oriented scholars of the Weimar era, for whom rationalization and the technologization of labor were causes for hope rather than worry. Without undue exaggeration one could say that he thought that he could give rationalization a human face.

The debate among advocates of natural scientific and "humanistic" (geisteswissenschaftliche) psychology (described in Part Two above) was by no means merely theoretical or ideological in nature. Despite their polemics against overspecialization in scholarship, many advocates of "humanistic" psychology in the 1920s had no difficulty with the idea of participating in the emerging expert society. Indeed, they claimed that their approaches were superior to those of the experimentalists not only because they assured a closer connection between psychology and philosophy, but also because they could provide real benefits to pedagogy and even for purely practical activities such as personnel selection.[54] From this perspective "humanistic" theories of "character" (Charakter) (i.e., personality) could be and often were understood as alternatives to "psychotechnical" diagnostics. As we have seen, Eduard Spranger's typological concepts were addressed at least implicitly to elite secondary school (*Gymnasium*) teachers. Others introduced explicitly hermeneutical styles of interpretation into the personnel selection of office workers, the "new employees" of the Weimar era. The key words in this field were "expression analysis" (*Ausdruckskunde*) and "physiognomics."

One of the best known advocates of such approaches was the anti-academic and extremely popular philosopher Ludwig Klages. Klages is known to intellectual historians as the author of a two-volume book entitled "The Mind as Adversary of the Soul" (*Der Geist als Widersacher der Seele*) and described as an anti-Semitic irrationalist and leading anti-modernist.[55] More important in this context are Klages's earlier writings on the psychology of handwriting and other forms of expression, which first established his reputation and popularity. Klages claimed that handwriting styles expressed basic personality characteristics. With the aid of handwriting analysis he sought to establish a style of personality diagnostics based on the recognition of unconscious expressions of a person's inner being. Klages vehemently argued that this approach was equal or superior to the technocratic style of "psychotechnics." As a sustainable alternative to the allegedly mechanical approach of "school (meaning: academic) psychology" and psychotechnics Klages offered trained intuition, which he claimed was suited to reveal "the consistent characteristic (*Eigenart*) beneath the ever changing actions of people, the true motives behind their masks of politeness."[56] Thus, Klages advocated an alternative professionalization of the psychologist's gaze. Indeed, handwriting analysts trained by Klages and others were actually employed either as consultants or even full time in numerous German personnel departments; and long after 1945 handwriting samples were required of job applicants for middle and upper-level employee positions in West Germany. Even so, their program was ridiculed and the validity of their approach disputed in the 1920s. As the cultural critic Siegfried Kracauer observed: "The graphologist who is entrusted with such expertise penetrates the employees' souls like a government spy in enemy territory."[57]

In this context other, more seriously considered approaches to a typological theory of personality developed by physicians were well received among psychologists. The most influential such effort was the so called "constitutional typology" (*Konstitutionstypologie*) of the Tübingen psychiatrist Ernst Kretschmer.[58] Kretschmer postulated three basic "constitutional" types of body shape: the leptosome (lean physique, more endurance than strength); athletic (broad shoulders, narrow hips, powerful muscles), and pyknic (distended belly, more fat than muscle, though not necessarily weak). Though he linked these types with different types of psychical illness, he emphasized that the body types were not in themselves pathological. All three types were in his view fully normal, and none was inferior or superior, healthier or sicker. He therefore avoided using terminology that could be interpreted as evaluative or racist.

Important in this context is a methodological point. Kretschmer's types were ideal types in the sense that they were not results of statistically derived frequency distributions of particular characteristics or bodily features. Although his types were based on measurements taken from the bodily features of psychically ill people, in Kretschmer's view such measurements alone were not sufficient to determine constitutional types. More important was the "artistic gaze" of the physician: "Everything depends on the entirely artistic, secure training of the eye. A schoolboy-like recording of single measurements without any idea or intuition of the complete form (*Gesamtaufbau*) will help us not at all. The measuring tape sees nothing. Using it will in and of itself never lead to the establishment of biological–type images (*Typenbilder*), which is our aim."[59] Empirical measurements could at best confirm what the holistic perception of the body had already grasped intuitively.

Here, too, as in the case of general psychology, the central point is the reliance on the "immediately given," a supposedly unmediated, intuitive gaze yielding holistic results. Thus, both the boundary between natural scientific and "humanistic" (*geisteswissenschaftliche*) methods and the line between expert knowledge and everyday psychology became blurred. Using the bridge of trained intuition and reliance on the "immediately given," the scientist's gaze approached that of the everyday person whom the scientists had originally thought to have been their object of study. In the process, the approach called "physiognomics"—the attempt to read off basic aspects of a person's character from facial expressions—acquired increased legitimacy in the 1920s, though it had been sneered at in respectable scientific and scholarly circles and left to soft-headed romantic outsiders before 1914.[60] However, as the example of Kretschmer shows, in this period attempts to decode both bodies and human personalities with such holistic tools did not necessarily lead to the sort of racist stigmatization indulged in by Clauß, Günther, and their associates.

Philipp Lersch, then a researcher in the psychological department of the Reichswehr, took yet another tack. Based on his practical work in officer selection, he developed a style of personality diagnostics in the early 1930s in which trained intuition ceased to be a radical alternative to "school (academic) psychology," (*Schulpsychologie*) as it had been for Klages, but became instead the methodological foundation for science based professional training.[61] Lersch carefully analysed the anatomical basis of expressive movements in the human face, for example, in order to observe and classify them more closely with the help of film clips. Bodily movements and expression formed for him a psychophysical, in his words "body-soul" (*körperseelische*) unity. Sometimes apparently evaluative descriptions such as "primitive" occur in Lersch's descriptions of facial expressions, and even in his descriptions of the people with such expressions. Nonetheless, he did not take the step to race theory, but remained within the framework of a general, though typological, personality and expression theory. It was on the basis of the use of this approach to personality diagnostics in officer selection for the Wehrmacht (and not Günther's racial studies, Clauß's "racial soul theory" or "psychotechnics") that German psychology would later achieve professional status under Nazism.[62]

Conclusion

The variety of approaches to psychological thought in Weimar culture could only be hinted at briefly here. Perhaps enough has been said to make clear that technoscientific aproaches like "psychotechnics" and holistic approaches to mind persisted alongside one another, and that both styles of thinking could be and actually were employed in psychological practice, although the golden years of "psychotechnics" were clearly limited to Weimar's "middle" period, like the brief moment of "new objectivity" (*Neue Sachlichkeit*) in the arts. In some approaches there was no separation between the normal and the pathological, or of the mental from the physical. In other cases, such as that of "race psychology," but also in less controversial approaches, world view and personality diagnostics were founded on just such distinctions, with decided preference for trained intuition as the preferred path to knowledge. Despite this wide variety of approaches, two trends stand out: the emphasis on the "immediately given" as a kind of anchor in a culturally insecure time, and the mobilization of the physiognomic gaze as an instrument of psychological expertise.

In their struggle with modernity, Weimar-era psychologists followed, in essence, two strategies: participating in the widespread revival of holistic thought—albeit from different philosophical and political standpoints—and taking active part in the rationalization of society. Both approaches were shot through with ambivalences, the first due to the ambiguities and complexities of holistic discourse itself, the second due to the inevitable culture clash between trained intuition as an alternative to allegedly mechanistic causal thinking and the demands of technocratic expertise.

Nonetheless, the tools of natural scientific psychology hardly disappeared from the "science of the soul." Textbooks of research method in psychology that emphasized hard science went through multiple editions in the late 1920s and early 1930s, at the very same time that Clauß' "racial soul doctrine" enjoyed similar popularity.[63] The challenge posed by scientific psychology's "humanistic" critics did not acquire cultural predominance in Germany until the Nazi period, and this was due less to ideological recastings of earlier approaches to suit the new regime—though there was plenty of that—than to the successful amalgamation of holistic "characterological" (that is, personality) theory and diagnostics with the demands of particular kinds of expertise, especially officer selection in the German military.[64]

Notes

1. Dorothy Ross, ed., *Modernist Impulses in the Human Sciences* (Baltimore: Johns Hopkins University Press, 1994); Mark S. Micale, ed., *The Mind of Modernism: Medicine, Psychology and the Cultural Arts in Europe and America, 1880–1940* (Stanford: Stanford University Press, 2004). Unfortunately, "psychology" in the later work is equated with psychoanalysis.

2. On holism's political affinities in Weimar medicine, see Anne Harrington, "Kurt Goldstein, Neurology of Healing and Wholeness: A Weimar Story" (25–45), and Cay-Rüdiger Prüll, "Holism and German Pathology (1914–1933)" (46–67), both in Christopher Lawrence and George Weisz, eds., *Greater than the Parts: Holism in Biomedicine, 1920–1950* (Oxford: Oxford University Press, 1998). See also the literature cited in Part Two.

3. See, e.g., Michael Neufeld, "Weimar Culture and Futuristic Technology: The Rocketry and Spaceflight Fad in Germany, 1923–1933," *Technology and Culture*, 31 (1990), 725–52; Peter S. Fischer, *Fantasy and Politics: Visions of the Future in the Weimar Republic* (Madison: University of Wisconsin Press, 1991); Herbert Mehrtens, *Moderne Sprache Mathematik* (Frankfurt am Main: Suhrkamp, 1990); Wolfgang Bialas and Georg Iggers, eds., *Intellektuelle in der Weimarer Republik* (Frankfurt a.M.: Lang Verlag, 1996); Sybilla Nikolow and Arne Schirrmacher, eds., *Wissenschaft und Öffentlichkeit als Ressourcen für einander. Studien zur Wissenschaftsgeschichte im 20. Jahrhundert* (Frankfurt a.M.: Campus Verlag, 2007); and the chapter by Cathryn Carson in this volume. Much of this work has yet to attract the attention of intellectual and cultural historians.

4. Lutz Raphael, "Die Verwissenschaftlichung des Sozialen als methodologische und konzeptionelle Herausforderung für eine Sozialgeschichte des 20. Jahrhunderts," *Geschichte und Gesellschaft*, 20 (1996), 165–93. On the role of experts, see Harold Perkin, *The Third Revolution: Professional Elites in the Modern World* (London: Routledge, 1996); on the emergence of a "knowledge society" in twentieth-century Germany, see Margit Szöllösi-Janze, "Wissensgesellschaft in Deutschland. Überlegungen zur Neubestimmung der deutschen Zeitgeschichte über Verwissenschaftlichungsprozesse," *Geschichte und Gesellschaft*, 30 (2004), 277–313.

5. For this distinction see Horst Gundlach, "Reine Psychologie, Angewandte Psychologie und die Institutionalisierung der Psychologie," *Zeitschrift für Psychologie*, 212 (2004), 183–99.

6. For contemporary discussions of these subjects, see, e.g., the relevant chapters in Emil Saupe, ed., *Einführung in die neuere Psychologie* (Osterwieck: A. W. Zickfeldt, 1928).

7. For more extensive discussions see Mitchell G. Ash, "Psychology in Twentieth-Century Germany: Science and Profession," in *German Professions, 1800–1950*, eds. Geoffrey Cocks and Konrad H. Jarausch (New York: Oxford University Press, 1990), 289–307; idem, "Psychologie in Deutschland um 1900: Reflexiver Diskurs des Bildungsbürgertums, Teilgebiet der Philosophie, akademische Disziplin," in *Konkurrenten in der Fakultät. Kulturwissenschaften um 1900*, eds. Christoph König and Eberhard Lämmert (Frankfurt a.M.: Fischer Taschenbuch Verlag, 1999), 78–93. For somewhat different views based in part on different definitions of the term "discipline," see Gary Hatfield, "Wundt and Psychology as Science: Disciplinary transformations," *Perspectives on Science*, 5 (1997), 349–82; Horst Gundlach, "Die Lage der Psychologie um 1900," *Psychologische Rundschau*, 55 (S1) (2004), 2–11.

8. Horst Gundlach, "Reine Psychologie, Angewandte Psychologie und die Institutionalisierung der Psychologie," cit. n. 5.

9. For further discussion see Monika Schubeis, "*Und das psychologische Laboratorium muss der Ausgangspunkt pädagogischer Arbeiten werden!*" *Zur Institutionalisierungsgeschichte der Psychologie 1890–1933* (Frankfurt a.M.: Peter Lang Verlag, 1990); Helmut Moser, "Zur Entwicklung der akademischen Psychologie in Hamburg bis 1945. Eine Kontrast-Skizze als Würdigung des vergessenen Erbes von William Stern," in *Hochschulalltag im "Dritten Reich": Die Hamburger Universität 1933–1945*, eds. Eckart Krause, Ludwig Huber und Holger Fischer (Berlin: D. Reimer, 1991), Teil II, 483–

518; Gerhard Benetka, *Psychologie in Wien. Sozial- und Theoriegeschichte des Wiener Psychologischen Instituts 1922–1938* (Vienna: Wiener Universitätsverlag, 1995); Georg Eckardt, "Der schwere Weg der Institutionalisierung: Wilhelm Peters," in *Psychologie vor Ort—ein Rückblick auf vier Jahrhunderte. Die Entwicklung der Psychologie in Jena vom 16. bis zum 20. Jahrhundert*, ed. Georg Eckardt (Frankfurt a.M.: Peter Lang Verlag, 2003), 337–402. Perhaps it is not entirely coincidental that many of these innovators were of Jewish background. For further discussion see Mitchell G. Ash, "Innovation, Ethnicity, Identity: German-Speaking Jewish Psychologists and Social Scientists in the Interwar Period," *Jahrbuch des Simon Dubnow Instituts*, 3 (2004), 241–68.

10. Kundgebung der Deutschen Gesellschaft für Psychologie, "Über die Pflege der Psychologie an den deutschen Hochschulen," in *Bericht über den XI. Kongress der Deutschen Gesellschaft für Psychologie* (Jena: Fischer, 1929), p. vii.

11. On Ach's role see Rainer Paul, "Psychologie unter den Bedingungen der 'Kulturwende'. Das Psychologische Institut 1933–1945," in *Die Universität Göttingen unter dem Nationalsozialismus*, eds. Heinrich Becker et al. 2nd exp. ed. (Munich: Saur, 1998), 499–522; here: p. 505.

12. Karl Bühler, *Die Krise der Psychologie* (Jena: Fischer, 1927). Expanded version of an article with the same title published in the journal *Kant-Studien* in 1926. For recent literature on the discourse of crisis in psychology during this period, see the special issue on the topic edited by Thomas Sturm in *Studies in History and Philosophy of Biological and Biomedical Sciences*, 43:4 (2012).

13. For a more widely focused discussion of Weimar-era crisis discourse, see Mitchell G. Ash, "Krise der Moderne oder Modernität als Krise? Stimmen aus der Akademie," in *Die Preußische Akademie der Wissenschaften zu Berlin in Krieg und Frieden, in Republik und Diktatur 1914–1945*, Wolfram Fischer, ed. (Berlin: Akademie-Verlag, 2000), 121–42; idem, "Multiple Modernisms? Episodes from the Sciences as Cultures, 1900–1945," in *Jewish Musical Modernism, Old and New*, ed. Philip V. Bohlman (Chicago: University of Chicago Press, 2008), 31–54.

14. William Stern, "Die psychologische Arbeit des 19. Jahrhunderts," *Zeitschrift für Pädagogische Psychologie*, 2 (1900), 329–52 and 413–36; here, p. 414.

15. Theodor Erismann, *Die Eigenart des Geistigen. Induktive und einsichtige Psychologie*, 2nd ed. (Leipzig: Quelle und Meyer, 1924).

16. Peter Gay, *Weimar Culture: The Outsider as Insider* (New York: Harper & Row, 1970), Chap. 4. For the context see Konrad H. Jarausch, "Die Krise des deutschen Bildungsbürgertums im ersten Drittel des 20. Jahrhunderts," in *Bildungsbürgertum im 19. Jahrhundert. Teil IV. Politischer Einfluss und gesellschaftliche Formation*, eds. Werner Conze and Jürgen Kocka (Stuttgart: Klett-Cotta, 1989), 180–205; Wolfgang Bialas, "Intellektuellengeschichtliche Facetten der Weimarer Republik," in *Intellektuelle in der Weimarer Republik*, eds. Wolfgang Bialas and Georg Iggers (Frankfurt a.M.: Lang, 1996), 13–30.

17. See Eckart Scheerer, "Organische Weltanschauung und Ganzheitspsychologie" (15–54), and Ulfried Geuter, "Das Ganze und die Gemeinschaft. Wissenschaftliches und politisches Denken in der Ganzheitspsychologie Felix Kruegers" (55–88), both in *Psychologie im Nationalsozialismus*, ed. Carl-Friedrich Graumann (Berlin: Springer-Verlag, 1985).

18. Max Wertheimer, "Untersuchungen zur Lehre von der Gestalt, I. Prinzipielle Bemerkungen," *Psychologische Forschung*, 1 (1921), 48–55; idem, *Über Gestalttheorie* (Erlangen: Verlag der Philosophischen Akademie, 1925). English: "Gestalt Theory," trans. N. Naird Alison, *Social Research* 11 (1944), 78–99.

19. For extensive discussion see Mitchell G. Ash, "Gestalt Psychology in Weimar Culture," *History of the Human Sciences*, 4 (1991), 395–415; idem, *Gestalt Psychology in German Culture 1890–1967: Holism and the Quest for Objectivity* (New York: Oxford University Press, 1995), esp. Chap. 17; Anne Harrington, *Reenchanted Science: Holism in German Culture from Wilhelm II to Hitler* (Princeton: Princeton University Press, 1996), Chap. 4; and Gary Hatfield, "Koffka, Köhler and the "crisis" in psychology," *Studies in the History and Philosophy of Biological and Biomedical Sciences*, Part C 43(2), 2012, 483–92.

20. Wolfgang Köhler, "Nachweis einfacher Strukturfunktionen beim Schimpansen und beim Haushuhn," *Abhandlungen der königlich Preußischen Akademie der Wissenschaften, physikalisch-mathematische Klasse*, 1918, Nr. 2; Idem, *Intelligenzprüfungen an Menschenaffen*, 3rd ed. (Berlin: Springer Verlag, 1973, first published 1917). For more extensive discussion, see Ash, *Gestalt Psychology*, Chap. 10.

21. Wolfgang Köhler, *Die physischen Gestalten in Ruhe und im stationären Zustand. Eine naturphilosophische Untersuchung* (Repr., Erlangen: Verlag der Philosophischen Akademie, 1924. First published 1920). For more extensive discussion, see Ash, *Gestalt Psychology*, Chap. 11.

22. Karl Duncker, "Über induzierte Bewegung," *Psychologische Forschung*, 12 (1929), 187–92, esp. 188–89. Cf. Kurt Koffka, *Principles of Gestalt Psychology* (New York: Harcourt Brace, 1935), 282 ff.; Ash, *Gestalt Psychology*, 234–35.

23. Mitchell G. Ash, "Gestalttheorie und logischer Empirismus," in *Hans Reichenbach und die Berliner Gruppe*, eds. Lutz Danneberg, Andreas Kamlah and Lothar Schäfer (Braunschweig: Vieweg, 1994), 87–100; Ash, *Gestalt Psychology*, 261, 294. For more detailed discussion see Steffen Kluck, *Gestaltpsychologie und Wiener Kreis. Stationen einer bedeutsamen Beziehung* (Freiburg: Alber, 2008).

24. Fritz K. Ringer, *The Decline of the German Mandarins: The German Academic Community, 1890–1933* (Cambridge, MA: Harvard University Press, 1969), 375–79.

25. Max Wertheimer, *Über Gestalttheorie*, cit. n. 18, 15–16, 23–24; cf. *Gestalt Theory*, also cit. n. 18, 85, 88, 91.

26. William Stern, *Studien zur Personenwissenschaft, I. Teil. Personalistik als Wissenschaft* (Leipzig: Barth, 1930), 18, cit. in Geuter, *Das Ganze und die Gemeinschaft*, p. 65.

27. Felix Krueger, *Über Entwicklungspsychologie* (Jena: Fischer, 1915).

28. Friedrich Sander, "Experimentelle Ergebnisse der Gestaltpsychologie," *Bericht über den 10. Kongress für experimentelle Psychologie* (Jena: Fischer, 1928), 1–88.

29. Felix Krueger, "Der Strukturbegriff in der Psychologie" (1923), repr. in idem, *Zur Philosophie und Psychologie der Ganzheit. Schriften aus den Jahren 1918–1940*, ed. Eugen Heuss (Berlin: Springer, 1953), here: 144. For further discussion of Krueger's folkish conservatism, see Geuter, *Das Ganze und die Gemeinschaft*.

30. It should be mentioned in passing that comparable controversies over the cultural content of research and professional practices took place in other countries as well. See, e.g., Trudy Dehue, *Changing the Rules: Psychology in the Netherlands, 1900–1945* (Cambridge: Cambridge University Press, 1995).

31. Karl Jaspers, *Psychologie der Weltanschauungen*, 3rd ed. (Berlin: Springer-Verlag, 1925. First published 1919). For further discussion of ideal typical theorizing, see David Kettler's chapter in this volume.

32. Eduard Spranger, *Lebensformen. Geisteswissenschaftliche Psychologie und Theorie der Persönlichkeit*, 3rd ed. (Halle: Niemeyer, 1922).

33. Eduard Spranger, "Die Frage nach der Einheit der Psychologie," *Sitzungsberichte der Preußischen Akademie der Wissenschaften*, Philosophisch-historische Klasse, 1926, 172–99.

34. Wilhelm Dilthey, "Ideen über eine beschreibende und zergliedernde Psychologie (1894)," repr. in Dilthey, *Gesammelte Schriften*, Vol. 5, 4th ed. (Göttingen: Vandenhoeck & Ruprecht, 1974), 139–240.

35. Jaspers, *Psychologie der Weltanschauungen*, esp. 159.

36. Ludwig Ferdinand Clauß, *Rasse und Seele. Eine Einführung in die Gegenwart* (Munich: Lehmann, 1926), esp. 27.

37. Clauß, *Rasse und Seele*, 24, 137 ff..

38. Hans F. K. Günther, *Rassenkunde des deutschen Volkes* (Munich: Lehmann, 1922); idem, *Kleine Rassenkunde des deutschen Volkes* (Munich: Lehmann, 1929). For further discussion see Michael Hau, *The Cult of Health and Beauty in Germany: A Social History 1890-1930* (Chicago: University of Chicago Press, 2003); Michael Hau and Mitchell G. Ash, "Der normale Körper, seelisch erblickt," in *Gesichter der Weimarer Republik. Eine physiognomische Kulturgeschichte*, eds. Sander Gilman and Claudia Schmölders (Cologne: Dumont, 2000), 12–31, here: pp. 19–20.

39. For examples and a brief discussion of Günther in this context, see Lorraine Daston and Peter Galison, *Objectivity* (New York: Zone Books, 2007), 338–40.

40. Gerhard Pfahler, *Vererbung als Schicksal. Eine Charakterkunde* (Leipzig: Barth, 1932).

41. Mitchell G. Ash and Thomas Sturm, "Die Psychologie in praktischen Kontexten—Einführende Bemerkungen," *Zeitschrift für Psychologie* 202 (2004), 177–82.

42. David Meskill, "Characterological Psychology and the German Political Economy in the Weimar Period (1919–1933)," *History of Psychology* 7 (2004), 3–19.

43. Hugo Münsterberg, *Psychologie und Wirtschaftsleben* (Leipzig: Barth, 1912); idem, *Psychology and Industrial Efficiency* (Boston: Houghton Mifflin, 1913). For further discussion see Andreas Killen, "Weimar Psychotechnics between Americanism and Fascism," in *The Self as Project. Politics and the Human Sciences*, eds. Greg Eghigian, Andreas Killen, and Christine Leuenberger, *Osiris* 22 (2007), 48–71.

44. Gabriele Wohlauf, "Moderne Zeiten—Normierung von Mensch und Maschine," in *Untersuchungen zur Geschichte der Psychologie und der Psychotechnik*, ed. Horst Gundlach (Munich: Profil, 1996), 147–64. For the wider context see Joan Cambell, *Joy in Work, German Work: The National Debate, 1800-1945* (Princeton: Princeton University Press, 1989); Anson Rabinbach, *The Human Motor: Energy, Fatigue and the Origins of Modernity* (Berkeley: University of California Press, 1992), Chap. 10; Mary Nolan, *Visions of Modernity: American Business and the Modernization of Germany* (New York: Oxford University Press, 1994).

45. Horst Gundlach, "Psychologie und Psychotechnik bei den Eisenbahnen," in *Untersuchungen zur Geschichte der Psychologie und der Psychotechnik*, ed. idem, 127–46; Michael Hau, "Sports in the Human Economy: '*Leibesübungen*,' Medicine, Psychology, and Performance Enhancement during the Weimar Republic," *Central European History*, 41 (2008), 381–412, esp. 400 ff..

46. Günter Spur and Wolfram Fischer, eds., *Georg Schlesinger und die Wissenschaft vom Farbrikbetrieb* (Munich: Hanser, 2000).

47. Fritz Giese, *Theorie der Psychotechnik* (Braunschweig: Vieweg, 1925).

48. Harold Perkin, *The Third Revolution*, cit. n. 4.

49. Nikolas Rose, "Engineering the Human Soul: Analysing Psychological Expertise," *Science in Context* 5 (1992), 351–369.

50. Killen, *Weimar Psychotechnics*, p. 63. For more extensive discussion see Alexandre Métraux, "Die angewandte Psychologie vor und nach 1933 in Deutschland," in *Psychologie im Nationalsozialismus*, ed. Carl Friedrich Graumann, cit. n. 16, 221–62, which is not cited by Killen.

51. Siegfried Jaeger, "Zur Herausbildung von Praxisfeldern der Psychologie bis 1933," in *Geschichte der deutschen Psychologie im 20. Jahrhundert*, eds. Mitchell G. Ash and Ulfried Geuter (Opladen: Westdeutscher Verlag, 1985), 83–112. On Kraepelin, see Rabinbach, *The Human Motor*, Chap. 7.

52. Kurt Lewin, *Die Sozialisierung des Taylor-Systems. Eine grundsätzliche Untersuchung zur Arbeits- und Betriebspsychologie* (Berlin: Weltkreis Verlag, 1920). Cf. Ash, *Gestalt Psychology*, Chap. 16, esp. 265.

53. Kurt Lewin, *A Dynamic Theory of Personality: Selected Papers* (New York: McGraw-Hill, 1935), Chap. 8; Joseph De Rivera, ed., *Field Theory as Human Science: Contributions of Lewin's Berlin Group* (Hillsdale, NJ: Gardner Press, 1976); Wolfgang Schönpflug, ed., *Kurt Lewin: Leben, Werk, Umfeld*, 2nd expanded ed. (Frankfurt a.M.: Lang Verlag, 2007).

54. For further discussion see Helmut Hildebrandt, *Zur Bedeutung des Begriffs der Alltagspsychologie in Theorie und Geschichte der Psychologie. Eine psychologiegeschichtliche Studie anhand der Krise der Psychologie in der Weimarer Republik* (Frankfurt a.M.: Peter Lang, 1991).

55. Ludwig Klages, *Der Geist als Widersacher der Seele*, 2 vols. (Leipzig: Barth, 1928–1930). Gay, *Weimar Culture*, 80; Walter Laqueur, *Weimar: A Cultural History* (New York: Harper Torchbooks, 1974), 101–2.

56. Ludwig Klages, *Die Grundlagen der Charakterkunde*, 4th ed. (Leipzig: Barth, 1926), 1.

57. Siegfried Kracauer, *Die Angestellten*, exp. ed. (Frankfurt a.M.: Suhrkamp, 1971, First published 1929), 22–23.

58. Ernst Kretschmer, *Körperbau und Charakter. Untersuchungen zum Konstitutionsproblem und zur Lehre von den Temperamenten*, 7th and 8th eds. (Berlin: Springer, 1929. First published 1921).

59. Kretschmer, *Körperbau und Charakter*, 7.

60. For examples see Hau and Ash, *Der normale Körper*.

61. Philipp Lersch, *Gesicht und Seele. Grundlagen einer mimischen Diagnostik* (Munich: Reinhardt, 1932).

62. Ulfried Geuter, *The Professionalization of German Psychology under Nazism*, trans. Richard Holmes (Cambridge: Cambridge University Press, 1992. First published 1984). Stefan Petri, "Personalauswahl zwischen Psychotechnik und Charakteranalyse. Die Kompetenzverschiebung der deutschen Militärpsychologie von 1914 bis 1942," *Zeitschrift für Psychologie*, 212 (2004), 200–211. This path to professionalization stands in sharp contrast to the increasing use of quantitative constructions of reliability that became predominant in other countries. See Theodore Porter, *Trust in Numbers* (Princeton: Princeton University Press, 1995). This was not, however, a German *Sonderweg*; Dutch psychology appears to have taken a similar path to professionalization via trained intuition. See Dehue, *Changing the Rules*.

63. See, for example, Richard Pauli, *Psychologisches Praktikum. Leitfaden für experimentell-psychologische Übungen*, 4th ed. (Jena: Fischer, 1930).

64. Geuter, *Professionalization*; Mitchell G. Ash, "Psychologie," in *Die Rolle der Geisteswissenschaften im Nationalsozialismus*, ed. Frank-Rutger Hausmann (Munich: Oldenbourg, 2002), 229–64; idem, "Psychologie," in *Kulturwissenschaften und Nationalsozialismus*, eds. Jürgen Elvert and Jürgen Nielsen-Sikora (Stuttgart: Franz Steiner Verlag, 2008), 823–62.

3

Legal Theory and the Weimar Crisis of Law and Social Change

John P. McCormick

Public lawyers in the Weimar Republic conceptualized the law as a novel means of performing the following pressing tasks that confronted state and society in the twentieth century: the regulation of an industrial economy, the amelioration of economic inequality and the negotiation of cultural disagreement. During the *Kaiserreich*, monarchically legitimated elites unilaterally executed comparable tasks. However, in the Weimar Republic, previously excluded social groups—for instance, those represented by the Catholic, Social Democratic, Communist and National Socialist parties—now vied with traditionally represented social forces in electoral and parliamentary fora to formulate and direct regulatory, redistributive, and socially integrative policy.

The renowned social democratic legal theorist, Hermann Heller (1891–1933), proposed accomplishing these tasks through a "social rule of law" (*sozialer Rechtsstaat*). The notorious conservative lawyer, and eventually Nazi jurist, Carl Schmitt (1888–1985), in typically dramatic fashion, defined the issue in more stark terms: namely, how to integrate, constitutionally, the newly enfranchised proletariat into the state. In general, most of the era's legal luminaries—Hans Kelsen, Richard Thoma, Hugo Preuß, Gerhard Anschütz, Heinrich Triepel, Erich Kaufmann, and others—analyzed the ensuing crisis of the Weimar Republic precisely in terms of a crisis of law accompanying a radical transition to the welfare state or *Sozialstaat*.[1]

This socio-legal crisis was clearly presaged by Max Weber's (1864–1920) late work, which generally cast such a long and deep shadow over so many spheres of Weimar's intellectual life. The opposition between abstractly formal and concretely specific aspects of legal matters identified by Weber became the intellectual standard with which his students and heirs in the legal profession grappled as they deciphered the fate of the law—and concomitantly the prospects for liberal and social democracy—during the Republic. In this essay, I trace the career of these distinct aspects of law, formal versus substantive, through the writings of various Weimar legal theorists, especially, Weber, Kelsen, Thoma, Heller, and Schmitt, highlighting their salience in the eventual collapse of Germany's first constitutional-social democracy.

Legal Positivism as the New Juridical Status Quo

Max Weber's best-known associations with Weimar are his "vocation" lectures and his political essays from the end of the Great War.[2] But Weber's attempt to elaborate a sociology of law in the early decades of the twentieth century, in writings such as his important commentary on Hermann Kantorowicz's (1877–1940) work,[3] and the various sections of his posthumously published *Economy and Society*,[4] convey in especially stimulating ways the dramatic implications of the emerging socio-legal problematic of the *Sozialstaat*. Even though Weber speaks in abstractly doctrinal and sociological terms, his analysis betrays a deep anxiety over problems confronting the rule of law in an emerging administrative and welfare state. One side of Weber's legal analysis, the more logically formal side, was taken up—with perhaps too little anxiety concerning its socio-historical adequacy—by the first legal theorist to rise to prominence in the interwar period, the Austrian jurist Hans Kelsen (1881–1973).

While not officially a student of Weber, Kelsen shared with Weber a neo-Kantian methodology and epistemology, which emphasized the formulation of highly refined, abstract categories with which the empirical world could be evaluated.[5] Kelsen, a brilliant left-liberal jurist, drafted the post-imperial Austrian constitution, served on the Austrian Republic's High Court, and spent the remainder of the Weimar epoch on Cologne's prestigious law faculty before fleeing Central Europe for safety and international acclaim abroad. Kelsen attempted to construct a highly formal constitutional system, focused primarily on the law's logical validity, that would allow the progressive social forces, for the very first time represented in Central European parliaments, to promote agendas enabling the regulatory and welfare state to address political and economic necessities effectively.[6] Within Kelsen's positivist framework, the law served as a democratic people's attempt to govern itself with as few institutional hurdles to majority rule as possible. This theorization of the abstract means—by which a society might freely, rationally and democratically regulate itself—gained Kelsen's jurisprudence wide renown for both rational sophistication and elegant presentation.

However, Kelsen's positivism was also frequently criticized as an ideological retreat from the pressing realities of the present into formalism—a retreat from the concrete specificities of regulation, redistribution and integration posed by the novel historical circumstances portended by the rise of the *Sozialstaat*. Critics charged that law and the state could not be posited, as Kelsen did, as the neutral translator of popular will into public policy. It was naïve, they argued, to think that law and the state did not or should not themselves substantively contribute to the shape of public policy. Both Heller and Schmitt, for instance, ridiculed Kelsen's theory as either an abdication from politics or an unwitting capitulation to its vicissitudes.[7]

To be sure, Kelsen admirably and brilliantly transformed the conservative legal positivism that prevailed in the German *Kaiserreich* by prioritizing the rationality of legal statutes promulgated in the post–Great War Austrian and German republics. In so doing, he also intellectually legitimated the popularly accessible institution responsible for creating statutes, the parliament; his theory posited parliamentary legislation in the new democracies as a progressive improvement over statute creation within the constitutional monarchies of the imperial era. But the parliamentary-generated statute positivism that Kelsen put in the place of the monarchically legitimated *Rechtsstaat*, or rule of law state, proved less than fully capable of addressing the normative-empirical tasks of the age. In the opening decades of the twentieth century, Kelsen placed legal theory in a predicament similar to the one in which Kant placed epistemology and ethics at the start of the nineteenth century: in both instances Kantianism stood incapable of guiding rational subjects precisely what to do in concrete circumstances, and remained largely silent on the more specific, appropriate institutional arrangements that might effectively facilitate such choices and actions.

As I explain more fully below, the writings of the liberal legal theorist Richard Thoma (1874–1957), and of the aforementioned social democrat Heller appear as more realistically progressive, if still undeveloped, solutions to the problem of a social rule of law appropriate for an emerging *Sozialstaat*. One of the Republic's greatest misfortunes, however, was the fact that its most brilliant diagnostician was Carl Schmitt, its fiercest and most perspicacious enemy.[8] Schmitt understood almost better than everyone else involved in these debates what was at stake in the regime's crises, and he consistently proposed the simplest and most feasible plans to solve them. "Solving" them for Schmitt, however, meant diverting the Weimar *Sozialstaat* crisis in the worst possible direction, one whose end entailed nothing less than the eclipse of law as such.[9]

In the following sections, I briefly sketch the problematic of a social rule of law defined in Weberian terms, as well as the Thoma/Heller attempt to recast that problematic in a constructive, progressive manner. I then devote the balance of the essay to the triumph of Schmitt's sinister exploitation of law's dire predicament in Weimar's emerging *Sozialstaat*.

The Weberian Problematic

Weber's "Legal Theory and Sociology," ostensibly a commentary on Kantorowicz's jurisprudence, is the effective template for Weimar debates over law and society. Quite famously, Weber begins the essay by declaring that observers can examine the basic building block of a legal system, the legal precept (*Rechtssatz*), either doctrinally or sociologically. That is, on the one hand, a legal precept may be evaluated in terms of its *meaning*: as "a general, hypothetical norm" that can be applied "correctly" to cases A, B, and C; or, on the other, in *factual* terms, particularly in terms of the "specific factual probability" that when real-world situations X, Y, and Z obtain, "factual consequences" will ensue.[10] The former criterion is an intellectual evaluation concerning the suitability of a particular concept for a certain discrete circumstance; the latter criterion is a calculable empirical prediction concerning state action in the world. Thus, there are two kinds of validity for Weber: correct interpretation, and the factual circumstances of enforcement or obedience. The first kind of validity, he suggests, pertains to the realm of the "ought," while the second is confined to the realm of the "is."[11]

But Weber does not want to hypostatize these alternatives of "ought" and "is," as more orthodox neo-Kantians, like Kelsen, often did. After all, as he reminds readers, the doctrinal aspect of law is not impervious to facts. There are "thousands of concrete circumstances" that affect whether a judge will arrive at a correct meaning of a norm in application, factors pertaining to the person of the deciding judge—the quality of his mind, the particularities of his education, the extent of his alcohol intake, etc.[12] Conversely, juridical descriptions derived from legal doctrine inform the way that the world is analyzed empirically. Weber suggests that the legal definition of the United States, for instance, although having no existence in empirical reality, is logically coherent, and hence valid, and, further, serves as an ideal-typical resource, "an orienting principle," for those who do in fact proceed to examine the world factually.[13]

But does Weber consider the status and relationship of these distinct yet mutually influencing approaches to be as unproblematic as they appear in this analysis? His next categorical opposition gives careful readers cause to wonder. Weber juxtaposes two kinds of adjudication or law finding: formal justice and Kadi justice, that is, logically based and consistently applied adjudication versus judgment that is not rationally justified and varies arbitrarily from case to case.[14] Weber is not nearly so objectively analytical, or value neutral, in his evaluation of these two types of justice that bear significantly on the initial distinction between formally doctrinal and factually sociological approaches to law. Invoking the words of Rudolph von Ihering, Weber signals a distinct moral affinity for the first type of justice: "form is the enemy of arbitrariness, the twin sister of *freedom*."[15] In other words, a doctrinally logical and consistently applied type of law is, to his mind, morally superior to law that is applied in an ad hoc fashion.

Indeed, when read in conjunction with *Economy and Society*, this early essay helps demonstrate Weber's torturous state of mind regarding the following state of affairs: increased economic regulation and socially demanded redistribution is converting the clear, consistent, formal law characteristic of the nineteenth century *Rechtsstaat* into a kind of arbitrary, ad hoc, Kadi justice within the *Sozialstaat*. The state, through decree-like types of legal measures, is now intervening into society to address individual circumstances of countless variety: dictating worker safety conditions, specifying the process for canning vegetables, establishing pensions, etc. This development imperils Weber's initial distinction between the two types of legal research. After all, *Sozialstaat* regulatory law is formulated such that there are infinite standards and criteria, many perhaps contradictory, by which an observer might determine whether a judge interprets a particular legal statement "correctly." What is the "correct" manner of legally specifying how peas should be canned?

As Weber remarked in the *Sociology of Law*, statutes formulated under the *Rechtsstaat* took a simple conditional form: they described state action that would ensue if an actor in society behaved in a particular way. On the contrary, *Sozialstaat* law takes the form of directives or measures: they over-specify the kinds of action that the state must perform. Thus, in such circumstances, observers often cannot easily reach consensus over the "correct" interpretation of the *Sozialstaat*'s legal precepts precisely because they are too concrete. Weber will go so far as to intimate that this "materialization," "deformalization" or "substantivization" of law within the *Sozialstaat* eliminates the very existence of legal precepts; he fears that incoherent state measures or edicts have completely supplanted precept-like statutes under the administrative and bureaucratic state.

Furthermore, Weber seems to be aware that the emerging *Sozialstaat* not only threatens the doctrinally coherent legal precept with extinction, it also jeopardizes the attempt in practice to operationalize his *sociological* approach to legal studies. It is, after all, much more difficult to observe and predict whether measures promulgated by the *Sozialstaat* are actually implemented or followed, or whether a precise kind of state action will ensue in circumstances when they are not. On the one hand, these measures are formulated in a semantically more vague manner than the conditional statements issued by the *Rechtsstaat*. On the other, the societal and state activity observed within the *Sozialstaat* present themselves as ongoing circumstances of indefinite temporal duration rather than as instances of clear and determinate cause and effect, as were the objects of legal activity under the liberal *Rechtsstaat*.

These realizations seem to impel Weber to consider legal *history* as a response to the ongoing crisis of the *soziale Rechtsstaat*. In "Legal Theory and Sociology," Weber states that legal historians must practice doctrinal analysis retroactively. They must convert legal material into the logical form of a legal precept and transport themselves back into the position of—literally, into the very "soul" of—the historical judge in order to observe how such a precept could have been applied correctly to a case in that earlier time. This, Weber avers, provides a standard by which to evaluate whether particular legal functioning was valid in a context different from one's own:

> If I have before me a "legal source." . . . be it a legal code, ancient legal sayings, a judgment, a private document, or whatever—I must necessarily first get a picture of it in legal *doctrine*, the *validity* of which legal precept it *logically* presupposes. I find this out by transporting myself back as far as possible into the soul of a judge of the time; and by asking how a judge of the time would have to decide in a concrete case presented to him.[16]

However, Weber suggests in *Economy and Society*—sometimes implicitly, sometimes explicitly—that it is nearly impossible to impute such a thing as a legal precept to, or derive doctrinal interpretation from, legal matter in historical circumstances that precede the development of the European *Rechtsstaat*. The rationally formulated statute was perfected within the modern *Rechtsstaat*, which was characterized by a separation between legislative and executive authorities. Indeed, Weber defines pre-modern patrimonialism and the patriarchal household precisely in terms of (a) an *absence* of discrete legal precepts (b) a merging of executive, legislative and judicial functions, as well as (c) a fusion of public and private spheres. Often in successive paragraphs, and even consecutive sentences, these patriarchal and patrimonial examples are associated directly with the *Sozialstaat* that was emerging before Weber's eyes in the Germany of his day.[17] Therefore, Weber's early Weimar legal writings demonstrate that the crisis of the rule of law and the *Sozialstaat* was not a crisis of *adjudication* alone, but also a crisis of the scholarly methods required to apprehend and analyze contemporary legal practice. In the ensuing years of the Republic, this is the situation with which Central European jurists desperately struggled.

Weber's immediate left-liberal and social democratic successors would attempt, in practice, to resolve these dilemmas that caused Weber such consternation at the outset of Weimar's novel experiment in mass democratic, social regulation. Liberal theorist, Richard Thoma, co-editor of and contributor to the most influential legal handbook of the era,[18] directly addresses the problem of combining the rule of law with administrative activity in an emerging welfare state.[19] Thoma seeks to ease the transition from traditional republicanism, on the one hand, where the form of a polity, even if popularly participatory, sets strict limits on its own shape and praxis, to, on the other, modern republicanism where participation facilitates a republic's consistent wholesale transformation through frequent, substantive constitutional reforms. Unlike the liberals of the *Kaiserreich* era, who had to sit still for social regulation promulgated on Bismarck's terms, Thoma enthusiastically extends such policy making to processes participated in by the entire people represented by competing mass parties.

Although progressively-inclined, Thoma does not open the distributive question as widely as Hermann Heller who explicitly raises the possibility of a "social *Rechtsstaat*."[20] Heller, the Social Democratic Party's most prominent jurist, understands the social *Rechtsstaat* as a rule of law regime in which democratic citizens would enjoy the requisite material means to ensure their full participation in the making of laws to which they were subject. Foreshadowing post-WWII arguments by progressive legal philosophers like Ronald Dworkin and Jürgen Habermas, Heller distinguishes between positive law, on the one hand, and principles of law on the other; a distinction in which necessary regulatory and redistributively driven deformalizations of statutory law could be justified to the extent that they satisfy the moral aspirations of a democratically organized society.[21]

As long as legal principles are fully articulated in constitutional norms generated by parliamentary majorities, Heller argues, the deformalization of individual statutes required to realize such principles need not, as Weber feared, result in either rational incoherence or pathological unaccountability. The interplay of statutes and principles, in society and in parliament, Heller hoped, would prevent formal law from masking concrete domination (especially, that of capital over labor) and, vice versa, keep concrete administrative measures from overwhelming the freedom of individuals (as conservative critics of the welfare state suggest they necessarily will).

But the dialectic to which Heller's theory aspires suffers from the lack of an appropriate sociological motor. His famous appeals to "social homogeneity" can neither reflect nor promote the requisite societal diversity necessary to prevent regulation and redistribution from becoming coercive. Without some robust way of translating society's diversity of voices into public policy through law, some social forces will inevitably force such policies on others. In this sense, Heller's problem is the inverse of Thoma's: the latter's theory is insufficiently egalitarian to engender the precise and extensive kind of regulation necessary to provide an adequate social safety net within an industrial society. Neither Heller's potentially coercive social uniformity nor Thoma's possibly exclusionary political contraction are appropriate for the task of formulating the representative, articulate and reflexive policies that can realize progressive social regulation; they still render society vulnerable to unintended consequences of state policies and accelerate a dangerous tendency to make dependent state clients out of democratic citizens. It would not be until years after the Weimar crisis, and the Republic's collapse, that the aspirations of Thoma and Heller would be realized, to some extent, in the institutions of the Federal Republic and the sociolegal theory of Habermas.[22]

To be sure, Habermas's highly influential book on the *Public Sphere* suggested that the Federal Republic did not necessarily constitute a progressive advance over the Weimar Republic, due to the Bonn Republic's deficiencies—specifically, limited political participation and moderately coercive corporatist tendencies.[23] Subsequently, however, Habermas would locate in the intersubjective, communicative-social potentials still latent within the post-WWII *Sozialstaat*, the motor by which regulation and redistribution could be legitimated, and their potentially pathological affects, reflexively ameliorated.[24] Through a deliberatively reinforced theory of solidarity, Habermas would greatly expand the participatory possibilities of Thoma's left-republicanism, and buttress and alleviate the, respectively, ineffectual and coercive aspects of Heller's notion of homogeneity.

Schmitt's Challenge to Legal Formalism

However, successful social democracy, to whatever extent it was realized after the war in the Federal Republic and in Habermas's legal-political philosophy, is a long way from the circumstances shadowed by Weber in which we left Thoma and Heller. In such circumstances, their wily adversary,[25] Carl Schmitt, would prevail. The right-wing jurist was something of a Weber devotee, attending both famous vocation lectures as well as Weber's address on "Parliament and Government in a Newly Ordered Germany." Of Weber's massive *Economy and Society*, Schmitt wrote, "the enormous sociological material for the conceptual development of jurisprudence in Max Weber's *magnum opus posthumum* has still to be tested"; and of the man himself, Schmitt later remarked, as an analyst of charisma, Weber was "a historian engaged in political theology."[26] It is only fitting then that Schmitt himself attempts to "test" the implications of Weber's sociology of law in a work originally dedicated to the great social scientist entitled *Political Theology*.[27]

Sniffing out the opportunity for state self-assertion in Weber's account of the supercession of the *Rechtsstaat*'s formal rule of law by the *Sozialstaat*'s deformalized law, throughout the Republic and beyond it, Schmitt incessantly sought to hasten the demise of the former. His aspirations for an authoritarian interventionist state that would intercede in society—*not* to address socio-economic injustice but to further aggrandize state power vis-à-vis liberal and leftist social forces—led him to support successive attempts at presidential coups by first Catholic, then Prussian aristocrats over and against the democratically elected parliament.

In his first great work of the Weimar era, *Political Theology*, Schmitt first and foremost elaborates his claim that all modern concepts of state and political philosophy are in fact secularized theological concepts. Even the liberal constitutional state—as is clear in the works of its intellectual founders, Hobbes, Bodin, and Spinoza—was grounded in significant ways on theological foundations. Schmitt insists that later liberals, like Kelsen, deny the theological dependence of the state by pretending that its legal-constitutional system functions as a machine that "runs itself." Schmitt argues that the indisputable fact of "the exception," the unpredictable but unavoidable phenomenon that escapes intellectual systematization and juridical codification, called for the acceptance of quasi-theological authority: a personalized sovereign empowered to make ultimate decisions for which reasons cannot be given. Liberal denial notwithstanding, Schmitt insisted, every concrete decision, whether exercised by a magistrate, police officer, social worker, judge, or the president himself, entails a moment of discretion that cannot be justified rationally or derived directly from the legal order. The unity and coherence of the state order depends, therefore, on some transcendent authority to which these decisions can be traced.

Political Theology urges readers to take seriously the transfer of political sovereignty from the monarch to the people occasioned by the revolutions of the late eighteenth century. Liberals presumed that the people could assume ultimate authority, while royal decision-making functions could be absorbed unproblematically by a system of positive laws.[28] With these two intellectual moves, enlightened revolutionaries hoped to secure "government of laws, not of men." But, as Schmitt explains, general laws cannot apply themselves; they cannot determine when or whether they are appropriate for particular cases. Furthermore, the entire, ordinary system of legal norms cannot itself, by definition, address what is not normal, what has not been circumscribed or predetermined by statute, that is, what is extraordinary.[29]

The need to distinguish the normal from the extraordinary, especially when the latter takes a form that threatens the state and legal order, raises afresh the question of authority. "Sovereign is he who decides the exception," Schmitt famously asserts.[30] Because the people as a whole cannot assemble and deliberate over the exception or what to do about it, Schmitt reaffiliates sovereignty with a personal, quasi-monarchic decision. Only a real person can decide most expediently "what constitutes the public interest or interest of the state."[31] The Enlightenment, it would seem, neither escaped the necessity of government by

men nor replaced it with the rule of laws as such. Schmitt concedes that a constitution may determine who acts in legally unanticipated circumstances, but not
when he acts or what he is to do in such moments. In this sense, the sovereign
must be unbound by the written constitution in significant ways—in fact, he
may suspend the constitution in its entirety if unforeseen emergency circumstances warrant it.

With characteristic cleverness, lest Schmitt's readers interpret this argument
as a pretext for an authoritarian coup against a constitutional government—like
the catastrophic one with which Schmitt would be associated a decade later that
signalled the Republic's collapse—he describes how his theories of sovereignty
and the exception validate and affirm the normal order. Schmitt suggests that
the exception actually helps define the normal order by delineating exactly
where normalcy ends, the point at which the thing-in-itself is not its other, the
border where it is distinguishable from its opposite. By definition, the ordinary
itself cannot determine its own limit; something, *someone*, part of, yet above the
normal order, must perform that task for it. "For a legal order to make sense, a
normal situation must exist, and he is sovereign who definitely decides whether
this normal situation actually exists. . . . [Thus] the exception reveals most clearly
the essence of the state's authority."[32]

Absent the exception, the normal would exist without a contrast; it would
lack an opposition to affirm and distinguish it. The exception poses a moment
of disruption that actually confirms what is essentially characteristic about the
norm. Arguing from analogy, Schmitt suggests that "the seriousness of an insight goes deeper than the clear generalizations inferred from what ordinarily
repeats itself."[33] The unprecedented originality of an intellectual epiphany or revelation demarcates the limit of a generally correct truism. Because the normal
without the exception amounts to mere endless repetition, more of the same,
Schmitt asserts that "the exception is more interesting than the rule."[34]

Here Schmitt's analysis, purportedly circumscribed by logic alone, begins to
blend with an aesthetic preference for, even celebration of, the exception. Although he insists that his position cannot be affiliated with Romanticism, he
does associate it with a "philosophy of concrete life," a way of thinking that he
claims is more "juridically" rational than the formal rationalism of the Enlightenment and the legal positivism of his day. Nevertheless, statements such as the
following certainly seem to border on the irrational: "In the exception the power
of real life breaks through the crust of a mechanism that has become torpid
by repetition."[35] This statement betrays Schmitt's profound anxiety over repetition, whether represented, on the one hand, by liberal fantasies that a positivist system of legal norms can function as a self-governing machine, or, by the
Soviet-Russian worship of mechanical reproduction within which humanity is
mere material to be manipulated. Toward the conclusion of *Political Theology*,
Schmitt associates the exception, likened to "a miracle" throughout the work,
as the occasion for an unavoidable choice between good and evil. Morality, he
insists, can be derived neither from an intellectual machine that runs itself nor
from a worldview that celebrates the technological transformation of nature—it

only emerges from unprecedented moments of divine intervention, or moments of human decision akin thereto.

Early in the work, Schmitt's arguments concerning regularity or repetition versus the exception seem more descriptive than prescriptive. There, he presents the exception as an inconvenient fact that liberals try at all costs to avoid; they speak endlessly about the "uninterrupted unity and order" of the legal system as if their insistence would simply make it so.[36] Because such thinking never reaches the existentially factual bottom line by confronting the facticity of the exception, and the consequent necessity of sovereignty, in Schmitt's estimation, legal positivism, despite all its technical precision, never rises to the level of genuine jurisprudence. "Methodological conjuring, conceptual sharpening, and astute criticizing are only useful as preparatory work. If they do not come to the point when arguing that jurisprudence is something formal, they remain, despite all effort, in the antechamber of jurisprudence."[37]

To believe that laws apply themselves, that facts can be absorbed automatically into the system of norms, is to deny, according to Schmitt, the importance of the person, and therefore humanity, in the realm of the juridical. When a judge, as a concrete personality, decides on a norm's relationship to an individual case, Schmitt declares, as if describing a priest presiding over the act of transsubstantiation, "a transformation takes place every time."[38] This transformation stands as far as logically possible from processes of mechanistic repetition and reproduction. The fact that norms do not apply themselves automatically to cases affirms the personality of the judge. For Schmitt, the process of adjudication affirms the sanctity of the human being in much the same way as does the act of God becoming human through incarnation, or bread and wine becoming body and blood through transsubstantiation. Each act of adjudication is a miniature miracle that affirms the transcendent power of human creativity, the ability to create something that had never existed before—but a power granted and sanctioned transcendentally by God.

Schmitt takes great pains to show that he is not importing theological principles from a premodern, prerational past into modern political thought. Modern state theory was originally infused with theology, so much so that his central claim, that modern political concepts are *secularized* theological ideas, is in fact an overstatement.[39] In early modern thought, when the omnipotent God became the sovereign, and the miracle became the exception, the concepts remained as theological as they were secular.[40] Early modern philosophers such as Hobbes and Bodin did not, according to Schmitt, simply retain the trappings of the theological in an ornamental fashion to legitimate a secular or atheistic agenda; they employed the theological because they were fully cognizant of the deficiencies of pure reason. Therefore, the premodern principles concerning concrete personality are not, according to Schmitt, the residues of superstition. Rather, they serve a function that anticipates the limits of abstractly formal rationality, and, as genuine attempts to preserve political unity in a way that affirms humanity, they represent a higher, juridical form of reason than the sheer legal positivism that would follow.

By the nineteenth century, according to Schmitt, the liberal heirs of Hobbes and Bodin were engaged in a vast effort to repress such theological notions as the exception and the sovereign. Instead, liberals posited a closed, gapless system, disruptable neither by unanticipated events nor by a sovereign's interventions.[41] According to Schmitt, they pretend either that the sovereign does not exist at all, or that either the people or their representatives in parliament can function as an ersatz sovereign. But the lacunae in rationalist thought reveal "systematic or methodological necessities" that demand the presence of sovereign power.[42] Thus, liberals like Kelsen are compelled to sneak through the back door the concretely decisive sovereign authority that they have pushed out the front. In moments when generality and regularity do not prevail in positivist jurisprudence, the sovereign state's concrete discretionary authority inevitably appears, despite liberal self-delusion, in the form of "lawgiver, executive power, police, pardoner, welfare institution."[43]

In light of such rational insufficiencies and intellectual dishonesty, Schmitt insists that it is deeply hypocritical of liberals to mock the efforts of scholars who theorize the concrete or organic personality of the state. How can liberals derisively liken the writings of a conservative organicist such as Otto von Gierke, et al., to disquisitions on the trinity, while Kelsen, himself, glosses over "the inner-heterogeneity" between his own Kantian epistemology and the democratic political values that he professes?[44] One ought not to deride the theological qualities of other thinkers, Schmitt suggests, while disregarding one's own leaps of faith. But beyond mere obliviousness to theological moments within their own intellectual systems, proponents of Enlightenment rationality exhibit a more dangerous propensity to lapse into complete irrationality. For Schmitt, because philosophies of "massive rationality" like liberalism (and, later, Marxism) eventually define *everything* as mere functions of deeper, fundamental processes, whether psychological or historical, they inevitably reduce their arguments to the level of absurdity.[45] Thus does Enlightenment reason devour itself.

When the systematic insufficiencies of Enlightenment reason and its latent tendency to become its opposite were finally apparent by the middle of the nineteenth century, more radical competitors appeared on the stage of European history. Liberalism and socialism, which still adhered to authority in some form—and therefore, unwittingly, to a political theology—gave way to more extremist movements that set as their goals the overcoming of order itself. Schmitt describes "radicals who opposed all existing order" and who directed, "with heightened awareness, their ideological efforts against the belief in God altogether, fighting that belief as if it were the most fundamental expression of the belief in any authority and unity."[46]

Liberals, left to their own devices, would offer no serious resistance to this atheistic anarchism. On the other hand, conservatives, such as Herder and Gierke, fared no better. In Schmitt's view, the traditionalism to which conservatives resorted in the face of the radically materialist "activist spirit" that emerged after 1789 and 1814 actually negated reason and encouraged passivity in the face of the historically unprecedented threat. Traditionalist conservatism, by emphasizing the organic, gradual, and natural, ultimately entails "an irrational rejection of every intellectually conscious decision."[47] It is not difficult to predict which adversary, reticent passivism or enthusiastic activism, would emerge victorious from a world-historical, life-and-death struggle.

In this spirit, Schmitt's *Roman Catholicism and Political Form* from the following year, 1923,[48] invites liberals, even anticlerical ones in the tradition of Lacordaire, Montalembert, and Tocqueville, to ally with the Church against the combination of atheistic anarchism, Slavic nationalism, and materialistic socialism taking root in revolutionary Russia. Liberals especially, Schmitt asserts, need Catholics to guide them with respect to the dire and unavoidable nature of the "exception": the exception is not only the logical gap that inevitably exists between general norm and concrete fact, a gap that Schmitt accentuated to highlight the deficiencies of legal positivism in *Political Theology*. More alarmingly, as *Roman Catholicism* makes clear, the "exception" is also the present historical epoch in which a decidedly nonliberal authority and order—one that in a historically unprecedented manner renounces all authority and order, all *theology*—has seized control of the vast empire on Europe's Eastern frontier and openly expresses a will toward world dominion.[49]

Schmitt and the Republic's Final Constitutional Crisis

Schmitt's *Crisis of Parliamentarism*, published in 1923,[50] is less restrained in its criticisms of liberalism than were either *Political Theology* or *Roman Catholicism* from the preceding months. According to Schmitt, liberal theory and practice have undermined the unity, the very *integrity*, of the state. Party politics in the legislature has fragmented the functioning of government; and law is now the outcome of secret bargaining, compromise, and even numerical coercion by particularist interests. Enlightened parliamentarians are no longer available to debate over the common good, having been replaced by hacks, who do the bidding of party bosses. Statutes are no longer the product of open, rational deliberation in the service of the nation at large or liberty in principle; rather, whatever power coalition controls the majority vote pushes through measures and directives reflecting their own particular vision of how society should be re-engineered.

Moreover, pluralism has rendered civil society not so civil: Liberals, conservatives, and social democrats barely interact with each other in legislative proceedings. And not long after Schmitt had first formulated his infamous friend/enemy theory of politics in *The Concept of the Political* from 1927,[51] paramilitary Fascist and working class organizations would again be clashing violently in the streets of German cities, even more intensely than they did in the Republic's early days. From those tumultuous first hours as the Republic emerged out of the ashes of the Prussian monarchy and humiliating defeat in the Great War to the near civil war circumstances of the Republic's last years, Schmitt's solution to its crises was fairly consistent: inflate the powers of the president against the parliament.[52] Because the president is directly elected by all the people—plebiscitarily—he, not the parliament, can re-enforce national homogeneity. Schmitt promotes this as a "democratic" solution to the social fragmentation engendered by liberal parliamentarism and pluralism. To this end, in a little studied but important 1928 essay on "The Liberal Rule of Law" Schmitt uses categorical elision and rhetorical manipulation to conjure structural or historical imperatives that his audience is warned not to resist lest the most alarming results ensue.[53]

To start, Schmitt conveniently jerry-rigs democracy, progressively conceived, right out of the core of the Weimar constitution, only to reintroduce it, fascistically reformulated, later on. He casually asserts that there is a fundamental constitutional continuity between the Reich and the Republic, and hence that the German state form has essentially remained the same before and after the war and abdication of the Kaiser. In actuality, the framers of the Weimar constitution and the general public understood the constitutional founding to entail the supersession of one regime type by another, monarchy by democracy. But Schmitt insists, counter-factually: "There is no break, no revolution in the strict legal sense between the old and the new form of the state."[54] Such an assertion lays the groundwork for the kind of functional-institutional equivalent of monarchy that Schmitt wishes to establish or revive within the Weimar context.

Schmitt snidely minimizes the genuine progressive achievement represented by the Weimar constitution: he charges that it is merely a "posthumous" document; it realizes the aspirations of 1848, not those of present struggles and necessities. Moreover, the constitution was not the product of a triumph achieved by the German bourgeoisie on their own, but merely a gift thrown into their lap after the defeat of the monarchy by foreign powers. Had the bourgeoisie itself destroyed or emasculated the monarchy, as had the French and British bourgeoisies previously, this might have signaled a "brilliant victory." But the Weimar constitution is one that has arrived too late and without any specifically German political virtue or vitality.[55]

Schmitt furthermore undermines the Weimar constitution's coherence, asserting that it reflects an indecisive middle way between East and West: the first part exhibits the "tradition of the liberal rule of law of 1789," and the second, with its social provisions, leans toward Bolshevism and the East.[56] The result is a semi-liberal constitution not up to the new historical situation of integrating the proletariat in, again, a specifically "German" manner. Schmitt asserts that the constitution is obsolete for the task of enabling a homogenous people "to achieve its political existence in a state," because it was designed to integrate the bourgeoisie who are educated and propertied, as opposed to the proletariat who are poor and uneducated: "Only the apparatuses and machines serving the old task of integrating the educated bourgeoisie remain available, even today," in the Weimar constitution.[57] In other words, nineteenth-century parliamentary structures, designed for rule of and by the bourgeoisie, have been overwhelmed by mass parties representing the industrial laboring classes.

Schmitt insists that the historical moment demands that the democratic potential of the constitution be accentuated and concomitantly that the working class be integrated materially into the state-order. In his view, the Weimar constitution offers the people "the opportunity to find a political form at all times—despite all restraints and safety valves and behind the barrier erected by the idea of the state under the liberal rule of law."[58] In other words, the democratic potential of the constitution must be "saved" from its liberal limitations and impositions. This right-, rather than left-wing appropriation of the working class is designed such that "the new significance of the proletariat [can] be mastered and the political unity of the German citizenry recreated."[59] This political unity would be achieved through the authority of a democratically elected president, who issues *Sozialstaat*-specific measures by fiat rather than *Rechtsstaat*-appropriate statutes—again, not for purposes of economic redistribution but rather for social coordination that enforces homogeneity.

This essay, published near the end of Weimar's relatively tranquil middle period, demurs on the specifics of how this is to be achieved. But during the Republic's final crisis, Schmitt would become even bolder. In *Legality and Legitimacy* from 1932, Schmitt uses the logic developed in *Political Theology* ten years before and the 1928 "Rule of Law" essay to further exploit the ideology of democracy, the structures of the administrative state and circumstances of civil war into an endorsement for presidential authoritarianism.[60] Only a Caesarist figure, Schmitt asserts, can motivate the uneducated and unpropertied masses into a vitally relevant and not fatally "posthumous" German state.

Schmitt attempts to elevate presidential emergency decrees issued under Article 48 of the constitution to a legal status equal with, or superior to, parliamentary statutes—even though the two are explicitly distinguished in the constitution. According to the latter, the *Reichstag* makes statutes of potentially enduring value while the president issues *Maßnahmen* or measures of expressly limited duration. But Schmitt suggests, clearly drawing on but inverting Weber's analysis examined above, that since parliamentary statutes have become more like measures in recent years, due to the pressures of mass parties involved in the construction of the *Sozialstaat*, it is not unreasonable to conceive democratically-legitimated presidential measures as *law*, not as law's opposite.[61] In terms that recall "the exception" from *Political Theology*, Schmitt declares that extraordinary circumstances lend decrees normative equality with—or rather, normative superiority over—statutes such that "law" now means a *measure* and *not* a statute.[62] The spiritual undertones that characterized works like *Political Theology* and *Roman Catholicism* reemerge as Schmitt remarks that the material or concrete quality of presidential decrees mean that "the extraordinary lawgiver can create accomplished facts in opposition to the ordinary legislature" which issues only abstract norms.[63] In other words, the president possesses a world-making, God-like, fiat of exceptional legislative-cum-executive authority.

Obviously, Schmitt's elevation of emergency measures to the status of law merges the law-making and law-applying tasks that are kept separate theoretically and institutionally in the *Rechtsstaat*.[64] Since the parliament has already reduced statutes to measures through economic regulation and redistribution, Schmitt intimates that the president might as well exert more legitimate decree-issuing power that will restore the force of law squandered by the parliament. After all, the president—elected by national plebiscite—more appropriately reflects and directs the will of the people. Schmitt hereby seizes ordinary party-pluralist or leftist *Sozialstaat* practice based in bargaining, compromise and, optimally, deliberation, aimed at progressive societal self-transformation, and he puts it in the service of an exceptional, right-wing imposition of order by unilateral action on the part of the executive branch.

Schmitt implies that most administrative measures issued by the *Sozialstaat* merely reflect the intentions of the particular party or interest group that lobbied for them; on the contrary, those issued by the president will purportedly reflect the will of the whole people. However, as the argument of *Legality and Legitimacy* unfolds, Schmitt consistently reveals this to be a theory of democracy that *disempowers* the people, and certainly, the working class on whose behalf *Sozialstaat* policy has been largely promulgated up to now. According to Schmitt's logic, if the people attempt to actually *participate* politically they will be merely represented by parties that supposedly threaten popular unity. But if they simply *acclaim* the president and his policies then they can be represented—indeed, embodied as a whole—because *he* is a whole: "for the extraordinary lawgiver of Article 48, the distinction between statute and statutory application, legislative and executive, is neither legally nor factually a hindrance; he combines both in his person."[65] It was, therefore, but a few steps from *Legality and Legitimacy* to Schmitt's endorsement of the Nazi seizure of power in 1933 and then to his 1935 essay on the "peculiarly German freedom" guaranteed by the Führer.[66] In the Republic's final days, Schmitt diligently worked for a political outcome in which an oligarchic clique would govern through President Hindenburg's emergency decrees. Once that failed, he helped draft the legislation by which Hitler gained access to power, and joined the NSDAP soon after the latter's consolidation of rule. Schmitt then publicly justified Hitler's murderous Röhm purge, the banishment of Jews from the legal academy, and Nazi plans for a German imperial *Grossraum* in Central-Eastern Europe. On the basis of these examples, the necessity of a substantive rather than a sham legal-democratic facilitation of participation and redistribution during the transition to the *Sozialstaat* could not be any plainer.

But the perverse legal-political logic exhibited by Schmitt's writings would not cease its continuous regression with these instances of his own malevolence. By 1941–42, the more radical NSDAP "jurists," Ernst Rudolph Huber and Reinhard Höhn, would be criticizing Schmitt's *Grossraum* theory of Nazi imperialism; they denounced Schmitt for failing to facilitate, in legal terms, sufficiently concrete, arbitrary, and physical domination by the Reich over its conquered subjects.[67]

Notes

Portions of this essay originally appeared, in a shorter and unrevised form, in "The Crisis of Constitutional-Social Democracy in the Weimar Republic," *European Journal of Political Theory* 1, no. 1 (2002): 121–28.

1. See Detlev Peukert, *The Weimar Republic: The Crisis of Classical Modernity*, trans. Richard Deveson (New York: Hill and Wang, 1992); Ulrich K. Preuß, "Die Weimarer Republik—ein Laboratorium für verfassungsrechtliches Denken," in *Metamorphosen des Politischen: Grundfragen der politischen Einheitsbildung seit den zwanziger Jahren* eds. Andreas Gödel, Dirk van Laak and Ingeborg Villinger (Berlin: Akademie Verlag, 1995),182–96; Mary Nolan, *Visions of Modernity: Fordism and Economic Reform in the Weimar Republic* (Oxford: Oxford University Press, 1994); and Young-Sun Hong, *Welfare, Modernity, and the Weimar State, 1919–1933* (Princeton: Princeton University Press,1998). Consult the review of Hong by Michael Geyer in the *Journal of Modern History* 72, no. 3 (September 2000): 832–34.

2. See Weber, "The Profession and Vocation of Politics," and "Parliament and Government in Germany Under a New Political Order" in Weber, *Political Writings*, eds. Peter Lassman and Ronald Speirs (Cambridge: Cambridge University Press, 1994), 309–69, and 130–271.

3. See Max Weber, "On Legal Theory and Sociology," in *Weimar: A Jurisprudence of Crisis*, eds. Arthur J. Jacobson and Bernhard Schlink (Berkeley: University of California Press, 2000), 50–54, hereafter LTS.

4. See Weber, *Economy and Society: An Outline of Interpretive Sociology* (1920), eds. Guenther Roth and Claus Wittich, 2 vols. (Berkeley: University of California Press, 1978), 311–13 and 641–899.

5. See Stanley L. Paulson, "The Neo-Kantian Dimension of Kelsen's Pure Theory of Law," *Oxford Journal of Legal Studies* 12 (1992), 311–32, and Dhananjai Shivakumar, "The Pure Theory of Law: Defending Kelsen on the Basis of Weberian Methodology," *Yale Law Journal* 105 (1996), 1383–1414. On the theoretical content and historical context of neo-Kantianism in Central Europe during this period see Thomas Willey, *Back to Kant: The Revival of Kantianism in German Social and Historical Thought, 1860–1914* (Detroit: Wayne State University Press, 1978).

6. See Hans Kelsen, *Introduction to the Problems of Legal Theory*, trans. Bonnie L. Paulson and Stanley L. Paulson (New York: Oxford University Press, 1992); as well as the selections from Kelsen's writings in Jacobson and Schlink, eds., *Weimar: A Jurisprudence of Crisis*, 57–62, 76–109.

7. For an analysis of all three legal theorists and their interactions and criticisms of each other in this era, see David Dyzenhaus, *Legality and Legitimacy: Carl Schmitt, Hans Kelsen and Hermann Heller in Weimar* (Oxford: Oxford University Press, 1997), and Peter C. Caldwell, *Popular Sovereignty and the Crisis of German Constitutional Law: The Theory and Practice of Weimar Constitutionalism* (Durham: Duke University Press, 1997).

8. See: John P. McCormick, *Carl Schmitt's Critique of Liberalism: Against Politics as Technology* (Cambridge: Cambridge University Press, 1997).

9. See William E. Scheuerman, *Carl Schmitt: The End of Law* (New York: Rowman & Littlefield, 1999).

10. LTS, 50.

11. LTS, 51.

12. LTS, 51.

13. LTS, 52.

14. LTS, 53.

15. LTS, 53, emphasis added.

16. LTS, 53.

17. See John P. McCormick, *Weber, Habermas and Transformations of the European State: Constitutional, Social and Supranational Democracy* (Cambridge: Cambridge University Press, 2007), chap. 3.

18. See Gerhard Anschütz and Richard Thoma, eds., *Handbuch des Deutschen Staatsrechts*, 2 vols. (Tübingen: J.C. Mohr, 1930–32). For Thoma's full biographical details, see Hans-Dieter Rath, *Positivismus und Demokratie: Richard Thoma, 1874–1957* (Munich: Duncker & Humblot, 1981).

19. See Thoma, "The Reich as a Democracy" (1930), in *Weimar: A Jurisprudence of Crisis*, eds. Jacobson and Schlink, 157–70.

20. See Heller, "Political Democracy and Social Homogeneity" (1928) and "The Essence and Structure of the State (1934), in *Weimar: A Jurisprudence of Crisis*, eds. Jacobson and Schlink, 256–64, 265–79 , here 250.

21. See David Dyzenhaus, "Hermann Heller: Introduction" in *Weimar: A Jurisprudence of Crisis*, eds. Jacobson and Schlink, 249–55 , here 252.

22. See McCormick, *Weber, Habermas and Transformations of the European State*, chap. 4.

23. See Habermas, *The Structural Transformation of the Public Sphere: An Inquiry into a Category of Bourgeois Society*, trans. Thomas Burger with Frederick Lawrence (Cambridge, MA: MIT Press, 1989), 48, 54, 80–82, 115, 148–49, 208–11.

24. See Habermas, *The Theory of Communicative Action, Vol. 1: Reason and the Rationalization of Society*, trans. Thomas McCarthy (Boston: Beacon Press, 1984), 19, 140–41, 190–92, 226, 243–71; *The Theory of Communicative Action, Vol. 2: Lifeworld and System: A Critique of Functionalist Reason*, trans. Thomas McCarthy (Boston: Beacon Press, 1987), 358–73; and *Between Facts and Norms: Contributions to a Discourse Theory of Law and Democracy*, trans. William Rehg (Cambridge, MA: MIT Press, 1996).

25. Heller and Schmitt opposed each other over the usurpation of Prussia's provincial authority by President Hindenburg's administration in the court case, "Preußen contra Reich" in 1932. See Dyzenhaus, *Legality and Legitimacy*, 206–10. Thoma composed one of the fiercest critiques of Schmitt's work in the Weimar period: see Thoma, "On the Ideology of Parliamentarism," in Carl Schmitt, *Crisis of Parliamentary Democracy*, trans. Ellen Kennedy (Cambridge, MA: MIT Press, 1985), 77–84.

26. G. L. Ulmen, *Politische Mehrwert: Eine Studie über Max Weber und Carl Schmitt* (Weinheim: VCH Acta humaniora, 1991), 178, 20–21.

27. See Schmitt, *Political Theology: Four Chapters on the Concept of Sovereignty* (1922), trans. George Schwab (Cambridge, MA: MIT Press, 1985), hereafter PT.

28. PT, 48-49.

29. PT, 6.

30. PT, 6.

31. PT, 6.

32. PT, 13.

33. PT, 15.

34. PT, 15.

35. PT, 15.

36. PT, 20.

37. PT, 21.

38. PT, 31.

39. PT, 36.

40. PT, 36.

41. PT, 36.

42. PT, 39.

43. PT, 38.
44. PT, 40-41.
45. PT, 43.
46. PT, 50.
47. PT, 54.
48. See Schmitt, *Roman Catholicism and Political Form*, trans. G. L. Ulmen (Westport, CT: Greenwood Press, 1986), 3–4, 13, 22.
49. See Schmitt, *Roman Catholicism*, 38.
50. See Schmitt, *Crisis of Parliamentary Democracy*, 1–50.
51. See the English translation of the full-length 1932 edition: Schmitt, *Concept of the Political*, trans. George Schwab (Chicago: University of Chicago Press, 2007).
52. See Ellen Kennedy, *Constitutional Failure: Carl Schmitt in Weimar* (Durham: Duke University Press, 2005).
53. Schmitt, "The Liberal Rule of Law" (1928), in *Weimar: A Jurisprudence of Crisis*, 294–300, hereafter LRL. See the fully elaborated version of these arguments in Schmitt, *Constitutional Theory* (1928), trans. Jeffrey Seitzer (Durham: Duke University Press, 2008).
54. LRL, 294.
55. LRL, 295.
56. LRL, 295.
57. LRL, 297.
58. LRL, 298.
59. LRL, 299.
60. Page numbers correspond to Carl Schmitt, *Legalität und Legitimität* (Munich: Duncker & Humblot, 1932); English renderings derive from Schmitt, *Legality and Legitimacy*, trans. Jeffrey Seitzer (Durham: Duke University Press, 2004); hereafter LL.
61. LL, 65.
62. LL, 66.
63. LL, 66.
64. LL, 67.
65. LL, 68.
66. See Schmitt, "The Constitution of Freedom," in *Weimar: A Jurisprudence of Crisis*, eds. Jacobson and Schlink, 323–25.
67. See the following three short but telling pieces: Huber, "Form and Structure of the Reich" (1941), "'Positions and Concepts': A Debate with Carl Schmitt" (1941); and Höhn, "Reich, Sphere of Influence, Great Power" (1942), in *Weimar: A Jurisprudence of Crisis*, eds. Jacobson and Schlink, 330–34.

4

The Legacy of Max Weber in Weimar Political and Social Theory

Dana Villa

I envy our American colleagues their political traditions which permit such a generous and (in the best sense of the word) liberal interpretation of Max Weber. We here in Germany, who are still seeking for alibis, would only too gladly follow them. But Weber's political sociology has had a different history here. At the time of the First World War he outlined a sketch of a Caesar-like leader-democracy on the contemporary basis of a national-state imperialism. This militant latter-day liberalism had consequences in the Weimar period which we, and not Weber, must answer for. If we are to judge Weber here and now, we cannot overlook the fact that Carl Schmitt was a "legitimate" pupil of Weber's. Viewed in the light of the history of influences, the decisionist element in Weber's sociology did not break the spell of ideology, but strengthened it.
—Jürgen Habermas in Heidelberg, Weber Centenary, 1964[1]

The reason I am no longer in politics, as you know, is because it is impossible to have politics in Germany as long as it is possible for madmen of the right and left to peddle their madness.
—Max Weber in May 1919[2]

Since the Second World War, Max Weber has been a convenient punching bag for those political theorists and philosophers who yearned to demonstrate the nihilistic consequences of a thoroughly "disillusioned" perspective in the moral-political sphere. While thinkers in the Frankfurt School tradition—Max Horkheimer, Herbert Marcuse, and the young Habermas—have been especially keen to point out the normative and political deficits of Weber's thought, theorists on the right have been no less eager to reveal the baneful consequences of so-called "value-free social science."[3] The basic line is easy enough to summarize: if we accept Weber's severe restrictions on the limits of reason or "science" to adjudicate amongst competing moral and political positions, we will find our-

selves without any rational guidance whatever when it comes to conflicting political ideologies and philosophies of life. This lack of guidance produces a de
facto "decisionism"—that is, a situation in which the citizen or political leader
is forced to make a leap of faith, a groundless commitment to *one* of the many
ideological "warring gods" demanding his worship. From here, Weber's critics
warn, it is but a short step to the kind of anti-liberal, radical politics that characterized the Weimar era and that led to Nazism in Germany. The logic is crude
but apparently compelling: if reason can't tell us that democracy is objectively
better than National Socialism or Communism, why not become a Nazi or a
Communist?

This particular gambit has become, by now, a hackneyed theme in the literature of political theory. That fact, however, has hardly impeded its popularity amongst partisans of an inflated Enlightenment idea of rationality on the
one hand or those who lean towards more Platonic, Aristotelian or Thomistic
models of practical reasoning on the other. Both camps have a vested interest in
portraying Weber's thought as the "beginning of the end" of the Western ideal
of just and rational society, an ideal that dates back to the Greeks. Such a society
was presumed (by the Greeks, Christian Natural Law, and the Enlightenment)
to be in accord with the dictates of a morally substantive reason. "Right reason"
prescribed universal laws and demonstrated the moral gap between truly just
norms and "merely positive" traditions, legal rules, or structures of domination.

As the critics like to point out, Weber's distinction between "facts" and
"values"—his rejection of the idea that there might be rationally demonstrable
"facts of value"—apparently dooms us to a merely empirical account of political
legitimacy; one in which democracy itself comes to be viewed as just another
form of political domination (albeit one in which the rulers are chosen by electoral means); one in which our most important political and moral commitments are beyond rational adjudication. Because this position is anathema, we
are better served, the critics say, by theoretical conceptions that maintain some
continuity between the "is" and the "ought," between the world of facts and the
world of values. Depending on the critic's political-philosophical predilections,
such continuity is usually established by either semi-Hegelian (dialectical) or
Aristotelian-Thomist means. Weber's "nihilistic" positivism is rejected, and the
crucial ideal of a rational and just society preserved.

What are we to make of this persistent line of attack? Does it hold water? Or
is it based, in the final analysis, upon a substantial misrepresentation of Weber's
political and theoretical positions?

Any attempt to answer this question must take account of several complicating factors, not least of which is the evolving (and often chaotic) political
situation within which Weber constructed his political sociology. The shifting
character of his political allegiances in the period 1895 (the height of the *Kaiserreich* and the year of Weber's *Freiburger Antrittsrede*) to 1920 (the year of Weber's death from pneumonia at age fifty-six) reflect this evolving situation. The
complex and changing distribution of emphasis in Weber's political position
from 1917 onwards is a case in point. Weber moves from a robust parliamen-

tarian stance in "Parliament and Government in Germany under a new Political Order"(1917) to what looks like an unqualified endorsement of plebiscitary *Führerdemokratie* in "Politics as a Vocation" (1919). This shift—emphasized by Habermas and by Mommsen's debunking 1959 critique in *Max Weber and German Politics*—has been the source of myriad confusions, especially with regard to the nature of Weber's commitment to liberal (constitutional) democracy. Was this commitment genuine, or was it merely situational and strategic?

This complication is linked to another, namely, the fact that two of the most gifted thinkers of the generation after Weber—Carl Schmitt and Georg Lukács—had deep intellectual ties to "the master." Lukács was a member of Weber's Heidelberg circle before the war, and his conversion to Marxism in 1918 (at age thirty-three) did little to diminish his reliance upon certain arch-Weberian ideas, such as rationalization. Schmitt, for his part, was also deeply indebted to Weber's thinking, particularly the idea that bureaucratization was gradually eliminating the space of politics, replacing it with administration and proceduralism.[4] This led Schmitt to focus on moments of "sovereign decision" in a manner parallel to, if not identical with, Weber's focus on charismatic leadership. Hence Habermas's characterization of Schmitt as a "legitimate pupil" of Weber—a characterization he later amended to something even stronger. On reflection, Habermas stated that Schmitt was more like a "natural son" of Max Weber.[5]

The present essay investigates these various charges and complexities. It begins by laying out the basics of Weber's theoretical and political positions, the better to assess the view that he was an unwitting godfather of Weimar anti-liberalism and political radicalism (section II). I then turn to discuss specific continuities and discontinuities between Weber and Schmitt (section III) and Weber and Luckács (section IV). My conclusion is that the discontinuities far outweigh the supposedly damning continuities. While Schmitt and Lukács undoubtedly learned much from Weber, their theoretical, practical and moral positions are irreconcilable with his, for reasons which are both clear and substantial. There is, in other words, no "slippery slope" that leads from Weber to the unbound (and often unprincipled) positions of either Schmitt or Lukács.[6] The nihilism, decisionism, and radicalism that supposedly flows from Weber's "disillusioned" perspective is, if not a total fabrication, a kind of legend, one eminently worth dismantling.[7]

Weber: Rationalization, Political Leadership, and Ideological Commitment

Weber's critics see his late emphasis on strong, charismatic leadership (the "Caesarist element" of mass democracy) as of a piece with his "negative" philosophy of history and his broader repudiation of rationalist-progressivist illusions. Weber famously viewed the history of the West in terms of rationalization and bureaucratization, the arc of his thought tracing a reduction of reason to instrumental or formal structures, as well as a corresponding constriction of individual freedom in both the private and the public spheres. The social evolution of the West had produced a bureaucratic state, an industrial capitalist economy characterized by purposive (means/end) rationality, and a formally rationalized legal system. Given the broad administrative tendency of this evolution, Weber viewed the socialist call for state control of the economy as clearly leading to less, not more, freedom:

> In theory one could probably conceive of the progressive elimination of private capitalism—although this is certainly not the trivial matter some littérateurs, who are unfamiliar with it, imagine it to be, and will quite certainly not be a consequence of this war. But assuming this were to be achieved at some point, what would it mean in practice? Would it perhaps mean the steel housing (*Gehäuse*) of modern industrial work would break open? No! It would mean rather that the *management* of businesses taken into state ownership or into some form of "communal economy" would also become bureaucratized. Is there any appreciable *difference* between the lives of the workers and the clerks in the Prussian state-run mines and railways and those of people working in large private capitalist enterprises? They are *less free*, because there is *no hope* of winning any battle against the state bureaucracy and because no help can be summoned from any authority with an interest in *opposing* that bureaucracy and its power, whereas this is possible in relation to private capitalism. *That* would be the entire difference. If private capitalism were eliminated, state bureaucracy would rule *alone*.[8]

The point of the above passage is not that capitalism guarantees freedom (Weber hardly thought that), but that the coming "rule by officials" would be made *even worse* if *one* set of administrators held what amounted to unchallenged sway. Since "the advance of bureaucratization is unstoppable," we are confronted, in Weber's view, with two very stark questions. First, "how is it *at all possible* to salvage any remnants of 'individual' freedom of movement *in any sense*, given this all-powerful trend towards bureaucratization?" And second, "how is democracy in even [a] restricted sense possible?" given the growth of what Weber calls the "enormous, crushing power" of state officialdom?[9]

Contra Tocqueville, the answer was not to be found in civil society associations (valuable though these were), nor even in political parties engaged in agonistic electoral competition. By the start of the twentieth century, political parties had themselves become bureaucratized entities, expressing in their own way the imperatives of this eminently successful form of social action and organization. As Weber stresses in "Politics as a Vocation," political struggle *could* be a source of greater freedom on such a constricted terrain, *but only if* a man of "genuine leadership capacity," charisma, and vocational responsibility came to stand at the head of the party and a mass following. The charismatic leader's "service to his cause" had, in Weber's view, the capacity to elevate the materialistic interests of his following. It also had the capacity to give direction to the party "machine," substituting meaning and new values for the "rule by officials." Given his political sociology, Weber's dialectic of bureaucratization and charismatic leadership is perfectly comprehensible, if not entirely persuasive. The problem is that his emphasis on the need for such leadership was repudiated by the course of German history. Hitler, to put it bluntly, had fulfilled Weber's hopes in the worst possible way. In Germany after World War II, "charisma" and "leadership" were permanently tainted by their association with the *Führerprinzip*. Thus, with hindsight, Weber's turn away from parliamentary institutions towards a "Caesarist leader" appears as a tremendous failure of political judgment—one enabled by a needlessly dystopic (not to say one-dimensional) idea of rationalization *qua* bureaucratization. Habermas's later insistence that rationalization is a "Janus-faced process," one with a communicative/political upside as well as an administrative-*Zweckrationalität* downside, looks almost predictable when placed in this context. The rule of law and a more deliberative form of democracy appear as the only viable alternatives to out of control bureaucratization and the "colonization" of the life-world by the "system." "Leadership" is off the table.

The problem with this familiar picture is that it takes Weber's sketch of a "Caesarist democratic leader" out of context, isolating it from his larger concern for authentic parliamentary government in Germany. A radical discontinuity is assumed between the Weber of 1917 and the Weber of 1919—a discontinuity based on the idea that the collapse of the *Kaiserreich*, and the massive problems of social, economic, and political restructuring it generated, led Weber to abandon parliamentary instrumentalities in favor of "strong leadership." There is a grain of truth to this. One can hardly read Marianne Weber's transcription of Weber's conversation with Ludendorff concerning the nature of democracy without recognizing a shift of focus.[10] However, Weber's intense and continuing concern with the political immaturity bequeathed Germany by Bismarck's "Caesarist leadership" should give us pause. What we are dealing with is not a *rejection* of one governmental form (parliamentary democracy) in favor of another (populism or *Führer-Demokratie*). Rather, we are dealing with is a redistribution of *emphasis* within a parliamentary-constitutional framework. We should read "Politics as a Vocation" not as an underdeveloped theory of "leadership democracy," but against the backdrop of Weber's parliamentary writings.

As is evident to even the most casual reader of "Parliament and Government in Germany," Weber was passionately committed to a strong parliament, one with robust powers of administrative oversight and inquiry, as well as legislative and budget responsibilities. Only a strong parliament could limit "rule by officials," and only a strong parliament could—through its electoral contests and committee work—serve as a training ground for individuals with genuine political (as opposed to bureaucratic) talents. After all, Weber observed, "it is *politicians* who must provide a counterbalance to the rule of officialdom."[11]

A strong parliament also provides a crucial avenues to the attainment of political maturity.[12] Through its debates and exercise of administrative inquiry and oversight, such a parliament tutors citizens in the workings of democratic-constitutional government, providing a stark contrast between a popular democracy (*Volksstaat*) and the kind of sham-constitutionalism of the authoritarian state (*Obrigkeitsstaat*) familiar from the *Kaiserreich*. Placed in a position of control over both the administration *and* the monarch, such a parliament is far more than a mere "talk shop." It is the genuine safeguard of democracy and the guarantee of a government liberated from the veils of "official secrecy."

Weber's defense of parliamentary and democratic elements in what would (nominally) remain a constitutional monarchy may strike the contemporary reader as overly functionalist and performance oriented, tone-deaf to liberalism's larger concern with the normative grounding of constitutional regimes in the rights of individuals and "the will of the people." Indeed, Weber was most concerned with creating a government that *worked* and that avoided the characteristic infirmities of the *Obrigkeitsstaat*. Public control of the administration; the reining in of the monarch; the cultivation of strong political leaders through committee work and elections—all these could be obtained by the transformation of parliamentary powers and practice. From Weber's *Realpolitik* perspective, the result would be a Germany no longer prey to the most vested of bureaucratic interests or the dilettantism of the monarch.

The collapse of the *Kaiserreich* brought about many of Weber's proposed reforms all at once—but at a great price.[13] The short-lived imperial government of Prince Max von Baden gave way to a revolutionary republic at the end of 1918. Weber, initially considered for Secretary of State and the responsibility of drafting a new constitution for the entire Reich (a commission ultimately given to Hugo Preuß), wound up being involved in only an unofficial capacity when it came to advising on new constitutional arrangements.[14] In January 1919, he gave his lecture on "Politics as a Vocation" at the University of Munich. It is in this text that Weber makes his most famous case for the charismatic "leading politician." This was followed—on February 25, 1919—by the article "Der Reichspräsident" in the *Berliner Börsenzeitung*, in which Weber argued strongly for direct popular election of the president of the Reich (in contrast to election by the newly established National Assembly).

These two pieces testify to Weber's belief that the new regime was in need of strong, popularly legitimated political leadership. The question is whether, in 1919, Weber wanted to reverse himself on parliamentary questions, abdicating positions for which he had previously argued strongly. Did Weber now view parliament as merely a selection mechanism—or institutional scaffolding—for the "leading politician"?

"Politics as a Vocation" is indeed remarkable in that the question of parliamentary or representative government is clearly a secondary (if not peripheral) concern) for Weber. The reason for this, I would suggest, is precisely that many of the strong parliamentary reforms Weber had argued for were now "facts on the ground." With these reforms at least formally in place, Weber was free to focus his attention almost entirely on the pressing question of political leadership. The famous set of alternatives Weber poses mid-way through the lecture— "There is only the choice between leadership democracy with a 'machine' [the bureaucratized party apparatus], and leaderless democracy"[15]—presupposes a continuity of representative institutions; it does not abolish them. One needs to remember that it is Gladstone, and not Napoleon I or Napoleon III, who is Weber's example of the "plebiscitary dictator on the battlefield of elections."[16]

What follows this apparently exhaustive either/or is an extended rumination by Weber on "what kind of a man must one be if he is to be allowed to put his hand on the wheel of history?" It is this part of "Politics as a Vocation" that attracts the most interest on the part of contemporary readers, and for obvious reasons. Focusing almost entirely on the *character* of the genuine political leader, Weber presents what, at first glance, looks like a highly Protestant-ized re-working of Machiavelli's *Prince*.[17]

In the opening sections of his lecture, Weber argues that *power* is indeed the commodity pursued by all genuine politicians. In the concluding section, he returns to Machiavelliian terrain by arguing for an ethic distinctive to politics. A *political* ethic is one that takes full account of the fact that "politics operates with very special means, namely, power backed up by *violence*."[18] It is in regard to this fundamental point that Weber reiterates one of Machiavelli's main arguments in *The Prince*, namely, that qualities that are genuine virtues in private life (such as charity, mercy, non-retaliation, and truthfulness) may well transmute into vices, becoming the source of untold harm if stringently adhered to in public-political life.[19]

Weber departs from Machiavelli, however, in emphasizing the tragic burden that every leading politician must bear. Again and again the political leader must face the fact that "good ends" can result from "morally dubious means." And he must face the equally unnerving fact that action rarely, if ever, achieves its intended goal.[20] Forced to contract with "diabolical powers" (power backed up by violence) and unsure whether what he intends will be brought about by his "guilty" means, the leading political actor only has his own sense of vocation, his own committed "service to a cause," to fall back on. If such service to a cause guides his actions, *then* his efforts and his use of power have meaning.

> The serving of a cause must not be absent if action is to have inner strength. Exactly what the cause, in the service of which the politician strives for power and uses power, looks like is a matter of faith. The politician may serve national, humanitarian, social, ethical, cultural, worldly or religious ends. The politician may be sustained by a strong belief in "progress"—no matter in which sense—or he may coolly reject this kind of belief. He may claim to stand in the service of an "idea" or, rejecting this in principle, he may want to serve external ends of everyday life. However, some kind of faith must always exist. Otherwise, it is absolutely true that the curse of the creature's worthlessness overshadows even the externally strongest political successes.[21]

With this insistence on the imperative of "faith"—on service to *some* cause or ideology—in place, Weber goes onto draw his justly famous contrast between an "ethics of ultimate ends" (in which the actor upholds certain ends or ideals, regardless of cost) and an "ethic of responsibility"(in which the political actor pays the greatest heed to costs, and takes personal responsibility for the "foreseeable results" of his action).[22]

However much we may prefer "responsibility for consequences" to the idealistic zealotry of an "ethic of ultimate ends," Weber's version of a distinctly political ethic ultimately merges the two. To sustain a career as a political actor, to give one's actions meaning and coherence and to merit the possibility of "placing one's hand on the wheel of history," one must be equal parts responsible politician and idealist. For only an idealist has a "cause"—even if that cause is a very "worldly" set of ends, e.g., social democracy. While Weber urges his student audience to own up to such responsibility—to their cause and its costs—he famously provides no criteria for deciding amongst the various political ideologies vying for their loyalty. The political actor—and only he—must *decide* which ideological "god or demon" is overlord, and then *serve* that god or demon. It is this emphasis on personal decision, combined with the "Caesarist element" in Weber's conception of political leadership, that most troubles his critics. Like Habermas, they see the former as a harbinger of irrationalism and the latter of fascism. Yet while Weber's emphasis on populist leadership comes late in his career, his emphasis on personal decision and the burden of choice has deeper roots. It is intimately connected to his broader theme of the disenchantment of the world (*Entzauberung der Welt*) and to his Nietzschean stress on what Weber called "the plain duty of intellectual honesty" in "Science as a Vocation" (1917).

In that lecture, Weber warned students against seeking answers to pressing moral and political questions from their professors. Contra the inflated claims of some of its practitioners, science and scholarship cannot rank or authoritatively evaluate practically-oriented worldviews. They have nothing to tell us about the meaning of the world or of life; they do not offer any instructions on how to live or how to act. At their best—that is to say, at their most self-conscious and intellectually honest—science and scholarship confront students with highly "inconvenient" facts, facts that complicate their various ideological commitments. When digested, such facts make a reflexive adherence to any given worldview virtually impossible.

Wissenschaft also confronts students with the inescapable question of the relation of ends and means. What *means* are demonstrably required to bring about various (ideologically specified) ends? What are the costs—human and material—entailed by such means? If the teacher is doing his job, the student will be forced to face such questions head-on. Confronted with "inconvenient facts" and the question of means and ends, the student will be forced to "give an account" of their conduct and commitment. This broadly Socratic, disillusioning effect amounts, Weber notes, to a kind of moral function. To ask for more than this—to pretend that *Wissenschaft* can offer authoritative answers to our deepest moral, political, and existential questions—is to fail to live up to the "plain duty of intellectual honesty." It would make one a demagogue, not a scholar.

None of Weber's recent critics would fault his plea for a political ethic of responsibility, nor would they dismiss his insistence on the importance of complicating "inconvenient facts." What they would fault is Weber's emphasis on unguided *decision*, an emphasis which animates both *Vocation* lectures. Whether we strive to be "leading politicians" or merely engaged citizens, the choice of our value commitments is left up to us. *Contra* much of the Western philosophical tradition, Weber asserts that reason—in its post-metaphysical, disenchanted form as specialized scientific inquiry—is incapable of providing anything like authoritative adjudication among competing political ideals and philosophies of life. One simply has to choose—preferably with one's eyes open to facts, no matter how inconvenient, and with a keen awareness of the costs involved.

It is this proto-existentialist aspect of the *Vocation* lectures that has enabled many, not just Habermas, to charge Weber with promoting an ethos of groundless commitment, one unmoored from any rational or deliberative constraints. Granted, there may well be no end-adjudicating "super-science" called Reason (or "right reason") as the tradition taught. Nevertheless, the critics point out, moral-political argument and commitment rely heavily on the giving and receiving of reasons—on the redemption of validity claims through a distinctly *communicative* form of rationality, one that militates against any and all "leaps of faith."

What would Weber say to the charge that he introduced a "decisionist element" into politics, and into German politics in particular, through his account of science and the "disenchantment of the world"? He might answer that acquaintance with inconvenient facts and the objective costs—both human and material—of any ideological program are amongst the most valuable contributions scholarship or "rational argumentation" can make to the elucidation of moral and political questions. At the end of the day, however, he would insist that there can be no comprehensive or "final" solution to questions about which political or moral perspectives we should take.

Science or reason cannot tell one to become a social democrat, a liberal, or a conservative, any more that it can tell one to become a Catholic, a Protestant, or a Jew. There are only more or less well-informed choices, more or less willingness to compromise when the various "gods" clash. As Weber wrote in "The Meaning of 'Ethical Neutrality' in Sociology and Economics," conflict "cannot be excluded from social life," however much rationalists from Socrates to Marx desired to curtail if not eliminate it. From Weber's point of view, the ineradicable nature of conflict is hardly a matter for untempered regret. The fact that classes, values, and ideologies are in conflict with each other serves to preserve a certain degree of individual choice and freedom in a world that, more and more, had come to resemble an "iron cage."

Schmitt: A "Natural Son"?

The Weberian emphasis on the ineradicable nature of struggle, combined with his focus on the state as a "relation of men dominating men" would seem, at first glance, to dovetail with Carl Schmitt's concept of the political. Schmitt emphasized the essentially antagonistic character of the political realm, focusing on the "sovereign capacity" of leaders to make the essential determination as to who was an enemy of the political association.[23] The "intimate relation" between the state and violence which Weber stresses at the beginning of "Politics as a Vocation" finds its echo in Schmitt's state-centric obsession with the "extreme case" (the possibility of war between two "fighting collectivities"). When we add to these similarities Weber's insistence on the fundamental irreconcilability of different values or ways of life (the "warring gods") and his insistence on the relative autonomy of the political sphere, we seem to have all the evidence we need to call Schmitt as a "natural son" of Weber.[24]

The surface similarity is, however, precisely that: a matter of surfaces. The moment we probe Schmitt's concept of the political, glaring and substantive differences reveal themselves.

First and most obviously, there is the matter of self-identification. Although Weber's political positions shifted markedly during his lifetime—from the belligerent, race-based expansionism of inaugural lecture at Freiburg in 1895 to his alignment with the German Democratic Party in 1918—he always identified with liberal commitments. To be sure, these commitments were more than balanced by a nationalism which, from the perspective of the present, looks extreme and highly dubious.[25] Yet the fact remains that Weber thought of himself as a liberal, while Schmitt's entire *oeuvre* has as its gravitational center a radical critique of liberalism and its presuppositions. Weber attempted to give liberalism a distinctively *German* form, one in sync with the nation's status as a *Machtstaat* comparable to France or England. Schmitt, in contrast, saw his job as revealing liberalism's various indefensible illusions—most notably, the "fantasy" of a world in which antagonism between states was sublimated into "ethical debate" and/or economic competition.[26]

Weber's brand of liberalism was, of course, free of this particular fantasy. Hence his disillusioned emphasis on the reality of conflict and on the state as an association characterized by the control of legitimate means of violence. However, the moment we interrogate Weber's idea of conflict or struggle we see a gap opening up between him and his "natural son." The full characterization he gives in 1917 in "The Meaning of 'Ethical Neutrality' in Sociology and Economics" (alluded to above) runs as follows:

> Conflict cannot be excluded from social life. One can change its means, its object, even its fundamental direction and its bearers, but it cannot be eliminated. There can be, instead of an external struggle of antagonistic persons for external objects, an inner struggle of mutually loving persons for subjective values and therewith, instead of external compulsion, an inner control (in the form of erotic or charitable devotion). Or it can take the form of a subjective conflict in the individual's own mind. It is always present and its influence is often greatest when it is least noticed, i.e., the more its course takes the form of indifferent or complacent passivity or self-deception, or when it operates as "selection." "Peace" is nothing other than a change in the form of the conflict or in the antagonists or in the objects of conflict, or finally the chances of selection.[27]

Conflict here is not only ineradicable, it is also ubiquitous. Weber's characterization, obviously indebted to Nietzsche, stretches conflict across the social, political and personal spectrum, and it does so in what can only be described as a highly metaphorical way.

In contrast to Weber, Schmitt's idea of antagonism is highly specified, finding its most authentic meaning in the fact of *combat*:

> Just as the term enemy, the word combat, too, is to be understood in its original existential sense. It does not mean competition, nor does it mean pure intellectual controversy nor symbolic wrestlings in which, after all, every human being is somehow always involved, for it is a fact that the entire life of a human being is a struggle and every human being symboli-cally a combatant. The friend, enemy, and combat concepts receive their real meaning precisely because they refer to the *real possibility of physi-cal killing*. War follows from enmity. War is the existential negation of the enemy [i.e., the group, association or state that has been determined to be an "existential threat" to "our" way of life].[28]

The Weberian idea of conflict stretching across all planes of life is here dismissed as a depoliticizing "symbolic" conception, one that draws our attention away from the fact that specifically *political* antagonism *always* implies "the real pos-sibility of physical killing"—that is, the "existential negation of the enemy."

This difference is amplified when we remember Weber's own more "political" determination of conflict and struggle. For Weber, electoral competition, parlia-mentary debate and maneuvering, and the perpetual tension between branches of government—parliament, administration and monarch—were all legitimate forms of political struggle and selection. While hardly blind to the "struggle be-tween nation-states," he did not reify that struggle as *the* quintessential case of *all* authentically *political* conflict. Indeed, for Weber, the "battlefield of elections" was as genuinely political (if not more so) than the literal battlefield that so fas-cinates Schmitt.

This difference points to another significant gap, this time regarding Weber and Schmitt's respective conceptions of the autonomy of the political. In his 1927 manifesto, *The Concept of the Political*, Schmitt lays out his own version of this au-tonomy. There is no denying that Schmitt's initial set up of the problem posed by the "autonomy of the political" owes much to Weber, specifically to the latter's the-sis concerning the "disaggregation of value-spheres." Modernization and secular-ization produce a separating out of life-spheres, with art, economics, politics, and science achieving a position of independence from the "grandiose rationalism of an ethical and methodical conduct of life which flows from . . . . religious proph-ecy."[29] The result, in Weber's formulation, is that "many old gods ascend from their graves; they are disenchanted and hence take the form of impersonal forces. They strive for power over our lives and again they resume their eternal struggle with one another."[30] Liberated from overarching theocratic control, the spheres of art, science, politics, and economics come to operate according to their own "laws," and in accord with their own (immanently generated) codes of conduct.

With this Weberian account of the relative autonomy of various life-spheres in the background, Schmitt asks whether, as in the cases of art and economics, there is a "special distinction which can serve as a simple criterion of the political and of what it consists."[31] The famous answer is that there is indeed such a specific (and specifying) distinction for the realm of the political: the distinction between friend and enemy.[32] This move restricts the sphere of the political to the field of potential antagonism between fighting collectivities—a restriction Weber would not have recognized. Moreover, where Weber cited the specificity of the political—its reliance on certain "characteristic means"—as reason to search for a distinctly political ethic, Schmitt cites it precisely in order to sever the link between ethics and politics—a link, it should be noted, that he deems characteristically "liberal" in nature.

This severing of ethics from politics is the fundamental strategic move in *Concept of the Political's* war on liberalism. According to Schmitt, liberalism depoliticizes by sublimating conflict into other (non-political) forms, such as economic competition and ethical debate. Its fundamental impulse is to "annihilate the political." This "annihilation" is accomplished by "an entire system of demilitarized and depoliticalized [*sic*] concepts," which succeed in covering over the relative frequency and determinative nature of the "extreme case," as well as the accompanying need for sovereign decision.[33] At least since Benjamin Constant's *De l'espirit de la conquête* (1814), liberalism has argued that the world is moving irrevocably away from a system of perpetually warring nation-states, and towards a global order of economic integration and competition, an order predicated on an increasingly universal and legally codified respect for human rights. Denying the existential priority of national identities, as well as the intrinsically "dangerous" character of man *qua* animal, liberalism encourages us to believe in an emergent world of perpetual peace, a peace enforced by ties of trade, international law, and a universal respect for humanity and the "rights of man."[34]

Schmitt's counter to Constant and liberalism's attempt to substitute the spirit of commerce for the spirit of war works on two levels. The first is logical-historical. No matter how far we have moved away from the inflamed particularities of the past, Schmitt argues, the emergence of an "enemy"—a threat to "our way of life"—is always present as a *possibility*. To be sure, the importance of friend/enemy decision may fade into the background during prolonged periods of peace and prosperity, such as Europe experienced between 1875 and 1914. Such periods incline us to view the state as secondary, as just one association among many (local, professional, religious, etc.). However, so long as there are *states*—so long as the political world is a "pluriverse" and not a "universe"—the *possibility* of the "extreme case" coming to pass remains intact.[35] According to Schmitt, the only way to genuinely eradicate this possibility would be for a world state to come into being.

It is in the course of musing on the implications of such a transformation that Schmitt reveals his second argument. This argument is robustly normative, if not exactly ethical, in character. The defining character of the nation-state is, in Schmitt's view, less its monopoly on legitimate violence than its possession of the *jus belli*, the "right to demand from its own members the readiness to die and unhesitatingly to kill enemies."[36] This right necessarily accompanies the state's duty of protection and its corresponding duty to determine who is friend and who is enemy. But suppose, for a moment, that the political "pluriverse" actually became a universe—that a "world state" came into being, one in accordance with liberal values. What then? Schmitt's answer takes us to the heart of his conception not only of the political, but of *identity* and *meaning* in a secular world:

> Were a world state to embrace the entire globe and humanity, then it would be no political entity and could only loosely be called a state. If, in fact, all humanity and the entire world were to become a unified entity based exclusively on economics and on technically regulating traffic, then it still would not be more of a social entity than a social entity of tenants in a tenement house, customers purchasing gas from the same utility company, or passengers traveling on the same bus. An interest group concerned exclusively with economics or traffic cannot become more in the absence of an adversary.[37]

With the elimination of the possibility of antagonism—a possibility inscribed in a world of nation-states—"what remains is neither politics nor state, but culture, civilization, economics, morality, law, art, entertainment, etc."[38] The "post-political world" realized by either a world state or globalization without limit would not only be a world without states and wars, but a world without any deep *identity*. To be a "we" at all, people need to be more than "tenants" occupying the same institutional edifice, or consumers buying goods from the same companies. They need to have a distinct *way of life*, one that can possibly be threatened by an alternative way of life. Such an alternative is concretely embodied in an *other* (potentially hostile) people.[39] To put the point in slightly different terms: the elimination of the "state of nature" between states and political groupings would leave us with a world composed merely of interest groups and consumers. It would not, however, leave any association—any way of life—worth fighting and dying for. Such a world, Schmitt implies, would simply not be worth living in.

Persons of broadly liberal sensibility would probably see the end of such ostensibly "deep" political identity as a small price to pay for the end of war. Yet we fool ourselves if we think nationalism, ethnic pride, and a reflexive patriotism are on the wane in our "enlightened" and globalized world. Most people, in most places, would find Schmitt's odd mix of Hobbes and Hegel (identity as a function of a hostile "other") right on the money. We think of ourselves as Americans, Chinese, Russians, Israelis, etc. first—not as Europeans, world citizens, or simple human beings. Schmitt's thesis regarding the existential importance of politically defined and defended group identities may be morally repugnant, but the vast majority frame their identities in accordance with it. And, as Schmitt implies, they would probably experience a world *without* such strong, politically-based group identities as a world devoid of much of its meaning.

I have dwelt on this point because it indicates another wide divergence between Weber and his erstwhile "disciple," Schmitt. For Weber, secularization and the retreat of theological worldviews capable of integrating the various life-spheres gives rise to the "warring gods" of modernity. These "gods"—the relatively autonomous spheres of modern social life, including art, economics, politics, science and religion—place conflicting demands on many if not all of us, conflicts that we have to negotiate in our everyday lives. The Weberian *topos* of conflict thus expresses one of the main characteristics of life in a fragmented modernity.

For Schmitt, the stresses created by "the old gods rising from their graves" are small potatoes compared to the *real* clash of values embodied in rival national "ways of life." Rather than focusing on the tensions between life-spheres, Schmitt concentrates on the one antagonism which, in his judgment, matters. This is the enmity between states or political groupings. It is hard to see how *this* radical narrowing of perspective—the literalization and politicization of both conflict and identity—can be seen as a "logical" or even legitimate product of Weber's broad problematic. Schmitt's sense of the friend/enemy groupings requires solidaristic identities, and so precludes the kind of internal fragmentation Weber sees as afflicting all social groups. When we add to this the fact that the "charismatic leader" is, first and foremost, a parliamentary politician who operates within the framework of party politics and constitutional restrictions, it becomes even harder to frame Schmitt's vision of politics as a natural outgrowth of Weber's political sociology.[40]

To this, the genealogist of Schmitt's thought might well respond along the lines suggested by Mommsen in 1959. Weber did not value parliamentary politics *in itself*, but only as a mechanism for the *selection* of strong leaders. This "instrumental" approach to parliament dovetailed with his hopes for the production of charismatic "leading politicians." These, according to Mommsen, would be "great demagogues" who would rule "on the strength of their personal qualities." Hence Mommsen's conclusion, reiterated by Habermas, that "Weber did not hesitate to carry the populistic leadership concept to its extreme conclusions."[41] The "extreme" meant a radical de-emphasis on popular political participation and on parliamentary-constitutional restrictions to the "great demagogue's" rule.

I think this characterization goes too far. Weber may have framed his endorsement of a "strong parliament" in terms of its capacity to generate a leading—and authentically political—elite. But *Parliament and Government* goes well beyond this merely instrumental rationale. As outlined above, a strong parliamentary system was, for Weber, the *sine qua non* for overcoming the authoritarian state (*Obrigkeitsstaat*) of the *Kaiserreich*. It brought transparency (at least in domestic affairs) where before there had be official secrecy; it provided essential control and interrogation of the administrative apparatus; and it served as an invaluable organ of political education for the electorate.

"Strong leaders" directly elected by means of a presidential system and representative institutions are by no means mutually exclusive. Weber—confronted by massive problems of post-war economic and social reconstruction—unsurprisingly stressed the need for such leadership in his last years.[42] The fact that "Politics as a Vocation" is sometimes read as a total rejection of the parliamentary system tells us more about ourselves—and the unfortunate tendency to interpret texts with 20/20 historical hindsight—than it does about Weber's actual position.[43]

Lukács: From Weber to Marx

The Hegelian Leninism of Georg Lukács presents us with an entirely different set of problems. Only the most promiscuous of commentators could conceivably call Lukács a "natural son" of Weber. "Legitimate pupil," on the other hand, may well seem warranted. Lukács's most important political-philosophical work, *History and Class Consciousness* (1923), owes almost as much to Weber as it does to Marx.[44] This is especially true of the central essay of the volume, "Reification and the Consciousness of the Proletariat." The early sections of this essay offer a profound reinterpretation of Marx's idea of commodity fetishism, one that expands this notion into the much broader social phenomenon of "reification." The latter idea—perhaps Lukács's single most important contribution to Marxist thought and social theory—is reached through the creative appropriation of Weber's concept of rationalization.

In *Capital*, "commodity fetishism" refers to what Marx considered a peculiarly capitalist phenomenon: social relations between men taking the "mystified" form of relations between things (commodities). Thus, instead of a class of factory owners confronting a hungry and exploitable class of workers whom they can hire for a pittance, we have the abstractions of "capital," "labor-power," and "exchange-value" engaging in a semi-inscrutable dance with one another. The human essence of the worker—his capacity to produce in an "all-sided" manner—is turned into a commodity, labor-power, which the capitalist purchases by means of an ostensibly "fair exchange" on the labor market. The "laws of the market" discovered by the early political economist (Smith, Ricardo, Say) all presuppose an extensive commodification of human beings and social life, one that veils relationships of hierarchy, power, and exploitation under the fluctuating relations of "fixed" and investment capital, rent, and available "labor power." The human dimensions of such relationships become a secondary and, strictly speaking, non-economic set of phenomena.

For Marx, the mystification born of commodity fetishism had important ideological consequences in that it created a picture of the world in which non-human entities interact according to their own intrinsic laws, mirroring the "eternal" laws of nature. The human creators of value, capital, and labor-power—the workers themselves—appear trapped by their own products, which have taken on a life of their own. The only way for this version of "The Sorcerer and His Apprentice" to have a happy ending—for the living abstractions to *serve* humanity rather than *enslaving* the vast majority—is for the workers to break out of the dance of abstractions presented by the classical economists. They can do this only if they grasp each and every "timeless" abstraction as a historically produced entity, part of a larger historically evolving totality: capitalism. Once the immanent tendencies of this dynamic totality are grasped by the working class (a process aided by theoreticians like Marx himself), they can recover their agency and begin to push this ever more social form of production towards its "logical" end—namely, a socialist society in which the means of production are held in common and the relations of production are egalitarian, voluntary, and transparent.

History and Class Consciousness in no way departs from this basic Marxian story. As noted above, its primary contribution is to read "fetishism" through the lens provided by the Weberian concept of rationalization. The resulting concept of "reification" no longer refers simply to commodification. Rather, it refers to the process by which an ever more developed division of labor creates "rational" and independent subsystems—not only in the economy, but in the social, legal, and political worlds as well. The "fragmented world of modernity," is one in which not only workers, but administrators, politicians, doctors, lawyers, judges, soldiers, officers, and scientists all find themselves separated from the "means of production" (whether these be offices, machines, weapons, laboratories or libraries).

Everywhere we turn, the independent artisan—or scholar, or physician, or warrior—has become a thing of the past. As Weber emphasized, a capitalist social formation demands the extension of rational administration and calculability to virtually all spheres of life. And, as Lukács points out, when this rationalization is complete (as it evidently is in the late modern age) "it seems to penetrate the very depths of man's physical and psychic nature."[45] The docile worker, the disciplined soldier, the "rational" administrator are one and all creatures of the specific institutions that mold them to be efficient cogs in the social machine.

For Lukács, then, Weberian rationalization is continuous with commodity fetishism. The basic phenomenon—in which direct social relationships, however hierarchical in nature, yield to rational and efficient administrative and economic forms—is the same. "Reification" is the term Lukács deploys to indicate *both* the rationalized independence of various social subsystems (each with their own "laws," logic, and patterns of development) and the character of the *consciousness* created by this pervasive rationalization. To be "objectified" by the labor market or the army, the health care or the legal system, is bad enough. But this familiar experience doesn't begin to reach the heart of the problem. Thanks to "reified consciousness" we are just as prone to objectify or commodify ourselves. Thus, on the one hand, we may well feel trapped by the "iron cage" comprised by such economic, legal, and administrative structures. On the other, however, we transform ourselves into the kind of entity that accepts and smoothly functions in the "completely administered world."[46]

How to regain a sense of agency in such a "mystified" (and seemingly unalterable) social world? How do we escape reified consciousness and subject our various creations—the productive apparatus, bureaucratic administration, "formal" rationality—to our wills? How, in short, is it possible for persons inhabiting a Weberian-Lukácsian world to empower themselves?

It is in response to questions like these that Lukács departs most radically from Weber. He rejects not only the latter's liberal politics, but the epistemological limits imposed by *verstehende* (or, interpretative) *Soziologie*. Weber's liberal concern with the diminishment of individual freedom, his methodological individualism, and his skepticism regarding the possibility of anything other than a self-consciously *constructed* (epistemologically modest) social science—all are viewed by Lukács as retrogressions when compared to the dialectical *truth* of the social process as discovered by Marx.

What is that truth? Its most basic structure is supplied by Marx's radical extension of Giambattista Vico's verum/factum thesis. Because, as a species, we have "made" history and the social world, we—humanity or its representatives—have the capacity to transform both. An essential precondition of such change is liberation from contemplative and neo-Kantian ideas of knowledge. The former approach models knowledge of the socio-historical world along the lines of the natural sciences. Following Descartes, it posits an ontological abyss between the scientific investigator (the subject) and the external reality (the object) he is examining. While the deficits of such an approach are less apparent in the natural sciences, they are, in Lukács's view, glaring when it comes to knowledge of society and history. For we are not merely observers, nor even participant observers, when it comes to history and society. We have, in a real sense, "made" both. Our understanding of this reality, and (thus) of ourselves, is both constituted by and transforms the very "object" under investigation.

As a result, how we understand history and society contributes mightily to how we structure—and potentially transform—both. If we comprehend the social realm as a functional nexus of relatively autonomous, "reified" subsystems (law, the market, bureaucracy, etc.), then we will view ourselves in a reified way, as mere "inputs" with the rigid factuality of the social machine. If, on the other had, we recognize our status as authors or producers of the social world; and if we see this world not as a set of independently operating systems, but rather as a dynamic, historically developing *totality*—*then* we will see that the apparently immoveable "facts" of our social universe are actually merely one stage in an ongoing process of social evolution.[47] The importance of Marx's reformulation of Vico's principle, according to Lukács, is that it reveals social knowledge to be intrinsically practical, with emancipatory implications. A "scientific" or merely contemplative conception of the social realm yields passivity in the face of seemingly brute facts. A dynamic or dialectical conception reveals us as (potentially) revolutionary transformers.[48]

Lukács has similar objections to methodologically self-aware or "constructed" versions of the *Geisteswissenschaften*, such as we find in Weber (sociology) or Dilthey (the historical and cultural sciences). While eschewing the natural sciences as a model, such neo-Kantian approaches make a point of circumscribing their respective "objects" in a highly artificial way. They exaggerate the fragmentation of modern society in order to make it more available to "specialized" scholarly disciplines. They also engage in the tortuous process of constructing methodically precise "ideal-types," insisting all the while on the gap between such definitions and the messier reality such constructed concepts are designed to illuminate. Finally, these "bourgeois" sciences presuppose what Lukács and the Western Marxist tradition view as an indefensible "value-neutrality." To be sure, they don't do this in a vulgar positivist manner. Weber, for example, hardly thought social "facts" were just out there, ready to discovered by the enterprising sociologist or economist operating "without presuppositions."[49] But he did think that the political and cultural presuppositions the investigator brings to his work could be comprehensively articulated—and thus prophylactically distinguished—from the actual phenomena under investigation.[50]

Such methodological precautions are, from Lukács's point of view, both misguided and disingenuous. They testify to the effective history of the Cartesian subject/object split, and to the continuing influence of Kant's distinction between knowable "phenomena" and the unknowable "noumena" (*Dinge an sich*), the things-in-themselves. Our claims to social and historical knowledge appear conditional and restricted only because we allow the Cartesian-Kantian heritage to bar us from grasping the *actual* historical and developmental process which creates the very "facts" (or "empirical data") confronting us. This heritage presents us with a frozen (or "reified") picture of social reality, one that can be comprehensively known only through painstaking specialization (a point Weber emphasizes again and again in his 1904 essay, " 'Objectivity' in Social Science and Social Policy"). But for Lukács—as for Hegel and Marx—the truth is to be found in the (dynamic and evolving) whole, and not in any fragment or part, no matter how intensively it is investigated.

Reclaiming a sense of one's own individual and collective agency, then, presupposes two things. First, it presupposes a theoretical-practical conception capable of grasping "reality as a social process" (something Weber's methodology does not give us).[51] Second, it presupposes a recognition that escape from a "reified" view of reality is possible only for members of that social class whose interests *as a class* are one with the *interests of humanity* as a whole. The bourgeoisie are incapable of escaping the "illusions" of reified consciousness and a fragmented world because their class interests and self-understanding actually *encourage* a contemplative attitude towards "social facts." They are, as both Marx and Lukács emphasize, barred from dialectical insight into the social process as a whole. The proletariat, on the other hand, can understand itself and its class aims only by transcending "the mechanical aggregate of individual historical events" and grasping "the totality of history" as itself a "real historical [i.e., practical] power."[52] Once it does this, the working class is able to realize its destiny as the "universal subject-object" of history—that is, as the constituted and constituting agent of social-historical reality.

The transcendence of the immediate world of frozen social "facts" by means of a dialectical grasp of the totality is precisely what makes the proletariat's recovery of its own agency possible. Driven, as no other class is, by its grim social situation to confront the way its members have been transformed into "mere things," the proletariat is primed to rebel against a reality that it experiences as literally dehumanizing. Their (collective) subjectivity awakened by the radical deprivation of their social condition, the proletariat is in principle open to a vision of reality as a dynamic social process. This vision is denied to the capitalist bourgeoisie (and bourgeois social scientists, like Weber) because of their superficially affirming place in the economic apparatus.[53] But with the help of theoretical allies like Marx and Engels, the working class comes to recognizes its historically constitutive role in the generation of humanity's productive forces and contemporary social reality. It sees through the "mystified" relations of capital to labor and the "thralldom to objects" that this mystification supports.

In all this, Lukács is glossing basic points found Marx's early "Contribution to the Critique of Hegel's *Philosophy of Right*" (with its philosophical deduction of an utterly dehumanized class with "radical chains") and *The German Ideology* (with its vision of humanity as demiurge that creates forces and structures that escape its control).[54] He goes well beyond Marx, however, by making explicit what could be called the "epistemologically privileged" standpoint of the proletariat. Whereas Weber had emphasized the partial and interpretative nature of causal explanation with respect to even the "smallest slice of [social] reality," Lukács devotes the lion's share of "Reification and the Consciousness of the Proletariat" to delineating why the "perspective of the proletariat" is not one perspective among many, but the privileged access point to truth itself. To repeat, this truth is broached in the form of a vision of society as dialectically mediated (interrelated and evolving) totality. Such a vision was originally laid out by Hegel, only to be subsequently "de-mystified" by Marx. "Humanity"—and its modern representative, the proletariat—is put into the place Hegel had reserved for his idealistic and demiurgic conception of *Geist*.

There are obvious problems—ontological, epistemological, political and methodological—with Lukács's argument. What are the implications of transforming the cognitive subject into a *social class*? Why should the concept of a dialectically-mediated "totality" grant us access to a non-perspectival "truth," as opposed to simply another standpoint from which interpret exceedingly complex social phenomena? Finally, isn't the epistemological privilege of the working class—its potentially illusion-free position in the social production process—actually reliant on its acceptance of the insight provided by its "bourgeois" theoretical allies (Marx and Engels) and—later—by the "vanguard" party organization (Lenin)?

The answers to these questions are readily apparent. If Weber hobbles his own investigations by adopting a dubious methodological individualism, Lukács swings in the opposite direction. He accepts as a matter of faith the Aristotelian/Hegelian insistence that the whole is prior to, and more "real" than, any part.[55] This ontological presupposition yields the conclusion that only the whole (or "totality") is true, as well as the partisan correlate that Marx had laid out a conceptually adequate account of this same "totality." This bit of theoretical dogmatism—evident on every page of Lukács's attacks on "the facts"—is directly related to his radical devaluation of concrete, empirical proletarian consciousness, and to his unqualified willingness to view the party as the guardian of truth.[56]

Considerations such as these take us back to Weber's "Science as a Vocation."

That lecture is nothing if not a plea for intellectual integrity in a time of crisis. To his audience's demand for an existentially meaningful conception of the scientific vocation, Weber responds with a deflationary account of the "progress" of Western *ratio* from the Greeks to the bourgeois epoch. At various points in its history, reason (as science or *episteme*) was held to be the way to true being (the Greeks), true art and nature (da Vinci and the Renaissance), the meaning of the world and God (the Reformation), or, simply, human happiness (the great technological achievements of the capitalist-bourgeois epoch).[57] It promised, in other words, to discover an authoritative answer to the question of the *meaning* of human existence, to the Tolstoyan question of "What shall we do and how shall we live?"

But it is precisely on this ground—the ground of worldly meaning, existential significance, and practical-ethical guidance—that modern science/reason at last reveals its impotence. The former illusions have been dispelled by an epochal arc of disenchantment. The fact that science gives no answer to the question "how to live and how to act" should, by now, be evident to all.[58] Viewed from a Tolstoyan perspective, science is "meaningless" as an activity. It cannot provide what it once unembarrassedly offered: authoritative ("rational") answers to our most pressing existential questions. As Weber famously wrote in "'Objectivity' in Social Science," "the fate of an epoch which has eaten of the tree of knowledge is that it must know that we cannot learn the *meaning* of the world from the results of its analysis, be it ever so perfect; it must rather be in a position to create this meaning itself."[59] Absent a built-in teleology of progress or doom that reason might somehow discover, there is only the continuing struggle of the "warring gods"— various faiths, ideologies, and life-spheres—in the newly "disenchanted" world.

"Science as a Vocation" is characterized by an astringent intellectual honesty.[60] It is precisely this honesty that Lukács rejects. The "correct" (Hegelian-Marxist) form of reason reveals not only the immanent teleology of "reality as a social process." It also—most emphatically—tells us "how to live and how to act" if we wish to actualize this *telos* (communism) and emancipate humanity. Like virtually all of Weber's subsequent critics (Habermas included), Lukács deems a thoroughly "disillusioned" idea of science and reason to be practically unacceptable and potentially "nihilistic." Shorn of its traditional end-adjudicating and *telos*-identifying functions, reason is not "reason" at all. It is "irrationalism," the corroding disease of the age and the abyss-like ground of fascism.[61]

Conclusion

In an interview with Steven Lukes, Isaiah Berlin once feigned ignorance of the fact that Weber had anticipated many of his primary points concerning moral pluralism and the indefensible "monism" of the Western philosophical tradition.[62] Like Weber, Berlin thought that when values or worldviews conflict, one simply had to chose (assuming, of course, a roughly equal acknowledgment of facts and costs). To pretend that other options were available—that reason, science, or nature might offer us an authoritative ranking of irreconcilable values or worldviews—was to pursue a "final solution" to life's problems. In Berlin's view, such "monist" ambitions animated the twentieth century's worst political catastrophes. They stand as bloody testimony what happens when political leaders, like the philosophers and theologians before them, assume that there must be one, and only one, "correct" answer to the question of how to live and how to act.

Given this substantive similarity on the question of moral pluralism and the unsustainable pretensions of a "value-ranking" rationalism, it is perhaps surprising that only Weber, and not Berlin, is charged with "decisionism" and "strengthening the spell" of ideology. One explanation for this state of is biographical/contextual. Berlin, of course, was a Russian Jew whose family narrowly escaped the Bolshevik revolution, a liberal political thinker who watched in horror as the tyrannies of left and right came to dominate the politics of the mid-twentieth century. Weber, on the other hand, was Germany's leading social and political thinker at the end of the first world war. He was enormously worried about by the emergence of the "madmen" of left and right in the early years of the Weimar Republic, even though he could not foresee the epic tragedy awaiting his country (however much foreboding he had about the future).

Berlin's historical acquaintance with the worst humanity had to offer led him to praise the liberal virtues of compromise and consensus, where possible. Weber, writing in what was, in effect, a different age, stressed the need to honestly and manfully stand up for one's ultimate commitments, all the while practicing (in the political realm, at least) an "ethic of responsibility." For obvious reasons, the latter position does not furnish a helpful ground for compromise. Weber's "leading politician" is a fighter. There is no getting around this fact. In this sense—and only in this sense—does Habermas's youthful critique ring true.

But what about Schmitt and Lukács? Isn't it plausible to view them as legitimate inheritors of the Weber's "decisionist" spirit, even if they did not share his liberal politics?

The short answer to this question is, simply, no. Whatever surface similarities exist between Weber and Schmitt—their nationalism, their joint emphasis on struggle, their apparently shared emphasis on leadership or "sovereign" power—pale when we take into account Schmitt's literalization of Weber's metaphorics of struggle, to say nothing of his restricted socio-political ontology of "us" and "them." The Schmittian vision reduces Weber's extraordinarily complex and qualified view of social and political life to one dimension: that of real or potential struggle between armed camps. Sovereign power—the power of decision as to who the enemy is and whether an emergency situation presents itself—is his most persistent object of fascination. Whatever Weber's reasons for emphasizing the importance of "leadership" in post–Great War Germany, such an underlying Hobbesianism was conspicuously lacking.

Lukács is even further removed from Weber's outlook. Wielding a rationalism that is both dogmatic and unapologetic, contemptuous of "facts" and unconcerned with costs, Lukács's Leninism led him to utterly disregard the Weberian imperatives of intellectual honesty and political responsibility. Whereas Weber tried to discern the physiognomy of a "disenchanted world" and a reason shorn of metaphysical pretension, Lukács (in effect) served the cause of re-enchantment. Historical teleology is resurrected as Truth itself. Whatever the merits of his reification thesis (and they certainly exist, as the work of the Frankfurt School has born out), the duality of "fact-based" mystification vs. holistic social truth restricts both its utility and its (potential) truth content.[63] Adorno's rejoinder to Hegel—"the whole is the false"—applies even more directly to Lukács's tortured theoretical efforts on behalf of the "universal subject-object" of history.

Notes

1. Habermas in *Max Weber and Sociology Today*, ed. Otto Stammer, trans. Kathleen Morris (New York: Harper & Row Publishers, 1971), 66.
2. Max Weber, *Max Weber-Gesamtausgabe*, eds. Horst Baier, M. Rainer Lepsius, Wolfgang J. Mommsen, Wolfgang Schluchter, and Johannes Winckelmann (Tübingen: Mohr Siebeck, 1986), 273.
3. See Max Horkheimer, *The Eclipse of Reason* (New York: Continuum, 1974), 6; Herbert Marcuse, "Industrialization and Capitalism" in *Max Weber and Sociology Today*, 133–51; and Habermas, 59–66 of the same volume. On the right, see Leo Strauss, *Natural Right and History* (Chicago: University of Chicago Press, 1959), chap. 2 and Alasdair MacIntyre, *After Virtue* (Notre Dame: University of Notre Dame Press, 1981), 24–25, where MacIntyre accuses Weber of "emotivism" *and* existentialism.
4. See, e.g., Tracy B. Strong, foreword to Carl Schmitt, *Political Theology* (Chicago: University of Chicago Press, 2005), xxiii.
5. As Stammer notes in his volume, "Following a friendly piece of advice, Professor Habermas said he thought afterwards [the Weber centenary conference in Heidelberg] 'a natural son' of Weber's to be a more appropriate expression" (Stammer, 66).
6. Schmitt was a National Socialist until 1936; Lukács a Leninist and more than occasional defender of Stalinism.
7. This is not to say that, morally and politically speaking, Weber's integrity is beyond impeachment. His nationalism was and is a persistent stain on his reputation, both as a social thinker and political actor. However, as I have pointed out in chapter 4 of *Socratic Citizenship*, it hardly follows from his ethos of disillusionment. See Dana Villa, *Socratic Citizenship* (Princeton: Princeton University Press, 2001).
8. Max Weber, *Political Writings*, eds. Peter Lassman and Ronald Spiers (New York: Cambridge University Press, 1994), 157.
9. Weber, *Political Writings*, 159.
10. See Marianne Weber, *Max Weber: A Biography*, trans. Harry Zohn (New York: John Wiley & Sons, 1975), 652–54.
11. Marianne Weber, *Max Weber: A Biography*, 178.
12. As Weber writes in "Parliament and Government," "Political maturity is not expressed in votes of no confidence, denunciations of ministers and similar spectacles of *unorganized* parliamentary rule in France and Italy, but rather in the fact that a nation is well informed about how its officials are *conducting their affairs*, so that it constantly controls and influences their work. The committees of a powerful parliament are the only possible places from which that educative influence can be exerted. In the end, officialdom as such can only gain from such an arrangement" (Weber, *Political Writings*, 180). It is interesting to compare what Weber says in this regard to what J. S. Mill wrote fifty years earlier in his *Considerations on Representative Government*. In that work, Mill defends representative assemblies precisely as "talk shops," i.e., as places of talk about "the great public interests of the country" where "every sentence represents the opinion either of some important body of persons in the nation, or of an individual in whom some such body has placed their confidence." The role of such assemblies, in Mill's view, is not to "do," but to "talk" and—thus—to help facilitate discussion of public affairs more broadly. "Doing" is, generally, to be left to the individual, or individuals, "specially trained to it" (J. S. Mill, *Considerations on Representative Government* in Mill, *Utilitarianism, On Liberty, and Considerations on Representative Government*, ed. H. B. Acton (London: Dent, 1984), 259–60.

Weber's conception of a "strong parliament"—obviously and explicitly modeled on the British case—is free of Mill's Hegel-like faith in the "trained intelligence" of civil service bureaucrats.

13. Mommsen, *Max Weber and German Politics*, trans. Michael S. Steinberg (Chicago: University of Chicago Press, 1984), 283.
14. Mommsen, "Politics and Scholarship: The Two Icons of Max Weber's Life" in Mommsen, *The Political and Social Theory of Max Weber* (Chicago: University of Chicago Press, 1989), 5.
15. Max Weber, "Politics as a Vocation" in *From Max Weber: Essays in Sociology*, eds. H. H. Gerth and C. Wright Mills (New York: Oxford University Press, 1958), 113.
16. Weber, "Politics as a Vocation," 106.
17. For a reading of "Politics as a Vocation" along these line, see Harvey Goldmann, *Politics, Death, and the Devil: Self and Power in Max Weber and Thomas Mann* (Berkeley: University of California Press, 1992), 163ff.
18. Weber, "Politics as a Vocation," 119.
19. Weber, "Politics as a Vocation," 119–20.
20. Weber, "Politics as a Vocation," 119, 117.
21. Weber, "Politics as a Vocation," 117.
22. Weber, "Politics as a Vocation," 120.
23. Carl Schmitt, *The Concept of the Political*, trans. and with an introduction by George Schwab (Chicago: University of Chicago Press, 1996), 26.
24. For Weber's version of the "autonomy of the political," see Peter Lassman, "The Rule of Man over Man: Politics, Power, and Legitimation" in *The Cambridge Companion to Max Weber*, ed. Stephen Turner (New York: Cambridge University Press, 2000), 84–90.
25. Weber's nationalism—like his liberalism—was a constant throughout his adult life. Thus, the dubious conflation of political economy and agricultural competition in West Prussia with the "struggle of nations" in the *Antrittsrede* is book-ended by Weber's declaration at the beginning of "Parliament and Government" that "anyone for whom the historical tasks of the German nation do not take *precedence*, as a matter of principle, over all questions of the *form* the state should assume . . . will not be open to the arguments advanced here." See Wolfgang J. Mommsen's "The Antinomical Structure of Weber's Thought" (in Mommsen, *Political and Social Theory of Max Weber*) for a sophisticated consideration of how the antinomy of nationalism/liberalism structured Weber's thinking.
26. Schmitt, *Concept of the Political*, 61.
27. Weber, "The Meaning of 'Ethical Neutrality' in Sociology and Economics," 26–27.
28. Schmitt, *Concept of the Political*, 33.
29. Weber, "Science as a Vocation," 148, 149.
30. Weber, "Science as a Vocation," 148, 149.
31. Schmitt, *Concept of the Political*, 26.
32. Schmitt, *Concept of the Political*, 27.
33. Schmitt, *Concept of the Political*, 71.
34. Schmitt, *Concept of the Political*, 70–71.
35. Schmitt's argument here is lent weight by recent pre-9/11 American experience. If nothing else, the 1990s appeared to be—from a narrow American perspective—proof of Constant's basic thesis, namely, that in the modern liberal order, commerce and not war will rule the world. 9/11 pierced that particular illusion, and brought Schmittian ways of thinking into the White House. The entire "war on Terror"

presupposes a world split into friends *or* enemies. A broader slice of Western experience–namely, that of Europe after the downfall of Napoleon–also suggests that Schmitt was on fairly firm ground when he attacked Constant's basic thesis. Two world wars, to say nothing of the traumas of decolonization, the Cold War, and numerous regional conflicts, underscore Constant's premature optimism as to what the future might hold.

36. Schmitt, *Concept of the Political*, 46.
37. Schmitt, *Concept of the Political*, 57.
38. Schmitt, *Concept of the Political*, 53.
39. Schmitt, *Concept of the Political*, 27.
40. Schmitt's defenders would no doubt say that his presidential system, grounded on Article 48 of the Weimar Constitution, mirrors much of what Weber had to say in his article on the *Reichspräsident*. They would also point to Schmitt's *Verfassungslehre* (1928) as evidence of a much more "liberal" Schmitt, one committed to a constitutional state and to preserving the Weimar Republic from extremist enemies (such as the Nazis and the KPD).
41. Mommsen, *Max Weber and German Politics*, 400–401.
42. See David Beetham, *Max Weber and the Theory of Modern Politics* (Cambridge: Polity Press, 1985), 232–33. Beetham notes a "decided shift in Weber's views" in the post-war years, a shift from the parliamentary focus of wartime writings like "Parliament and Government" to an emphasis on a directly elected president and "strong leadership." Such a shift is apparent but–like Beetham and unlike the early Mommsen–I think no either/or is implied with respect to the larger questions of representative government and the continuing need for popular political education.
43. Another, but by no means unimportant, point against the "charismatic leader"/Hitler slippery slope thesis comes in the form of Weber's "ethic of responsibility" for foreseeable consequences. If there is one example of political leadership utterly without such responsibility, it is surely Hitler, who was more than willing to see the German people disappear once they had "let him down."
44. Georg Lukács, *History and Class Consciousness: Studies in Marxist Dialectics*, trans. Rodney Livingstone (Cambridge, MA: MIT Press, 1971).
45. Lukács, *History and Class Consciousness*, 101.
46. The importance of both Weber and Lukács for "classic" Frankfurt School theory is self-evident here.
47. See Lukács, "What is Orthodox Marxism?" in *History and Class Consciousness*, 1–26.
48. Lukács, "What is Orthodox Marxism?," 6–13.
49. See Max Weber, "'Objectivity' in Social Science and Social Policy" in Weber, *The Methodology of the Social Sciences*, trans. and eds. Edward Shils and Henry Finch (New York: Free Press, 1949), 72–79.
50. Weber, "Objectivity," 81–84.
51. Lukács, *History and Class Consciousness*, 13.
52. Lukács, *History and Class Consciousness*, 152.
53. Lukács, *History and Class Consciousness*, 150.
54. See Karl Marx, "Contribution to the Critique of Hegel's *Philosophy of Right*: Introduction" and *The German Ideology*, both in *The Marx-Engels Reader*, ed. Robert Tucker (New York: Norton, 1978), 64 and 161, respectively.
55. See Leszek Kołakowski's discussion of this point in his *Main Currents of Marxism* (New York: W. W. Norton, 2005), 998–1001.
56. Kołakowski, *Main Currents of Marxism*. 1011–12.

57. Weber, "Science as a Vocation," 140–43. Cf. Nietzsche's parallel account ("How the 'Real World' becomes a Fable") in *Twilight of the Idols*, trans. R. J. Hollingsdale (New York: Penguin Books, 1979).

58. Weber, "Science as a Vocation," 143.

59. Weber, "'Objectivity' in Social Science and Social Policy," 57.

60. See chapters 3 and 4—on Nietzsche and Weber, respectively—of my *Socratic Citizenship* (Princeton: Princeton University Press, 2001) for an elucidation of the underlying "ethos of disenchantment" in the two thinkers.

61. See Georg Lukács, *The Destruction of Reason*, trans. Peter Palmer (Atlantic Highlands: Humanities Press, 1981), 614–619. Cf. Horkheimer, *Eclipse of Reason* and Leo Strauss, "What is Political Philosophy?" in Strauss, *"What is Political Philosophy? and other Studies* (Chicago: University of Chicago Press, 1988). Also Leo Strauss, *Natural Right and History* (Chicago: University of Chicago Press, 1953), chapter 2.

62. Isaiah Berlin, "In Conversation with Steven Lukes," *Salmagundi* no 120 (Fall, 1998), 102–03.

63. For a latter day assessment of the meaning and utility of reification, see Axel Honneth, *Reification: A New Look at an Old Idea* (New York: Oxford University Press, 2008).

Part II

Philosophy, Theology, Science

5

Kulturphilosophie in Weimar Modernism

John Michael Krois

The Weimar Republic was one of the most fertile epochs in German philosophy, and its effects are still being felt today. The call for "new thinking" was shared by otherwise disparate approaches. The phenomenologists (Edmund Husserl, Max Scheler, and Martin Heidegger) sought to find the "beginnings" of knowing in pre-scientific phenomena while thinkers at the forefront of what would later be known as analytic philosophy (Gottlob Frege, Rudolf Carnap, and Hans Reichenbach) found a new approach to philosophy in the analysis of language. A third approach took its starting point from the fact of culture and sought to find a new orientation for philosophy in the study of the historical world. For reasons that will become apparent, this movement, known as "Kulturphilosophie" (the philosophy of culture), was often regarded as a more conservative approach to philosophy. But *Kulturphilosophie* was less unified than the other movements and cannot be easily classified, although certain *theoretical* approaches stand out that can be identified with representative figures: Heinrich Rickert, Georg Simmel, and Ernst Cassirer. Histories have been written about phenomenology and analytic philosophy, but *Kulturphilosophie* awaits such a treatment. The following seeks to highlight what was characteristic of *Kulturphilosophie*.

The abdication of the Kaiser had a parallel in philosophy. The belief that philosophy could grasp the world in a system, formulated by a single thinker, had been the target of polemics since Arthur Schopenhauer and Friedrich Nietzsche. Both regarded Hegelianism as the chief example of this kind of philosophy and rejected it vehemently, especially Hegel's apotheosis of reason. For them, and for many German philosophers in the Weimar era, the world was not the manifestation of reason nor could human beings be understood only in such terms. Since the nineteenth century science and technology made continuing strides toward explaining nature, and their prestige in the university grew accordingly. Science seemed to offer a better model of rationality than the traditional philosophical concept of "reason." But the rejection of traditional systematic philosophy gradually raised a problem: what did philosophers have to contribute to knowledge that the empirical sciences did not? The answer that emerged was simple: if philosophy could not explicate the nature of things in general as it had previously done, it could instead explicate knowledge itself. "Erkenntnistheorie," the theory of knowledge, became the catchword in the nineteenth century philosophy. Eduard Zeller, in a famous lecture of 1862, proclaimed that "Erkenntnistheorie," the theory of knowledge, was the future of philosophy. Philosophers had always discussed knowledge, but now it became the central issue from which philosophy derived its own justification.[1]

But the rise of the theory of knowledge led to a new kind of system: the mental organization of experience. The Neo-Kantian movement regarded Kant as the founder of the theory of knowledge *avant la lettre*, and they believed that by reconsidering Kantianism in light of modern developments in logic and science they would be able to distill its essence, "purifying" it so to speak by stripping it of the dated and contingent aspects of its presentation that it had received at Kant's hands. Neo-Kantianism was already a well establishing way of thinking before the upheavals of the Weimar era, yet German philosophers could not escape from the shadow of Kant, so the attempts to reorient philosophy were defined in many ways by how thinkers sought to revise or overcome Kantianism. This was especially true for early "Kulturphilosophie."[2]

The philosophy of culture, like phenomenology and analytic philosophy, was supposed to be an alternative to traditional metaphysical philosophy. "Philosophy of culture" is not a perfect translation of "Kulturphilosophie," even though it is correct. The term "Kultur" was an embattled concept in Germany during the Weimar republic, and the English word "culture" masks what the controversy was about. Since ancient times philosophers assumed that human activity was inconstant, so that culture was never considered a proper topic for philosophy. This began to change in the eighteenth century. The word "culture" comes from Latin (*cultura* originally was used in conjunction with the activity of growing crops: agriculture). Cicero used it in a figurative sense as *cultura animi*, the culture of the mind, envisioning a combination of philosophical thinking and rhetoric, a combination alien to ancient Greek thinking, which kept theoretical contemplation separate from action. Although the notion of culture involves activity, the German word "Kultur" came to be associated in the course the nineteenth century with the care and preservation of the past, a meaning that has been traced back to the Berlin philologist Friedrich August Wolf.[3] Taken in this sense, *Kultur* was concerned only with enduring things and so was associated with art, religion, and philosophy—Hegel's three forms of "absolute Mind." *Kultur* was contrasted to the supposedly more material aspects of social life—the technical, scientific, and political. This restricted meaning of the term *Kultur* is not evident in the English term "philosophy of culture."[4]

In contrast to this conservative conception of *Kultur* the first great historian of culture in the German-speaking world, Jacob Burckhardt, regarded *Kultur* as that which constantly acts to modify and dissolve whatever is stable in life. In his masterpiece, *Die Kultur der Renaissance in Italien* (1860), he dealt with dynasties of political rulers, the mechanics of waging war, universities and schools, domestic economy, festivals, the position of women, the rediscovery of classical antiquity, and all manner of things that brought change.[5] Both of these conceptions of culture—the conservative and the active—can be found in German *Kulturphilosophie*, and for a time they shared an uneasy coexistence.

The heyday of *Kulturphilosophie* in Germany can be followed in the career of the journal that was its chief organ—*Logos: Internationale Zeitschrift für Philosophie der Kultur*. Although this journal's main editor, Heinrich Rickert, was the chief representative of a particular school of *Kulturphilosophie*, the journal's orientation was not limited to his perspective and its scope was international. *Logos* was initiated by a group of five doctoral students, three of whom were from Russia, who had worked with Wilhelm Windelband and Rickert, Windelband's successor in Heidelberg. The journal began publishing in 1910 and acquired an illustrious editorial board including the philosopher Edmund Husserl, the jurist Otto von Gierke, the historian Friedrich Meinecke, the art historian Heinrich Wölfflin, and—as a counterweight to the neo-Kantian philosopher Heinrich Rickert—Georg Simmel. It also came to include the sociologist Max Weber, the protestant theologian Ernst Troeltsch, and the philosopher Ernst Cassirer, among others. *Logos* published a host of significant essays ranging over a wide range of topics including Husserl's " Philosophy as a Rigorous Science," Erwin Panofsky's first publication of his theory of Iconology, or the first German study of the philosopher Alfred North Whitehead.[6] But in 1933 the journal's title was changed to *Zeitschrift für Deutsche Kulturphilosophie: Neue Folge des Logos* (Journal for German Philosophy of Culture: New Series of Logos). With this change in the masthead, the attempt to think philosophically about culture in an "International" manner came to an end.

In the history of philosophy as shaped by the ancient Greeks and Christianity the human ability to effect the world or to shape history were not important topics. The goal was either to grasp the ahistorical forms behind appearances or to grasp history's set course defined by the appearance of Christ and his second coming and the Last Judgment. In the eighteenth century the historical nature of human existence became a topic of philosophical reflection in a new way. Thinkers like Giambattista Vico, Johann Gottfried Herder, David Hume, and Jean-Jacques Rousseau conceived of the human world as a human creation, as made and remade historically. Time became an important element in human nature, humans could make or misshape their own nature. The belief that there is such a thing as "progress" in history and that humans could reform social life was the basis of the eighteenth-century Enlightenment. The greatest philosopher of the era, Kant, was the inspiration for many philosophers of culture but neither Kant nor any other eighteenth-century philosopher used the term philosophy of culture. In his widely read *Lehrbuch der Geschichte der Philosophie* (1892) Wilhelm Windelband (1848–1915) focused in the section about the European Enlightenment on what he called the "Kulturproblem," by which he meant the question whether intellectual perfection contributed to the morality and happiness. With the rise of *Kulturphilosophie*, the concept of culture was transformed from a mere "problem" to a methodological conception. Windelband's own programmatic essay on "Kulturphilosophie und transcendentaler Idealismus" made the link to Kant explicit. Kant, on this reading, was the originator of the philosophy of culture—a belief widely held by philosophers of culture. Kant's analysis of universal, ahistorical transcendental consciousness was reinterpreted in a way that was supposed to make cultural variation possible, without abandoning its unchanging normative character. Windelband's conception of "culture" was so vague that it seemed like a banality: "the totality of whatever human consciousness is able to make out of the given by virtue of its being determined by reason."[7]

Heinrich Rickert (1863–1936), took a more epistemological approach to history by seeking to explicate the methodology of historical knowledge. Like the Berlin philosopher Wilhelm Dilthey (1833–1911) before him, Rickert sought to explicate and justify the historical methods in the humanities (Rickert spoke of "Kulturwissenschaften," Dilthey of "Geisteswissenschaften") in contrast to the natural sciences. Rickert's distinction between the generalising methods in science versus the individualising methods in the humanities did not stir continuing controversy as did Dilthey's emphasis on the difference between causal "explanation" and historical "understanding." Rickert's distinction does not hold up to closer scrutiny since some natural sciences, such as geology, are concerned with understanding specific objects historically, such as fossil finds, whereas general regularities, such as styles, are the topic of study in the humanities too.[8]

Kulturphilosophie was closely affiliated with the notion of *Kulturkritik*, the questioning of the value of culture in general or in particular instances. The most famous example of German *Kulturkritik* was Nietzsche's study "On the Use and Abuse of History for Life" (1873), in which he called into question the value of historical memory. Sometimes *Kulturkritik* and *Kulturphilosophie* were hard to distinguish. The first major publication with the word *Kulturphilosophie* in its title dealt with the value of culture rather than offering a theory: Ludwig Stein's *At the Turn of Century: Outline of a Philosophy of Culture* (1899). Stein's aim was to develop what he called a "philosophy of the west European-American cultural system," that would give a reasoned argument for the optimism and enthusiasm for progress that he sensed "at the turn of the century" in the rise of modern technology. By 1918, after the catastrophe of the World War, this mood was replaced by widespread pessimism, and Oswald Spengler's best-selling *The Decline of the West* (*Der Untergang des Abendlandes*, 1918) offered instead a fatalistic conception, which gave a dispensation from responsibility.[9] These kinds of popular "Kulturphilosophie," which openly professed optimistic or pessimistic sentiments, were merely dogmatic worldviews. Other thinkers of the Weimar era, such as Walter Benjamin or Siegfried Kracauer, were able to combine *Kulturkritik* and more general philosophical reflections on culture and history. This is also true of the founders of so-called "critical theory" in philosophy, Max Horkheimer and Theodor Adorno. All of these thinkers considered themselves cultural critics rather than philosophers of culture, as did most of the thinkers motivated by Marxian conceptions rather than a Kantian perspective. They spoke of society—"Gesellschaft"—rather than "culture," a term which for them had become associated with conservativism. A characteristic statement of this perspective, Herbert Marcuse's 1937 essay "The Affirmative Character of Culture" characterized *Kultur* as a concept inhibiting activity and reform because it elevated the mind to a sphere above history. Culture became a sphere of unchanging values, above the practical world of "civilization."[10]

One of the thinkers whose conception of culture seemed to fit this conception was Heinrich Rickert. Rickert sought to make Kant's philosophy more concrete without abandoning his ahistorical conception of the conceptual organization of experience. Rickert sought to find a way around history by establishing the timeless "values" (*Werte*) that supposedly guided cultural activity. Rickert defined *Kultur* as "the totality of real objects, to which generally recognized values or meanings (*Sinngebilde*) constituted by them adhere, and which are maintained out of care for these values."[11] These particular cultural values were measured against such higher, unchanging values of truth, goodness, and beauty, which philosophy elaborates. These values taken together constituted what might be called Culture with a capital "C."

In striking contrast to this conception of *Kulturphilosophie*, Georg Simmel (1858–1918) explicated culture as the source of change. Simmel, who spent most of his life at Berlin as a low income university lecturer, was also the university's most successful teacher, whose classes filled the largest auditorium. Simmel dealt with culture in detail, emphasizing such disruptive factors such as urbanization ("The Metropolis and Mental Life"), the role of women in society, and especially the cultural impact of money. Simmel's magnum opus, *The Philosophy of Money* (1900), was not about economics, but the effects that the institution of money has on all manner of human relations, and how it accelerated social processes.[12] Simmel was noted for his micrological studies of everyday topics such as fashion from which he could draw far-reaching conclusions. Whereas Rickert appealed to the notion of transcendental determinations of thought in a Kantian sense, Simmel found no more stable conception for his philosophy than *Leben* or "life," but the designation of "Life philosophy" hardly does justice to Simmel's multifaceted work. Simmel was led to develop a "tragic" conception of culture, for while he claimed that it is characteristic of human life to produce cultural forms and to strive for freedom, these very productions result in restrictions and limitations to life. In this process of cultural production the individual is increasingly subjected to the ossification of the objective forms of culture leading inevitably to alienation.

Ernst Cassirer's approach to the philosophy of culture differed from both Rickert's ahistoricism and Simmel's more sociological conception. Culture, he claimed, is based upon symbolism. Today, there is a broad consensus among cultural theorists of all persuasions (Umberto Eco, Roland Barthes, Pierre Bourdieu, Clifford Geertz, to name only a few) as well as physical anthropologists that symbolism makes culture possible. Cassirer's conception of symbolism influenced or anticipated many of these approaches, but his emphasis on expressive meaning is unique.

Cassirer has been called "the last philosopher of culture."[13] This is true in the chronological sense that his approach to culture was the last to be developed before the Nazi era, but also in the sense that with Cassirer the paradigm of *Kulturphilosophie* was extended beyond culture. After 1933, in Swedish exile, he developed what he termed the doctrine of *Basisphänomena*, by which he explicated the realities that precede culture.

Cassirer came to philosophy from an initial interest in literature, but as a student his theoretical concerns did not fit the biographical and philological orientation that were typical of German literature studies in the late nineteenth century. As a student in Berlin he took Simmel's course on Kant in the Summer of 1894, which introduced him also to Neo-kantian schools of thought. Simmel's mention of the Marburg school, led Cassirer study in Marburg, where he wrote his dissertation on Descartes under the guidance of Hermann Cohen and Paul Natorp.

Cassirer spent most of the first decades of his career in Berlin, where he published his pathmaking theoretical work *Substanzbegriff und Funktionsbegriff* (1910).[14] This book dealt with logic, not culture, but it led Cassirer to a new way of understanding the "order of things" that enabled him to understand culture in a new way. The focal point of discussion was the most fundamental category in Western philosophy: the idea of "substance"—the self-identical substratum or entity supporting the different characteristics or features of an object. Cassirer argued that this category assumes what it is supposed to explain: the unitary basis by which particulars are subsumed under classes. Instead of beginning with the idea of substance, Cassirer compared the unity in concepts with a function in the mathematical sense of the law constitutive of a series: F (a,b, c, . . .). Identity is a matter of inclusion in a series as defined by a particular function. Concepts depend upon the category of relation, hence phenomena can be grasped in reference to innummerable relations, and not by reference to a single "essence" or substantial form. Regarded from the standpoint of the theory of knowledge, this meant that the world was no great chain of Being, no hieararchy of forms, rather countless serial orders exist simultaneously. Even before Cassirer aligned himself with *Kulturphilosophie*, he had already rejected the logical basis of what later cultural theorists referred to as pejoratively as "essentialism." *Subtance and Function* was a logical study, but Cassirer would later explicate this criticism of hierarchical orders in historical studies of the Renaissance. He showed, for example, how Machiavelli eliminated the notion of hierarchies in his treatment of political power, but Cassirer's most influential studies of this topic dealt with Shakespeare and what he termed "Renaissance humor" which attacked the scholastic hiearchical world view by laughter. These writings would later so impress the Russian critic Bakhtin that he reproduced many of Cassirer's discussions in his own works without indicating that they were quoted or giving the source.[15]

Cassirer came to the philosophy of culture from studies on the history of philosophy, especially on Leibniz. Whereas the traditional aim of systematic philosophy of establishing conceptual unity in phenomena by means of reason, Cassirer came to espouse the opposite view: "It is the task of systematic philosophy—which goes far beyond that of the theory of knowledge—to liberate our view of the world from one-sidedness." Following Leibniz, he rejected monism and dualism in favor of what he referred to as Leibniz's "pluralistic universe" composed of "dynamic" unitary realities. The thesis of Cassirer's first book, *Leibniz's System*, was that Leibniz's philosophy offered a logical vindication of qualitative individuality. With Leibniz, the idea of rigid, fixed form was supplanted by the idea of "development." "Form" then means "continuity in development," so that individuality and generality are no longer opposites. This emphasis on qualitative individuality, which Cassirer derived from his interpretation of Leibniz put his philosophy closer to Simmel's concerns than to Rickert's and nearer to Leibniz than to Kant.[16]

Cassirer spent the First World War in Berlin, where he lectured at the university and taught in schools to replace teachers fighting on the front, but in 1916 he was given a more important war assignment, when he was put in charge of the French language section of the War News Office (*Kriegspresseamt*). There he was responsible until 1918 for a team of military readers that gleaned foreign language newspapers for information to help the German war effort and assuage public opinion. This work was daily, even on Sundays, and he was decorated for it at the end of the war. But unlike his own teachers and numerous other German philosophy professors, Cassirer wrote no tracts favoring the war and he signed no declarations in support of it. During this time he wrote a large essay that appeared in two parts in the journal *Logos* that gives insights into his experience at the Press office. This essay, "Hölderlin und der deutsche Idealismus" began with a discussion of mythology in eighteenth-century aesthetic theories. Cassirer distinguished poetry from myth by the fact that art is "aesthetically liberated." It can be moving but does not take possession of the reader, who retains a degree of freedom and distance from his or her emotions. Art occupies a sphere between elementary mythic experience and enlightened rational thought. Poetry that instills people to act has become myth. The essay concludes with a discussion of the meaning of sacrificial deaths, as in Hölderlin's "Der Tod des Empedokles." Here for the first time he speaks about mythic thought as a form of life and not as a literary phenomenon. The final pages are dedicated to what he calls the "tragedy that characterizes every finite existence" (*Tragik, die jedem endlichen Sein anhaftet*). Cassirer ends with the observation that the efforts of the Idealist philosopher Hegel seek to give individual existence a place in the whole, but that Hölderlin is the more convincing, for he lets the individual and the general remain tragically opposed to one another so that the loss is unredeemable.[17] As the head of the French newspaper unit, Cassirer was one of the best informed about the reality of the battle at Verdun in 1916 with its sea of hundreds of thousands of dead and all the other military disasters that characterized modern warfare.

After the war Cassirer was offered the professorship in philosophy at the newly founded University of Hamburg, where he began teaching in 1919. On November 27, 1920 the course of Cassirer's intellectual career was changed when he visited the research library of "Kulturwissenschaft" or Cultural Science founded by Aby Warburg. Warburg himself was at a Sanitarium in Switzerland under treatment for a nervous breakdown following World War I, so on this first visit Cassirer was shown the library's holdings and its unique organization by its deputy director, Fritz Saxl. This visit affected Cassirer profoundly and changed the direction of his philosophy. Nearly ten years later, in Cassirer's memorial address after Warburg's death in October of 1929 he recalled this first visit and how he recognized that the library was not the work of a mere scholar, but the result of Warburg's attempt to master the dangers that threatened him: the library's focus was the human struggle against the deepest threats to freedom and existence. For Warburg and his library of "Kulturwissenschaft," culture was not the result of reason's organization of the given, but the attempt to ward off fear and the threats that endanger mankind. In this conception, culture begins with certain symbolic activities—magical and other rituals—that cannot be subsumed under reason, yet have a logic. In his memorial speech Cassirer recalled that he understood the library and its creator immediately, adding: "I was overcome by the violent force of what emanated from both, before I ever saw Warburg or spoke a word with him." After the library moved to London in 1933, where it was incorporated into the University of London as "The Warburg Institute," he was able to visit it frequently from Oxford where he was a guest professor at All Souls until he left for Sweden in 1935. In 1936 he called the Warburg library the "Archimedean point of my entire philosophy."[18]

Cassirer did not abandon his earlier approach to philosophy, but he reconsidered its foundations. He continued his research on the philosophy of modern physics, later writing a book-length study on causality in quantum physics to compliment his earlier study of Einstein's theory of relativity. But he now saw that science and knowledge demanded a new philosophical basis that went beyond the theory of knowledge. At this juncture Cassirer took a step that still has not lost its shock value for most philosophers or interpreters of Cassirer's thought. Beginning with "The Form of the Concept in Mythic Thought" in 1921 until his death in 1945 Cassirer wrote a series of studies that detailed how culture stemmed from and so depended upon mythic thought.[19] Mythic thought derives from symbolism, not articulated reason, so philosophy needed to begin with pre-scientific, pre-verbal thinking, which originated from acting in the world, not theoretical reflection: "Not mere observation, but rather actions provides the middle point from which, for human beings, the intellectual organization of reality takes its beginnings."

The basic premise of Cassirer's philosophy is that the existence of reason presupposes the reality of symbolism, not the other way around. Cassirer's replacement of the concept of "reason" with that of "symbolism" was no minor revision to the Western philosophical tradition. The problem with the philosophical tradition was not that philosophers venerated reason, but that they ignored the body and so separated reason from action and emotion. Cassirer maintained that symbolism is already found in non-verbal and non-propositional forms of meaning— such as facial expression, gesture, and ritual—all of which depend upon the body for their articulation. Cassirer stated as a matter of principle that "The relation between body and soul represents the prototype and model for a purely symbolic relation." By this he meant that the ability to understand and communicate by gesture and to perform rituals together depend upon public actions and these are the basis for the symbolic functions which make culture possible.

This led Cassirer to criticize and lump together all philosophies of intuition or immediacy, from Bergson to Heidegger, and any theory that envisions reality as a lost paradise of immersion, to be mistaken: human existence, even in the sense of bodily experience never is pre-symbolic. To lack all "symbolic pregnance" would entail being without any kind of meaning at all and so to be unconscious. On Cassirer's theory of symbolism even bodily feeling is symbolically pregnant because it is expressive of kinds of qualities: "Qualities of the tactile sense—qualities such as hard and soft, rough and smooth—arise only through motion, so that if we limit tactile sensations to a single moment, they can no longer be discerned as data." Cassirer's theory of symbolism was set out in his main work, *The Philosophy of Symbolic Forms*, which appeared in three volumes in 1923, 1925, and 1929.[20]

In the midst of writing this work, after the completion of the first and second volumes, he discovered the work of Goldstein and Gelb and the significance of neuropathology. The *limitations* to symbolic processes offered a window on its otherwise unnoticed basic functions. For example, Cassirer was particularly struck by the similarity between the spatial orientation that one of Goldstein's patients displayed and Hans Volkelt's account of a spider's relationship to its own net. The slightest change in a detail could disorient the spider, which could not recognize prey placed directly into its net. A ritual procedure of action by the spider was necessary for it to perceive that something was prey; it could not just be recognized as such. So too a patient suffering from aphasia could only perceive details by including them in complete ritualized actions of their own. Goldstein's patient was able to knock on a door, but a knocking action, by itself, without the ritualistic context of knocking on a real door was impossible for him to produce. Cassirer's research on "The Pathology of Symbolic Consciousness" showed how neurological pathologies not only could limit a person's capacity to think in an abstract categorical manner, but also affected their personality, their relations to themselves and to others.[21]

The discussions of expressive meaning in the *Philosophy of Symbolic Forms* culminate in the concept of *symbolische Prägnanz*. According to this doctrine, there can be no such thing as elementary atemporal phenomena, neither of the sort that Carnap called "Elementarerlebnisse"—momentary cross sections of a holistic empirical experience— nor in the sense of Husserl's phenomenological conception of hyle, the "matter" of phenomenological reality. What philosophers—and not just philosophers—usually call "sensation" or "intuition" is really a symbolic phenomenon. At this level symbolism has nothing to do with cultural conventions, allegory or any literary conception; it begins with the bodily sensation of touch. With each volume of *The Philosophy of Symbolic Forms* Cassirer was led more and more from cultural to anthropological concerns. The development was further spured also by a new colleague, who came to the University of Hamburg in 1925, the theoretical biologist Jakob von Uexküll.

In 1929 the German national minister of education, Leo Kestenberg, asked Cassirer to contribute to a volume about art and modern technology, *Kunst und Technik*. Kestenberg, who is known for his reform of music education, was confronted with the problem of how to cope with the impact of the new electronic media on the arts, and asked a host of prominent figures to write on the relationship of technology and art. *Kunst und Technik* appeared in 1930. Cassirer's extensive essay dealt with the problem of technology in general and in the context of the historical situation of its rapid spread in the 1920s. Other contributors including the composer Ernst Krenek and the filmmaker Walter Ruttmann ("Berlin: Die Symphonie der Großstadt") dealt with recorded music, film, and radio.[22] Cassirer had already dealt with the topic of "Technik" in the second volume of his *Philosophy of Symbolic Forms: Mythic Thought*. There he showed that technology and cult practices originated together. Knowledge of the use of fire and even the domestication of animals derived from cult practices. "Form und Technik" is Cassirer's longest published essay, and its argument cannot be reconstructed briefly, but one point is outstanding in the context of the Weimar discussion of *Kultur*. For Cassirer, technology is and always was integral to "Kultur." In the Weimar era technology, like natural science and politics, was considered to be mere "Zivilisation," not "Kultur." The divorce of *Zivilisation* and *Kultur*, which seems apolitical, actually was a part of a highly political ideology. This distinction drove a wedge between Germany, which possessed "Kultur," and Western Europe, especially England and France, which were identified with "Zivilisation." The debate surrounding *Kultur* and *Zivilisation* took various paths during the Weimar era, but none had such a fatal effect on the Weimar Republic itself, as the contention that parliamentary democracy itself was a "Western," un-German, kind of government. This claim, reiterated again and again, emphasized that such democracies were typical of England and France. This contention eroded support for democratic government in the most radical way, denying its legitimacy and so adding alienation to the sense of loss after the German regent, the Kaiser, abdicated in 1918. In this way the contention that culture was fundamentally different from civilization, aided directly in the destruction of the Weimar Republic from within.

There were some notable attempts to repudiate this claim, such as Thomas Mann's lecture "On the German Republic," but they were few. German academics who were not directly opposed to the Republic accepted it without welcoming it. These so-called "Vernuftrepublikaner"—republicans out of reason—were not prepared to defend democratic institutions when the Nazis assumed power. As Cassirer himself recalled: "In the first days, shortly after Hitler's rise to power, I heard very often from the lips of educated people, of scholars or philosophers, the ominous words 'History has spoken.' They were repeated time and again. Men who had by no means been in favour of the national-socialistic party suddenly changed their minds. The political success was regarded by them to be the incontrovertible proof of its 'truth' and 'right,' an irrevocable judgment of history, a decree of fate."

From the beginning Cassirer was a genuine supporter of the Weimar Republic. Asked to give an address at the Hamburg City Hall in 1928 in celebration of the founding of the republic, he lectured on "The Idea of the Republican Constitution."[23] His lecture was not merely ceremonial, it offered an argument against the claim that republican government was "Un-German" by detailing how in fact the idea of republican government had originated in Germany, in the philosophy of Leibniz, and showing how other German thinkers including Kant embraced it. Cassirer's claim that Leibniz's philosophy combined the concept of unique individuality with that of a system of interrelations and so served as the metaphysical model for a republic government was not new; he had already developed this argument in 1900 in his book *Leibniz's System*. As rector of the University of Hamburg for the academic year of 1929–30 Cassirer organized the first—and only—university celebration of the Republic. In his address on this occassion he argued for a conception of the state as a space in which opposites were able to exist together. Cassirer engaged in a host of other activities, giving lectures and publishing essays, including a two-part essay in a journal of international affairs in 1931, criticizing directly the supposed opposition between German *Kultur* and the "West," but by this time a way of thinking had set in that was immune to argument.

Cassirer, who more than anyone had made the study of mythic thinking a central topic of philosophy, realized too late what it meant for mythic thought to return in the modern world. Cassirer had argued that mythic thinking is rooted in forms of life, in action, not in ideas or language, and this meant that mythic beliefs are impervious to argument: "It is beyond the power of philosophy to destroy the political myths. A myth is in a sense invulnerable. It is impervious to rational arguments; it cannot be refuted by syllogisms."

In *The Myth of the State*, Cassirer's last book, he claims that mythic thought can always return in times of crisis when the critical forces of culture—intellectual, ethical, and artistic—are insufficient to limit its appeal and emotional force, but that the Third Reich represented something else that was new in the political world. The National Socialists, using modern technical media, were able to control the minds of an entire nation by a combination of the oldest and most modern aspects of culture, which he called the "technique of myth." This involved techiques of ritualization and a special, emotive use of language. *The Myth of the State* appeared posthumously in 1946, with important omissions, that were published in 2008.[24]

In *The Logic of the Cultural Sciences* (1941) Cassirer agreed with Simmel that a fundamental opposition exists in the cultural tendencies towards preservation and renewal, which leads to constant inner tensions and conflicts: "Nevertheless, this drama of culture never becomes a complete 'tragedy of culture.' For just as little as there is an ultimate victory so there is no ultimate defeat. The opposing forces increase with one another rather than destroying each other."[25] The philosophy of culture arose in the eighteenth-century Enlightenment with its criticism of superstition and striving for reform through reason. Cassirer's philosophy of culture sought to renew this Enlightenment project, but without its emphasis on "reason": "For us, the word 'reason' (Vernunft), has long since lost its unequivocal simplicity even if we are in essential agreement with the basic aims of the philosophy of the Enlightenment." Cassirer's own philosophical ethos is most obvious in his book *The Philosophy of the Enlightenment* (1932). He holds up as a model Diderot, who called superstition a "worse insult" to God than atheism because ignorance is not as far from truth as prejudice is. He leaves no doubt where he stands, agreeing explicitly with Bayle, that it is "impossible to justify the use of force for the sake of religion," to which Cassirer adds that "Every literal interpretation of the Bible must therefore be rejected which commands us to act contrary to the first principles of morality." Toleration, Cassirer declares, is not laxiety or indifference, but a sign of humility, in contrast to those who tolerate only their own opinion and disallow all others. The most compact statement of Cassirer's enlightenment ethos is found in his definition of culture in *An Essay on Man* (1944): "Human culture taken as a whole may be described as the process of man's progressive self-liberation."[26] This was not meant as a statement about a constant "march of history," but described a process, demanding constant individual effort in which reversions are always possible. Cassirer's justification for this view was the theory of symbolism, which makes it possible for humans to liberate themselves from fear, repression and ignorance.

Cassirer's revision of the classical definition of humanity as "animal rationale" to "animal symbolicum" did not entail rejecting the *normative* ethical concept of rationality, only it required recognizing the inadequacy of attempts to comprehend human beings or human culture as based on reason—an admission that has been difficult for political philosophers. Rituals, gestures, poetic speech, depiction, art, religion, and historical narratives possess an elementary symbolic importance in human culture that cannot be grasped in terms of "reason." The way people habitually live and act is itself of great (expressive) symbolic import. Cassirer emphasized the primacy of action over language and the ritual or cult value that adheres to ways of acting. This is why even the strongest arguments remain abstract in the face of traditional ways of doing things. The central claim of *The Myth of the State*, that myth is immune to argument, poses deep problems to political philosophy that remain unsolved.

In the "philosophy of symbolic forms," myth and religion, art, history, technology, and science do not "contradict" one another—they move in entirely different dimensions of symbolism: expressive, representative, or significative. Their unity as kinds of symbolism does not diminish or resolve their differences. The task for *Kulturphilosophie* is not to look for unity, but to show how it is possible to switch perspectives: "It is the task of systematic philosophy—which goes far beyond that of the theory of knowledge—to liberate our view of the world from one-sidedness." The affirmation of multiple perspectives is one of the hallmarks of Modernism, and it is one of the ways *Kulturphilosophie* contributed to Weimar Modernism.

Notes

1. Eduard Zeller, "Über Bedeutung und Aufgabe der Erkenntnistheorie," in *Vorträge und Aufsätze: Zweite Sammlung* (Leipzig: Fues, 1887), 489–95.
2. For a general overview of the turn to culture in relation to the neo-Kantian movement, see Peter E. Gordon, *Continental Divide: Heidegger, Cassirer, Davos* (Cambridge, MA: Harvard University Press, 2010), esp. 19–22, and 52–64.

3. Friedrich August Wolf, *Prolegomena zu Homer, 1795,* trans. Grafton, Most, and Zetzel (Princeton: Princeton University Press, 1985), and also see Anthony Grafton, "Prolegomena to Friedrich August Wolf," *Journal of the Warburg and Courtauld Institutes* 44 (1981), 103–9.

4. See, e.g., Norbert Elias, *The Civilizing Process: Sociogenetic and Psychogenetic Processes,* trans. Edmund Jephcott, rev. ed. (Oxford: Blackwell, 2000), esp. Chap. 1, "The Sociogenesis of the Antithesis between *Kultur* and *Zivilisation,*" 9–11.

5. Jacob Burckhardt, *The Civilization of the Renaissance in Italy* (Penguin Classics) trans. S.G.C. Middlemore (New York: Penguin, 1990), originally published under the title: *Die Kultur der Renaissance in Italien: ein Versuch* (1860).

6. Edmund Husserl, "Philosophie als strenge Wissenschaft," *Logos* 1 (1911), republished in book form (Frankfurt am Main: Vittorio Klostermann, 1981). In English: Husserl, *Phenomenology and the Crisis of Philosophy,* trans. Quentin Lauer (New York: Harper Torchbooks, 1965).

7. Wilhelm Windelband, "Kulturphilosophie und transzendentaler Idealismus" *Logos* 1, 2 (1911), 186–96.

8. Heinrich Rickert, *Kulturwissenschaft und Naturwissenschaft,* 2nd ed. (Freiburg i.B.: J.C.B. Mohr, 1910).

9. On Oswald Spengler's theory of historical decline, see the essay by Charles Bambach in this volume.

10. Herbert Marcuse, "The Affirmative Character of Culture," in *Negations: Essays in Critical Theory,* ed. idem (London: Free Association Books, 1988), 88–133.

11. Heinrich Rickert, *Kulturwissenschaft und Naturwissenschaft* (Tübingen: J.C.B. Mohr, 1910), 89

12. Georg Simmel, "The Metropolis and Mental Life, in *Simmel on Culture: Selected Writings,* eds. David Frisby and Mike Featherstone (London: Sage Publications, 1997), 174–85; and Simmel, *The Philosophy of Money,* ed. David Frisby, 2nd ed. (New York: Routledge, 1990).

13. Edward Skidelsky, *Ernst Cassirer: The Last Philosopher of Culture* (Princeton: Princeton University Press, 2008).

14. Ernst Cassirer, *Substance and Function and Einstein's Theory of Relativity,* trans. William Curtis Swabey and Marie Collins Swabey. (Chicago: Open Court, 1973).

15. Ernst Cassirer, *The Individual and the Cosmos in Renaissance Philosophy,* trans. Mario Domandi (New York: Dover, 2000).

16. Ernst Cassirer, *Leibniz' System in seinen wissenschaftlichen Grundlagen,* in Cassirer, *Gesammelte Werke,* Band 1 (Hamburg: Meiner Verlag, 1988).

17. Cassirer, "Hölderlin und der deutsche Idealismus" in *Aufsätze und kleine Schriften 1902–1921,* eds. Birgit Recki and Marcel Simon (*Cassirer, Gesammelte Werke,* Band 9) (Hamburg: Meiner Verlag, 2001), originally in Cassirer, *Idee und Gestalt: Goethe, Schiller, Hölderlin, Kleist,* 2nd ed. (Berlin: Bruno Cassirer, 1921).

18. Cassirer, "Critical Idealism as a Philosophy of Culture" in *Symbol, Myth, and Culture. Essays and Lectures of Ernst Cassirer, 1933–1945,* ed. D. P. Verene (New Haven: Yale University Press, 1979), 64–94.

19. Ernst Cassirer, *Die Begriffsform im Mythischen Denken* (Leipzig: Teubner, 1922).

20. Ernst Cassirer, *Philosophie der symbolischen Formen. Erster Teil: Die Sprache* (Berlin: Bruno Cassirer, 1923); *Philosophie der symbolischen Formen. Zweiter Teil: Das mythische Denken.* Berlin: Bruno Cassirer, 1925); *Philosophie der symbolischen Formen. Dritter Teil: Phänomenologie der Erkenntnis* (Berlin: Bruno Cassirer, 1929); translated as *The Philosophy of Symbolic Forms. Volume One: Language* and *The Phi-*

losophy of Symbolic Forms. Volume Two: Mythical Thought (both from New Haven: Yale University Press, 1955). Volume 3 translated as *The Philosophy of Symbolic Forms. Volume Three: The Phenomenology of Knowledge.* (New Haven: Yale University Press, 1957).

21. On Cassirer's analysis of pathological consciousness, see the discussion in Peter E. Gordon, *Continental Divide: Heidegger, Cassirer, Davos* (Cambridge, MA: Harvard University Press, 2010), 254–56.

22. For a fuller discussion, see John Michael Krois, "Introduction" in Cassirer, *Symbol, Technik, Sprache: Aufsätze aus den Jahren 1927–1933,* eds. Ernst Wolfgang Orth, John Michael Krois, and Josef M. Werle (Hamburg: Meiner, 1985), xxi.

23. Cassirer, *Die Idee der Republikanischen Verfassung: Rede zur Verfassungsfeier am 11 August 1928* (Hamburg: Friederichsen, de Gruyter und Co., 1929).

24. Cassirer, *The Myth of the State* (New Haven: Yale University Press, 1946); for the later notes and omissions, see Cassirer, *Nachgelassene Manuskripte und Texte. Band 9. Zu Philosophie und Politik, mit Beilagen,* eds. John Michael Krois und Christian Möckel (Hamburg: Felix Meiner, 2008).

25. Cassirer, "The 'Tragedy of Culture,'" in *The Logic of the Cultural Sciences*, trans. S. G. Lofts (New Haven: Yale University Press, 2000), 103–28; quote from 124.

26. Cassirer, *An Essay on Man.* (New Haven: Yale University Press, 1944), 228.

6

Weimar Philosophy and the Fate of Neo-Kantianism

Frederick Beiser

January 30, 1933, the day Hindenburg made Hitler Chancellor, was fateful for German philosophy as well as German politics. The collapse of the Weimar Republic on that day also marks the end of neo-Kantianism in Germany. Neo-Kantianism had become so closely associated with Weimar that its fate would be sealed with the Republic itself. The Weimar Constitution had enshrined the liberal and democratic values of Kant's philosophy, and on solemn public occasions prominent neo-Kantians would defend the Republic. Thus Ernst Cassirer, the most eminent of the neo-Kantians, gave a public address at the University of Hamburg on August 1928 celebrating the Republic's ninth anniversary.[1] But with the National Socialist rise to power, Cassirer was forced to flee. His exile was symbolic. For when Cassirer fled Germany, neo-Kantianism went with him. Since then, there has been no major neo-Kantian philosopher in Germany.

The golden age of neo-Kantianism was from 1860 to 1910.[2] In those happier decades, to have a rigorous philosophical training, and to be at the cutting edge of the discipline, meant attending the dominant neo-Kantian universities: Marburg, Strassburg, Göttingen, Heidelberg and Berlin. The movement was divided into three main schools: the Marburg school, whose chief protagonists were Hermann Cohen (1842–1918), Paul Natorp (1854–1924), and Ernst Cassirer (1874–1945); the Southwestern, Baden, or Heidelberg school, whose major exponents were Wilhelm Windelband (1848–1915), Heinrich Rickert (1863–1936), and Emil Lask (1875–1915); and the neo-Friesian school in Göttingen under the leadership of Leonard Nelson (1882–1927).[3] Though it did not have the eminence of Marburg, Göttingen, Strassburg or Heidelberg, Berlin too eventually became a centre of neo-Kantianism in the late nineteenth and early twentieth centuries, when Friedrich Paulsen (1896–1901), Alois Riehl (1894–1924), and Benno Erdmann (1851–1924) held chairs there.[4]

Since the end of the Great War, neo-Kantianism had been in drastic decline. By then most of its leaders were either dead or decrepit. Though Nelson, Rickert and Cassirer were still active, they were fighting rear-guard actions. At the dawn of the Republic, the movement was under siege, surrounded by hostile forces: the pragmatism of Pierce, James and Dewey; the *Lebensphilosophie* of Nietzsche, Simmel and Dilthey; the existentialism of Dostoyevsky, Kierkegaard and Jaspers; the positivism of Schlick, Neurath and Carnap. Cassirer's famous dispute with

Heidegger at Davos in 1929 was really the last stand of neo-Kantianism. It was surely an ominous sign of the times that the youth attending that conference were more sympathetic with Heidegger than Cassirer.[5]

Why did neo-Kantianism decline? How do we explain the demise of such a deeply rooted and widespread intellectual movement? We could simply say its leaders grew old and died; but that begs the question why no one came to replace them. We could also say it was due to the Nazi rise to power; but exile and oppression explain only the *death* of neo-Kantianism, not its *decline*. If we wish to explain that decline, things get complicated. We have to consider several factors: its internal intellectual development, its response to hostile intellectual forces, and the cultural crises at the close of the Great War.

Neo-Kantianism withered partly for philosophical, partly for cultural reasons. Philosophically, it ran into aporias that it could not resolve and enemies that it could not refute. Culturally, it was at odds with the *Zeitgeist*, with all the profound disillusionment and pessimism that came in 1918 with defeat and the loss of a great proportion of the younger generation. For many, neo-Kantianism had become indelibly associated with the "ideas of 1914," which had been deeply discredited by 1918.[6] Although the neo-Kantians were, to be sure, not the only advocates of the war, some of their most prominent spokesman—Windelband, Cohen and Natorp—had been especially vocal, indeed fanatical, on its behalf. Furthermore, the cultural optimism of neo-Kantianism—its belief in the inevitable progress of civilization toward ideals of reason–had been shattered by the experience of the war, which seemed to vindicate the darkest cultural pessmimists.

The fate of neo-Kantianism had been sealed by three intellectual forces that dominated the cultural climate of Weimar: historicism, nihilism and pessimism. They were spoken of as "forces of darkness," which worked like a cancer, sapping moral and intellectual foundations. The talk of crisis, so common to the age, would invariably allude to one or more of them. Weimar did not create these monsters; it inherited them. They arose at the end of the eighteenth century as a reaction against the pride and pretensions of the Enlightenment. From the very beginning these forces had been hostile to Kant's philosophy, which was widely considered the epitome of the Enlightenment. When Heidegger debated with Cassirer at Davos, he was, sometimes unwittingly, the spokesman for these deeper and darker forces, which stealthily and steadily coiled their way inside him.

It sounds like a cliché to write of neo-Kantianism beset by forces of darkness. There is even an old story told about the fate of neo-Kantianism during the Weimar years: that it represented the path of reason, that it was the sensible *via media* between the extremes of right and left, that it was murdered by irrationalist fanatics.[7] My aim here, however, is not to retell this story, still less to rationalize the cliché. Rather, my task is to play *advocatus diaboli* and to defend the forces of darkness.[8] Upon examination, they prove much less dark and much more rational than they are often made out to be. And that old story will prove to be a myth. It is philosophically problematic because neo-Kantianism could not effectively justify the democratic and moral values of the Weimar Constitution. And it is historically inaccurate, because the great reaction against neo-Kantianism arose less because of its support for Weimar than because of its support for the Great War. Let me then proceed to examine each force of darkness, to show its noble origins and ancestry. Let me clear each of the charges of "irrationalism," and let me show why the neo-Kantians could not defeat it. The reader, who is now judge and jury, needs to see why these forces reigned over the intellectual atmosphere of Weimar.[9]

Historicism

"Historicism," in the sense relevant here,[10] is the doctrine that human nature, thought, and value depend upon their specific historical and cultural context, so that they are not eternal and universal but changing and local. The belief in universal and eternal moral, religious, and aesthetic values is therefore illusory, arising from "ethnocentrism," the belief that the values of one's own culture and age are valid for all humanity. Historicism thus brought into question any attempt to justify universal or eternal human values, whether that of Platonism, Christianity, or the natural law tradition. Understandably, Friedrich Meinecke, one of the formost historians and exponents of historicism declared it "one of the greatest revolutions in human thought."[11]

Historicism was both cause and effect of the rise in history as an academic discipline in the eighteenth and nineteenth centuries. It finds its first fledgling expression in the writings of Friedrich Herder and Justus Möser, who both stressed how human nature, thought and value are embedded in, and inseparable from, their specific historical context.[12] The doctrine acquired a name, and became feared, however, only at the close of the nineteenth century.[13] It was then that its relativistic implications began to become clear and to unnerve nearly everyone. "Historicism" (*Historismus*) became virtually synonomous with "relativism." While virtually every historicist before then was blind to, or reluctant to admit, these implications, Nietzsche shouted them from the rooftops in his 1878 *Human, All Too Human* (*Menschliches, Allzumenschliches*).[14] *Épater le bourgeoisie* was always a guiding principle of his thought, and never did he have more fun applying it than in taunting *Bürgertum* with relativism. According to his new "historical philosophy," there are no eternal truths or values, because all truth and value arises from historical causes. Though the first to espouse relativism, Nietzsche was not the last. Dilthey flirted with a kind of relativism, which seemed the inevitable consequence of his "historical critique of reason," whose aim was to expose the a-historical pretensions of philosophy.[15] Though he struggled against these relativistic implications, he never succeeded in disarming them, leaving that task to his students.[16] What Dilthey refused to acknowledge, Spengler preached as gospel. In his 1918 *Der Untergang des Abendlandes*, one of the most influential books of the Weimar era, he declared that the only appropriate philosophy for his age was a historical skepticism whose task is to undermine the pretensions of philosophy to eternal and universal truth.[17] He then went on to declare that the Kantian philosophy, too, had only a relative truth, being little more than an expression of eighteenth century European values.[18]

The relativism openly proclaimed by Nietzsche and Spengler sent tremors throughout Weimar. It became common in the 1920s to write about "the crisis of historicism" or even "the spiritual crisis of the age."[19] No one was more disturbed by this crisis than the neo-Kantians. As heirs of the Enlightenment, they firmly believed that culture should rest upon universal values, and that it is the central task of philosophy to justify them. The neo-Kantian response to the crisis is best illustrated by Wilhelm Windelband, who throughout his career battled against historicism.[20] The main problem with historicism, Windelband argued, is that it confuses the distinction between the *quid juris?* (what right?) and *quid facti?* (what fact?).[21] The *quid juris?* concerns the question: What *evidence* or *justification* do I have for a belief? The *quid facti?* involves the question: What are the *causes* for a belief? Historicism confuses these questions—so the criticism goes—because it reasons that if a belief arose under certain historical conditions, then its validity is limited to them. But this is an obvious *non sequitur.* Even though the idea of a republican constitution grew in fifth-century Athens, its validity is not limited to that time and place. Although Christianity arose at the end of the Roman Empire, it does not follow that it has no message for us today. Such examples make clear that the validity and genesis of a belief are very different matters. To determine its validity is to assess the *reasons* for it, which is very different from determining its *causes.* Thus the historicist's relativism was a bogeyman, a mere logical fallacy, the result of a failure to observe the most basic logical distinction.

The neo-Kantians had another diagnosis of the ills of historicism. They held that all forms of historical criticism—whether Nietzsche's "genetic critique," Dilthey's "historical critique of reason" or Spengler's "historical skepticism"—rest upon a basic misunderstanding of the "transcendental."[22] All Nietzsche's diatribes against the Kantians' noumenal world, all Dilthey's polemics against the "bloodless" transcendental subject, all Spengler's warnings about a naïve European ethnocentrism, had confused the "transcendental," which determines the second-order conditions of *knowledge* of objects, with the "transcendent," that is, some kind of mysterious object beyond the limits of experience. Blind to the distinctive second-order status of transcendental discourse, the historicists had hypostasized these conditions, as if they implied the existence of some kind of mysterious entity (viz., noumena or things-in-themselves). But there is no such implication at all, the neo-Kantians insisted. The transcendental has a purely epistemological meaning and purpose, and it involves no metaphysical commitment to the existence of a peculiar kind of thing. Again, then, the historicists revealed their philosophical crudity and naivité.

These strategies go some way toward restraining historicism. They show that it goes beyond its limits in drawing relativistic conclusions. Yet they do not go far enough, for they make no positive case for universal and necessary values. They show at most the *possibility* of such values, not their *reality*, let alone *necessity*. To establish the existence of such values, the neo-Kantians had nothing better to fall back upon than Kant's formal criterion of morality. This criterion is his famous "categorical imperative," which states in its standard formulation "Act only on that maxim that you can will as a universal law."[23] By the early twentieth century, however, the problems with this criterion were well known, indeed notorious. The chief problem is that it seemed "empty," i.e., so general and formal that *all* policies and practices, whether moral or immoral, could satisfy it. The criterion demands only universalizability, consistency as a general law; but even immoral policies and practices are universalizable or consistent when generalized.

The standard Kantian response to this problem was to stress the second formulation of the categorical imperative: "Always act so that you treat humanity as an end and never merely as a means."[24] This criterion is indeed more successful in ruling out immoral policies and practices, which often involve exploiting people or taking advantage of them. However, it still does not answer the question *why* we should treat people as ends in themselves. This demand is moral rather than logical, for there is no inherent contradiction in treating people as means toward ends. Ultimately, then, the Kantian faces a dilemma: if the criterion is formal, it is empty; if it has content, it cannot demonstrate its rationality.

Whatever the ultimate merits of Kant's criterion, our only task is to see what contribution the neo-Kantians made toward solving these basic problems. It is precisely here, however, that they reveal their weakness. For they made no headway in re-formulating or strengthening Kant's criterion; and they otherwise had no better strategy to provide a rational foundation for morality. Consider the following examples:

In *Kant's Grounding of Ethics* (1877), Cohen saw the solution to the problem of formalism in a substantial criterion of morality he called "the community of rational beings," which is essentially the Kantian "kingdom of ends" where all people treat one another as ends in themselves.[25] Although such a criterion would perhaps solve the problem of emptiness, Cohen did not explain why we should act on it, or why the ideal of an ethical community is "rational."

In his "On the Principle of Morals" (1883),[26] Windelband admitted that the fundamental principle of morality, as expressed in the categorical imperative, is only formal, and that its specific content is relative and historical, depending on the specific time and place. He argued that we could give a more specific account of our duties *if* we presuppose a definite ideal of the highest good; then it is only a question of determining which are the most effective means toward that ideal. However, he admitted that this ideal could not be demonstrated and that it would vary with history.

In his *Philosophy of Right* (*Rechtsphilosophie*) (1905),[27] Emil Lask sketched a programme for jurisprudence that would be the *via media* between the relativism of the historical school of law and the metaphysics of the natural law tradition. That middle path was the philosophy of value of Windelband and Rickert. This philosophy could address the *quid juris?*, which had been evaded by the historical school, and it would not require the metaphysics of the natural law tradition. But Lask stopped short of showing how this programme could be fulfilled; he does not treat, by his own admission, the methodology for a philosophy of value.

Last but not least, there were Heinrich Rickert's attempts to solve the problem. In his 1902 *The Limits of Concept-Formation in the Natural Sciences* (*Die Grenzen der naturwissenschaftlichen Begriffsbildung*), Rickert proposed a transcendental ethics that would determine the universal and necessary conditions for having values at all; but he conceded that, because these conditions are very general and formal, their content would have to derive from history.[28] Then, in his 1904 *Problems in the Philosophy of History* (*Probleme der Geschichtsphilosophie*), he had another proposal: a philosophy of history that would show how the universal principles of morality appear in the constant purposes and common ends of different cultures in world history; but he recognized that history alone proves nothing about universal values (because empirical premises cannot yield universal conclusions, and because nothing about what *is* the case determines what *ought* to be the case), and so he admitted that their real proof would have to come from metaphysics.[29] In his later years Rickert admitted failure: he argued that there cannot be any proof for the principles of morality; and he sharply distinguished between *ethical* value, which depends on the will and practice, and *logical* validity, which is the province of reason.[30]

It would be pointless to add to this list, though it would be easy to do so. As it stands it should be more than sufficient to show the deficiencies of neo-Kantianism in dealing with the problem of the foundation of value. But, as the neo-Kantians fumbled and stumbled, powerful voices spoke out against them. One was Max Weber, who (notwithstanding his professed alliance with the Heidelberg neo-Kantians Windelband and Rickert) declared that ultimate values are simply a matter of choice, and that they are based upon tradition or charisma.[31] Another was Georg Simmel, who argued at length that the Kantian criterion is empty, and that "moral pluralism" is a fundamental fact of modern life.[32] And there was the young Heidegger, who taught that there could be no higher rational foundation for *Dasein*, that everyone had to live within historical circumstances.

Once we consider these problems, it becomes hard to accept the view that neo-Kantianism represented the standpoint of reason in Weimar. To be sure, it stood for constitutionalism, republicanism and basic human rights. But why are these values the only rational ones? Why does a rational being accept them alone? To that basic question the neo-Kantians still had no convincing answer.

Nihilism, or Kirilov's Resurrection

Nihilism, in the broad sense of believing in nothing and having no allegiances, haunted cultural life in Weimar. This gaunt shrouded figure usually stood in the background, lurking in dark alleyways and corners. Nevertheless, she was all too familiar, all too feared. Anarchists would invoke her name in committing terrorist acts; and Dadaists would appeal to her in exhibiting urinals and snowshovels. To the bourgeoisie, anarchists and Dadaists were "irrational" extremists.

But truly sensitive souls knew better. They found it hard to believe in anything in the 1920s. After all, Europe had just immolated herself in the name of her highest cultural ideals. Was it not better, then, to have no ideals at all? Was not nihilism the safest and kindest policy? Was it not, in short, the most rational reaction to an irrational world?

Nihilism came from a venerable family line. She was all too German, as German as *Bratwurst und Sauerkraut*. She was born and bred in the cradle of German culture, in Weimar and Jena in the late eighteenth century. And, appropriately enough for our present theme, she first came on the scene to respond to the cultural crisis created by Kant's philosophy, whose radical criticism seemed to annihilate traditional religion, metaphysics and theology. It was Jacob Hermann Obereit, an eccentric hermit, who first introduced her in 1787 in his "critical fairy drama" *Der wiederkommende Lebensgeist der verzweifelten Metaphysik*, where the character "Nihilisme" stands for the "*Vernichtungs-Geist,*" that is, the destructive critical spirit of Kantian philosophy.[33] Friedrich Heinrich Jacobi then reintroduced her in his 1799 *Brief an Fichte*,[34] where "nihilism" now referred to the ultimate result of the critical philosophy: that we have no right to believe in the existence of anything. According to the critical philosophy, Jacobi argued, we should believe in nothing but the existence of appearances, where these appearances are nothing more than "representations in us." We have no right to believe in the independent existence of God, the external world, other minds, even our own selves! Of course, Kant also postulates the existence of the thing-in-itself; but for that he has no warrant whatsoever, because it exists beyond possible experience and he limits all knowledge to experience.[35]

Nihilism continued to be a sulking presence throughout the nineteenth century. She appears in macabre fashion in 1805 in Bonaventura's chilling *Nachtwachen,* where we learn from a wild assortment of bizarre characters—a night watchman, Hamlet and Ophelia, a clown, a starving poet—that that there is no ultimate reality, that life has no meaning whatsoever, and that it is better not to be than to be.[36] She re-appears in 1845 in Stirner's frightening *Der Einzige und sein Eigenthum* (*The Ego and Its Own*),[37] where we are encouraged to believe in nothing, nothing at all except the reality and authority of our own will. The very title of Stirner's preface appeals to the spirit of nihilism: "*Ich hab 'Mein Sach' auf Nichts gestellt.*" He then proceeds to argue that, just as long as I will them, murder and rape are fine.

Nihilism again came knocking at the door in the late 1880s when Nietzsche wrote about her in his notebooks.[38] Nihilism is usually associated with him, though the theme was already a century old by the time he came to it, and though his reflections are tame compared to his predecessors. Nietzsche defined nihilism in a more narrow ethical sense: the doctrine that life has no value or meaning because it has no purpose. Though this was an accurate formulation of one theme in the tradition, it missed others, especially the epistemological theme of Obereit, Bonaventura, and Jacobi. Because Nietzsche has so often been taken as the source of nihilism, the important epistemological theme and its anti-Kantian intentions have been forgotten.

Because of this loss of meaning, the neo-Kantians had no clear conception of nihilism, which they would sometimes confuse with relativism or pessimism. They wrote no explicit refutation of it, and there are few references to it in their writings.[39] Yet there can be little doubt that they would, in principle, have been deeply opposed to it. It is necessary to reconstruct, therefore, what their stance toward nihilism would have been.

To respond to nihilism in the ethical sense, the neo-Kantians' only needed to apply some of Kant's basic principles to the question of life's meaning. Their antidote for nihilism would consist in the recognition of our human autonomy and creativity, our power to live by our own self-imposed rules, our capacity to create the very world in which we live. The Kantian diagnosis of the problem of nihilism would then be that the nihilist has still not shaken off the legacy of medieval theology, according to which the meaning of life must come from the divine providential order. When the nihilist finds there is no evidence for the existence of God, he falls into despair, believing that his life can no longer have any meaning at all. What he fails to realize is that the meaning of life has to be created by us and cannot be given to us. Rather than seeing human beings as the ultimate source of the moral order, he hypostasizes that order, as if it were an objective realm to which we have to conform. If, however, he were to become self-conscious of his spontaneity and creativity, he would see that he, not God, is the source of the moral world order, and that his destiny lies in his own hands. This solution to the problem of nihilism is only in keeping with the primary mission of the critical philosophy: the self-awareness of human freedom through the exposure of hypostasis.

This response to nihilism could be effective only under one condition: that the autonomous Kantian subject can be the source of moral principles, the legislator of universal and necessary norms. We have already seen, however, that the neo-Kantians had failed to demonstrate this. Given the emptiness of practical reason, Kantian ethics is more likely to promote rather than prevent nihilism. For if we accept that the will is the source of the moral law, i.e., that human beings are autonomous in the sense that they should obey only those laws that they make, and if it turns out that there is no rational criterion to distinguish between right and wrong, then the will stands under no constraints at all. What I will to do is right—just because I will it. This was just the radical position Stirner had proclaimed in *Der Einzige und sein Eigenthum*. Having begun from perfectly Kantian premises, though having lost faith in the categorical imperative, he drew the perfectly correct conclusion that his own will is the source of the law. "Whatever is right to me, is right."[40] Thus the Kantian Prometheus became a monster, a creature like Kirilov in Dostoevsky's *The Devils*. Believing that his own will is the source of the law, Kirilov saw himself as master over the right to live or die; and to prove his point, he shot himself.

What about nihilism in the epistemological sense, the nihilist charge that Kant's philosophy gives us no reason to believe in the existence of anything? Here too the neo-Kantians were in trouble. Ever since Jacobi first voiced this objection in 1799, it had been a challenge for the Kantian. All that seemed to lie between Kantian appearances and the realm of nothingness was Kant's postulate of the thing-in-itself, whose inconsistency was notorious. Rather than trying to save this last remnant of hard reality in the Kantian system, the neo-Kantians did their best to eliminate it. It is a striking feature of neo-Kantianism—in both its Marburg and Southwestern forms—that it is intent on removing the thing-in-itself. Applying Kant's programme for converting "constitutive principles" (i.e., those that postulate some entity) into "regulative" ones (i.e., those that prescribe some task or goal), both Cohen and Windelband had interpreted the thing-in-itself in regulative terms, so that it became a goal or ideal of knowledge.[41] Thus the thing-in-itself is not an entity beyond experience but simply the ideal of a complete knowledge of experience.

The nihilist aspect of neo-Kantian epistemology is no less apparent in its attitude toward the self. The subject of knowledge has no more title to existence than the object. For the neo-Kantians, the transcendental subject, that is, that self that is the condition of all experience, is little more than a hypostasis or abstraction. They stressed that we should not reify this subject, as if it were a noumenal entity. Cohen and Windelband saw it as little more than a placeholder for ideas, hypotheses or intersubjective norms, while Rickert construed it as an abstraction or theoretical construct for the purposes of understanding the conditions of experience.[42]

Nothing in neo-Kantianism seemed to vindicate more the charge of nihilism than the philosophy of science of the Marburg school. In his 1910 *Substance and Function* (*Substanzbegriff und Funktionsbegriff*) the most sophisticated work on the philosophy of science in all neo-Kantianism, Ernst Cassirer argued that the object of modern science is essentially a construction, the product of our own creative rational activities.[43] It was naive of a positivist or an empiricist to think that a scientific theory corresponds to given facts. A fact or object is really nothing more than "a totality of constants," that is, a determinate weight, mass, voltage, where these constants depend upon the system of measurement and quantification which is created by the intellect.[44] A theory cannot be verified or falsified by its encounter with bare facts, which do not exist, but only by its consequences and coherence with other constructions.

All these developments seem to prove rather than disprove the charge of nihilism. For if there is no thing-in-itself, no transcendental subject, no enduring substance, one might plausibly conclude that there is little left but passing impressions, or, as Jacobi put it, representations that represent nothing? Yet the neo-Kantian still had a last defense against these worries. He would point out that, just as the nihilist had not outgrown the old theology, so he had not liberated himself from the old epistemology, that is, the transcendental realist standard of truth as the correspondence of a representation with a thing-in-itself. The nihilist was at bottom a hidden transcendental realist, who feared that losing his old standard would lead to skepticism. The neo-Kantian would argue, however, that dropping that standard implies no skepticism whatsoever. We can explain knowledge in terms of the conformity of representations with rules and norms, and we do not need to do so in terms of their correspondence with entities. Indeed, if we do not abandon the old realist way of explaining knowledge, then we really do fall into skepticism, for the simple reason that the correspondence of a representation with an independent reality is impossible to confirm. Like the historicist, then, the nihilist had failed to understand the distinct logical status of norms or rules. These, and not any kind of entity, whether Platonic archetype or thing-in-itself, are the means and methods by which we validate knowledge.

However plausible, this argument was too abstract to convince the nihilist. The nihilist is really a melodramatic transcendental realist who screams "cheat" and "swindle" whenever he is deprived of reality, the world that exists independent of his consciousness. Kant's "empirical realism" will never satisfy the nihilist, because he demands something more solid and substantial than mere appearances, which are ultimately only "representations in us." The empiricist realist insists that these appearances conform to rules, that they strictly follow universal and necessary laws; but that really does not matter to the nihilist, who insists that they are still only representations. The neo-Kantian had reduced "lived experience" to nothing more than a law-like, norm-governed, dream.

Pessimism, or the Ghost of Jean-Jacques

Pessimism, it could be argued, was the dominant *Zeitgeist* of Weimar. It permeated all aspects of its life, culture, politics, and philosophy. The bars, bordellos, cinemas and nightclubs were so popular in part because people had to escape its grip and distract themselves. Pessimism in those dark days was the belief that life is in decline, that things are only going to get worse and that little or nothing can be done about it. This belief was closely tied with nihilism, though hardly identical with it. While the nihilist thinks that life has no meaning at all, that it is neither good nor evil, the pessimist is bleaker still: he complains that it is dominated by evil. The nihilist has no values and ideals, and therefore finds existence worthless and meaningless; but the pessimist has values and ideals, it is just that he believes they will be thwarted, because of either the mechanisms of life or the laws of history. The source of the pessimist's *Weltschmerz* was often a theory of history. History teaches us, he would say, that there is no such thing as progress, that people do not approach greater happiness or perfection, no matter how hard they try. History is like the labor of Sisyphus: with great effort we roll the ball up the hill only for it to roll back down again. And we must not imagine Sisyphus happy.

That pessimism became so pervasive and popular in Weimar was almost inevitable. A nation that had just sacrificed most of its youth for a futile cause, that stood on the brink of civil war, that had to pay enormous reparations when it was already bankrupt, that was defenseless against occupation by foreign armies, was unlikely to face the future with robust optimism. It was a sign of the deep pessimism of the times that Spengler's *The Decline of the West* (*Der Untergang des Abendlandes*) became such a best seller in 1918.[45] His theory of history had somehow captured the public mood. Spengler preached that there is no such thing as progress in history, that all nations go through organic cycles, so that decline is as inevitable as ascent, and that right now the end of Western dominance is near. "We cannot alter the fact that we have been born at the beginning of the Winter of civilization," he wrote in one of his gloomier lines.[46] Hand-in-glove with this bleak prophecy, which the War seemed only to confirm, went a strong relativistic message: that Europe should cease to regard its culture and values as the apex of history.

Unlike nihilism, pessimism was no native German plant. Its modern father was Swiss, the prodigal son of Geneva, Jean-Jacques Rousseau. His first discourse, conceived in a flash of inspiration while walking from Nanterre to Paris in 1749, threw down a provocative challenge to the Enlightenment: that its belief in progress is illusory, because the arts and sciences are not improving, but corrupting morals.[47] Compared to the state of nature, Rousseau argued, life in civilization was a bad bargain, for its artificiality, competition and inequality inevitably involve the loss of innocence, integrity and independence. All movement toward greater civilization was therefore not progress but regress, an actual worsening of the human condition.

Reaction to Rousseau's discourse came quickly in Germany. Shortly after its publication, Lessing discussed it with Moses Mendelssohn, who immortalized their conversations in his 1756 *Sendschreiben an den Herrn Magister Lessing in Leipzig*.[48] That was the start of a longstanding battle against Rousseau among the *Aufklärer*, who never ceased to feel threatened by him.[49]

Not the least of Rousseau's opponents was Kant himself. His famous 1784 essay on world history, *Idea for a Universal History from a Cosmopolitan Point of View* (*Idee zu einer allgemeinen Geschichte in weltbürgerlicher Absicht*), was not least a response to Rousseau's pessimism.[50] The nub of Kant's reply to Rousseau is that the workings of nature inevitably lead history toward the ideals of freedom and equality of a republican constitution, which is a better condition for mankind than the state of nature, where we never develop our powers of reason. Kant's theory of history is based upon his "teleological theory of nature," according to which everything in nature works toward the full realization of all the natural capacities of man. The mechanism by which nature achieves this end is the "unsocial sociability" of mankind, which consists essentially in competition among individuals for prestige, power, and property (*Ehrsucht, Herrschsucht, Habsucht*). The result of such competition is that people are forced to develop their natural capacities. Kant admits that without this mechanism "man would live an Arcadian pastoral existence of perfect concord, self-sufficiency and mutual love," which was the very ideal of Rousseau's state of nature. But in that idyll they would not develop their powers, so that they would be "as docile as the sheep they tended." Though the price of civilization is the loss of a simple pastoral happiness, the reward is the development of humanity's power of reason. Thus the very mechanism that Rousseau saw as a source of civilization's discontent—competition and the workings of *amour propre*—Kant saw as the source of civilization's beneficence. His argument against Rousseau was a brilliant twist of the dialectical knife; but he was also ambiguous about the status of his teleology. Why should one accept that nature works through history? And why assume that there is always a progressive development? In response to such questions Kant hedged; he declined to demonstrate his teleology, realizing that this would involve him in metaphysics. He ends his essay by making its teleology a regulative idea: if we at least believe in providence and act on it, we can make it come true.[51]

Philosophers in the Kantian tradition shared Kant's basic optimism, even if they did not accept the details of his theory of history. They reaffirmed his belief in progress; his hope that humanity, through constant striving and effort, could at least approach, if not attain, the ideals of a republican constitution. They were less willing to accept, however, Kant's teleology. Not ready to rest their faith in nature or providence, which they saw as a residue of the old theology, they believed instead in the power of the human will and the efficacy of direct action. Man had to take control over his own fate, and he could not wait for providence or nature to do things for him. If people would only work together in political associations, they could transform the political order. The *locus classicus* for this response to Rousseau's cultural pessimism is the fifth of Fichte's famous lectures on *The Vocation of the Scholar* (*Die Bestimmung des Gelehrten*),which became the standard for the entire neo-Kantian generation.[52] Here Fichte argued that we should see moral corruption as the result of a *specific* culture and state—that of the *ancien régime*—and not as the result of culture and the state in general. While Rousseau pined for the lost golden age of the state of nature, where men lived in peace, justice and harmony, he should have realized that this is achievable only in a republican constitution. What he saw in the past we should now put in the future as a goal for human striving. No one believed more passionately than Fichte in the powers of the human will and striving to change and transform its world. It was his radical Promethean faith—not Kant's belief in providence—that entered into the pulse of the neo-Kantian tradition.[53]

There is something noble and inspiring about that faith, which is the ultimate *credo* of the optimist. Yet, in that great debate between Rousseau and the Kantians, between pessimists and optimists, history came down firmly on the side of Rousseau and the pessimists. Faith in progress and the creative powers of man came to grief in the Great War. Rousseau's core thesis—that science and technology are not improving but destroying morals—found its stunning and spectacular confirmation on the battlefields of Verdun and the Somme. For here the latest science and technology was used on a grand scale to murder an entire generation of young men. Poison gas, machine guns, tanks, airplanes and howitzers—these were the legacy of science, these were the triumph of civilization. In the face of the vast spectacle of the slaughtered, the ghost of Jean-Jacques could only weep and mutter "I told you so."

The trauma of the Great War was a source of deep disillusionment, on all sides but especially in defeated Germany. Who could believe in progress, in the value of culture, in the creative powers of man, amid all the destruction and slaughter? The war had exacted the utmost effort, the utmost sacrifice from an entire nation. And to what end? The nihilists had a word for it: nothingness. That was the only accurate term to describe the self-annihilation of a nation, not to mention the fate of 1.7 million young men, who now mouldered in mass graves. In the face of such shocking trauma it was only natural that neo-Kantian optimism would have lost its credibility and authority.

Yet, for the neo-Kantians, the results of the Great War were even more dire. The reaction against them was all the more severe—all the more passionate, all the more personal—because it was directed against not only their doctrines but also their deeds. For, with few exceptions,[54] the neo-Kantians joined in the hysteria of 1914, and they enthusiastically supported the cause of the war. They did everything in their power to join the war effort and to defend the German cause.[55] Cohen and Natorp wrote propaganda; Riehl and Windelband signed the *Aufruf der 93*; and Lask paid the ultimate tribute: he fell on the Eastern Front on May 1915.

What especially incriminated the neo-Kantians is that their propaganda was particularly prominent, pervasive, and pernicious.[56] In article after article, in pamphlet after pamphlet, in lecture after lecture, they preached that this was a just and necessary war. It was not a war for the sake of colonies, commercial advantage, or empire—the interests of France, England, and Russia—but a war for the sake of the ideal. And the philosopher who represented the ideal was, of course, Immanuel Kant. Kant was the father of German idealism; and German idealism became the rationale for the war. The sage of Königsberg, it seemed, had supplied just the right kind of idealism to justify bravery, patriotism, and personal sacrifice. For was it not Kant who had placed the value of the ideal above happiness, and who had taught that duty is categorical and that obligation is absolute, whatever the personal cost? It was indeed Kant who taught the youth to march bravely in front of machine guns, to sit in trenches through bombardments, and to bear their wounds with pride.

Nowhere can we see more clearly how Kant's philosophy was put into service than in the war-time essays of Paul Natorp, which extol German soldiers for their willingness to sacrifice themselves for the sake of the ideal.[57] The ideal was an end in itself, an eternal value, whereas the individual was only a fleeting appearance and instrument for its realization. While Kant had faith in humanity because of the public's enthusiasm for the French Revolution, Natorp now believed that the enthusiasm of August 1914 gave reason to restore that faith.[58] Every German soldier had to face a terrible choice: duty or life, the ideal or personal existence. Natorp knew in 1914 that this generation of heroes would choose the former option; but they knew in 1918 that they should have chosen the latter.

No claim should be made against Kant because of the misdeeds of his followers. Indeed, a strong case can be made that the neo-Kantians had abused their great teacher, for his pacifism and cosmopolitanism did not sit well with their belligerent nationalist propaganda. Cohen and Natorp did somersaults to disguise the glaring discrepancy, endorsing the paradoxical thesis that war is sometimes the only path to peace and international understanding.[59]

"World history is the world court" (*"Die Weltgeschichte ist das Weltgericht"*) Schiller once said, which means *inter alia* that moral judgment has to be *ex post facto*.[60] If that is so, the sentence against the neo-Kantians cannot be mild. The ancient charge against Socrates had been that he *corrupted* the youth; but the modern charge against the neo-Kantians would have to be much more severe: they *sacrificed* the youth.[61]

Such, in sum, is the brief of *advocatus diaboli*. His aim has been only to remind contemporary neo-Kantians, in the name of the sacrificed, of the history they tend to forget: that in Weimar, neo-Kantianism was associated not only with the cause of reason but also with the war-hysteria of August 1914. If neo-Kantianism was the victim of extremist forces in 1933, it itself had been an extremist force in 1914. If the disillusioned listened to such "irrational" forces as historicism, nihilism and pessimism, that was ultimately because they were much more rational than neo-Kantianism. *Advocatus diaboli* now leaves the court, grateful for his reader's patience and the opportunity to defend historicism, nihilism and pessimism. So often maligned, something had to be said in their behalf. No one should doubt that more can be said in behalf of the neo-Kantians. But we leave that for another occasion.

Notes

1. Ernst Cassirer, *Die Idee der Republikanischen Verfassung: Rede zur Verfassungsfeier am 11. August 1928* (Hamburg: de Gruyter, 1929).
2. The best study of neo-Kantianism is Klaus Köhnke, *Entstehung und Aufstieg des Neukantianismus* (Frankfurt: Suhrkamp, 1986). There is an English translation by R. J. Hollingdale: *The Rise of Neo-Kantianism* (Cambridge: Cambridge University Press, 1991), though it is not to be recommended. The translation eliminates all notes and bibliographical aids, and the nearly 200 pages of documentation of the original, which are indispensable to any serious scholar.
3. On the Marburg school, see Ulrich Sieg, *Aufstieg und Niedergang des Marburger Neukantianismus* (Würzburg: Königshausen & Neumann, 1994). Unfortunately, there is no counterpart history for the Southwestern school. On the neo-Friesian school, see Arthur Kronfeld, "Geleitworte zum zehnjährigen Bestehen der neuen Friesschen Schule" in *Das Wesen der psychiatrischen Erkenntnis* (Berlin: Springer, 1920), 46–65; and Erne Blencke, "Zur Geschichte der neuen Friesschen Schule," *Archiv für Geschichte der Philosophie* 60 (1978), 199–208. Though the Friesian school is neglected by standard histories, the group surrounding Nelson was especially eminent. Among its members were the theologian Rudolf Otto (1869–1937), the psychiatrist Arthur Kronfeld (1886–1941) and the Nobel Prize winner Otto Meyerhoff (1884–1951). The group published their own journal, *Abhandlungen der Fries'schen Schule, Neue Folge* (Göttingen: Vandenhoeck & Ruprecht, 1907–37), 6 vols. New histories of the Southwestern and neo-Friesian schools are desiderata of future research.
4. On neo-Kantianism in Berlin, see Volkert Gerhardt, Reinhard Mehring and Jana Rindert, *Berliner Geist, Eine Geschichte der Berliner Universitätsphilosophie bis 1946* (Berlin: Akademie Verlag, 1999), 179–93.
5. On that dispute see Peter Gordon, *Continental Divide: Heidegger, Cassirer, Davos* (Cambridge, MA: Harvard University Press, 2010); and Michael Friedman, *A Parting of the Ways: Carnap, Cassirer, and Heidegger* (Chicago: Open Court, 2000).

6. The ideas of 1914 were "duty-order-justice," which were to replace "liberty-equality-fraternity," the ideas of 1789. Kant was the main source for the idea of duty. See Rudolf Kjellén, *Die Ideen von 1914* (Leipzig: Hirzel, 1915), 39.

7. This assessment appears explicitly in Thomas E. Willey, *Back to Kant: The Revival of Kantianism in German Social and Historical Thought, 1860–1914* (Detroit: Wayne State University Press, 1978), 10, 179–80.

8. I should stress that my standpoint here is entirely forensic. I realize fully that much more could, and should, be said in the neo-Kantians' behalf. Their advocacy of democratic socialism against Marxist and National-Socialist ideology was admirable. On that development, see the collection of essays edited by Helmut Holzhey, *Ethischer Sozialismus* (Frankfurt: Suhrkamp, 1994). A proper discussion of this topic exceeds the boundaries of the present article.

9. For an opposing perspective, see Peter Gay, *Weimar Culture* (New York: Harper & Row, 1968). I agree with Gay that "outsiders" were "insiders" in Weimar. Despite his pretensions, Gay is entirely on the side of the Weimar establishment because he assumes that its constitution represents the standpoint of "reason." See, e.g., pp. 23–24, 45. He does not defend this assumption, which begs every question.

10. On the problems of defining "historicism" and its several senses, see my *The German Historicist Tradition* (Oxford: Oxford University Press, 2011), 1–6.

11. Friedrich Meinecke, *Die Entstehung des Historismus* (Munich: Oldenbourg, 1965), 1.

12. On the decisive role of Herder and Möser in founding the historicist tradition, see Meinecke, *Die Entstehung des Historismus,* 303–444.

13. It is difficult to find a historicist thinker before Nietzsche who embraces relativism. Herder discusses the problem in his early fragment "Von der Verschiedenheit des Geschmacks und der Denkart unter den Menschen," *Werke,* ed. Martin Bollacher et.al. (Frankfurt: Deutscher Klassiker Verlag, 1985), I, 149–60. But Herder himself would struggle against relativism in all his major historical works.

14. Friedrich Nietzsche, *Menschliches, Allzumenschliches* §§1, 2, 96–97, in *Sämtliche Werke, Kritische Studienausgabe,* eds. G. Colli and M. Montinari (Berlin: de Gruyter, 1967–77), II, 23–24, 92–94.

15. See his 1883 *Einleitung in die Geisteswissenschaften,* in *Gesammelte Schriften,* eds. Karlfried Gründer and Frithjof Rodi (Göttingen: Vandenhoeck & Ruprecht, 1961), I, xvii–xx, 116. In his later years Dilthey struggled with the issue of relativism and attempted to overcome it. See his "Das geschichtliche Bewußtsein und die Weltanschauungen," *Schriften* VIII, 3–71.

16. See the late undated series of manuscripts entitled "Das geschichtliche Bewusstsein und die Weltanschauungen," *Schriften* VIII, 3–71. In his seventieth birthday address, Dilthey admitted that he had not solved the problem of relativism, leaving that task to his students. See *Schriften* V, 9.

17. Oswald Spengler, *Der Untergang des Abendlandes* (Munich: Beck, 1919), I, 61.

18. Ibid, I, 25, 29–30.

19. See Ernst Troeltsch, "Die Krise des Historismus," *Die neue Rundschau* 33 (1922), 572–90; Karl Heussi, *Die Krisis des Historismus* (Tübingen: Mohr, 1932); Karl Joël, *Die philosophische Krisis der Gegenwart* (Leipzig: Meiner, 1922); and Arthur Liebert, *Die geistige Krisis der Gegenwart* (Berlin: Pan Verlag, 1923). On the theme of crisis, see Charles Bambach, *Heidegger, Dilthey, and the Crisis of Historicism* (Ithaca: Cornell University Press, 1995).

20. On Windelband's struggle against historicism, see my "Historicism and neo-Kantianism," *Studies in History and Philosophy of Science* 39 (2008), 554–64.

21. See Windelband, "Was ist Philosophie?," in *Präludien: Aufsätze und Reden zur Philosophie und ihrer Geschichte*, 9th ed. (Tübingen: Mohr, 1921),I, 24, 29. Windelband explicitly turns this point against historicism in his *Einleitung in die Philosophie*, 2nd ed. (Tübingen: Mohr, 1920), 210.

22. See, for example, Rickert, *Der Gegenstand der Erkenntnis*, 6th ed. (Tübingen: Mohr, 1928), 95–104. The *locus classicus* for the neo-Kantian concept of the transcendental is Hermann Cohen, *Kants Theorie der Erfahrung* (Berlin: Dümmler, 1871).

23. Kant, *Grundlegung zur Metaphysik der Sitten*, IV 421. (Akademie Ausgabe)

24. Ibid, IV, 429.

25. Hermann Cohen, *Kants Begründung der Ethik* (Berlin: Dümmler, 1877), 184, 198–99.

26. See *Präludien* II, 161–94, esp. 164, 166, 172, 182, 191, 193–94.

27. See Emil Lask, *Rechtsphilosophie* (Heidelberg: Winter, 1905). Republished in *Gesammelte Schriften*, ed. Eugen Herrigel (Tübingen: Mohr, 1923), I, 275–331.

28. Heinrich Rickert, *Die Grenzen der naturwissenschaftlichen Begriffsbildung* (Tübingen: Mohr, 1902), 731–72. Rickert made some attempt to sketch this transcendental ethics in his "Vom System der Werte," *Logos* 4 (1913), 295–327.

29. See his *Die Probleme der Geschichtsphilosophie*, 3rd ed. (Heidelberg: Winter, 1924), 142–58, esp. 14548.

30. See his "Über logische und ethische Geltung," *Kant-Studien* 19 (1914), 182–220, cited p. 207. Rickert would later prove to be a harsh critic of what he called "intellectualism," i.e., the attempt to prove values through logical or rational means. See his "Das Leben der Wissenschaft und die griechische Philosophie," *Logos* 22 (1923/24), 303–39.

31. See Max Weber, "Der Sinn der 'Wertfreiheit' der soziologschen und ökonomischen Wissenschaften," and "Wissenschaft als Beruf," in *Gesammelte Aufsätze zur Wissenschaftslehre*, ed. Johannes Winckelmann (Tübingen: Mohr, 1973), 507–8, 604–5.

32. See especially his much neglected early work, *Einleitung in die Moralwissenschaft*, in *Georg Simmel Gesammtausgabe*, ed. Ottheim Rammstedt (Frankfurt: Suhrkamp, 2005), IV, 70–102, 348–402.

33. Jacob Obereit, *Der wiederkommende Lebensgeist der verzweifelten Metaphysik* (Berlin: Decker und Sohn, 1787), 14.

34. Friedrich Heinrich Jacobi, *Werke*, eds. Friedrich Roth and Friedrich Köppen (Leipzig: Fleischer, 1816), III, 1–57.

35. This was the sum and substance of Jacobi's "Ueber den transcendentalen Idealismus," which appears in his "Beylage" to his *David Hume, Werke* II, 291–310.

36. *Nachtwachen. Von Bonaventura.* (Penig: Dienemann, 1805). Bonaventura was a pseudonym. The author is now believed to be August Klingemann (1777–1831).

37. Max Stirner (alias for Caspar Friedrich Schmidt), *Der Einzige und sein Eigenthum* (Leipzig: Wigand, 1845). On Stirner, see my "Max Stirner and the End of Classical German Philosophy," in *Politics, Religion and Art: Hegelian Debates*, ed. Douglas Moggach (Evanston, IL: Northwestern University Press, 2011), 281–300.

38. Friedrich Nietzsche, *Nachgelassene Werke: Der Wille zur Macht. Versuch einer Umwerthung aller Werthe* (Leipzig: Naumann, 1901).

39. Rickert discusses "nihilism" (*Nihilismus*) at the close of his *Die Grenzen der naturwissenschaftlichen Begriffsbildung* (Tübingen: Mohr, 1913), 642–43, though it is conflated with relativism. Another implicit reference is in Windelband's "Kritische oder Genetische Methode?," in *Präludien* II, 117. Here he discusses a nihilist position under the label of "relativism."

40. *Der Einzige und sein Eigenthum* (Stuttgart: Reclam, 1972), 208.

41. See Cohen, *Kants Theorie der Erfahrung* (1871), 252, 258; and Windelband, *Prinzipien der Logik* (Tübingen: Mohr, 1913), 58–60.

42. On the tendency toward elimination of the subject in the Marburg school, see Siegfried Marck, "Die Lehre vom erkennenden Subjekt in der Marburger Schule," *Logos* 4 (1913), 364–86. On Windelband's interpretation of the transcendental subject, see "Kulturphilosophie und transzendentaler Idealismus," *Präludien* II, 283; and "Was ist Philosophie?," *Präludien* I, 47; and *Einleitung in die Philosophie*, 255. On Rickert's account of the transcendental subject, see *Der Gegenstand der Erkenntnis*, 95–104.

43. Ernst Cassirer, *Substanzbegriff und Funktionsbegriff* (Berlin: Cassirer, 1910). See especially Cassirer's critique of positivism in chapter 4. He admits that there is a circularity to science: that we identify facts only through the theories they are to test (p. 194); and he concedes that there is no way to escape the circle of constructions of scientific theory (p. 196). In general, Cassirer's theory of science was in the service of the later Cohen's epistemological principles, whose "logical idealism" aimed to eliminate entirely the given element of experience (see p. 130).

44. Ibid, 196.

45. The *Jubiläumsausgabe* of Spengler's book, which was published in 1929 to celebrate the first decade of its publication, notes on the title page: "*Anlässlich des hundertsten Tausend.*"

46. Spengler, *Untergang des Abendlandes* I, 59.

47. Jean Jacques Rousseau, *Discours sur les sciences et les arts*, *Œuvres complètes* (Paris: Gallimard, 1964), III, 1–30.

48. Moses Mendelssohn, *Gesammelte Schriften, Jubiläumsausgabe,* ed. Fritz Bamberger et.al. (Stuttgart-Bad Cannstatt: Frommann, 1929), II, 81–109. Mendelssohn translated Rousseau's second discourse into German in 1756. His translation is in *Schriften* VI/2, 61–202.

49. Throughout its history the Kantian tradition would battle other forms of pessimism, not least that of Schopenhauer. On this episode, see Köhnke, *Entstehung und Aufstieg des Neukantianismus*, 327–336. Because Schopenhauer's pessimism is more relevant to the 1870s than Weimar, I do not discuss it here.

50. Kant, *Schriften* VIII, 15—31.

51. Ibid, VIII, 27, 29, 30–31.

52. Fichte, *Sämtliche Werke*, ed. I. H. Fichte (Berlin: Veit, 1845–46), VI, 335–46.

53. On the enormous influence of Fichte on neo-Kantianism, see Köhnke, *Entstehung und Aufstieg*, 179–94; and Hermann Lübbe, *Politische Philosophie in Deutschland* (Munich: Deutscher Taschenbuch Verlag, 1974), 194–205.

54. The exceptions were Leonard Nelson and Ernst Cassirer. On Cassirer's attitude toward the war, see Sieg, *Aufsteig und Niedergang*, 391–92.

55. On the role of the Marburg neo-Kantians in the war, see Sieg, *Aufstieg und Niedergang*, 373–92.

56. To get the measure of the pervasiveness of Kantian themes in wartime propaganda, see Klaus Schwabe, *Wissenschaft und Kriegsmoral: Die deutschen Hochschullehrer und die politischen Grundfragen des Ersten Weltkrieges* (Göttingen: Musterschmidt Verlag, 1969), 24, 30, 35, 38, 43–45.

57. See Paul Natorp, *Der Tag des Deutschen* (Hagen: Otto Rippel, 1915).

58. Ibid, 89.

59. See Natorp, *Der Tag des Deutschen*, 97; and Cohen, "Vom ewigen Frieden," in *Deutsche Weihnacht, eine Liebesgabe deutscher Hochschüler* (Kassel: Furche, 1914), and "Kantische Gedanken im deutschen Militarismus," *Frankfurter Zeitung und*

Handelsblatt 60, January 9, 1916, 1–2. These articles are reprinted in *Hermann Cohen Werke*, eds. Helmut Holzhey, Julius Schoeps, and Christoph Schule (Hildesheim: Olms, 1997), XVI, 311–18 and XVII,135–46.

60. Friedrich Schiller, "Entsagung," in *Schillers Werke, Nationalausgabe*, eds. Julius Petersen and Gerhard Fricke (Weimar: Böhlaus Nachfolger, 1943), I, 168.

61. I agree entirely with the sentiment of Ulrich Sieg, who writes (in *Aufstieg und Niedergang des Marburger Neukantianismus*, 377) of the Marburg Neo-Kantians: "Die jungen Menschen wurden das Opfer eines Idealismus, der ihnen nicht zuletzt von ihren Universitätslehrern vermittelt worden war" ("The young people were the victims of an idealism which had been imparted to them not least by their university instructors"). Like Sieg, I take issue with Hermann Lübbe, *Politische Philosophie in Deutschland* (Munich: Deutscher Taschenbuch Verlag, 1974), 171–75.

7

Weimar Philosophy and the Crisis of Historical Thinking

Charles Bambach

The Great War and Historical Thinking

In an essay on the relevance of tragedy for understanding modern existence, the German poet Friedrich Hölderlin (1770–1843) writes on what he calls "the calculable law" that legislates the pattern and movement of tragic destiny.[1] Tragedy needs to be understood in terms of a "counter-rhythmic rupture" or "caesura," Hölderlin claims; a rupture that sunders the continuity of temporal progression and provides a break in the jointure of experience and expectation. As a break in, with, and against time, the caesura functions as the "pure word" of poetic insight into the human experience of time as history. On the basis of this Hölderlinian insight, the French philosopher Philippe Lacoue-Labarthe contends that "a caesura would be that which, within history, interrupts history and opens up another possibility of history, or else closes off all the possibility of history."[2] As he construes it, "the history of the 20th century is marked by the scission of Auschwitz, the caesura of our times." Lacoue-Labarthe is hardly alone in singling out Auschwitz as a kind of metonymic shorthand for the experience of disruption that characterizes the twentieth-century experience of history. Given the power of this metonymy it is easy to forget that before Auschwitz there was another caesura that definitively broke the line of continuity that forms the history of modern Europe and that left its indelible mark on the consciousness of an earlier generation—the caesura of the Great War. Into a middle-class world of order and stability, the brutal fact of millions of casualties had ruptured the historical narrative of progress and optimism that had reigned over European life in the pre-war epoch. The unspoken bourgeois faith in both the meaning and coherence of history had been shattered. The Great War brought in its wake a profound disillusionment with the pre-war liberal worldview of academic *Bildung* and a heightened awareness of the power and necessity of "destruction" for any project aimed at cultural renewal.

As the combatants returned home from the front in 1918 to a Germany wracked by economic and political turmoil, the generational mood grew at once bleak and ominous. Two popular books published in Munich in 1918 perfectly captured this mood: Paul Ernst's *The Collapse of German Idealism* and Oswald Spengler's *The Decline of the West*. Each in its own way constituted an assault on the reassuring platitudes of pre-war culture. One year later the Swiss theologian Karl Barth published *The Epistle to the Romans* that, like Spengler's book, expressed a radical rejection of the historicist faith in the meaning of history and an awareness of a profound crisis in the foundations of German *Bildung* and *Wissenschaft*. Each of these works acknowledged the caesura of the Great War as initiating a crisis-mentality that was to pervade all areas of learning and culture in the Weimar era. The catastrophe of 1918/19—the loss of the war, the abdication of the Kaiser, the socialist revolutions on the streets in Berlin and Munich, the assassinations of Karl Liebknecht and Rosa Luxemburg, the Versailles Treaty—helped to bring about the collapse and dissolution of the old Wilhelmine order. *Destruktion, Abbau*—demolition, dismantling, and destruction—all became the watchwords of social and intellectual change.

As part of this generational transformation, nineteenth-century authors such as Kierkegaard, Nietzsche, Overbeck, and Dostoevsky grew newly relevant to the Weimar generation as it sought to navigate through "the crisis of learning" that dominated German intellectual life. In this climate of crisis, philosophers such as Rudolf Pannwitz wrote *Die Krisis der europäischen Kultur*, which was followed by Arthur Liebert's *Die geistige Krisis der Gegenwart*; in 1921 Herrmann Weyl wrote an essay on "The New Crisis in the Foundations of Mathematics," which was followed the next year by Johannes Stark's *The Present Crisis in German Physics*, Joseph Petzold's "Concerning the Crisis of the Causality Concept," and Albert Einstein's popular article "On the Present Crisis in Theoretical Physics." Within every discipline of both the natural and human sciences, the foundations of learning were under assault. As Liebert expressed it,

> The task of my work is not to substantiate or present any of the arbitrary crises of contemporary life, no matter how staggering a force it may possess. Rather, it is to expose *the* crisis of our time and of the whole contemporary worldview and temper of life, viz., the concept and meaning of all the individual crises and the common intellectual and metaphysical source by which they are conditioned and from which they are nourished.[3]

This consummate crisis of all crises lay, for Liebert, in "the fatal historical skepticism and relativism nourished by historicism."[4]

One of the most prominent German philosophers of this generation, Ernst Troeltsch, came to understand this cultural crisis of learning in Weimar as the epiphenomenal expression of an underlying "crisis of history itself in its innermost structure," a crisis of "relativism that paved the way for the seismic upheaval of values."[5] The war had leveled many of the old metaphysical structures of German historical thinking and had undermined the transcendental-absolute standards of measure provided by the Kantian-Hegelian philosophy of history. As Troeltsch put it, "the contemporary crisis of historicism is a deep, inner crisis of our time; it is not merely a scholarly or scientific problem but a practical problem of life." The older tradition of classical historicism that embraced a rigorously empirical model of research knew no value relativism. It was, rather, committed to the ethical unfolding of God's ultimate plan that manifested itself in

Ranke's divinatory *Weltgeschichte,* Humboldt's spiritual *Ideen,* Droysen's "moral powers," and Hegel's Christological revelation of *Geist.*

Yet, as Troeltsch well understood, "the world war and the revolution provided a lesson in historical perception filled with the most terrible and frightful violence."[6] The foundations of the old order had been shattered and the new generation of survivors stood in a precarious space "between the times," as the Protestant theologian Friedrich Gogarten put it. Like Troeltsch, Gogarten claimed that "the historicizing of all of our thinking has been carried out today to the extent that it has become impossible for any of our ideas to escape it. This historicizing threatens to abolish absolutely every idea that requires a norm or might tend to be a norm itself" since every measure, standard, criterion, and law is thereby relativized. "Our question then is not whether the historicizing of all thinking has actually occurred . . . but whether the historicizing that actually did take place is valid."[7]

For Gogarten, Barth, and other proponents of Weimar "crisis theology," the breakdown of historical norms and values had led to a "permanent *Krisis* of the relation between time and eternity."[8] Seizing on the moment of sterility and spiritual exhaustion within German culture as an opportunity to effect a post-Nietzschean "reevaluation of all values," Barth called for a radical dismantling of the old foundations. As Gogarten expressed it:

> It is the destiny of our generation to stand between the times. We never belonged to the period presently coming to an end; it is doubtful whether we shall ever belong to the period which is to come. . . . So we stand in the middle—in an empty space. We belong neither to the one nor to the other . . . therefore, we were jubilant over Spengler's book. It proves, whether or not it is true in detail, that the hour has come in which this refined, intelligent culture through its own intelligence, discovers the worm in itself, the hour in which trust in progress and culture receives the death blow. And Spengler's book is not the only sign. Whoever reads can find it in nearly every book and essay.[9]

In this void "between the times" the work of Spengler, Barth, and Gogarten came to signify a "crisis of historicism": not merely of the empirical research paradigm of practicing historians, but rather a crisis in the foundations of historical thinking, of Nietzsche's question about whether history itself has any meaning for life. It is this crisis that came to shape German historical thinking in decisive ways during the Weimar era, especially in the work of four philosophers of history— Oswald Spengler (1880–1936), Ernst Troeltsch (1865–1923), Heinrich Rickert (1863–1936), and Martin Heidegger (1889–1976).

Spengler's *The Decline of the West*

Spengler's book *The Decline of the West* appeared in the summer of 1918 as the reality of German defeat in the Great War was beginning to seem inevitable. It became an overnight success among the reading public, leading quickly to a second printing and in 1922 to a second volume that expanded Spengler's analysis of Western decadence into a wider consideration of non-Western cultures. The impact of the work on the Weimar cultural scene was seismological. Written in a highly idiosyncratic, rhetorical style marked by presumptive authority and self-aggrandizing pronouncements, Spengler assumed the Nietzschean mantle of the cultural prophet. Drawing on a morphological theory of organic cultural development, Spengler put forward a metaphysical interpretation of history modeled on the biological processes of the life-cycle. All cultures, he claimed, follow the same cyclical pattern of birth, development, maturation, senescence, and death. Each embodies its own unique "form" that develops according to biological principles, archetypes that follow a specific life-course and pass through "a series of stages that must be traversed, and traversed moreover in an ordered and obligatory sequence."[10]

If previous ages sought to grasp history according to the principles of the natural sciences, Spengler saw these attempts as bankrupt since they merely perceived dead forms according to "mathematical law." Against this whole tradition of thinking, Spengler embraced the Goethean principle of *analogy* as a way "to understand living forms" which held "the key to understanding our own future." On this basis he claimed "for the first time to venture the attempt at predetermining history" and of offering "a new outlook on *history, a philosophy of destiny* and indeed the first of its kind" (emphasis in original).

Looking at the previous historiography of world history, Spengler identified two fundamental approaches, which he termed "the world-as-nature" and "the world-as-history." Within the first vision the world is formulated in a rigid, mechanical way in terms of laws, systems, causality, and "the logic of space." Within the second, however, the world appears as an organic process of becoming, governed by "the logic of time." Against the doctrine of causality, Spengler juxtaposed a vision of destiny, which was "the word for an inner certainty that is not describable." "Real history," he asserts, "is heavy with destiny but free of laws."[11] It does not focus merely on the past as what has already become (*das Gewordene*), but on its meaning as part of a destiny marked by becoming (*Werden*). Through "intuitive vision" and the poetic grasp of Goethean analogy, the historian comes to understand the "living forms" of history that hold within their arcane order the key to historical destiny. And only this destiny is "the authentic mode of existence of the originary phenomenon, that in which the living idea of becoming unfolds itself immediately to the intuitive vision."

From this perspective Spengler looks back on the Western European tradition of historiography and faults it for what he calls its Ptolemaic arrogance, designating itself as "the natural center of the historical system" and relegating all other cultures to a subaltern status as mere "footnotes" to the grand pageant of European world dominion. Against this vision Spengler seeks instead to initiate a "Copernican turn" in world history that

> admits no sort of privileged position to the Classical or Western (Faustian) culture as against the cultures of India, Babylon, China, Egypt, Arabia,

Mexico—separate worlds of dynamic being which in point of mass count for just as much in the general picture of history as the Classical, while frequently surpassing it in point of spiritual greatness and soaring power.

In attacking the blatant Eurocentrism of Western historiography, Spengler finds its categorical subdivision of history into ancient-medieval-modern an "incredibly jejune and *meaning-less* scheme"; one that prevents us from grasping the deep spiritual significance of culture which is "the originary phenomenon of all past and future world-history."

Like so many other German thinkers of the Great War generation (Sombart, Scheler, Mann, Jünger), Spengler identifies *Kultur* as the spiritually authentic inner essence of a people that expressed its organic relation to time as the vital expression of its *soul*. As cultures grow, however, they pass through inevitable stages of development on their way to full flowering, decline, and death. Once a culture moves past its vital inner stage its destiny is to become a *Zivilisation*, the external, artificially constructed, mechanical expression of the living culture on its way to extinction. If *Kultur* can be metaphorically expressed as the living soil of a *Volk* tended by a bucolic shepherd-poet, then *Zivilisation* can be understood as an asphalt road built by a mathematically-trained engineer. Spengler's prophetic analysis of the decline and degeneration of a Faustian culture that had lost its "soul" in the calculative rationality of a technological civilization played well in the post-war epoch of skepticism and radical uncertainty.

In an era beset with anxieties about its fundamental values and future direction, Spengler enjoyed enormous success, even as he was vilified and mocked by the very mandarin establishment that he criticized in *The Decline of the West*. Yet his relationship to the classical historicist tradition that came under assault in the generation of the Great War is far more complex and contradictory than many of his peers realized. Spengler resolutely assaulted the historicist image of the Rankean scholar who dispassionately collected archival data according to an empirical method of sober, scholarly detachment. For him, the contemplative Rankean historian drawn by the alexandrine pleasures of archival research was nothing less than a passive observer, unable to act decisively or create anything vital. This passive scholar-fact-collector functioned merely as one of Nietzsche's "eunuchs [who] watch over the great historical world-harem."[12] Spengler's repudiation of the life-denying neutrality of historical observation in favor of a Nietzschean will to life show him as a poignant critic of German historicism.

And yet the whole ethos of *The Decline of the West* was marked by historicist principles that shaped its conception, aims, and execution. For example, although Spengler was critical of the Eurocentric bias of most contemporary history, he nonetheless shared the historicist prejudice that only in Western Europe—the Faustian culture—was the human being predestined to understanding history.[13] Like Ranke, Humboldt, Droysen, Dilthey, and Troeltsch, Spengler believed that the human being could only be grasped in terms of its historicity, not in universal concepts. And like them he understood that the highest values of a culture did not derive their value from their participation in timeless Platonic forms, but rather were relative to the cultures that produced them. Spengler's commitment to these two principles—the belief in "the radical breakdown of supra-temporal systems of norms and the increasing knowledge that we must understand ourselves as historical beings right to the core of our humanity"—mark him as a philosophical historicist.[14]

Indeed Spengler's whole view of world history was shaped by the philosophical historicism of Johann G. Herder (1744–1803), who maintained that human life needs to be understood in its historical *individuality* as a process of *development*. Cultures rise and fall much as flowers bloom and decay; each needs to be viewed in its own context. Herder had understood human life as historical *individuality* to its core, as a process of *development* that unfolds over time much as in the realm of biological growth and decay. A similarly historicist insight shaped Spengler's whole view of world history. Hence he could claim, "There are no eternal truths. Every philosophy is an expression of its own—and only its own—time. . . . . Truths are truths only in relation to a particular form of humanity."[15]

Spengler even extends this historicist insight into the realm of mathematics, claiming, "There is not, and cannot be, number as such. . . . The style of any mathematic . . . depends wholly on the culture in which it is rooted." Given this relativist perspective, he abandons the notion of a progressive, unified, and teleologically-driven historical process that culminates in either the advancing perfection of the human species (Herder) or in spirit's progress in the consciousness of freedom (Hegel). As he views it, each culture within world history has its own isolated meaning and does not affect other cultures in any profound way; rather, each follows its own unique historical destiny to fulfill its vital possibilities. The history of cultures reveals itself to Spengler as something discreet, discontinuous, and relative; it resists all attempts at universal synthesis. Hence, he affirms "the historically relative character" of each form of life, privileging none above any other since amongst different cultures "there are different truths. The thinker must admit the validity of all, or of none."[16]

This leads him to abandon any notion of purpose, design, or goal that inheres within human history: "humankind has no aim, no idea, no plan, any more than the species of butterflies or orchids. 'Humanity' is a zoological concept or an empty word . . . , [a species] that grows with the same sublime aimlessness as the flowers of the field." In the final verdict, not only are there no supra-historical values according to which we might be able to judge the progress of culture, but the very process of history is a Heraclitean river of coming-to-be and passing-away without any enduring ground. In this sense Spengler claims that "the history of humanity has no meaning (*Sinn*) whatever."

Out of the suffering and absurdity of the Great War, Spengler forms a tragic view of history "full of joy precisely in respect to the gravity of human destiny." For those who seek a higher moral order to the wayward happenings of national conflicts, Spengler offers no consolation: "history has nothing to do with human logic. A thunderstorm, an earthquake, a flowing stream of lava that randomly destroys life are much like the fundamental events of world history": they happen without plan or direction. Given this state of affairs it is imperative that we take on the Nietzschean virtues of hardness and severity, since "he who does not experience history as it truly is—namely as something tragic that is pervaded by destiny, something that (in the eyes of those who worship the useful) is therefore without meaning, goal, or morality—he is not in a position to make history."[17] Out of this nihilistic interpretation of history as a Heraclitean conflict of opposites without higher unity, Spengler constructs a posture of tragic fatalism. In doing so he draws on Nietzsche's notion of *amor fati* ("love of fate"), that affirms only that which is "necessary."

If classical historicism affirmed both a *method* for the intuitive understanding of individual historical development *and* a *faith* in history as something meaning-filled and purposive, then Spengler can be understood, as Detlef Felken argues, as "a renegade of historicism."[18] For though his whole physiognomic method for intuitively understanding the individual phenomenon within its larger historical development had its roots in Ranke, Humboldt, and Herder, his morphological insights into history as a mythic construction of human will without metaphysical direction nonetheless mark him as a disaffected, faithless apostate from the historicist tradition. On the one hand, like most historicists he attempts to foster a rigorously scientific form of methodological objectivity; on the other, he tendentiously embraces the principles of a Nietzschean-Heraclitean life-philosophy that has its roots in the right-wing anti-modernism of Weimar culture. Hence, Spengler embraces a "biological ethics" that affirms strength and disdains weakness.[19]

Moreover, Spengler contends that "the history of humanity is the eternal struggle between the ethos of a master-animal on the prowl and that of a weak-animal pursued as prey."[20] In this biologistic vitalism that raises "life" and "becoming" to the highest of values, to "the primordial facts of eternal blood that is one and the same as the eternally recurrent cosmic stream," Spengler falls victim to the same relativistic appeal of *Weltanschauung* that precipitated the crisis of historical relativism from which he sought to extricate himself.[21] In Spengler's deep-rooted contradictions between the glorification of "life, race, the triumph of will to power" on the one hand *and* the historicist commitment to scholarly-scientific principles of historical rigor on the other, we can locate some of the deepest antinomies of the Weimar era—the irreconcilable tension between *Leben* and *Wissenschaft* (life and science), values and objectivity, relativism and a yearning for meta-historical truth. This conflict of worldviews would get played out in dramatic fashion in the debate between two of the most prominent philosophers of the Weimar era, the Baden Neo-Kantian philosopher Heinrich Rickert and the Heidelberg philosopher of history Ernst Troeltsch.

Rickert and Troeltsch: *Wissenschaft* and *Weltanschauung*

For both Rickert and Troeltsch the crisis of the 1920s took shape as a "crisis of history in its innermost structure . . . that prepared the way for a relativism that led to the breakdown of values."[22] Historicism had brought with it not only a "shattering of all eternal truths," but had also led to the formation of a new *Welt-anschauung* that developed in response to the older tradition of "naturalism" that embraced the philosophical principle that universal laws govern the world of nature (and, by extension, human society and culture). For Troeltsch, the "crisis of historicism" was not, however, to be understood as a recent response to the political upheaval and intellectual ferment of post-war German culture. These effects were merely epiphenomenal; the genuine roots of the crisis lay in both the history of philosophy and, more particularly, in the philosophy of history. As Troeltsch saw it, Spengler's book stood as the culmination for long-developing historicist tendencies; it merely reflected the mood of the time and rather than offering a solution to the crisis of relativism had merely intensified it. Inasmuch as Spengler's morphological construction of various cultures often veered into an ideological defense of German right-wing nationalism, this undermined in an egregious way the value of its *Wissenschaft*. Moreover, its fashionable pessimism offered no real hope for overcoming the problems of relativism but merely exacerbated its generation's "spiritual exhaustion."[23] In an effort to find some measure of truth amidst the unending pluralism of individual values, Troeltsch focuses his energy on a scientific-scholarly "conception of historical values from which we have to think and construct the coherence of history."[24] Only by committing ourselves to the rigors of *Wissenschaft* can we hope to understand the problem of values that might lead to the "formation of a contemporary cultural synthesis out of the historical heirloom, a task for which it is irrelevant whether one's place in the development of culture is one of ascent or decline."

In Troeltsch's view, Spengler's *Decline of the West* had shifted the focus of its generation onto the problem of German culture's health or sickness, while failing to confront the genuine question: "how, from the realm of the historically relative, to find the path to valid cultural values?" While Troeltsch would agree with Rickert about the need to separate the methodological realms of natural science and history and to locate such a difference precisely in their different approaches to the problem of "value," Troeltsch insisted that value itself be grasped historically, and not only in terms of logic. His debate with Rickert over precisely this issue would decisively shape the very terms of the historicist question in the Weimar era.

Heinrich Rickert would concur with Troeltsch that the anarchy of convictions, beliefs, and ideologies that pervaded Weimar culture posed a threat to genuine scientific philosophy. In an effort to counter what he perceived as the destructive effects of life-philosophy, Rickert sought to develop a theory of universal values that would overcome the specious appeal of worldview-philosophy for the rigors of scientific philosophy. In an article that he composed describing his own work, Rickert claimed:

> philosophy originally goes by the name of *Wissenschaft* . . . It is the concern of the theoretical human being. Only he, with his logical thinking, is capable of forming concepts to comprehend all being, while the "whole" person with his perceptions, desires, feelings, with his "life" (Nietzsche) and "existence" (Kierkegaard) continually remains confined to his par-

ticular 'world.' Scientific philosophy must, therefore, renounce any claim to provide that which one infelicitously terms *Weltanschauung* . . . which precludes any theoretical grounding or logical validity. . . . Only by providing this universal conceptual basis can philosophy overcome the individual-historical limitations of an existential and emotional form of *Weltanschauung*-thinking.[25]

Amidst the Weimar crisis of historical thinking with its uncertainty about how to overcome the reigning anarchy of values that threatened philosophy, theology, history, and the other so-called human sciences, Rickert turned to Kant so as to ground a universally valid system of values that would merit the name of a *philosophical* method. For Rickert, "Every problem of universal *Weltanschauung* and of life is transformed for us into a problem of logic and of epistemology."[26]

In an effort to address the crisis of historical thinking in Weimar, Rickert began by challenging the fundamental canon of historical research adopted by practicing historians. What distinguished history from nature, he claimed, was not its content or subject matter, but the aims of its particular method. As the basis for his critique he relied on the fundamental distinction worked out by his teacher, Wilhelm Windelband (1848–1916), between the *nomothetic* or generalizing method of natural science and the *idiographic* or individualizing method of history. Windelband's underlying scheme seemed to him fundamentally sound and useful; yet it struck him as too broadly drawn and inexact to serve as the grounding principle of a rigorous Neo-Kantian epistemology of history. Rickert's response was to reformulate the old *Natur/Geist* division in the sciences along more rigorously logical lines by presenting a new schema of *Natur*- and *Kulturwissenschaften* that hoped to complete Kant's unfinished project of rigorous scientific knowledge. If Kant had defined nature as "the existence of things so far as they are determined according to universal laws," Rickert now sought to define culture as the existence of things so far as they are determined by values.[27] On this reading, the ultimate difference between the natural and historical sciences could not properly be framed as a problem of taxonomic classification (as Windelband had done), but as one of logical "concept formation."

Concept formation, as Rickert understood it, denotes the process of structuring, ordering, and making rational the sensory data provided to consciousness in the world of reality. In unvarnished terms, reality comes to us as an infinite manifold of discrete, irrational sensory data without any fixed temporal or spatial limits. In this sense "empirical reality proves to be an *immeasurable manifold* which seems to become greater and greater the more deeply we delve into it and begin to analyze it and study its particular parts. For even the 'smallest' part contains more than any mortal man has the power to describe."[28] How then, Rickert asks, can we come to any genuinely scientific knowledge of the world if, in our attempts to discover universal laws, we only come to grasp an "infinitesimally small" part of reality? How, in a world where "everything is different from everything else," and heterogeneity confronts us everywhere, do we come to grasp scientific-universal truth?[29]

Rejecting the epistemological realism of correspondence theory, Rickert claims in good Kantian fashion that we can never know the thing in itself—hence, any attempt to set up a correspondence between knowledge claims and reality is doomed to failure. Scientific knowledge does not aim at a reproduction of reality, but rather, selects out of the infinite stream of possibilities some aspect of that reality that accords with values that the researcher deems worthy of pursuing. These values are, however, not coextensive with the reality that they organize and imbue with meaning. Values do not "exist" in any concrete sense; they neither possess material substance nor occupy space in the world of being, they are instead based on formal principles. Their ground is logical or axiological, not ontological—reality "is," values are "valid" (*Seiendes "ist," Werte "gelten"*). Human beings make sense of the immeasurably complex heterogeneity of the world by reducing its complexity via concepts that, in turn, are formed by values. Concepts simplify reality; they reduce to manageable proportions the mass of phenomena that the mind encounters, transforming the "real" into the "valuable" via a concept formation that distinguishes the essential from the inessential.

In Rickert's scheme the process of concept formation depends ultimately on the goal that one seeks in selecting essential elements from the stream of reality. This goal, in turn, shapes the objects that one selects. In every interpretation of reality, he claims, there exists a formal difference: either one focuses on the general characteristics that one particle of reality has in common with another, or one focuses on the differences between particles. The one approach defines the logical aims of the natural sciences, the other, the axiological procedures of history. Science can either be generalizing, nomothetic, and law-seeking or it can be individualizing, idiographic, and particular. It cannot be both at the same time. Hence, the task of the philosopher is to logically explain the problem of concept formation as it helps to shape the principles of selection that reign in the natural and historical sciences. The natural scientist has an interest in the individual phenomenon only as an example of a universal law. But the historian seizes upon this individuality because of its relation to a cultural value. And yet Rickert realized that by grounding his logic of historical science in the problem of values he was opening himself to charges of historical relativism. How could science, which strove for objectivity, be grounded in value, which reflected subjective aims and ideals? How could one reconcile the subjective realm of historical experience with the objectivity of historical science?

Determined to secure the objectivity of history by means of his conceptual logic, Rickert focused on two problems. First, he claimed that we need to distinguish logically the valuation (*Wertung*) of facts from the scientific task of relating such facts to values (*Wertbeziehung*). Valuations are unquestionably subjective; relating facts to values, however, need not be: "on the contrary, practical valuation and theoretical reference to values are two logically *distinct* acts."[30] An historian can identify a specific action (the execution of Louis XVI) as essential to the history of the French Revolution without acknowledging that such an act either promoted or impeded the attainment of a specific cultural value (political freedom). "Valuations must always involve *praise* or *blame*. To *refer* to values is to do neither." Secondly, he claimed, we can guarantee the objectivity of historical science if our theoretical value-reference is undergirded by referring it to transcendental values that obtain independently of any subjective evaluation: "the fact that *cultural values are universal* in this sense is what keeps concept formation in the historical sciences from being altogether *arbitrary* and thus constitutes the primary basis of its 'objectivity.' What is historically essential must be *important* not only for this or that particular historian, but for *all*."

Within Rickert's logic of concept formation, universal-transhistorical values served as transcendental norms (Kant's *Sollen*) by which to measure cultural reality (*Sein*) in terms of its scientific relevance. As valid (*geltend*) rather then real (*seiend*), values do not exist as such but find expression in cultural spheres such as religion, art, the state, community, economic practices, ethical precepts, and the like. In this distinction between cultural values (whose ground is transcendental) and cultural objects (whose expression is historical) Rickert was convinced he had found the means to overcome the crisis of historicism and its anarchy of values. In his work, which attempted to derive a full-blown philosophy of history from his logical analysis of historical-cultural concept formation, Rickert sought to demonstrate how ahistorical values could serve as the logical ground for a transcendental subject who stood opposed to the empirical-psychological subject of the historical world.

In pursuing an ahistorical solution to problems of historical and cultural relativism, Rickert turned to the Kantian notion of an ethical imperative that transcended history. As he always maintained, "history was in no position to solve philosophical problems for itself."[31] The answers must come from philosophy. In actual practice, Rickert maintained, the historical subject attempts to concretize ethical demands by bringing to fruition certain projects and aims that we call "culture." In all of these endeavors we seek ultimately to reconcile the gap between the "is" and the "ought," between meaningless being and meaning-laden history. Such a reconciliation can never be completed, however, because of the unbridgeable gulf between the reality of history and the ideality of value. And yet the meaning of historical life is grounded in the attempt to overcome this gulf and achieve a universal value—a task that is "insoluble," (*unauflöslich*) according to Rickert.

Consequently, the philosophy of history never succeeds in proffering final truth. The values that it attempts to systematize serve as exemplars of a "Kantian *Idee* whose realization becomes the goal for all cultures that must, nonetheless, labor under the knowledge that theirs is a never-ending task."[32] The historian's goal of relating facts to universal values, then, becomes a Kantian expression of freely pursuing an ethical imperative that seeks to bridge the chasm between what is and what ought to be. In recognizing the primacy of freedom as an ethical imperative within science itself—and in freeing science from the realm of strict necessity—Rickert believed he had provided Troeltsch and his generation with a lasting solution to the crisis of historicism.

Historicism Deconstructed: Heidegger, *Kairos*, and Historicity

Rickert's Neo-Kantian approach to the problems of historical relativism proved problematic at best. Even sympathetic readers such as Troeltsch and Meinecke found Rickert's attempt to ground historical study in a timeless system of absolute validity to be deeply flawed. The most devastating critique of Rickert's work, however, came from his former student at Freiburg, Martin Heidegger. Heidegger claimed that in his attempt to measure "the values of the past against what *should* be," Rickert had appealed to suprahistorical values that denied the historicity of human experience.[33] That history was essentially past history and not something "there" in the present for the historian waiting to be "known" was something that Rickert had wholly overlooked. In effect, the reality of temporal distance did not constitute a logical problem in Rickert's theory of concept-formation. By defining history as something "past," held there for contemplation by the researcher, Rickert had forgotten the original meaning of history as a form of temporality that shapes human life.

More critically, however, in defining the problem of history in terms of methodology and logic, both Rickert and Windelband had "trivialized and distorted" the fundamental insight of Wilhelm Dilthey that "authentic historical being is human *Dasein*."[34] As Heidegger would continuously emphasize, "Dasein" is nothing other than the temporal process of relating to, caring for, and concerning oneself with, the being that one has been, a being whose very sense of having been is something that emerges out of *Dasein*'s projection of itself as futural, as being that is always to come. It is this hermeneutic projection of futural possibilities out of its own interpretation of its past (having been), that constitutes *Dasein*'s essentially historical character or "historicity." As Heidegger explained in his magnum opus, *Being and Time* (1927): "Having-been [*Gewesenheit*] arises from the future in such a way that the future that has been [*gewesene*] (or better, is in the process of having been [*gewesende*]) releases the present from itself. We call the unified phenomenon of the future that makes present in the process of having-been, *temporality*."[35]

By reframing Rickert's epistemology of historical logic, Troeltsch's commitment to ethical values, and Spengler's diagnosis of cultural decline into a question concerning historical temporality, Heidegger achieved nothing less than a radical reformulation of German historicism. By turning his philosophical attention away from questions of method, aim, and teleology, Heidegger was able to show how the very debates about historical values in terms of objectivity and relativity were misguided: "what is philosophically primary is not a theory of concept-formation and historical science nor the theory of historical knowledge, nor even the theory of history (*Geschichte*) as the object of historical science (*Historie*). Rather, what is primary is the interpretation of authentic historical *being* in its historicity."[36] By grasping the fundamental happening of history not as historical science (*Historie*) but as historicity, Heidegger succeeded in transforming the meaning of history from a question of logical method or scientific research to an ontological exploration of human being-in-the-world:

"Philosophy will never get to the root of what history is so long as it analyzes history as an object of contemplation for a method. The enigma of history lies in what it means *to be* historical."[37]

Unlike his contemporaries Spengler, Troeltsch, or Rickert, Heidegger did not approach the question of history from within the rubrics of "world history," "ethics," or "historical logic." Rather, Heidegger understood it in terms of an experience of temporality that he found buried in the earliest Christian texts of Saint Paul (and his later Protestant interpreters, Luther, Schleiermacher, and Kierkegaard): an experience of originary Christian faith as a matter of concrete life that needs to be *enacted* rather than merely contemplated.[38] In this situation of primordial Christian faith, defined by a radical uncertainty about the time of the "coming of the Lord" (*parousia*), Heidegger offered a critique of the reigning ontology of Western metaphysics that grasps "being" in terms of its standing presence as a substance (*ousia*). Against this religious background Heidegger developed his own unique reading of the crisis of historicism that uncovered the aporia at the heart of the historicist debate: the fundamental incompatibility of the Greek idea of being and the Christian experience of time.

Because, Heidegger argued, traditional historicism thinks of its object in terms of the static ontology of permanent presence that defines the model of the natural sciences, it misses the hermeneutical relation to time as temporality, as the enactment of futural possibilities within the present situation against the historical possibilities bequeathed to us by/through the past. The primordial Christian experience of time enunciated by Saint Paul in the *Letter to the Thessalonians*, however, points to a different understanding of time than the chronological succession of moments organized as a narrative of "contents." Paul thinks of time not as the objective time (*chronos*) of history but as the experiential time (*kairos*) of enactment, the hopeful waiting towards a future whose coming is expressed in the Christian eschatological proclamation, "thy kingdom come." In this theological turn toward the radically contingent life-experience of "the time of faith," Heidegger uncovered a phenomenological indication of temporality that challenged the timeless validity of transcendental values that sustained Rickert's entire project.

The Pauline insight into the kairological character of time opened to Heidegger the dynamic context of life in all its historical contingency and in terms of its concrete possibilities. The hopeful anticipation of the *parousia* is marked by the situation of decision, of the need to actualize the eternal in the here and now, to enact faith historically. Pauline time does not measure the historical situation against the static time of eternity as what will come at the end of time. Rather, it focuses on one's comportment to the coming itself, a question of "how" one waits. This originary Christian experience of life within the historical situation of a "coming" that cannot be grasped as incremental units of mathematical or calendrical time led Heidegger to see that the reality of time is nothing measurable, quantifiable, thingly, or present-at-hand, but involves one within a horizon of possibility and caring that marks the phenomenon of existence.

Existence (from the Latin *sistere* "to stand" and *ex* "out, out from") is now thought as a "standing out from" the present-at-hand world of beings into the openness and possibility of being itself. With this understanding of time as a nexus of possibilities or unity of horizons, Heidegger made a fundamental break with the ontological tradition of standing presence that had fateful consequences for his interpretation of historicism. Here Heidegger de-structured the traditional historicist concept of time as a succession of fixed "now" points to reveal a kinetic movement of temporal possibilities within a unified horizon—a unity that had been sundered by metaphysics into the separate categories of past-present-future.

Heidegger's early Pauline interpretation of temporality would reappear in a fuller way in his critique of historicism in *Being and Time* (1927). Drawing on his readings of late nineteenth-century philosophers of historical consciousness such as Nietzsche, Dilthey, and Count Paul Yorck von Wartenburg, Heidegger put forward a reading of historicity that he defined as "the being of the historical," one that would transform the question-frame (*Fragestellung*) of historicism from one about "values" and relativity to one about the ontology of historical existence.[39] The historicist tradition culminated in a crisis of relativism precisely because it was caught within a subject-object metaphysics that defined history according to the same Cartesian-Kantian metaphysics of presence as the natural sciences. In Heidegger's reading, the historicist project was misconceived from its very foundations, ensnared as it was in the contradictory goals of developing an objective science for subjective life experience. Hence, Heidegger claimed, before the crisis of historicism could be properly addressed, historians and philosophers would need to break free of the subject/object aporia that had governed Western philosophy from Descartes through Dilthey.

Heidegger sought to do this by recasting the historicist's *epistemological* question about the objectivity of historical knowledge as an *ontological* question about the meaning of historical *being*. Historicists like Ranke sought meaning in the past itself as an objective process, purposeful and with direction; Rickert located it, conversely, in the transcendental operations of consciousness that related the historical individual to logical meaning itself. Troeltsch embraced an ethics of conscience and Europeanism; Spengler preached the gospel of decline. But Heidegger rejected all these conflicting alternatives as falling into the same either/or categories of subjective *Weltanschauung* and objective *Wissenschaft*. Genuine historical meaning could never be found "in" history as a temporal process, he claimed, but only in the temporality and historicity of historical existence. In this sense historical inquiry would need to be understood as something other than a movement backward in time; rather, it would need to disclose the possibilities of what *Dasein* could be futurally on the basis of what it had already been. As Heidegger explained in *Being and Time*:

> If historical science which arises from authentic historicity reveals through retrieval the Dasein that has-been-there in its possibility, then it has already made manifest the universal in the singular. The question of whether historical science has as its object merely the succession of singular and "individual" events or "laws" is mistaken at its root. The theme of historical science is neither a singular happening or something universal floating

above but the factically existent possibility that has been. This possibility is not retrieved as such (that is, understood in an authentically historical sense) if it gets perverted by the power of a supratemporal model. Only factically authentic historicity can disclose past history as a resolute fate that, through retrieval, strikes home the force of what is possible in factical existence—that is, in its futurity that comes toward [*zu-kommt*] existence. Historical science, then . . . does not take its departure from the present . . . . but discloses itself temporally in terms of the future.[40]

Ultimately, Heidegger's ontological insight into the historicity of human *Dasein* brought to awareness the fundamental aporias of the German historical tradition, especially its practice of interpreting historical life in terms of the same metaphysics of presence that reigned over the study of nature. For this insight Heidegger would draw on the work of Count Yorck who had insisted that "the entire psycho-physical datum is not one that *is*, but one that lives; this is the essential point of historicity."[41] The historicist tradition had proceeded as if the present-at-hand being of nature (which is) were no different from the present-at-hand "facts" of historical life. But in unreflectively applying the ontic categories of nature to the ontological phenomena of history, historicism had missed what was most essential about historical existence—namely, its historicity. In the end, Heidegger would claim, "the rise of the problem of 'historicism' is the clearest indication that historical science manages to alienate Dasein from its authentic historicity."

In the 1930s Heidegger would take up his interpretation of authentic historicity and its relation to the "fateful destiny of Dasein" in terms of a political commitment to National Socialist community, a commitment rooted in the same privileging of kairological time as his earlier interpretation of primordial Christian temporality. For Heidegger this kairological dimension of time would find its most proper expression in Hölderlin's notion of the festival that founds anew the time of the community, a celebratory time of political-philosophical meaning that Heidegger construed as the authentic time of German destiny. This kairological reading of historicity would find its echo in a very different political register in the Marxist writings of Walter Benjamin, who would maintain that "the genuine conception of historical time rests entirely upon the image of redemption."[42] For Benjamin the messianic, redemptive meaning of history that underlies Marxism must be read "not as written history, but as festively enacted history."[43] In this shared rejection of the "homogeneous, empty time" of historical narrative that relates "the sequence of events like the beads of a rosary" both Benjamin and Heidegger would lay the philosophical groundwork for the "End of History" debate that would decisively break with the metaphysical presuppositions of German historicism.[44]

Notes

1. Friedrich Hölderlin, *Essays and Letters on Theory* (Albany: SUNY Press, 1988), 109.
2. Philippe Lacoue-Labarthe, *Heidegger, Art and Politics* (Oxford: Blackwell, 1990), 46.
3. Arthur Liebert, *Die geistige Krisis der Gegenwart* (Berlin: Pan-Verlag, 1924), 7–9.

4. Arthur Liebert, *Die geistige Krisis der Gegenwart*, 7–9.

5. Ernst Troeltsch, "Die Krisis des Historismus," *Neue Rundschau* 33 (June 1922), 584–86.

6. Ernst Troeltsch, *Der Historismus und seine Probleme* (Tübingen: Mohr, 1922), 6.

7. Friedrich Gogarten, "Historicism" in *The Beginnings of Dialectical Theology*, ed. James M. Robinson (Richmond: John Knox Press, 1968), 343–54.

8. Karl Barth, *Epistle to the Romans* (Oxford: Oxford University Press, 1989), 10–11.

9. Friedrich Gogarten, "Between the Times," in *The Beginnings of Dialectical Theology*, ed. Robinson, 277–80.

10. Oswald Spengler, *The Decline of the West*, I (New York: Knopf, 1926), 4,26,3, xiv (hereafter DW); *Der Untergang des Abendlandes*, I (Munich: Beck, 1924), 4,35,3,viii (hereafter UA) (translation altered).

11. Spengler, DW, I: 118, 121, 16–18, 105; UA, I: 153, 157, 21–23, 146.

12. Friedrich Nietzsche, *Untimely Meditations* (Cambridge: Cambridge University Press, 1983), 84.

13. Spengler, DW, I: 15; DW, II: 294/UA, I: 19; UA, II: 361.

14. Walter Schulz, *Philosophie in der veränderten Welt* (Pfullingen: Neske, 1977), 492.

15. Spengler, DW, I: 41, 46, 59/UA, I: 55, 61, 78-79.

16. Spengler, DW, I: 23, 25, 21; DW, II: 44/UA, I: 30–32, 27–28; UA, II: 38.

17. Spengler, *Jahre der Entscheidung* (Munich: Deutscher Taschenbuch Verlag, 1961), 39.

18. Detlev Falken, *Oswald Spengler: Konservativer Denker zwischen Kaiserreich und Diktatur* (Munich: Beck, 1988), 66

19. Walter Schulz, *Philosophie in der veränderten Welt*, 579.

20. Oswald Spengler, *Urfragen* (Munich: Beck, 1965), 344.

21. Spengler, DW, II: 507/UA, II: 633.

22. Ernst Troeltsch, "Die Krisis des Historismus," 584.

23. Ernst Troeltsch, *Gesammelte Schriften, IV: Aufsätze zur Geistesgeschichte und Religionssoziologie* (Tübingen: Mohr, 1925), 681.

24. Ernst Troeltsch, *Der Historismus und seine Probleme*, 4,ix.

25. Heinrich Rickert, "Selbstdarstellung" in *Philosophen–Lexikon*, eds. Werner Ziegenfuss and Gertrud Jung (Berlin: de Gruyter, 1950), 346.

26. Heinrich Rickert, *Die Grenzen der naturwissenschaftlichen Begriffsbildung* (Tübingen: Mohr, 1929), 11.

27. Immanuel Kant, *Prolegomena to Any Future Metaphysics* (New York: Bobbs-Merrill, 1950), 42.

28. Heinrich Rickert, *Science and History* (Princeton: Van Nostrand, 1962), 32.

29. Ibid., 321.

30. Ibid., 89, 90, 97.

31. Rickert, *Die Grenzen der naturwissenschaftlichen Begriffsbildung*, 697.

32. Heinrich Rickert, *Die Probleme der Geschichtsphilosophie* (Heidelberg: Winter, 1924), 119.

33. *Ibid.*, 131.

34. Martin Heidegger, *History of the Concept of Time* (Bloomington: Indiana University Press, 1985), 17/ *Prolegomena zur Geschichte des Zeitbegriffs* (Frankfurt: Klostermann, 1979), 20; Martin Heidegger, "Wilhelm Dilthey's Research and the Struggle for a Historical Worldview" in *Supplements*, ed. John van Buren (Albany: SUNY Press, 2002), 167.

35. Martin Heidegger, *Being and Time* (Albany: SUNY Press, 1996), 300 (hereafter BT); *Sein und Zeit* (Tübingen: Niemeyer, 1949), 326 (hereafter SZ).

36. Ibid.

37. Martin Heidegger, *The Concept of Time* (Oxford: Blackwell, 1992), 20; *Der Begriff der Zeit* (Tübingen: Niemeyer, 1989), 26.
38. Martin Heidegger, *Phenomenology of Religious Life* (Bloomington: Indiana University Press, 2004), 72; *Phänomenologie des religiösen Lebens* (Frankfurt: Klostermann: 1995), 103.
39. Heidegger, "Wilhelm Dilthey's Research," 159.
40. Heidegger, BT: 360-361/SZ: 395.
41. Heidegger, BT: 366/SZ: 401; BT: 361/SZ: 396.
42. Walter Benjamin, *The Arcades Project* (Cambridge, MA: Harvard University Press, 1999), 479; *Gesammelte Schriften V* (Frankfurt: Suhrkamp, 1982), 600.
43. Walter Benjamin, "Paralipomena to 'On the Concept of History,'" in *Selected Writings* (Cambridge, MA: Harvard University Press, 2003), 404.
44. Walter Benjamin, "Theses on the Philosophy of History" in *Illuminations* (New York: Schocken, 1969), 263–64.

8

Weimar Theology

From Historicism to Crisis

Peter E. Gordon

As if in a compulsive repetition of the First World War's apocalyptic violence, the brief lifespan of the Weimar Republic saw some of the most earthshaking revolutions in the study of religion. To recall only the era's most prominent scholars will drive the point home: Barth, Otto, Bultmann, Brunner, Gogarten, Tillich, Buber, Rosenzweig, Bloch, Benjamin, Hirsch—the list is by no means complete. If we then widen our scope to consider the many theologians and religious philosophers who either prepared the way for this explosion or emerged from its ruins, we may be tempted to conclude that Germany in the early decades of the twentieth century was the true birthplace of modern religion. Yet there is something paradoxical in the attempt to fasten religious ideas to a particular moment in history. A commonplace of theological discourse is that history serves merely as a theater for the irruption of a non-historical truth. And it turns out that it was precisely this paradox—the relation of the eternal to time—that became one of the key preoccupations of Weimar theology. In what follows I provide a survey of the major movements. As we shall see, an intellectual drama that opened with the subdued efforts in both historical criticism and historical sociology of religion would pass through a revolution of anti-historicism, rising to a crisis with various trends in dialectical theology and religious existentialism, and reaching an inconclusive end in bitter factionalism and political disarray.[1]

The Nineteenth-Century Inheritance

"Theology has *always* been modern," observed Franz Overbeck in 1873, "and for that very reason has also, by its very nature, *always betrayed Christianity*."[2] Although his contributions to theological debate belong to an earlier age, the example of Overbeck (1837–1905) may remind us that what we habitually see as a distinctively interwar crisis in German theology had noteworthy antecedents in the nineteenth century. A professor of the New Testament at the University of Basel and a close friend to Friedrich Nietzsche (for some five years, in fact, they lived one floor apart in the same house in Basel), Overbeck shared with Nietzsche the fear that modern culture suffered from a surfeit of historical knowledge. Overbeck was especially outraged by the historicizing impulses of liberal Protestant theology. In his 1873 manifesto, "How Christian is Our Present-Day Theology?" he condemned "historical Christianity" as little more than a pastiche of dogmatism and apologetics that had no relation to the genuine message brought to humanity by Christ.[3]

To understand Overbeck's antipathies toward the main currents of historical theology it is helpful to recall the period of anti-theological debate in the earlier nineteenth century, when left-Hegelians such as Ludwig Feuerbach and David Friedrich Strauß had deployed the tools of historical and philosophical criticism to develop a purely anthropological interpretation of Christian doctrine. In his *The Life of Jesus* (1835–36) Strauß called upon the methods of historical analysis to dismantle what he saw as the myth of Christ's divinity. Meanwhile, in his 1841 *The Essence of Christianity,* Feuerbach took a more philosophical approach to argue that the very idea of a transcendent God was the consequence of humanity's self-alienation, an error he believed would eventually give way to a purely anthropocentric religion.[4] From Overbeck's perspective such efforts merely served to demonstrate the chasm between authentic Christianity and any of its historically conditioned doctrines. "[O]riginal Christianity," he explained, no more expected to have a theology than it expected to have any kind of history on this earth."[5]

The movement of historical theology that so incensed Overbeck was indeed the dominant trend in late-nineteenth-century Protestant theology, its fortunes epitomized by Adolf von Harnack (1851–1930).[6] A scion of the Ritschlian school and dedicated practitioner of the so-called "higher criticism," Harnack was perhaps the most accomplished and publicly acclaimed theologian of Germany's fin-de-siècle. In his popular lectures, *Das Wesen des Christentums* (1900), Harnack declared that in answering the question, "What is Christianity?" he would resort only to historical explanations, excluding both apologetics and religious philosophy.[7] As Harnack explained, "we cannot form any right estimate of the Christian religion unless we take our stand upon a comprehensive induction that shall cover all the facts of its history."[8] Jesus Christ and his disciples "were situated in their day just as we are situated in ours; that is to say, their feelings, their thoughts, their judgments and their efforts were bounded by the horizon and the framework in which their own nation was set and by its condition at the time. Had it been otherwise, they would have not been men of flesh and blood, but spectral beings."[9] Harnack nonetheless struggled against the premises of his own method to sustain some vision of the essence of Christianity, a doctrine that was "simple and sublime." Christianity, he wrote, meant "one thing only: Eternal life in the midst of time, by the strength and under the eyes of God."[10] To be sure, this was an extraordinary confession for a theologian who retained primary allegiance to the historical methods of the higher criticism. For as Harnack admitted, "In history absolute judgments are impossible."

> History can only show how things have been; and even where we can throw light upon the past, and understand and criticize it, we must not presume to think that by any process of abstraction absolute judgments as to the value to be assigned to past events can be obtained from the results

of a purely historical survey. Such judgments are the creation of feeling and of will; they are a subjective act.[11]

The liberal-historicist method popularized by Harnack was not without its detractors. Overbeck, in the second edition of his controversial book, *How Christian is our Present-Day Theology?* snarled that Harnack's "book of the century" had demonstrated "far more vividly the 'insignificance' of Christianity than its 'essence.'"[12] Generally speaking, however, in the years that led up to the First World War the historicizing trend in Protestant theology encountered little opposition and only grew in vigor. Harnack himself would survive well into the 1920s to launch vehement salvos against Karl Barth and kindred theologians who sought to question liberal-historicist methodology.[13] But intellectual movements often forge the tools for their own burial. The historicist tendencies of the later nineteenth century would eventually spawn a distinctive school of *Religionsgeschichte* that more or less dispensed with the apologetic elements that persisted in the higher criticism. Before we can comprehend the anti-historicist rebellion we therefore need to gain a deeper understanding of the historical and sociological trends it challenged.

The History and Sociology of Religion

To appreciate the earlier traditions that proved most consequential for the development of Weimar theology one must first consider the foundational theorists in the sociology and history of religion—Weber, Troeltsch, and Simmel. Of these three the longest shadow was cast by Max Weber (1864–1920), who for many years held the Chair in Law and Economics at the University of Heidelberg before his departure for Munich in 1919, where he lived just long enough to assist in the establishment of Germany's new Republic.

Weber's *The Protestant Ethic and the Spirit of Capitalism* surely ranks among the greatest monuments in the sociology of religion. Published in two installments (in 1904 and 1905), the book sets out to explain the peculiar genesis of a practical style of behavior or "ethic" that distinguished the early heroes of entrepreneurial capitalism in the West. Now it is crucial to note (against a great many later misconceptions) that Weber did not claim to have discovered the causes of capitalism as such. Instead he was interested to *understand* (in the interpretative sense of *Verstehen*) the idiosyncratic genesis of a behavioral disposition common to ideal-typical representatives of *early-modern* capitalism. Their characteristic ethic of methodical self-abnegation (famously articulated by Benjamin Franklin in *Poor Richard's Almanack*) seemed to suggest that early merchant capitalists saw accumulation as an end in itself beyond any possible advantage in power or worldly gratification. For Weber the emergence of this seemingly non-rational ethic of worldly asceticism at the very inception of economic rationalization in the West was a historical puzzle of immense significance: it demanded a hermeneutic inquiry into the motivational forces behind early capitalism.

Hence the importance of Protestantism. Though a reconstruction of the characteristic attitudes of Western Christian sects toward capitalist accumulation, Weber noted that whereas Catholicism condemned the passion for economic gain as *cupiditas*, and Lutheranism remained similarly bound to a pre-Reformation attitude of hostility toward the marketplace, Calvinist Protestantism alone eventually found a way to reconcile its religious doctrine with an affirmation of economic gain. The clue to this reconciliation lay in the Calvinist doctrine of predestination, according to which the believer's preordained status as damned or redeemed was utterly unknown and unknowable, as it was the sovereign decision of the *deus absconditus*—a wholly transcendent and inscrutable God. But this doctrine proved so intolerable to Calvin's fellowship that over the course of several generations, lay preachers introduced a subtle modification in the founder's doctrine: Although one could not hope to increase one's chances for salvation through works it was nonetheless possible to regard worldly success as a *sign* of one's prior election.

With this amendment in place, even the most pious of Protestants now found that economic achievement afforded a powerfully religious consolation. To be sure, in one's economic behavior one had to obey the properly Calvinistic attitude of asceticism. But the doctrinally-sanctioned application of this anti-sensualistic disposition to economic gain created that distinctive ethic of "worldly asceticism" that became so widespread amongst the Protestant merchant classes in the Netherlands, England, and North America. Herein lay the historical connection—between the "Protestant ethic" of worldly asceticism and disposition of methodical accumulation and deferred gratification that happened to be most conducive to success in a capitalistic enterprise. Weber hastened to note that this connection was not a unidirectional causality—it was merely an "elective affinity" or *Wahlverwandtschaft* (a term he borrowed from Goethe's novel of romantic liaisons). Merchants found in Protestant doctrine a higher consolation for their behavior, while Protestants found in capitalistic entrepreneurialism a material satisfaction for their religious longing. The genius of Weber's sociological interpretation was to suggest that this largely subjective affinity grounded in theological need served as the objective sociological foundation for the flourishing of the modern economy. Yet his study ended on a bitter note with the observation that, with the gradual rationalization of economy and society, modern capitalism turned against its irrationalistic supports and began to work on its own, with a machine-like indifference to spiritual purposes. In the twentieth century, Weber wrote, the Protestant ethic had reached its end:

> The Puritan wanted to work in a calling; we are forced to do so. For when asceticism was carried out of the monastic cells into everyday life, and began to dominate worldly morality, it did its part in building the tremendous cosmos of the modern economic order. This order is now bound to the technical and economic conditions of machine production which totally determine the lives of all the individuals who are born into this mechanism, not only those directly concerned with economic acquisi-

tion, with irresistible force. Perhaps it will so determine them until the last ton of fossilized coal is burnt. In Baxter's view, the care for external goods should only lie on the shoulders of the "saint like a light cloak, which can be thrown aside at any moment." But fate decreed that the cloak should become an iron cage. . . . Since asceticism undertook to remodel the world and to work out its ideals in the world, material goods have gained an increasing and finally an inexorable power over the lives of men as at no previous period in history. Today the spirit of religious asceticism . . . has escaped from the cage. But victorious capitalism, since it rests on mechanical foundations, needs its support no longer.[14]

The drama of this conclusion was that it both extolled Protestantism for its historical achievements yet denied it any further efficacy for the present. "The idea of duty in one's calling," wrote Weber, "prowls around in our lives like the ghost of dead religious beliefs."[15]

This overall conception of the history of religion as a process of increasing rationalization gained further precision in Weber's comparative studies in the sociology of world religions.[16] Even today Weber's contributions to the comparative sociology of religion remain more or less unsurpassed. (It was in fact Weber himself who first used the term *Religionssoziologie*.[17]) It should be noted that Weber followed the hermeneutic principle that understanding social action requires an empathic reconstruction of the inner sense (*Sinn*) of action from the agent's point of view, and for this reason Weber remained more or less immune to any kind of materialist reductionism that would dismiss the contents of religious belief as epiphenomena.[18] Yet a definite fatalism governed his conception of religious history. In his November 1917 address to a students in Munich, "Science as a Vocation" (*Wissenschaft als Beruf*) he painted a grim portrait of the modern West as the terminal stage in a pan-historical process of rationalization that had emptied the cosmos of all meaning. Religion had once promised a total normative system. But the meaningful whole had now shattered, leaving the occident to cope with the relativistic chaos of warring gods—a predicament summarized in the memorable phrase, "the disenchantment of the world" (*die Entzauberung der Welt*). Weber acknowledged that many of his contemporaries lacked the courage this condition required. Instead they sought after substitute modes of quasi-religious consolation, whether in art or in politics. But he feared the consequences of such experimentation. Artists who persisted in the monumental style even while they lacked the robust conviction that had inspired the medieval cathedrals, could build only "miserable monstrosities." Similarly, those who contrived to found new religions without the gift of genuine prophecy would only breed fanaticism. Weber's message was clear: A scholar truly dedicated to his vocation must accept, for the sake of intellectual honesty alone, that the great age of religious conviction was irrevocably past.[19]

Embedded in this narrative was the normative judgment that in the modern world religion could no longer furnish either ethical or socio-political guidance. It followed that religion had retreated to the wholly private realm of groundless and inarticulate conviction. Furthermore, because moderns now saw the cosmos as governed by (in principle) intelligible law, religion was compelled to abandon its early-modern alliance with systems of cosmological and scientific explanation. In his essay, "The Social Psychology of the World Religions" Weber explained that the modern age only sharpened the contrast between religion and reason where it had not vanquished religion entirely: "The general result of the modern form of thoroughly rationalizing our conception of the world and our way of life—theoretically and practically, intellectual and purposively—has been that religion has been shifted into the realm of what is—from the standpoint of the intellectual articulation of a worldview—the irrational."[20]

But the sociology of religion did not always lead into a cul-de-sac of historical fatalism. A moderate variant was developed by Ernst Troeltsch (1865–1923), who worked alongside Weber at the University of Heidelberg from 1894 until 1915, when he moved to Berlin to assume a prestigious post as professor in religious, social and historical philosophy. Although Troeltsch, like Weber, was primarily interested in the this-worldly effects of religious doctrine, he eschewed the vision of disenchantment that concluded Weber's historical narrative. "The rise of Christianity," Troeltsch observed, "is a religious and not a social phenomenon. For although religion is interwoven with life as a whole, in development and dialectic it has an independent existence."[21] Yet Troeltsch was nonetheless convinced that Christianity was best grasped through its historical and social manifestations. His monumental work, *The Social Teaching of the Christian Churches* (published in two volumes in 1911) painted Christianity on a vast historical canvas according to its "intrinsic sociological idea."[22] For Troeltsch as for Weber, the peregrinations of Christianity across time culminated in the modern phenomenon of an "ascetic Protestantism" that emerged when Calvinism adapted itself to "modern bourgeois-capitalistic civilization," by extolling both a radically interiorized individualism and the world-transformative activity of methodical labor.[23] Yet unlike Weber, Troeltsch saw modern religion in a rather more charitable light. He admitted that the historicizing methods of *Religionssoziologie* posed a serious challenge to the traditionalist idea of eternal revelation.[24] But he drew back from Weber's more relativistic conclusions, and he remained confident that comparative and historical scholarship would finally vindicate Christianity as the supreme truth toward which all religious history was heading.[25]

Although we cannot officially register him as a participant in Weimar sociology of religion, the sociologist and cultural critic Georg Simmel (1858–1918) authored many essays on religion—most of them published in the first two decades of the twentieth century—that furnished a rich legacy to later theorists. A Berlin-born Jewish convert to Protestantism, Simmel trained at the University of Berlin and taught there until 1914, when he was granted a full professorship at the University of Strasbourg. Simmel was widely admired by his students and his academic peers—Weber tried, unsuccessfully, to secure him a professorship at Heidelberg. Although he was a peripatetic intellectual, his multidisciplinary approach helped to lay the groundwork for the still-developing discipline of German sociology, and it was through a specifically sociological lens that he scrutinized both the doctrines and worldly significance of religious phenomena. At the urging of Martin Buber (whose own philosophy of religion will be addressed below), Simmel composed the sustained essay entitled simply "Religion," that was published first in 1906 and with revisions in 1912.

The sustained essay on religion exemplifies Simmel's characteristic concern for *social form*. Following the philosophical precepts of neo-Kantianism, Simmel conceived of religion in much the same way as his French counterpart Émile Durkheim (whose *The Elementary Forms of Religious Life* also appeared in 1912): Religion is a structure of dualistic concepts, attitudes, and emotions that are correlative to social forms. There is a strong analogy, Simmel claims, between an individual's behavior toward God and his behavior toward society. In both cases the individual feels himself at once distinct yet unified with and dependent upon the object. The characteristically dualistic emotional attitudes are also the same: Toward God and toward society the individual feels simultaneously a vital contest of emotions, love *versus* alienation, despair *versus* trust. Religiosity, which only occasionally hardens into religion *simpliciter*, is therefore a crucial element in social cohesion: obedience to a superior person is founded upon both faith in their goodness and fear of their punishment. The basic forms of social life are thus easily understood according to the religious analogy:

> The relationship of the devoted child to its parents, of the enthusiastic patriot to his country, of the fervent cosmopolite toward humanity; the relationship of the worker to his insurgent class or of the proud feudal lord to his fellow nobles; that of the subject to the ruler under whose control he is, or of the true soldier to his army—all these relationships, with their infinite variety of context, seen from the psychological point of view have a common tone that can be described only as religious.[26]

Simmel's ready appeals to religion as an *analogy* for social form raised the question of whether he deemed religion *in itself* as *nothing more than* a human attitude. As a sociologist Simmel declared that such a question was beyond his competence. "[W]e are dealing here solely with the structural meaning of religion," he wrote, adding that he could not offer "any statement regarding the objective, supra-psychological existence of the objects of religion." Some readers might resent having their sacred beliefs exposed to the cool light of sociological analysis. But Simmel denied that his methods subtracted from the authenticity of religious belief. "Many still feel that an ideal loses its attraction, that the dignity of an emotion is degraded if its origin is no longer an incomprehensible miracle, a creation out of nothing—as if comprehension of its development affected the value of a thing." For Simmel such fears only betrayed an inner weakness of conviction: "The subjectivity, certainty, and emotional depth of such religiousness surely must be limited, if the knowledge of its origin and development endangers or even makes the slightest different in its worth."[27]

Although Simmel insisted that his task was merely to understand religion and not to dissolve it, the methods of sociological analysis and historical criticism nonetheless left many critics discontented: Was religion truly nothing more than a repertoire of social forms and historical effects? Were the findings of sociology exhaustive? If so, then no confessions of scholarly neutrality could conceal the irreligious consequences of scholarly research. If not, then the actual phenomenon of religion remained opaque to a merely sociological inquiry. A similar complaint was addressed to the so-called "higher criticism." Didn't the historical study of the Bible impugn its originality and therefore the authenticity of revelation? Simmel's anticipatory rejoinder suggests he appreciated the force of these objections. Weber was even more direct. In "Science as a Vocation" he spoke with contempt of the individual "who cannot bear the fate of the times." To such a man Weber counseled that "one must say, may he rather return silently, without the usual publicity build-up of renegades, but simply and plainly. The arms of the old churches are opened widely and compassionately for him. After all, they do not make it hard . . ." Weber professed to admire those heroes of "absolute conviction" who refused to be shaken from their belief. But the grim lesson of his own historical sociology was that religion in its metaphysical substance was no longer compatible with the modern age. A true scholar had to discern the relativity of value spheres and the correlative breakdown of metaphysical absolutes. The solace of religion remained possible but only for those who failed to recognize the objective meaninglessness of the heavens. Weber's philosophy of history, in other words, presupposed atheism. This implicit kernel of irreligion would help to provoke the great rebellions of Weimar theology, as we shall see.

Theologies of Crisis

The first and most memorable cry for revolution against the liberal-historicist study of religion came from Karl Barth (1886–1968), the son of a Swiss Reformed pastor who was intimately familiar with the principles of liberal Protestant theology. Barth had studied with both Harnack in Berlin and, at the Phillips-Universität in Marburg, with Wilhelm Hermann, a prominent theologian of the Ritschlian school who promoted Schleiermacher's definition of religion as experience. Barth's reaction against his teachers was due in part to his feelings of disillusionment when Harnack issued a public statement at outbreak of war in 1914 that declared God the "only possible ground and author" of Germany's military mission. For Barth this was a scandalous confusion of divine and human purposes, and it cast in doubt the entire tradition of nineteenth-century theology descending from liberal experientialism. What this tradition had forgotten, in Barth's view, was the radical chasm that separated God's transcendent reality from human experience. When nearly all of Barth's teachers (including Hermann) signed a manifesto in support of Germany's war aims, Barth suffered a major blow: "An entire world of theological exegesis, ethics, dogmatics, and preaching, which up to that point I had accepted as basically credible, was thereby shaken to the foundations, and with it everything which flowed at that time from the pens of the German theologians."[28]

Even during the war, Barth remained an outspoken pacifist and socialist, signs of the nonconformist persona that would distinguish him throughout his life. In the Swiss village of Safenwil where he had been appointed pastor in 1911 (and where his sermons often bewildered his congregation) Barth began to develop the foundations for a radically different kind of theology, emphasizing most of all the radical gulf between humanity and God. In 1918 he published the first edition of *The Epistle to the Romans* (*Der Römerbrief*), which he then revised for a second edition in 1922. The book was in outward form a line-by-line commentary on Paul's letters to his Christian fellowship in Rome. But in fact it was passionate manifesto of theological rebellion, a call for readers to cast off the accumulated weight of the liberal-historicist tradition so as to confront anew the unconditional truth of divine revelation. In his prefatory remarks Barth declared that although he saw merit in the historical-critical method of Biblical interpretation, he could not trouble himself with investigations that saw Paul merely as "a child of his age." Recalling Overbeck, Barth explained that his predecessor's challenge to the liberal theologians still retained its validity: historical criticism risked losing sight of the truth of Christianity. "History," wrote Barth, is

> the display of the supposed advantages of power and intelligence which some men possess over others, of the struggle for existence hypocritically described by ideologists as a struggle for justice and freedom, of the ebb and flow of old and new forms of human righteousness, each vying with the rest in solemnity and triviality. Yet one drop of eternity is of greater weight than a vast ocean of finite things. Measured by the standard of God the dignitaries of men forfeit their excellence and their serious importance—they become relative; and even the noblest of human moral and spiritual attainments are seen to be what they really are—natural, of this world, profane, and 'materialistic.' The valleys are exalted and the high hills made low.[29]

Barth's disillusionment with all historical categories may seem to align *The Epistle to the Romans* with a great many of the other theological and political texts of the post-war era. But unlike anti-liberal exponents of historical pessimism such as Oswald Spengler, and unlike sociologists of disenchantment such as Simmel and Weber, Barth wished to clear away the fog of historical reasoning—to see "through and beyond history"— only in order to better fix his sights on the eternal spirit.[30] "If the Epistle is to be treated seriously at all," Barth argued, then it must begin with one assumption only, that "God is God."[31]

Yet one could argue that this utter disregard for historical categories ironically drove Barth to embrace a similarly bleak vision of history as evacuated of meaning. Indeed, Barth's image of an utterly transcendent God seemed to *presuppose* rather than challenge the Weberian vision of the modern world as a mechanistic system lacking any sources of immanent purpose. Commenting on Paul's question in *Romans* 3, 1–4 concerning the matter of Jewish election— "What advantage then hath the Jew?"—Barth was driven to conclude that from the eschatological point of view no merely human advantage or effort held any value whatsoever:

If everything be under the judgment of God, is there, seriously considered, any *advantage*? Are not all the advantages of particular salvation or peace simply obliterated? Are there in history any high points which are more than large waves upon the stream of transitoriness, thick shadows where all is shadow? Is there any connexion between those impressions of revelation which may be discovered in the events of history or in the spiritual experiences of men, and the actual revelation of the Unknown God Himself?[32]

Following this logic with strict consistency, Barth distinguished between two accounts of revelation, which we might call revelation as experience and revelation as event. As an experience, revelation denoted the merely human reception of divine intelligence. Only as an event did revelation retain its theological importance as the self-unveiling of God. To mistake the experience for the event, Barth believed, was the cardinal error of liberal-historicist theology and the experientialist tradition from which it emerged. As Barth explained, "if divinity be so concreted and humanized in a particular department of history—the history of religion or the history of salvation—God has ceased to be God."[33]

Still, it is worth noting that Barth appreciated the difficulty of sustaining the absolute distinction between experience and event: For without some worldly manifestation in human experience how could one speak of revelation at all? Barth's answer was that the very experience of revelation was also an experience of its radical inadequacy. "All experience bears within it an understanding by which it is itself condemned," he explained," and "all time bears within it that eternity by which it is dissolved."[34] This belief in a strong disjunction between personal faith and social-historical reason marked Barth as a participant in the interwar revival of interest in Kierkegaard, from whom Barth drew inspiration for his idea of an "infinite qualitative distinction" between time and eternity. Theology, Barth insisted, must commence with and must sustain its awareness of this chasm: "God is in heaven and thou art on earth."[35]

The emphasis on a radical separation between God and humanity earned Barthian movement the epithet "crisis theology" (after the Greek word *Krisis*, or separation), although the term inevitably acquired the more evocative sense of crisis as a pivotal moment fraught with danger. Among Barth's earliest allies was Friedrich Gogarten (1887–1967), a young theologian of Barth's generation who had studied with both Harnack and Troeltsch. A pastor in a Thuringian village, Gogarten was eventually appointed in 1931 as a professor of systematic theology at Breslau, and then in 1935 in Göttingen. His 1917 book, *Religion from Afar* stands as one of the earliest signs of the Kierkegaard-revival in Weimar thought, and it announces the concern for an I-Thou relation that would remain throughout the interwar period one of Gogarten's most distinctive themes.[36] But his earliest and perhaps most famous essay appeared in 1920 in the esteemed Christian journal, *Die Christliche Welt*. Entitled "Between the Times," the essay presented a frontal assault on the older generation of liberal-Protestant theology, which Gogarten faulted for conflating religion and social-historical progress. "We have all entered so deeply into the human that we have lost God," Gogarten wrote. "We can no longer deceive ourselves and mistake the human for the divine." In this situation of religious and civilizational crisis, hope for smooth advance into yet another historical phase was no longer justified: "The times have fallen apart," he explained. "*We* stand between the times."[37]

Taking the theme of religious and historical crisis as their point of departure, Gogarten joined in 1922 with the other exponents of crisis-theology, Karl Barth and Emil Brunner, to found a new theological journal under the name *Zwischen den Zeiten* (*Between the Times*), which was to remain throughout the decade a leading organ for the movement now known officially as "dialectical theology." Gogarten continued to sharpen his theological weapons for an assault on Troeltsch's liberal-Protestantism and the broader values of "culture-idealism" that extolled purely human capacities. He repeatedly faulted Troeltsch for confusing religion and history. "Here we begin our opposition," he wrote in 1926,

> because here is where modern man's "religion" beings: man's belief in himself, his belief in the soul and its "formation" of the world. Here the godlessness of modern man is covered by a significant, pious garment: culture-formation, the attempt of modern man to create a religion with the help of a high-flying ethical ideology. In this religion man is God.[38]

But Gogarten's labors were hardly confined to polemic. Building upon the works of Ferdinand Ebener and Eberhard Grisebach, and appealing to a Kierkegaardian analysis of the relation between the individual and God, Gogarten would spend much of the 1920s working up a distinctive theory of human experience as a relation between "I" and "Thou."[39] For Gogarten the human being was uniquely a *creature* who depends upon the other for its very being. The human being thus exists in the mode of *von-dem-Anderen-sein* (being-from-the-other) while human life is structured as *mit-dem-Anderen-sein* (being-with-the-other). Today much of what was original in this theory has fallen into neglect, due in part to the greater prominence of the "I-Thou" philosophy developed by Gogarten's contemporary, Martin Buber.[40]

Almost immediately the movement of dialectical theology acted as a catalyst, polarizing the field of Weimar theology and radically redefining the terms of debate. While many theologians (especially of the younger generation) rejoiced in what they considered a vigorous challenge to the moribund academicism of liberal-historicist scholarship, the very extremism of the Barthian distinction between God and world struck some critics as dangerously Manichean. Adolf Harnack, notwithstanding his advanced age, struck back with great ferocity, warning in a 1923 letter that Barth's emphasis on the absolute transcendence of God would end in "Gnostic occultism." Theology had to remain wedded to "historical-critical study" or it risked falling into a romanticism of paradox and eventual unintelligibility. "Is there any other theology," Harnack asked, "than that which has strong ties and is in a blood-relationship with science in general?"[41]

Nor was the movement of dialectical theology in agreement on all points. Dissension became especially pronounced between Barth and Emil Brunner,

the third member of the *Zwischen den Zeiten* triumvirate. In 1924 Brunner
assumed a prestigious chair at the University of Zurich as a professor of systematic and practical theology, and in 1927 he published *Religionsphilosophie
protestantischer Theologie*, summarizing key themes of the dialectical theologians. But summary is rarely uncontroversial. Already Brunner's exposition
touched upon a critical fault line in the movement: For wasn't revelation not
only a divine event but also an appeal to humanity? And could one speak
of an absolute distinction between God and man if the event of revelation
implied a relation between them? "There is no such thing as revelation-in-
itself," Brunner explained. "Revelation is not a thing, but an act of God, an
event involving two parties; it is a personal address."[42] By 1934 the disagreement between Barth and Brunner was now explicit. Whereas Barth sought
to retain the radical separation of God and humanity, Brunner allowed for a
relation between them. The same relationism animated Brunner's conception
of scripture. As it is revealed to humanity, Brunner, wrote, scripture is a "piece
of the world [that is] at anyone's disposal, even though the fact of its being a
revelation is not at anyone's disposal."[43] In his zeal to sustain God's radical otherness Barth failed to explain how revelation could ever penetrate the worldly
sphere and how humanity could ever be expected to grasp God's purposes.
Humanity, Brunner explained, must exhibit some capacity for receiving what
revelation entails even if it is merely a "capacity for words." Barth, Brunner
complained, "acknowledges only the act, the event of revelation, but never
anything revealed."[44]

Needless to say, Barth deemed Brunner's relationism an unacceptable compromise, as it seemed to collapse both divine transcendence and human finitude
onto a common metaphysical terrain. In a 1934 rejoinder, entitled simply "No!"
Barth accused Brunner of succumbing to a dangerous species of "natural theology" that awarded humanity its very own power in the drama of revelation. Nor
was this a merely theological scandal. Brunner's willful confusion of God and
man, Barth warned, ultimately posed a greater threat to the Christian faith than
those contemporary theologians who had signed a blood-pact with National Socialism or had even endorsed the heretical movement of the pro-Nazi German
Christians.[45]

Dialectical theology was without question the most transformative theological movement of the interwar era, and its seismic effects would continue
to reverberate throughout the twentieth century. But even those who admired
the movement continued to harbor certain reservations concerning the radicalism of its trademark themes. In a letter written from prison (5 May 1944),
the Lutheran pastor and founder of the anti-Nazi Confessing Church Dietrich
Bonhoeffer observed that "Barth was the first theologian to begin the criticism
of religion, and that remains his great merit." The irony, however, was that his
critique of liberal historicism appealed to an absolutistic idea of religion that
allowed for neither interpretation nor criticism. In Bonhoeffer's words, the Barthian account of revelation was therefore "positivist" even while it imagined its
own perspective as "a law of faith."[46]

From Experience to Existence

Notwithstanding its initial vigor, crisis theology proved to be only one among the several revolutions that would transform interwar German theology. Even before Barth had announced his bold critique of experientialism, a different sort of experientialist theology was being developed by Rudolf Otto (1869–1937), a professor of Protestant theology who secured a full professorship in Marburg in 1917. If Otto's contributions seem to forbid synopsis, this is perhaps because his work sits at the crossroads between various schools, combining a Schleiermacherian definition of religion as non-conceptual experience with a neo-Kantian method that purports to explain the transcendental rules governing all understanding of religious phenomena.

Otto's most celebrated, but also contested book appeared in 1917 under the elaborate title, *The Holy—On the Irrational in the Idea of the Divine and its Relation to the Rational.*[47] Its central message was that religious experience has an irrational aspect that escapes all doctrinal categorization. This is the experience of an encounter with the holy as *numinous*. At once terrifying and fascinating, the numinous in Otto's view is the defining category of religious experience and as such it is *sui generis*, irreducible to any other categories of explanation be they historical, sociological, psychological, or aesthetic. The paradoxical quality of Otto's effort is due to the fact that he subjects this apparently mysterious phenomenon to a rigorous and scholarly analysis inspired by neo-Kantian philosophy. Indeed, Otto retained an abiding philosophical affinity for the Kantian logic that had also inspired Ernst Troeltsch, who had first formulated the notion of a "religious *a priori*" in a 1905 essay.[48] From this Kantian premise Otto derived his methodological belief that the defining categories of religious experience must each possess their own intrinsic logic. The holy, therefore, was not to be confused with specific notions of the good or with an ethical relation. It was a unique[ly] original feeling-response," and as such "ethically neutral," although it could be filled in with "ethical meaning" just as Kant's a priori categories could be "schematized" so as to readied for spatio-temporal application. The holy was in its essence an experience of a *mysterium*, an awe-filled encounter with the "wholly other."[49]

Although his analysis of the numinous as an irreducibly religious category may bear some resemblance to the theme of absolute otherness that so inspired his Barthian contemporaries, Otto cleaved to precisely the sort of experientialism the dialectical theologians despised. For critics such as Rudolf Bultmann (also at Marburg), certain trace elements in Otto's inquiry pointed the way toward a more viable philosophy of religion; but Otto's analysis represented only a partial and incomplete movement beyond the liberal theologies of experience that had dominated Protestant theology since Schleiermacher.[50] As Bultmann observed, one cannot fathom the genuine event of revelation is one categorizes it as "feelings" of the numinous or creaturely dependency: "Even in the numinous, man does not become aware of God, but only of himself. And he is deceived if he interprets the numinous as the divine, even when his frightful shuddering is a blessed experience. For then he always asks only about himself and not really about something that lies beyond him."[51]

A more powerful trend of the 1920s—as vigorous and distinctive as dialectical theology—is the diverse constellation of existential theologians that included both Rudolf Bultmann and Paul Tillich. The son of a Lutheran minister, Rudolf Bultmann (1884–1976) studied theology in Tübingen, Berlin, and Marburg, and eventually secured a full professorship at Marburg in 1921, where he remained until his retirement thirty years later. In a 1956 autobiographical reflection Bultmann explained his admiration for the dialectical theologians: In "this new theological movement, it was rightly recognized, as over against the 'liberal' theology out of which I had come, that the Christian faith is not a phenomenon of the history of religion, that it does not rest on a 'religious a priori' (Troeltsch), and that therefore theology does not have to look upon it as a phenomenon of religious or cultural history." By contrast, "the new theology had correctly seen that Christian faith is the answer to the word of the transcendent God."[52] But it would be misleading to regard Bultmann as a partisan of dialectical theology. In his 1921 *History of the Synoptic Tradition* he demonstrated his scholarly acumen for "form-criticism," a method of historically-informed biblical criticism that scrutinizes the biblical text to distinguish between original narrative forms and later accretions.[53] He elaborated on this technique in his 1926 study, *Jesus*, where he tried to peel away the merely historical life of Jesus from his genuine "teaching."[54]

But Bultmann's true originality is associated with his later attempt to radicalize the distillatory method of form-criticism in order to create a species of existential theology.[55] One could only discern the true core of the New Testament, Bultmann claimed, if one engaged in an interpretative-critical process of "demythologization" that distinguishes the *kerygma* (Christ's true teaching) from the *mythos* (the elaborately figurative and poetic language stemming from ancient cosmology). Unlike the school of historical criticism, Bultmann did not develop this technique only in order to develop a more accurate portrait of historical Christianity. Instead he wished to salvage an existential and perennially valid dimension of New Testament teaching from the mythical and historically invalidated husks that moderns could no longer find credible. For historical Christianity remained encased in a mythic cosmology: "The world [in this mythic conception] is a three-storied structure, with the earth in the center, the heaven above, and the underworld beneath. Heaven is the above of God and of celestial beings—the angels. The underworld is hell, a place of torment." Bultmann granted that such mythic constructs served an important role: "The real purpose of myth," he observed, "is not to present an objective picture of the world as it is, but to express man's understanding of himself in the world in which he lived." But this still entailed that Christianity's myths could not be affirmed in a literal fashion. They were only a figurative means for expressing theological truths concerning human existence, "man's awareness that he is not lord of his own being."[56]

As a colleague to the philosopher Martin Heidegger (who was at Marburg between 1923 and 1928), Bultmann found himself strongly drawn to the themes associated with existential analysis. So it is perhaps unsurprising that when Bultmann demythologized the New Testament he found at its kerygmatic core an ensemble of religious truths remarkably coincident with existentialism. In his 1929 essay on "The Concept of Revelation in the New Testament," Bultmann defined revelation as "that opening up of what is hidden which is absolutely necessary and decisive for man if he is to achieve 'salvation' or authenticity." Revelation in this sense was primarily a disclosure to humanity of its own existential finitude and only secondarily a divine act. For Bultmann the cardinal significance of revelation lay in its being "the means whereby we achieve our authenticity, which we cannot achieve by our own resources. Therefore, to know about revelation means to know about our own authenticity—and, at the same time, thereby to know of our limitation."[57]

Because the demythologized kerygma so closely resembled existentialist doctrine it was only natural that some critics would accuse Bultmann of bending the New Testament to his own philosophical purposes. The accusation was all the more deadly because Heideggerian existentialism was widely deemed an atheistic philosophy and hence incompatible with Christianity. In a 1930 rejoinder to one such critic, Bultmann denied that his demythologizing method involved any distortion because Christianity was always and only to be grasped within the bounds of human existence. It was therefore only natural that theology would permit itself to be "referred by philosophy to the phenomenon itself." "Theology does indeed 'repeat' the work of philosophy," Bultmann explained, "and it must repeat it if what happens in the Christian occurrence that is realized in faith, in 'rebirth', is not a magical transformation that removes the man of faith from his humanity."[58]

Bultmann's defensive rejoinder prompts the question as to whether the philosopher Martin Heidegger (1889–1976) can be considered an exponent of German interwar theology *stricto sensu*. While the label seems dubious Heidegger nonetheless merits our attention here, not only because his existential phenomenology left a deep imprint on Bultmann but also because many interpreters have noted that, even after his conscious break from traditionalist Catholicism, the philosopher continued to draw upon the rhetoric and the pathos (though not the metaphysical substance) of Christian doctrine. Although he abandoned his training as a Jesuit novice, in a 1921 letter the young philosopher could still described himself as a "Christian Theo-*logian*"[59] His early writings from this era exhibit the uncertain pathos of a newly atheistic philosopher who was nonetheless struggling to preserve some bond to religion. His 1921 seminar on *The Phenomenology of Religious Life* may strike the reader as an especially transitional work insofar as religious experiences such as conversion and repentance (as recounted by Saint Augustine) are lifted free of their doctrinal contents and transfigured into formal categories for phenomenological analysis. But one could argue that the formalizations are still grounded in the phenomena they purportedly shift into the language of philosophical "indication," and that even in his later years Heidegger never entirely surrendered his religiously-derived belief that philosophy (as Socrates says in the *Theateatus*) begins with wonder. This Greco-pagan insight, amplified in both Scholastic philosophy and medieval

Christian mysticism, still moved the mature Heidegger to define questioning as "the piety of thinking."[60]

During his time at Marburg Heidegger worked out details of his existential ontology both in his many seminars and, in 1927, in his *magnum opus, Being and Time*. While he would never outright reject Bultmann's appropriation, Heidegger accepted the application of his ideas to theology only with reluctance. In the 1928 lecture, "Phenomenology and Theology," he observed that "*faith*, as a specific possibility of existence, is in its innermost core the mortal enemy of the *form of existence* that is an essential part of *philosophy*." Whereas philosophy was the name for *ontology* (a formal inquiry into Being), theology was merely *ontic* in that it was a "positive" science that concerned itself with matters of fact. For Heidegger it followed that the idea of a "Christian philosophy" was no more coherent than the idea of a square circle. Yet he granted that philosophy could nonetheless speak to theology by working out the "pre-Christian" or ontological meaning of basic theological concepts via the method of "formal indication." The concept of sin, for example, though theological in content, could be grasped as a positive manifestation of the ontological phenomenon of *guilt*, a phenomenon that belonged to the essential structure of human existence.[61] In a gesture that would remain characteristic throughout his later career, Heidegger insisted on the *priority* of ontological inquiry even while he granted that this procedural and existential precedence still allowed for religious faith as (at least) a factual *possibility* within human life. This argument seemed to accord with Bultmann's understanding of Christian existentialism as an inquiry that borrowed only its formal procedures from Heideggerian phenomenology even while it injected these procedures with the crucial articles of Christianity.

The existentialist theology developed by Paul Tillich (1886–1965) was of an altogether different character. The son of a Lutheran pastor, Tillich served as an army chaplain in the First World War and emerged from the experience with an enduring commitment to socialism. In 1920 he joined the "Kairos circle"—a small weekly discussion group for intellectuals and theologians organized around the journal, *Blätter für religiösen Sozialismus* (published from 1920–1927).[62] During his Weimar years and before his exile to the United States, Tillich held professorships at several universities, including Marburg, where he counted both Bultmann and Heidegger among his colleagues. Of his years there Tillich would later recall:

> During the three semesters of my teaching [in Marburg] I met the first radical effects of the neo-orthodoxy on theological students: cultural problems were excluded from theological thought; theologians like Schleiermacher, Harnack, Troeltsch, Otto, were contemptuously rejected; social and political ideas were banned from theological discussions. The contrast with the experiences in Berlin was overwhelming, at first depressing and then inciting: a new way had to be found.[63]

Although Tillich shared the crisis-theologians' general hostility toward the conformist tendencies of nineteenth-century *Kulturprotestantismus*, he could not share their generalized suspicion of all social meaning, in which he detected a license for political quietism. Tillich's own theology exhibited an uncommon breadth of influences.

His starting premise was the Kierkegaard-inspired idea that the human being by his very nature thirsts for ultimate meaning. If one harkens to its message this ultimacy must shatter any merely institutional or historical frameworks and can only be defined as a "breaking-in of the unconditioned."[64] Like Barth, Tillich in principle rejected any attempts to collapse the distinction between the conditioned and the unconditioned; between the human and the divine. But Barth's fulminations against the liberal Protestant establishment had led Barth, Tillich believed, into a "one-sided" dialectic of absolute transcendence. Unlike Barth, for whom theological absolutism seemed to preclude social engagement, Tillich insisted that any genuine acknowledgment of the unconditioned must also necessarily burden humanity with ethical-political responsibility.[65] The ultimate concerns of religion could not be severed from the ultimate concerns of humanity. In his 1926 book, *The Present-Day Religious Situation*, Tillich argued that capitalism was itself to blame for injecting modern society with indifference toward the ultimate. Capitalism, he wrote, lacks any trace of "self-transcendence, of the hallowing of existence."[66] Given his emphatic commitment to political criticism, Tillich also retained a somewhat more generous attitude toward history as the sphere in which human beings seek ultimate meaning. "Religion lasts as long as man lasts," Tillich observed. "It cannot disappear in human history, because a history without religion is not *human* history, which is a history in which ultimate concerns are at stake."[67]

Tillich was an enduring and outspoken voice on the political left: Already in 1922 in the essay "Kairos" Tillich advocated a form of religious socialism. In 1929 when he joined the philosophy faculty at the University of Frankfurt, Tillich found a close ally in the Marxian philosopher and social theorist Max Horkheimer (who, the next year, was appointed director at the Institute for Social Research in Franfurt). Tillich also received and approved the habilitation on Kierkegaard by Horkheimer's younger associate, Theodor Adorno.[68] In his "Ten Theses" published in 1932, Tillich warned that National Socialism promised only a new paganism that the Protestant churches must condemn without qualification. An ideology of "blood and race" stood in starkest contrast to the Christian ideal of a single God bound to a single and united humanity. "A Protestantism that is open to nationalism and repudiates socialism," Tillich warned, "is on the verge of once again betraying its mission to the world."[69] Following his public statement of opposition to the Nazis in *The Socialist Decision* (1932), Tillich was ejected from his Frankfurt chair and eventually found a new home in North America, where he achieved increased fame as the author of both popular tracts and numerous volumes of systematic theology.[70]

Philosophies of Judaism

If we turn our attention to Jewish thought, we can discern in the Weimar years a similar pattern of rejection and innovation—a rebellion against inherited patterns of nineteenth-century cultural synthesis and novel strains of anti-historicism and existentialism that turned increasingly toward theological-political solutions. Notwithstanding their manifold disagreements, the most prominent Jewish philosophers of the Weimar years—Martin Buber, Franz Rosenzweig, and Walter Benjamin—all shared a single and burning dissatisfaction with the late nineteenth-century synthesis of Judaism and Kantianism epitomized by the philosophy of Hermann Cohen, the founder of neo-Kantianism at Marburg whose final work, *Religion of Reason out of the Sources of Judaism* was published posthumously in 1919.

Cohen's religious philosophy was imprinted with a stringent idealism. It extolled Judaism as a religion of cosmopolitan-rationalist universalism that had vanquished all traces of pagan sensualism and mythology. In a departure from his earlier writings on religion (where he seemed to suggest it could serve only a subordinate role as a conceptual annex for ethics) in *Religion of Reason* Cohen now claimed that religion possessed concepts of its very own whereby it injected the generalistic reasoning of ethics with individualistic content: Ethics is addressed to humanity without differentiation, but religion discloses each person as a discrete "thou" (*Du*) whose nonfungibility as a suffering being is thereby acknowledged.[71] Correlative to the uniqueness of the individual, Cohen argued, was the uniqueness of God as a transcendent "idea" (in Kant's terminological sense of an idea of reason) stripped of all sensualism or worldly attributes. The love of God was therefore love of the highest idea and one's duty to God was realized through the pursuit of justice. For the love of God, declared Cohen, "roots out all quietism."[72]

For the generation of Jewish philosophers who emerged in the 1920s and early 30s, the memory of Hermann Cohen's *Religionsphilosophie* remained quite powerful, even if it was most often the model they wished not to emulate but to overcome. The ambivalence of Cohen's legacy is especially noticeable in the case of Franz Rosenzweig (1886–1929), whose major philosophical work, *The Star of Redemption* (first published in 1921) both borrows and utterly transforms certain elements of Cohen's system. For Rosenzweig as for so many of his contemporaries, the catastrophic events of the Great War brought a thoroughgoing disillusionment with the idealistic philosophical traditions of the nineteenth century. His book begins with a memorable vision of an unnamed human being crawling through the trenches in a condition of mortal terror. With this overture Rosenzweig announces his major theme—that philosophy has no relevance if it cannot speak to the needs of the human being as a creature of fear and trembling. Religion, too, must cast off its idealistic trappings to address its essential elements—God, Man, and World— in this-worldly terms. As a system of religious philosophy *The Star* must explain how its cardinal themes—creation, revelation, and redemption—gain concrete significance and interconnection only within the bounds of lived temporality. In this way the *Star* attempted to recapture the experience of unity (or *Allheit*) that idealism failed to achieve: in revelation God reaches out to the individual who then turns to the neighbor and eventually to the collective. In redemption the human being strives to anticipate divine justice through worldly exertion and communal life. Rosenzweig's idea of revelation obviously drew from Cohen's model of a "correlation" between human being and God—an "I-Thou" relation also developed by Gogarten and Buber. But Rosenzweig abandoned Cohen's idealism and turned instead toward what he called "the earthly path of revelation."[73]

Although we might for convenience describe *The Star* as a specimen of religious existentialism, it also indulges in a speculative philosophy of religious history. Perhaps because in his adulthood he had considered conversion, Rosenzweig retained an unusual sensitivity for both Judaism and Christianity as complementary but nonetheless distinct modes of religious life. To Christianity he assigned the task of building the redeemed kingdom by means of historical and political action, while to Judaism he awarded the strange role of standing still in history—as if to embody in its very inaction the peace of an already-redeemed world. Christianity was therefore in Rosenzweig's imaginative language a religion of the "line," Judaism a religion of the "point." In a section of *The Star* entitled "World Peace," Rosenzweig describes the nations of the world as captives to the idea of a holy war according to which history may be advanced via violence toward its ultimate perfection. The Jew alone, Rosenzweig claims, withdraws from the logic of political violence because he cannot regard history as a theater for the realization of human salvation. For the Jew lives *already* at the end point toward which all nations strive. The Jew alone, therefore, "does not wait for world history to unroll its long course to let him gain what he feels he already possesses in the circuit of every year," an experience of divine immediacy, "the perfect community of all with God."[74] The dualistic logic of Rosenzweig's philosophical system thus effects an uneasy truce between historicism and anti-historicism—on the one hand embracing history for politicized Christianity, on the other hand disowning its significance for a depoliticized and non-territorial conception of Judaism.

Throughout the later 1920s Rosenzweig embarked on a cooperative project of translating the Hebrew Bible into German—the fruits of this exercise still read even today as a startling illustration of aesthetic modernism. His partner was the Viennese-born Martin Buber (1878–1965), who, well before the First World War, had already made his name as a passionate advocate for Zionism and Jewish cultural renewal. The neo-romantic character of his nationalist appeals (especially in the 1911 "Three Speeches on Judaism") earned Buber widespread attention as a spokesman for the left wing of the Zionist movement. The very same neo-romanticism shaped his mystical and hagiographic anthologies of Hasidic lore such as *The Legend of the Baal Shem* (1908).[75] But in the years following the war the mystical themes gave way to a theory of dialogue, first presented in the 1923 book *I and Thou* (*Ich und Du*).

There are two modes of human encounter, Buber claimed, the "I-it" encounter between the self and the objectified thing, and the "I-Thou" encounter between the self and another being whose subjectivity is fully acknowledged. For most of our lives we remain in the mode of the I-it, only rarely rising to the genuine heights of the I-Thou. But human life only achieves its true purpose in the encounter with others. "The *It* is the eternal chrysalis, the *Thou* the eternal butterfly."[76] The relation to the *Thou* is direct, wholly present, an encounter rather than merely an experience. For an experience has characteristics that can be itemized and possessed by a solitary being. Such characteristics dissolve the unity of the *I-Thou,* which is a "primary word" that permits itself to be spoken "only with the whole being," and can never be achieved with instrumental intent by means of sheer will. "The *Thou* meets me through grace," Buber explains. Nor am I primarily a self who only encounters the *Thou* in some *a posteriori* fashion. It is rather only through the *Thou* that I am brought into one's genuine selfhood (a claim that recalls Cohen's theory of correlation): "I become through my relation to the *Thou*," Buber writes. "As I become *I*, I say *Thou*."[77]

The I-Thou relation appears with its greatest intensity in love, whether it is the exclusive love of one person for another or a generalized love that embraces the whole world:

> Love ranges in its effect through the whole world. In the eyes of him who takes his stand in love, and gazes out of it, men are cut free from their entanglement in bustling activity. Good people and evil, wise and foolish, beautiful and ugly, become successively real to him; that is, set free they step forth in their singleness, and confront him as *Thou*. In a wonderful way, from time to time, exclusiveness arises—and so he can be effective, helping, healing, educating, raising up, saving. Love is responsibility of an *I* for a *Thou*. In this lies the likeness—impossible in any feeling whatsoever—of all who love, from the smallest to the greatest and from the blessedly protected man, whose life is rounded in that of a loved being, to him who is all his life nailed to the cross of the world, and who ventures to bring himself to the dreadful point—to love all men.[78]

By the end of the 1920s Buber would turn his attention increasingly to the cause of Jewish nationalism, and he emigrated to Palestine in 1938. An ardent Zionist, he was equally passionate in his criticism of the Zionist movement's right flank for its failure to acknowledge standards of justice transcending the goal of national self-assertion. Buber would eventually assume prominence in the 1930s in *Brit Shalom*, the left-Zionist group that advocated bi-nationalism. But already in 1921 he despaired that "we [had] hoped to save Jewish nationalism from the error of making an idol of the people:

> We have not succeeded. Jewish nationalism is largely concerned with being "like unto all the nations," with affirming itself in the face of the world without affirming the world's reciprocal power. It too has frequently yielded to the delusion of regarding the horizon visible from one's own station as the whole sky. It too is guilty of offending against the words of that table of laws that has been set up above all nations: that all sovereignty becomes false and vain when in the struggle for power it fails to remain subject to the Sovereign of the world, who is the Sovereign of my rival, and my enemy's Sovereign, as well as mine.[79]

Buber and Rosenzweig were only two but perhaps the most prominent of the many Jewish philosophers who devoted their attention primarily to Judaism as a resource for philosophical and cultural renaissance.[80] Other equally accomplished thinkers in the German-Jewish milieu, such as Georg Lukács and Ernst Bloch (both of them early members of Max Weber's Heidelberg circle) exhibited a more pronounced engagement with left-political or socialist causes, embracing an aesthetic and anarchistic temperament that Lukács called "romantic anti-capitalism."[81] In *The Spirit of Utopia* (1921) the German-Jewish philosopher Ernst Bloch (1880–1959) ranged freely across themes of Gothic architecture and chiliastic religion as spiritual resources for his highly heterodox conception of revolutionary Marxism.

But surely the most famous German-Jewish philosopher to work at the troubled boundary-line between Judaism and Western Marxism was the literary and cultural critic Walter Benjamin (1892–1940). An assimilated child of Berlin's Jewish bourgeoisie, Benjamin was an unlikely candidate for revolutionary politics and no less plausible as an authority on Judaism. But through his friendship with Gershom Scholem (1897–1982) he was introduced to the Kabbalah, the half-forgotten tradition of Jewish mysticism and messianic hope that Scholem was just beginning to recover for scholarly attention. A number of Benjamin's writings betray the influence of the Kabbalah, hidden or acknowledged, but most often brought into an explosive combination with ideas derived from Marxism.

One of the earliest samples is the enigmatic text known as the "Theological-Political Fragment" (a title given by Benjamin's Frankfurt School colleague Theodor Adorno and probably written in 1920 or 1921), in which Benjamin nourishes a longing for a future messiah even while he condemns profane history. "Only the Messiah himself completes all history," Benjamin writes,

> in the sense that he alone redeems, completes, creates its relation to the messianic. For this reason, nothing that is historical can relate itself, from its own ground, to anything messianic. Therefore, the Kingdom of God is not the telos of the historical dynamic; it cannot be established as a goal.[82]

The "Fragment" arguably anticipates the anti-historicist theory of messianic politics that Benjamin would elaborate with intensely metaphoric pathos in the essay "On the Concept of History," a text he completed in spring, 1940 shortly before his suicide. In this remarkable work Benjamin meditates upon the significance of Paul Klee's painting, *Angelus Novus*, and discerns in it a conflict between "empty" or historicist time and "messianic time." The angel's face is turned toward the past. "Where we perceive a chain of events, he sees one single catastrophe which keeps piling wreckage upon wreckage and hurls it in front of his feet." The figure of the angel personifies the redemptive practice of the historical materialist who must "brush history against the grain" so as to resist the triumphalist historicism that would silence those vanquished by history. In this allegory one may discern the traces of a theological conviction, but it has been transfigured into a "weak messianic power" whose only redemptive efficacy is the anamnistic remembrance of past suffering.[83] Whether Benjamin's philosophy is driven by genuinely religious energies or whether the messianic imagery serves merely as illustrative husk for profane revolutionary belief remains unclear. But in either case we can detect in his writings the very same mutual entanglement of apocalyptic hope and historical despair that marks so much of Weimar theology.

The Descent into Political Theology

With the Nazi seizure of power Weimar theologians were confronted with a difficult choice, between various stratagems of compromise with the new regime or the far more challenging path of outright resistance. Few chose the latter. A more typical case was that of Friedrich Gogarten, whose disdain for political liberalism eventually drove him into the arms of nationalist revolution. In his 1932 *Political Ethics*, Gogarten extolled the state as a divine gift, and also affirmed that "the law of God is met *in* the law of the nation (*Volk*)." In 1933 Gogarten allied himself briefly with the German Christians, the racialist movement that sought an ideological reconciliation between Christianity and National Socialism. His *Political Ethics* earned Gogarten bitter denunciation from several prominent theologians and philosophers. Martin Buber charged Gogarten with having collapsed all problems of personal ethics into politics, thereby denying the genuinely religious dimension of human experience which requires an encounter between the individual and God. As Buber observed, "no philosophical concept of the State [and] likewise no theological concept of the State leads beyond the reality of the human person in the situation of faith. None leads beyond his responsibility—be he servant or emperor—for the body politic as man in the sight of God."[84] Meanwhile, Karl Löwith suggested that Gogarten's political orientation bore a strong resemblance to the doctrines of political decisionism articulated by exponents of the Weimar right such as Carl Schmitt and Heidegger.[85] Finally, in a dramatic 1933 letter Karl Barth announced his "Farewell" from Gogarten and the circle of *Zwischen den Zeiten*, rebuking his former colleague for conflating the law of God and the law of the nation.[86] In Barth's judgment, German Christianity was the illogical consequence of a longstanding error reaching back to the nineteenth century that had imbued political history with divine purpose. "I cannot see anything in German Christianity," he explained, "but the last, fullest, and worst monstrosity of Neo-Protestantism."[87]

Another case of pro-Nazi enthusiasm was that of the Lutheran theologian Emanuel Hirsch (1888–1972), a student of Harnack and a leading exponent in the Kierkegaard-revival who already trumpeted his hostility for the Republic as early as its founding.[88] A vocal critic of dialectical theology, Hirsch disdained the Barthians most of all for their denial of history and their indifference toward the "sacred bonds" of earthly community. In 1934 Hirsch published a systematic defense of the new regime. "We evangelical Christians," he wrote,

> can thankfully and honorably give ourselves to, and in the spirit of cooperation and support affirm the movement which is now fundamentally

transforming our nation-stately *Nomos* and *Logos*. We can do this, as no one can, out of an inner accountability before the Lord of history, and with the consciousness that in his Word and Gospel there exists a power with us and over us, that stands with majestic truth over all changes and movements of nation-state life.[89]

Hirsch's political manifesto ignited a storm of controversy. Paul Tillich lashed back with a series of letters in which he faulted Hirsch for sacralizing the German nation and thereby abolishing the "reserve" (*reservatum*, i.e., independence from worldly authority) that Christianity must practice if it is to retain its true character.[90]

But cases of extravagant enthusiasm were hardly the rule. Like most academics, the more common stratagem among theologians during the Third Reich was a morally dubious retreat into political quietism and "inner migration." Even Karl Barth was criticized for his failure to speak out with greater force against Nazi anti-Semitism.[91] Yet credit is surely due to Barth—and to him perhaps most of all—for launching the opening salvo of German evangelical resistance against National Socialism. In June 1933 Barth published his manifesto, "Theological Existence Today" (*Theologische Existenz Heute*) a copy of which he actually sent to the *Führer*. In May of the following year a group of theologians signed the Barmen Declaration, an official statement of the Confessing Synod that brought together leading members of the main evangelical orders in an unambiguous rebuke of the German Christian movement. Composed chiefly by Barth (but with the cooperation of Dietrich Bonhoeffer and others) the Declaration condemned German Christianity as a catastrophic rupture with the true faith: Its first article rejected any allegiance to "events, powers [and] historic figures" other than the "one Word of God." The fifth article explicitly rejected the Hitler cult as "the false doctrine that apart from the ministry, the church could . . . give itself or allow itself to be given special Leaders vested with ruling authority."[92] Needless to say the new regime did not welcome such criticism. Tillich had already been dismissed from his professorship. Barth remained in Switzerland. Bonhoeffer left Germany briefly in 1933 for a pastorship in London, only to return two years later. Soon afterwards, the Nazi-approved evangelical Bishop Theodor Heckel forbade him from teaching in Berlin, and, after a brief sojourn in the United States, Bonhoeffer returned to Germany to join the anti-Hitler resistance. He was arrested in 1943, and, after a year and a half in Tegel prison, he was executed.

The lessons of this drama remain unclear. Notwithstanding cases of occasional heroism, the political denouement of Weimar theology may strike us as a scandal. But from the theological point of view it is surely too thick with ambiguity to warrant any certain verdicts in matters of doctrinal controversy. Nevertheless, across the spectrum of theological themes we have surveyed here, one can make out a few general patterns: theological radicalism was grafted onto political pessimism; rebellion against the liberal-historicist teaching of the nineteenth century was transformed into apocalyptic and anti-historical doctrines on both the left and the right; God was expelled from the social-historical matrix only to return with even more irresistible authority as the numinous or the wholly other or—perversely—as the *Volk*. But we should be wary of reading history as a theological argument. The drama of Weimar theology neither vindicates the Barthians in their anti-historicism nor condemns their historical naïveté. But perhaps it yields at least a non-theological lesson—that theology is what human beings make of it. Eternity must reveal itself in time after all.

Notes

1. For their critical comments on earlier drafts of this essay I owe a debt of gratitude most of all to my former colleague Ronald Thiemann, Bussey Professor of Theology, Harvard Divinity School. Thanks as well to my co-editor, John McCormick.
2. Franz Overbeck, *How Christian is our Present-Day Theology?* trans. Martin Henry (London: Continuum International, 2005). A translation of Overbeck's famous text, *Über die Christlichkeit unserer heutigen Theologie* (1873, 2nd ed., 1903), quoted from the "Postscript," 193.
3. Overbeck, *How Christian is our Present-Day Theology?*
4. David Friedrich Strauß, *Das Leben Jesu kritisch bearbeitet* (Tübingen, 1835–36); translated into English by George Eliot as *The Life of Jesus, Critically Examined* 3 vols. (London: John Chapman, 1846); Ludwig Feuerbach, *Das Wesen des Christentums* (1841), in English translation, also by George Eliot, as *The Essence of Christianity* (London: John Chapman, 1854).
5. Overbeck, *How Christian is our Present-Day Theology?*, 33.
6. For more on Harnack and the historical background of ninetheenth-cenutry German theology see the excellent study by Thomas Albert Howard, *Protestant Theology and the Making of the Modern German University* (Oxford: Oxford University Press, 2006).
7. Adolf von Harnack, *What is Christianity? Sixteen Lectures Delivered in the University of Berlin during the Winter-Term 1899–1900*, trans. Thomas Baily Saunders (New York: G.P. Putnam's Sons, 1901), 6.
8. Harnack, *What is Christianity?*, 11.
9. Harnack, *What is Christianity?*, 13.
10. Harnack, *What is Christianity?*, 9
11. Harnack, *What is Christianity?*, 19.
12. Overbeck, *How Christian is our Present-Day Theology?*, 194.
13. See, e.g., *Adolf von Harnack,* "Revelation and Theology: the Barth-Harnack Correspondence" in *Adolf Von Harnack: Liberal Theology at its Height*, ed. Martin Rumscheidt (London: Collins Liturgical Publications, 1989).
14. Max Weber, *The Protestant Ethic and the Spirit of Capitalism* (orig. 1905; English, New York: Scribner's Press, 1958), 181–82. I am quoting here from the Talcott Parsons translation, which, despite numerous inaccuracies, remains the canonical English-language version.
15. Weber, *The Protestant Ethic, 182*.
16. Perhaps the most intriguing was the monograph on ancient Judaism, See Max Weber, *Das Antike Judentum*, originally published in the *Archiv für Sozialwissenschaft* (1917–18), reprinted in *Gesammelte Aufsätze zur Religions-soziologie* (Tübin-

gen: J.C.B. Mohr, 1921). In English as *Ancient Judaism*. trans. and ed. H. H. Gerth and Don Martindale (Glencoe: Free Press, 1952).

17. Ephraim Fischoff, "Translator's Preface," in Max Weber, *The Sociology of Religion* (Boston: Beacon Press, 1963), xx. Originally published as "Religionssoziologie" in the posthumous collection, *Wirtschaft und Gesellschaft* (Tübingen: J.C.B. Mohr (Paul Siebeck), 1922).

18. "The external courses of religious behavior are so diverse that an understanding of this behavior can only be achieved from the viewpoint of the subjective experiences, ideas, and purposes of the individuals concerned—in short, from the viewpoint of the religious behavior's 'meaning' (*Sinn*)." Quoted from Max Weber, *The Sociology of Religion*, 1.

19. Max Weber, "Science as a Vocation" in *The Vocation Lectures,* eds. David S. Owen and Tracy Strong (Indianapolis: Hackett Publishers, 2004), 1–31. For an analysis of the relationship between religion and science in Weber's famous address, "Science as a Vocation," see Peter E. Gordon, "German Existentialism and the Persistence of Metaphysics," in *Situating Existentialism*, eds. Jonathan Judaken and Robert Bernasconi (New York: Columbia University Press, 2012). 65–88. A similar statement on religion can be found in Max Weber, "Religious Rejections of the World and their Directions," and "The Social Psychology of the World Religions," in *From Max Weber*, eds. H. H. Gerth and C. W. Mills (New York: Oxford University Press, 1958), 323–59 (esp. 355) and 267–301.

20. Weber, "The Social Psychology of the World Religions," 281.

21. Ernst Troeltsch, *Die Soziallehren der christlichen Kirchen und Gruppen* (Tübingen: J.C.B. Mohr (Paul Siebeck), 1912); in English as *The Social Teaching of the Christian Churches,* 2 vols., trans. Olive Wyon (Chicago: University of Chicago Press, Midway Reprints, 1976), I, 43.

22. Troeltsch, *The Social Teaching of the Christian Churches*, I, 34.

23. Troeltsch, *The Social Teaching of the Christian Churches*, II, 625.

24. See Ernst Troeltsch, "The Crisis of Historicism," *Die Neue Rundschau* 33 (1922), 572–90; and the more elaborate *Der Historismus und seine Probleme* (Tübingen: J.C.B. Mohr, 1922).

25. For this claim in particular, see Ernst Troeltsch, "The Place of Christianity Among the World Religions," in Troeltsch, *Christian Thought: its History and Application,* ed. Baron F. von Hügel (New York: Meridian Books, 1957), esp. 43–63. Also see Troeltsch, *The Absoluteness of Christianity and the History of Religions*. trans. David Reid, 2nd ed. (Richmond, VA, 1971). A helpful discussion can be found in Sarah Coakley, *Christ without Absolutes: A Study of the Christology of Ernst Troeltsch.* (Oxford: Clarendon Press, 1988).

26. Simmel, "Religion," in *Essays on Religion*, ed. and trans Horst Jürgen Helle (New Haven: Yale University Press, 1997), 137–214; quotation from 160–61.

27. Simmel, "Religion," 214.

28. Karl Barth, "Concluding Unscientific Postscript on Scheiermacher," in *The Theology of Schleiermacher*. trans. Geoffrey W. Bromiley (Grand Rapids, MI: Wm. B. Eerdmans Publishing, 1982), 264. Quoted in Gary Dorrien, *The Barthian Revolt in Modern Theology: Theology without Weapons* (Louisville, KY: Westminster John Knox Press, 2000), 38.

29. Karl Barth, *Epistle to the Romans*, trans. Edwyn Hoskyns, 6th ed. (New York: Oxford University Press, 1968), 77.

30. Barth, *Epistle*, 1–3.

31. Barth, *Epistle*, "Preface to the Second Edition," 11.
32. Barth, *Epistle*, 78.
33. Barth, *Epistle*, 79.
34. Barth, *Epistle*, 79.
35. Barth, *Epistle*, 10.
36. Friedrich Gogarten, *Religion weither* (Jena: Diederichs, 1917), esp. 14–15.
37. Friedrich Gogarten, "Zwischen den Zeiten," *Die Christliche Welt* (1920), 375; reprinted in translation as "Between the Times," in *The Beginnings of Dialectical Theology*. ed. James M. Robinson (Richmond, VA: John Knox Press, 1968), 277–82.
38. Friedrich Gogarten, *Illusionen: Eine Auseinandersetzung mit dem Kulturidealismus* [Illusions: A Discussion with Culture-Idealism] (Jena: Diederichs, 1926), as quoted in Larry Shiner, *The Secularization of History: An Introduction to the Theology of Friedrich Gogarten* (New York: Abingdon Press, 1966), 199.
39. For Gogarten's influences, see Gogarten, *Von Glauben und Offenbarung* (Jena: Diederichs, 1923).
40. For Buber's remarks on Gogarten, see Buber, *Die Schriften über das dialogische Prinzip* (Heidelberg: Lambert Schneider, 1954), 296.
41. Harnack, "Fünfzehn Fragen an die Verächter der wissenschaftlichen Theologie unter den Theologen," in Harnack, *Aus der Werkstatt des Vollendeten*, ed. Axel von Harnack (Giessen: A. Töpelmann,1930), 51–54. Quoted in Thomas Albert Howard, *Protestant Theology and the Making of the Modern University* (New York: Oxford University Press, 2009), 414.
42. Emil Brunner, *Religionsphilosophie protestantischer Theologie* (1927); translated as *The Philosophy of Religion from the Standpoint of Protestant Theology*. trans. A.J.D. Farrer and Bertram Lee Woolf, 2nd English ed. (London: James Clarke & Company, 1958), 32. Quoted in Gary Dorrien, *The Barthian Revolt* (Louisville, KY: Westminster John Knox Press, 2000), 111.
43. Quoted in Dorrien, *The Barthian Revolt*, 120.
44. Quoted from Brunner, "Nature and Grace: A Contribution to the Discussion with Karl Barth," in *Natural Theology: Comprising "Nature and Grace" by Professor Dr. Emil Brunner and the Reply "No!" by Dr. Karl Barth*, trans. Peter Fraenkel (London: Geoffrey Bles, 1946), 48.
45. For a discussion, see Dorrien, *The Barthian Revolt*, 110, and 120–24.
46. Dietrich Bonhoeffer to Eberhard Bethge (5 May 1944), in *Letters and Papers from Prison*. Eberhard Bethge, eds. and trans. Riginalf Fuller et al. (New York: Macmillan, 1971), 286. As quoted in Dorrien, *The Barthian Revolt*, 154.
47. Rudolf Otto, originally entitled *Das Heilige—Über das Irrationale in der Idee des Göttlichen und sein Verhältnis zum Rationalen*. Translated as *The Idea of the Holy: An Inquiry into the non-rational factor in the idea of the divine and its relation to the rational*, trans. John W. Harvey (New York: Oxford University Press, 1923).
48. Ernst Troeltsch, *Psychologie und Erkenntnistheorie in der Religionswissenschaft* (Tübingen: J.C.B. Mohr, 1905). For a discussion see Todd A. Gooch, *The Numinous and Modernity. An Interpretation of Rudolf Otto's Philosophy of Religion.* (Berlin: Walter de Gruyter, 2000), 52–63.
49. Otto, *The Holy*, 6.
50. See the criticism by Bultmann in "Die liberale Theologie und die jüngste theologische Bewegung," in *Glauben und Verstehen*, 9th ed., vol. 1 (Tübingen: Mohr (Siebeck), 1993), 22; as cited by Gooch, *The Numinous and Modernity*, 3.
51. Gooch, *The Numinous and Modernity*, 68.

52. Rudolf Bultmann, "Autobiographical Reflections," in Bultmann, *Existence and Faith: Shorter Writings of Rudolf Bultmann*, trans.Schubert M. Ogden (New York: Meridian Books, 1960), 283–88; quotation from 288.

53. Bultmann, *Die Geschichte der synoptischen Tradition* (Göttingen: Vandenhoeck & Ruprecht, 1921); *History of the Synoptic Tradition* (San Francisco: Harper, 1976).

54. Bultmann, *Jesus and the Word*, trans. L.P. Smith and E.H. Lantero (New York: Scribner, 1980).

55. Rudolf Bultmann, *Neues Testament und Mythologie : das Problem der Entmythologisierung der neutestamentlichen Verkündigung*. 2nd ed. (1st ed. 1941), ed. Eberhard Jüngel, *Beiträge zur evangelischen Theologie; Bd. 96* (München: Chr. Kaiser, 1985).

56. Bultmann, "New Testament and Mythology," in *Kerygma and Myth*, vol. 1, ed. Hans Werner Bartsch (New York: Harper and Row, 1961), 1–2.

57. Bultmann, "Der Begriff der Offenbarung im neuen Testament" (Tübingen: J.C.B Mohr, 1929); reprinted as "The Concept of Revelation in the New Testament," in Bultmann, *Existence and Faith*, 58–91; quotations at 59 and 62.

58. Bultmann, "Die Geschichtlichkeit des Daseins und der Glaube: Antwort an Gerhardt Kuhlmann," *Zeitschrift für Theologie und Kirche* 11 (1930), 339–64; translated as "The Historicity of Man and Faith" in *Existence and Faith*, quoted from 95–96.

59. Heidegger to Löwith, letter as quoted in *Im Gespräch der Zeit*, vol. 2: *Zur philosophischen Aktualität Heideggers*. eds. Dietrich Papenfuss and Otto Pöggeler. (Frankfurt: Klostermann, 1990), 27–32.

60. Heidegger, "The Question Concerning Technology," in *The Question Concerning Technology and Other Essays*, trans. William Lovitt (New York: Harper Perennial, 1982), 35.

61. Martin Heidegger, "Phenomenology and Theology," in *Pathmarks*, ed. William McNeill (New York: Cambridge University Press, 1998), 39–62; 52.

62. Werner Schüßler, "Tillich's Life and Works," in *The Cambridge Companion to Paul Tillich*, Russell Re Manning, ed. (Cambridge: Cambridge University Press, 2008), 13–17.

63. Tillich, "Autobiographical Reflections of Paul Tillich," in *Theology of Paul Tillich*, ed. C. W. Kegley and R. W. Bretall (New York: Macmillan, 1961); quoted in Werner Schüßler, "Tillich's Life and Works," 3–18, 7.

64. Paul Tillich, "Kairos" in *Main Works / Hauptwerke*, vol 4, ed. J. Clayton (New York: de Gruyter, 1987), 55–57.

65. This theme grew especially pronounced in later years, especially during the Second World War, when Tillich criticized Barth for opposing fascism on apolitical grounds: "It was not the common fight of people of all religions and creeds against the National-Socialist distortion of humanity that interested him, but the defense of the church as the finger pointing only to heaven and not to earth." Tillich, "Trends in Religious Thought that Affect Social Outlook," in *Religion and the World Order*, ed. F. Ernest Johnson (New York: Harper and Brothers, 1944), 24–25.

66. Paul Tillich, *Die religiöse Lage der Gegenwart* (Berlin: Ullstein, 1926).

67. Paul Tillich, "Vertical and Horizontal Thinking," in *The American Scholar* 15, no. 1 (1945–46), 103.

68. See Robert Hullot-Kentor, "Foreword," in Theodor W. Adorno, *Kierkegaard: Construction of the Aesthetic*, trans. Robert Hullot-Kentor (Minneapolis: University of Minnesota Press, 1989), xi–xii.

69. Paul Tillich, "Zehn Thesen," first published in *Die Kirche und das Dritte Reich. Fragen und Forderungen deutscher Theologen*, ed. Leopold Klotz (Gotha: Klotz, 1932), 126–28.

70. Paul Tillich, *Die sozialistische Entscheidung.* (Potsdam, A. Protte, 1933).

71. For a discussion see Peter E. Gordon, *Rosenzweig and Heidegger: Between Judaism and German Philosophy* (Berkeley: University of California Press, 2003), 54–66.

72. Hermann Cohen, *Religion of Reason out of the Sources of Judaism*, 52.

73. Franz Rosenzweig, "The New Thinking," eds. and trans. Alan Udoff and Barbara Ellen Galli (Syracuse: Syracuse University Press, 1999), 67–105; 92.

74. Franz Rosenzweig, *Der Stern der Erlösung*, 4th ed. (Frankfurt am Main: Suhrkamp, 1993), 368; in English as *The Star of Redemption*, trans. William W. Hallo (Notre Dame, IN: University of Notre Dame Press, 1985), 331.

75. Martini Buber, *Drei Reden über das Judentum* [Three Speeches on Judaism] (Frankfurt a.M.: Rütten & Loening, 1911); *Die Geschichten des Rabbi Nachman* (Frankfurt a.M.: Rütten und Loening, 1906); *Die Legende des Baalschem*, 2nd. ed., [1st ed. 1908] (Frankfurt a.M.: Rütten & Loening, 1916).

76. Martin Buber, *Ich und Du* (Leipzig: Insel-Verlag, 1923); in English as *I and Thou* trans.Walter Kaufmann (New York: Continuum, 2004), 21.

77. Buber, *I and Thou*, 17.

78. Buber, *I and Thou*, 19–20.

79. Martin Buber, "Nationalismus," in *Kampf um Israel* (Berlin: Schocken Verlag, 1933), 225–42; first delivered as a spoken address at the Twelfth Zionist Congress, Karlsbad (5 September 1921); reprinted in Martin Buber, *Israel and the World* (New York: Schocken Books, 1948).

80. See Michael Brenner, *The Renaissance of Jewish Culture in Weimar Germany* (New Haven: Yale, 1998).

81. For a general survey of the phenomenon, see Michael Löwy, *Redemption and Utopia: Jewish Libertarian Thought in Central Europe. A Study in Elective Affinity* (Stanford: Stanford University Press, 1992).

82. On the problems of dating the fragment, see the editorial note 306n1, in Walter Benjamin, *Selected Writings*, vol. 3, 1935–1938, ed. Michael Jennings (Cambridge, MA: Harvard University Press, 2002), 305–6.

83. Walter Benjamin, "On the Concept of History" in *Walter Benjamin: Selected Writings; Volume 4* (Cambridge, MA: Harvard University Press, 2003), 389–400.

84. Martin Buber: *Between Man and Man* (London: Kegan Paul, 1947), 93.

85. Karl Löwith, "Der okkasionelle Dezisionismus von C. Schmitt," in Karl Löwith, *Gesammelte Abhandlungen; zur Kritik der geschichtlichen Existenz* (Stuttgart: Kohlhammer, 1960), 93–126; see esp. 214–26.

86. Karl Barth, "Abschied," *Zwischen den Zeiten* (1933), 538–39.

87. Quoted from Eberhard Busch, *Karl Barth: His Life from Letters and Autobiographical Texts.* trans. John Bowden (London, S.C.M. Press, 1976), 229–30.

88. See Emanuel Hirsch, *Deutschlands Schicksal: Staat, Volk, und Menschheit im Lichte einer ethischen Geschichtsansicht* (Göttingen: Vandenhoeck & Ruprecht, 1920). For further information see Robert P. Ericksen, *Theologians under Hitler: Gerhard Hittel, Paul Althaus, and Emanuel Hirsch* (New Haven: Yale University Press, 1985).

89. Emmanuel Hirsch, *Die gegenwärtige geistige Lage im Spiegel philosophischer und theologischer Besinnung: Akademische Vorlesungen zum Verhältnis des deutschen Jahres 1933* (Göttingen: Vandenhoeck & Ruprecht, 1934), 153; quoted in A. James Reimer, *The Emanuel Hirsch and Paul Tillich Debate: A Study in the Political Ramifications of Theology.* Toronto Studies in Theology, Vol. 42 (Lewiston: Edwin Mellen Press, 1989).

90. Paul Tillich, "Die Theologie des Kairos und die gegenwärtige geistige Lage: Offener Brief an Emanuel Hirsch," *Theologische Blätter* 11, no. 13 (November 1934), 305–28. The second letter appeared in the same journal in May 1935.

91. By Paul Tillich, for example. For a summary see Dorrien, *The Barthian Revolt*, 143.

92. Quoted from *Karl Barth: Theologian of Freedom*, ed. Clifford Green (Minneapolis: Augsburg Fortress, 1989), 222–23.

9

Method, Moment, and Crisis in Weimar Science

Cathryn Carson

Weimar intellectuals were notoriously riven, divided along every possible line. Yet there was one thing that arguably held them together: their sense of living in a particular moment—experiencing it, and simultaneously describing and theorizing it. That commonality is one reason the label "Weimar thought" feels so reasonable: those intellectuals' sense of their moment as a natural unity, as well as our sense of it as an appropriate analytic construction. It feels reasonable, that is, as long as we look at intellectuals preoccupied with historical creations like human institutions and culture. But intellectuals preoccupied with science?

Rather than shaped moment by moment, the history of modern science looks monotonic, as long as positivity is taken as science's governing ideal. That is, as long as science is seen as the methodical cumulation of positive knowledge, each setback looks like an unfortunate accident, each triumph like a dispensable milepost along a progressive course that is essentially foreordained. If the dynamic of science is really driven by nature, it can only incidentally be affected by being embedded in human affairs. If its foundational assumptions stand outside of time, there is no room for singling out the present by diagnosing a moment of crisis.

And yet in Weimar-era science, the diagnosis of present crisis *was* startlingly available. It was repeated across multiple disciplinary discourses; it was made use of by scientists and non-scientists in sometimes similar ways. The notion of a far-reaching methodological crisis, which in fact first gained intellectual content in the Weimar Republic, challenged inherited conceptions of science as far as these were uninterested in human time scales. More than that: Revolutions underway, foundations being called into question—these ways of depicting science's presumed instability resonated with intellectuals' accounts of Weimar's *other* crises. Were the sciences somehow converging with other movements of thought? Exactly the possibility implied by convergence—that science did not take its lead from nature alone—was among the most provocative of ideas being explored in Weimar discussions surrounding natural science. Since then, and this is not a coincidence, it has become one of the leitmotifs of the discipline of the history of science.

This chapter examines how a self-consciously "Weimar science" came together, meaning how the Weimar moment was experienced and theorized by intellectuals preoccupied with science. We start with an introduction to the natural scientific enterprise as it was pursued in the Wilhelmine and Weimar eras. Against this backdrop we can highlight several developments in the life sciences, mathematics, and physics that attracted critical notice. Showing how disputes over these matters intersected, even lapped over the borders of professional science, we can see how they resonated with contemporary philosophical contention. To close, we pick out two responses that shared a desire to stake a claim on a scientific present: calls associated with logical empiricist philosophy to create a unified worldview based on science, and attempts by intellectual historians, philosophers, and some scientists to understand science itself as irreducibly situated in historical time.

The Scientific Enterprise

When Weimar intellectuals talked about natural science (*die Naturwissenschaft*), they typically took their lead from the version they saw with their own eyes—not the natural philosophy of Galileo or Newton, not the natural history of Linnaeus or Cuvier, but the full-blown modern science that came together in their time. In its modern form, science had grown up in Germany with other fields in the philosophical faculty of the university system, rapidly expanding since the mid-nineteenth century. Unlike many scholarly disciplines, however, science had secured footholds in territory inaccessible to most other fields of intellectual life. The great age for founding scientific institutions was the *Kaiserreich*. The medical faculties and *Technische Hochschulen*, industrial research departments and testing laboratories, public health institutions and government bureaus all contributed to science's institutional and financial base. So by the early twentieth century, the German research system's high-water mark extended from the university to industry to the state. Its institutional innovations—such as the Imperial Physical Technical Institute, carrying out work on physical standards, or the Kaiser Wilhelm Society for advanced research at the nexus of government, industry, and pure science—were widely admired and emulated abroad.[1] But even as that assessment honored intellectual advances, it pointed to a highly ambivalent fact: science might make obeisance to ideals of disinterested contemplation, but it gained underwriting largely because it promised technically useful results. The "scientific age" famously called out by the inventor Werner von Siemens had more than ideal values at stake. That is, the diverse interests to which the scientific enterprise responded signaled the breadth of demands placed by a modernizing society on natural science.[2]

Science's admirers and practitioners often called on a rhetoric of intellectual and practical triumph. And by the early twentieth century they certainly had reason: By their day the terrain of scientific knowledge had been carved up into knowable territories, with disciplines and subdisciplines defined by materials and methods. Physical chemistry, immunology, fluid mechanics, genetics, and the countless other specialties staked out by this era still provide the basic architecture of the scientific enterprise. The seemingly limitless refinement of the technologies of inquiry made it possible to inspect a nerve cell, graph a heart's electrical rhythm, or discriminate the frequencies of light sent out by a collection of atoms. Above all else, perhaps, systematic investigation of nature had begun paying off in tangible ways. Advances in bacteriology and medical research were beginning to make their mark on the public welfare, and the physical sciences were increasingly counted on for economic returns. Whole branches of industry such as electrical technology had been erected on scientific grounds, while Germany's global dominance in trade-critical fields like organic and inorganic chemicals owed an immense debt to in-house industrial research.

Systematic collection of data, analytic disaggregation, and experimental investigation were coming to look like a royal road to secure, objective knowledge. The public language of triumph that scientists often relied on was probably matched by some inner belief in the inherent progress of empirical investigation. In one domain after another, science promised to reveal new mechanisms and explanations, while overarching theories like evolution or thermodynamics could offer a scientific worldview to replace more conventional sources of meaning. By the late Wilhelmine era, certainly, a number of such systems were on display, advocated by figures such as Ernst Haeckel (1834–1919, evolutionary monism), Wilhelm Ostwald (1854–1932, energeticism), and Ernst Mach (1834–1916, phenomenalism or positivism). Whether a kind of routine faith in scientific practice really brought scientists to commit to a full-fledged philosophical system—materialism, naturalism, scientism, and so on—is not entirely clear. But these systems came to stand for the scientific worldview, at least for observers on the outside. They certainly gave the methodology or findings of the sciences a uniquely authoritative status. And whether or not scientists necessarily believed that science *was* uniquely authoritative, that was a good description of the way they actually worked. In the laboratory or the field, after all, only certain kinds of procedures counted in generating reliable knowledge.

This was a feature of science that troubled some observers. To practice natural science, and practice it well, no grand philosophical commitments were needed, just fidelity to some presumably prescriptive procedure. By narrowing its vision and keeping its focus, science seemed to guarantee a kind of automatic technical progress. Science staked its case on empirical effectiveness. And next to empirical effectiveness, what else mattered? Even when the rhetoric of science was not overtly imperialistic, it still came across as unresponsive to other epistemic claims. Here was one reason science was received ambivalently in the larger cultural sphere. Scientific statesmen could take on the mantle of humanistic learning—well into the twentieth century, the path to a university doctorate in science still led through the *Gymnasium*—but the scientist of caricature was not the classically educated man of broad culture. Instead he was the epistemological parvenu, lacking in historical depth or good tone. In assessments of this sort there was sometimes a strain of romantic antimodernism, painting the scientist as a brash creature of this loathsome modern world, in league with industrialization, alienated from humanity and nature, respecting only hard, cold facts. This line of criticism was hardly countermanded by scientists' public alliance with captains of industry who were remaking the world as a resource for economic exploitation—or, for that matter, by their patriotic service in the Great War (think only of that great new invention the chemists delivered, poison gas).[3]

Still, it was not just romantic antimodernists who looked back over science's path and thought something had been lost. As Max Weber (1864–1920) famously commented in his 1919 lecture "Science as a Vocation,"

> Who—aside from certain big children who are indeed found in the natural sciences—still believes that the findings of astronomy, biology, physics, or chemistry could teach us anything about the *meaning* of the world? If there is any such "meaning," along what road could one come upon its tracks? If the natural sciences lead us to anything in this way, they are apt to make the belief that there is such a thing as the "meaning" of the universe die out at its very roots.[4]

Weber was not chastising the natural sciences for disenchanting the world. Disenchantment was inevitable, the natural result of all lines of modern scholarly work. (Weber's "science" here is *Wissenschaft* at large.) Still, when Weber needed to describe the force that drove disenchantment, he took his terms from contemporary natural science: human efforts to eliminate the universe's mysterious forces and subject it to rational control. Most early twentieth-century commentators on science, whatever perspective they adopted, more or less shared a default narrative. Science was on the march victorious, unstoppable in its material and intellectual conquests—whether that fact was greeted with cheering, dismay or stoic reserve.

So the rhetoric of unstoppable scientization was compelling, and among those speaking about science, it was probably the most common figure of speech. Curiously, it did not necessarily describe the ordinary practice of science in the Weimar era. Not only had science become a more routine profession by this time—far more fine-grained technical work than grand vistas of intellectual progress—but its forward march hardly unfolded so smoothly when viewed from the mundane struggles of its practitioners to keep it afloat. The gap between triumphal rhetoric and on-the-ground difficulties was a hallmark, in fact, of the Weimar Republic, which may partly explain why the period was so extraordinarily productive for intellectual commentary on science.[5] During Weimar's periods of fiscal contraction, the institutions of science, too, had to deal with funding cutbacks and sharply limited purchasing power. Many scientific leaders harbored profound skepticism that a democratic polity would support their venture as generously had imperial governing elites. After the lost war, too, international scientific organizations excluded Germany as late as the mid-1920s. This came at just a time when the surging successes of other national scientific communities (the United States and Soviet Union, among other previously marginal places) seemed to announce that German supremacy was on its way out.

The inverse of the narrative of triumph, then, was a narrative of crisis. Crisis was a challenge to any discipline that assumed its foundations were stable; and that, by default, was the assumption science made. Yet crisis was not solely a negative word. In Weimar culture at large, when commentators evoked a crisis they meant not only that the old patterns of thought were failing; they also implied that new ones might be beginning to emerge.[6] In funding or in politics, scientific statesmen wished crisis away. But intellectually, certain scientific disciplines (not all of them) welcomed it. A moment of crisis reopened the time horizon. It suggested that the future would not just be more of the past—a past that looked uniformly progressive and, just for that reason, stagnant. In the words of one theorist,

> In the natural science of the present day we are witnessing a strange and disturbing spectacle. It is as though the grand sweep of its historical development, stretching from its beginnings in early Greek times up to the turn of the twentieth century, had received a check. The foundations of our thought and investigation, hitherto regarded as assured, have collapsed. . . . Some years ago this state of affairs could be regarded as the break-down of Western science. But the remarkable developments which have recently been coming to fruition . . . suggest a totally different interpretation: we can see in the present state the raw and as yet unsettled early phase of a new step in scientific thought.[7]

The Sciences of Life

Ludwig von Bertalanffy (1901–1972), the author of these words, was one of Weimar's spokesmen for a coming revolution in science. That he spoke as a biologist hardly surprised his contemporaries. More, perhaps, than any other interwar science, biology seemed ripe for transformative change. It was expanding its reach on seemingly every possible front—the elucidation of cellular structures and processes, whole-organism development and behavior, species-level questions of inheritance and evolution. If there were a domain of natural science, moreover, that promised immediate consequences for human culture, it was biology, as the pervasiveness of biological thinking in contemporary social and political discourse made clear.[8]

The no-holds-barred growth of the life sciences in the early twentieth century was made possible by sharpened tools and techniques for investigating living organisms. Responding to a spectacular proliferation of research strategies, biology had developed an array of subspecialties. Each of these had its own practitioners, journals, and institutions—and its own canons of demonstration, among which real dissension reigned. In fact, university professorships continued to be designated by specific biological disciplines: physiology, neurology, bacteriology, botany, zoology, comparative anatomy, and so on. The word "biology," which was just beginning to be used broadly in these years, suggested a unity that was hardly to be seen on the ground. One trend of the day was the rhetorical celebration of experimental biology, continuing a fin-de-siècle contest between so-called descriptive-comparative strategies and "modern" experimentalist approaches. But even experimentalism had multiple variants. When the Kaiser Wilhelm Institute for Biology, a shaping institution of the Weimar era, was dedicated in 1916, struggles over disciplinary leadership were written into its founding mission. Devoted to experimental studies carried out under five division directors—Carl Correns (1864–1933), Hans Spemann (1869–1941), Richard Goldschmidt (1878–1958), Max Hartmann (1876–1972), and Otto Warburg (1883–1970)—the institute's work initially sat at the intersection of genetics with developmental biology and embryology, along with a strong dose of biochemical investigation.[9]

The sheer accumulation of empirical knowledge of living systems and mechanisms was stunning. It was overshadowed only by some scientists' conviction that critical questions were scarcely beginning to be framed. The very heterogeneity of the field left some of them disturbed: what unified intellectual structure could mediate claims about conflicting approaches and meld these disciplines into a coherent scientific view of life? One conspicuous feature of Weimar science was the presence of institutions and forums where problems like these could be argued out. A "theoretical biology," for instance, might address fundamental questions of evidence and argumentation across the spectrum of the life sciences, yoking together philosophical reflection with hard-won empirical knowledge. That was the project of von Bertalanffy and others who, loosely connected with one another, published in the monograph series *Abhandlungen zur theoretischen Biologie* (*Treatises on Theoretical Biology*), launched in 1919 by the developmental biologist Julius Schaxel (1887–1943). Theoretical biology likewise found a platform—as did many other general-interest topics in the sciences—in the young periodical *Die Naturwissenschaften*, a venue for wide-ranging discussions across scientific specialties, founded 1913 under the editorial guidance of the broad-minded Arnold Berliner (1862–1942).[10]

The aim of theoretical biology, as it was programmatically articulated in these forums, was not just to systematize existing knowledge, but to give real direction to scientific practice. How far it succeeded in that ambition is still unclear. One reason: even though its advocates tried to mark their distance from armchair speculation, for many scientists this was still too much philosophy and too little science. But in the context of the life sciences, one thing "philosophy" meant was simply a degree of self-consciousness about experimental method and explanatory strategy. In practice, theoretical biologists who called for disciplinary self-consciousness were usually criticizing what they considered the field's unquestioned consensus: mechanistic materialism. That is, they were arguing it was a methodological mistake to assume that the phenomena of life could be adequately explained by reducing them the mechanical operation of parts governed by physical and chemical causality, as the pioneers of the nineteenth century's new approaches had demanded. In reaction, various strains of antireductive holism marked much Weimar discussion about the proper direction of biology—at least, among that set of practitioners who did not proceed with chemical and physical reduction as a matter of course. Instead the advocates of methodological reflection urged that new scientific concepts were needed at higher levels of study, namely, tissues, organs, and whole organisms. Sometimes they also took a critical stance towards strict Darwinian theories of inheritance and evolution by natural selection (which, it bears noting, put them in sympathy with many other biologists of the time).[11]

Setting the tone for much of the discussion in this vein, Hans Driesch (1867–1941) had begun thinking about organismal development while experimenting on sea urchin embryos. Driesch believed that if science was to succeed in capturing an individual organism's development, it had to think at a level above cellular processes, introducing a nonmaterial principle that governed development as a whole. He named his directive principle "entelechy" (a term he borrowed from Aristotle) and around it he elaborated a neo-vitalist biology. Likewise, Driesch's colleague Jakob von Uexküll (1864–1944) developed an interest in holistic co-ordinating principles, in his case starting not from embryology, but from questions of sensation and reflex action. Von Uexküll devised ways of describing an organism's relations to its environment (its *Umwelt*) that stood above physiology, operating on an organizationally higher plane. Describing the adaptation of organism to environment was of course a critical task in multiple subfields of biology, so von Uexküll was touching upon questions also prominent in Darwinian thinking. In part because his approach was not tied to specific organisms in their material realization, his arguments would later capture attention far beyond his biologist colleagues. And among Weimar's younger generation, Ludwig von Bertalanffy worked out his own antireductive argument. Without campaigning against materialism (as did Driesch and von Uexküll), von Bertalanffy began exploring the possibility of abstract ("system") descriptions of organismic processes. Physical and chemical laws held in living beings, he thought; but that hardly meant that other levels of concepts and explanations were unnecessary. Von Bertalanffy would eventually make his name as the originator of General Systems Theory, which was taken up in information theory and cybernetics.[12]

Questions of mechanism and reduction were pointed enough when sea urchins eggs were the subject—even though in all of these cases, the particular organism under study served a stand-in for organic life at large. One particular organism still mattered more than the others. Inescapably, scientific methodology took on an intense charge when human beings came into biological view. By the 1920s, a broad range of natural scientific disciplines, from endocrinology to labor physiology, had asserted their relevance for the human body. Adjudicating their claims was a matter of real practical significance, in no small part because therapeutic interventions were built on the shifting foundations of this new biomedicine; and for reasons of politics and profession as well as of science, the Weimar Republic was a period of massive medical contestation.[13] And the mind? Along with the development of psychosomatic (mind-body) medicine and Gestalt psychology—see Mitchell Ash's chapter in this volume—new questions in brain function were opened up for investigation in concentrated research programs as in the Kaiser Wilhelm Institute for Brain Research. Reaching public attention in part through studies of brain-damaged war veterans, in part through deliberate work at the boundary between the laboratory and the public, the wired, connected brain of Weimar neuroscience captured a broader cultural imagination. The material conditioning of consciousness and subjectivity, of course, was a critical point of contact of the natural with the human and cultural sciences.[14]

Holism and antimechanism were scientific strategies. Political discourse and cultural production show they were also intellectual preoccupations at large. Were these strains of life science somehow responsive to a sense of the moment? No one who knows the cultural history of the Weimar Republic will miss its ambivalence vis-à-vis its inheritance from the *Kaiserreich*. The advocates of a methodologically renovated biology shared that attitude. The self-satisfied triumphal rhetoric that science, too, had adopted was turned back on itself.

Mathematics and Physics

The emergent sense of crisis was hardly limited to the life sciences. In Weimar a crisis of foundations was equally perceptible in the seemingly secure domains of mathematics and physics. This other crisis, in fact, was accompanied by disputes that were, if anything, even more trenchant. After all, the mathematicians and physicists supposedly *had* shared foundations, while the biologists lacked them. The disciplinary pillars of mathematics and physics that were coming under attack by the 1920s undergirded an impressive conceptual edifice—though one already showing its own small cracks. We can look at the strife here, too, as a series of debates over method, and thus over what could count as an authoritative, completed system of knowledge. For that reason it makes sense to include mathematics among the natural sciences, even if one of the points under dispute was exactly its relation to the empirical world.

By the Weimar period, mathematics in Germany had striking successes to its credit, both in pure technical results and in openings to practical application. At the same time, disagreement about the nature of the discipline had been stirring for some time; and it was no small matter, nor was it confined to esoteric parts of the field. The so-called *Grundlagenstreit* (conflict over foundations) can be traced back to the nineteenth-century unsettlement of Cantor's set theory, which called into question any kind of naïve basis for mathematics. In Cantor's wake a round of alternative proposals were advanced to put the discipline on a new footing. On one side of the debate in Germany was the towering figure of David Hilbert (1862–1943) and his collaborators, who put forward a vision of mathematics consisting purely in formal symbolic manipulation and sought to formalize all of it in an axiomatic structure. On the other side, critics led by the Dutch mathematician L.E.J. Brouwer (1881–1966) insisted that mathematics define its terrain in terms of constructions in the mathematician's mind and step back from concepts not constructible in that way—even if large chunks of earlier mathematics, once considered justified, now went by the wayside.

In 1921 a polemical essay by Hermann Weyl (1885–1955) formally announced the advent of "the new foundational crisis in mathematics." Weyl marked his own change of allegiance to Brouwer (he had been a student of Hilbert) by calling for a revolutionary new approach. In the highly public tug-of-war between Hilbert's formalism and Brouwer's intuitionism that played out in the German-speaking mathematical community over the next decade, intuitionism was indeed sometimes presented as a radical revision of so-called classical mathematics, willing to pay the price for leaving that secure world behind. However, Hilbert had no less of a claim to be the torch-bearer of modernity. He tried to guarantee the integrity of mathematics' axiomatic formalization while cutting its symbols loose from outside reference and reconstructing their use as a kind of linguistic game. Hilbert's ambition to carry out the axiomatization of all of mathematics set Kurt Gödel (1906–1978) on the path to proving his famous incompleteness theorems, work he carried out in Austria and published in 1931.[15]

As for physics, whatever outsiders imagined to be its triumphal program of mechanical reduction, by Weimar the discipline had in fact moved toward a more complicated stance. Coming out of the nineteenth century, its fundamental challenge was in fact how to hammer together its *different* theoretical structures: alongside Newtonian mechanics, also electromagnetism and thermodynamics. Electromagnetic theory after Faraday and Maxwell had made physicists more comfortable operating with abstract field notions, which stood at a distance from Newtonian matter-in-motion, while statistical mechanics had grown in plausibility as a stand-alone approach to physical explanation, rewriting thermodynamics (the science of heat and energy) by trading exact mechanical knowledge at a low level for powerful statistical laws at a high one. By the *fin de siècle*, disputes over electromagnetic and energetic alternatives to a mechanical world picture crossed with a phenomenological shift among some practitioners (phenomenological in the scientific sense: merely describing the phenomena). This shift let theorists continue making elaborate explanatory structures, so long as they understood them as models or analogies, a challenge to ontological commitment *tout court*. Certainly, ordinary experimental research—measuring thermal conductivity of solids, deciphering optical properties of materials, describing transmission behavior of electromagnetic waves in the atmosphere—could proceed largely untouched by foundational dispute. However, starting around the turn of the century, some relatively small problems at the boundaries of particular domains of physics grew to be seen as forcing revisions in the methodological commitment of scientists, not to mention any kind of physical world picture at large.[16]

The sense of crisis that some physicists evoked in the 1920s actually came from the cumulation of two distinct provocations. Einsteinian relativity and quantum mechanics overlapped only slightly in application. Historically, however, they were interpreted into a coherent series of challenges; and along the way, classical physics was marked out as the supposed consensus from which they broke.[17] Relativity, to begin with, responded initially to certain conceptual unclarities in electromagnetism in relation to mechanics. Addressing these seemingly formal theoretical problems, relativity ended up reworking the framework of mechanics itself. In 1905, looking to bring a kind of invariance into the equations of electromagnetism, Albert Einstein (1879–1955) proposed to treat space and time as bound together in an abstract four-dimensional unity. Space and time could be transformed into one another—in ways, in fact, that depended on how an observer was moving through them. In creating this hybrid Einstein dispensed with any absolute space and time, as well as their operational consequence, an ether against whose backdrop physical processes (electromagnetic or otherwise) would unfold. This move was abstractly disconcerting, although any new effects only showed up when material bodies were moving near the speed of light. In 1915 Einstein went further by suggesting that spacetime was deformed near heavy bodies, bringing about deviations from Euclidean geometry. As conceptually unsettling as that was, too—gravity as a warping of the space-time fabric?—it was even more remote in its observable consequences, which showed up only for extremely heavy masses and huge, even cosmological distances. Thus the theory initially attracted little public attention in its 1905 version (called "special relativity")—nor, in fact, in its 1915 expansion ("general relativity"). In November 1919, however, that would change. A tiny but important deviation from previous theories was announced in results of a British expedition to measure the bending of starlight around the sun in a total eclipse. Coming amid the chaos of revolution and the new Weimar Republic, Einstein's confirmation made his four-dimensional non-Euclidean universe into a cultural fascination.[18]

For its part, quantum theory originated at the interface between electromagnetism and thermodynamics. Early work on the quantization (discreteness) of light and energy by Max Planck (1858–1947) and Albert Einstein certainly posed problems for established physical theory. However, it was first in the early 1920s, in the hands of a new group of theorists, that the quantum came to appear threatening to the theoretical edifice as a whole.[19] The focus of this contention was the quantum theory of atomic structure, whose leading figures were the Danish physicist Niels Bohr (1885–1962) and two doyens of modern theoretical physics in Germany, Arnold Sommerfeld (1868–1961) and Max Born (1888–1970). Atomic structure forced quantum considerations into mechanics, since the subatomic construction of atoms—electrons moving in space and time—stood at the center of its practice. Arguing from the failure of modeling to account for the frequencies of light emitted by atoms, Bohr and Born propagated the idea that atomic-scale phenomena required a radical departure from past theory: if not abandoning space-time pictures inside the atom, then constructing a new mechanics for it. When Werner Heisenberg (1901–1976) created quantum mechanics in 1925, he believed he was doing just that.[20]

Crisis, then, was resolved by breaking through to a new order. The interpretative consequences that came in the wake of quantum mechanics—uncertainty and limits to physical knowledge, acausality and the solely statistical nature of the theory's predictions, restrictions on objectivity and a new role for the observer—felt to its apostles like a price they were willing to pay. Others were far less persuaded. Erwin Schrödinger (1887–1961) in fact developed, independently of Heisenberg, an alternative account that handled everything that Heisenberg's mechanics could, just far more conveniently, and came with less of an epistemological price (as long as one was ontologically willing to dissolve matter into an assemblage of waves). Thus the later 1920s were a high point of methodological contention. The strongest resistance to Bohr-Heisenberg came from other physicists who understood quantum mechanics as well as anyone, but held up a different standard of what counted as science. When Planck or Einstein raised questions, they were concerned above all that canons of scientific explanation (cause and effect, objective reality) were being too readily sacrificed.[21]

If Heisenberg's and Schrödinger's formalisms delivered the same results, then on what basis could one choose between them? In practice, test cases and thought experiments shut down many objections to the Bohr-Heisenberg line. But some of the work, interestingly, was done by implicitly historical arguments. Quantum mechanics was presented as a departure from nineteenth-century classical physics, in a multi-step process beginning with relativity theory. Just as relativity abandoned absolute space and time, so quantum mechanics gave up physical values independent of the act of observing; just as relativity pulled back from Euclidean strictures, so quantum mechanics loosened causality from deterministic to probabilistic. And just as relativity introduced new notions as science moved into one domain outside ordinary experience, so quantum mechanics brought in its own concepts as it entered another.[22] That is, the historical advancement of science did not proceed linearly; its practitioners had to be prepared to renounce old strategies and bring in new approaches.

Skeptics had other historical questions—whether quantum mechanics, for one thing, rather than being grounded in scientific necessity, was actually derivative of a Weimar intellectual environment hostile to mechanical causality.[23] As hard as that question is to answer, one thing is clear: many of the founders of quantum mechanics were invested in themes that preoccupied other scientific theorists of crisis. Stepping outside of physics, Bohr and Heisenberg both believed, like von Bertalanffy, that organized living beings called for scientific concepts that stood independent of physics and chemistry. That is, they took quantum mechanics to drive home the point that *all* theories were appropriate to particular scales and levels of organization. Without denying a material basis for organic phenomena, they argued for the conceptual irreducibility of biology to physics. Methodological reductionism could be called into question from the bottom up, not just the top down.[24]

Questions of Method and Knowledge

In Weimar, as we have seen, the life sciences, mathematics, and physics all witnessed disputes over foundations. But what was at stake was not necessarily foundations in a material or metaphysical sense. Rather than affinities between specific ideas—neovitalism, intuitionism, indeterminacy—what held these varied disciplinary developments together was the demand for methodological reflection. Behind all the specific proposals, the biggest issue up for debate was the route to trustworthy knowledge.

Thus a series of historically specific conjunctions delineated the very possibility of "Weimar science." Those who spoke of a revolutionary moment shared, first of all, the belief that nineteenth-century scientific strategies were showing their limits in practice. That is, the triumphant progress of science was not going to continue on its inherited basis, in whatever way that nineteenth-century framework was defined. Self-consciousness was needed, and self-conscious change. It should be no surprise that concern for methodological and epistemological reflection went hand-in-hand with the spectacular ascent of self-consciously theoretical sciences.[25] Second, theorists of crisis worked by criticizing past foundational attempts. Implicitly or explicitly, they thereby acknowledged the possibility that even in science, foundational attempts could go *wrong*. Looking back on the period, Heisenberg would observe: "It is not by chance that the development that led to this end [in quantum mechanics] no longer took place in a time of belief in progress. After the catastrophe of the First World War one understood outside of scholarship as well that there were no firm foundations for our existence, secure for all time."[26] And third, they shared the sense of witnessing, in their own day, a critical moment in the scientific enterprise. After the massive acceleration that characterized the *Kaiserreich*, empirical knowledge was being generated at a rate never remotely approached in the past. Statesmen of science complained about rampant specialization and loss of a unified picture. Yet this was more than nostalgia for a coherent world now lost. The crying need was for reflection to help with what Hans Reichenbach (1891–1953) described at the end of the 1920s as the "necessary form of modern productivity in the sciences . . . this machine age knowledge" that left scientists with little time for philosophical analysis—the same situation Martin Heidegger (1889–1976) apostrophized more critically as "the tendency of science to become entangled in its facts."[27]

Reichenbach's and Heidegger's comments suggest, of course, how powerfully these observations resonated outside the community of natural scientists. And here especially, we see how well natural science fit with central preoccupations of the Weimar intellectual mainstream. Advocates of a new science joined in attacking the bogeyman of positivism, understood as a kind of methodological *un*-self-consciousness. In the background, for those aware of it, was the turn-of-the-century discussion around Dilthey, Windelband, Rickert, Cohen, and Natorp over the character of *Wissenschaft*, specifically, the distinct strategies attributed to the natural sciences. The central role of the phenomenology of Edmund Husserl (1859–1938), too, can hardly be overestimated; it sometimes seems that every Weimar contributor to debates over science had spent time in Husserl's orbit. By the 1920s these arguments had ramified into sharply marked-out positions in philosophical debates over the future of neo-Kantianism or rising alternatives to it. It bears underlining that philosophers' arguments scarcely registered with many scientific practitioners. However, to those scientists interested in theorizing Weimar science, connections were many and dense on the ground.

For the life sciences, *Lebensphilosophie* opened an obvious door, though what difference it actually made it is harder to say. Driesch's neo-vitalism can certainly be understood in *lebensphilosophischen* terms. However, during the Weimar period Driesch occupied a chair in philosophy and to a great many scientists seemed to have left science behind. For active professional biologists,

Kant functioned as a more familiar touchstone for reflective musings in essays and public addresses.[28] And plenty of philosophers seized on what the biologists were saying. Heidegger devoted extensive space to Driesch and von Uexküll in his late-1920s lecture courses; Ernst Cassirer (1874–1945) was profoundly responsive to ideas coming out of theoretical biology. The strain of philosophical anthropology, too, that was carried by Max Scheler (1874–1928) and Helmuth Plessner (1892–1995) played off the life sciences.[29] As has recently been pointed out sheerly by listing journal publications, the philosophy of biology was part of German-language philosophy of science from the start.[30]

Among mathematics, physics, and philosophy, ultimately, the connections were no less tight. Husserl was just the most visible of a good number of philosophers who had trained in mathematics before moving on, sometimes via the halfway house of logic, to other, more conspicuously philosophical concerns. It is true that a minority of practicing physicists and mathematics had serious grounding in philosophy. However, those who did tended to be attracted to foundational problems in mathematics or in the theoretical part of physics. They found that the scientific crises of the day spoke to pressing concerns about space, time, and perception; realism, idealism, or formalism; and the possibility of objective empirical knowledge.[31] Hermann Weyl, for one, carried his admiration for Husserlian phenomenology not just into his mathematical work, but also his famous text on relativity theory (*Raum, Zeit, Materie*). In the discussion surrounding relativity, indeed, many of the participants were hard to sort into professional camps. While Einstein was clearly a physicist and Cassirer a philosopher, there was Moritz Schlick (1882–1936), a Planck Ph.D. who moved into philosophy, and Rudolf Carnap (1891–1970), whose Jena dissertation was too physical for many philosophers and too philosophical for many physicists.[32] Arguments over the Kantian *a priori* in relativity then carried over, sometimes in bowdlerized form, to quantum mechanics, where statistical causality or objectivity became good topics for debate. The possibility that quantum physics could reflect on the conditions of possibility of its knowledge even briefly inspired Heidegger, against his own grain, to hold up Bohr and Heisenberg as exemplars of a science that could think. The significance of Weimar's *Grundlagenkrisis* for the thinking of Heidegger, no less than Husserl, is beginning to come into view.[33]

A Scientific Philosophy?

Out of Weimar-era exchanges over scientific knowledge and method, there emerged two critically influential intellectual movements outside the empirical sciences. The first has already been signaled via the participants in the relativity discussion. As a philosophical program, logical empiricism (sometimes called logical positivism) was firmly anchored in 1920s disputes over the future of neo-Kantianism in an age of onrushing natural science. Logical empiricism was not just the work of the Vienna Circle, as it is sometimes presented. In Berlin, Hans Reichenbach stood at the center of a dense network of contacts that was formalized in the Society for Empirical (later Scientific) Philosophy. Rather than a monolithic movement borne by professionally certified philosophers, logical empiricism in Weimar was a venue for exchanges—between scientists of varied backgrounds who believed they might have something to learn from one another, and philosophers who considered the empirical sciences to be the overwhelming innovative force in contemporary intellectual life. Among the speakers in the Berlin Society's lecture series were logicians, biologists, psychologists, mathematicians, and physicists, along with philosophers of different persuasions. Reichenbach and Rudolf Carnap, by then in Vienna, together edited the journal *Erkenntnis* starting in 1930. *Erkenntnis* quickly became another venue for a relatively wide range of reflections on the method and significance of science.[34]

Because of the logical empiricists' later reputation as dismissive of all philosophy ("metaphysics") except their own, and of all intellectual endeavors except the hardest of natural sciences, it has been too easily forgotten how tightly knit they initially were into the broader debates of their day.[35] The Vienna Circle has recently been opened up to a wider range of historical preoccupations; the Berlin group awaits comparable attention. It is already clear, however, that it was not just new foundational efforts in physics or mathematics that attracted logical empiricists' attention. Biology belonged to their interests, too. We now know a great deal about some of the logical empiricists' openness to seeing affinities between their project and architectural modernism (*Neue Sachlichkeit/Bauhaus*), a range of left reform movements, even Frankfurt School social theory. If this was a scientific philosophy for a scientific age, the term "scientific" was expansively defined.[36]

Putting Science into Historical Time

There is a final contribution of Weimar to our thinking about science, a contribution that often goes unremarked. That era of methodological reflection, with its talk of revolution and crisis, began fitting science into human historical timescales. Weimar ideas about the temporality of science seemed initially to stay confined to German-speaking Central Europe, which is not where the history of science, as it is practiced today, has usually looked for its disciplinary roots.[37] All the same, the connections are curious and significant, reminding us that today's ways of speaking about science's history have historical origins of their own.

One sort of historical attentiveness showed up in initiatives toward a historically minded sociology of science. Practitioners of an emergent sociology of knowledge—Helmuth Plessner, for instance—took their lead from what they saw all around them in contemporary science. Less interested in the social structures of the scientific profession per se, and more in how those structures fit into their historical moment, Plessner gave analytic grounding to perceptions like Reichenbach's of a linkage between the contemporary pursuit of science and the mechanized progress of rationalized industrial organization. In fact, Plessner intimated that the orientation of modern science (he might have said: modern physical science) to predictability, objectivity, and mathematization put its contemplative side in lockstep with its practical use. As much as the theoretical arguments advanced by Karl Mannheim (1893–1947), whose remarks on the perspectivity of knowledge in *Ideology and Utopia* attracted much attention in Weimar (and later played out in complicated ways in one kind of sociology of scientific knowledge), it was accounts like Plessner's, growing out of philosophical anthropology, that influenced Weimar's sense of the researcher's historical world.[38]

Other theorists, equally interested in the contemporary scientific enterprise, felt driven to characterize the grand historical arc of science. When Oswald Spengler (1880–1936) wrote *The Decline of the West*, he certainly fit in this camp, speculating as he did on the ongoing crisis in mathematics and science.[39] But so did other intellectuals who, though they became less of a popular sensation, had significantly more influence on later understandings of science. It seems likely that the portrait of scientific modernity that can be found equally in Heidegger and the Frankfurt School, just taking shape as Weimar passed away, owed much to what they believed they saw in their present: an overwhelmingly positivist science bereft of reflection, as long as it satisfied instrumental demands for practical use. Reading their own moment partially, then generalizing it backward, these authors were practicing their own kind of history of the present. When they tried to capture the essence of science, after all, they were most interested in scoping out the potential for change that the current crisis might still contain.[40] Their narrative resonated with others that had come together in Germany since the turn of the century. The story of the birth of modern science with Descartes, Galileo, and Newton, whether it was Cassirer or Husserl who told it, became *the* central narrative of the history of science. None of these accounts focused on individual facts, discoveries, or theories. Attuned to the crisis at hand, they spotlighted the emergence of the new science's methodological and epistemological stances. And in all of their narratives—and, most influentially for historians, in the work of Husserl's one-time student Alexandre Koyré (1892–1964)—science appeared to arise at the same time, by the same processes, as the rest of Western modernity. Their accounts allowed (in fact, insisted) that science's dynamic could only effectively be grasped by coupling it to human history at large.[41]

This was a quite different kind of history from that which scientists had told earlier, as examples of which Mach's critical histories come to mind.[42] Yet in the eyes of its practitioners, the impetus for the new human history of science was hardly external to science. It was the lesson of recent developments *within* science itself. In his Frankfurt School monograph on the origins of the bourgeois world picture, Franz Borkenau (1900–1957) expressed the reason most powerfully: Displaying notions of lawfulness, causality, or mathematization, he wrote, as

> impermanent, historically conditioned forms of thought . . . might have been taken even a few decades ago as an attack on the most certain knowledge we have. It cannot be conceived that way any longer, since the most recent development of physics has put into doubt the foundational categories of modern natural science and thereby shown their historical impermanence.[43]

In fact, this point of view was not foreign to the logical empiricists, who held up natural science as a model for knowledge.[44] And while far from universal among practicing scientists, the position was not totally outré. Some scientists, marking the removal of earlier strictures, found it methodologically and epistemically compelling to historicize the knowledge they had helped to create.[45] For those who lived through the crisis, it felt reasonable to expand their own experience to the history of science at large.

Just like Weimar itself, this moment of historical-methodological reflection had its end. With stunning effectiveness, the Third Reich dispersed the participants and shut down their intellectual exchange.[46] Many of the ideas they were debating did poorly in exile, absent either the neo-Kantian prehistory or the backdrop of intradisciplinary disputes over method. However, by indirect routes, Weimar thinking about scientific revolution found new audiences, even when its historical provenance was forgotten along the way.[47]

Notes

1. Alan Beyerchen, "On the Stimulation of Excellence in Wilhelmian Science," in *Another Germany: A Reconsideration of the Imperial Era*, eds. Jack R. Dukes and Joachim Remak (Boulder: Westview, 1988), 139–68; Margit Szöllösi-Janze, "Science and Social Space: Transformations in the Institutions of *Wissenschaft* from the Wilhelmine Empire to the Weimar Republic," *Minerva* 43, no. 4 (2005), 339–60.

2. Werner von Siemens, "Das naturwissenschaftliche Zeitalter," in *Forschung und Fortschritt: Festschrift zum 175 jährigen Jübilaum der Gesellschaft deutscher Naturforscher und Ärzte*, ed. Dietrich von Engelhardt (Stuttgart: Wissenschaftliche Verlagsgesellschaft, 1997), 167–74.

3. Russell McCormmach, "On Academic Scientists in Wilhelmian Germany," in *Science and its Public: The Changing Relationship*, eds. Gerald Holton and William A. Blanpied (Dordrecht: D. Reidel, 1976), 157–71; Paul Forman, "Weimar Culture, Causality, and Quantum Theory, 1918–1927: Adaptation by German Physicists and Mathematicians to a Hostile Intellectual Environment," *Historical Studies in the Physical Sciences* 3 (1971), 1–115; Wolfgang J. Mommsen, "Kultur und Wissenschaft im kulturellen System des Wilhelminismus: Die Entzauberung der Welt durch Wissenschaft und ihre Verzauberung durch Kunst und Literatur," in *Kultur und Kulturwissenschaften um 1900*, eds. Gangolf Hübinger, Rüdiger vom Bruch, and Friedrich Wilhelm Graf, vol. 2, *Idealismus und Positivismus* (Stuttgart: Franz Steiner, 1997), 24–40.

4. Max Weber, "Science as a Vocation," in *Essays in Sociology*, trans. and eds. H. H. Gerth and C. Wright Mills (New York: Oxford University Press, 1946), 129–56, on 142.

5. For an entrée see Rüdiger vom Bruch and Brigitte Kaderas, eds., *Wissenschaften und Wissenschaftspolitik: Bestandaufnahme zu Formationen, Brüchen und Kontinuitäten im Deutschland des 20. Jahrhunderts* (Stuttgart: Franz Steiner, 2002).

6. Moritz Föllmer and Rüdiger Graf, eds., *Die "Krise" der Weimarer Republik: Zur Kritik eines Deutungsmusters* (Frankfurt: Campus, 2005).

7. Ludwig von Bertalanffy, *Modern Theories of Development: An Introduction to Theoretical Biology*, trans. J. H. Woodger (London: Oxford University Press, 1933), 1.

8. Eugenics and racial hygiene have been well-explored. See Paul Weindling, *Health, Race, and German Politics between National Unification and Nazism, 1870–1945* (Cambridge: Cambridge University Press, 1989); Sheila Faith Weiss, "The German Race Hygiene Movement," *Osiris* 3 (1987), 196–236; Robert Proctor, *Racial Hygiene: Medicine under the Nazis* (Cambridge, MA: Harvard University Press, 1988); Peter Weingart, Jürgen Kroll, and Kurt Bayertz, *Rasse, Blut und Gene: Geschichte der Eugenik und Rassenhygiene in Deutschland* (Frankfurt: Suhrkamp, 1988).

9. A good introduction is Ulrich Sucker, *Das Kaiser-Wilhelm-Institut für Biologie: Seine Gründungsgeschichte, seine problemgeschichtlichen und wissenschaftstheoretischen Voraussetzungen* (Stuttgart: Franz Steiner, 2002); in English see Jonathan Harwood, *Styles of Scientific Thought: The German Genetics Community, 1900–1933* (Chicago: University of Chicago Press, 1993).

10. Manfred D. Laubichler, "Mit oder ohne Darwin? Die Bedeutung der Selektionstheorie in der Konzeption der Theoretischen Biologie in Deutschland vom 1900 bis zum Zweiten Weltkrieg," in *Darwinismus und/als Ideologie*, eds. Uwe Hoßfeld and Rainer Brämer (Berlin: Verlag für Wissenschaft und Bildung, 2001), 229–62; Christian Reiß, "No Evolution, No Heredity, Just Development—Julius Schaxel and the End of the Evo-Devo Agenda in Jena, 1906–1933: A Case Study," *Theory in Biosciences* 126, no. 4 (2007), 155–64.

11. For background see Kurt Bayertz, Myriam Gerhard, and Walter Jaeschke, eds., *Weltanschauung, Philosophie und Naturwissenschaft im 19. Jahrhundert* (Hamburg: Felix Meiner, 2007).

12. Anne Harrington, *Reenchanted Science: Holism in German Culture from Wilhelm II to Hitler* (Princeton: Princeton University Press, 1996); Garland E. Allen, "Mechanism, Vitalism and Organicism in Late Nineteenth and Twentieth-Century Biology: The Importance of Historical Context," *Studies in History and Philosophy of Science C* 36, no. 2 (2005), 261–83; Jonathan Harwood, "Weimar Culture and Biological Theory: A Study of Richard Woltereck," *History of Science* 34 (1996), 347–77. Von Bertalanffy's biological theorizing is still in need of historical attention.

13. Anson Rabinbach, *The Human Motor: Energy, Fatigue, and the Origins of Modernity* (New York: Basic Books, 1990); Cay-Rüdiger Prüll, "Holism and German Pathology (1914–1933)," in *Greater Than the Parts: Holism in Biomedicine, 1920–1950*, eds. Christopher Lawrence and George Weisz (New York: Oxford University Press, 1998), 46–67; Carsten Timmermann, "Constitutional Medicine, Neoromanticism, and the Politics of Antimechanism in Interwar Germany," *Bulletin of the History of Medicine* 75 (2001), 717–39.

14. Michael Hagner, ed., *Ecce Cortex: Beiträge zur Geschichte des modernen Gehirns* (Göttingen: Wallstein, 1999); Cornelius Borck, *Hirnströme: Eine Kulturgeschichte der Elektroenzephalographie* (Göttingen: Wallstein, 2006); in English, Cornelius Borck, "Electricity as a Medium of Psychic Life: Electrotechnological Adventures into Psychodiagnosis in Weimar Germany," *Science in Context* 14, no. 4 (2001), 565–90; Andreas Killen, *Berlin Electropolis: Shock, Nerves, and German Modernity* (Berkeley: University of California Press, 2006). On the methodology of psychology, Michael Hagner, "Naturphilosophie, Sinnesphysiologie, Allgemeine Medizin: Wendungen der Psychosomatik bei Viktor von Weizsäcker," in *Der Hochsitz des Wissens: Das Allgemeine als wissenschaftlicher Wert*, eds. Michael Hagner and Manfred Laubichler (Zürich: Diaphenes, 2006), 315–36; Mitchell Ash, *Gestalt Psychology in German Culture, 1890–1967: Holism and the Quest for Objectivity* (Cambridge: Cambridge University Press, 1995).

15. Paolo Mancosu, ed., *From Brouwer to Hilbert: The Debate on the Foundations of Mathematics in the 1920s* (New York: Oxford University Press, 1998); Herbert Mehrtens, *Moderne Sprache Mathematik: Eine Geschichte des Streits um die Grundlagen der Disziplin und des Subjekts formaler Systeme* (Frankfurt: Suhrkamp, 1990); Jeremy Gray, *Plato's Ghost: The Modernist Transformation of Mathematics* (Princeton: Princeton University Press, 2008); Dirk van Dalen, *Mystic, Geometer, and Intuitionist: The Life of L.E.J. Brouwer*, vol. 2, *Hope and Disillusion* (Oxford: Oxford University Press, 2005); Richard Zach, "Hilbert's Program," in *The Stanford Encyclopedia of Philosophy* (Fall 2008 ed.), ed. Edward N. Zalta, http://plato.stanford.edu/archives/fall2008/entries/hilbert-program/.

16. J. L. Heilbron, "Fin-de-siècle Physics," in *Science, Technology, and Society in the Time of Alfred Nobel*, eds. Carl Gustaf Bernhard, Elisabeth Crawford, and Per Sörbom (Oxford: Pergamon, 1981), 51–73. Theodore M. Porter, "The Death of the Object: 'Fin de siècle' Philosophy of Physics," in *Modernist Impulses in the Human Sciences, 1870–1930*, ed. Dorothy Ross (Baltimore: Johns Hopkins University Press, 1994), 128–51; Richard Staley, "The Fin de Siècle Thesis," *Berichte zur Wissenschaftsgeschichte* 31, no. 4 (2008), 311–30. For a recent entry point into statistics, see Deborah R. Coen, *Vienna in the Age of Uncertainty: Science, Liberalism, and Private Life* (Chicago: University of Chicago Press, 2007).

17. Suman Seth, "Crisis and the Construction of Modern Theoretical Physics," *British Journal for the History of Science* 40, no. 1 (2007), 25–51; Richard Staley, "On the Co-Creation of Classical and Modern Physics," *Isis* 96 (2005), 530–58; Richard Staley, *Einstein's Generation: The Origins of the Relativity Revolution* (Chicago: University of Chicago Press, 2008).

18. Points of entry are Albert Einstein, *Relativity: The Special and the General Theory* (New York: Penguin, 2006); Gerald Holton and Yehuda Elkana, eds., *Albert Einstein: Historical and Cultural Perspectives* (Princeton: Princeton University Press, 1982).

19. A general, if somewhat technical, introduction is Helge Kragh, *Quantum Generations: A History of Physics in the Twentieth Century* (Princeton: Princeton University Press, 1999).

20. Two culturally attentive biographies are Nancy Greenspan, *The End of the Certain World: The Life and Science of Max Born, the Nobel Physicist who Ignited the Quantum Revolution* (New York: Basic, 2005); David C. Cassidy, *Uncertainty: The Life and Science of Werner Heisenberg* (New York: W. H. Freeman, 1992). See also Suman Seth, *Crafting the Quantum: Arnold Sommerfeld and the Practice of Theory, 1890–1926* (Cambridge, MA: MIT Press, 2010).

21. Arthur Fine, *The Shaky Game: Einstein, Realism, and the Quantum Theory* (Chicago: University of Chicago Press, 1986); Mara Beller, *Quantum Dialogue: The Making of a Revolution* (Chicago: University of Chicago Press, 1999).

22. E.g., Werner Heisenberg, "Recent Changes in the Foundation of Exact Science," in *Philosophical Problems of Quantum Physics* (Woodbridge, CT: Oxbow Press, 1979), 11–26.

23. Forman, "Weimar Culture, Causality, and Quantum Theory"; Cathryn Carson, Alexei Kojevnikov, and Helmuth Trischler, eds., *Weimar Culture and Quantum Mechanics: Selected Papers by Paul Forman and Contemporary Perspectives on the Forman Thesis* (London: Imperial College Press, 2011).

24. Niels Bohr, "Light and Life," in *Essays 1932–1957 on Atomic Physics and Human Knowledge* (Woodbridge, CT: Oxbow Press, 1963), 3–12; Werner Heisenberg, *Ordnung der Wirklichkeit* (Munich: Piper, 1989), available in an ongoing translation project as "Reality and its Order" at http://werner-heisenberg.unh.edu/t-OdW-english.htm.

25. Seth, "Crisis and Construction"; Manfred D. Laubichler, "Allgemeine Biologie als selbständige Grundwissenschaft und die allgemeinen Grundlagen des Lebens," in *Der Hochsitz des Wissens: Das Allgemeine als wissenschaftlicher Wert*, eds. Michael Hagner and Manfred Laubichler (Zürich: Diaphenes, 2006), 185–205.

26. Werner Heisenberg, "Die Beziehungen zwischen Physik und Chemie in den letzten 75 Jahren," in *Gesammelte Werke / Collected Works*, eds. Walter Blum, Hans-Peter Dürr, and Helmut Rechenberg, vol. C.I (Munich: Piper, 1984), 387–93, on 389.

27. Hans Reichenbach, *The Philosophy of Space and Time*, trans. Maria Reichenbach and John Freund (New York: Dover, 1958), xiii; Martin Heidegger, *The Fundamental Concepts of Metaphysics: World, Finitude, Solitude*, trans. William McNeill and Nicholas Walker (Bloomington: Indiana University Press, 1995), 217.

28. Driesch veered into parapsychology; he also published on *Relativitätstheorie und Weltanschauung* (Leipzig: Quelle & Meyer, 1930). Along with Driesch and von Uexküll, Max Hartmann has been studied in detail: Heng-An Chen, *Die Sexualitätstheorie und "Theoretische Biologie" von Max Hartmann in der ersten Hälfte des zwanzigsten Jahrhunderts* (Stuttgart: Steiner, 2003), chap. 11.

29. On Cassirer, who is attracting ever more attention, see John Michael Krois, "Ernst Cassirer's Philosophy of Biology," *Sign Systems Studies* 32, no. 1–2 (2004), 277–95; Gregory B. Moynahan, "Ernst Cassirer, Theoretical Biology, and the Clever Hans Phenomenon," *Science in Context* 12, no. 4 (1999), 549–74; Barend von Heusden, "Jakob von Uexküll and Ernst Cassirer," *Semiotica* 134 (2001), 275–92; for Scheler and Plessner, who are still under-studied, see Max Scheler, *Die Stellung des Menschen im Kosmos* (Darmstadt: Reichl, 1928); Helmuth Pleßner, *Die Stufen des Organischen und der Mensch* (Berlin: de Gruyter, 1928).

30. Jason M. Byron, "Whence Philosophy of Biology?" *British Journal for the Philosophy of Science* 58 (2007), 409–22.

31. For illustrations see Theodore Kisiel, "On the Dimensions of a Phenomenology of Science in Husserl and the Young Dr. Heidegger," *Journal of the British Society for Phenomenology* 4 (1973), 217–34; Peter Eli Gordon, "Realism, Science, and the Deworlding of the World," in *The Blackwell Companion to Phenomenology and Existentialism*, eds. Hubert L. Dreyfus and Mark A. Wrathall (Oxford: Blackwell, 2006), 425–44; Volker Peckhaus, *Hilbertprogramm und kritische Philosophie: Das Göttinger Modell interdisziplinärer Zusammenarbeit zwischen Mathematik und Philosophie* (Göttingen: Vandenhoeck & Ruprecht, 1990).

32. Hermann Weyl, *Space—Time—Matter*, trans. Henry L. Brose (London: Methuen, 1922); Michael Friedman, "Carnap and Weyl on the Foundations of Geometry and Relativity Theory," *Erkenntnis* 42 (1995), 247–60. For good overviews see Thomas Ryckman, *The Reign of Relativity: Philosophy in Physics, 1915–1925* (Oxford: Oxford University Press, 2005); from the side of physics, Klaus Hentschel, *Interpretationen und Fehlinterpretationen der speziellen und der allgemeinen Relativitätstheorie durch Zeitgenossen Albert Einsteins* (Basel: Birkhäuser, 1990). For consequences in the philosophy of science see Don Howard, "Einstein and the Development of Twentieth-Century Philosophy of Science," in *The Cambridge Companion to Einstein*, eds. Michel Janssen and Christoph Lehner, forthcoming.

33. Michael Stöltzner, "Die Kausalitätsdebatte in den *Naturwissenschaften*: Zu einem Milieuproblem in Formans These," in *Wissensgesellschaft: Transformationen im Verhältnis von Wissenschaft und Alltag*, eds. H. Franz, W. Kogge, T. Möller, and T. Wilholt (Bielefeld: Institut für Wissenschafts- und Technikforschung, 2001), 85–128. On Heidegger see Cathryn Carson, "Science as Instrumental Reason: Heidegger,

Habermas, Heisenberg," *Continental Philosophy Review* 42 (2010), 483–509; Cathryn Carson, "Modern or Antimodern Science? Weimar Culture, Natural Science, and the Heidegger-Heisenberg Exchange," in *Weimar Culture and Quantum Mechanics*, 523–42. Heidegger's 1935 reference to Bohr and Heisenberg is found in "Modern Science, Metaphysics, and Mathematics," in *Basic Writings*, ed. David Farrell Krell (San Francisco: Harper Collins, 1993), 267–305, on 272.

34. Dieter Hoffmann, "The Society for Empirical/Scientific Philosophy," in *The Cambridge Companion to Logical Empiricism*, eds. Alan Richardson and Thomas Uebel (Cambridge: Cambridge University Press, 2007), 41–57; Lutz Danneberg, Andreas Kamlah, and Lothar Schäfer, eds., *Hans Reichenbach und die Berliner Gruppe* (Braunschweig: Vieweg, 1994).

35. Michael Friedman, *A Parting of the Ways: Carnap, Cassirer, and Heidegger* (Chicago: Open Court, 2000).

36. Veronika Hofer, "Philosophy of Biology around the Vienna Circle: Ludwig von Bertalanffy, Joseph Henry Woodger and Philipp Frank," in *History of Philosophy of Science: New Trends and Perspectives*, eds. Michael Heidelberger and Friedrich Stadler (Dordrecht: Kluwer Academic, 2002), 325–33; Byron, "Whence Philosophy of Biology?"; Peter Galison, "Aufbau/Bauhaus: Logical Positivism and Architectural Modernism," *Critical Inquiry* 16, no. 4 (1990), 709–52; Angela Potochnik and Audrey Yap, "Revisiting Galison's 'Aufbau/Bauhaus' in Light of Neurath's Philosophical Projects," *Studies in History and Philosophy of Science* 37 (2006), 469–88; Hans-Joachim Dahms, "*Neue Sachlichkeit* in the Architecture and Philosophy of the 1920s," in *Carnap Brought Home: The View from Jena*, eds. Steve Awodey and Carsten Klein (Chicago: Open Court, 2004), 357–75; Hans-Joachim Dahms, *Positivismusstreit: Die Auseinandersetzung der Frankfurter Schule mit dem logischen Positivismus, dem amerikanischen Pragmatismus und dem kritischen Rationalismus* (Frankfurt: Suhrkamp, 1994).

37. For the Anglophone discipline see, e.g., Margaret W. Rossiter, ed., *Catching up with the Vision: Essays on the Occasion of the 75th Anniversary of the Founding of the History of Science Society*, Supplement to *Isis* 90 (1999); Jan Golinski, *Making Natural Knowledge: Constructivism and the History of Science* (Chicago: University of Chicago Press, 1995). A separate French tradition starting from Gaston Bachelard and Georges Canguilhem has more affinities to Weimar discussions. A point of entry is David Hyder, "Foucault, Cavaillès, and Husserl on the Historical Epistemology of the Sciences," in *Science and the Life-World: Essays on Husserl's "Crisis of European Sciences,"* eds. David Hyder and Hans-Jörg Rheinberger (Stanford: Stanford University Press, 2010), 177–98.

38. Helmuth Pleßner, "Zur Soziologie der modernen Forschung und ihrer Organisation in der deutschen Universität," in *Versuche eine Soziologie des Wissens*, ed. Max Scheler (Munich: Duncker & Humblot, 1924), 407–25; Max Scheler, *Die Wissensformen und die Gesellschaft: Probleme einer Soziologie des Wissens* (Leipzig: Der Neue Geist, 1926); Karl Mannheim, *Ideology and Utopia: An Introduction to the Sociology of Knowledge*, trans. Louis Wirth and Edward Shils (New York: Harcourt, Brace, 1946); David Frisby, *The Alienated Mind: The Sociology of Knowledge in Germany 1918–1933* (London: Heinemann, 1983); David Kaiser, "A Mannheim for All Seasons: Bloor, Merton, and the Roots of the Sociology of Scientific Knowledge," *Science in Context* 11 (1998), 51–87.

39. Oswald Spengler, *The Decline of the West*, trans. Charles Francis Atkinson (New York: Knopf, 1926).

40. Martin Heidegger, "The Age of the World Picture," in *The Question Concerning Technology and Other Essays*, trans. William Lovitt (New York: Garland, 1977), 115–154;

Max Horkheimer, "Notes on Science and the Crisis," trans. Matthew J. O'Connell, in *Critical Theory: Selected Essays* (New York: Continuum, 1999), 3–9; Carson, "Science as Instrumental Reason."

41. A sometimes unreferenced starting point is Ernst Cassirer, *Das Erkenntnisproblem in der Philosophie und Wissenschaft der neueren Zeit* (Berlin: Bruno Cassirer, 1906–7). For other examples and discussion see Edmund Husserl, *The Crisis of European Sciences and Transcendental Phenomenology: An Introduction to Phenomenological Philosophy*, trans. David Carr (Evanston, IL: Northwestern University Press, 1970); Dermot Moran, "Husserl and the Crisis of the European Sciences," in *The Proper Ambition of Science*, ed. M.W.F. Stone and Jonathan Wolff (London: Routledge, 2000), 122–50; Hyder and Rheinberger, eds., *Science and the Life-World: Essays on Husserl's 'Crisis of European Sciences*; Alexandre Koyré, *Études galiléennes* (Paris: Hermann, 1939), as interpreted in Yehuda Elkana, "Alexandre Koyré: Between the History of Ideas and the Sociology of Knowledge," *History and Technology* 4 (1987), 111–44. On other contributors to the idea of a "Scientific Revolution" see H. Floris Cohen, *The Scientific Revolution: A Historiographical Inquiry* (Chicago: University of Chicago Press, 1994).

42. Ernst Mach, *The Science of Mechanics: A Critical and Historical Account of Its Development*, trans. Thomas J. McCormack (Chicago: Open Court, 1902); compare even Hans Driesch, *The History and Theory of Vitalism*, trans. C. K. Ogden (London: Macmillan, 1914).

43. Franz Borkenau, *Der Übergang vom feudalen zum bürgerlichen Weltbild: Studien zur Geschichte der Philosophie der Manufakturperiode* (Paris: Libraire Félix Alcan, 1934), vi.

44. Elisabeth Nemeth, "Logical Empiricism and the History and Sociology of Science," in *The Cambridge Companion to Logical Empiricism*, eds. Alan Richardson and Thomas Uebel (Cambridge: Cambridge University Press, 2007), 278–302; specifically addressing Reichenbach, Alan W. Richardson, "Science as Will and Representation: Carnap, Reichenbach, and the Sociology of Science," *Philosophy of Science* 67 Supplement (2000), S151–S162.

45. E.g., Erwin Schrödinger, "Is Science a Fashion of the Times?" and "Physical Science and the Temper of the Age," in *Science and the Human Temperament*, trans. James Murphy (London: Allen & Unwin, 1935), 66–85 and 86–106; Heisenberg, "Reality and Its Order" or *Ordnung der Wirklichkeit*.

46. On the redefinition of "theoretical" as "Jewish" science see Alan D. Beyerchen, *Scientists under Hitler: Politics and the Physics Community in the Third Reich* (New Haven: Yale University Press, 1977).

47. For Thomas Kuhn's uptake of Koyré and Ludwik Fleck see *The Structure of Scientific Revolutions*, 2nd ed. (Chicago: University of Chicago Press, 1970), vii–viii. On Fleck's relation to the Weimar debates, see esp. Cornelius Borck, "Message in a Bottle from 'the Crisis of Reality': On Ludwik Fleck's Interventions for an Open Epistemology," *Studies in History and Philosophy of Biological and Biomedical Sciences* 35 (2004), 447–64; Hans-Jörg Rheinberger, "Zur Historizität wissenschaftlichen Wissens: Ludwik Fleck, Edmund Husserl," in *Epistemologie des Konkreten: Studien zur Geschichte der modernen Biologie* (Frankfurt: Suhrkamp, 2006), 21–36; Hans-Jörg Rheinberger, "On the Historicity of Scientific Knowledge: Ludwik Fleck, Gaston Bachelard, Edmund Husserl," in *Science and the Life-World: Essays on Husserl's "Crisis of European Sciences*," 164–76; Eva Hedfors, "Fleck in Context," *Perspectives on Science* 15, no. 1 (2007), 49–86.

Part III

Aesthetics, Literature, Film

10

Walter Benjamin, Siegfried Kracauer, and Weimar Criticism

Michael W. Jennings

At first tentatively, and then beginning in 1926 with a new focus and resolve, Walter Benjamin and Siegfried Kracauer set out to reinvent German cultural criticism as a form. Their writings do not simply mirror the new set of preoccupations and circumstances that characterize cultural criticism in the Weimar Republic: no other writers were so instrumental in setting its agenda and defining its formal means and strategies. Kracauer and Benjamin virtually invented the criticism of popular culture. In the early years of their shared project, essays on popular culture stand alongside appreciations and interpretations of high culture; as they become more confident, the essays move freely between the high and the low.[1] In books and essays such as *One Way Street* and "Surrealism" (Benjamin) and "The Mass Ornament" and "Photography" (Kracauer), the two writers reinvent cultural analysis as a specific form of the critique of the new urban metropolis. And in doing so, they formulate what is arguably the most compelling theory of modernity ever to arise from cultural criticism.

In the decade between 1924 and 1934—the year of the first drafts of the great montage text *A Berlin Childhood around 1900*—Benjamin's writings changed radically.[2] Before 1924, Benjamin had written precisely one piece on contemporary literature, an unpublished essay on Paul Scheerbart; his criticism had focused instead on the German literary tradition from the seventeenth to the early nineteenth centuries. He had produced studies of Goethe, of Friedrich Hölderlin, of the Romantic theory of criticism, and, finally, his *Habilitationsschrift*, or second dissertation, on the German baroque *Trauerspiel* or "play of mourning." Each of his writings in the years 1912–1924 represents a contribution to an integrated, if highly esoteric and even refractory theory of criticism; as Benjamin's friend, the great student of the Kabbalah Gershom Scholem put it, each of these works describes a philosophy of its object. For all its idiosyncrasy, though, Benjamin's early theory of criticism draws on a number of the dominant critical paradigms of its era—all of which were still widely practiced in the early years of the Weimar Republic. The most important of these was the great tradition of philology that ran from Friedrich Schlegel to Friedrich Nietzsche—the intensive, often brilliantly intuitive engagement with texts in all their particularity.[3] Nearly as important was Benjamin's implicit allegiance to the tradition of *Geistesgeschichte* advocated by Wilhelm Dilthey and his followers: crudely put, the notion that cultural objects are expressions of a *Weltanschauung* or *Zeitgeist*.[4] It is too seldom acknowledged that Benjamin was, early and late, a historicist critic. More specifically, Benjamin's approach to specific cultural objects was given its decisive shape by his reading of the work of the first Viennese School of art criticism that formed around Alois Riegl. Riegl's influential idea of the *Kunstwollen* (will to art) is broadly indebted to Dilthey, insofar as the *Kunstwollen* indicates the manner in which the form of specific works of art, as the product of the general volition of a society at a particular moment, gives access to the essential structure of that society.[5] One additional broad horizon needs to be mentioned here: the early work occured within the context of what Lukács called "Romantic Anti-Capitalism:" that broad current of thought that drew on a set of values that predated the rise of urban commodity capitalism in the nineteenth century for the central elements of its critique.[6]

Benjamin, Kracauer, and the Criticism of Popular Culture

Beginning in 1924, though, the tenor, form, and object of Benjamin's criticism changed radically as he turned his attention and his energies in precipitously new directions: to contemporary culture (with an emphasis not just on major works and authors, but on popular forms and on what we might call everyday modernity), to Marxist politics, and to a career as a journalist and wide-ranging cultural critic.[7] These three central aspects of Benjamin's turn in 1924 have received varying attention: the turn to Marxism is very well documented and plays a role in nearly every reading of the life and work;[8] the failed academic career and the decision to pursue a career as a freelance cultural critic has, surprisingly, remained undervalued;[9] but the shift from German Romanticism and its predecessors to contemporary European culture—and especially to popular culture and the theory of media—which is in many ways the most momentous decision for Benjamin in the 1920s, remains a black hole in Benjamin scholarship. At first haltingly, and then, beginning in 1926, with a vengeance, Walter Benjamin turned his thought and writing to Europe, to the modernist and avant-garde culture being produced in France and the Soviet Union, and especially to popular culture and modern media, something Benjamin and his friend Siegfried Kracauer in some ways invented as a field of serious investigation. His range in the period is astonishing: between 1926 and 1931, Benjamin produced essays on children's literature, toys, pedagogy, gambling, graphology, pornography, folk art, outsider art, food, the culture of health and hygiene, and a wide variety of media including film, radio, photography, and the illustrated press. Writing for some of the most prominent weeklies and monthlies in Germany, he had established himself by the late 1920s as a visible and influential commentator on cultural matters. He did not, however, invent Weimar criticism by himself: his development as a critic is inseparable from his growing intellectual friendship with Siegfried Kracauer.

After several years of architectural practice, Kracauer (1889–1966) had in 1921 joined the staff of the *Frankfurter Zeitung*, one of Germany's most prominent newspapers, as a reporter assigned to local and regional events such as exhibitions, conferences, and trade fairs. Then as now, this is not a prime assignment for a young reporter. By the time Benjamin first met him in the summer of 1923, Kracauer had seemingly moved past this base and established himself as the newspaper's principal writer on the role of the German intellectual in a period of cultural crisis. The essays Kracauer published in 1922 and 1923 concentrate on two issues. First, the role of classical German humanism—the German "ideal of humanity" propagated by German idealist philosophy from Kant to Hegel under conditions of modernization, and second, the ecumenical religious revival in the years after the war. In essays such as "Those Who Wait," "The Group as Bearer of Ideas," and "The Crisis of Science," Kracauer portrayed a cultural and philosophical tradition falling dizzyingly into crisis as its shared values were challenged. His own adherence to the values of the humanistic tradition was as much at stake here as was the more general situation of the German intellectual, but Kracauer in 1923 had no notion of any possible resolution of the crisis.

With the publication of the essay "Travel and Dance" in the *Frankfurter Zeitung* on March 15, 1925, however, Kracauer showed that he was on the way to a mode of analysis that could aid in the comprehension of new social forms. The essay focuses on popular forms—travel and dance as "spatio-temporal passions"—that have become, on Kracauer's reading, modes of coping with the boredom and sameness of life in modern society: travel is reduced to a pure experience of a space that is "less deadeningly familiar" than the everyday, while dancing, as a "representation of rhythm," deflects attention from chronological sequence toward the contemplation of time itself.[10] This is for Kracauer a process of formalization: the "intrinsic value" of things is effaced as the appearance of phenomena such as travel and dance are subjected to changes that have no relation to the things themselves (K 67). "Travel and Dance" is a key transitional essay for Kracauer in a number of ways. It shows him turning toward forms and artifacts of everyday modernity and deriving from them revelatory information as to the character of daily life. Yet the essay still bears the traces of his earlier, frankly idealist work: it is a lament for the loss of the "real person . . . [who] resists being dissolved into space and time," and is instead "committed to eternity," oriented "toward the Beyond in which everything in the Here would find its meaning and conclusion" (K 68–69). Under the conditions of modernity, in a world that "desires nothing other than the greatest possible technologizing of all activities," humans are forced to lead a "double existence," attempting to exist "simultaneously within space and at the threshhold of a supra-spatial endlessness" (K 69–71). In the concluding pages of the essay, Kracauer argues that humans are increasingly denied even this doubleness as the forces of technology, rationalization, and mechanization conspire to constrain every attempt to transcend the spatio-temporal as mere form: "access to the sphere they seek is blocked and thus their demand for reality can express itself only inauthentically." Travel and dance would thus seem to be representative forms of inauthenticity, mere substitutes "for the sphere to which they have been denied access" (K 70). While Kracauer never denies this, he also invests them with a "theological significance: they are the essential possibilities through which those in the grip of mechanization can live (albeit inauthentically) the double existence that is the foundation of reality" (K 71). In sounding this note of deep ambiguity, Kracauer in "Travel and Dance" sets the tone that will dominate not just his analysis of modernity, and not just that of Benjamin, but of the entire institution of the "Frankfurt School" with which he was affiliated. In the years to come, Kracauer, in essays with titles such as "Cult of Distraction," "Analysis of a City Map," "Calico World," and "The Little Shopgirls go to the Movies," would offer a series of brilliant analyses and critiques of contemporary culture. His gaze was particularly attuned to Berlin's diverse and frenetically active leisure world: spectacles with Tiller girls, movies, shopping, bestsellers. Perhaps the signal accomplishment of these essays is the reorientation of Weimar's critical gaze toward a series of surface phenomena that had, in traditional culture, been dismissed as ephemeral and, well, superficial.

A critical aspect of the manner in which Kracauer—and Benjamin—directed their gaze toward the new world of the modern capitalist metropolis did not originate with them. The distanced, critical attitude toward the modern metropolis began as a peripatetic, optically oriented phenomenon: as *flanerie*.[11] Kracauer and Benjamin were inveterate walkers in Berlin, Frankfurt, and Paris; and both of them acknowledged the German master of the discipline, Benjamin's friend Franz Hessel. "That strolling absolves you from your more or less wretched private existence," Hessel writes, "is its most incomparably charming aspect. You keep company, you communicate with an array of alien circumstances and fates. The true stroller is made aware of this by the remarkable fright that he senses when he suddenly encounters an acquaintace in the dream city of his flanerie and quite simply becomes, with an abrupt jolt, a determinate individual once again."[12] If Hessel emphasized the "pure, aimless pleasure" of such optics, Benjamin, typically, lent a sharper edge to his analysis: for him, the figure of the Parisian flaneur that has come down to us through Baudelaire's poetry and the painting of the impressionists was nothing less than the "mythological ideal type" of modern subjectivity.[13] Whatever their differences, though, the spontaneously framed optical insight into a particular aspect of city life emerged as a central aspect of Weimar cultural criticism, shaping not merely its repertoire of objects, but its very form.

It is thus instructive to compare one of Benjamin's first efforts at the criticism of contemporary popular culture to "Travel and Dance." Benjamin had long been a consumer of popular culture: he was an avid reader of detective novels and he and his wife Dora had assembled a remarkable collection of illustrated children's books. Only now though, in his exchanges with Kracauer, does Benjamin begin to discern a path down which he could turn his personal obsessions, such as detective novels and children's books, into objects of serious consideration.[14] The essay "Old Forgotten Children's Books" draws not only on the Benjamin's lovingly assembled collection, but on Benjamin's long-standing interest in the child's "inner life" and the moral and cognitive formation that proceeds from it. Benjamin was intensely interested in the history of pedagogy in Germany, and the little essay contains a brief history of the role of children's books in that development—the first of many analyses of the problem. Yet the most important contribution of the essay is the highly speculative distinction he draws between the child's reactions to color illustrations and to woodcuts. Color illustrations are related, on this view, to the developing inner life of the child. "After all, the role of children's books is not to induct their readers directly into the world of objects, animals, and people—in other words, into so-called life. Very gradually their meaning is discovered in the outside world, but only in proportion as they are found to correspond to what children already possess within themselves. The inward nature of this way of seeing is located in the color, and this is where the dreamy life that objects lead in the minds of children is acted out. They learn from the bright coloring. For nowhere else is sensuous, nostalgia-fee contemplation as much at home as in color" (SW I 410). The woodcut, though, is the "polar complement" to the color illustration: "the plain prosaic illustration leads him out of himself. The compelling invitation to describe, which is implicit in such pictures, arouses the child's desire to express himself in words. And describing these pictures in words, he also describes them by enactment." The dichotomy drawn here between a dreamlike, fluid interiority and an active agency in the world of course recalls Kracauer's notion of a "double existence." It is striking that, in their first forays into the world of popular culture, both friends see in the object of popular culture an important bridge or fulcrum between older notions of human interiority and a newer emphasis on a fully vested agency in the world—however delusory both terms of the dichotomy might prove under the conditions of modernity.

As the parallels in these essays show, Benjamin was in frequent touch with Kracauer at critical points in the formation of his new idea of criticism: at first by letter and then, in 1926, through frequent personal contact in France. Kracauer's laying bare of the materiality and exteriority of the city, its commonplace objects, surfaces, and surface structures, brought about fundamental changes in Benjamin's work. During the time in Paris, their correspondence takes on a new intensity as they begin to share their unpublished work with one another. Benjamin thus points repeatedly to a new "convergence" between his approach and style and that of Kracauer. After praising Kracauer's "Das Mittelgebirge" (Central German Uplands), he writes "As you continue to pursue the clichés of the petit bourgeois stagings of dream and longing, I believe that wonderful discoveries lie ahead of you and we will perhaps meet one another at the one point at which I've been taking aim with all my energy for the last year: the postcard. You will perhaps also someday write that redemption of stamp collecting for which I've been waiting so long without wanting to dare undertake it myself" (III 177). In writing to his friend about his experiences of Paris, Benjamin thus emphasizes that he is attempting to first approach the city in its "exteriority": its street layout, transportation systems, its cafes and newspapers. It was Kracauer, then, who showed Benjamin how a theory like his, apparently suited only to the refractory objects of a mandarin cultural elite, might open up the world around him.

Denkbild and "Little Form"

For both writers, though—and especially for Benjamin—the turn to the popular brought with it a reconsideration of what it meant to write criticism in a po- litically and historically responsible fashion. The first sign of a major change is a new directness and openness in Benjamin's writing. The major works of the early 1920s—"Goethe's Elective Affinities" and *The Origin of German Tragic Drama* (*Trauerspiel*)—are frequently considered among the most difficult, hermetic texts in the canon of twentieth century criticism. An exchange with Kracauer written in Paris in 1926 confirms Benjamin's awareness of the urgency of a new directness and transparency: "that which is meant has emerged more clearly in my writings in the course of time. There is really nothing that can be more urgently important for a writer" (B III 180). Fortunately, we have been left with a precise record of the gradual change in Benjamin's style and focus: the montage book *One Way Street* was composed between 1924 and 1926 and offers not just a snapshot of the new prose form that would dominate Benjamin's Weimar criticism, the *Denk- bild* or figure of thought, but a virtual user's manual of the new critical writing. The book, first published in 1928, consists of sixty short prose pieces; these differ wildly in genre, style, and content. There are aphorisms among the texts, and jokes and dream protocols. There are also descriptive set pieces: cityscapes, land- scapes, mindscapes. There are portions of writing manuals; trenchant contempo- rary political analysis; prescient appreciations of the child's psychology, behavior, and moods; decodings of bourgeois fashion, living arrangements, and courtship patterns that anticipate the Roland Barthes of *Mythologies*; and, time and again, remarkable penetrations into the heart of everyday things, what Benjamin would later call the "exploration of the soul of the commodity."

Many of the pieces in *One Way Street* first appeared in the feuilleton section of newspapers and magazines: the medium in which they appeared played a decisive role in the shaping of the prose form on which the book is based. The feuilleton had been introduced in French political journals and newspapers in the nineteenth century. Although the feuilleton was in some ways the forerun- ner of the arts and leisure sections of today's newspapers, there were significant differences: First, rather than a separate section, the feuilleton appeared on the bottom third of most pages of the paper, demarcated by a printed line (feuilleton pieces are commonly said to appear "unter dem Strich" or "below the line" in German); second, it consisted mainly of cultural criticism and of serial publica- tions of longer literary texts, but also included significant quantities of other material, including gossip, fashion commentary, and a variety of short forms— aphorisms, epigrams, quick takes on cultural objects and issues—often referred to as "glosses." In the course of the 1920s, a number of prominent writers shaped their writing practice in order to accommodate it to the feuilleton; the "kleine Form" or "little form" that resulted came rapidly to be identified as the primary mode of cultural commentary and criticism in the Weimar Republic. The writer Ernst Penzoldt defined the subject matter of the "little form" in the following way: "poetic observations of the small and big world, daily experience in all its charm, fond strolls, curious encounters, moods, sentimental chatter, glosses and things of that sort."[15] By the late years of the Weimar Republic, the "little form" had in fact become pervasively identified as the cognate form of metropolitan modernity. In the 1931 novel *Käsebier conquers the Kurfürstendamm* (*Käsebier erobert den Kurfürstendamm*) by Gabriele Tergit, the publisher of a Berlin daily offers the writer Lambeck the opportunity to write on a regular basis about Berlin. "He was tempted. It would be pleasant to be able to bring his experiences, couched in cultured prose, directly to someone else for once, rather than simply storing them up. . . . Lambeck said, 'Allow me to consider your proposal from the ground up; I just don't know whether the little form suits me or not.' "[16]

The form certainly suited Walter Benjamin. The first section of *One Way Street*, "Filling Station," is a call to arms for the little form. "Significant literary effectiveness can come into being only in a strict alternation between action and writing; it must nurture the inconspicuous forms that fit its influence in active communities better than does the pretentious, universal gesture of the book—in leaflets, brochures, articles, and placards. Only this prompt language shows itself actively equal to the moment" (I 444). In a series of rapid claims in the sections to come, Benjamin privileges the fragment over the finished work ("the work is the death mask of its conception"), improvisation over "competence" ("all decisive blows are struck with the left hand"), and waste products and detritus over the carefully crafted (children bring together "materials of widely different kinds in a new, intuitive relationship") [I 459, 447, 450]. Traditional forms of writing were, for Benjamin, simply no longer capable of surviving in capitalist modernity—let alone of providing the framework for meaningful insights into its structure, functioning, and effects. "Script—having found, in the book, a refuge in which it can lead an autonomous existence—is pitilessly dragged out into the street by advertisements and subjected to the brutal heteronomies of economic chaos" (I456). As these oppositions imply, Benjamin was convinced that any criticism worth the name was animated by "a moral question": "the critic is the strategist in the literary struggle" (I 460).

As these remarks indicate, Benjamin's new understanding of his writing was decisively shaped by his growing political consciousness. Driven not merely by the developments of the years following World War I, but by his reading—and especially his reading of Georg Lukács's *History and Class Consciousness*—and his relationship to the Latvian Communist theater director Asja Lacis, Benjamin had in 1924 begun to formulate a political position within the broad outlines of European Marxism. As he wrote to his friend Scholem, "anyone of our generation who feels and understands the historical moment in which he exists in this world, not as mere words, but as a battle, cannot renounce the study and the praxis of the mechanism through which things (and conditions) and the masses interact" (B III 159). The exact shape of that Marxism remains, almost a century later, a matter of intense debate.[17] Like many aspects of Benjamin's thought, his communism is a "mobile and contradictory whole," a position characterized by "paradoxical reversal": a reversal that is "ruthless and radical" and that allows one "not to decide once and for all, but to decide at every moment. . . . If I were to join the Communist Party one day. . . . my stance, in regard to the most important things, would be always to proceed radically and never with an eye to consequences" [B IV 412].

And Benjamin was just as clear in *One Way Street* that his new political convictions could be enacted only in a new prose form. In the short pieces in *One Way Street*, Benjamin for the first time experimented with a form that he would call the *Denkbild* or figure of thought. The section titled "Manorially Furnished Ten-Room Apartment" is one of the first fully realized examples of the form.

> The furniture style of the second half of the nineteenth century has received its only adequate description, and analysis, in a certain type of detective novel at the dynamic center of which stands the horror of apartments. The arrangement of the furniture is at the same time the site plan of deadly traps, and the suite of rooms prescribes the path of the fleeing victim. That this kind of detective novel begins with Poe—at a time when such accommodations hardly yet existed—is no counterargument. For without exception the great writers perform their combinations in a world that comes after them, just as the Paris streets of Baudelaire's poems, as well as Dostoevsky's characters, existed only after 1900. The bourgeois interior of the 1860s to the 1890s—with its gigantic sideboards distended with carvings, the sunless corners where potted palms sit, the balcony embattled behind its balustrade, and the long corridors with their singing gas flames—fittingly houses only the corpse. "On this sofa the aunt cannot but be murdered." The soulless luxury of the furnishings becomes true comfort only in the presence of a dead body. Far more interesting than the Oriental landscapes in detective novels is that rank Orient inhabiting their interiors: the Persian carpet and the ottoman, the hanging lamp and the genuine dagger from the Caucasus. Behind the heavy, gathered Khilim tapestries, the master of the house has orgies with his share certificates, feels himself the eastern merchant, the indolent pasha in the caravanserai of otiose enchantment, until the dagger in its silver sling above the divan puts an end, one fine afternoon, to his siesta and himself. This character of the bourgeois apartment, tremulously awaiting the nameless murderer like a lascivious old lady her gallant, has been penetrated by a number of authors who, as writers of "detective stories"—and perhaps also because in their works part of the bourgeois pandemonium is exhibited—have been denied the reputation they deserve. The quality in question has been captured in isolated writings by Conan Doyle and in a major work by A. K. Green. And with *The Phantom of the Opera*, one of the great novels about the nineteenth century, Gaston Leroux has brought the genre to its apotheosis.

Benjamin here re-conceives the short prose text. Most obviously, it is an example of a prose that has earned him the reputation as one of the foremost stylists of the twentieth century. As a producer of memorable sentences, his only real competitors in German are Franz Kafka and Robert Musil. Benjamin's critical prose has a lapidary quality, a beauty and trenchancy of expression, but especially the ability to generate multivalence from an extreme economy of means. Perhaps more importantly, it reconceives the short prose piece in a way that effaces generic boundaries: the figure of thought is at once a literary, philosophical, journalistic, and critical form.[18] At the heart of even the most rigorously philosophical *Denkbild* is a literary, figurative core. As Gerhard Richter has observed, the *Denkbild* as a form comes down from Nietzsche's famous dictum in "On Truth and Lie in an Extra-Moral Sense": "What, then, is truth? A mobile army of metaphors, metonyms, and anthropomorphisms—in short, a sum of human relations which have been enhanced, transposed, and embellished poetically and rhetorically, and which after long use seem firm, canonical, and obligatory to a people: truths are illusions about which one has forgotten that this is what they are."[19] Benjamin's figurative evocation of the bourgeois interior is the ground on which this *Denkbild* stands; and the imputation of orientalist fantasies to the bourgeois inhabitant—he is an eastern merchant, an indolent pasha—verges on the literary form of narrative monologue. Yet, for all the beauty and surprise of its prose, the *Denkbild* is finally organized by philosophical concepts: those of the fetishism of commodities and of phantasmagoria.[20] The orientalist fantasies are not just played out within the environment: they are generated by it, as the commodities in the room exert a malign influence on the human sensory and cognitive capacities. The literary detective is the necessary antidote, as he brings his powers of ratiocination to bear on the decoding of a thoroughly irrational space.[21] The *Denkbild* is thus the realization and home of a mode of thought that is always radical and—embedded as it is in an argument that is rarely linear or discursive but instead takes the form of a constellation or montage—freed of the burden of "direct consequences." The exigencies of feuilleton publication were of course hardly the only influence on the new form. In rethinking the small form as the *Denkbild*, Benjamin draws on the long tradition of the European aphorism, and especially its great German practitioners such as Lichtenberg and Nietzsche, as well as the Romantic fragment as theorized by Friedrich Schlegel and Novalis.[22] And, more proximately, Benjamin's conception of the form and in particular its function in a broader cultural ensemble is decisively shaped by his involvement in the Berlin avantgardes of the early 1920s.[23]

Weimar Criticism

For Benjamin and Kracauer alike, the *Denkbild* came to serve as the nodal unit in their subsequent writing. Even apparently discursive essays reveal themselves on closer inspection to be montages, or to use the term increasingly favored by Benjamin, "constellations" of fully formed, often hermetic units: figures of thought. Using this new critical form, they produced, in the second half of the 1920s, a series of critical essays that, taken together, comprise a theory of modernity that has proven among the most influential in the last century. Although by far the greatest volume of Benjamin's critical production in these years continued to appear as the "little form" in newspapers and magazines, he also produced a series of longer essays such as "Surrealism" and "On the Image of Proust" (both 1929), "Karl Kraus" and "Little History of Photography" (both 1931), and "Experience and Poverty" (1933)—and, especially in the English-speaking world, Benjamin's reputation as the leading Weimar critic is based on these essays. Kracauer's seminal essays from this period—"Photography" and "The Mass Ornament" (both 1927), "Farewell to the Linden Arcade" (1930)—have failed to gain the same status, but are in many ways the equal of Benjamin's work.[24] There is a compelling reason to discuss these two bodies of work together: throughout the second half of the 1920s, the two writers were exchanging ideas and commenting on one another's work. After 1926, Kracauer began to take defining concepts and theories from Benjamin's early work and apply them to the high and low culture of the Weimar Republic in new and sometimes astonishing ways. Although his creative misprisions of Benjamin are widespread, they are particularly important in the cluster of essays at the heart of Kracauer's great collection *The Mass Ornament*. And in turn, Kracauer's refunctioning of these Benjaminian concepts is particularly important for Benjamin's own work; and no essay was more important for Benjamin than Kracauer's great essay "Photography." In what follows I offer a reading of that essay and of Benjamin's great assessment of surrealism, hoping to offer a kind of reading guide for other canonical essays of Weimar criticism.

In Kracauer's essay, the action seems to be anywhere else but in a modern medium such as photography. Truth, after all, resides elsewhere, as Kracauer is at pains to tell us—in fact, photography is not only said to be indifferent to truth, it is finally nothing more than "a jumble that consists partly of garbage" (K 51). Worse, it is deeply complicit with the most degraded practices of capitalist society: "In the hands of the ruling society, the invention of illustrated magazines is one of the most powerful means of organizing a strike against understanding" (K 58). Photography would seem, then, to be complicit with anti-rational forces and thus in part accountable for the spread of a pernicious mythological thinking. Insofar as the opening pages of "Photography" take photographic practice at all seriously, they seem to do so only in terms of the purported temporal authenticity of photography's reference. "Although time is not part of the photograph like the smile or the chignon, the photograph itself . . . is a representation of time" (K 49).

The traditional work of art, by contrast—and here Kracauer mainly intends painting—is a privileged locus of meaning. Painting is uniquely capable of representing what Kracauer calls "memory images" or "monograms," moments of time remembered that are shot through with significance. And these images are related in an important way to truth.

> Truth can be found only by a liberated consciousness which assesses the demonic nature of the drives. The traits that consciousness recollects stand in a relationship to what has been perceived as true, the latter being either manifest in these traits or excluded by them. The image in which these traits appear is distinguished from all other memory images, for unlike the latter it preserves not a multitude of opaque recollections but elements

that touch upon what has been recognized as true. All memory images are bound to be reduced to this type of image, which may rightly be called the last image, since it alone preserves the unforgettable. The last image of a person is that person's actual *history.* . . . This history is like a *monogram* that condenses the name into a single graphic figure which is meaningful as an ornament. (K 51)

These last images, these monograms are represented in the painting as their *meaning* takes on spatial appearance—whereas in a photograph, the mere spatial appearance of an object *is* the only meaning to which it can possibly obtain. The object represented in a painting is "permeated by cognition" (K 52) in a way unobtainable to the photograph. This is obviously good work if we can get it: Kracauer's ideal painter creates works of art in which reside a truth content that "outlasts time."

But, as Brecht was wont to remind us, *die Verhältnisse sind nicht so—* conditions today just aren't like that. Modern consciousness is anything other than a "liberated consciousness" capable of discerning truth. And Kracauer has a rather precise idea of how conditions actually are: "One can certainly imagine a society that has fallen prey to a mute nature which has no meaning no matter how abstract its silence. The contours of such a society emerge in the illustrated journals" (K 61). In this apparently witty *aperçu* resides the insight fundamental to Kracauer's mature work, and to Benjamin's as well: that the conditions that obtain in their historical period are nowhere directly accessible to human cognition—they emerge, if ever, only in highly mediated and abstracted form. As allegories, in photographs.

In perhaps the densest section of a very refractory essay, Kracauer engages, through direct reference to Benjamin's book on the *Trauerspiel*, in the debate on symbol and allegory that had played so significant a role in the shaping of the modern German cultural tradition. He begins by aligning the memory image, or monogram, with the symbol. Symbols are, in Kracauer's phrase, "dependent upon natural conditions, a dependence that determines the visible and corporeal expression of consciousness" (K 60). In epochs in which nature comes wholly to dominate consciousness, however, "symbolic presentation becomes *allegory*" (K 60). It is interesting to note that Kracauer, like Benjamin, distances himself from the more rigid teleologies of Ernst Bloch and Lukács, adopting a view of historical expression indebted to Riegl and even to a certain extent to Wilhelm Worringer.[25] Just as the art of the Vienna Genesis emerged as not just characteristic of its age, but as its only historically responsible expression, so too does allegory, for Benjamin and Kracauer, become the only responsible trope of modernity. And in Kracauer's essay, photography is defined as an allegorical practice, in essence, the primary expression of the *Kunstwollen* of modernity.

If, though, photography can capture only "the residuum that history has discharged" (K 55), of what exactly is it expressive? In Kracauer's view, photography is uniquely charged with the laying bare of a nature from which human consciousness has wholly departed. A nature that is at once inimical and highly seductive, at once "the sum of what can be subtracted" from the human being *and* something more appealing to consciousness even than images. "The more decisively consciousness frees itself from [its natural] contingency, in the course of the historical process, the more purely does its natural foundation present itself to consciousness. What is meant no longer appears to consciousness in images; rather, this meaning goes toward and through nature" (K 60). Kracauer attempts here to create a post-Weberian vocabulary for what is still the process of *Entzauberung* or disenchantment; he is careful to avoid the vocabulary of commodification, reification, and second nature then under rapid development in the wake of Lukács's *History and Class Consciousness*. Yet what Kracauer means with the notion of the "pure presentation" of nature to consciousness is not far either from Lukacs's notion of second nature or from the discourse of phantasmagoria that had begun to play a role in the discussions between Adorno and Benjamin by 1927. The assumption common to all three positions is that the human sensorium confronts an environment that appears to be coherent, meaningful, and given, but that is in fact the objective manifestation of networks of fetishized commodities which, working together, serve to disorient and denature the human sensory and cognitive abilities. Considered in its relationship to a "foundation of nature devoid of meaning," photography thus performs central epistemological tasks, in that it is capable of raising to the level of consciousness the conditions that actually obtain. Or, as Kracauer puts it, "It is the task of photography to disclose this previously unexamined *foundation of nature*" (K 61–62). It does so through a particular form of consonance between its mechanisms and the age in which it arises. "No different from earlier modes of representation, photography, too, is assigned to a particular developmental stage of practical and material life. It is a secretion of the capitalist mode of production. The same mere nature which appears in photography flourishes in the reality of the society produced by this capitalist mode of production" (K 61). Photography is, in the phrase Benjamin uses to describe the *Trauerspiel* in its relationship to its age, "historically responsible," in that it is, in its brokenness, thoroughly symptomatic of the conditions that produced it.

But, more importantly, photography serves, much as had Benjamin's early criticism, as a form of mortification or annihilation of its object.[26] "A shudder runs through the view of old photographs. For they make visible not the knowledge of the original but the spatial configuration of a moment; what appears in the photograph is not the person but the sum of what can be subtracted from him or her. The photograph annihilates the person by portraying him or her, and were person and portrayal to converge, the person would cease to exist" (K 57). Photography produces—and does not merely represent—a "disintegrated unity," a "ghost-like reality" that is unredeemed. "The photograph gathers fragments around a nothing." Or, in a recurrent figure from the text, the "inert world" is revealed, dormant in its cocoon. As a nearly random set of little dots, which is only another term for a spatial representation, a photograph presents elements in space "whose configuration is so far from necessary that one could just as easily imagine a different organization of those elements" (K 56). If for Benjamin, in allegory anything can mean anything else, in Kracauer's conceptualization of photography the image as spatial representation is susceptible to a particular recombinatory logic. But that logic is societal, and not metaphorical. Kracauer imagines that that same society that has fallen prey to a mute nature, if relentlessly exposed to the mortification of the photographic image, might fail to endure. This, it seems to me, is the meaning of Kracauer's enigmatic slogan-eering for photography as the "go for broke—va banque—game of history" (K 61). Giving ourselves up to photographs means, for Kracauer, our acceptance of the possibility that the world as we know it could be brought to its end—by photographs. It could be revealed as a heap of garbage and simply cease to have the kind of meaning that alone ensures its perpetuation.

It is against the background of Kracauer's essays that Benjamin's own canonical works from the late 1920s must be read. In "Surrealism: The Last Snapshot of the European Intelligentsia," Benjamin argues that surrealism is too important to be understood as an art movement: it is instead a position statement on the "crisis of the intelligentsia," an attack on the "humanistic concept of freedom" that might enable a "decision" on the part of the alert reader (IV 207). He thus intertwines his reading of surrealism and its predecessors (Rimbaud, Lautréamont) with a series of remarks on the history of anarchist revolt; on this reading, Bakunin becomes a proto-surrealist. Benjamin shows that the often jejeune communist posturings of the surrealists are in fact much less important than their aesthetic practices, which prove to be the key to a systematic displacement of the bourgeois subject and his potential incorporation in a new "body and image space" (IV 217). How, though, can the surrealist refunctioning of dream and revery be revealed as a political weapon?

Benjamin starts from a rather obvious reading of surrealist poetry, showing that it came to encompass everything with which it came in contact: "Life seemed worth living only where the threshold between waking and sleeping was worn away in everyone as by the steps of multitudinous images flooding back and forth." In highly coded language, though, Benjamin extends this reading, showing that the surrealist dream-state and the way in which poetry was "exploded from within" were themselves the key to the escape from the phantasmagoria of life under capitalism. Intoxication as a "fruitful, living experience," "allowed these people to step outside the charmed space of intoxication" and to deal with experience "and not with phantasms" (IV 208). Paradoxically enough, revery and intoxication—usually held to be illusory states of consciousness—provide the means of recognizing and countering the pervasive delusion imposed upon the modern world by urban commodity capitalism. Benjamin dubbed these states "profane illumination," a concept he elaborates on the basis of a reading of André Breton's novel *Nadja*. Breton's poetic prose, in evoking what he himself calls "the marvelous," dissolves the boundary between our existence and the spaces in which we move and so breaks down an important barrier to the rise of a genuine political consciosness in the bourgeosie. In yet another paradoxical reading, love itself, as the primary incorporation of the marvelous or profane illumination in the novel, ensures that the lover attains a new approach to things—those recalcitrant, commodified props that otherwise remain distant, on the stage of capitalist phantasmagoria.

And the Paris of the surrealists is for Benjamin the very embodiment of the capitalist dream world. At the heart of Benjamin's reading is a particular relationship to material things. Yet the essay's central thesis, on the political potentials of things, remains enigmatic. "[Breton] was the first to perceive the revolutionary energies that appear in the 'outmoded'—in the first iron constructions, the first factory buildings, the earliest photos, objects that have begun to be extinct, grand pianos, the dresses of five years ago, fashionable restaurants when the vogue has begun to ebb from them" (IV 210). Just how, and under what circumstances, the perception of obsolescence can become "revolutionary experience" is never articulated in "Surrealism."[27] Benjamin hints at a general answer when he asserts that the "trick by which this world of things is mastered . . . consists in the substitution of a political for a historical view of the past" (IV 210). The assumption of a communist viewpoint is, in other words, the precondition for the attempt to "win the energies of intoxication for the revolution" (IV 215). The essay closes with a kind of apocalyptic fervor that recurs at key points in some of Benjamin's most important pieces.[28] Profane illumination of the sort evoked by surrealism *may* initiate us to an "image space" within which a new collective body might be formed. Just as Kracauer had found in photography the means for the revelation of the deep meaninglessness of the capitalist world, Benjamin finds in surrealism the precondition for a "dialectical annihilation" of the individual, the present society, and its mode of production. Only then might the "innervation" of the bodily collective occur, an innervation that itself might lead to that transcendence of reality foreseen in the *Communist Manifesto*.[29]

Theodor W. Adorno—a close friend of Kracauer's, an intellectual ally of Benjamin's, and another of the twentieth century's most powerful thinkers—long ago pointed to Benjamin's inability to think "without a basis, in an amateur way." He meant that Benjamin's ideas were always built up off of the concrete reading of a text, an image, a form, or a medium. He might well have included Kracauer in his observation. These two writers set the tone for a new mode of criticism in the Weimar era: the analysis of aesthetic objects, high and low, gave rise, bit by bit, not just to a bracing critique of capitalist society, but to a comprehensive, if highly condensed and truncated, theory of modernity and of modernism. In the years following the demise of the Weimar Republic, Benjamin, Kracauer, and their friends and collaborators in the "Frankfurt School," laboring in exile, worked more systematically to construct just such a theory. The extent to which these efforts consisted in the unpacking of key ideas and formulations from the Weimar criticism produced by Benjamin and Kracauer is nothing short of astonishing. Kracauer produced his best-known work, *From Caligari to Hitler: A Psychological History of the German Film* (1947), in America during World War II. Benjamin himself spent much of the decade of the 1930s in Paris the attempt to finish his *Arcades Project*, his analysis of Paris as the original site of urban commodity capitalism. And Adorno and Max Horkheimer, the Director of the Institute for Social Research, composed *The Dialectic of Enlightenment*

(1944/1947), undoubtedly the major product of the Frankfurt School, in New York in the early 1940s. One example of the relationship between these major works and the Weimar essays of Benjamin and Kracauer will have to stand for the many examples that show that it took years for some of Europe's most powerful minds to work out the implications of their ideas. In the essay "The Mass Ornament," Kracauer proposes that the historical process is "a process of demythologization:" "it may be that nature, increasingly stripped of its magic, will become more and more pervious to reason" (K 80). He goes on to make a powerful claim. Capitalism's "core defect" is that "it rationalizes not too much but rather *too little*" (K 81). In an important sense, Adorno and Horkheimer's massive work is nothing more than the attempt to work out the implications of that sentence.

Notes

1. The best concise introduction to the cultural politics of high and low remains the introduction to Andreas Huyssen's *After the Great Divide: Modernism, Mass Culture, Postmodernism* (Bloomington: Indiana University Press, 1986), vii–xii.
2. For a biography of Benjamin, see Howard Eiland and Michael Jennings, *Walter Benjamin: A Critical Life* (Cambridge, MA: Harvard University Press, 2013).
3. See especially Nikolaus Wegmann, "Was heißt einen klassischen Text lesen? Philologische Selbstreflexion zwischen Wissenschaft und Bildung" in *Wissenschaftsgeschichte der Germanistik im 19. Jahrhundert*, eds. Jürgen Fohrmann and Wilhelm Voßkamp (Stuttgart: Verlag J.B. Metzler, 1994), 334–450.
4. Benjamin had hoped to publish his great essay on Goethe's *Die Wahlverwandtschaften* in the Deutsche *Vierteljahresschrift für Literaturwissenschaft und Geistesgeschichte*, the leading organ of Dilthey's school; the journal had been founded by Paul Kluckhohn and Erich Rothacker, two followers of Dilthey, in 1923.
5. On Benjamin's reading of Riegl, see Michael W. Jennings, *Dialectical Images: Walter Benjamin's Theory of Literary Criticism* (Ithaca: Cornell University Press, 1987), 152–63; and Thomas Y. Levin's "Walter Benjamin and the Theory of Art History: An Introduction to 'Rigorous Study of Art'," *October* 47 (Winter 1988), 77–83.
6. See esp. Michel Löwy, "Naphta or Settembrini: Lukács and Romantic Anticapitalism," in Judith Marcus and Loltan Tarr, eds., *Georg Lukács: Theory, Culture, and Politics* (New Brunswick, NJ: Transaction, 1989), 189–206.
7. Despite these changes, there is a fundamental continuity in Benjamin's theory and practice of criticism. For many years, Benjamin scholars observed a rigid dichotomy between his early "Romantic" work and his late "Marxist" work. See Michael W. Jennings, *Dialectical Images*, for the first systematic demonstration of the continuities between the early and late work, what one might call the "unity thesis." Uwe Steiner's *Die Geburt der Kritik aus dem Geiste der Kunst: Untersuchungen zum Begriff der Kritik in den frühen Schriften Walter Benjamins* (Würzburg: Königshausen & Neumann, 1989), by concentrating on the key transitional years in the mid-1920s, first articulated a number of the key aspects of this continuity.
8. See Uwe Steiner, *Walter Benjamin*, 72–79.

9. The most important study of the role of the feuilleton in the shaping of the new criticism remains Eckart Köhn, *Strassenrausch: Flanerie und kleine Form. Versuch zur Literaturgeschichte des Flaneurs bis 1933* (Berlin: Das Arsenal, 1989).

10. Siegfried Kracauer, "Travel and Dance" in *The Mass Ornament*, ed. and trans. Thomas Y. Levin (Cambridge, MA: Harvard University Press, 1995), 65, 66. All further references to the essays in this volume are indicated in the text as K plus page number.

11. The canonical treatment of the critical role played by flanerie in Paris and in the modern metropolis in general is Benjamin's "The Paris of the Second Empire in Charles Baudelaire," in *Walter Benjamin, Selected Writings Volume Four 1938–1940*, eds. Howard Eiland and Michael W. Jennings (Cambridge, MA: Harvard University Press, 2003), 3–92. All further references to Benjamin's *Selected Writings* are indicated in the text by volume and page number.

12. Hessel, "Die Kunst spazieren zu gehen" in *Ermunterung zu Genuß, Sämtliche Werke*, vol. 2, 434. On Hessel and Weimar flanerie more generally, see Anke Gleber, *The Art of Taking a Walk: Flanerie, Literature, and Film in Weimar Culture* (Princeton: Princeton University Press, 1999).

13. Rob Shields, "Fancy Footwork: Walter Benjamin's Notes on Flanerie" in *The Flaneur*, ed. Keith Tester (London: Routledge, 1994), 67.

14. In a letter to Kracauer, Benjamin reveals himself as the only commentator in the history of the detective genre to view it from the perspective of the doctrine of the humors: he remarks to Kracauer that the detective himself fits "remarkably uncomfortably" in the old scheme, yet that he shares qualities not just with the melancholy, but with the phlegmatic. Walter Benjamin, *Gesammelte Briefe*, 6 vols. (Frankfurt: Suhrkamp Verlag, 1995–2000), III, 147. All further references to Benjamin's letters are indicated in the text as B plus volume and page number.

15. Ernst Penzoldt, *Lob der kleinen Form*, quoted in Köhn, 9.

16. Tergit, *Käsebier erobert den Kurfürstendamm* (Frankfurt: Krüger, 1977), 35. Quoted in Köhn, 7.

17. Two early readings shaped this debate: Frederic Jameson's critical stance, which identifies Benjamin as a reluctant convert suffused with nostalgia for bourgeois high culture, and Terry Eagleton's radical stance, which sees in Benjamin's work, beginning already with the book on the Trauerspiel, an exemplary deployment of Marxist thought in cultural criticism. Fredric Jameson, "Walter Benjamin: Or, Nostalgia," in *Marxism and Form* (Princeton: Princeton University Press, 1971), 60–82 and Terry Eagleton, *Walter Benjamin, or Towards a Revolutionary Criticism* (London: New Left Books, 1981). For a contemporary reckoning, see T. J. Clark, "Should Benjamin Have Read Marx?," *boundary 2* 30, no. 1 (Spring 2003), 31–49.

18. For a treatment of the *Denkbild* that compares Benjamin's practice to that of Theodor Adorno, Ernst Bloch, and Siegfried Kracauer, see Gerhard Richter, *Thought-Images: Frankfurt School Writers' Reflections from Damaged Life* (Stanford: Stanford University Press, 2007).

19. Friedrich Nietzsche, *The Portable Nietzsche*, ed. and trans. Walter Kaufmann (New York: Penguin 1982), 46–47.

20. For a fuller consideration of the role played by commodity fetishism and phantasmagoria in *One Way Street*, see Michael W. Jennings, "Trugbild der Stabilität: Weimarer Politik und Montage-Theorie" in Klaus Garber, ed., *Global Benjamin*, Internationaler Benjamin-Kongreß 1992 (Munich: Wilhelm Fink Verlag, 1999), I, 517–28.

21. For a more extensive analysis of rationality and irrational spaces, see Tom Gunning, "The Exterior as Interieur: Benjamin's Optical Detective," *boundary* 2 30, no 1 (Spring 2003), 105–30.

22. On the aphorism and the fragment in *One Way Street*, see Detlef Schöttker's "Nachwort" to the volume of the new critical edition of Benjamin's *Werke und Nachlaß* devoted to *Einbahnstraße* (Frankfurt: Suhrkamp Verlag, 2009), 554–71.

23. For an analysis of the role played by avantgardist forms such as Dada photomontage and constructivist assemblage, see Michael W. Jennings, "Walter Benjamin and the European Avantgarde" in *The Cambridge Companion to Walter Benjamin,* ed. David Ferris (Cambridge: Cambridge University Press, 2004), 18–34.

24. If Kracauer had possessed the same stylistic gifts as Benjamin, he would certainly by now have attained that equal status. Whatever differences the reception history of these two writers might suggest, though, one astonishing fact stands out: these essays, which constitute some of the most challenging and suggestive writing about culture in the twentieth century, appeared without exception in popular newspapers and magazines.

25. On Benjamin's relationship to Riegl and Worringer, see Michael Jennings. "Walter Benjamin and the Theory of Art History" in, *Walter Benjamin 1892–1940: Zum 100. Geburtstag,* ed. Uwe Steiner (Bern: Peter Lang, 1992), 77–102.

26. On criticism as annihilation or mortification, see Jennings, *Dialectical Images,* 164–211.

27. It takes Benjamin until 1935, in fact, before he can extend this initial aperçu into a fully theorized explanation (in the first full exposé of his unifinished masterwork of the 1930s, *The Arcades Project*): "Corresponding to the form of the new means of production, which in the beginning is still ruled by the form of the old (Marx), are images in the collective consciousness in which the new is permeated with the old. These images are wish images; in them the collective seeks both to overcome and to transfigure the immaturity of the social product and the inadequacies in the social organization of production. At the same time, what emerges in these wish images is the resolute effort to distance oneself from all that is antiquated—which includes, however, the recent past. . . . In the dream in which each epoch entertains images of its successor, the latter appears wedded . . . to elements of a classless society. And the experiences of such a society—as stored in the unconscious of the collective— engender, through interpenetration with what is new, the utopia that has left its treaces in a thousand configurations of life, from enduring edifices to passing fashions" ("Paris, Capital of the Nineteenth Century" [III 33–34]).

28. Compare, for example, the section "To the Planetarium" in *One Way Street*, the conclusion of the essay "Experience and Poverty," and the section "The Moon" in *A Berlin Childhood around 1900.*

29. For a brilliant account of Benjamin's elaboration of the concept of innervation, see Miriam Bratu Hansen, "Room for Play," *October* 109 (Summer 2004), 3–45.

11

Writers and Politics in the Weimar Republic

Karin Gunnemann

The founding of the Weimar Republic brought to an end the previous Empire's restrictions on free artistic expression, and during the twenties many writers and artists gained a new appreciation for the public and political efficacy of their work. More than ever before in the history of German culture, art was recognized as having the potential for powerfully influencing political ideology and social change. The handful of authors discussed here are in no way representative of the whole of the Weimar Republic with its outstanding variety of literary works. Many artists chose the stage for its immediacy of communicating their message and for their notion that theater had an important part to play in bringing about a better, often socialist world. Weimar theater would easily deserve a whole chapter, including the Marxist playwright Bertolt Brecht with his theory and creation of "epic theater" as a "wake-up-call" for the complacent bourgeois spectator.

Two writers who help illustrate the often troubled relation between literature and politics in the Weimar Republic are Kurt Tucholsky and Heinrich Mann. Both made the cause of democracy for Germany into the central theme in their writing. Tucholsky (1890–1935) was foremost a polemical political journalist, a humorist, and a writer of satiric poetry for the cabarets of Berlin. No ills of the Republic escaped his witty scrutiny, but when the Republic failed he ended his life in despair. Heinrich Mann (1871–1950) was both a prolific writer of fiction and one of Germany's leading political essayists. In response to the cultural changes of the twenties, he developed a new aesthetic for fiction that helped him preserve his utopian ideal of a democratic Germany. Both authors were famous during their time, though neither is well-remembered in the English-speaking world today. Alfred Döblin (1878–1957) expressed his criticism of post-war German society with greatest success in *Berlin Alexanderplatz*. The Dada-inspired formalist experimentation in this novel has earned him a permanent place in the canons of Weimar modernism. And finally there is the virtuosic storyteller and master of the German language, Thomas Mann (1875–1955). Thomas serves as an instructive case in his struggle to reconcile the new republican form of government with the German intellectual and historical tradition. More specifically, he is a representative of those writers who had great difficulty in moving away from their aesthetic and autonomous view of literature to a more "democratic" way of writing. Thomas's life and work display some of the reasons why Germany had difficulty in adopting the democracy so enthusiastically embraced by both his own brother and Tucholsky.

Brothers in Conflict

The chaotic political and social situation in Germany in November 1918, and the following year compelled many serious artists to take sides and help guide the people through this painful confusion. The tone and content of the intense debates about the role of literature in politics was set in part by the earlier famous "Bruderzwist" (fraternal dispute) between Heinrich und Thomas Mann in 1916 concerning Germany's role in the First World War. Insight into their controversy is essential for understanding their very different participation in the politics of the Weimar Republic.

Both Heinrich and Thomas left their prestigious bourgeois home of Lübeck at an early age. For about two decades they stayed personally and artistically close as they wrote in the fashion of Aestheticism, the main literary movement of the time, and were caught up in the general intellectual frenzy over the ideas and writings of Friedrich Nietzsche. They both hailed the German philosopher's vicious criticism of the bourgeoisie as hardworking but intellectually lazy. Thomas especially agreed with Nietzsche's idea of the superiority and isolation of the artist in society, and he also identified with Nietzsche's view that all cultural greatness was apolitical, if not anti-political. Also important for Thomas at this time were Arthur Schopenhauer's cultural pessimism and his metaphysical reflections on death. Alongside these two philosophers, Thomas found inspiration in what he termed the "sublime morbidity"[1] of Richard Wagner's (1813–1883) music.

Heinrich's artistic development took a very different direction. He discovered the moral and intellectual basis for his evolving democratic commitment chiefly in French philosophers and writers such as Voltaire, Rousseau, Balzac, and Zola. Heinrich was inspired by the Scandinavian critic Georg Brandes's inquiries into the relation between eighteenth-century liberal writers and the French Revolution. Just as the French philosophers of the Enlightenment had helped to bring about the French Revolution, so too it was the task of the present-day intellectual to help nourish liberatory political values. The function of art was to change the world. Looking back on his life Heinrich remembered his decision at the age of twenty-five to write social novels about contemporary life in Germany because German society did not know itself.[2]

Thomas felt some envy at Heinrich's liberal acceptance of modernity, but he confessed to his brother that his persistent sympathy with themes of decay hindered him from any similar reconciliation.[3] The outbreak of the First World War shook Thomas from his admitted political lethargy to take a vehement stand favoring the preservation of German "culture" against the onslaught of Western "civilization." In September 1914, and in January/February 1915, Thomas published two shockingly chauvinistic articles in which he called the war a "holy disaster" but also a "cleansing act," an opportunity to free Germany from the moral undermining through the "revolutionary intellect" and the "destructive reason" of the West. Germany, he believed, was destined to win the war. As "the most important people of Europe today," the rest of the world would have to pay attention to this heroic and "daemonic" country in the years to come.[4]

Heinrich was so outraged at his brother's nationalistic pronouncements that he immediately countered them with the aggressively political but also very personal essay, "Zola."[5] He modeled his composition on the nineteenth-century French writer's "J'accuse" through which Zola had helped achieve the release in 1898 of the innocent prisoner Dreyfus (the anti-Semitic Dreyfus Affair). For Heinrich the war was the final and most disastrous consequence of the German national power-state as it had been conceived in the nineteenth century. He predicted that Germany would lose this war because democracy was the political truth and its realization in Germany inevitable. Only in a democracy could humankind achieve the indubitable ideals of compassion, justice, and freedom for the persecuted and the poor. In the longest section of the essay, Zola-Heinrich elaborated his theory of the novel as social and moral action and identified the novelist as teacher of democracy.

Heinrich's essay deeply wounded Thomas who rightly discerned in it an attack not only on his person but on his work as an artist and on the whole of German culture. Thomas responded in 1918 with the nearly six hundred pages-long work, *Die Betrachtungen eines Unpolitischen* (*The Reflections of a Nonpolitical Man*).[6] Armed with the spiritual weapons of Schopenhauer, Nietzsche, and Wagner, Thomas fought against his brother's notion that the spirit should become politicized in the name of freedom. He defended his own anti-political romanticism by declaring that the Germans were by nature apolitical. He viewed Germany's move toward becoming a republic as a "spiritual-political invasion of the West," a turn to anarchism, barbarism, and a general mediocrity, a "democratic equalization" that would destroy "this country of music" with its special standing in Europe as a "people of the soul." Against his brother's demand that the artist-intellectual be political, Thomas insisted that the purpose of the artist-intellectual was to portray life's uncertainties, passions, non-reason, and "old primordial thoughts." He also heaped various insults upon his brother and one in particular, the term *Zivilisationsliterat* (civilization's literary man), stuck with Heinrich throughout the 1950s in West Germany. By the time Thomas was finishing the book at the end of 1917, it was clear to him that Germany was losing the war and that Germany's transformation into a republic was now inevitable. As he was writing the introductory chapter to the *Reflections*, he looked back and asked himself with a typical, almost appealing irony whether throughout these intensive conservative arguments he had not at least in part been writing in favor of Germany's "progress," namely, "democracy." The *Reflections* were widely read and helped intensify the public controversy over the relationship between literature and political engagement at the beginning of the republic. It placed Thomas in the limelight of political debate throughout the twenties and it remained the intellectual standard by which he would be judged by many, even as he changed, albeit with some reluctance, from a nationalist conservative into a social democrat by the end of the Weimar era.

Never before in German history had the possibility of an effective involvement of intellectuals in politics looked more promising than in November 1918. Kurt Hiller, an activist among the expressionist writers and a great admirer of Heinrich Mann, had organized the multi-city Political Councils of Intellectual Workers which were to cooperate with the Councils of Workers, Soldiers and Peasants. Though modeled on the communist Workers' Councils further to the east, they differed substantially insofar as they rejected revolution as a political solution. Instead they aimed to establish peace between the radical factions and to prepare the way for a parliamentary government.

Heinrich agreed to work in the Munich Council alongside Kurt Eisner, the chief architect of the short-lived socialist Free State of Bavaria. As chairman of the Political Council of Intellectual Workers, Heinrich gave a number of important addresses.[7] He declared the so-called November Revolution of 1918 a moral event, an opportunity for Germany to join the rest of the world which had long before adopted the ideas of freedom and justice in their constitutions. The most important task now was the enlightenment of the future voters in order to prevent a relapse into reactionary politics. The aim of the revolution, Heinrich proclaimed, was the creation of a "state of spiritual well-being" and not, as with the communists, the victory of one class over another. Heinrich assumed, naïvely but with great passion, that workers and intellectuals shared the same interests. He hoped that the Councils would help establish a socialist people's state, reconciling class differences, dismantling the monopoly economy, and creating a democratic culture in order to guard against the threat of anti-democratic Bolshevism. While starvation and violence played havoc with the livelihood of most people, Heinrich appealed for inspiration to the democratic traditions from 1848, and also acknowledged Woodrow Wilson's Fourteen Points to make the world "safe for democracy."

To Heinrich, the goal of popular democratic education was so urgent that in December 1919, he assembled a "textbook" that provided his readers an historical context for social democratic thought. The volume *Macht und Mensch* (Power and Humanity), which he dedicated "To the German Republic,"[8] was a collection of his most important political essays since 1910. In a long piece called "Kaiserreich und Republik" (Empire and Republic) which he wrote for the volume, Heinrich for the first time declared himself an active social democrat. He suggested that the solution for a viable democracy lay in the equalization of the social classes. Only if both social extremes, the proletariat and the new bourgeoisie, met in the middle and joined in their common interest in work and acquisition, could a broad petit-bourgeoisie of head-and-hand workers develop. A future-directed ethic of individual responsibility of all people working toward the common good was the basis for any democracy.

Heinrich Mann's utopian goal of a classless bourgeois society was clearly born out of despair at Germany's post-war turmoil. Notwithstanding his evident lack of insight into the factionalism and class-division that plagued industrial society and post-war Germany especially, some critics praised him as a champion of German democracy. Such acclaim was due mostly to the 1918 publication of Heinrich's most famous novel, *Der Untertan,* which he had completed before the outbreak of the First World War.[9] The serialization of the book in the weekly journal *Zeit im Bild* was stopped on August 1, 1914 (the day Germany mobilized for war), because the publishing house feared censorship and did not want to risk offending the public during a moment of intense patriotism. In the novel, Heinrich had mercilessly exposed the Wilhelmian power state with its subjects who were not only willing to serve it but were eagerly trying to imitate the political hypocrisy of the *Kaiser* in their own lives. When *Der Untertan* was finally published, it created a sensation. The violent responses to the novel give further evidence for Germany's political fragmentation at the time. But among the literati who most praised the novel was Kurt Tucholsky (1890–1935), who, in his review for the prestigious journal *Die Weltbühne,* declared that this was the way Germany should fight to get rid of the German spirit of the *Untertan.*[10] Two years later Tucholsky ranked Heinrich's *Macht und Mensch* as the most important book in this time of transition.[11]

The Five Voices of Kurt Tucholsky

When Berlin was still the imperial capital of the German Reich, Tucholsky was already well regarded as a keen critic of theater, literature, and film, and also as a formidable opponent of the person and policies of the *Kaiser.* A true Berliner, Tucholsky was an acerbic and witty writer for whom recklessness and provocation were second nature. During the Weimar years Tucholsky directed his merciless criticism mostly against both the military and the judiciary, whose corruption and incompetence he had witnessed firsthand as a law student in Berlin between 1909 and 1915. As he was preparing for a career as a defense lawyer, he discovered that his greater talent lay in social satire and cultural criticism, modes of writing in which he could express his political passion and exercise both his sense of humor and his keen sense for language (including a facility with various dialects). Above all, essays and poems gave Tucholsky the freedom to play with fictitious names. He used nicknames for all of his personal friends, and for himself he invented four pseudonyms, each representing a particular style and perspective. This "joyful schizophrenia"[12] permitted him to express his often contradictory views with playful and self-reflexive irony.

Tucholsky first developed his four authorial personae as a ruse to trick the readers of *Die Weltbühne* into believing that the contributions in this small weekly were written by different authors. Peter Panter, Tucholsky's first alter ego, had the main function of keeping his creator honest, scolding him whenever he was tempted to make concessions to society. Theobald Tiger, when not sleeping, wrote witty verses and famous chansons for various Berlin cabarets. Ignaz Wrobel was an acid, bespectacled, red-headed man whose very name was grating to the ears and hence was the preferred mouthpiece for the author's most aggressive criticism. The fourth persona was Kaspar Hauser, a bewildered man who opened his eyes after the war and "beheld a world he did not understand." He represented Tucholsky's melancholy side, who said of himself that all his life he was trying "to learn to laugh without crying."[13] Working together like the five fingers on a single hand, Tucholsky and each of his personae loved democracy and conspired to attack the remainders of an antiquated Prussianism.[14]

Tucholsky responded to the rampant violence of the early post-war years with a furious literary output. Between 1918 and 1920, he published hundreds of essays and poems alone under the pseudonymous "revolutionaries" Ignaz Wrobel and Theobald Tiger. His main goal was to make the German population aware of the powerful resurgence of the "archaic authority" of the military, a serious moral danger for the young republic. Unperturbed by the potential backlash from those he attacked, Tucholsky condemned the Prussian officers as a "fossil class." He noted that eight months had passed since the end of the war, sufficient time for the more serious crimes of the degenerate military to have been brought to trial. Instead everything was "working at the old pace."[15] The right-wing Kapp Putch in the early spring of 1920 caused Tucholsky to intensify his attacks on the government. He accused the Social Democrats of sleeping through sixteen months of dire warnings about the old officers who, having returned from the war "undefeated in battle" (such was the official lore), now feared the end of their privileged position in the Prussian conservative army and the dissolving of the Officer's Corp. Since they no longer had an external enemy to combat, they created an internal one for the purpose of self-preservation.[16] In his essay, "Militärbilanz" (Taking Stock of the Military), Tucholsky discussed the government's failure to punish those who had committed treason through participation in the Kapp Putch. He gave concrete examples of republicans who were pushed out of government positions in favor of members of the old officer corps, and he concluded with a call for strict compliance with the Versailles Treaty (a reference to the size of the army and an immediate disbandment of all local military groups).[17]

Repeatedly the reactionary press attacked Tucholsky for "foul[ing his] own German nest" by criticizing the new Republic. In March 1919, he responded to this accusation with an essay in *Die Weltbühne*, entitled, "Wir Negativen" (We Nay-Sayers), which, in a rare moment of candor, he signed with his own name.[18] As a representative for "intellectually independent men," he expressed disdain for those who suggested that approval was due to the persistently antidemocratic bourgeoisie, to the hypocritical and still power-hungry army officers, to the bloated bureaucrats and the politicians who lacked all spiritual focus and were influenced by big business. He reminded his adversaries that it was the task of the intellectuals to assure that Germany regain the world's respect. The purpose of their criticism was to sweep out "with an iron broom . . . whatever has been and is rotten and born of evil in Germany."

The breadth of Tucholsky's literary talents was amazing. Beside his daily work as a highly effective journalist, Theobald Tiger wrote and sometimes composed music for the most famous singers of the most notorious cabarets in Berlin. Even before the war Tucholsky had discovered the cabaret and theater as an arena for venting his more humorous social criticism. Once wartime censorship was lifted, the satiric cabaret again became popular as a venue for both entertainment and political-cultural dissent. Tucholsky was an ideal contributor. While not all of his lyrics were political, among the most moving were those that addressed the miseries of war and the promise of peace. The name Theobald Tiger quickly became one of the most popular in the cabaret world of the early twenties.

Politics and the Magic Mountain

Thomas Mann, meanwhile, responded to the politics of the day in a fashion altogether different from both Heinrich or Tucholsky. Until National Socialism became a true menace Thomas remained remote from political events and preferred to engage them as he had done in the *Betrachtungen,* by relating them to expansive matters of German culture and personal concerns of intellectual integrity. Insight into Thomas's complex feelings concerning the political events of the Republic's fledgling years has been greatly helped by the publication of his diaries from 1918–1921 in which he recorded his daily activities in minute and sometimes trivial detail.[19] But they also show that Thomas kept abreast of the daily papers even while he continued to study an overwhelming number and variety of books in preparation for his emergent novel, *Der Zauberberg* (*The Magic Mountain*).[20] As he neared its completion in the mid-twenties, he was inclined to experience anything concerning politics as an intrusion upon his creative labor.

Focusing on the diaries, Hans Wisskirchen has shown how various remarks concerning the early Republic mixed with assorted remarks on literary texts found their way into the finished version of *The Magic Mountain,* published in 1924.[21] As Wisskirchen argues, Thomas quickly recognized the necessity to come to terms with the political reality after the war: He knew that the imperial order was irretrievably broken. Now the urgent question was how best to integrate the new political reality into his own personal life, and how to explain that reality in continuity with German intellectual history. Wisskirchen comes to the most astonishing but convincing conclusion that Thomas's initial wish to keep everything spiritual, national, and philosophical cleanly separated from politics found its political reality in the communist revolution. In March 1919, Thomas wrote, "My sympathy grows for the healthy, humane, national, anti-ententist, *anti-political* (his italics) that is in Spartacism, Communism, Bolshevism."[22] To be sure, Thomas's remarks about the nature of the communist revolution were confused at best, but his enthusiasm for communism was fueled by his dislike for the intellectual ideals of the French Revolution which he associated with his brother, and by his hatred for what he called the "Entente-Imperialism" of the West, exemplified in the humiliating Treaty of Versailles. As early as November 1918, he had confided to his diary that as much as he was horrified at the thought of mob rule, his hatred for the triumphant "rhetoric-bourgeois" (a term he had used for Heinrich) was so great that he wished for the Bolshevization of Germany.[23] Thomas understood the revolutionary events in the first months of the republic as a new August 1, 1914; a national uprising against the western democracies in the form of communism and in union with Russia. Thomas's diaries show that he continued to have an elitist regard for Germany which he hoped would reclaim a new kind of political and cultural *Sonderweg*, or "special path." He envisaged for Germany a socialism that emphasized its nationalist character, and lay between a social democracy and a bourgeois democracy, superior to "the plutocracy of the West."[24]

Wisskirchen shows how Thomas Mann worked these political observations into his fiction. He identifies the complex figure of the Jesuit Naphta in *The Magic Mountain* as an especially good illustration of Thomas's changing attitude toward the Republic in the years up to 1924.[25] In passages written before Thomas had fully accepted Weimar democracy as an historical necessity, Naphta argues as a religious "medieval communist" for a "dictatorship of the proletariat" that will unite spirit with power. But as Thomas lost confidence in the communist cause, and at the same time became increasingly alarmed by the brutality of the radical right, Naphta's arguments changed. In the name of political reaction Naphta now became the fierce opponent to Settembrini, the novel's representative of enlightenment principles. In the pedagogical struggle over the young protagonist Hans Castorp, Naphta borrows slogans of the right conservative revolution of the early twenties. He proclaims humanism's demise and the advantages of "moral chaos." He calls for "absolute order! Iron commitment! Rape! Obedience! Terror!"

Thomas Mann's technique of mingling fiction with responses to political events is especially striking in the address he gave at the memorial service for the foreign minister Walther Rathenau, who was murdered in June 1922, at the hands of right-wing militarists. Paraphrasing Settembrini, Thomas condemned nationalistic youth for "embracing not individualism, but community, not freedom, but unconditional order and terror." In an indirect self-accusation Thomas blamed the German tradition of cultural education (*Bildung*) with its emphasis on individual development as a major obstruction to implementing democracy.[26]

Rathenau's murder spurred the pedagogue in Thomas to appeal directly to the conscience of Germany's youth. In October 1922, he addressed university students in Berlin in honor of the sixtieth birthday of the writer Gerhard Hauptmann (1862–1946), who was hailed as the cultural representative of Germany even though his groundbreaking Naturalist plays had been written at the end of the previous century.[27] Thomas, choosing "Von deutscher Republik" (About the German Republic)[28] as his topic, tried to convince the young people, most of them ardent nationalists, that democratic government was not a foreign (French or English) intrusion but could be understood as a continuation of the German political tradition. The speech conveys how Thomas himself had to work hard to arrive at this conclusion. His reconciliation with Heinrich, in January 1922, when Heinrich was seriously ill, may have contributed to his change of heart. To be sure, Thomas was faced with a dilemma: Just four years earlier in his *Reflections* he had condemned "democracy" as Western and un-German. How could he possibly try to convince his audience of the opposite without being called "a traitor?" But Thomas denied he had changed his mind, assuring his audience that he had only adjusted his views to the responsibilities of the day. While his young audience shuffled their feet in protest, Thomas insisted that the *Reflections* was intended as "a provision against the destruction of the essential fabric" of the nation, an attempt by a "conservative" to preserve German culture in its humanistic tradition. The democratic republic was the continuation of this German tradition. In calling democracy a form of humanism Thomas tried to connect the present form of government to both Gerhart Hauptmann's early concern for social justice, and the ideas of the poet Novalis and German Romanticism. Democracy, Thomas explained, was nothing else but the legal form of humanism, the unification of the national, political, and cultural life of a country. The state was undoubtedly the highest level of what it meant to be human, challenging people to accept personal responsibility for their political future and to abandon a national feeling of superiority. Democracy, Thomas concluded, was not only a moral necessity, it was Germany's "fate."

Even though there are no diaries to prove this point, critics agree that it was one of Thomas's intentions to work the major topics of his speech on the new republic into *The Magic Mountain*. In spite of his early insistence on the separation between art and politics, Thomas was proud of his keen sense for politics in his novels[29] and wanted to be understood as a writer of timely chronicles and a mapper of the psychology of his epoch. Given Thomas's stated intention, it is understandable if the reader of *The Magic Mountain* expects to find in this novel the rebuttal of some of the more conservative statements he had made in his prewar writings, a greater acceptance of democratic ideals, and lessened attention to the theme of death and decay. This expectation is intensified by the portrayal of the protagonist, Hans Castorp, who undergoes a process of education not unlike the one found in the genre of the German *Bildungsroman*. Significantly, although Castorp's story takes place mostly before the First World War, Mann insisted that he had already learned the war's deepest lessons.

Castorp has gladly become a patient in an international sanatorium for tuberculosis on the "magic mountain" in Switzerland. This house of the sick represents European civilization before the First World War in its feverish activities, sick inside but strident outside, corrupt and without moral direction. Castorp, as representative of this pre-war society, becomes infatuated with the institution's timelessness and the preoccupation with disease permeating it. Two pedagogically inclined patients, Naphta, a nihilist, and Settembrini, a literatus and humanist modeled on Heinrich, engage Castorp in high-minded intellectual debates about all aspects of human life. Naphta preaches a mixture of asceticism, communist ideology and terror while Settembrini tries to persuade Castorp to consider the validity of reason and work in the service of moral progress which, he says, are the same as "democracy." Castorp listens and tries to argue, but it is through a dream that he seems to learn a less confusing lesson. The dream occurs about two-thirds of the way through the novel, and Thomas makes clear that the conclusions Castorp draws from it are the essence of the book. He writes in italics: *"For the sake of kindness and love man should not grant death dominium over his thoughts."* For a brief moment, Castorp has understood that only reason supports loving thought and communities. When faithfulness to death and clinging to the past dominate our thinking and action, they create only "wickedness, dark voluptuousness and misanthropy."[30]

Neither the lessons of Naphta and Settembrini nor these insights from his dream take hold in Castorp, making him take responsibility for his actions or letting go of his fascination for the morbid "hermetic magic" of the sanatorium. With obvious delight, Thomas describes how Castorp develops a new passion for listening to classical music that transports him into a "blissful dream-like state" and frees him from the usual imperatives of life such as, "justify yourself!" and the "Western command to action."[31] Castorp's favorite piece is Schubert's song of the *Lindenbaum* with its voluptuous intonation of love and death. Castorp is aware of but not deterred by the fact that the song expresses the "sympathy with death," the very "sickness" about which Settembrini had warned him. When, at the vague ending of the novel, the First World War breaks out like a "thunderbolt," Castorp is catapulted from the "magic mountain" to serve as a volunteer in the German army without having made a moral decision about this action. In mindless excitement Castorp marches in mud-heavy boots into the senseless killing, humming to himself the song of the *Lindenbaum*. He is ready to die and the author admits there is little chance that he will survive the carnage.

Thomas's narrative device of using finely wrought irony to describe events and characters enabled him to detach himself from the action of the novel and from making binding moral judgments about his characters. But clearly, by the time Thomas had finished his long book, his move toward becoming an active proponent of the Weimar Republic had come no further than to criticize pre-war society harshly for its nihilistic pessimism, to give voice to a humanist democracy through Settembrini's debates, and to hint at a vague premonition of a love to come that might eventually unite all of humanity. When the novel was criticized as depicting "a world hostile to life," Mann admitted that indeed, Castorp was "emotionally and spiritually in love with death (mysticism, Romanticism)." Against his critics he argued that although he himself was no Settembrini, his fascination with the complexity of individual lives and the metaphysical rather than with the social did not make him hostile to life.[32] In 1924, Thomas was still far from able to commit himself to the Weimar Republic. This is clear in the article he wrote the same year in honor of the fifth anniversary of the republic. Here he dismissed the important document of the Weimar Republic with the derogatory term, "parchment of Weimar," and when he discussed its content, he based his judgment not on contemporary circumstances but on the nineteenth century poet Hölderlin with his dream of a German revolution.[33]

Defenders of the Republic

The difference between Thomas's engagement with the Weimar Republic at this time and that of his brother is striking. A year earlier on the fourth anniversary of the Constitution, Heinrich had used his so-called "Dresden Address"[34] as an occasion to launch a vicious attack on the government's inaction in the face of the disastrous economic situation in 1923. While granting various responsible factors, Heinrich chiefly blamed the concentration of capital in the hands of "blood-gorging" profiteers who made the German people work for them and then diverted the funds of their labor to foreign consumers. The shackles of capitalist despotism had replaced military absolutism, and the parliamentary parties were now influenced by the "dictatorship of the greediest." The Reichstag itself was a "house of ghosts." But Heinrich also blamed himself and fellow artist-intellectuals for their "criminal weakness" in failing to recognize this situation. Heinrich urged the working classes to place their trust now in "the men who think," the intellectuals, who regarded them as moral beings to whom they were responsible.

Tucholsky, meanwhile, focused his criticism of the republic on its corrupt judiciary. He demanded a "ruthless cleansing of the justice system from all monarchic elements."[35] Because of his legal training, Tucholsky felt compelled to observe court procedures, witnessing first-hand the notorious difference in treatment of left- and rightwing offenders. In an essay under his own name, he attacked the German courts for their handling of the attempted murder of the famous publisher and Jew, Maximilian Harden, in July 1922. The trial of the hired murderers was a farce. Harden was the "accused" and allowed to leave; his two would-be murderers were condemned to a few years in prison, but the German nationalistic instigators of the murder went free, justifying their deed by saying that fifty per cent of the German people stood behind them. Such judicial perversions gave a green light for more political murders, Tucholsky warned. "Tear away the false blindfold from this figure of Justice! We no longer have any justice."[36] It is little wonder that he received anonymous threats on his life calling him a traitor and a "poison-spitting Jew."

By the end of the 1923, however, Tucholsky had grown dispirited. His main artistic weapon, satire, could only succeed in a society of shared values and goals, for which words had agreed-upon meanings and change remained a real possibility. But the material and moral devaluation of the nation, now riven by political division, had reached a point where Tucholsky believed that communication through satire had been rendered powerless. Discouraged, he left Germany for Paris in April of 1924, though remaining active: He warned of the dangers of German militaristic demagogy and worked toward improved understanding between France and his native land. While he continued, if sporadically, as author of polemics on the current political situation, he would return to Germany only as a visitor in the years between 1924 and his death in 1935.

Heinrich Mann, too, was moved to reconsider the meaning of his political interventions and his status as an artist in these times of economic crisis. As he continued to battle the injustices of the so-called Republic, he reassured himself and his readers in numerous public statements that "spirit" (*Geist*), represented by artists and intellectuals, had to survive as an ideal and as "the steering power toward goals which lay beyond the material."[37] He was convinced that if the structure of society changed, art forms must also change in order to continue to communicate and teach these goals. When the *Literary Review,* a New York journal, asked him for remarks on "Intellectual Germany in 1923," Heinrich had criticized contemporary German writers for their escapism into "exotic, historic, fantastic, or mythical pieces" in order to distract their readers who were discouraged by the present political situation.[38] But at the end of 1923, in an attempt to be newly effective, he used those same popular literary means himself in his three so-called "inflation stories." Unlike those he had criticized earlier, however, these stories have an analytical origin and are in their drastic narrative anything but escapism. They are based on six extended essays in which Heinrich tried to analyze the underlying causes of Germany's economic crisis. He argued that business had become a quasi-religion in Germany to the point of taking on grotesque dimensions. Heinrich depicted this morbid, fantastic situation especially successfully in the short story "Kobes"[39] which is a satirical allegory of the Weimar Republic during the inflation. The figure of Kobes, a hydra-like phantom, is modeled after Hugo Stinnes, the prototype of the predatory capitalist in the early twenties. As a representative of the "active businessman" Kobes defines himself as the "symbol of German democracy." He is the envy, but also the death of the middle class. Communicating by radio only, the "Führer" Kobes gives orders to his lieutenants which bear shocking resemblances to those Hitler will broadcast in years to come. With this story, which has been called "more horrifying than Orwell's *1984*,"[40] Heinrich showed his ability to catch a momentous mood of the time, and his skill and willingness to adjust his artistic medium and creative expression to the tastes of contemporary readers. Through violent scenes and a fast-paced narrative style Mann wanted to move his young readers to recognize the evil power of mass propaganda and be alarmed by authority wielded without responsibility.

As Heinrich was searching for new art forms through which he could continue the moral and political education of contemporary readers, he developed a special interest in popular fiction (such as the detective stories of the British writer, Edgar Wallace), in the cinema with its attraction to young viewers, and in literature associated with the thoroughly modern art movement, the *Neue Sachlichkeit* (New Objectivity). He admired the enthusiastic energy with which many of the contemporary youth identified themselves with this matter-of-fact art form, but he was also alarmed by the way young people embraced the often soulless views of the world depicted by the *Neue Sachlichkeit* artists.[41] For the purpose of the moral instruction of future democratic citizens, Heinrich was willing to continue making remarkable artistic concessions to the aesthetic taste of his young contemporaries. In a letter to Tucholsky, who was at the time despairing about the usefulness of art in a time of mass culture, Heinrich suggested that writing fairy tales might be an appropriate literary genre.[42] He recalled how his French models, Balzac and Hugo, in a time of similar social and political crisis, had written social novels based on reality but then in critical passages had opened up the plot to visionary moments of moral instruction for the future of humankind. Between 1927 and 1930 Heinrich wrote a trilogy of social novels each of which is composed around a moral maxim, essential for a future working democracy: "learn to be responsible," "learn to endure," and "learn to be joy-ful."[43] In 1928, his brash didactic musical "Bibi,"[44] written in the style of the *Neue Sachlichkeit*, was performed in Berlin with the famous actress Trude Hesterberg.

With the same energy with which he wrote fiction, Heinrich was involved in battling those political forces that threatened to destroy the Republic. Like Tucholsky, he watched with alarm the failure of the judiciary system, and he fought with increasing urgency and courage against capital punishment.[45] When the government passed a new law censoring publications it deemed "filth" or "rubbish," Heinrich addressed the prosecuting attorney directly, reminding him that such a law would be irrelevant to the lives of poor youth who were far more damaged by the harsh realities of living in public mass quarters than by reading trashy literature.[46] With the novelist Alfred Döblin, Heinrich worked on a new textbook for the Prussian school system that would include attention to labor and popular experience rather than celebrating Germany's heroic past. The last socialist minister of education approved the book, but there was not enough interest to justify publication.

Döblin's Experiments in Form: Dada, Interior Monologue, Montage

Alfred Döblin (1878–1957) was among the left-wing writers who from the very beginning stressed the important role of the writer for the politics of the new republic. In 1921 he observed that "The poet should not become politicized, but the state must—this is our demand—become humanized and cultivated to the greatest degree."[47] Working as a medical doctor in a psychiatric practice in the proletarian Eastern sections of Berlin, Döblin gathered everyday material for his writings while also studying philosophy. Although he began as an Expressionist writer (he helped found this movement before the First World War), during his nearly sixty years he produced an astonishing array of works whose themes and styles vary from the realistic to the fabulous. In 1929 he published his best known work and the perhaps most innovative novel of the Weimar years overall, *Berlin Alexanderplatz. Die Geschichte vom Franz Biberkopf* (Berlin Alexanderplatz: The Story of Franz Biberkopf).[48] Never before in German literature had the realism of the modern metropolis with its dynamism and moral chaos been portrayed in such mythic proportion and in a style of writing that corresponded so intimately to its content. The protagonist, Franz Biberkopf, a Berlin proletarian and crimi-nal, makes repeated attempts to become a "new man," but each time he thinks he has wrested himself free of his past he finds himself thrown back once again into the quagmire of Berlin's brutal underworld.

In the novel Döblin adopted the realist collages of the Dadaists whose work he admired. To narrate the bewildering tale of Biberkopf's ruin he resorted to a patchwork of different narrative devices. He mixed the multi-perspectivism of events, including interior monologue, mostly written in colloquial language and Berlin slang, with ironic games and jarring contrasts in topic and tone. The novel is a dazzling montage of disconnected details of objects and experiences associated with the confusion of city life. Its protagonists, inhabitants of a bewildering urban landscape, are overwhelmed by the simultaneity of bits of unrelated information: scraps of newspaper articles, statistics, ordinances, stock market reports, and the jumble of overheard conversation.

Of his controversial book Döblin explained that it first emerged from his close observation of post-war German society when it had been, in fact, difficult to determine who was a criminal and who was not. The philosophical underpinning of the novel had come from his daily encounter as a physician with a new type of human being who experienced life in the big city as a buffeting between extremes of order and chaos. At the novel's end, Biberkopf, through his encounter with death and an excruciating cleansing process of the self, comes to see that life is not a consequence of fate but a rough mixture of "sugar and filth" which calls for personal assessment and responsibility. Apathetic confusion and the reduction of politics to simplistic slogans attractive to gullible citizens like himself must be replaced by a life in which people want "to know" and to "change" their situation. In an interior monologue, addressing his "Dear Fatherland," Biberkopf reassures it:"you can relax, I have my eyes wide open and cannot easily be fooled."[49] Marxists who had hoped that Döblin would be a champion for their cause were right when they stridently criticized the novel. Clearly, *Alexanderplatz* is not a work that propagates one political view over another. Döblin's message on the last page, writing about the old world that must collapse in the "morning breeze" to give way to "a new freedom" is highly ambiguous. It could be a reference to Biberkopf's rebirth as a man who now accepts responsibility for his own life and that of his country, but it is equally likely that it refers to Biberkopf's awareness of large troops "on their way to war" marching through the streets of Berlin in 1928. If so, Döblin would be depicting here with biting irony his alarm about the pressing power of fascism with its premonition of an early death.

Meanwhile, Thomas Mann's involvement with politics remained mostly mediated by culture. In 1927, he published the essay "Kultur und Sozialismus" (Culture and Socialism)[50] where he admitted that, when he tried to define "democracy," he did not have "Parteienwirtschaft" in mind (a derogatory term for party politics) but instead a combination of German culture and socialist politics. He saw a "German solution" in a union between Greece and Moscow, a society in which Karl Marx would have read Friedrich Hölderlin. Only as he watched with increasing concern as the National Socialists gained in power did Thomas's writings turn gradually from their idealism to address the reality of contemporary events. Between 1928 and 1932 he focused his energy on the celebratory responses to his nomination for the Nobel Prize in literature in 1929, and he worked intensively on his multi-volume "biblical-mythological tale" about Joseph and his brothers.[51] During the last years of the Republic he went on frequent and tightly scheduled reading tours to introduce his budding novels to readers throughout the German-speaking countries of Europe.

After 1929 Tucholsky lived in exile in Sweden. Distance and his deep depression about the political situation in Germany, however, did not diminish his intense attacks on social and political events. One of his most successful works of the time was a book provocatively entitled *Deutschland, Deutschland über alles.* It was a collaboration with the Dada artist John Heartfield, best known for his photomontage.[52] As early as 1912 Tucholsky had recognized the powerful function of photography for the class struggle.[53] Now, in 1929, Tucholsky chose selections from Heartfield's aggressive political and satirical photomontages to intensify some of the disturbing *seelische Situationen* (mental situations) he himself had experienced in the life of the Weimar Republic. He expressed his disgust by adding clever and often contrasting captions to Heartfield's stark images. The topics of the book include the glaring class differences, the inhumane justice system, the pompous bureaucrat, and the devastation of war. One of the more comical combinations of picture and text mocks the alleged impotence of the legislature. The photograph shows a proud and angry little cockatoo with ruffled crest and screeching beak to which Tucholsky gives the title, *Der Reichstagsabgeordnete* (The Reichstag Representative) and then the caption, "We will force the government . . . !"[54] The last section of the book, entitled "Heimat," is Tucholsky's declaration of love to the country of pristine nature and beautiful buildings: "We have the right to hate Germany—because we love it."[55]

As Tucholsky watched the brutality with which the National Socialists increasingly dominated public life and proclaimed Germany's right to world domination, he remarked that satire had an "upper" and a "lower" boundary and that Germany's fascist forces were too low to shoot at.[56] Nevertheless, he viciously ridiculed them from a distance in a number of chansons that were sung in the Berlin cabarets during the winter of 1930–31. As Harold Poor notes, it is both "curious and even tragic" that Tucholsky's hostility against the National Socialists also led him to severely criticize the Jews.[57] In a letter written seven months before his death, Tucholsky called the Jews a "slave-people" who deserved their persecution since they had made peace with ghetto life long ago.[58] Throughout his life he claimed that Judaism had little meaning for him since he had already "seceded from Jewry" in 1911. But the fierceness with which he attacked the Jews for their submission to Nazi ordnances can only be understood as coming from someone who perhaps still harbored a special if suppressed attachment to the Jewish people. Ironically, even as he expressed contempt for the Germanized Jew, his Jewishness only intensified the Nazis' hatred for him.

Conclusions

Of the four writers interpreted here, only the two Mann brothers continued to work for the political future of Germany through and beyond the Weimar Republic. Watching as National Socialism destroyed all possibilities for reaching the moral and political ideals for which he had fought, and exhausted by his physical ailments, Tucholsky committed suicide in 1935. Throughout his life he had struggled with his own identity and in finding a clear orientation for his own life. The invention of pseudonyms for himself was playful but it was also a device permitting him to avoid commitment to one point of view and allowing an ironic distance between himself and the events around him. His satirical approach to life and art caused him to vacillate between extremes, between love and hatred for Germany, the country with which he so closely identified. Alfred Döblin was a left-wing intellectual who actively participated in many attempts to democratize Weimar culture. However, his early disappointment in the revolution, his deep distrust of the effectiveness of the Social Democrats, and his dislike for the communist movement, prevented him from becoming politically active. His novel *Berlin Alexanderplatz* attests to his unique familiarity and sympathy with the plight of the working class but he depicts the frightful metropolis more as a sociological phenomenon than as a battleground for the social classes. The novel demonstrates Döblin's emphasis on the importance of the insightful, responsible individual over the pressures of conformity to a political system,[59] but in the figure of the transformed and repenting Franz Biberkopf, Döblin expressed his fascination with the metaphysical and mystical over the political.

Heinrich and Thomas Mann, on the other hand, became ever more vocal in their public statements as the Republic disintegrated and the Nazis gained in power. Although Thomas did not speak out strongly against National Socialism before 1930, he was one of the first writers to comment on the political threat of Fascism in Germany.[60] By 1930 he understood it to be his personal obligation not only to warn the German people, and especially Germany's youth, of the danger of the National Socialists and their anti-liberal radicalism, but to serve as a representative for Germany in international efforts at peaceful cooperation. He traveled frequently to France and participated in a number of meetings of international organizations.

In the fall of 1930, Thomas made the (for him) unusual gesture to request to speak in Berlin about the terrifying gains the National Socialists had made in the September elections. He opened his speech "Deutsche Ansprache: Ein Appell an die Vernunft" (German Address: An Appeal to Reason)[61] by questioning his own legitimacy, as an artist and as "a son of the German bourgeoisie," to address a political topic. The answers he gave show the enormous distance he had come in his understanding of politics and of the role of the artist in public life. Art, he explained, was the sphere in which the contrast between idealism and socialism was transcended. At this time of social and political crisis, when thousands of people were suffering, the artist's first allegiance belonged to the community into which he had been born. The outcome of the September elections, Thomas argued, was not simply the result of the current economic crisis but reflected the general frame of mind of the German people, whose susceptibility to political irrationality and National Socialism was only partially due to the festering resentments of the Versailles Treaty. Thomas indicated that the political place of the German bourgeoisie today was at the side of the Social Democrats; only in union with the socialists could the bourgeoisie be assured of their "beloved values: freedom, spirituality, culture." And only the socialists could fulfill three important tasks: Improve the social economic life of the working class, preserve the threatened democratic form of government, and defend a foreign policy of understanding and peace. Nazi intruders tried to disrupt the speech, and at its end Thomas had to be conducted from the auditorium through a secret back door. Through these and many more public statements Thomas became a preferred target of fascist reprisal. When Hitler's henchmen came looking for him in February 1933, he had left on a long-planned reading tour abroad. But he continued a well-informed and intensive critique of National Socialism throughout his long exile and even after the end of the war.

Of the four authors discussed here, Heinrich's assessment of Hitler and his Nazi followers proved the most prophetic. A fine example is the essay "Die deutsche Entscheidung" (The German Decision), which was published in Germany, Luxembourg, and Prague in 1931/1932.[62] Heinrich alerted his readers to Hitler's clever psychological method for gaining power "legally." But, did the German people not notice, Heinrich asked, "that one could conquer, rob, take away rights with the help of votes?" Did the Germans not even have a healthy instinct for self-preservation like animals do when they are led to the slaughtering block? Together with other artists and intellectuals, Heinrich thought that the only possible means of combating the threat of a National Socialist dictatorship was for the Socialist and Communist Parties to form a coalition—a desperately unrealistic proposition, of course, in light of the long-standing mistrust and mutual animosity between the two major parties on the left. A few days before the 1932 election, in which the National Socialist party more than doubled its membership in parliament, Heinrich urgently warned in print that the National Socialist party was neither national nor social. Behind Hitler's twaddle about "breeding a master-race" lay a false nationalism and plans for a vast blood bath. "They will have to gas the masses. Do you call this love for a nation!" Heinrich wrote.[63] In repeated addresses in Paris, he pleaded for French-German cooperation and warned of the next war as "the end of our civilization."[64]

Heinrich's last literary attempt to help his country resist fascism and war is a puzzling document. The long essay "Das Bekenntnis zum Übernationalen" (Confession to Supranationalism) appeared in the last uncensored edition of the prestigious journal, Die Neue Rundschau, in December 1932, only weeks before Hitler came to power.[65] Heinrich now declared that economically, politically, and morally the time for the nation-state had ended. National Socialism was the extreme consequence of the irrational nationalism that had seized Europe since the nineteenth century, and which monopoly capitalism had helped to enflame. He called on his fellow intellectuals to confess their allegiance to building a State of Europe before it was too late. Heinrich predicted that the world had become too weak for war, and that the irrational era would expire toward 1940. He was convinced that the German people had learned from the years of their struggle with the values of democracy and were ready to join a United States of Europe.

Evoking a "new age of reason" against the "facts of life" even while the Nazi terror was already at the door may seem bizarre. Like his brother, Heinrich was now bending historical realities to fit his ideal vision. Yet his perspective soon changed: Only three days after he had crossed the French border in flight from the Nazis, Heinrich published his first anti-fascist essay in the French newspaper, *Dépêche de Toulouse* (February 25, 1933). He was preparing himself for a long battle, his six-year role as spokesman for Germans in French exile and as mediator among several of the international political groups combating National Socialism. Meanwhile, he was also writing what would be a highly praised two-volume novel about the French King Henri IV, a moral-historical parable of tolerance which he composed as a utopian alternative to the German situation[66] A letter to the young son of his French friend Félix Bertaux summarizes Heinrich's stubborn view of the artist and Germany's political future: "For my own part I cannot say I am altogether convinced of the future victory of reason: I have seen it fail too many times. But as long as one is alive it would be stupid to give up hope."[67]

Notes

1. Thomas Mann, "Deutsche Ansprache: Ein Appell an die Vernunft," *Gesammelte Werke*, vol 11 (Oldenburg: Gerhard Stalling AG, 1960), 881.

2. H. Mann, "Theater der Zeit," *Sieben Jahre: Chronik der Gedanken und Vorgänge, 1921–1928* (Berlin: Paul Zsolnay Verlag, 1929), 267.

3. Thomas Mann and Heinrich Mann, *Briefwechsel 1900–1949* (Frankfurt a.M.: S. Fischer, 1984), 48 and 127; *Letters of Heinrich and Thomas Mann, 1900–1949* (Berkeley: University of California Press, 1998).

4. T. Mann, "Gedanken im Kriege," "Friedrich und die grosse Koalition," *Politische Schriften und Reden*, vol. 2 (Frankfurt a.M.: Fischer Bücherei, 1968), 7–65.

5. H. Mann, "Zola," *Geist und Tat: Franzosen 1780–1930* (Berlin: Gustav Kiepenheuer Verlag, 1931), 153–261.

6. T. Mann, *Die Betrachtungen eines Unpolitischen* in *Gesammelte Werke*, vol. 12 (Frankfurt a.M.: S. Fischer Verlag, 1960), 9–589; *Reflections of a Nonpolitical Man* (New York: Frederick Ungar Publishing Co., 1983).

7. H. Mann, "The Meaning and Idea of the Revolution," in *The Weimar Republic Sourcebook*, eds. Anton Kaes, Martin Jay, and Edward Dimendberg (Berkeley: University of California Press, 1994), 38–40.

8. H. Mann, *Macht und Mensch: Essays* (Frankfurt a.M.: Fischer, 1989).

9. H. Mann, *Der Untertan* (Frankfurt a.M.: Fischer Taschenbuch Verlag, 1991). The first English edition with the title *The Patrioteer* was published in New York in 1921. Two more translations, one American (*Little Superman*) and one English (*Man of Straw*), appeared in 1945 and 1947 respectively. The title of the only in-print English translation is *The Loyal Subject* (New York: Continuum International Publishing Group, 1998).

10. Kurt Tucholsky, "Der Untertan," *Gesammelte Werke*, vol. 2 (Reinbek bei Hamburg: Suhrkamp, 1975), 63–67.

11. Tucholsky, "Macht und Mensch," 359–62.

12. Tucholsky, "Start," *Gesammelte Werke*, vol. 5, 434–36.

13. Michael Hepp, *Kurt Tucholsky* (Reinbek bei Hamburg: Rowohlt Taschenbuch Verlag, 1998), 111.

14. Tucholsky, "Wir alle fünf," *Gesammelte Werke*, vol. 3, 267–69.

15. Tucholsky, "Militaria," vol. 2, 8–38, 263–72.

16. Tucholsky, "Kapp-Lüttwitz," vol. 2, 294–301.

17. Tucholsky, "Militärbilanz," vol. 2, 306–15.

18. Tucholsky, 52–57. "We Nay-Sayers," in Kaes, *Sourcebook*, 96–100.

19. Thomas Mann, *Tagebücher 1918–1921*, ed. Peter de Mendelssohn (Frankfurt a. M.: S. Fischer Verlag, 1979). Thomas Mann's diaries were opened in 1975, twenty years after his death. They are an important source for new Thomas Mann scholarship. The *Tagebücher 1918–1921* stand by themselves. Mann destroyed all earlier diaries. The next set dates from 1933 and goes to his death in 1955.

20. T. Mann, "Der Zauberberg," *Gesammelte Werke*, vol. 3; *The Magic Mountain* (New York: Knopf Publishing Group, 2005).

21. Hans Wisskirchen, *Zeitgeschichte im Roman: Zu Thomas Manns "Zauberberg" und "Doktor Faustus"* (Bern: Francke Verlag), 1986.

22. T. Mann, *Tagebücher*, 175–76. Entry from March 22, 1919.

23. T. Mann, *Tagebücher*, 84–85. Entry from November 19, 1918.

24. T. Mann, *Tagebücher*, 73–74. Entry from November 12, 1918.

25. Wisskirchen, *Zeitgeschichte*, 65–83.

26. T. Mann, "Geist und Wesen der Deutschen Republik. Dem Gedächtnis Walther Rathenaus," *Gesammelte Werke*, vol. 11, 853–60.

27. Gerhart Hauptmann, *Three Plays: The Weavers, Hannerle and the Beaver Coat* (Long Grove, IL: Waveland Press, 1991).

28. T. Mann, *Gesammelte Werke*, vol. 11, 811–52; "The German Republic," in Kaes, *Sourcebook*, 105–9.

29. Hans Rudolf Vaget, "Ein unwissender Magier? Noch einmal der politische Thomas Mann," *Thomas-Mann-Studien: Siebenunddreissigster Band* (Frankfurt a.M.: Vittorio Klostermann, 2007), 135.

30. T. Mann, *Gesammelte Werke*, vol. 3, 989.

31. T. Mann, *Gesammelte Werke*, vol. 3, 898.

32. Helmut Koopmann, ed., *Thomas-Mann-Handbuch* (Stuttgart: Alfred Kröner Verlag, 1990), 421.

33. T. Mann, "Zitat zum Verfassungstag," *Gesammelte Werke: Reden und Aufsätze*, vol. 12, 630–34.

34. H. Mann, "Dresdner Rede," in *Diktatur der Vernunft* (Berlin: Verlag Die Schmiede, 1923), 66–75. The speech was immediately translated into English for publication in the October–November–December issue of 1923 of the Boston journal *The Living Age*.

35. Tucholsky, "Die zufällige Republik," *Gesammelte Werke*, vol. 3, 219–24.

36. Tucholsky, "Prozess Harden," *Gesammelte Werke*, vol. 3, 296–304.

37. H. Mann, "Gräber des Geistes öffnen sich," *Sieben Jahre*, 483–88.

38. H. Mann, "Intellectual Germany in 1923," *New York Evening Post Literary Review* (8 December 1923), 343.

39. H. Mann, "Kobes," *Ausgewählte Erzählungen* (Zürich: Diogenes Verlag, 1964), 173–216.

40. R.W. Linn, "Heinrich Mann and the German Inflation," *Modern Language Quarterly* 23 (1962), 81.

41. H. Mann, "Zeit und Kunst," *Sieben Jahre*, 542–47.

42. Deutsche Akademie der Künste zu Berlin, *Heinrich Mann 1871–1950: Werk und Leben in Dokumenten und Bildern* (Berlin: Aufbau-Verlag, 1971), 212.

43. H. Mann, *Mutter Marie* (Berlin: Paul Zsolnay Verlag, 1927). *Eugénie oder die Bürgerzeit* (Berlin: Paul Zsolnay Verlag, 1928). *Die große Sache* (Berlin: Paul Zsolnay Verlag, 1930).

44. H. Mann, *Sie sind jung* (Berlin: Paul Zsolnay Verlag, 1929), 131–211.

45. H. Mann, "Justiz: Jakubowski," *Sieben Jahre,* 520.

46. "Letzte Warnung," *Sieben Jahre,* 297.

47. Alfred Döblin, "Der Schriftsteller und der Staat," *Die Glocke* 7, no.7 (16 March 1921); Kaes, *Sourcebook,* 288–90.

48. Döblin, *Berlin Alexanderplatz: Die Geschichte vom Franz Biberkopf* (Zürich: Walter-Verlag, 1996), translated as *Berlin Alexanderplatz: The Story of Franz Biberkopf,* ed. Eugene Jolas (New York: Continuum International Publishing Group, 2003).

49. Döblin, *Berlin Alexanderplatz,* 454.

50. T. Mann, *Gesammelte Werke,* vol. 12, 639–49.

51. T. Mann, *Die Geschichten Jaakobs* (Berlin: S. Fischer Verlag, 1933); *Der junge Joseph* (Berlin: S. Fischer Verlag 1934); *Joseph in Ägypten* (Vienna: Bermann-Fischer Verlag, 1936); *Joseph der Ernährer* (Stockholm: Bermann-Fischer Verlag, 1943).

52. Tucholsky, *Deutschland , Deutschland über alles* (Reinbek bei Hamburg: Rowohlt Verlag, 1992); *Deutschland, Deutschland über Alles: A Picture Book* (Amherst: University of Massachusetts Press, 1972).

53. Tucholsky, "Mehr Fotografien!" *Gesammelte Werke,* vol. 1, 47.

54. Tucholsky, *Deutschland,* 29.

55. Tucholsky, *Deutschland , 231.

56. Harold L. Poor, *Kurt Tucholsky and the Ordeal of Germany, 1914–1935* (New York: Charles Scribner's Sons, 1968), 198.

57. Poor, *Ordeal of Germany,* 213.

58. Tucholsky, *Ausgewählte Briefe, 1913–1935* (Reinbek bei Hamburg: Rowohlt Verlag, 1962), 325–26.

59. Kaes, *Sourcebook , 357.

60. T. Mann, "Goethe und Tolstoi: Fragmente zum Problem der Humanität," *Gesammelte Werke,* vol. 9, 169.

61. T. Mann, 870–90; "An Appeal to Reason," Kaes, 150–59.

62. H. Mann, "Die deutsche Entscheidung," *Das öffentliche Leben* (Berlin: Paul Zsolnay Verlag, 1932), 305–11.

63. H. Mann, "Wir wählen," *Das öffentliche Leben,* 256–62.

64. H. Mann, "La Guerre Prochaine," *Das öffentliche Leben,* 274–76.

65. H. Mann, *Essays: Zweiter Band* (Berlin: Aufbau-Verlag, 1956), 496–528. A long excerpt from this essay appeared in *Heart of Europe: An Anthology of Creative Writing in Europe 1920–1940,* eds. Klaus Mann and Hermann Kesten (New York: L. B. Fischer, 1943) under the title "The Supernational Manifesto."

66. H. Mann, *Die Jugend des Königs Henri Quatre* (Düsseldorf: Claassen Verlag, 1976). *Die Vollendung des Königs Henri Quatre* (Düsseldorf: Claassen Verlag, 1976).

67. Heinrich Mann and Félix Bertaux, *Briefwechsel 1922–1948* (Frankfurt a. M.: S. Fischer Verlag, 2002), 277–78.

12

Aesthetic Fundamentalism in Weimar Poetry

Stefan George and his Circle, 1918–1933

Martin A. Ruehl

For its issue of 13 July 1928, the editorial board of the German weekly *Die litera-rische Welt* asked a number of writers and public figures to describe the role that Stefan George (1868–1933) had played in their personal development. That so many of the printed replies were positive can perhaps be put down to the fact that they were published on the occasion of George's sixtieth birthday.[1] Their emphatic and often rapturous tone, however, calls for further comment—as does the fact that the vast majority of respondents chose to describe George's influence in intellectual, rather than aesthetic or cultural terms. After all, George was known primarily for his literary output, a handful of volumes of highly formalized lyrical poetry, notably *Das Jahr der Seele* (1897) and *Der Siebente Ring* (1907). Many contemporaries ranked this poetry, in its originality and impact, with that of Goethe and Hölderlin. The numerous tributes in the *Literarische Welt*, however, suggest that in the aftermath of the First World War, it was not so much George the poet, but George the prophet of a "New Man" who captivated a younger generation of *Bildungsbürger*. George had taught this generation the insufficiency of the modern, scientific-materialist worldview and powerfully reminded them of the importance of heroism, "the beautiful life" (*das schöne Leben*), and Germany's unique world-historical calling. For most of the respondents, George was a "Dichter" (poet) as well as a "Denker" (thinker), and, if anything, his impact had been greater in the realm of thought. One noted the "strange, almost exceptional fact" that even though he had "only expressed himself in books of verse," George's significance in the field of contemporary German literature was "negligible" compared to the "deep and lasting" influence he had exerted on Germany's "intellectual life."[2]

There can be little doubt that George and the coterie of followers he gathered around himself since the early 1900s, the so-called *George-Kreis* or George Circle, intended to have an intellectual impact some time before the Weimar era. One of their house journals, launched in 1910, bore the programmatic title *Jahrbuch für die geistige Bewegung*, indicating that the Circle saw itself not just as a counter-cultural, but also as a "counter-intellectual" movement, in radical opposition to the "official" *Zeitgeist* of Wilhelmine Germany. Even before the First World War, members of the Circle had voiced their critical distance to contemporary academic scholarship, their different educational ideals, and their hope for comprehensive spiritual renewal. It was only in the Weimar period, however, when George became an iconic figure and his disciples played a more prominent role in public debates, that the ideas and ideals of the Circle came to have a palpable effect in German intellectual life.

In the wake of the Great War, which he, unlike so many other German intellectuals, had denounced from the start,[3] George acquired a kind of cult following that extended well beyond the small group of acolytes—never more than twenty—who made up the core of his Circle.[4] After only a brief introductory meeting with him, the political economist Kurt Singer rhapsodized about George in a letter to the Jewish philosopher Martin Buber, remarking that his life had become ever more imbued with the conviction that "no man incarnates the divine more purely and more creatively" than George; in the eyes of Singer, George both chanelled "all the great intellectual currents" of his age and at the same time promised its total "renewal."[5] The twenty-nine-year-old Walter Benjamin would wait for hours outside Heidelberg Castle just to catch a glimpse of "the Master" ("der Meister"),[6] as George was reverently addressed by his followers,[7] and possibly developed his concept of "auratic art" in the light of George's poetry and personality.[8] In an entry for the *Encyclopaedia Judaica* (1928) Benjamin noted the particular appeal of the George Circle to assimilated German-Jewish intellectuals with a more "conservative" political outlook.[9] Gentiles seemed no less mesmerized. Albert Speer reports how in the early 1920s, he witnessed George on his way to the Heidelberg Castle, radiating "dignity and pride and a kind of priestliness. . . . The great religious preachers must have had such an effect upon people, for there was something magnetic about him."[10]

Yet George's reach went deeper and wider. His exhortation, in the opening lines of a poem from *Der Stern des Bundes* (1914)—"Who once has circled the flame / Always shall follow the flame!"—became something like a mantra for the German youth movement (*Wandervogel*) and, subsequently, the Hitler Youth,[11] thus partly confirming Georg Lukács's prediction of 1908 that George's seemingly cold and exclusive compositions would one day become *Volkslieder*.[12] According to Benjamin, his poems provided a legitimation and "sanctuary" for those scions of the German middle class who had become alienated from the bourgeois ways of their parents' generation.[13] They even inspired the anti-bourgeois rhetoric of the socialist revolutionaries in the Munich Soviet Republic (April–May 1919), who turned George's apocalyptic vision "Einzug"—"Full is the time / Awaken with a dark rumble / What so far has slumbered untouched"[14]—into one of their marching songs.[15] But George affected the German middle-class youth not just through his poetry. Throughout the 1920s, his educational ideals, notably his critique of scientific positivism and his call for a holistic form of *Bildung*, based on the ancient Greek model of the master-disciple relationship and designed to inspire the vital, creative impulses of a new intellectual elite, influenced the teaching and research agendas in the humanities faculties of various German universities. The inscription over the entrance of the new auditorium erected at Heidelberg University in 1930/31, "To the Living Spirit" ("Dem lebendigen Geist"), chosen by the noted *Germanist* Friedrich Gundolf, George's long-time favorite disciple, encapsulated these ideals and demonstrated their increasingly prominent position in German academe.[16]

The impact that George and his Circle had on the development of *Geisteswissenschaften* in the Weimar period was particularly pronounced. With his intellectual biography of Goethe (1916), Gundolf had set a precedent for a new type of scholarship that aimed at the vivid (*anschaulich*) representation of historical personalities in their essential totality (*Gestalt*), discarding the dissecting, analytical gaze of the "scientist" and turning the great individuals of the past into myths and models for the present.[17] Ernst Bertram, like Gundolf a scholar of German literature and, since 1906, an associate of the Circle, took a similar approach in his critically acclaimed (and hugely popular) *Nietzsche: Versuch einer Mythologie*, which appeared with the Circle's house publisher Georg Bondi in 1918. Ernst Kantorowicz, who joined the Circle in 1919, introduced its mythopoeic methods to the field of medieval history with his best-selling biography of the Hohenstaufen emperor Frederick II. Like Bertram's *Nietzsche*, Kantorowicz's *Kaiser Friedrich der Zweite* (1927) was published by Georg Bondi, adorned on the cover and title page with a spinning swastika, the emblem reserved for the Circle's scholarly books or *Geistbücher*, and, lacking both footnotes and a bibliography, ostentatiously addressed to a non-academic audience. More distant associates of the Circle such as Hans-Georg Gadamer incorporated central aspects of George's thinking into their philosophical systems.[18] Karl Jaspers thought that the mystical elements of Martin Heidegger's early writings bore the imprint of the George Circle.[19] Karl Reinhardt, Walter F. Otto, Paul Friedländer, and Werner Jaeger, four classical scholars who transformed the discipline of *Altertumswissenschaft* in the 1920s and 1930s, all drew, to varying degrees, on George in their critique of the new brand of positivist philology inaugurated by Wilamowitz and in their reinvention of "the classical" as an educational ideal.[20]

Even skeptical observers like Kurt Tucholsky acknowledged George and his Circle as epicentres of the intellectual revolutions that shook Germany after the First World War.[21] Max Weber, though he disapproved of George's mysticism and his tendency towards self-deification,[22] greatly admired his personality and took seriously his critique of science.[23] According to George's most recent biographer, Weber's notion of "charismatic rule" was partly formed by his impression of George's role in the Circle.[24] In the early 1920s, Thomas Mann, well aware that they viewed him as a second-rate author,[25] nonetheless believed that "truth and life" could only be found in the sphere of George and his followers. As he confided in his diary on 1 August 1921: "I would not know where to look for any positive opposition to the hopelessness of modern civilization and of intellectualistic nihilism if not in [George's] doctrine of the body and the state ["Lehre des Leibes und des Staates"]. This realization is not hindered by the fact that I, too, must consider myself opposed."[26] The essayist Friedrich Sternthal described this oppositional stance in slightly different terms. In his contribution to the anniversary edition of the *Literarische Welt* of July 1928, Sternthal remarked that George's mission was to restore to German society the sense of community ["Bindung"] it had lost in the wake of the Protestant Reformation and to save it from the two types of materialism represented by American capi-talism and Soviet communism, respectively.[27]

Since the beginning of the twentieth century, George and his followers had thought of themselves as representing what they called "the Secret Germany" ("das geheime Deutschland")—a kind of nucleus or avant-garde that would bring about their country's cultural and intellectual rebirth in its moment of greatest need. With the military defeat of 1918, that moment seemed to have arrived. The Weimar years were the "times of chaos" ("Zeiten der Wirren") that George invoked in one of his last poems, entitled "Der Dichter in Zeiten der Wirren," first published in 1921 and then incorporated in the final cycle *Das Neue Reich* of 1928. For the members of the Circle, these times represented both a moment of crisis and a moment of opportunity to perform their redemptive task. If their self-consciously guarded esoteric status prevented them from truly becoming "insiders" of the Weimar Republic, they nonetheless ceased being the "outsiders" they had been in the Wilhelmine era[28] and actively penetrated the public sphere, a process that was doubtless aided by the fact that a relatively large number of them occupied exalted positions in German academe. It was in the Weimar period, at any rate, that George emerged as a new "König im Reich des Geistes," as Sternthal put it,[29] and claimed a central place in Germany's intel-lectual landscape.

If 1918 marked a turning point in the history of the Circle, 1933 marked an end-point of sorts. Hitler's seizure of power in January had already driven a wedge between the Jewish and non-Jewish disciples. When their Master, who had obliquely acknowledged his role as the spiritual "ancestor" of the new re-gime,[30] died in December of that year, his Circle quickly dissolved. Some mem-bers embraced National Socialism; others emigrated; yet others, notably Claus and Berthold von Stauffenberg, eventually joined the resistance. None of these choices, as Ulrich Raulff has shown,[31] can easily be explained in terms of George's teachings. Subsequent efforts to revive the spirit of the Circle, for instance Wolf-gang Frommel's foundation of the literary journal *Castrum Peregrini* in 1951, proved fruitless. Despite its relatively loose structure and its wide dispersion in other networks, the Circle ultimately revolved around the charismatic figure of George to such an extent that the latter's end also spelt the end of the former.

For a variety of reasons, it thus makes sense to consider the writings of Ste-fan George and his disciples under the rubric "Weimar thought." Yet hardly any scholars have done so to date. With one important exception,[32] none of the major historians of Weimar Germany discuss the ideas of the George Circle in any de-tail.[33] In the works of Peukert, Mommsen, Schulze, and Winkler, the Circle does not feature at all.[34] Bußmann's early survey of Weimar thought, similarly, fails to mention George and his followers.[35] There are only passing references in the classic intellectual histories by Mosse, Stern, and von Klemperer as well as the more recent studies by Phelan, Barnouw, and Durst.[36] The few historians who comment on the place of the George Circle in the intellectual landscape of Wei-mar Germany tend to locate it on the right of the political spectrum. Eric Weitz and Richard Evans, for instance, have described the thinking of the Circle as "conservative."[37] Others have associated it with the ideas of the so-called Conservative Revolution.[38] In his acclaimed study of the Circle, Robert Norton has gone a significant step further, arguing that George helped create "the psychological, cultural, and even political climate that made the events in Germany leading up to and following 1933 not just imaginable, but feasible."[39]

My aim in the following is to challenge—or at least modify—these readings. The role that George and his Circle played in Weimar thought cannot be reduced to that of conservative "critics of modernity" and much less to that of progenitors of the Third Reich. George, who rejoiced at the revolutionary unrest during the early years of the Weimar Republic and explicitly called himself a "revolutionary,"[40] was hardly a conservative. Nor can he be labelled a "cultural pessimist" (F. Stern), imbued as he was with the hope for the imminent rebirth of European civilization out of a revived German spirit. Unlike Oswald Spengler, Arthur Moeller van den Bruck, Othmar Spann, Ernst Niekisch and other representatives of the Conservative Revolution, he and his disciples did not conceive of this revival primarily in political terms. For the members of the Circle, the "crisis of classical modernity" (D. Peukert) could not be solved by re-creating the authoritarian structures and the borders of Bismarck's empire or by returning to some idyllic, pre-industrial form of *Gemeinschaft* (community); nor could it be overcome by establishing a *völkisch* or racist utopia.

George and his Circle, to be sure, rejected the Weimar Republic as comprehensively and radically as any ideologues of the Conservative Revolution and the *völkisch* Right—or, for that matter, the Communist Party (KPD). The form that their rejection took, however, was quite distinctive and arguably unique in the context of Weimar thought. Though they were compatible with certain tenets of National Socialism, the ideas of the George Circle were hardly identical with it or necessarily conducive to its later ascendancy. All things considered, they are best described as a variant of what Stefan Breuer has called "aesthetic fundamentalism,"[41] that is, the quasi-religious belief in the wholesale renewal of an utterly corrupt modern civilization through the redemptive power of art, or, to put it in Weberian terms: the re-enchantment of a thoroughly rationalized world through the charisma of a new poet-prophet-god. For the members of the Circle, that aesthetic redeemer, of course, was none other than George himself. George's verse, they believed, had the power not just to transform their own lives, but also—and partly through their example—to bring about the cultural-spiritual revival of Germany and ultimately the rest of Europe.

Though the George Circle was acutely critical of those aspects of modernity they considered detrimental to culture (materialism, rationalism, "scientism," democratization, "massification," and so on), Breuer overstates the anti-modern dimension of their aesthetic fundamentalism. The palingenetic vision of the Circle,[42] as will be argued here, was inspired less by an outright rejection of modernity than by the conception of an alternative modernity. In sharp contrast to many *völkisch* and neo-Romantic theorists of the Weimar era, George and his followers did not hold up as their ideal a medieval *Ständestaat*, let alone the pre-Christian, pre-Roman "barbarism" of the ancient Germanic tribes. At the

same time, their aesthetic concerns made them extremely wary of modern technology, which set them apart from "reactionary modernists" like Ernst Jünger
and Werner Sombart.[43] The numerous studies of the George Circle published
in Germany over the past fifteen-odd years, in particular the works by Groppe,
Braungart, Kolk, Karlauf, and Raulff, have given us a more complex, nuanced
understanding of the Circle's critique of modernity and its relation to other intellectual currents of the Weimar period, including National Socialism.[44] There has
been a tendency in some of the recent German-speaking scholarship, however,
to downplay the anti-democratic, illiberal, and racist elements of the Circle's
worldview and to present the Master and his disciples as largely unpolitical,
cosmopolitan humanists.[45] This interpretation of Georgean thought is no less
misleading than the "proto-Nazi" one. Insofar as it was directed against specific institutions of the Weimar Republic, the aesthetic fundamentalism of the
George Circle had decidedly political implications. My goal in this essay is to
investigate these implications without losing sight of the Circle's larger cultural
concerns and its ideological distance from the thought of the *völkisch* as well as
the fascist Right.

In the following, I will provide a brief survey of the Circle's main contributions to several key Weimar debates: about Germany's national identity in the
aftermath of her military defeat, the relative merits of a *Staatsnation* (a nation
defined by its political structures) as opposed to those of a *Kulturnation* (a nation defined by its cultural achievements), the post-Nietzschean dichotomy between "science" and "life," the call for a redemptive "Tat" (deed) as well as a
redemptive "Täter" (man of action), and the notion of a trans-European Reich
under German hegemony, which numerous Weimar intellectuals invoked as an
antithesis to the Versailles settlement. The Circle's interventions in these debates
were not presented in any systematic or axiomatic manner, but in the highly al-
lusive idiom of George's poetry and the aureate, at times oracular language that
characterized the works of most of his followers. Some critics insist that any attempt to distil specific, topical doctrines out of these writings is bound to fail or
at least to do gross injustice to their irreducible complexity and ambiguity. Others point out that there was so much ideological diversity within the Circle that
one cannot speak of a shared set of beliefs voiced by its different members, let
alone a single, unified dogma known as "Georgean thought."[46] These are important provisos that necessarily qualify a generalizing intellectual historical assessment of the Circle such as the present one—but they do not invalidate it. As one
of the most distinguished scholars in the field reminds us: if it is accepted that
George "controlled, authorized, and authenticated" the principal publications of
his followers and that a follower only qualified as such inasmuch as he adhered
to the Master's views, then it is possible to reconstruct certain core tenets of the
Circle by examining a selection of its most prominent texts.[47]

This essay combines a close reading of George's own poetic utterances,[48]
which represented a kind of gospel in the eyes of his disciples, with a more contextual examination of several important writings by his followers to arrive at a
critical assessment of what might be viewed as the two foundational concepts or

idées mères that determined the specific forms the Circle's aesthetic fundamentalism took in the Weimar years: first, the idea of a Secret Germany, a crucial feature of the Circle's palingenetic nationalism,[49] which grew out of their earlier notion of a *welthaltig* or world-containing *Deutschtum* (Germanness); second, the idea of the Reich, which reveals some of the more straightforwardly political aspects of Georgean thought since 1918 as well as its resonances with certain aspects of National Socialist ideology.

The following sections tackle these two themes in turn. The first examines the increasingly nationalist notion of Germanness that George and his followers espoused after World War I and its complex relation to their self-perception as the embodiment (or harbingers) of a Secret Germany; it also investigates their conception of the poet as seer, teacher, and leader, which informed the Georgean program of comprehensive renewal, and highlights its fundamentally aesthetic concerns. The second section discusses Kantorowicz's popular 1927 biography of the medieval emperor Frederick II to map out the Circle's vision of Europe as a trans-national, and at the same time identifiably German Reich. The essay concludes with a few general observations on the distinctive place these two ideas—of a Secret Germany and the Reich—occupied in the realm of Weimar thought and their ambivalent legacies.

Secret Germany and Weimar Germany: Redefining *Deutschtum* after the Great War

In the 1890s and 1900s, George's ideal of a "Roman Germany" ("römisches Deutschland") stood in sharp contrast to the nationalist orthodoxy of the Second Reich. His celebration of the South in *Der Teppich des Lebens* (1899) and *Der Siebente Ring*[50] represented an implicit critique of the prussophile patriotism inaugurated by intellectuals like Heinrich von Treitschke, who, in the aftermath of Bismarck's bitter struggle with Catholicism in the 1870s, the so-called *Kulturkampf*, denounced Rome as the ultramontane enemy of the Reich and demanded the elimination of all Latin influences for the sake of German cultural autonomy.[51] While Treitschke's followers glorified the Hohenzollern and their colonization of the Slavonic and Baltic lands, the George Circle exalted the Holy Roman Empire of the Hohenstaufen dynasty. For the former, the symbol of Germanness was the *furor teutonicus* of Hermann the Cheruscan (16 BC–AD 21);[52] for the latter, it was the restrained, classical beauty of a thirteenth-century equestrian statue in Bamberg Cathedral, the so-called "Bamberger Reiter," whom Kantorowicz would call a "Germanic type" in his *Kaiser Friedrich der Zweite*.[53]

After 1918, this cosmopolitan spirit became mixed with more narrowly patriotic sentiments. The experience of the Great War and its aftermath—Versailles, the war guilt debate, reparations, the occupation of the Rhineland and the Ruhr area—evidently aroused the national passions of the *Georgeaner*. As one of the younger disciples, the political economist Edgar Salin, remarked in his memoirs, the "outlawing" of the German people during the War and even more after Versailles was depressing and unbearable for the members of the Circle. "In the years 1919–32 more clearly than ever before," therefore, "the path of honour pointed in a very similar direction for the German friends of the Poet [i.e., George] and the German people."[54] In particular, Friedrich Wolters, who after George's alienation from his one-time favorite Friedrich Gundolf in the mid-1920s became a central figure in the Circle, began to strike a much more politicised and assertively patriotic note in his publications, celebrating Goethe as a national poet and glorifying Germany's struggle against her Latin ("welsch") enemies over the centuries, from the Investiture Controversy to the Franco-Prussian War.[55]

Although George remained critical of Wolters's political activism,[56] both his poetic and his private utterances reveal the extent to which he, too, began to develop a more patriotic vision of Germanness.[57] If his earlier works had been indebted to the spirit of Hölderlin and Nietzsche, the models for George's new collection of poems, *Das Neue Reich* (1928), seemed to be Arndt and Fichte. Seeing his own vocation as "poet of the Germans,"[58] George prophesied Germany's purification from shame, her coming rebirth and her universal mission: "that one day the heart of the continent shall redeem the world."[59] This rebirth, he declared in "Der Dichter in Zeiten der Wirren," written in 1918 and originally published in 1921,[60] could only come after a comprehensive destruction of the old order. It would be brought about by

> A young generation that measures man and thing once more
> With genuine yardsticks · that both with beauty and with gravity
> Rejoicing in its singularity · proudly detached from others
> Renounces both the cliffs of brazen arrogance
> And shallow swamps of false fraternization
> That spewed out what is brittle cowardly and tepid
> That through its sacred dreaming doing and suffering
> Begets the only one who helps the Man. [61]

The context of the passage implies that this young generation ("jung geschlecht") hails from Germany, indeed that it is identical with the new generation of disciples that George began to gather around himself after the First World War, in which six of his erstwhile followers had perished. The emphasis on their singularity and their immunity from all outside influences ("vor Fremdem stolz") is notable, as is the critical allusion to the—in George's eyes, false—ideals of the French Revolution ("erlogner brüderei"). Perhaps because, as a native of the region, he was offended by their occupation of the Rhineland,[62] the Master, who had been deeply influenced by French symbolist poetry in the 1890s, now began to show signs of Francophobia, at one point even demanding that "these French be exterminated."[63] Deeply worried by what he perceived to be the Americanization of German culture in the Weimar years, George prophecied the "destruction of all true nations" through the "victory of the Anglo-American standard ant" ("Sieg der angloamerikanischen Normalameise"). Americanization meant "antification" ("Verameisung"), he remarked, and would eventually result in the "total degradation of humanity" ("die völlige entseelung der menschheit").[64]

In the aftermath of the First World War, George re-evaluated another component of his earlier cosmopolitan conception of *Deutschtum*, the German "Drang nach Süden."[65] Even more notable are his frequent diatribes against the Curia and the "clerics," which stand in sharp contrast to the largely pro-Catholic sentiments the Circle expressed around the turn of the century. Edith Landmann, who played Eckermann to George's Goethe for much of the 1920s, recalls his lashing out bitterly against the Catholic church, decrying its "lack of interest" in Germany and in European culture in general.[66] Bismarck, Wilhelm II and "Prussianness" on the other hand, George now saw in a more positive light, observing, evidently with an eye on the last of the Hohenzollern, that "a bad emperor is still better than no emperor at all."[67]

In the Weimar period, the Circle also seems to have become more preoccupied with the question of race. In 1920, one of the new disciples, the classicist Kurt Hildebrandt, published a treatise on racial hygiene, entitled *Norm und Entartung des Menschen*.[68] George apparently felt ambivalent about the idea of a state-directed eugenic policy,[69] but nonetheless defended Hildebrandt's book against the criticism of Salin.[70] Wolters spoke of the "inferior races" of the French in his 1923 pamphlet "Der Rhein unser Schicksal" and extolled the "holiest herd of our race" in his *Blättergeschichte*.[71] George seems to have conceived of this herd in European rather than German terms.[72] It was the "white kin"[73] of Western Europe that, he believed, had to be saved from the "yellow apes" of Asia,[74] as well as from miscegenation with the African races. According to George, the decline of the French was due to interracial marriages,[75] or what he called "blood shame" ("Blut-schmach") in his 1917 poem "Der Krieg."[76] The racial divide, for him, lay between Europe on the one hand and Africa as well as Asia (to which he apportioned Russia) on the other, but not between Germanic and "welsch," or Aryan and Semitic, peoples.

This does not mean that George, as is sometimes claimed,[77] was philosemitic—and neither, for that matter, were his disciples.[78] On the contrary, given the large number of Jews among George's immediate entourage (they included Karl and Hanna Wolfskehl, Friedrich and Ernst Gundolf, Berthold Vallentin, Ernst Morwitz, Edith and Julius Landmann, Erich von Kahler, Edgar Salin, Wilhelm Stein as well as Gertrud and Ernst Kantorowicz),[79] expressions of anti-Semitism in the Circle were surprisingly numerous. The Master himself, though he declared that all loyal disciples, whether Catholic, Protestant or Jew, were "of his race,"[80] yet remarked that Jews were "different people" who did not "experience things as deeply as we do." He would never allow them, he told Ernst Robert Curtius, to comprise the majority in the Circle.[81] Hildebrandt reports that already during the First World War, George described Jews as "agents of decomposition" in the political and the intellectual sphere and expressed his dissatisfaction with "their attitude."[82] As for the disciples, there were not infrequent antisemitic remarks *intra muros*, especially from the "third generation" (Max Kommerell, Johann Anton, Woldemar Uxkull-Gyllenband),[83] sometimes with regard to other Circle members.[84] Kommerell, George's youthful favourite in the second half of the 1920s, noted with some satisfaction that his antisemitism was proverbial in the Circle.[85]

Hildebrandt recalls the anti-Jewish tendencies of the "nationally oriented" disciples,[86] probably an allusion to the sub-groups around Wolters in Marburg and
Kiel.[87] Wolters's biography of George, the so-called *Blättergeschichte*, compiled
over a decade and a half and published in 1930, with the Master's explicit ap-
probation, as the official history of the Circle, downplayed the contributions of
Jewish disciples (most notably that of Friedrich Gundolf) and was regarded as
anti-Semitic by many readers.

In view of the growing prominence of Wolters and his adherents as well as
George's implicit endorsement of their attitude, it seems fair to say that in the
post-war era the members of the Circle began to embrace a more nationalist
conception of *Deutschtum*. The birth of the new republic in the shadow of defeat,
the humiliating terms of the Treaty of Versailles, and the experience of Weimar
mass culture obviously led them to re-assess their earlier cosmopolitan ideal of
a "Roman Germany." The anti-Catholic polemics, the diatribes against "die Wel-
schen," the positive reassessment of Prussia, the heightened concern with racial
issues—this was Germanness in a new key. In his 1930 review of Max Kommerell's book *Der Dichter als Führer in der deutschen Klassik*, Walter Benjamin
observed that the notion of a "Secret Germany" had been incorporated into the
ideological arsenal of the German Right, where the magic cap ("Tarnkappe")
of the George Circle hung next to the steel helmet ("Stahlhelm") of the neo-
conservatives and the National Socialists.[88]

An otherwise perceptive commentator on George and his Circle, Benjamin seems to be off the mark here. The new notion of *Deutschum* espoused
by the *Georgeaner* in the Weimar era was hardly congruent with the *völkisch*
ideas of the radical Right. It was always counter-balanced by a broader, universal vision and the understanding that Germany belonged to a larger European,
indeed Mediterranean civilization. Next to the shining armour of the German
emperors, George invoked the cedar trees of the Orient; next to Baldur he saw
Apollo.[89] The tirades of Wolters and Elze against France and Rome were offset
by Vallentin's and Gundolf's paeans to Napoleon and Caesar.[90] And despite the
more narrowly political attacks on Versailles and Weimar, there remained the
wider concern with the aesthetic regeneration of Europe. As George remarked
to Hildebrandt shortly after the end of the First World War, his only hope was
now "the revival of Europe out of the German spirit."[91] The ideological distance
between the Circle and more aggressively nationalistic groups like the Conservative Revolution is thrown into relief by the notion of a Secret Germany.

"Das geheime Deutschland" was an in-house term used by members of the
George Circle to refer both to themselves and to the "Dichter und Helden" of
the past whom they venerated, for instance Hölderlin and the Hohenstaufen
emperor Frederick II, but also non-German figures such as Dante and Napoleon.[92] The term first appeared in a 1910 essay by Karl Wolfskehl, one of George's
original associates, who described George's poetry as the manifestation of a different, "secret" Germany, distinct from the apparent, "public" Germany that was
the Wilhelmine Empire.[93] Norbert von Hellingrath, like Wolfskehl an early associate of George's, invoked the concept in his 1915 lecture on "Hölderlin und

die Deutschen."[94] George himself chose the title "Geheimes Deutschland" for one of the poems he composed in the early 1920s, whose final stanza alludes to the "protective slumber" in which the Secret Germany rests, hidden for a long time in a "deep innermost shaft" ("in tiefinnerstem schacht") beneath a "sacred earth," to emerge one day and to decide the fate of the nation, indeed of human civilization.[95] But the notion of a Secret Germany represents a kind of leitmotiv throughout his poetic oeuvre, at least since the publication of *Der Teppich des Lebens* in 1899.

In the earlier poems, the Secret Germany is described as a small, selective group of men, imbued with a higher calling and touched by (or at least in correspondence with) a divine entity.[96] It is contrasted, repeatedly and favorably, with "the masses" which are depicted as obsessed with material possessions dismissed by the poet, alternatively, as "wust" (debris), "tand" (bric-a-brac) and "flitter" (frippery).[97] Alongside materialism, the other great evil of the present age that the members of the Secret Germany have to resist is empty intellectual speculation, a mode of scientific or scholarly inquiry that has lost touch with life and is blind to the divine. These modern forms of intellectualism and scientism the poet denounces as "flimsy fabrications of the brain" ("dünnes hirngeweb").[98] The Secret Germany is to provide an antidote to this "twin poison" ("doppelgift") of materialism and intellectualism which threatens to destroy modern man. In *Der Stern des Bundes*, the masses cry out when they realize the worthlessness of their possessions and their scientific understanding of the world:

> What can we do before we're smothered by our own detritus
> Before our self-created phantoms sap our brain?[99]

The implicit answer to this question proffered in the early poems is that "they," viz., the masses, cannot do anything to alter their fate, but there is the hope that modern civilization can yet be saved by the select few, that is, the members of the Secret Germany, whom George at times associates explicitly with the members of his Circle. Their hidden presence within society promises redemption, the coming of a new world, a "reich des Geistes" (realm of the spirit), as George calls it in the third book of *Der Stern des Bundes*, juxtaposing the spiritualism and idealism of his followers with the intellectualism and materialism of their age. The circle of disciples has been transformed by the experience of the new Georgean god ("Maximin")[100] into an ideal *Lebensgemeinschaft* (living community) or Staat (state) that constitutes of nucleus or germ with the potential to transform, in its turn, their surroundings and thus bring about nation-wide regeneration.

Before the First World War, George seems to have regarded this process of wider regeneration as imminent and he seems to have conceived of it in more expansive, European terms. When he speaks of "The new people awakened by thee [i.e. Maximin],"[101] he appears to have in mind not just the German people. The poem "Franken" in *Der Siebente Ring* evokes a wider realm, beyond contemporary national boundaries, modelled on the Carolingian Empire. "Die Gräber in Speier," similarly, alludes to the Holy Roman Empire of the Middle Ages which included large parts of present-day Germany, France, and the Mediterranean South. In the poems published after the First World War, by contrast, George appears less sanguine about the prospects of wider regeneration and he identifies the Secret Germany more narrowly with the features of his fatherland, which he now praises as the country where "the radiant Mother first revealed her true countenance" to the "decayed and decadent white Race." Germany, he says in the same poem ("Der Krieg"), is "too beautiful" that foreign intruders should "ravage" it and despite the recent military misfortunes, it is still so full of "promise" that it "will not die."[102]

The post-war poems are different also insofar as they describe the masses in considerably more negative terms. They now seem to represent an obstacle to, rather than an object of, the great task of cultural transformation to be undertaken by the Secret Germany. There are earlier instances, to be sure, of this kind of rhetoric in George's verse. Already in "Die tote Stadt,"[103] he had condemned the people simply for their profusion ("your very number is sacrilege") and in *Der Stern des Bundes* he had announced:

> Tens of thousands must be smitten with the holy madness
> Tens of thousands must be destroyed by the holy plague
> Tens of thousands by the holy war.[104]

Such images of violence and destruction, however, become more prominent in the cycle *Das Neue Reich*, where George enunciates his fundamentalist critique of modern society in a more militantly apocalyptic idiom. In the first of the "Sprüche an die Toten," for instance, he describes the process of catharsis necessary for the coming of the new age as a violent purging of the German nation from internal as well as external corruption:

> When one day this race will have cleansed itself of disgrace
> Will have thrown off the shackles imposed by their oppressor
> Will feel nothing inside but the hunger for honour
> Then the field of battle, full of endless graves, will be alight with a bloody
>   glow[105]

In "Der Dichter in Zeiten der Wirren," George suggests that even the horrendous bloodletting of the First World War was only a prelude to a much greater crisis which alone will bring about genuine, fundamental change:

> An even sharper ploughshare must slash the soil
> An even thicker haze must threaten the air[106]

These lines leave little doubt that death and destruction were an integral part of George's palingenetic vision after 1918. They show George, the self-appointed critic and "judge" ("Richter") of his time at his most fundamentalist. But they must be read in conjunction with other utterances in *Das Neue Reich*, which indicate that his notion of palingenesis was hardly "ultranationalist," as Roger Griffin and other scholars have claimed.[107] "Der Dichter in Zeiten der Wirren," "Der Krieg," and "An die Toten" are complemented by various poems that evoke rebirth and renewal as gradual, cultural-spiritual processes rather than violent, militant ones. In "Goethes letzte Nacht in Italien" and "Hyperion," for instance, George depicts his own role as poet-prophet in the context of a longer, German literary tradition that is attached to classical "maass" (measure or proportion) and conceives of Germany's cultural regeneration in terms of her fusion with the heritage of ancient Greece. Many of the "Sprüche," especially those "An die Lebenden," reiterate central motifs of the earlier verse: the transformative power of the Circle, the sense of a community based on love and the charisma of the Master, the poet's role as educator towards the beautiful life. Indeed, it is only through the poet and his community of disciples, George implies, that redemption can come. The poet, not the politician (Hindenburg is briefly alluded to in "Der Krieg"), will bring about meaningful change: through his inspired, prophetic words, his exemplary life and *Gestalt*, and through his followers. If George regarded himself as a "leader" ("Führer") in the sense that his one-time favorite Kommerell had portrayed Hölderlin as a leader in *Der Dichter als Führer in der deutschen Klassik*, and if he regarded his Circle as a "state" ("staat"), then these terms should be understood metaphorically. George doubtless wanted his works and his Circle to have a political effect—but he did not want to bring about this effect by political means, since he viewed the sphere of politics as inherently subordinate, epiphenomenal to the sphere of *Geist* in which the actual transformations were to take place. All the necessary solutions were first discovered in the realm of *Geist*, he remarked to Ernst Robert Curtius in 1919; political events inevitably lagged behind.[108] The Secret Germany was not a political entity, then, but, despite its own ambitions and pretensions, first and foremost a kingdom of the spirit.

His "germanocentric" turn in *Das Neue Reich* notwithstanding, George's ideal of a Secret Germany also remained a predominantly European construct. Again and again, he associates it with the borderlands of Germany and with the former territories of the Holy Roman Empire. The central stanza of "Goethes letzte Nacht in Italien," for instance, describes a wine harvest in the Rhineland, the region in which George had grown up and in which Latin and Germanic cultural influences historically converged:

> There by the Roman wall the frontier of the Reich
> I had a vision of my secret homeland [*heimliches muttergefild*][109]

The Roman wall is a reference to the *limes*, which marked the boundaries of the Roman empire, and George seems to imply that the "heimliches muttergefild" evoked by the lyrical "I" (Goethe) is identical with the Secret Germany. The word "weidicht" (denoting an area, generally near a river or a lake, grown with willow trees) in "Der Krieg" also recalls the Rhineland.[110] In "Burg Falkenstein," too, German and Latin, North and South are united.[111] George's vision in this poem, as Ray Ockenden observes, "embraces the whole of Germany as well as the Mediterranean south."[112] Even in the later verse, thus, George's notion of a Secret Germany continued to reflect some of his early francophilia and his medievalizing nostalgia for a trans-national Reich centred around the Rhenish heartland of the former Carolingian Empire.

All these features of the Secret Germany—its European expansiveness, its spiritual nature, its cultural concerns, and in particular its elitism—indicate the extent to which the palingenetic nationalism of the George Circle was different from that of the *völkisch* Right, with its racist populism, and that of the Conservative Revolution, with its statist authoritarianism. They also indicate that the Circle's notion of poetic leadership based on pure charisma was distinctive from—and potentially more radical than—the uneasy fusion of charismatic *Führertum* and bureaucratic governance established by National Socialism.[113] The idea of a Secret Germany throws into relief what was aesthetic and what was fundamentalist about the Circle's aesthetic fundamentalism, an ideological configuration that was quite unique in the context of Weimar thought.

Imperium Teutonicum or Pan-Europa? The Idea of the Reich

If George's poetry suggests the European, universalist dimensions of the Circle's ideal of cultural renewal, the hero-worshipping biographies composed by his disciples in the 1920s indicate the limits of the Circle's cosmopolitanism and the ways in which their idea of a Reich lent itself to certain expansionist notions of German hegemony in Europe. The most influential of these biographies was Ernst Kantorowicz's *Kaiser Friedrich der Zweite* (1927).[114] Introduced to George by Woldemar Uxkull-Gyllenband, who quickly became his intimate associate,[115] Kantorowicz belonged to the third generation of disciples, many of whom, notably Max Kommerell, Johann Anton, and Walter Elze, belonged to the so-called Marburg Circle, a sub-group of the George Circle that had crystallized around Friedrich Wolters. Although it echoed some of the Circle's earlier cosmopolitan ideas, his book *Kaiser Friedrich der Zweite* was composed, to a great extent, in the new, more stridently nationalistic key sounded by Wolters and his followers.[116]

Distributed by Georg Bondi and adorned with the signet reserved for the *Geistbücher* in the Georgean series *Blätter für die Kunst*, a curved swastika, Kantorowicz's book was a certified product of the George Circle. George himself had suggested a biography of the medieval emperor, insisting that Frederick's history be written "as the myth of the entire [German] nation's longing for the unification of North and South."[117] And the Master played a crucial role in the conception, production and publication of *Kaiser Friedrich*.[118] Alongside Bertram's *Nietzsche*, Kantorowicz's biography was also one of the most popular works composed by a member of the Circle.[119] It thus not only provides insight into the vision of the Reich within the Circle, but also offers some clues about the reception of that vision amongst the educated elites of Weimar Germany.

For George in the 1920s, Frederick II no longer just embodied the people's yearning for the unification of North and South, he also represented an essentially German heroic figure.[120] Like so many other aspects of his *Weltanschauung*, George's conception of the Middle Ages changed after the First World War. His early poem "Die Gräber in Speier," first published in 1903, had invoked the glory of the Holy Roman Empire in order to denounce the Second Reich with its undignified ruler Wilhelm II.[121] In 1928, by contrast, he presented the medieval emperors as the warlike harbingers of a once-more heroic Germany, mythical figures announcing the violent rebirth of their country. He now spoke of "our emperors" and of the Hohenstaufen in particular as part of a specifically German historical legacy.[122] As he told Vallentin in October 1924: "There is nothing comparable to the glory of the Staufen in the history of any other people."[123]

Kantorowicz's Frederick, to be sure, was still in many respects a foreign figure. His relations with the Orient took a prominent place in *Kaiser Friedrich* and so did his programme to renew the former Roman Empire, the *renovatio imperii Romanorum*.[124] Kantorowicz frequently emphasised Frederick's Mediterranean attributes—his Roman spirit,[125] his exotic entourage, his strong affinities with Sicily—and made much of the civilising influence his *romanitas* had on Germany. His Hohenstaufen hero often seems less one of "our emperors" than an embodiment of the unification of German and Roman blood that George had celebrated in *Der Stern des Bundes*.[126] Indeed, he at one point calls Frederick a "Roman of Swabian blood."[127] At the same time, he presented the emperor as an essentially German figure. Frederick's Reich, for Kantorowicz, was more than just an attempt at a renewal of the Roman Empire. It also formed the backdrop to the birth of the German nation and symbolized Germany's potential to rule the West.

For Kantorowicz, Frederick's reign as emperor (1220–1250) marked the cultural and political apex of the Holy Roman Empire as well as the Empire's German lands, the so-called *Regnum Teutonicum*. In the 1920s, a number of medieval historians, notably Georg von Below, had argued that the Hohenstaufen emperors' involvement in Lombardy had decisively impeded the subsequent political and economic development of a Central European nation state and that Frederick II's policy in particular had fatefully decentralized Germany. Against the weight of such academic authorities and indeed most of the historical evidence, Kantorowicz not only defended Frederick II's Imperial policy, but actually reinterpreted it as "the deepest possible fulfilment of the [German] national project then possible."[128] Even though he subordinated, at least *prima facie*, Germany to his Italian lands, Frederick, Kantorowicz contended, had very definite plans for the establishment of a more centralized German nation. With a few bold strokes of his mythographic brush, Kantorowicz radically redrew the image of Frederick II's German policy in the popular imagination and presented him as nothing less than "the emperor of the fulfillment of the German dreams" ("der End- und Erfüllungskaiser der deutschen Träume"), who had "in a higher sense completed the one German Reich."[129]

As father of the German Reich and ingenious antagonist of the popes, the Hohenstaufen emperor emerged like a medieval Bismarck from the pages of *Kaiser Friedrich*. In the evocative final paragraph of his book, Kantorowicz in fact alluded to the Iron Chancellor as the Reich's "greatest vassal." There is a strong sense, indeed, that the so-called "ideas of 1871," no less than the "ideas of 1914," informed his biography of Frederick II. The empire Kantorowicz envisioned in 1927, however, was not the one founded by Bismarck in 1871 or the one for which he himself had taken up arms in 1914. Like other Weimar ideologues of the Reich such as the right-wing Catholic (Rechtskatholik) Martin Spahn and the Conservative Revolutionary Arthur Moeller van den Bruck,[130] Kantorowicz conceived the new Reich in much grander dimensions. The reference to Bismarck at the end of the book actually seems to have been less a form of praise than a reminder that the Hohenzollern Empire was not the final fulfillment of Germany's imperial yearning, and that Frederick's Reich had yet to emerge: the Reich's greatest vassal (Bismarck) and the "greybeard" (Wilhelm I), we read here, only realised the *kleindeutsch* dreams centering on the "grizzled sleeper" (the mythic figure of Barbarossa in the Kyffhäuser),[131] but the "Lord of the Beginning" (Frederick II) and his "Volk" (the German people in its "welthaltig" totality) remained unredeemed.[132]

The Reich invoked at the end of *Kaiser Friedrich*, to be sure, cannot easily be identified with any particular political programme. Its extensions, like those of the Secret Germany, seemed to correspond "à aucune géopolitique réelle,"[133] and hardly provided the basis for specific irredentist claims. There is some evidence, however, that the Georgean *Reichsidee* underlying the Hohenstaufen biography had a more concrete revisionist dimension than most of today's critics allow[134] and that the idealized image of the Hohenstaufen "world empire" projected in *Kaiser Friedrich* functioned as a weapon in the Circle's polemics against Weimar.[135] The symbol of this empire was the Roman eagle emblazoned on the yellow Imperial banners at Frederick's triumphal procession through Cremona after the Battle of Cortenuova (1237), which Kantorowicz, significantly, portrayed as a victory of German arms.[136] Weimar, on the other hand, stood for Germany's defeat and humiliation, territorial loss and financial bondage at the hands of the enemy, most notably France. The lament that the Germans had failed to clean "the bloodstained eagle"[137] had unmistakably political implications: to undo Weimar and Versailles and to realize the first "ewigdeutsche" possibility, the Reich. In this respect, the eagle resembled the phoenix, the potent symbol of rebirth and renewal that Kantorowicz would go on to study in his later magnum opus, *The King's Two Bodies*.[138]

Insofar as it referred back to Rome—as opposed to Prussia—the eagle also carried imperialist, expansionist connotations. Just as Frederick II had revived the universal *imperium Romanum*, the new Reich would revive the trans-European legacy of the Holy Roman Empire, transcending the *kleindeutsch* boundaries of Bismarck's nation-state. In Frederick's *renovatio* plans, the German lands had evidently played a secondary role at best, as a reservoir of mercenaries for his campaigns in Northern Italy. For the author of *Kaiser Friedrich*, however, Frederick's renewal of the old "Weltstellung" of imperial Rome had equally renewed Germany's universal role. Only in the larger geopolitical arena of Frederick's Reich could the German universal capacities manifest themselves. Through Frederick, he asserted, the entire Imperium, not just the lands north of the Alps, could be German.[139] Although he made much of its Southern orientation, Kantorowicz left no doubt that the Holy Roman Empire was also the empire of the German nation, a vehicle for the realization of the German European mission. In accordance with the large majority of neo-Ghibellines in the 1920s, he embraced a *Reichsidee* that was supranational, but at the same time deeply germanocentric.[140]

Scholars like Abulafia and Landauer contend that Kantorowicz's references to Germany's "Welthaltigkeit" do not so much imply the possibility of German continental hegemony as a truly European, universal conception of Frederick and his Reich.[141] There are a number of passages in *Kaiser Friedrich* that support this contention. For instance, Kantorowicz says of Frederick's empire that there was no subjection of other nations by any one nation, just an alliance of all monarchs and all people of Christendom under the Roman Emperor. At another point, he even calls medieval Europe an "egalitarian community of peoples" ("gleichberechtigte Völkergemeinschaft"), which Frederick, no less than Dante, had envisioned.[142] Yet one should not make too much of the universalism that reverberates in these passages.[143] "Welthaltigkeit," for Kantorowicz, did not mean "Weltbürgertum" (cosmopolitanism) and the Georgean vision of a European Reich he developed in *Kaiser Friedrich* ultimately accommodated the notion of German supremacy.[144] This is evident when Kantorowicz, echoing Dante's *De monarchia*, refers to Frederick as "dominus mundi,"[145] the absolute universal ruler above other kings. At the beginning of his book, he had already applauded Henry VI's "German world rule" ("deutsche Weltherrschaft") which reduced all other European nations, most notably France and England, to the status of vassal states. Throughout *Kaiser Friedrich*, he exalted Frederick's empire, like Henry VI's, over the individual monarchies of thirteenth-century Europe.[146] The anachronistic comparisons between Frederick and Napoleon, between the Hohenstaufen empire and the "Napoleonic world kingdom," are revealing in this context.[147] The reference to Frederick's Reich as a "great Central European empire" ("großes mitteleuropäisches Imperium") is another telling turn of phrase. Ever since Paul de Lagarde's *Deutsche Schriften* (1878),[148] "Mitteleuropa" had been a synonym for German supremacy on the continent, whether in Friedrich Naumann's more federalist, economic plans,[149] the aggressively annexationist claims of the Pan-Germans during the First World War, or the irredentist rhetoric of the Weimar historian Wilhelm Schüßler, who called for a drastic revision of the boundaries imposed on Germany by the Treaty of Versailles and the recuperation of "German national space" ("deutscher Volksraum") in Eastern and South Eastern Europe.[150] Like Schüßler, Spahn, and other contemporary theoreticians of "Mitteleuropa," Kantorowicz legitimized these German claims to European leadership with reference to the Middle Ages, when Germany was the "land of emperors" France only the "land of monarchs."[151]

In the context of these contemporary debates on *Mitteleuropa* and the Reich, the political contours of Kantorowicz's "universalism" become more readily apparent. His insistence on the "Roman" or "welthaltig" dimension of Germany under Frederick II's rule reflect the essential tension at the heart of the Georgean idea of the Reich: the pan-European vision of a unified, transnational empire—

and the belief in Germany's mission to lead the West.[152] Marc Bloch traced this germanocentric interpretation of the Holy Roman Empire in the 1920s back to the imperialist legacy of Wilhelmine Germany. *Weltpolitik*, as the French medievalist shrewdly observed, went hand in hand with an acute nostalgia for medieval *Weltherrschaft*. "It might not be impossible even today," Bloch wrote in 1928, "to trace [the effects of the *Reichsidee*] in certain undercurrents of German patriotism that reveal a fundamental will to power."[153] For Bloch, Kantorowicz's "nationalisme historique" evidently belonged to these undercurrents. [154]

One year after Kantorowicz's *Kaiser Friedrich*, George published his last collection of verse under the title *Das Neue Reich*. A number of poems in the cycle allude to a secret realm or empire (the German word *Reich* can mean both in English), but only one of them directly refers to "das Neue Reich." At the end of "Der Dichter in Zeiten der Wirren," George describes how a man of action, a *Täter*, emerges from a new elite and violently terminates the "times of chaos."

> He breaks the chains and on the ruins he creates
> Order he drives the lost ones home
> Into the realm of eternal law where the great is once more great
> Lord once more lord · Discipline once more discipline · he fixes
> The true symbol on the national [*das völkische*] banner
> He leads through storm and eerie signals
> Of the red dawn his loyal horde to the work
> Of the bright day and plants the New Reich.[155]

When five years later the *völkisch* banner, emblazoned with the swastika symbol, was carried triumphantly through the streets of Berlin to celebrate the so-called "Seizure of Power," many readers of this poem believed that the Third Reich proclaimed by the Nazis was the realization of the New Reich prophecied by George. At the end of 1933, shortly after George's death, a Nazi paper ran the headline "George the Prophet—Hitler the Führer."[156] Earlier that year, Walter Benjamin had posited a similar relation. "This much I believe I have realized," he told his friend Gershom Sholem in a letter of June 1933, "if ever God punished a prophet by fulfilling his prophecy, then that is the case with George."[157]

Epilogue: "George-Hitler-Stauffenberg"— Reconsidering the Vanishing Points of the Circle

With this last comment, too, Benjamin offered a strangely skewed, one-sided assessment. To be sure, it is possible—Robert Norton has done this very effectively—to read the intellectual legacies of the Circle *sub specie 1933*, as it were. Seen from that vantage point, the aesthetic fundamentalism of George and his followers belongs to the pre-history—the "intellectual origins"—of National Socialism. That so many members of the Circle, including the Master himself, reacted positively to Hitler's seizure of power lends considerable weight to such a reading.

Although he refrained, until his death in December of that year, from a public statement on the new rulers, George hardly disapproved of the Nazi takeover. On the one hand, he called the Nazis henchmen ("Henkersknechte," literally: "hangman's assistants")[158] and declined the honorary position they offered him in the section for poetry of the Prussian Academy of the Arts, the so-called "Dichterakademie." At the same time, however, he let them know through Ernst Morwitz that he welcomed the fact that the Academy was "now nationally oriented" and pointed to his own spiritual influence on the new national movement.[159] The large majority of George's remarks *intra muros* during this period suggest that he did indeed welcome certain aspects of National Socialism.[160] In March 1933, he told Edith Landmann that now for the first time he was hearing his views "echoed from outside."[161] Hildebrandt recalls that George wanted to avoid everything that would have brought him into opposition to National Socialism—except for his loyalty to the best of his Jewish followers.[162] And even this loyalty was limited. Although he regretted the fate of individual friends, such as Kantorowicz's troubles at Frankfurt,[163] the Master condoned the brutality of Nazi antisemitism.[164] When his oldest and most prominent Jewish disciple, Karl Wolfskehl, came to see him in Minusio in October 1933, obviously with the intention to get him to publicly speak out against Hitler's Germany, George refused to receive him.[165]

For many of George's followers—including Ludwig Thormaehlen, Kurt Hildebrandt, Walter Elze, and Albrecht von Blumenthal—National Socialism was not just an echo, but the actual realization of their Master's ideas.[166] In July 1933, Woldemar Uxkull-Gyllenband hailed the Nazi takeover as the manifestation of George's "revolutionary ethos." George, Uxkull-Gyllenband declared, had heralded the new Germany through which, just as previously through the Holy Roman Empire, the "heart of the continent" ("des Erdteils Herz") would once again redeem the world.[167] Berthold Stauffenberg confessed in 1944 that, initially at least, he had for the most part supported the basic ideas of National Socialism: the notion of "leadership" ("Führertum"), coupled with that of a "healthy hierarchy" ("gesunde Rangordnung"), as well as the "principle of race" ("Rassegedanke").[168] Until the summer of 1942, as Peter Hoffmann has shown, the Stauffenberg brothers viewed Nazi Germany if not as a manifestation, then at least as a harbinger of the New Reich announced by George.[169]

Even some of the Jewish members of the Circle were willing to consider that possibility. In a letter from October 1932, Wolfskehl reproached the other Jewish disciples for their readiness to welcome National Socialism as the ideology of national renewal. They would wholeheartedly join, he lamented, "the 'great national movement'," if a "disgusting accident did not hold them back."[170] Thomas Mann made a similar remark in 1934, but, surprisingly, singled out Wolfskehl himself as one of the Jewish followers of George who had "paved the way" for the "anti-liberal turn" and who would "easily adapt himself" to Hitler's Germany, if the Nazis let him.[171] According to Hildebrandt, Jewish as well as Gentile members of the Circle supported Nazism as a bulwark against communism.[172] In 1932, Berthold Vallentin gave a Jewish friend the following explanation for his support of the Nazis: "We have to think of Germany, not ourselves."[173]

At least initially, the biographer of Frederick II allowed himself to think along similar lines. On 10 July 1933, Kantorowicz wrote George:

"May Germany become as the Master envisioned it!" And if the recent events are not just a travesty of that vision, but actually the true path to its realization—then everything shall turn out well. And then it won't matter if the individual can walk along on this path—or rather: may walk along—or if he must, instead of applauding, stand aside. "Imperium transcendat hominem," declared Frederick II, and I would be the last one to contradict here. If one is not allowed access to the "Reich" by the Fates—and as a "Jewish or coloured person," as the new twin expression has it, one is necessarily excluded from a state founded on purely racial criteria—then one has to muster the amor fati and take decisions accordingly.[174]

Clearly, Kantorowicz was still reluctant to identify Nazi Germany with the ideals of the Secret Germany: he prefaced his remarks with a crucial conditional clause and put the word "Reich" in inverted commas. But ultimately, he, too, was prepared to view the recent events as a path to the realization of the Germany prophecied by George.[175]

There is ample evidence, then, to suggest that 1933 indeed represents a "vanishing point" of sorts for the brief history of Georgean ideas that has been sketched here.[176] Regarding the contributions that George and his followers made to Weimar thought solely from this perspective, however, seriously distorts their meaning. In his celebrated study on George's "after-life," Ulrich Raulff has shown that certain ideas of Circle—in particular, its pedagogical theories and its European conception of Germanness—remained influential long after the Second World War and shaped the political culture of West Germany.[177] But one could also point to the German resistance against Hitler, especially—though not exclusively—the bomb plot of July 1944, as part of the Circle's "alternative" intellectual legacy.[178] As early as November 1933, Kantorowicz had voiced his opposition to the new regime in a noticeably Georgean idiom. His "re-inaugural" lecture at the Goethe University in Frankfurt (with which he temporarily reclaimed the professorship he had lost due to the anti-Semitic "Civil Service Law" of 7 April 1933), eloquently entitled "Das Geheime Deutschland," was not only a courageous defence of key Georgean concepts like the Secret Germany and the New Reich against their appropriation by National Socialist ideologues, but also a first attempt to denounce National Socialism in terms of these concepts.[179]

Ten years later, Claus von Stauffenberg, similarly, began to conceive of his plan to oppose Hitler in Georgean terms. In an oath he drafted on the eve of his assassination attempt with his brother Berthold, Claus projected an image of a future, post-Nazi Germany that reverberated with George's ideas about rulership ("Herrschaft") and service ("Dienst"), discipline ("Zucht") and sacrifice ("Opfer"), his notion of a natural hierarchy or rank-ordering ("naturgegebene Ränge"), and his rejection of egalitarian democracy ("die Gleichheitslüge"). Echoing George's philhellenist credo, the Stauffenberg brothers remarked that it was their successful fusion of *Deutschtum* and hellenism that entrusted the

Germans of all European peoples with a leading role in the mission "to lead the community of Western nations towards a more beautiful life."[180] Stauffenberg's associates report that in the weeks leading up to his attempt, he repeatedly recited to himself passages from George's poem "Der Widerchrist," which warned that the works of the devil were often barely distinguishable from those of God.[181] In a more general, but no less important way, Stauffenberg's decision to defy and, eventually, kill Hitler seems to have been inspired by Georgean notions such as heroism, nobility of spirit, the Master's belief in a decisive, redemptive *Tat*, and his original insistence that the mission of the Secret Germany was to stand in opposition to the "public" Germany.

If George's vision of a Secret Germany and a new Reich conditioned some members of the Circle to espouse National Socialism, it also inspired others not just to renounce, but to actively and heroically resist it. For a number of scholars, 1933 represents the natural terminus and *telos* of the ideas formulated by George and his followers. For these scholars, Hitler's seizure of power marks the arrival of "the Man" and the *Täter* whom George had announced in his late poems. But the ideas of the Circle could also be considered in light of the *Tat* that Stauffenberg performed in July 1944. Both dates—1933 and 1944—furnish possible vanishing points for the story of the Circle told here. As Sebastian Haffner remarked more than thirty years ago, the three names "George—Hitler—Stauffenberg" denote an important chapter in modern German intellectual history.[182] It is a chapter that suggests not so much the "failure of illiberalism" in Weimar thought,[183] but its radical ambivalence and open-endedness.

Notes

1. *Die literarische Welt* 4, 28, (13 July 1928). George's birthday fell on the previous day, 12 July.
2. Conrad Wandrey, "Stefan George," *Die literarische Welt* 4, 28 (1928), 1–2, here 1. Wandrey's doctoral dissertation of 1910 had been published under the title *Stefan George* (Strasbourg: Heitz, 1911). On these and other contemporary reactions to George see David Midgley, "The Absentee Prophet: Public Perceptions of George's Poetry in the Weimar Period," in *A Poet's Reich: Politics and Culture in the George Circle,* eds. Melissa Lane and Martin A. Ruehl (Rochester: Camden House, 2011), 117–29.
3. See Stefan George, "Der Krieg" [1917], in: Stefan George, *Gesamt-Ausgabe der Werke. Endgültige Fassung,* 15 vols. (Berlin: Georg Bondi, 1927–34), IX, 27–34, here 30: "It is not fitting to rejoice: there will be no triumph / Just many downfalls without dignity" ("Zu jubeln ziemt nicht: kein triumf wird sein / Nur viele untergänge ohne würde"). Stefan Breuer, *Ästhetischer Fundamentalismus: Stefan George und der deutsche Antimodernismus* (Darmstadt: Wissenschaftliche Buchgesellschaft, 1995), 73–77, notes that George, unlike most of his disciples, condemned the Great War from the start and saw nothing regenerative or redemptive in it. This is confirmed by Edgar Salin, *Um Stefan George: Erinnerung und Zeugnis,* 2nd ed. (Munich: Helmut Küpper vormals Georg Bondi, 1954), 260. See also Friedrich Wolters, *Stefan George und die Blätter für die Kunst: Deutsche Geistesgeschichte seit 1890* (Berlin: Georg Bondi, 1930), 439–40.

4. In this and the following four paragraphs I draw on material from the introduction, co-authored with Melissa Lane, to Lane and Ruehl, *A Poet's Reich*, 1–4.

5. Kurt Singer to Martin Buber, 5 February 1916: see Martin Buber, *Briefwechsel aus sieben Jahrzehnten: 1897–1965*, 3 vols., ed. Grete Schaeder (Heidelberg: Lambert Schneider, 1972–75), I, 416–17. See also Michael Landmann, *Figuren um Stefan George*, vol. II (Amsterdam: Castrum Peregrini Presse, 1988), 62.

6. See Walter Benjamin, "Über Stefan George" [1928], in Walter Benjamin, *Gesammelte Schriften*, eds. Rolf Tiedemann and Hermann Schweppenhäuser, 7 vols. (Frankfurt a.M.: Suhrkamp, 1972–99), II/2, 622–23.

7. See Stefan George, *Tage und Taten. Aufzeichnungen und Skizzen* [1933] (Düsseldorf: Helmut Küpper vormals Georg Bondi, 1967), 55: "Deshalb o dichter nennen dich genossen und jünger so gerne meister weil du am wenigsten nachgeahmt werden kannst und doch so grosses über sie vermochtest."

8. See Wolfgang Braungart, "Walter Benjamin, Stefan George und die Frühgeschichte des Begriffs der Aura. Anmerkungen mit Blick auf die Geschichte des fotografischen Portraits," *Castrum Peregrini* 230 (1997), 38–51 (38); and Günter Heintz, "Der Zeuge: Walter Benjamin," in Günter Heintz, *Stefan George: Studien zu seiner künstlerischen Wirkung* (Stuttgart: Hauswedell, 1986), 310–45 (340).

9. Benjamin, *Gesammelte Schriften*, II/2, 812.

10. Albert Speer, *Inside the Third Reich* (New York: Macmillan, 1970), 36.

11. George, *Gesamt-Ansgabe der Werke*, VIII, 84. For the popularity of the poem's first two lines ("Wer je die flamme umschritt / Bleibe der flamme trabant!") in the *Wandervogel* and the Hitler Youth see, e.g., Heinz Schreckenberg, *Erziehung, Lebenswelt und Kriegseinsatz der deutschen Jugend unter Hitler: Anmerkungen zur Literatur* (Münster: Lit Verlag, 2000), 195.

12. Georg Lukács, "Die neue Einsamkeit und ihre Lyrik: Stefan George," in Georg von Lukács, *Die Seele und die Formen: Essays* (Berlin: Egon Fleischel, 1911), 176.

13. See Benjamin, "Über Stefan George," 623; and Walter Benjamin, "Rückblick auf Stefan George," [1933] in: Benjamin, *Gesammelte Schriften*, III, 399.

14. George, *Gesamt-Ausgabe der Werke*, VI/VII, 62. The poem powerfully evokes the millennarian mood that characterizes much of George's verse and his palingenetic ideal of renewal through destruction, both of which would have appealed to anarchists like Erich Mühsam and Gustav Landauer who played a prominent role in the so-called *Münchner Räterepublik*.

15. See Manfred Riedel, *Geheimes Deutschland. Stefan George und die Brüder Stauffenberg* (Cologne: Böhlau, 2006), 107.

16. See Eike Wolgast, *Die Universität Heidelberg, 1386–1986* (Berlin: Springer Verlag, 1986), 139–40.

17. On Gundolf's conception of biography and historiography see Ulrich Raulff, "Der Bildungshistoriker Friedrich Gundolf," in Friedrich Gundolf, *Anfänge deutscher Geschichtsschreibung von Tschudi bis Winckelmann*, ed. Edgar Wind (Frankfurt a.M.: Fischer, 1992), 115–54.

18. That George left a deep mark on Simmel is already evident in Georg Simmel, "Stefan George: Eine kunstphilosophische Betrachtung," *Die Zukunft* 6 (1898), 386–96. On Simmel and George see Breuer, *Ästhetischer Fundamentalismus*, 169–83; Günther Freymuth, "Georg Simmel und Stefan George," *Neue deutsche Hefte* 17, 3 (1970), 41–50; Carola Groppe, *Die Macht der Bildung. Das deutsche Bürgertum und der George-Kreis 1890–1933* (Cologne: Böhlau, 1997), 160–82; and Michael Landmann, "Georg Simmel und Stefan George," in *Georg Simmel und die Moderne. Neue Interpretationen*

und Materialien, eds. Heinz-Jürgen Dahme and Otthein Rammstedt (Frankfurt a.M.: Suhrkamp, 1984), 147–73. Gadamer acknowledges his debts to George in Hans-Georg Gadamer, "Stefan George (1868–1933)," in: *Die Wirkung Stefan Georges auf die Wissenschaft: Ein Symposium*, ed. Hans-Joachim Zimmermann (Heidelberg: C. Winter, 1985), 43–47. See also Hans-Georg Gadamer, "The Verse and the Whole," in: *Gadamer on Education, Poetry, and History: Applied Hermeneutics*, eds. Dieter Misgeld and Graeme Nicholson (Albany: State University of New York Press, 1991), 83–92, and Hans-Georg Gadamer, "Under the Shadow of Nihilism," in: *Gadamer on Education*, 111, where he calls George "the most significant artist in the German tongue in the last hundred years." On Gadamer and George see, e.g., Robert R. Sullivan, *Political Hermeneutics: The Early Thinking of Hans-Georg Gadamer* (Philadelphia: University of Pennsylvania Press, 1989), 27, 48.

19. See Karl Jaspers, *Notizen zu Martin Heidegger* (Munich: Piper, 1978), 58, 62, 103, 107. Charles Bambach, *Heidegger's Roots: Nietzsche, National Socialism, and the Greeks* (Ithaca: Cornell University Press, 2003), 219–20 points out that Heidegger's reading of Hölderlin and Nietzsche was also conditioned by the George Circle.

20. See, e.g., Uvo Hölscher, "Strömungen der deutschen Graezistik in den zwanziger Jahren," in *Altertumswissenschaft in den 20er Jahren: Neue Fragen und Impulse*, ed. Hellmut Flashar (Stuttgart: Franz Steiner Verlag, 1995), 65–85.

21. See Kurt Tucholsky, "Radio Censorship" [1928], in *The Weimar Republic Sourcebook*, eds. Anton Kaes, Martin Jay, and Edward Dimendberg (Berkeley: University of California Press, 1994), 604.

22. Heinrich Rickert had drawn Weber's attention to George as early as 1897, but it was only after his nervous breakdown in 1898 that Weber began to appreciate George's poetry: see Marianne Weber, *Max Weber. Ein Lebensbild* (Tübingen: Mohr/Siebeck, 1926), 463.

23. See Wolf Lepenies, *Die drei Kulturen: Soziologie zwischen Literatur und Wissenschaft* (Frankfurt a.M.: S. Fischer, 2002), 342. See also Folker Reichert, *Gelehrtes Leben: Karl Hampe, das Mittelalter und die Geschichte der Deutschen* (Göttingen: Vandenhoeck & Ruprecht, 2009), 175.

24. Thomas Karlauf, *Stefan George: Die Entdeckung des Charisma* (Munich: Blessing, 2007), 410–18. In his intellectual biography of Max Weber, Joachim Radkau argues, similarly, that George provided a model for Weber's notion of the charismatic leader: see Joachim Radkau, *Max Weber: A Biography* (Cambridge: Polity Press, 2009), xv, 295, 394. On Weber and George see also the perceptive comments in Lepenies, *Die drei Kulturen*, 311–57.

25. George revealed his dislike of Thomas Mann on various occasions: see, e.g., his letter to Ernst Glöckner of June 1921, in which he urged the recipient to break off all contact with Mann, "einem gemeinen und gefährlichen kerl [*sic*]." Stefan George to Ernst Glöckner, 12 June 1921, Stefan George Archiv, Württembergische Landesbibliothek, Stuttgart (Abschrift Ernst Glöckner). On George and Mann see Hans Albert Maier, *Stefan George und Thomas Mann: Zwei Formen des dritten Humanismus in kritischem Vergleich* (Zurich: Speer-Verlag, 1947); Friedhelm Marx, "Der Heilige Stefan? Thomas Mann und Stefan George," *George-Jahrbuch* 6 (2006/7), 80–99, and Robert Norton, *Secret Germany: Stefan George and his Circle* (Ithaca: Cornell University Press, 2002), 621–22.

26. Thomas Mann, *Tagebücher 1918 bis 1921*, ed. Peter de Mendelssohn (Frankfurt a.M.: Fischer, 1979), 249.

27. Friedrich Sternthal, "Zu Georges Politeia," *Die literarische Welt* 4, 28 (1928), 5–6, here 5. See Midgley, "The Absentee Prophet," 120–21.

28. Peter Gay is one of the few historians to do justice to the important contributions that George and his Circle made to the shifts in German culture and thought during the Weimar period: see Peter Gay, *Weimar Culture: The Outsider as Insider* (New York: Harper and Row, 1968), 46–70.

29. Sternhall, "Zu Georges Politeia," 6.

30. Stefan George to Ernst Morwitz, 10 May 1933; quoted in Peter Hoffmann, *Claus Schenk Graf von Stauffenberg und seine Brüder* (Stuttgart: Deutsche Verlags-Anstalt, 1992), 117.

31. See Ulrich Raulff, *Kreis ohne Meister: Stefan Georges Nachleben* (Munich: C. H. Beck, 2009), 30–187, 527–29.

32. See Gay, *Weimar Culture*, 46–70.

33. It is notable that neither George nor any of his disciples are represented in Kaes et al., *The Weimar Republic Sourcebook*.

34. See Detlev Peukert, *The Weimar Republic: The Crisis of Classical Modernity* (London: Penguin, 1993); Hans Mommsen, *The Rise and Fall of Weimar Democracy* (Chapel Hill: University of North Carolina Press, 1996); Hagen Schulze, *Weimar: Deutschland 1917–1933* (Berlin: Bärsch, 1982); Heinrich August Winkler, *Weimar, 1918–1933: Die Geschichte der ersten deutschen Demokratie* (Munich: C. H. Beck, 1993).

35. See Walter Bußmann, "Politische Ideologien zwischen Monarchie und Weimarer Republik. Ein Beitrag zur Ideengeschichte der Weimarer Republik," *Historische Zeitschrift* 190, 1 (February 1960), 55–77.

36. See George Mosse, *The Crisis of German Ideology: Intellectual Origins of the Third Reich* (New York: Grosset & Dunlap, 1964), 205–12; Fritz Stern, *The Politics of Cultural Despair: A Study in the Rise of the Germanic Ideology* (Berkeley: University of California Press, 1974), 88, 149n, 158n, 171; Klemens von Klemperer, *Germany's New Conservatism: Its History and Dilemma in the Twentieth Century* (Princeton: Princeton University Press, 1968), 44–45, 71; Anthony Phelan, *The Weimar Dilemma: Intellectuals in the Weimar Republic* (Manchester: Manchester University Press, 1985), 40, 51, 63; Dagmar Barnouw, *Weimar Intellectuals and the Threat of Modernity* (Bloomington: Indiana University Press, 1988), 126; David C. Durst, *Weimar Modernism: Philosophy, Politics, and Culture in Germany, 1918–1933* (Oxford: Lexington Books, 2004), 204. There are no references to the George Circle in Kurt Sontheimer, *Antidemokratisches Denken in der Weimarer Republik: Die politischen Ideen des deutschen Nationalismus zwischen 1918 und 1933* (Stuttgart: Deutscher Taschenbuch-Verlag, 1978) and Jeffrey Herf, *Reactionary Modernism: Technology, Culture, and Politics in Weimar and the Third Reich* (Cambridge: Cambridge University Press, 1984).

37. See Eric Weitz, *Weimar Germany: Promise and Tragedy* (Princeton: Princeton University Press, 2007), 338; and Richard Evans, *The Coming of the Third Reich* (London: Penguin, 2004), 411–12. See also Raimund von dem Bussche, *Konservatismus in der Weimarer Republik: die Politisierung des Unpolitischen* (Heidelberg: Universitätsverlag Winter, 1998), 22.

38. See Martin Travers, *Critics of Modernity: The Literature of the Conservative Revolution in Germany, 1890–1933* (Bern: Peter Lang, 2001), 81-82; and Roger Woods, *The Conservative Revolution in the Weimar Republic* (London: St. Martin's Press, 1996).

39. Norton, *Secret Germany*, xvi.

40. Ernst Robert Curtius, "Stefan George im Gespräch," in Curtius, *Kritische Essays zur europäischen Literatur* (Bern: A. Francke, 1950), 153, 157.

41. Breuer, *Ästhetischer Fundamentalismus*. See also Stefan Breuer, *Moderner Fundamentalismus* (Berlin 2002) 73–137. For a critical assessment of Breuer's interpretation see Frank Schirrmacher, "Dies ist der Pfeil des Meisters: Der Staat des Dichters Stefan George, der Verrat und der ästhetische Fundamentalismus. Aus Anlaß der Studie von Stefan Breuer," *Frankfurter Allgemeine Zeitung* (14 November 1995), L1.

42. On palingenesis as a mythic notion signifying national rebirth or renewal out of destruction see Roger Griffin, *The Nature of Fascism* (London: Routledge, 1991), 32–36.

43. For the concept "reactionary modernism" see Herf, *Reactionary Modernism*, 1–18. For Herf's discussion of Jünger and Sombart, respectively, as "reactionary modernists" see ibid., 70–109, 130–52

44. See Groppe, *Die Macht der Bildung*; Wolfgang Braungart, *Ästhetischer Katholizismus: Stefan Georges Rituale der Literatur* (Tübingen: Niemeyer, 1997); Rainer Kolk, *Literarische Gruppenbildung. Am Beispiel des George-Kreises 1890–1945* (Tübingen: Niemeyer, 1998); Karlauf, *Stefan George*; Raulff, *Kreis ohne Meister*. See also Michael Petrow, *Der Dichter als Führer? Zur Wirkung Stefan Georges im "Dritten Reich"* (Marburg: Tectum-Verlag, 1995); and *Stefan George: Werk und Wirkung seit dem "Siebenten Ring,"* eds. Wolfgang Braungart, Ute Maria Oelmann, and Bernhard Böschenstein (Tübingen: Niemeyer, 2001).

45. See, e.g., *Wissenschaftler im George-Kreis: Die Welt des Dichters und der Beruf der Wissenschaft,* eds. Bernhard Böschenstein, Jürgen Egyptien, Bertram Schefold, and Wolfgang Graf Vitzthum (Berlin: Walter de Gruyter, 2005), 3–12, and Riedel, *Geheimes Deutschland*, 169–70. See also *Das Ideal des schönen Lebens und die Wirklichkeit der Weimarer Republik: Vorstellungen von Staat und Gemeinschaft im George-Kreis,* eds. Roman Köster, Werner Plumpe, Bertram Schefold, and Korinna Schönhärl (Berlin: Akademie-Verlag, 2009); and *Stefan George: Dichtung, Ethos, Staat,* eds. Bruno Pieger and Bertram Schefold (Berlin: Verlag Berlin-Brandenburg, 2010).

46. See, e.g., Raulff, *Kreis ohne Meister*, 26, 56–57, and Böschenstein et al., *Wissenchaftler in George-Kreis*, 4, 7–8.

47. Peter Hoffmann, "The George Circle and National Socialism," in Lane and Ruehl, *A Poet's Reich*, 287–317 (287).

48. It should be noted, in this context, that George's original poetic output in the Weimar years was very small. Apart from the small volume *Drei Gesänge* (1921), George only published the cycle *Das Neue Reich* (1928), which mainly contained poems composed before 1918.

49. On the concept "palingenetic ultra-nationalism" see Griffin, *The Nature of Fascism*, 26–43.

50. For George's praise of Italy in these early collections see Elisabeth Gundolf, "Stefan George und der Nationalsozialismus," in Elisabeth Gundolf, *Stefan George: Zwei Vorträge* (Amsterdam: Castrum Peregrini, 1965), 52–76 (60–63); Bernhard Böschenstein, "Stefan George und Italien," *Jahrbuch des freien deutschen Hochstifts* (1986), 317–33; and Emmy Rosenfeld, *L'Italia nella poesia di Stefan George* (Milan: Malfasi, 1948).

51. See, e.g., Heinrich von Treitschke, "Unsere Aussichten," *Preußische Jahrbücher* 44 (1879), 559–76; Heinrich von Treitschke, *Historische und politische Aufsätze*, 4th ed. (Berlin: S. Hirzel, 1871); and Heinrich von Treitschke, *Zehn Jahre deutscher Kämpfe: Schriften zur Tagespolitik* (Berlin: G. Reimer, 1879). On Treitschke's nationalistic views see Walter Bußmann, *Treitschke: sein Welt- und Geschichtsbild*, 2nd ed. (Göttingen:

Muster-Schmidt, 1981); and Ulrich Langer: *Heinrich von Treitschke. Politische Biographie eines deutschen Nationalisten* (Düsseldorf: Droste, 1998).

52. In the eyes of nineteenth-century German nationalists, Hermann's victory over the Roman military commander Varus in the Battle of the Teutoburg Forest (9 AD) prevented the "Latinization" of Central Europe and marked the beginning of a uniquely German historical trajectory: see Klaus von See, *Barbar, Germane, Arier. Die Suche nach der Identität der Deutschen* (Heidelberg: Winter, 1994), 31–60; *Arminius und die Varusschlacht: Geschichte—Mythos—Literatur*, eds. Rainer Wiegels and Winfried Woesler (Paderborn: Schöningh, 1995); and Werner M. Doyé, "Arminius," in *Deutsche Erinnerungsorte*, eds. Étienne François and Hagen Schulze, 3 vols. (Munich: C. H. Beck, 2001), III, 587–602.

53. Ernst H. Kantorowicz, *Kaiser Friedrich der Zweite* (Berlin: Georg Bondi 1927), 77. In his radio lecture "Deutsches Papsttum" (written 1933, broadcast 1935), Kantorowicz again invoked Bamberg as a symbol of a classically restrained, "Apollonian" Germany: Ernst Kantorowicz, "Deutsches Papsttum," *Castrum Peregrini* 12 (1953), 7–24 (9). Claus Schenk Graf von Stauffenberg, who entered the Circle in May 1923, apparently bore a close physical resemblance to the statue in Bamberg and the members of the Circle jokingly referred to him as "der Bamberger Reiter": see Michael Baigent and Richard Leigh, *Secret Germany: Claus von Stauffenberg and the Mystical Crusade against Hitler* (London: J. Cape, 1994), 119. The Circle also associated the Stauffenberg brothers with the Hohenstaufen dynasty of the Middle Ages: see Hoffmann, *Stauffenberg*, 52, 61.

54. Salin, *Um Stefan George*, 143–44.

55. See Friedrich Wolters, *Vier Reden über das Vaterland* (Breslau: Ferdinand Hirt, 1927); Friedrich Wolters and Walter Elze, *Stimmen des Rheins* (Breslau: Ferdinand Hirt, 1923); and Friedrich Wolters, *Die Bedingungen des Versailler Vertrags und ihre Begründung* (Kiel: Max Tandler, 1929). Wolters's politics and his increasingly dominant position in the Circle are discussed by Groppe, *Die Macht der Bildung*, 213–89. See also Claude David, *Stefan George: Son œuvre poétique* (Lyons: I.A.C., 1952), 361–63, and Martin A. Siemoneit, *Politische Interpretationen von Stefan Georges Dichtung* (Frankfurt a.M.: Peter Lang, 1978), 23–40.

56. For George's critical remarks about Wolters's participation at a Schlageter celebration see Berthold Vallentin, *Gespräche mit Stefan George 1902–1931* (Amsterdam: Castrum Peregrini, 1967), 72. George's distance to Wolters is palpable in their correspondence: see Stefan George and Friedrich Wolters, *Briefwechsel 1904–1930*, ed. Michael Philipp (Amsterdam: Castrum Peregrini,1998). On their relationship see Michael Philipp's "Einleitung" to this edition of the *Briefwechsel*, 1–61; and Michael Philipp, "Wandel und Glaube. Friedrich Wolters—Der Paulus des George-Kreises," in Braungart et al., *Werk und Wirkung*, 283–99.

57. Petrow, *Der Dichter als Führer?*, 1, as well as Salin, *Um Stefan George*, 145–46, contend that Wolters's opinions did not reflect George's. But Vallentin reports that in April 1931, George expressed his admiration for Wolters's development in the 1920s, and Kurt Hildebrandt recalls that George and Wolters were united in their nationalist attitude since the breakdown of 1918: see Vallentin, *Gespräche mit Stefan George*, 136; and Kurt Hildebrandt, *Erinnerungen an Stefan George und seinen Kreis* (Bonn: Bouvier, 1965), 119. See also David, *Stefan George*, 362. George's amendments to Wolters's history of the Circle, the so-called *Blättergeschichte*, suggest that the Master often took an even more extreme position than Wolters: see Friedrich Wolters, "Frühe Aufzeichnungen nach Gesprächen mit Stefan George zur 'Blättergeschichte,'" *Cas-*

trum Peregrini 225 (1996), 5–62 (12). Michael Philipp's comparison of Wolters's early 1913 manuscript with the 1930 final version of the *Blättergeschichte* impressively demonstrates the increasing nationalisation of the Circle after the First World War: see Wolters, "Frühe Aufzeichnungen," 15–16.

58. Salin, *Um Stefan George*, 264. For George's political aspirations during and after the First World War see Volker Dürr, "Stefan George und Gottfried Benn im europäischen Kontext: Politische Aspekte der ästhetizistischen Tradition," in *Das Stefan-George-Seminar 1978 in Bingen am Rhein. Eine Dokumentation*, eds. Peter Lehmann and Robert Wolf (Bingen: Gesellschaft zur Förderung der Stefan-George-Gedenkstätte im Stefan-George-Gymnasium Bingen e.V., 1979), 48–59 (56–57).

59. George, *Gesamt-Ausgabe der Werke*, IX, 39: ". . . dass einst / Des erdteils herz die welt erretten soll." See also Wolters, *Stefan George*, 440–43.

60. Stefan George, *Drei Gesänge: An die Toten; Der Dichter in Zeiten der Wirren; Einem jungen Führer im ersten Weltkrieg* (Berlin: Georg Bondi, 1921).

61. George, *Gesamt-Ausgabe der Werke*, IX, 39: "Ein jung geschlecht das wieder mensch und ding / Mit echten maassen misst das schön und ernst /Froh seiner einzigkeit vor Fremdem stolz / Sich gleich entfernt von klippen dreisten dünkels / Wie seichtem sumpf erlogner brüderei / Das von sich spie was mürb und feig und lau / Das aus geweihtem träumen tun und dulden / Den einzigen der hilft den Mann gebiert."

62. See David, *Stefan George*, 362. George was born in Büdesheim near Mainz, spent much of his childhood and youth in Bingen and later frequently stayed in Heidelberg.

63. Salin, *Um Stefan George*, 262. See also Edith Landmann, *Gespräche mit Stefan George* (Düsseldorf: Helmut Küpper vormals Georg Bondi, 1963), 150.

64. See Karlauf, *Stefan George*, 420.

65. For George's changed view of Italy see Vallentin, *Gespräche mit Stefan George*, 87; and Landmann, *Gespräche*, 98, 107.

66. Landmann, *Gespräche*, 178, 182.

67. Hildebrandt, *Erinnerungen*, 228, citing George: "Ein schlechter Kaiser ist besser als gar kein Kaiser!"

68. Kurt Hildebrandt, *Norm und Entartung des Menschen* (Dresden: Sibyllen-Verlag, 1920). The book was published without the signet of the Circle—but with the explicit approval of George and Wolters; see Hildebrandt, *Erinnerungen*, 113–14.

69. Cf. Salin, *Um Stefan George*, 248, and Hildebrandt, *Erinnerungen*, 115, 124.

70. This is confirmed by Salin, *Um Stefan George*, 248.

71. See Wolters, "Der Rhein unser Schicksal," in Wolters, *Vier Reden*, 139; and Wolters, *Stefan George*, 440.

72. He was disappointed, however, by Austria's failure to "Germanize" Bohemia: Vallentin, *Gespräche mit Stefan George*, 64, citing George (8 February 1922).

73. George, *Gesamt-Ausgabe der Werke*, IX, 33. See Landfried, *Stefan George*, 219–21.

74. "Only when the yellow apes come," George remarked to Karl Wolfskehl during the First World War, "I'll grab a rifle": Salin, *Um Stefan George*, 260.

75. See Ernst Morwitz, *Kommentar zu dem Werk Stefan Georges* (Munich: Helmut Küpper vormals George Bondi, 1960), 419.

76. George, *Gesamt-Ausgabe der Werke*, IX, 30. This at least is Ernst Morwitz's interpretation of the word: Morwitz, *Kommentar*, 419–20; but cf. Katherina and Momme Mommsen, "'Ihr kennt Eure Bibel nicht!' Bibel- und Horaz-Anklänge in Stefan Georges Gedicht 'Der Krieg,'" *Castrum Peregrini* 34 (1985), 42–69.

77. See, e.g., Hans Liebeschütz, "Ernst Kantorowicz and the George Kreis," *The Leo Baeck Institute Yearbook* 9 (1964), 345–47 (346); and Ralph E. Giesey, "Ernst H. Kantorowicz:

Scholarly Triumphs and Academic Travails in Weimar Germany and the United States," *The Leo Baeck Institute Yearbook* 30 (1985), 191–202 (193).

78. On George's attitude towards Judaism and Jews see Geret Luhr, *Ästhetische Kritik der Moderne: Über das Verhältnis Walter Benjamins und der jüdischen Intelligenz zu Stefan George* (Marburg a.d. Lahn: Verlag Literaturwissenschaft, 2002); and *"Verkannte brüder"?: Stefan George und das deutsch-jüdische Bürgertum zwischen Jahrhundertwende und Emigration*, eds. Gert Mattenklott, Michael Philipp, and Julius H. Schoeps (Hildesheim: G. Olms, 2001).

79. Elizabeth Gundolf, "Stefan George und der Nationalsozialismus," in Gundolf, *Stefan George: Zwei Vorträge* (Amsterdam: Castrum Peregrini, 1965), 52–76 (69), calculates that almost half of the 35 German contributors to the *Blätter für die Kunst* were Jewish or of Jewish background. See also Yakov Malkiel, "Ernst Kantorowicz," in *On Four Modern Humanists: Hofmannsthal, Gundolf, Curtius, Kantorowicz*, ed. Arthur R. Evans Jr. (Princeton: Princeton University Press, 1970), 146–219 (178).

80. Salin, *Um Stefan George*, 244, 249, citing George: "der wirklich von meiner Rasse ist."

81. Quoted in Hoffmann, *Stauffenberg*, 501.

82. K. Hildebrandt to A. Brodersen, 7 January 1935; quoted in Hoffmann, *Stauffenberg*, 502 n. 53.

83. These younger members played an increasingly central role in the Circle since the mid-1920s. According to Hoffmann, *Stauffenberg*, 76–77, between 1925 and 1930 Kommerell and Anton were closest to George, who lost interest during this time in his older Jewish friends. See also Groppe, *Macht der Bildung*, 654–57.

84. See Hoffmann, *Stauffenberg*, 501–2.

85. M. Kommerell to J. Anton, 24 December 1930; quoted in Hoffmann, *Stauffenberg*, 493.

86. Hildebrandt, *Erinnerungen*, 120.

87. These included Max Kommerell, Johann and Wolfgang Anton, Walter Elze, and Rudolf Fahrner. See Groppe, *Macht der Bildung*, 273–76.

88. See Benjamin, *Gesammelte Schriften*, III, 259.

89. George, *Gesamt-Ausgabe der Werke*, IX, 57, 34.

90. See Berthold Vallentin, *Napoleon* (Berlin: Georg Bondi, 1923); Friedrich Gundolf, *Caesar. Geschichte seines Ruhms* (Berlin: Georg Bondi, 1924).

91. Hildebrandt, *Erinnerungen*, 105. Cf. ibid., 125, 164, 165. See Landfried, *Stefan George*, 219–21.

92. See Eckhart Grünewald, *Ernst Kantorowicz und Stefan George. Beiträge zur Biographie des Historikers bis zum Jahre 1938 und zu seinem Jugendwerk "Kaiser Friedrich der Zweite"* (Wiesbaden: Franz Steiner Verlag, 1982), 74–80. For a more detailed analysis of the genealogy and significance of the concept see Hans-Christof Kraus, "Das Geheime Deutschland. Zur Geschichte und Bedeutung einer Idee," *Historische Zeitschrift* 291, no. 2 (2010), 385–417.

93. See Karl Wolfskehl, "Die Blätter für die Kunst und die neuste Literatur," *Jahrbuch für die geistige Bewegung* 1 (1910), 1–18 (14–15).

94. See Norbert von Hellingrath, *Hölderlin-Vermächtnis. Forschungen und Vorträge. Ein Gedankenbuch zum 14. Dezember 1936* (Munich: F. Bruckmann, 1936), 123–53 (124–25).

95. George, *Gesamt-Ausgabe der Werke*, IX, 60–65, here 65.

96. My reading of these poems relies on Raymond Ockenden, "Kingdom of the Spirit: The Secret Germany in Stefan George's Later Poems," in Lane and Ruehl, *A Poet's Reich*, 91–117 (91–99).

97. George, *Gesamt-Ausgabe der Werke*, IX, 28, 39.

98. George, *Gesamt-Augsabe der Werke*, IX, 39.

99. George, *Gesamt-Ausgabe der Werke*, VIII, 31.

100. Maximin was the name George posthumously gave to Maximilian Kronberger, a Munich youth and aspiring poet whom George tried to attract to his Circle from January 1903 onward. The following year, at the age of sixteen, Kronberger died unexpectedly of meningitis. After his death, George stylized him into the god-like figure Maximin. The cult of Maximin became a central integrative element of the Georgean *Lebensgemeinschaft* and the Circle's redemptive promise, especially after the publication of *Der Siebente Ring* in 1907. See Norton, *Secret Germany*, 335–51, and Claus-Artur Scheier, "Maximins Lichtung: Philosophische Bemerkungen zu Georges Gott," *George-Jahrbuch* 1 (1996/1997), 80–106.

101. George, *Gesamt-Ausgabe der Werke*, VIII, 91.

102. George, *Gesamt-Ausgabe der Werke*, IX, 33.

103. George, *Gesamt-Ausgabe der Werke*, VI/VII, 31.

104. George, *Gesamt-Ausgabe der Werke*, VIII, 31.

105. George, *Gesamt-Ausgabe der Werke*, IX, 114.

106. George, *Gesamt-Ausgabe der Werke*, IX, 38.

107. See Roger Griffin, ed., *Fascism* (Oxford: Oxford University Press, 1995), 101–2.

108. Curtius, "Stefan George im Gespräch," 157.

109. George, *Gesamt-Ausgabe der Werke*, IX, 10.

110. George, *Gesamt-Ausgabe der Werke*, IX, 33. See Ockenden, "Kingdom of the Spirit," 100.

111. See George, *Gesamt-Ausgabe der Werke*, IX, 54–57.

112. Ockenden, "Kingdom of the Spirit," 100.

113. See Breuer, *Ästhetischer Fundamentalismus*, 450.

114. The following discussion of Kantorowicz's work draws on material from Martin A. Ruehl, "'In this Time without Emperors': The Politics of Ernst *Kantorowicz's Kaiser Friedrich der Zweite* Reconsidered," *Journal of the Warburg and Courtauld Institutes* 63 (2000), 187–242.

115. See E. Kantorowicz to S. George, 7 September 1925 and 27 July 1930, Stefan George Archiv, Stuttgart, Akte Ernst Kantorowicz.

116. See Groppe, *Macht der Bildung*, 284, 655. Kantorowicz himself was probably never very close to Wolters. In a letter to Ernst Morwitz from September 1926, he actually condemned Wolters's signing of nationalist and *völkisch* appeals, whereby "things that clearly stand above all parties are being pulled . . . into the dirt of one party": E. Kantorowicz to E. Morwitz, September 1926, Stefan George Archiv, Stuttgart, Akte Ernst Kantorowicz.

117. Morwitz, *Kommentar*, 230.

118. On George's active involvement in the production of *Kaiser Friedrich* see Edgar Salin, *Ernst Kantorowicz 1895–1963* (Privatdruck, 1963), 5; Ludwig Thormaehlen, *Erinnerungen an Stefan George* (Hamburg: Ernst Hauswedell, 1962), 227–28; Grünewald, *Kantorowicz und George*, 57–80, 149–57; Norton, *Secret Germany*, 664–70; and Karlauf, *Stefan George*, 549–53, 558–62.

119. It went through four editions between 1927 and 1936, selling more than 12,000 copies—a remarkable success for a scholarly work, especially during the Great Depression: see Grünewald, *Kantorowicz und George*, 156. According to Horst Fuhrmann, these numbers do not even fully reflect "the deep lasting impact" the work had on the German *Bildungsbürgertum* in those years: H. Fuhrmann, "Die Heimholung des Ernst Kantorowicz," *Die Zeit* (22 March 1991), 49.

120. Berthold Vallentin, *Gespräche mit Stefan George, 1902–1931* (Amsterdam: Castrum Peregrini, 1961), 50–51 (11 January 1920): "wesenhafte deutsche heroische Erscheinung."

121. George, *Gesamt-Ausgabe der Werke*, VI/VII, 22–23. See also Klaus Landfried, *Stefan George: Politik des Unpolitischen* (Heidelberg: Lothar Stiehm, 1975), 69–75.

122. George, *Gesamt-Ausgabe der Werke*, IX, 57. This interpretation of George's poem "Burg Falkenstein" relies on the commentary in Morwitz, *Kommentar zu dem Werk*, 436–39.

123. Vallentin, *Gespräche mit Stefan George*, 77. See also Edith Landmann, *Stefan George und die Griechen: Idee einer neuen Ethik* (Amsterdam: Castrum Peregrini, 1971), 130.

124. George's "Karlen- und Ottonen-plan" alluded to this program of renewal.

125. Kantorowicz, *Kaiser Friedrich*, 377: "römischer Geist."

126. George, *Gesamt-Ausgabe der Werke*, VIII, 43: "Eur kostbar tierhaft kindhaft blut verdirbt / Wenn ihrs nicht mischt im reich von korn und wein."

127. Kantorowicz, *Kaiser Friedrich*, 355.

128. Kantorowicz, *Kaiser Friedrich*, 75. Cf. ibid, 353: "die letzte Vollendung des alten Reiches der Deutschen."

129. Kantorowicz, *Kaiser Friedrich*, 74, 351, 197, 354.

130. On Spahn and the Reich see Gabriele Clemens, *Martin Spahn und der Rechtskatholizismus in der Weimarer Republik* (Mainz: Matthias-Grünewald-Verlag, 1983), esp. 98–144. For Catholic conceptions of the Reich in this period see K. Breuning, *Die Vision des Reiches: Deutscher Katholizismus zwischen Demokratie und Diktatur 1929–1934* (Munich: Max Hueber Verlag, 1969). See Arthur Moeller van den Bruck, *Das ewige Reich*, 3 vols, ed. Hans Schwarz (Breslau: W.G. Korn, 1933-35). For the appropriation of the Middle Ages by the authors of the Conservative Revolution see Joachim H. Knoll, "Der autoritäre Staat. Konservative Ideologie und Staatstheorie am Ende der Weimarer Republik," in *Lebendiger Geist. Hans-Joachim Schoeps zum 50. Geburtstag von Schülern dargebracht*, ed. Hellmut Diwald (Cologne and Leiden: E.J. Brill, 1959), 200–24.

131. Probably a punning allusion to Wilhelm I's sobriquet "Barbablanca."

132. Kantorowicz, *Kaiser Friedrich*, 632. Both Grünewald, *Kantorowicz und George*, 80, and Karlauf, *Stefan George*, 553, identify "des Kaisers Volk" with the George Circle. Grünewald, similarly, interprets Kantorowicz's *amor patriae* in his Halle speech of 1930 as love for the Secret Germany: Eckhart Grünewald, "Sanctus amor patriae dat animum—ein Wahlspruch des George-Kreises?," *Deutsches Archiv für Erforschung des Mittelalters* 1 (1994): 89-103, esp. 101–03. *Kaiser Friedrich* , however, was not just an esoteric "Geistbuch," but also a patriotic appeal to the German people. It was, as Kantorowicz later told Salin, full of hopes both for the victory of the Secret Germany *and* for the "renewal of the German nation through the vision of its greatest emperor": Salin, *Ernst Kantorowicz*, 9.

133. Alain Boureau, *Histoires d'un historien: Kantorowicz* (Paris: Gallimard, 1990), 41.

134. See, e.g., Raulff, *Kreis ohne Meister*, 324; Malkiel, "Ernst Kantorowicz," 146–219; Petrow, *Der Dichter als Führer?*, 123–28; and Giesey, "Ernst H. Kantorowicz," 198.

135. For the anti-republican implications of the *Reichsidee* see Sontheimer, *Antidemokratisches Denken*, 280–306.

136. See Kantorowicz, *Kaiser Friedrich*, 400.

137. Kantorowicz, *Kaiser Friedrich*, 620. According to a folk legend, an eagle had trailed his wing in the blood of the dead Konradin and thus stained soared again to heaven. Kantorowicz combined this image of the unavenged Hohenstaufen with the notion of a German Vespers.

138. See Ernst Kantorowicz, *The King's Two Bodies: A Study in Medieval Political Theology* (Princeton: Princeton University Press, 1957).

139. Kantorowicz, *Kaiser Friedrich*, 389–90, 74, and 89.

140. For the neo-Ghibelline conception of the Reich and its expansionist agendas see Wolfgang Hardtwig, "Von Preußens Aufgabe in Deutschland zu Deutschlands Aufgabe in der Welt. Liberalismus und borussianisches Geschichtsbild zwischen Revolution und Imperialismus," *Historische Zeitschrift* 231, 2 (1980), 265–324.

141. See David Abulafia, "Kantorowicz, Frederick II and England," in *Ernst Kantorowicz: Erträge der Doppeltagung,* eds. Robert Benson and Johannes Fried (Stuttgart: Franz Steiner Verlag, 1997), 124–43 (132), and Carl Landauer, "Ernst Kantorowicz and the Sacralization of the Past," *Central European History* 25, 2 (1994), 1–25 (7–8).

142. Kantorowicz, *Kaiser Friedrich*, 353, 522.

143. Note that at the end of the last quotation, Kantorowicz implicitly distinguishes Frederick's "Genossenschafts-Staat" from the League of Nations. His contempt for the latter institution is evident in "Deutsches Papsttum," 8.

144. See Heinrich August Winkler, *The Long Shadow of the Reich: Weighing Up German History* (London: German Historical Institute, 2002).

145. This was the heading of his book's penultimate chapter.

146. Kantorowicz, *Kaiser Friedrich*, 17 and 12.

147. Kantorowicz, *Kaiser Friedrich*, 444.

148. See Paul de Lagarde, "Die nächsten Pflichten deutscher Politik" (1886), in Lagarde, *Deutsche Schriften*, 5th ed. (Göttingen: Dieterich, 1920), 440–42. George greatly admired Lagarde: see Landmann, *Gespräche*, 50. On the concept of "Mitteleuropa" see Henry C. Meyer, *Mitteleuropa in German Thought and Action, 1815–1945* (The Hague: Martinus Nijhoff, 1955), Reinhard Frommelt, *Paneuropa oder Mitteleuropa: Einigungsbestrebungen im Kalkül deutscher Wirtschaft und Politik 1925–1933* (Stuttgart: Deutsche Verlags-Anstalt, 1977), Hans-Dietrich Schultz, "Deutschlands 'natürliche' Grenzen. 'Mittellage' und 'Mitteleuropa' in der Diskussion der Geographen seit dem Beginn des 19. Jahrhunderts," *Geschichte und Gesellschaft* 15, 2 (1989), 248–281, and Rainer Eisfeld, "*Mitteleuropa* in Historical and Contemporary Perspective," *German Politics and Society* 28 (Spring 1993), 39–52.

149. See Friedrich Naumann, *Mitteleuropa* (Berlin: G. Reimer, 1915), 40–42, where Naumann invokes the Holy Roman Empire as a model for "Mitteleuropa."

150. See Sontheimer, *Antidemokratisches Denken*, 292–97; Bernd Faulenbach, *Ideologie des deutschen Weges: Die deutsche Geschichte in der Historiographie zwischen Kaiserreich und Nationalsozialismus* (Munich: C. H. Beck, 1980), 82–85.

151. Kantorowicz, *Kaiser Friedrich*, 349, 520.

152. Arvid Brodersen, *Stefan George: Deutscher und Europäer* (Berlin: Verlag die Runde, 1935) provides an insightful commentary on this tension. See also Richard Faber, "Third Reich and Third Europe: Stefan George's Imperial Mythologies in Context," in *A Poet's Reich*, eds. Lane and Ruehl, 251–69.

153. Marc Bloch, "The Empire and the Idea of the Empire under the Hohenstaufen," Lectures delivered at Strasbourg in the academic year 1927–28, in *Land and Work in Mediaeval Europe: Selected Papers by Marc Bloch*, trans. J. E. Anderson (London: Routledge, 1967), 41.

154. Marc Bloch, "Bulletin Historique: Histoire d'Allemagne (Moyen Age)," *Revue historique* 158 (1928): 108–58, here 157. Bloch mockingly mentioned Kantorowicz's anglophobic description of Otto the Welf in this context.

155. George, *Gesamt-Ausgabe der Werke*, IX, 39: "Der sprengt die ketten fegt auf trümmerstätten / Die ordnung · geisselt die verlaufnen heim / Ins ewige recht wo grosses wiederum gross ist / Herr wiederum herr · zucht wiederum zucht · er heftet / Das wahre sinnbild auf das völkische banner / Er führt durch sturm und grausige signale / Des frührots seiner treuen schar zum werk / Des wachen tags und pflanzt das Neue Reich."

156. *Der Angriff*, 5 December 1933; quoted in Norton, *Secret Germany*, 740.

157. Walter Benjamin, *Gesammelte Briefe*, eds. Christoph Gödde and Henri Lonitz, 6 vols. (Frankfurt am Main: Suhrkamp, 1995–98), IV, 237.

158. See Hoffmann, *Stauffenberg*, 118. For George's ambivalent attitude toward National Socialism see Thormaehlen, *Erinnerungen*, 282–83.

159. Stefan George to Ernst Morwitz, 10 May 1933; quoted in Hoffmann, *Stauffenberg*, 117.

160. See ibid., 111, 116–20.

161. Landmann, *Gespräche*, 209: "Über das Politisch-Aktuelle sagte [George] mir in Berlin . . . es sei doch immerhin das erste Mal, dass Auffassungen, die er vertreten habe, ihm von aussen wiederklängen."

162. Kurt Hildebrandt to Arvid Brodersen, 7 January 1935; quoted in Hoffmann, *Stauffenberg*, 119.

163. See Hildebrandt, *Erinnerungen*, 232.

164. See Landmann, *Gespräche*, 209. See also Michael Landmann, *Erinnerungen an Stefan George. Seine Freundschaft mit Julius und Edith Landmann* (Amsterdam: Castrum Peregrini, 1980), 50.

165. See Landmann, *Erinnerungen*, 50.

166. Hoffmann, *Stauffenberg*, 107–28, Groppe, *Macht der Bildung*, 651–76, Karlauf, *Stefan George*, 611–37, Raulff, *Kreis ohne Meister*, 30–188, provide the most thoughtful discussions of the Circle's reaction to the Nazi takeover. See also David, *Stefan George*, 363–69, and Wolfgang Graf Vitzthum, "Stefan George und der Staat," in *Festschrift für Martin Heckel zum 70. Geburtstag*, eds. Karl-Hermann Kästner, Knut W. Nörr, Klaus Schlaich (Tübingen: Mohr Siebeck, 1999), 915–39.

167. Woldemar Uxkull-Gyllenband, *Das revolutionäre Ethos bei Stefan George* (Tübingen: J.C.B. Mohr, 1933), 8.

168. Quoted in *"Spiegelbild einer Verschwörung": Die Opposition gegen Hitler und der Staatsstreich vom 20. Juli 1944 in der SD-Berichterstattung. Geheime Dokumente aus dem ehemaligen Reichssicherheitshauptamt*, ed. Hans-Adolf Jacobsen, 2 vols (Stuttgart: Seewald, 1984), I, 447–48. Berthold Stauffenberg then went on to say that the regime had turned almost all of these ideas into their opposite: ibid., 448.

169. Hoffmann, *Stauffenberg*, 449. For the "konservatives Großmachtdenken" of the resistance groups around Canaris and Beck and their ideal of a Europe under German leadership see Hermann Graml, "Die außenpolitischen Vorstellungen des deutschen Widerstandes," in *Der deutsche Widerstand gegen Hitler. Vier historisch-kritische Studien*, eds. Walter Schmitthenner and Hans Buchheim (Cologne: Kiepenheuer & Witsch, 1966), 5–72 (37-39).

170. Karl Wolfskehl to Albert Verwey, 26 October 1932: quoted in Groppe, *Macht der Bildung*, 664.

171. Thomas Mann, *Tagebücher 1933–1934*, ed. Peter de Mendelssohn (Frankfurt a.M.: S. Fischer, 1977), 473 (15 July 1934).

172. Hildebrandt, *Erinnerungen*, 231. Cf. Thormaehlen, *Erinnerungen*, 283.

173. Quoted in Hildebrandt, *Erinnerungen*, 231.

174. Ernst Kantorowicz to Stefan George, 10 July 1933, Stefan George Archiv, Stuttgart, Akte Ernst Kantorowicz.

175. Like Kantorowicz, Edith Landmann was not sure whether the Nazi seizure of power could be seen as a realization of George's utopia. "Should we be horrified by this parody of the New Reich that is being enacted by the Third Reich," she wrote in a circular to the Jewish members of the Circle in 1933, "or should we . . . welcome these bastards of the New Reich as the ones we have been longing for for such a long time, who will cleanse the earth from the old debris and plough up the the soil so that its true sons can later farm it?" Edith Landmann "An die deutschen Juden, die zum geheimen Deutschland hielten," (1933), Leo Baeck Institute, New York, Stefan George Collection, no. AR 1038, 1.

176. On the concept of the "vanishing point" see Helmut Walser Smith, "The Vanishing Point of German History: An Essay on Perspective," *History & Memory* 17, 1/2 (2005), 269–95.

177. See Raulff, *Kreis ohne Meister*, 428–97.

178. The two most important recent studies to read Stauffenberg's opposition to Hitler in light of his attachment to the ideals of the George Circle are Karlauf, *Stefan George*, 530–80, and Riedel, *Geheimes Deutschland*, 198–221. For a critical response to this reading see Robert Norton, "Lyrik und Moral," *Die Zeit* (16 July 2009), 48. See also Raulff, *Kreis ohne Meister*, 420–27.

179. See Ernst Kantorowicz, "Das Geheime Deutschland" (as presented at Frankfurt University on 14 November 1933), in Benson and Fried, *Ernst Kantorowicz*, 77–93. Kantorowicz conceived his lecture at least partly as a response to the pro-Nazi pronouncements given earlier that year by Uxkull-Gyllenband and Ernst Bertram: see Eckhart Grünewald, "'Übt an uns mord, und reicher blüht was blüht!': Ernst Kantorowicz spricht am 14. November 1933 über das 'Geheime Deutschland'," in Benson and Fried, *Ernst Kantorowicz*, 57–76, here 63–64.

180. Quoted in Hoffmann, *Stauffenberg*, 396–97.

181. See George, *Gesamt-Ausgabe der Werke*, VI/VII, 55–57, here 56: "Kein werk ist des himmels das ich euch nicht tu / Ein haarbreit nur fehlt und ihr merkt nicht den trug / Mit euren geschlagenen sinnen." ("There is no heavenly work that I cannot do for you / You are barely able to notice the deceit / With your degraded senses")

182. Sebastian Haffner, *Anmerkungen zu Hitler* (Munich: Kindler, 1978), 26.

183. On the "failure of illiberalism" see Fritz Stern, *The Failure of Illiberalism: Essays on the Political Culture of Modern Germany* (New York: Knopf, 1972). Following Detlev Peukert's revisionist foray, a number of recent scholars have called into question the conventional narrative of Weimar's "failure": see, e.g., Peter Fritzsche's influential article "Did Weimar Fail?," *Journal of Modern History* 68 (1996), 629–56. For insightful comments on the contingency and openness of Weimar thought see *Die "Krise" der Weimarer Republik. Zur Kritik eines Deutungsmusters*, eds. Moritz Föllmer and Rüdiger Graf (Frankfurt a.M. and New York: Campus, 2005),and Rüdiger Graf, *Die Zukunft der Weimarer Republik: Krisen und Zukunftsaneignungen in Deutschland 1918–1933* (Munich: R. Oldenbourg, 2008). See also the pertinent remarks in Benjamin Ziemann, "Weimar was Weimar: Politics, Culture and the Emplotment of the German Republic," *German History* 28, 4 (2010), 542–71, esp. 553–6 and 564–571.

13

Weimar Film Theory

Sabine Hake

Weimar film theory today is closely identified with three names: Siegfried Kracauer, Béla Balázs, and Rudolf Arnheim. However, a return to the archives reveals that their contributions are more accurately located in the space between
criticism and theory and can only be understood through the entire historical constellation: the various institutional contexts, aesthetic categories, social
practices, and cultural traditions that constituted film as a discursive object;
the competing functions of film as mass-produced commodity, art form, and
propaganda tool that informed critical practices; and the changing positions of
film in relation to other art forms, mass media, and modes of perception and
experience.

Theorizing Film, Debating Modernity

Thus marked as a site of contestation and negotiation, the new medium of film
allowed critics to address key issues of Weimar modernity: the threat of rationalization, mechanization, standardization, and homogenization; the ambivalent promises of Americanization and modern consumer culture; the leveling
of social differences as well as the erosion of the high/low culture divide. Above
all, writing about film meant confronting the modern masses in their changing
manifestations from the working-class audiences of the 1910s to the white-collar
audiences of the early 1930s. Two terms, *Kino* and *Film*, illustrate the underlying
issues and the gradual change in perspective: The earlier term *Kino* (cinema)
still connected the spectacle of technical innovation provided by *Kinematogra-
phie* (cinematography) to the popular diversions found in the *Kintopp* (flickers
or nickelodeon). Accordingly, the shift from *Kino* to *Film* during the 1920s announced a growing interest in aesthetic qualities and artistic possibilities and
laid the foundation for the absorption of film's socially disruptive effects into
the formal qualities of film as a work of art.[1] Yet this linguistic tension between
socio-psychological and aesthetic approaches and persistent anxieties about cinema's politics of emotion remained a constitutive element of Weimar writings
on film and distinguished them from contemporaneous debates in France, Italy,
and Britain.

There is no doubt that Weimar discourses on film would not have developed without the enormous productivity and artistic vision of the period's leading film directors, producers, actors, screenwriters, cinematographers, and set designers. The expressionist film of the early 1920s, which inspired Rudolf Kurtz's treatise on *Expressionismus und Film* (Expressionism and Film, 1926), served as an important reference point in the critical reception of what since has become known as Weimar art cinema. Its main representatives—Ernst Lubitsch, Fritz Lang, F. W. Murnau, and G. W. Pabst—inspired critics to introduce questions of film authorship and style and argue for the inclusion of film among more established art forms. Famous film stars from Charlie Chaplin to Asta Nielsen allowed their learned fans to examine the fundamentally different status of the human body and, hence, of acting in the cinema and to consider the emergence of a new universal language based on gestures and facial expressions beholden only to the laws of looking. The global reach of the Hollywood film industry and its highly standardized products and the enthusiastic reception of the so-called Russian films with their innovative approach to montage prompted calls for a uniquely German cinema of quality based on an artisanal mode of production. Meanwhile, the politicization of filmmaking in the later 1920s necessitated an urgent reconsideration of the relationship between film and ideology and the conditions of film production under capitalism. Last but not least, the arrival of the sound film in 1927 forced critics to revisit earlier statements claims about film's inherent laws and to pay closer attention to the interrelation between art and technology.

However, it would be unproductive to see Weimar film criticism and theory solely as an engagement with contemporary film production and to organize historical overviews only around formal categories such as camerawork, lighting, editing, and mise-en-scène. In ways that will become very clear in the essay's second part, writing about film in the 1920s and early 1930s involved above all a direct confrontation with the consequences of modernization and the manifestations of modernity in everyday life: As a new public sphere, the cinema announced the triumph of a democratic mass society over the rigid class structures of the pre-war period, but it also contributed to the disappearance of local, regional, and national differences. As a popular entertainment, the cinema offered new sensations, pleasures, and distractions while aestheticizing the experience of acceleration, fragmentation, and shock. As a modern mass medium, the cinema embodied the shift from literary to visual culture, the leveling of distinctions between high and low culture, and the increasing cross-fertilization among art forms (literature, theater, music, opera, dance) and mass media (photography, broadcasting). And as a mode of experience, the cinema established spatio-temporal models and socio-psychological structures that had as much in common with older popular diversions as with new forms of simulation and commodification, including flanerie.

In order to understand the overdetermined nature of Weimar writings on film, we must first take account of its origins in the Wilhelmine period and recognize the strong continuities between the pre-war and post-war years. All of the major arguments and debates started during the 1910s, such as the composition of film audiences and the pleasures of movie-going, the potential uses of film in education and propaganda, the institutional relationship between film and the other arts, the ascendancy of the longer narrative film and the introduction of the star system, and the changing affinities of the new medium with the aesthetic paradigms of realism and illusionism, visual spectacle and narrative continuity.

Trade journals played an important role in establishing film as a discursive object at the intersection of technology, industry, and aesthetics. The first articles on film style and technique accompanied the emergence of the longer narrative film as the dominant practice (against an early cinema of attractions) and promoted entertainment as the main function of cinema (against the competing models of art and education). Early film criticism developed out of film advertisement, an influence that survived in the preoccupation with film's effect on the spectator (i.e., as reception aesthetics) which in turn informed critics' treatment of its double status as art and commodity. Trade journals such as *Der Kinematograph* (1907–37) and *Lichtbildbühne* (1908–40) provided information for, and exchanges between, all three branches of the film industry—production, distribution, and exhibition—and supported efforts for more public recognition, economic regulation, and favorable legislation on the local, regional, and national level. The first reviews still acknowledged all aspects of the cinematic apparatus, with the spectacle of the apparatus and the attractions on the screen taking equal space and with the physical pleasures and sensationalist effects of the event emphasized. Yet the rise of the *Kinodrama* (cinema drama), which focused on melodramatic and sentimental stories and often featured Asta Nielsen and Henny Porten in the leading roles, and the promotion of the early *Autorenfilm* (author's film), which offered screen adaptations of literary classics as well as contemporary works by Gerhart Hauptmann, Hermann Sudermann, and Max Halbe, called for an aesthetically informed criticism that established clear categories of evaluation aimed at middle-class audiences and their different modes of cultural consumption. The adaptation and subsequent reception of Paul Lindau's *Der Andere* (The Other, 1913), with the famous Albert Bassermann in the title role, marked a milestone in the desired embourgeoisement of cinema.

Around 1909, the first film reviews appeared in daily newspapers and cultural journals, with Kurt Pinthus's 1913 article on *Quo vadis?* commonly cited as the first serious film review.[2] While the majority of reviewers still perceived film as an assault on class sensibilities and moral values, a growing number acknowledged its unique qualities: the emphasis on action, sensation, and adventure, the affinities with childhood and dream, and the similarities with myths and fairytales. Of special relevance, many agreed, were the cinema's "pure kinetics" and "optical lyrics," qualities that, according to Paul Wegener and others, made it particularly suited for the traditions of the fantastic and its challenges to everyday perception.[3]

Within the conceptual dyads that organized the discourses of film from the 1910s to the 1930s, the cinema invariably occupied the site of otherness. It stood for industrial class society rather than organic community, modern civilization rather than traditional culture, the global entertainment industry rather than national culture and heritage. Consequently, the cinema was both denounced and celebrated as the preferred form of entertainment for the lower classes and cited as the clearest indication of their great susceptibility to mass manipulation as well as mass mobilization; hence the many polemics about the dangers of movie addiction and the pleasures of scopophilia. For cinema reformers such as Hermann Halter and Walter Conrad, the audience usually functioned as a stand-in for the modern masses and their alleged threat to the established social and political order. By contrast, writers celebrated the cinema as either an instrument of aesthetic innovation and social change (e.g., Yvan Goll, Else Lasker-Schüler) or an agent of cultural and national decline (e.g., Franz Pfemfert).

The social composition of the audience, the conditions of collective reception, and the affective dimensions of film spectatorship were a concern in all contributions. Art historian Herbert Tannenbaum, the author of *Kino und Theater* (Cinema and Theater, 1912) and regarded by some scholars as the first German film theoretician, described the movie audience as a model of cultural diversity and social harmony and praised the cinema as the quintessential modern *Gesamtkunstwerk*. Yet realizing these inherent qualities, he concluded, required "the attention and contribution of all those who see themselves as the intellectual leaders of our nation."[4] Emilie Altenloh's groundbreaking study, *Zur Soziologie des Kino* (On the Sociology of Cinema, 1914), was the first to draw attention to the social heterogeneity of audiences and consider the implications of cinema as an alternative public sphere especially for women and young people. The notion of *Schaulust* (visual pleasure or scopophilia, to use the scientific term) also played a key role in explaining the otherness of the filmic experience and its potentially subversive effects. Visual pleasure stood for irrational forces, unconscious drives, and social and sexual transgressions. Not surprisingly, the cinema's function as a "substitute for dreams," to evoke Hugo von Hofmannsthal's 1921 essay, drew attention to the much-discussed crisis of meaning and the problem of modern alienation and inspired the utopias and dystopias of cinema that linked all contributions to larger questions of politics and society.

The two most important contributions of the Wilhelmine period to the emerging discourses of film were the literary debate on the cinema, the *Kinodebatte*, and the cinema reform movement; both continued throughout the 1920s. Inseparable from expressionist literature and, later, expressionist film, the cinema debate brought together a group of young writers, including Goll, Pfemfert, and Lasker-Schüler, who turned to film for creative inspiration while reaffirming the aesthetic superiority of literature. The categories of idealist aesthetics and the traditions of German classicism (e.g., Lessing's *Laokoon* on the difference between poetry and sculpture, Schiller on the theater as a moral institution) played a key role in working out the social and cultural implications. References to "eternal truth," "artistic value," and "good taste" established an explanatory model and interpretative framework and aided the transformation of "the flickers" into a respectable middle-class diversion. Meanwhile, representatives of the historical avant-gardes incorporated certain filmic techniques (e.g., Döblin's *Ki-*

noismus) into their own work, confirming the equation of film with a modernist sensibility. In *Das Kinobuch* (The Cinema Book, 1912), Kurt Pinthus brought together film scenarios by Walter Hasenclever, Else Lasker-Schüler, Max Brod, and others to demonstrate in what ways the new medium resisted conventional definitions of the work of art and instead incorporated older traditions of comedy, fantasy, and mass spectacle.

In all cases, the polemical declarations by film's friends and enemies were also animated by professional concerns: fears about the decline of book culture and the future place of intellectuals as the arbiters of taste; awareness of the increased competition between cinema, theater, and other performing arts; and uncertainty about the employment opportunities for writers in the film industry.[5] Two essays illustrate the opposing positions of elitism and populism: Alfred Döblin's 1909 polemic on "The Theater of the Little People," which locates the provocation of cinema in the base instincts and unconscious drives of the urban masses, those who "want to be touched, titillated, shocked, and then burst out into laughter," and Carlo Mierendorff's 1920 manifesto "If I Had the Cinema!," which similarly describes the cinema as a means of survival for the masses but already emphasizes its empowering qualities; his conclusion: "He who has the cinema will rule the world."[6]

Three features were of particular concern for the literary intelligentsia: the specific conditions of mass reception, the industrial mode of production, and film's artistic ambitions. Positions wavered between enthusiastic declarations about film as the basis for all future art and emphatic statements that film would never become an art. Normative poetics became the preferred mode of explanation and, hence, discursive co-optation in dealing with the problem of, to cite Benjamin, "the work of art in the age of mechanical reproduction." Focusing primarily on the longer narrative film, writers passionately debated the differences between film and theater or film and literature, fearing border crossings but also welcoming cross-fertilizations. Emphasizing the sheer physicality of film acting, some envisioned closer ties to dance and pantomime; for yet others the cinema's popular quality and communal nature brought it closest to folklore, with the term promising the much-desired reconciliation of tradition and modernity. The most innovative approaches emphasized the photographic quality of the moving image and developed film's formal means out of its technical limitations; which at the time meant: its silence. As the first to argue in this vein, Georg Lukács, in a 1913 essay on "Thoughts on an Aesthetic for the Cinema" even declared the lack of language as film's primary stylistic principle and located its affective and cognitive rewards in the tension between presence and absence organized by the photographic image.

A similar tension between the utopia of social harmony and the diagnosis of class strife informed the writings of the *Kinoreformer* (cinema reformers), a loosely defined group of conservative educators, pastors, lawyers, civil servants, and media activists most active during the early 1910s. Deeply concerned about the pitfalls of modernization, they saw the cinema as both the cause and the solution to the crisis of nation and society. Accordingly, for them, the utopias of cinema were found not in aesthetic experiences but in the project of national education. Sociological, pedagogical, legislative, and mass-psychological perspectives dominated their writings. The most pressing issues for the cinema reform movement were the effect of "trash and smut" on the nation's youth, the need for stricter and more consistent censorship laws, and the more effective use of cultural films (e.g., about geography, biology, ethnography, medicine) in educational settings. Through media initiatives, film was to be transformed into a tool of social reconciliation and national renewal. Only a strong national cinema, the cinema reformers believed, could stop the disintegration of society and reunite all classes and generations under the unifying force of German nationalism.

Almost all reformers were categorically opposed to the film drama and what they perceived as its dangerous manipulation of fantasy and desire. Whereas the infamous Karl Brunner limited his campaigns against the *Schundfilm* (trashy film) to issues of film censorship, others emphasizes the benefits of (Catholic) media education for the nation's youth. The reformist journal *Bild and Film* and the Lichtbühnen-Bibliothek monograph series allowed Hermann Häfker, Willi Warstat, Adolf Sellmann, and Albert Hellwig to disseminate such media pedagogical ideas and promote the reformist political agenda. In *Das Kino in Gegenwart und Zukunft* (The Cinema of the Present and the Future, 1920), Konrad Lange summarized many of the film political positions of the cinema reformers: opposition to the dominant model of illusionism and sensationalism and support for documentary forms that explored film's inherent affinity with the natural world, rejection of the binary structures (e.g., of good vs. evil, rich vs. poor) that aligned the filmic imagination with the specter of class struggle and promotion of a national cinema able to envision an alternative to capitalism and internationalism.

Weimar film criticism at its best managed to mediate between the goals of film advertising and marketing and the expression of aesthetic judgment in the tradition of literary criticism. In trade journals such as *Film-Kurier* (1919–44), the first to be published on a daily basis, Willy Haas, Lotte Eisner, and Hans Feld reconciled the economic interests of the film industry with widespread calls for the artistically ambitious film. In national newspapers such as *Frankfurter Zeitung*, *Vossische Zeitung*, and *Berliner Börsen-Courier*, film reviews became a regular part of the *Feuilleton*, with Herbert Ihering setting new standards for the kind of writing that reflected the progressive, democratic spirit of the young republic. In *Die Weltbühne* and *Der Querschnitt*, Hans Siemsen and Rudolf Kurtz argued repeatedly about the role of film criticism as a privileged site for working through the contradictions of mass culture and modernity. Alfred Polgar, Alfred Kerr, Kurt Tucholsky, and Benjamin von Brentano shared a strong belief in the transformative power of cultural critique. Even when they attacked the low quality of contemporary productions or, as did Polgar and Kerr, insisted on the superiority of the theater, they always acknowledged that film had become a legitimate cultural practice.

The politicization of cultural life especially in the later years of the Weimar Republic had a profound effect on film criticism. Critics on the left and right focused increasingly on the relationship between film and ideology and debated the uses of film as political propaganda. Even leftwing publications overcame their disdain for popular entertainment to take on four film-related projects: critique of the big-budget UFA (Universum Film AG) productions as reactionary and nationalistic, promotion of the Russian films and their revolutionary message, support for proletarian filmmakers in Germany, and analysis of the relationship between mainstream cinema and bourgeois ideology. Willi Münzenberg's pamphlet *Erobert den Film!* (Conquer the Film!, 1925) on "this effective and vital means of propaganda and agitation" captured best the mixture of practical advice (e.g., on leftist media initiatives), political activism (e.g., in the fight against censorship), and ideology critique (e.g., of the *Fridericus* films) found in the film reviews of the KPD daily, *Die Rote Fahne,* and *Film und Volk,* the official publication of the left-liberal Volksverband für Filmkunst.[7]

Yet with the exception of Lu Märten, the first critic to develop a materialist aesthetic based on the characteristics of the cinematic apparatus, leftist film critics remained beholden to the naturalist paradigm and its underlying assumptions about the transparency of filmic representation and the centrality of character identification. The same could be said about film criticism on the right, which continued the cinema reformer's emphasis on film as a non-narrative medium, while adding an increasingly strident nationalistic, racist, and anti-Semitic tone. Thus in Hans Buchner's *Im Banne des Films* (Under the Spell of Film, 1927), cinema comes to signify all the supposed pathologies of Weimar society: consumerism, materialism, capitalism, internationalism, Americanism, and so forth. The strong continuities between pre-1933 and post-1933 writings especially in relation to questions of nation and race are especially evident in the work of Oskar Kalbus whose early proposals for film as propaganda found plenty of applications during the Third Reich.

Film criticism was part of a larger discursive constellation that contributed to the dissemination of film consciousness into all areas of cultural life. This process was both accelerated and validated by plays and novels set in the film world, film adaptations of famous literary texts, the increasingly popular books to the film, and a new brand of sensationalist journalism about the film world and its celebrities. Film directors such as Ewald André Dupont and Urban Gad published how-to manuals, established writers from Hanns Heinz Ewers to Carl Zuckmayer wrote film scenarios, Alfred Döblin incorporated filmic montage techniques into his famous 1929 modernist city novel, *Berlin Alexanderplatz,* and even Bertolt Brecht, in *Der Dreigroschenprozess* (Three Penny Trial, 1931), used his legal problems with the Nero-Film in the wake of the G.W. Pabst adaptation of his famous 1928 *Dreigroschenoper* (music: Kurt Weill) to debunk the myth of film authorship and deconstruct the conditions of filmmaking under capitalism.

Through all of these discursive interventions, film emerged as the founding site of modern mass culture, and "cinema man," in the terminology of the times, became the embodiment of the mass individual. Nowhere are the implications more apparent than in the popular treatises that diagnosed the power of cinema over all areas of modern life and identified its real and imaginary subject effects.

Typical of the resultant middlebrow theorizing, Curt Morek's popular *Sittenge-schichte des Kinos* (The Cinema's History of Manners and Morals, 1926) no longer approached film through a comparison with literature and theater but celebrated its origins in the variety, the circus, and the fairground. Concerned neither with aesthetic enjoyment nor moral edification, film according to Morek appealed to, and engaged, an entirely different set of pleasures, among them the need for sensation, stimulation, distraction, and, as "one of the most powerful human drives," *Schaulust*.[8] Some of his contemporaries offered even more sweeping scenarios of cultural renewal or decline, with the most embarrassing examples found in the kind of populist treatises that combined philosophical speculation with political invective. Ilja Ehrenburg in *Die Traumfabrik* (The Dream Factory, 1931) located the attractions of cinema in the psychological mechanisms of lack, desire, and compensation that allowed the Hollywood studio system to exploit the new media technology for its own purposes. His conclusion: "During the day—the running conveyer belt; at night—the cinema. That is the law of being."[9] Similarly linking the cinema to Americanization, René Fülöp-Miller's *Die Phan-tasiemaschine* (The Fantasy Machine, 1931) described film as "the industrialized satisfaction of psychological needs" and, for that reason, far removed from the spheres of real art.[10] Focusing on cinema as an instrument of massification, Hans Buchner in *Im Banne des Films* (Under the Spell of Film, 1927) warned that "the marriage of Art and Technology" would only succeed under the guidance of a strong individual. Similarly concerned with social and cultural leveling, Curt Wesse in *Großmacht Film* (Superpower Film, 1932) saw the future of cinema between two alternatives: the redemptive experience of community and the dangerous forces of totalitarianism—precisely the terms used by the Nazis to justify the *Gleichschaltung* (forced coordination) of the film industry in 1933.

Growing public interest in film as the most important art form of the twentieth century and acute awareness among the cultural elites of film's threat to established categories of aesthetic analysis also found expression in two kinds of theoretical writing: philosophical treatises in the tradition of normative aesthetics and critical reflections on film as an ally of modernism and the avant-garde. The best example for the dominant philosophical tradition is Rudolf Harms, who in *Philosophie des Films* (Philosophy of Film, 1926) used a system of aesthetics inspired by his teacher Johannes Volkelt to define film's stylistic means out of its technical limitations and collective modes of production and reception. Pursuing a more speculative approach, Walter Bloem's *Die Seele des Lichtspiels* (The Soul of the Motion Picture, 1922) and Georg Otto Stindt's *Das Lichtspiel als Kunstform* (The Motion Picture as an Art Form, 1924) claimed that the process of mechanical reproduction needed to be shrouded in spiritual qualities in order to lift film to the level of art, made possible for Bloem through the stylization of the pro-filmic event and for Stindt through the stylistic will of the director. Taking a very different approach, modernists such as Guido Bagier in *Der kommende Film* (1928, The Coming Film) and Hans Richter in *Filmgegner von heute—Filmfreunde vom morgen* (Enemies of Film Today—Friends of Film Tomorrow, 1929) embraced film's connection to the machine aesthetics and located

its aesthetic concerns in the formal exploration of movement and rhythm and the explosion of the space-time continuum.

Three Models of Weimar Film Criticism: Kracauer, Balázs, Arnheim

The film theoretical writings of Siegfried Kracauer, Béla Balázs, and Rudolf Arnheim cannot be understood outside the larger discursive formations that situated the new mass medium within Weimar culture and modernity. Yet by moving beyond the conceptual impasses of idealist aesthetics and normative poetics, these three thinkers developed models of film analysis and cultural critique that sometimes were ahead of their times and that continue to resonate with contemporary concerns.

Kracauer, Balázs, and Arnheim belonged to two generations of Central European intellectuals (born between 1884 and 1904) profoundly influenced by the First World War and the Russian Revolution. Sharing a Jewish middle-class background, they believed deeply in the power of cultural critique, but pursued their interests outside the professional culture of scholarship and the academy. Their preference for essayist writing must be explained through its ability to capture best the fragmentation, impermanence, and perspectivism of modern life. The philosophical and political movements of the turn of the century left a indelible mark on their conceptualization of film, with their reflections on experience and the life world informed by *Lebensphilosophie*, and Georg Simmel in particular; with their understanding of modern mass society indebted to Max Weber, Georg Lukács, and Karl Marx; and with their interest in perception and spectatorship influenced by both Bergsonian vitalism and Freudian psychoanalysis, and, in the case of Arnheim, the Gestalt psychology of Wolfgang Köhler, Max Wertheimer, and Kurt Lewin.

Of the three theorists discussed here, Siegfried Kracauer went furthest in reading film as an integral part of modern life and expanding the filmic experience toward other phenomena such as urbanism and consumerism. Not surprisingly, his Weimar writings have become most closely associated with theories of modernity and mass culture that, as in Walter Benjamin's famous 1936 essay, *The Work of Art in the Age of Its Technical Reproducibility*, develop their categories of analysis out of the conditions of mechanical reproduction and, as Theodor W. Adorno in "The Culture Industry," a chapter from *Dialectic of Enlightenment* (1947), correlate film to the capitalist mode of production. However, Kracauer's Weimar writings distinguished themselves from Critical Theory in two significant ways: through his belief in the emancipatory power of modern mass culture and the aesthetic contribution of vernacular modernism.

In giving voice to the legitimate entertainment needs of the urban masses, Kracauer enlisted sociological, phenomenological, and vitalist categories to study such diverse phenomena as architecture, fashion, sports, product design, urban planning, exhibition culture, middlebrow literature, and white-collar society. The constitutive tension among empiricism, phenomenology, and allegorization in his highly suggestive readings of surface phenomena must be regarded as the productive principle through which new critical methods and insights become possible. Approaching film as a privileged perspective on modernity, Kracauer uses terms such as distraction, pleasure, and experience to move beyond the critical binaries of idealist aesthetics (e.g., text vs. context, production vs. reception, surface vs. depth) and map the unstable configurations of modern life in their own terms. On the one hand, this analysis of surface phenomena allows him to uncover the contradictions of mass society and to consider the possibility of "redemption of physical reality" through film. On the other, his comments on the social function of film are predicated on the insight that reality is a construction and that the daydreams of society—and hence, the social and political imaginary—can be studied best through the conventional stories, stereotypical characters, and escapist fantasies depicted on the screen.

Precisely this constitutive difference between lived experience and filmic reality and its myriad manifestations in filmic genres and styles defines the organizing principle behind his critical practice. From 1921 to 1933, Kracauer worked for the liberal *Frankfurter Zeitung*, writing film reviews as well as articles on a wide range of cultural phenomena; in addition, he published several sociological studies and two autobiographical novels. As head of the newspaper's Berlin office after 1930, he witnessed firsthand the politicization of film during the last years of the Weimar Republic, an experience that resulted in a more sobering view of mainstream cinema, ideology, and capitalism. In numerous reviews he remained highly critical of the artistic ambitions of the Weimar art film and generally faulted German productions for their mediocrity and shallowness. He reserved his praise for the exploration of sensation, adventure, and suspense in the popular Hollywood films and the exploration of radical politics and aesthetics in the critically acclaimed Russian films. Throughout formal and technical questions became relevant only in relation to the ideological functions performed by them. Consequently, the arrival of film sound troubled him only because the additional of dialogue put an end to the indeterminacy of meaning that safeguarded the silent film against the incursions, via language, of bourgeois ideology; hence his hope that the sound film, in principle, "could afford the possibility of wresting away life in all of its totality from transitoriness and imparting it to the eternity of images."[11]

Two essays in particular capture the originality of Kracauer's method of reading modern mass culture: "The Cult of Distraction" (1926) and "The Mass Ornament" (1927). Theorizing distraction, he rejects the conventional view of distraction as inferior, which is predicated on a sharp high/low culture divide, and insists instead on the significance of the ephemeral and the contingent in making sense of the phenomena of modern life. Given his training as an architect, it is hardly surprising that it is the changes in motion-picture theater architecture and design that reveal to him the gradual embourgeoisement of cinema: from the early flickers and their working-class origins to the motion picture palaces that numb their audiences with their "*Gesamtkunstwerk* of effects." Similarly, it is the ornamental choreography of the Tiller Girls as an allegory of Taylorism that allows him to define his critical method: "An analysis of the simple surface manifestations of an epoch can contribute more to determining its place in the historical process than judgments of the epoch about itself."[12]

The vacillation between the defense of modern mass culture against elitist attitudes and bourgeois notions of high art and the attack on mainstream culture as escapist and reactionary manipulation appears at its most pronounced in Kracauer's sociological writings on film audiences and his closely related texts on film spectatorship and the cult of distraction. The historical alliance of film culture and white-collar culture, first diagnosed in *Die Angestellten* (1924, White-Collar Workers), enabled him to assert the legitimacy of white-collar workers' need for forms of entertainment that reflected their experiences of social mobility and economic uncertainty. Making the cinema "their shelter for the homeless," the white-collar workers sought out forms of entertainment "that radically aim at a form of distraction that unmasks the disintegration instead of masking it."[13] Associated with social and cultural leveling, they became the model of "the *homogeneous cosmopolitan audience* that, from the bank director to the sales assistant, from the diva to the typist, is of *one* mind."[14] While aware of the fundamental transformations of class society as the unacknowledged reference point behind all debates on the mass psychology of cinema, Kracauer adhered to rather conventional notions of gender when he used women audiences to complain about the surrogate emotions and escapist functions of mainstream cinema. In "The Little Shopgirls Go to the Movies" (1927), he uses women's alleged higher susceptibility to media images to identify the central problematic of contemporary culture, the disappearance of the real: "Film story and reality usually correspond to each other because typists model themselves after the examples from the screen; perhaps the most hypocritical examples are stolen from life."[15]

Especially in his film reviews from the last years of the Weimar Republic, Kracauer made it very clear that an emancipatory mass culture depended on democratic structures and institutions. Confronted with the rise of nationalist, reactionary, and anti-Semitic forces, he retreated from his earlier utopianism concerning mass culture and focused instead on its ideological function. Rejecting the distinction between entertainment and propaganda as deceptive, he paid particular attention to the tendentious films (e.g., the *Fridericus* films) that offered their political message in historical costume. Yet the mass-produced comedies and melodramas were no less dangerous politically because they perpetuated the false distinction between public and private life and infused their formulaic stories with hidden political messages. Confronted with the full might of the culture industry, Kracauer resorted to traditional categories of evaluation; but he never gave up on the utopia promise of cinema as liberating and emancipatory. Whether this promise could be translated into real social change depended not only on filmmakers and their audiences but also on film critics and their readers.

The Hungarian-born Balázs started out as a critic writing countless reviews for the Viennese daily *Der Tag*, which provided the basis for his first book, *Der sichtbare Mensch oder die Kultur des Films* (Visible Man, 1924). Like many contemporaries, he celebrated the art of Chaplin and Nielsen, analyzed the popular

Hollywood productions and critically acclaimed Russian films, closely followed the rise of the expressionist film and the making of a popular genre cinema, and lent his professional expertise to the most detailed questions of film technology and technique. An interest in older literary forms and popular diversions, a fascination with transitional states and threshold experiences, and an affinity for the experiences of regression found in childhood and dream align all of his creative endeavors with traditions presumably purged from modernity's enlightened worlds: namely the irrational, the mythological, the intuitive, and the non-linguistic and non-cognitive. Thus the new mass medium provided him with an important model of multimediality and aesthetic hybridity for all of his creative projects: as a film critic writing for daily newspapers, cultural magazines, and trade journals, as a literary author and opera librettist with an interest in fairytales and folk motifs, and as a screenwriter whose credits include the controversial G. W. Pabst adaptation of Brecht's *Dreigroschenoper* (The Threepenny Opera, 1931) and a contentious collaboration with Leni Riefenstahl on *Das blaue Licht* (The Blue Light, 1932).

The Visible Man has been described as an actor's theory and a poetics of the close-up, but is more fully understood through Balázs's use of physiognomy in explaining the perceptual, affective, and experiential qualities of cinema. Part training manual in visual literacy, part confessions of a cinephile, the book represents the first attempt to explain film's mass appeal through its unique ability to dissolve the boundary between the audience and the world of the film; which also means, the boundary separating art and life. Film, for Balázs serves as an instrument of reconciliation: between tradition and modernity, between individual and mass, and between the discourses of folk and class. His belief in the formative effect of spectatorship and, hence, in the redemptive power of film is evident already in the opening statement that "film is the folk art (*Volkskunst*) of our century. . . . Not in the sense, unfortunately, that it arises out of the people's spirit (*Volksgeist*) but that the people's spirit arises out of it [i.e., film]."[16]

In contrast to Kracauer, who reads the legitimate entertainment needs of the urban masses as part of a progressive, emancipatory mass culture, Balázs turns to older narrative traditions and highlights film's debts to the tradition of myths, legends, and fairytales. Accordingly, film's main contribution to the shift from a literary print culture to a new/old visual culture lies in "making human beings visible again," which means: reinstating them as the subjects and objects in the expressive regimes of visibility. The creation of "the first international language, the language of facial expressions and body gestures,"[17] is predicated on the development of film as a dialogic process and symbolic act, the recognition of physiognomy as a cognitive and aesthetic device, and the emphasis on the central role of expressive movement (*Ausdrucksbewegung*) in the making of meanings. Expressive movement, of course, suggests an expanded definition of physiognomy that applies equally to the animate and inanimate world, that acknowledges the filmic image as meaningful as well as legible and that locates in the phenomenological and hermeneutic qualities of physiognomy the promise of both spiritual redemption and political emancipation.

Written in response to the new sound technology and the increasing politicization of film, *Der Geist des Films* (The Spirit of Film, 1930) approached the question of reception from the perspective of class and discusses film more explicitly as a product of capitalist industry and bourgeois ideology. Reflecting on the double meaning of *Einstellung*, Balázs now asserted: "Every image suggests a point-of-view (*Einstellung*), every point-of-view suggests a relationship, and not just a spatial one. . . . That is what every camera position stands for a particular human [i.e., ideological] position."[18] As a consequence, his writings came to be defined by the tension between the utopian potential of film as a modern folk art and its actual limitations under capitalist modes of production. Until realizing their full potential, presumably under socialism, most films would therefore address themselves to a petty bourgeois mentality, a mentality that for Balázs found expression in a conception of social reality defined by individual agency, cult of family and private life, and a fatalistic view of history and politics.

In formal terms, *The Spirit of Film* also allowed Balázs to move beyond the aesthetics of the individual shot, especially the close-up, and its occasional conflation with screen acting and the pro-filmic event (i.e., mise-en-scène, lighting, camerawork). Partly in response to a critique by Eisenstein, he now focused on a wide range of editing techniques and discusses the dramaturgy of the sound film in relation to spatiotemporal relations, narrative strategies, and genre conventions. The new possibilities of sound were integrated into his unifying concept of physiognomy and its privileged position between communication and expression as the two primary functions of film. Balázs remained nonetheless committed to the primary of storytelling and rejected the experimental film as a fetishizing of technology, a position that put this Marxist critic in sharp opposition to the materialist aesthetics of Benjamin and Brecht.

Fairytales provided an important model for Balázs's conceptualization of early cinema as a public sphere and allowed him to extend his dream of a universal (or international) visual culture into the realm of social and political practices.[19] As the modern form of storytelling, film carried forward the older, communal traditions evoked by Benjamin in his theoretical romance with the figure of the storyteller and acknowledged by Balázs in his deeply nostalgic engagement with folk culture. Yet as a modern mass medium, film for the latter also compensated for the modern experience of fragmentation and shock by providing the audience with an illusory sense of oneness and unity through the symbolic universalism of physiognomy. For this reason, his characterization of film as modern folklore must be seen as an attempt simultaneously to validate and contain the medium's otherness within an established discursive paradigm, namely that of folk, and to utilize this tradition for the mobilization of the modern masses as film's designated object and subject, producer and consumer. Because of such conceptual incommensurabilities between the discourses of folk and class and their mediation through the affective and cognitive regimes of spectatorship and physiognomy Balázs's film theoretical work has often been dismissed as incoherent, inconsistent or compromised. Yet with their contradictions and nonsynchronicities, his film theoretical writings today also offer a historical model that resists the familiar binaries of early film studies—passive vs. active, affirmative vs. resistant, bourgeois vs. proletarian—and opens up the cinema and its discourses toward the corporeal regimes of sensation, affect, and experience.

The name of Rudolf Arnheim is usually associated with formalist theories of art and perception, a view encouraged by the author when he purged all Weimar references from the 1957 English re-edition from his main contribution to classical film theory, *Film als Kunst* (Film as Art, 1932). Like Balázs and Kracauer, Arnheim started out as a film critic writing countless reviews for *Die Weltbühne* and similar left-liberal publications and participating actively in the political debates of the late Weimar years. However, university studies with Max Wertheimer early on also directed his scholarly interests toward the laws of visual perception and the dynamics of art and technology. Especially the Gestaltist notion that the whole is more than the sum of its parts and that each part is determined by the intrinsic laws of the whole allowed him to approach concrete questions of film style and technique as part of a larger theory of visual perception. Arnheim saw himself not as a formalist but a materialist in the sense of *Materialtheorie*, to be defined as "a theory meant to show that artistic and scientific descriptions of reality are cast in modes that derive not so much from the subject matter itself but from the properties of the material—or *Material*—employed."[20]

Consequently, Arnheim's contribution cannot be contained within the formalist camp of classical film theory but must be seen as a critical working-through of the various formalist, cognitive, media theoretical, and ideology critical approaches that gave rise to Weimar discourses on film. Most surprising for this later advocate of film art, his film reviews from the 1920s express unabashed love for genre films and strong contempt for art films. While Chaplin and Garbo embodied for him the unlimited possibilities of the silent film, he evinced little patience for either the material excesses of UFA's cinema of quality, as personified by Lang, or the theoretical indulgences of an Eisenstein or Pudowkin. His enthusiasm for the formulaic *Konfektionsfilm* (i.e., genre film) betrayed his firm belief in an evolutionary model that saw in the codification of spatiotemporal relations the beginnings of a future film art based not on artistic ambitions but formal explorations. To underscore his point, he adamantly rejected the notion that film should always provide pleasure and called for a clear separation between art and entertainment. He polemically asserted, "that film is not an art of the masses (*Massenkunst*), except in the sense that quantity (*Masse*) must be generated at the box office."[21] Similarly he rejected his colleagues' preoccupation with matters of content (e.g., plot synopses and narrative themes) and insisted that film form had to always be regarded as an expression of material-specific qualities rather than psychological dispositions or aesthetic traditions.

Above all, Arnheim believed that all arts developed their inherent laws out of their technical limitations. Consequently, the sound film represented to him a betrayal of the medium's original promise: of training new modes of perception, of rediscovering the visual world, and of promoting visual literacy. The addition of sound returned film to the aesthetics of the proscenium stage and stifled its artistic ambitions with a perfunctory naturalism. Even the distinction between the sound film (*Tonfilm*) as the mere recording of an audiovisual source and the complete film (*Komplettfilm*) with its cacophony of dialogue, music, and sound effects failed to assuage his concerns about the artistic and social consequences of this new aesthetics of simulation. Held together by this principled opposition to the sound film, Arnheim's conception of film as a medium of mechanical reproduction involved two lines of argumentation: the one directed against mere imitations of physical reality, the other oriented toward a reconfiguration of art and reality: "What distinguishes this reproductive art?" he asked. "That reality represents itself. . . . The fact that reality represents itself only shows us where we have to look for the specific characteristics of this new art. Its strength lies in *representation*, and its specific formal means originate in the representation from a *particular perspective* and through a *particular selection*."[22]

As a result, *Film as Art* overcomes the contradictions defining film as modern art, mass entertainment, and cultural commodity through an exclusive focus on the relationship between art and perception.[23] Its main points can be summarized as follows: not all films should be considered art; film cannot be reduced to mechanical reproduction; filmic perception differs from normal perception; and the aesthetic qualities of an art form develop out of its inherent limitations. Arnheim's formalist tendencies are most pronounced in his detailed discussion of the differences between camera and human eye; by contrast, his observations on the constancies of size and shape are influenced by Gestalt psychology. Under headings such as "The Projection of Solids Upon a Plane Surface," "Reduction of Depth," "Lighting and the Absence of Color," "Delimitation of the Image and Distance From the Object," "Absence of the Space-Time Continuum," and "Absence of the Nonvisual World of the Senses," the book offers a scientific explanation of the transformation of the visible world through the perspective of the film camera and, based on these processes, outlines how the laws of visual perception can be translated into aesthetic qualities. Individual case studies privilege the photographic qualities of the image, with framing, lighting, and perspective as its most important formal means; the sensations of movement and speed are acknowledged in comments on the kinesthetic effects on the body. Moving from the single shot to the possibilities of editing, Arnheim highlights formal elements such as duration, similarity, contrast, synchronism, and asynchronism. In contrast to the proponents of Soviet-style montage (such as Sergei Eisenstein or Vsevolod Pudovkin), he counts editing among the standard elements of film language and its continuous refinement as the foundation of classical realist cinema (e.g., through the shot/reverse shot pattern and the narrative function of fade-in/fade-out).

In the context of Weimar critical thought, Arnheim's preoccupation with technology and technique must be read as an attempt both to avoid the then-ongoing political instrumentalization of cinema and to defend the artistic qualities of film against its commercial exploitation. Even while he denied that the work of art was indeed determined by social and economic forces, he explicitly linked the retreat to escapist fare to the crisis of the German film industry and the worldwide economic depression. And even if he showed little interest in questions of narrative, he remained acutely aware of the ideological function of conventions and stereotypes. Hence his conclusion concerning standard genre films: "Almost all of these films contain, whether consciously or unconsciously, a certain tendency in their story [*sic*]." It is a tendency found not in any particular themes or messages but located "in the position from which the things of this world are viewed, the selection of stories and their underlying moral standards as one-sided."[24] Elsewhere Arnheim admitted that film manipulates the audience, making sure "that dissatisfaction does not explode in revolutionary action, but dissipates into dreams of a better word."[25] With this surprisingly radical statement, the 1932 German original of *Film as Art* construed the rise of film art as conditioned by changes in the social order, whereas the later American edition closes with somber predictions about the demise of the silent film and the ascendancy of the despised complete film. The difference furnishes stark evidence that the history of classical film theory depends much on proper translations, and also confirms that film theory is an ongoing process whose continued relevance requires revisionist rereadings and repeated returns to the archives.

Conclusion: The Legacy of Weimar Film Theory

The reception of Weimar film theory as an integral part of Weimar culture and classical film theory has been inextricably linked to the Third Reich and the experience of exile. Kracauer and Arnheim left Germany for the United States, where they continued to write on film in the context of Cold War culture, with the former focusing his efforts on film propaganda and the latter pursuing research in cognitive psychology. Arnheim expanded his formal inquiries on film form toward a general theory of perception, *Art and Visual Perception: A Psychology of the Creative Eye* (1954), that exerted a strong influence on post-WWII abstract art and experimental film and confirmed his place in the formalist tradition in classical film theory. Kracauer's exile writings are inextricably linked to two works, *From Caligari to Hitler: A Psychological Study of the German Film* (1947), which analyzes Weimar films for their prefascist tendencies, and *Theory of Film: The Redemption of Physical Reality* (1960), which asserts the medium's inherent affinity with the realist aesthetics. Whereas Kracauer's contribution to classical film theory has for the longest time been equated with theories of realism, the recent rediscovery of his Weimar essays on cinema and the cult of distraction has drawn attention to his close ties with the Frankfurt School and the embeddedness of his writings in the larger constellations of Weimar mass culture and modernity. By contrast, Balázs's decision to move to the Soviet Union and, later, to Hungary, limited his reception in the English-speaking world to a 1952 translation of *Theory of Film: Character and Growth of a New Art* (1945). Yet, surprisingly, his anthropocentric film theory has most recently attracted the attention of a Deleuzian-inspired theory of the moving image and has been appropriated by cognitive scholarship on cinema, perception, and affect—evidence that Weimar film theory and its three main representatives are still relevant today.

Notes

1. Sabine Hake, *The Cinema's Third Machine: Writings on Film in Germany 1907–1933* (Lincoln: University of Nebraska Press, 1993). This essay summarizes ideas presented in greater detail in the book; it was written in 2006 and does not reflect research published since.
2. Kurt Pinthus, "Quo vadis-Kino? Zur Eröffnung des Königpavillion-Theaters," reprinted in *Kino-Debatte: Texte zum Verhältnis von Literatur und Film 1909–1929*, ed. and introduction by Anton Kaes (Munich: Max Niemeyer, 1978), 72–75. For another annotated collection of texts, also see Jörg Schweinitz, *Prolog vor dem Film: Nachdenken über ein neues Medium 1909–1914* (Leipzig: Reclam 1992).
3. Paul Wegener, "Neue Kinoziele," reprinted in *Kein Tag ohne Kino: Schriftsteller über den Stummfilm*, ed. Fritz Güttinger (Frankfurt a.M.: Deutsches Filmmuseum, 1984), 341–50. For a comprehensive overview of the literary responses to the cinema, also see, by the same author, the companion volume *Der Stummfilm im Zitat der Zeit* (Frankfurt a.M.: Deutsches Filmmuseum, 1984).
4. Herbert Tannenbaum, *Kino und Theater* (Munich: Max Steinbach, 1912), 36.
5. Heinz-B. Heller, *Literarische Intelligenz und Film: Zu Veränderungen der ästhetischen Theorie und Praxis unter dem Eindruck des Films 1910–1930 in Deutschland* (Tübingen: Max Niemeyer, 1984). For greater emphasis on the Wilhelmine years, see Helmut H. Diederichs, *Anfänge deutscher Filmkritik* (Stuttgart: Robert Fischer & Uwe Wiedlerroither, 1986).
6. Alfred Döblin, "Das Theater der kleinen Leute" and Carlo Mierendorff, "Hätte ich das Kino," reprinted in *Kino-Debatte*, 37 and 146.
7. Willy Münzenberg, *Erobert den Film! Winke aus der Praxis für die Praxis proletarischer Filmpropaganda* (Berlin: Neuer Verlag, 1925), 88. A comprehensive overview of leftist writings on film can be found in Gertraude Kühn, Karl Tümmler, and Walter Wimmer, eds., *Film und revolutionäre Arbeiterbewegung in Deutschland 1918—1932. Dokumente und Materialien zur Erweiterung der Filmpolitik der revolutionären Arbeiterbewegung und den Anfängen einer sozialistischen Filmkunst in Deutschland*, 2 vols. (Berlin/GDR: Henschel, 1975). Also see Richard Weber, ed., *Arbeiterbühne und Film: Zentralorgan des Arbeiter-Theater-Bundes Deutschlands* (Cologne: Gaehme Henke, 1974).
8. Curt Moreck, *Sittengeschichte des Kinos* (Dresden: Paul Aretz, 1926), 63.
9. Ilja Ehrenburg, *Die Traumfabrik: Chronik des Films* (Berlin: Malik, 1931), 32.
10. René Fülöp-Miller, *Die Phantasiemaschine: Eine Saga der Gewinnsucht* (Leipzig: Paul Zsolnay, 1931), 31.
11. Siegfried Kracauer, "Tonbildfilm (1928)," in *Schriften 2 (Von Caligari bis Hitler)*, ed. Karsten Witte (Frankfurt am Main: Suhrkamp, 1979), 411. On Kracauer, see Heide Schlüpmann, "Phenomenology of Film: On Siegfried Kracauer's Writings of the 1920s," *New German Critique* 40 (1987), 97–114.
12. Siegfried Kracauer, "Das Ornament der Masse," in *Das Ornament der Masse*, afterword by Karsten Witte (Frankfurt am Main: Suhrkamp, 1977), 67. For an English translation, see *The Mass Ornament: Weimar Essays*, ed. and trans. Thomas Y. Levin (Cambridge, MA: Harvard University Press, 1995). For a collection of additional articles on film, see Siegfried Kracauer, *Kino: Essays, Studien, Glossen zum Film*, ed. Karsten Witte (Frankfurt am Main: Suhrkamp, 1974).
13. Kracauer, "Kult der Zerstreung," in *Das Ornament der Masse*, 317.
14. Kracauer, "Kult der Zerstreung," in *Das Ornament der Masse*, 313.

15. Kracauer, "Die kleinen Ladenmädchen gehen ins Kino," *Das Ornament der Masse*, 280.

16. Béla Balázs, *Der sichtbare Mensch oder die Kultur des Films*, afterword by Helmut H. Diederichs (Frankfurt a.M.: Suhrkamp, 2001), 10. The first English translation appeared recently in *Béla Belázs: Early Film Theory. "Visible Man" and "The Spirit of Film,"* trans. Rodney Livingstone, ed. Erica Carter (New York: Berghahn, 2010). For a collection of his journalistic writings, see Béla Balázs, *Schriften zum Film*, 2 vols., eds. Helmut H. Diederichs, Wolfgang Gersch, and Magda Nagy (Munich: Carl Hanser, 1982). On Balázs, see David Bathrick, "Der ungleichzeitige Modernist: Béla Bálazs in Berlin," in *Filmkultur zur Zeit der Weimarer Republik*, ed. Uli Jung and Walter Schatzberg (Munich: Saur, 1992), 26–37; and Gertrud Koch, "Béla Balázs: The Physiognomy of Things," *New German Critique* 40 (1987), 167–78.

17. Balázs, *Der sichtbare Mensch*, 22. On the centrality of physiognomy, also see Massimo Locatelli, *Béla Balázs: Die Physiognomie des Films* (Berlin: Vistas, 1999).

18. Balázs, *Der Geist des Films*, afterword by Hanno Loewy (Frankfurt a.M.: Suhrkamp, 2001), 30.

19. Quoted by Hanno Loewy, *Béla Balázs—Märchen, Ritual und Film* (Berlin: Vorwerk 8, 2003), 34.

20. Rudolf Arnheim, Preface to *Film as Art*, selections from the 1933 British translation of *Film as Art*, with new preface by the author (Berkeley: University of California Press, 1957), 2. A fiftieth anniversary edition was published in 2006.

21. Arnheim, "Die traurige Zukunft des Films (1930)," in *Kritiken und Aufsätze zum Film*, ed. Helmut H. Diederichs (Munich: Hanser, 1977), 17. The anthology has been published in English as *Film Essays and Criticism*, trans. Brenda Benthien (Madison: University of Wisconsin Press, 1997). For a more recent selection of his Weimar writings, see *Die Seele in der Silberschicht: Medientheoretische Texte. Photographie—Film—Rundfunk*, ed. Helmut H. Diederichs (Frankfurt a.M.: Suhrkamp, 2004).

22. Arnheim, "Film und Funk (1933)," in *Kritiken und Aufsätze zum Film*, 22.

23. Arnheim, *Film as Kunst* (Munich: Hanser, 1977). On Arnheim, see Gertrud Koch, "Rudolf Arnheim: The Materialist of Aesthetic Illusion—Gestalt Theory and Reviewer's Practice," *New German Critique* 51 (1987), 167–78.

24. Arnheim, *Film als Kunst*, 193.

25. Arnheim, *Film als Kunst*, 194.

14

The Politics of Art and Architecture at the Bauhaus, 1919–1933

John V. Maciuika

Introduction: The Kaleidoscope of Weimar Art

The birth of social democracy out of the ashes of a defeated, delegitimized Wilhelmine Empire galvanized the German art world as never before. Artists at Walter Gropius's experimental Bauhaus school and in such diverse avant-garde art movements as Expressionism, Cubism, Dada, and Constructivism reflected a broad consensus that the pre-war empire had proved an absolute failure. The Kaiser, the government, the aristocracy, the military, big business, and the bourgeoisie were all seen as complicit in a corrupt system unable to cope with the many challenges of industrial modernity.

Like a shifting kaleidoscope, artistic production during the Weimar era dazzled with unexpected forms, ever-shifting conceptual variety, and ideological diversity. At one extreme Richard Huelsenbeck, the leader of a new, politically radical "anti-art" movement known as Berlin Dada, denounced all artistic conventions, and indeed all nationalist and materialist values associated with the collapsed Wilhelmine Empire. Huelsenbeck and fellow Dada artists like Hannah Höch and George Grosz wanted to awaken people to the fact that "Art, regarded from a serious point of view," was "a large-scale swindle." This was especially true in Germany, where

> the most absurd idolatry of all sorts of divinities is beaten into the child, in order that the grown man and taxpayer should fall on his knees when, in the interest of the state or some smaller gang of thieves, he receives the order to worship some 'great spirit.' . . . Art should altogether get a sound thrashing, and Dada stands for the thrashing with all the vehemence of its limited nature.[1]

The aggressive politics of Berlin's "Club Dada" distinguished it from the movement's counterparts in Zurich, Paris, or New York. Signature early artworks such as Hannah Höch's visually riotous anti-Establishment collage, *Cut with a Dada Kitchen Knife through the Last Beer-Belly Weimar Cultural Epoch* of 1919–20, for example, featured an orgy of superimposed mass media clippings: here a contemplative Albert Einstein partially obscured by wheels in one eye and a locomotive and giant grasshopper emerging from his head, there an uncanny visage of Kaiser Wilhelm with his mustache replaced by an upside-down, miniature human figure (Figure 14.1). These images floated among jostling crowds, buildings, and dozens of other faces of famous and unknown figures suspended at every angle. Appearing throughout were cut out letters and phrases such as "the great Dada," "the anti-Dada," and "invest your money in Dada."

Höch's collage was just one notorious expression of Dada revulsion at the modern era's destructive tendencies. An unsettling techno-humanoid sculpture by George Grosz and John Heartfield, entitled *Der wildgewordene Spießer Heartfield* (The Middle-Class Philistine Heartfield Gone Wild [Electro-Mechanical Tatlin Sculpture]) of 1920, similarly aimed to detonate false consciousness, to shock viewers into greater awareness of capitalism, industrialism, and militarism run amok. Their work featured an uncanny one-legged mannequin with an illuminated Osram lightbulb in place of a head, a revolver in place of a shoulder

Figure 14.1. Hannah Höch, *Cut with a Kitchen Knife through the Last Weimar Beer-Belly Cultural Epoch in Germany*, collage, 1919. *Source*: Nationalgalerie, Staatliche Museen zu Berlin. © 2012 Artists Rights Society (ARS), New York / VG Bild-Kunst, Bonn.

and arm, and a knife, fork, and embroidered Prussian Order of the Black Eagle on its chest, among other objects. "The highest art," explained Huelsenbeck and his colleague Raoul Hausmann in their "Dada Manifesto," "will be that which in its conscious content presents the thousandfold problems of the day, the art which has been visibly shattered by the explosions of last week, which is forever trying to collect its limbs after yesterday's crash."[2] Heartfield's mutilated mannequin, still somehow holding a weapon and decorated with a medal of honor and a lightbulb head, starkly illuminated the human toll exacted by capitalism, imperial dynastic leadership, and blind patriotism. Supported by such art, Berlin Dada's political program sought "the international revolutionary union of all creative and intellectual men and women on the basis of radical Communism."[3]

Berlin Dada's revolutionary fires dimmed amid internal partisan bickering and the group's ambivalent relationship to its political mission in 1923–24. Not all radical artists, moreover, proved as extreme. Käthe Kollwitz, a talented graphic artist and sculptor, emerged from the war to become the first woman to earn the title of professor in the Prussian Academy of Fine Arts in 1919. The horrible experience of the war and the loss of her younger son Peter, killed in the trenches in 1914, strengthened Kollwitz's commitment to left-wing causes. Her stirring graphic "cycles" depicted injustices against workers, while emotionally powerful sculptural works dramatized the war-induced human suffering of mothers, sons, and families.

Kurt Schwitters, an artist whose application to join Berlin Dada Huelsenbeck rejected in 1918, became an influential Weimar innovator in his own right. Cobbling together such "junk" (Schwitters's term) as wood, metal, string, coins, and the fragment "MERZ" cut from a sign for the "KOMMERZ UND PRIVATBANK," Schwitters fashioned a poetic collage, or "MERZ-picture," from the fragmentary remains of post-war material culture. "I named all my pictures the MERZbilder as a species," Schwitters explained, "because I could not define them with the older conceptions like Expressionism, Futurism, or whatever. . . . Later I expanded the title MERZ, first to include my poetry, and finally to all my relevant activities. Now I call myself MERZ."[4] In the shifting kaleidoscope of Weimar art, a word like "commerce" (KOMMERZ) divided to form a "MERZ picture." A further turn of the conceptual wheel, and "MERZ" subsumed all of Schwitters's literary and artistic output—and, finally, even the name of the artist himself.

New Art for a New Nation

From the Berlin Dadaists' point of view, Schwitters's work was insufficiently radical and too "bourgeois"—too forgiving, that is, toward a culture that framed, displayed, sold, and circulated artworks in a capitalist economy. To the young architect and Bauhaus founder Walter Gropius, who had fought in and survived the war, the German Empire and bourgeois culture certainly deserved plenty of blame. However, like Schwitters and contrary to Berlin Dada, the architect believed art still had a powerful role to play in reviving German culture within existing socioeconomic structures. Gropius's article, "The Free People's State," published in 1919 in the *German Revolutionary Almanac*, condemned the prewar regime while reengaging long-standing pre-war debates about which Germans were the rightful "bearers of culture." Gropius stated:

> Capitalism and power politics have made our generation creatively sluggish, and our vital art is mired in a broad bourgeois philistinism. The intellectual bourgeois of the old Empire—tepid and unimaginative, mentally slow, arrogant and incorrectly trained—has proven his incapacity to be the bearer of German culture. His benumbed world is now toppled, its spirit is overthrown, and is in the midst of being recast in a new mold.[5]

Weimar artists and fellow soldier-survivors like George Grosz would give visual expression to such "broad bourgeois philistinism" in an array of startling paintings, drawings, and caricatures. Gropius, for his part, was reacting to blows he had suffered as a junior member of Germany's premier pre-war design association, the Deutscher Werkbund. In the *German Revolutionary Almanac* Gropius inveighed against an older generation of architects, artists, and designers who in his view had collaborated with government and big industry in a kind of unholy imperial alliance—one whose policies had catapulted the nation into war and ultimate defeat in the First World War. As early as 1911, August Bebel, a founder and pillar of the Social Democratic Party, had denounced runaway militarism in the Reichstag and proclaimed the "twilight of the bourgeois world" (*Götterdämmerung der bürgerlichen Welt*).[6] Following the November 1918 revolution, new social forms, and even socialism itself, seemed much closer to becoming reality. Speaking to Bauhaus artists and students shortly after he opened his new school in April 1919, Gropius observed:

> We find ourselves in a colossal catastrophe of world history, in a transformation of the whole of life . . . Before the war we put the cart before the horse and wanted to drag art backward into the public sphere by means of organization. We designed artistic ashtrays and beer mugs, and in that way hoped to work up to the great building . . . That was an incredible presumption upon which we were shipwrecked, and now things will be reversed. No large spiritual organizations, but small, secret, self-contained societies, lodges . . . [7]

To Gropius and many other young artists and architects, it seemed that real opportunities for post-war progress in society lay in reviving the crafts, fine arts, and architecture by combining them in one school, the "unified arts school" (*Einheitskunstschule*), a type of institution that had been a frequent topic of discussion and debate in Germany both before and during the war.[8]

New artistic developments, however, proved threatening to members of the Wilhelmine old guard such as Wilhelm von Bode, who was still active as the venerable director of Berlin's museums in the Prussian Ministry of Culture. Von Bode had initially approved, in principle, of unified art schools that would combine the fine and applied arts. He had likewise approved the Belgian artist

Henry van de Velde's nomination of Walter Gropius to succeed him as director of the Weimar school of applied arts.[9] Von Bode drew the line, however, at the promotion of such movements as Expressionism and Cubism, whose radicalism he considered a threat to the established German social and cultural order. Gropius's Bauhaus, he believed, ranged too far into experimental territory.

Debates over the future of the arts and artistic education thus assumed special importance from Weimar Germany's very beginning. On the political Right, cultural rebirth often meant reconnecting with perceived German "traditions," without the low regard for the Wilhelmine Empire and the critique of the sociopolitical structures so criticized by Communists, Social Democrats, and other Left progressives. On the Left, post-war reconstruction offered an opportunity for fresh beginnings in both art and social organization. In short, since the arts had long been understood as partly constitutive of society, *and* since Germany was rebuilding along modern, democratic lines, the types of art encouraged by the state signaled the type of modern society post-war Germans were setting out to create.

Yet any truly radical break with the past—even after a cataclysm of the magnitude of the First World War—proved extremely difficult to realize. Dadaists, for example, championed collage and montage as the "new medium," although Cubists such as Pablo Picasso and Georges Braque had pioneered modernist collages before the war. The Expressionists, who initially dominated such newly formed artists' groups as the "Art Soviet" (*Arbeitsrat für Kunst*, or Workers' Council for Art) and the closely aligned November Group, likewise had roots extending back to the early years of the twentieth century.

The idea that a particular social class could serve as a model for societal and cultural leadership had a pre-war origin as well. Where post-war Social Democrats would promote the working class, older reform-minded architects such as Hermann Muthesius, the influential vice president of the Deutscher Werkbund design association and, by 1914, a veritable mortal enemy of the young Gropius, had championed the educated middle class (*Bildungsbürgertum*) as Germany's true "bearers of culture" before the war. Muthesius's famous 1903 polemic, an essay that campaigned to replace imitative "style-architecture" with an authentic middle-class "building art," had declared:

> As the bearer of new ideas, the new spiritual aristocracy arises, which this time stems from the best of the middle class rather than the hereditary aristocratic elements, and this especially clearly signals the new and enlarged goal of the movement: the creation of a contemporary middle-class art. . . . The goal remains sincerity, straightforwardness (*Sachlichkeit*), and a purity of artistic sensibility, qualities that avoid all secondary considerations and superficialities. . . . If from the labyrinth of the arts of the last hundred years we are ever again to succeed to artistic conditions that bear even a remote similarity to the great epochs of the history of art, then architecture must assume leadership in the community of the arts.[10]

Whereas Muthesius's pre-war Deutscher Werkbund based the modernization of German design culture and the "spiritualization of German work" (*Durchgei-*

stigung der deutschen Arbeit) on the example of the hard-working middle class, after the war Gropius and the Workers' Council for Art turned to the working class and its social democratic leadership for fresh inspiration.[11]

Progressive artists and architects wasted no time in articulating visions for a new society to supplant the defunct Wilhelmine Empire. By Christmas of 1918, the youthful and idealistic architect Bruno Taut had published "A Program for Architecture," later condensed into an influential Worker's Council prospectus.[12] Taut advocated "a complete revolution in the spiritual realm" and a policy of melting down the old regime's public monuments. Gropius, who replaced Taut as director of the Workers' Council in early 1919, would soon adapt his predecessor's language for his own "Bauhaus Program." Taut, meanwhile, proposed designs for elaborate crystalline mountain-top settlements of colored glass along with grandiose "earth-crust architecture" for Germany's dawning socialist society, presenting them in such illustrated books as *Alpine Architecture* (1919), *The Dissolution of Cities* (1920), and *The City Crown* (1920).[13]

Visionary utopias proliferated in the wake of war, but like the word "utopia" itself—which of course means "no place" in the original Greek—Taut's Alpine projects remained unbuilt "paper architecture." His aspirational colored glass constructions made for exciting viewing at post-war Workers' Council exhibitions in Berlin like the "Exhibition for Unknown Architects" of April 1919 and "New Architecture" of May 1920. Yet however much sympathetic art lovers admired the florid crystalline and biomorphic forms by Taut, Wenzel Hablik, Hermann Finsterlin, and the brothers Hans and Wassili Luckhardt, precious little could be built in the fiscal wasteland of the immediate post-war moment. Their works gave powerful visual expression to the sentiments captured in the 1919 Worker's Council prospectus all the same:

> We know that the feeling of brotherhood that arises out of this kind of communal work—an architecture which, thanks to the many hands contributing to it, will burst into magnificent bloom—is capable of producing in the soul of man that which we all of us long for: the true spirit of socialism. . . . Man, in going about his business, is transformed.[14]

Post-war paper architecture, manifestoes, exhibitions, and the letters exchanged among architects in such groups Taut's "Crystal Chain" helped feed this idealistic spirit of the new. The architects Hans Poelzig and Erich Mendelsohn scored two early built successes in the Expressionist mode with the realization of Poelzig's Great Theater (*Grosses Schauspielhaus*) completed in 1918–19 in Berlin, and Mendelsohn's Einstein Tower, an observatory completed between 1918 and 1921 in Potsdam. The cavernous performance hall of Poelzig's Great Theater overwhelmed visitors with its vast, domed space hung with 1200 wired-plaster stalactites. Recalling Islamic *muqarnas* decoration at the wondrous Alhambra palace in Granada, Spain, the concentric rings of stalactites could be lit in various ways to produce a panoply of colorful and "cosmic" effects. Though some criticized it as overdecorative and others complained of its lack of functional purpose, Poelzig defended his building for its Expressionist exuberance: "It is

Figure 14.2. Erich Mendelsohn, Einstein Tower Observatory, Potsdam, 1918–21. *Source*: Gustav Adolf Platz, *Die Baukunst der Neuesten Zeit* (Berlin: Propyläen Verlag, 1927), 390.

still better," he declared, "to do violence to the purpose and create a true work of art than to let the purpose, i.e., cold reason, get the better of you."[15]

Erich Mendelsohn, by contrast, designed the curvaceous, concrete-covered brick masses of his Einstein Tower to fulfill every necessary practical purpose for the telescope, the laboratory, and the scientists' accommodations within. His highly sculptural Expressionist tower with its projecting appendages appeared crouched like a modern sphinx atop a hill overlooking Potsdam (Figure 14.2). Mendelsohn's balance of practicality and Expressionist form seemed a fulfillment of the dictum expressed by the radical Dutch architect J.J.P. Oud in his 1921 article, "On Future Building Art and Its Architectonic Possibilities," in which Oud insisted that "A feeling for life must guide art, not the tradition of form."[16]

The Bauhaus as a Bastion of Social and Artistic Idealism

Ambitious architects of the generation of Taut and Mendelsohn, most of them in their 30s in the immediate post-war era, sensed unprecedented opportunities to express this new "feeling for life" in architectural form. No one, in fact, better embodied or articulated this feeling than Walter Gropius. Descended from an established Berlin family that included such successful architects as his great uncle, Martin Gropius of the nineteenth-century "Schinkel School," Walter Gropius experienced a meteoric rise to prominence through a combination of ambition, charisma, and organizational ability. By early 1919, at the age of only thirty-five, Gropius not only directed the Workers' Council for Art, he also established Weimar Germany's earliest and most progressive art school of the new type, the "Unified Art School," in the Weimar Bauhaus.[17] His early Bauhaus colleague, the American-born German painter Lyonel Feininger, wrote: "He works till three in the morning, hardly sleeps, and when he looks at you, his eyes are like stars. I'm sorry for anyone who can't gather strength from him."[18]

Although he would later conceal his considerable debts to pioneering pre-war schools of applied arts and design, Gropius put his own stamp on the idea of the unified art school.[19] As in the Workers' Council and the November Group, organizational leadership in the Bauhaus fell to architects, although artists far outnumbered them in all three organizations. Long accustomed to translating lofty artistic aspirations into the earthbound materials of concrete, bricks, and mortar, architects had the practical foresight to organize the applied arts and fine arts under the architectural banner.

Borrowing from the writings of fellow Workers' Council members Otto Bartning and Bruno Taut, Gropius's Bauhaus Program maintained the applied arts and fine arts as independent entities within a larger unified whole. The school's lengthy official title, "The State Bauhaus in Weimar (Combined former Grand Ducal Academy of Art and former Grand Ducal School of Applied Arts)," expressed this separation. [20] Approving the school's new name on 12 April 1919, the Thuringian government opened the school with modest beginnings and no official fanfare.[21] Weimar, home to such Enlightenment figures as the German literary greats Goethe and Schiller, was now also home to Germany's most experimental art school. Whereas in bigger cities like Berlin artists and educators had grown accustomed to radical artistic ideas, in the much quieter town of Weimar such innovations hardly met with universal enthusiasm. Many residents, proud of their town's palaces, gardens, and canonical literary heroes, wished to preserve Weimar as a unique center of traditional Germanness.

Setting its sights on the higher purpose of rebuilding German society, Gropius's Bauhaus Program refined the spirit and language of the Workers' Council for Art prospectus. In a four-page curriculum and mission statement, Gropius idealized the medieval German past, a time when builders' lodges and artisans' guilds collaborated with artists, sculptors, and architects to erect such communal structures as the Gothic cathedral. Even the name "Bauhaus" fortified the modern school's mythical ties to medieval lodges by evoking the ancient German word "Bauhütte," a medieval guild of craftsmen and building-trades workers.

Extolling craft as the "ancient source" of all artistic activity (exactly as Muthesius had done in 1903), the Bauhaus Program promoted egalitarian unity in the collaborative process of forging new, collective works of art and architecture.[22] With the crafts as their unifying base, the arts would experience a revival analogous to the social democratic ideal of workers reviving German society from below. As Gropius observed in his essay for the German Revolutionary Almanac, "New, intellectually undeveloped levels of our people are rising from the depths. They are our chief hope."[23] Like Berlin Dada, Dutch Neoplasticism, or the experiments of Constructivist art schools in Moscow, the Workers' Council for Art and the early Bauhaus tended to regard the upper-class and bourgeois worlds with suspicion: in their push for industrial concentration, military expansion, and capitalist development, leading Wilhelmine members of these classes had propelled Germany into the disastrous world war. The working classes, represented at least symbolically at the Bauhaus by craftsmen and, over time, by industrial designers, offered inspiration for the development of a socially relevant new art. This art would in turn support a new and authentic social order, one that required new aesthetic principles as well as novel forms.

Students enrolling at the Bauhaus therefore began their studies by taking a bracing, six-month introductory course (*Vorkurs*) designed to unburden them of art historical baggage and unleash individual creative potential. The next level of study involved mastering an individual craft of their choice, with the aid of practical instructional workshops in woodworking, ceramics, book binding, weaving, metalworking, and sculpture. Only upon successful completion of this stage, lasting from one to three years, would students be allowed to contribute toward the "ultimate" artistic goal, the fully realized building, which stood like a bull's eye at the center of the Bauhaus curriculum diagram (Figure 14.3). As Gropius explained in his 1923 publication, "Theory and Organization of the Bauhaus," the aim was "a center for experimentation which will try to assemble the achievements of economic, technical and formal research and to apply them to problems of domestic architecture in an effort to combine the greatest possible standardization with the greatest possible variation of form."[24] When the faculty expanded in the early 1920s, leading artists like Paul Klee, Wassily Kandinsky, and Oskar Schlemmer taught courses in painting, art theory, typogra-

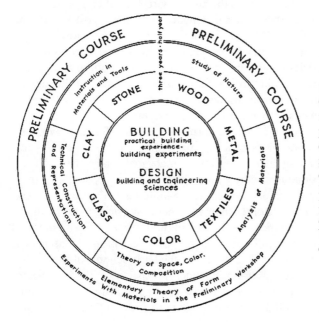

Figure 14.3. Bauhaus Curriculum Diagram, 1923. The typical student progresses from the outer to the innermost ring over several years of study. *Source*: Herbert Bayer, Walter Gropius, Ise Gropius, eds., *Bauhaus 1919–1928* (New York: Museum of Modern Art, 1938), 23.

phy, and set design, while over time the school collectively explored a variety of performance-based media, including music and experimental theater. Architecture, considered by Gropius to be the "mother of all the arts" after John Ruskin's dictum of half a century earlier, did not become an official Bauhaus department until the school relocated with new energy and funding in Dessau in 1927.

Rather than representing any particular philosophy, style, or precisely defined approach to design, the Bauhaus was always "an idea," as the school's third and final director, the architect Ludwig Mies van der Rohe, famously characterized it. That is, the school was always the idealistic, collective product of its influential faculty and individualistic students, whose experimental inclinations were given direction and focus by the school's three successive directors. Thus Gropius, the director from 1919 to 1928, presided over the Bauhaus's initial (and, thanks to hostile conservatives in the legislature, chronically underfunded) crafts and Expressionist phases in the early 1920s. By 1923, he adopted a fresh, Constructivist-influenced school slogan, "Art and Technology: A New Unity," which became the title of the Bauhaus's first major design exhibition in the summer of 1923. In developments discussed further below, the Swiss architect Hannes Meyer assumed the directorship between the years 1928 and 1930 and reoriented the school to a scientific Marxist program of simple, affordable, practical furnishings and architecture. Mies van der Rohe, in turn, realized his "idea" for the school as director between 1930 and the school's closure in 1933: he abandoned Meyer's Marxism and focused students instead on the systematic and rigorous practice of architecture.

While a synthesis of the crafts, fine arts, and architecture quickly emerged as Walter Gropius's modern Bauhaus ideal, in reality early antecedents for this principle could be found as far back as the ancient Greek Parthenon and, as the Bauhaus Program noted, in the medieval cathedral. But in the post-war desire for collective German rebirth, it became easier to imbue ancient notions with fresh significance and renewed possibility. Had not the quintessential modern poet, the bohemian Charles Baudelaire, memorably defined modernity as a particular blending of new and old? In his classic essay of 1863, "The Painter of Modern Life," Baudelaire wrote: "By 'modernity' I mean the ephemeral, the contingent, the half of art whose other half is eternal and immutable."[25]

As if drawing on Baudelaire's timeless formula, Gropius's *Bauhaus Program* exuded confidence in modernity's endless capacity for renewal from the bedrock of tradition. Its opening lines read: "The ultimate goal of all artistic activity is the building. To decorate it was once the noblest task of the visual arts, they were indissoluble components of the great art of building." Adapting architect Otto Bartning's revival of the nomenclature of medieval society, the Bauhaus Program replaced such academic titles as "student" and "professor" with the medieval "apprentice," "journeyman," and "master." These idealistic designations set the school apart from the art academies and applied arts schools of recent decades.[26] Embellishing the very Workers' Council prospectus quoted earlier in this chapter while eliminating its direct references to socialism, Gropius concluded the Bauhaus mission statement on a high note, proclaiming: "Let us collectively desire, conceive, and create the new building of the future, which will be everything in one structure: architecture and sculpture and painting, which, out of the millions of hands of crafts workers, will one day rise towards heaven like the crystal symbol of the new and coming faith."[27]

Gropius's rich imagery invoked at once the medieval, communally constructed German cathedral and a "new faith" in the architecture of Expressionists like Taut, Poelzig, and Mendelsohn. The multivalent *Bauhaus Program* further connected the crafts "base" of medieval society to the new social order, a social democratic majority analogous to "the millions of hands of crafts workers," whose constructions would rise toward heaven. As its earliest promotional document, the *Bauhaus Program* gained international attention, attracting idealistic young students and faculty—or "apprentices" and "masters"—from across German-speaking Central Europe.

Gropius invited Lyonel Feininger, the first artist he hired as a Bauhaus master, to design a visually compelling cover for the Bauhaus Program. Feininger rendered the "crystal symbol of the new and coming faith" in the form of a dramatic Cubist-Expressionist woodcut, entitled "Cathedral" (Figure 14.4). Like other Expressionists before him, Feininger consciously employed an artistic medium

Figure 14.4. Lyonel Feininger, "Cathedral," Cover of Bauhaus Program of 1919, woodcut. *Source*: Herbert Bayer, Walter Gropius, Ise Gropius, eds., *Bauhaus 1919–1928* (New York: Museum of Modern Art, 1938), 17.

developed in the Middle Ages, the wood-cut, to infuse his modern imagery with a kind of primitivist power. His "Cathedral" presents the front elevation of a building comprising three gabled portals, three levels of flying buttresses, and three towers, all topped by three stars emitting bright rays of light. This vertically organized set of triads is highly suggestive of the Holy Trinity, a cornerstone of Christian doctrine frequently symbolized in the interior "triforium" and clover-leaf "trefoil" ornaments of actual medieval cathedrals. At the same time, the tri-angle of stars radiating light above the building seems to suggest the applied and fine arts organized under the leadership of architecture, here given a notably cosmological significance.

Feininger's Cubist-Expressionist rendering struck a precise visual balance between the image of a Gothic cathedral and a more modern, updated "crystal symbol." Experts in Gothic architecture such as Steven Murray have observed that "triple towers in the western frontispiece of a Gothic cathedral"—like those shown in Feininger's wood-cut—"never occur in reality . . . there is [also] no precedent for the lateral portals having their own roof structure projecting out beyond the body of the building [and] no precedent for flyers [flying buttresses—J.M.] against towers."[28] Feininger, who had a life-long fascination with churches and was known to paint up to two-dozen versions of individual church buildings that captured his interest, seems to have given a modern, Expressionist twist to familiar Gothic architectural forms to better suit the Bauhaus Program's blend of tradition and modernity.

However, and like the Bauhaus school itself, Feininger's jagged, Cubist-Expressionist lines and pulsating emanations of light, structure, and shadow expressed an aesthetic that could easily offend conservative artists wedded to stricter academic traditions. Amid the divisive politics of post-war Germany, many conservatives saw avant-garde art not as the dawning of a promising new age, but as fundamentally threatening to an established social order. Precisely that which inspired youthful avant-garde seekers of new aesthetic truths, in other words, was prone to offend those who remained suspicious of experimen-tation in virtually all its forms.

Although Feininger seldom taught on a regular schedule—especially after his popularity brought financial independence in the mid-1920s—he was one of very few Bauhaus masters who remained with the school for the full duration of its turbulent fourteen-year existence. He was beloved by students and fellow masters alike for his openness, geniality, and fresh artistic vision. For no one viewing Gropius's and Feininger's collaboration on the *Bauhaus Program* could mistake the school for anything other than a state-sponsored campaign to place the crafts, fine arts, and architecture on a fresh footing. Appealing to Germans' sense of their culture's historical achievements in the Middle Ages, and deftly skipping over any debts the school owed to Wilhelmine precedents, the Bau-haus became a veritable poster child for social democratic efforts to rebuild a war-torn country and refashion German society. The question was whether the school could present new aesthetic forms in the crafts, fine arts, and architecture in ways that Germans of all political persuasions could embrace.

Bauhaus Battles for Survival

By modeling the Bauhaus as a small community or "lodge" of masters and apprentices, Gropius put behind him his bitter pre-war experiences in the troubled national design organization, the Deutscher Werkbund. Between 1912 and 1914 the Werkbund had succumbed to a takeover by the national government and its leading architectural representative, Hermann Muthesius. The latter only surrendered his national leadership position when the failing war effort eliminated prospects for any government-coordinated collaboration between artists and industry in the field of industrial and commercial design.[29] Now, in the wake of his own harrowing wartime experiences as a sergeant major in the German military, Gropius tapped into the idealized model of the medieval artists' community to set his experimental school apart from major urban power centers. For its initial phase in 1919–20, the Bauhaus represented a parable of a harmonious German society in which practitioners of the crafts, fine arts, and architecture cooperated in a purer, less mediated, and realizable form of artistic production.

Yet promises of communal harmony proved elusive. If the founding of the progressive Weimar Bauhaus aroused the ire of the town's cultural conservatives, the school also suffered early attacks from a less expected quarter: its own student body. During the first full semester of instruction in the fall of 1919, thirteen students—or some five percent of a total student body of 231—resigned en masse in protest over the *Bauhaus Program* and its curricular innovations. Bauhaus masters' executive committee meeting minutes (unavailable to Western scholars until the end of the Cold War) help to reconstruct the students' actions and motivations. According to meeting minutes from December 18 and 20, 1919, Walter Gropius and the director of the Weimar School of Building Trades, Paul Klopfer, attended a special assembly called by Weimar's Free Association for City Affairs (*freie Vereinigung für städtische Interessen*) to discuss the Bauhaus and "the new art in Weimar" on December 12. There, the minutes record, the chair of the meeting, a Dr. Emil Kreubel, leveled attacks against the Bauhaus that Gropius and Klopfer "successfully parried."[30] The architectural historian Barbara Miller Lane (who used German newspaper clippings to reconstruct parts of this meeting) recounts Kreubel's comparison of Cubist and Expressionist painting to the artistic output of patients at a mental hospital. As Kreubel denounced the school for being a "Spartacist-bolshevist institution," individual agitators in the audience added catcalls of "Jewish art" and "foreigners."[31] Perhaps most disturbingly, a Bauhaus student named Hans Gross then rose and "Unfortunately made a speech to the gathering against the trends embodied by the State Bauhaus. This was all the more surprising," the minutes continue, "because Gropius had coincidentally encountered Gross on the afternoon of the special assembly, and Gross had explained that he thoroughly approved of the goals of the State Bauhaus and was prepared to follow Gropius through thick and thin."[32]

Ensuing executive committee discussions make clear that among Bauhaus students, Gross had initiated the "circulation of an anti-Semitic petition on which his own name failed to appear." He also delivered a "German nationalist party speech which, prepared in longhand, was read at a public gathering of students on Friday, December 11."[33] What emerges from heated executive committee discussions is that Gross denounced both the foreign and Jewish representation at the Bauhaus as "un-German," a tactic common enough among the xenophobic far right. Here Gross joined those right-wing Germans who consoled themselves for Germany's loss of the First World War not by viewing the Wilhelmine Empire as a collective failure to master the challenges of industrialization, urbanization, and modern social integration, as many on the left did. Rather, the right accused German Jews and left-wing "traitors" at home of undermining Germany's war effort, producing the "Dolchstosslegende": the legend that Jews and the left had "stabbed Germany in the back," thereby causing the German Empire to lose the war. In his speech at the meeting Gross had further claimed that Bauhaus assignments in the fall 1919 semester, which focused on the making of toys and other three-dimensional objects, were preparation for a ban on the venerated artistic tradition of easel painting. Gross's public assault and resignation from the school with a dozen other students made plain how closely arguments about modern art and cultural production were tied to political orientation, definitions of German identity, and conceptions of the future direction of German art and social development.

The masters' executive committee submitted an immediate, detailed written rebuttal—a carefully worded blend of defense and offense—to the Weimar Culture Ministry officials overseeing the school. The document refuted Gross's specious assertions and included an exact breakdown of the 231 students enrolled at the Bauhaus in 1919, by nation of origin: 210 Germans, fourteen Austrian Germans, two Bohemian Germans, three Baltic Germans, and two Hungarian Germans. The two elected student representatives were not foreigners, as Gross maintained, but were in fact Germans of Austrian extraction. The only traitorous and "un-German" behavior at the Bauhaus, the masters' rebuttal emphasized, was that of the student Hans Gross himself. Gross trafficked in deliberate untruths, deception, and false denunciations, and was a disgrace to the school and to other Bauhaus students who were "especially qualified, including some who participated in the war and achieved officers' rank."[34]

The Bauhaus painters Lyonel Feininger and Johannes Itten thereafter signed a public statement affirming that they had every intention of continuing to practice and teach the art of easel painting in their studios and classrooms. A second statement, signed by all members of the Bauhaus masters' executive committee, forbade student participation in political activity "regardless of which side" or ideological persuasion, "on penalty of expulsion."[35] Seeking to dampen sustained criticism in the local and national press, Gropius withdrew from the Workers' Council and the November Group after overseeing the former merge with the latter on December 17, 1919, in the midst of the Bauhaus controversy. Gropius thereafter maintained a safe distance from left-wing organizations and would, in fact, insist at every opportunity that the Bauhaus was "unpolitical."

Not a single one of his enemies listened. Despite Gropius's increasing propensity to argue in the 1920s that art should be regarded as occupying a realm separate from politics, and notwithstanding the resolute avoidance of any official political involvement by himself or his school, the Bauhaus remained a right-wing target. For his part, Gropius promoted the school tirelessly in a blizzard of press articles. The frequency of his public lectures, moreover, led the architectural historian Winfried Nerdinger to characterize Gropius as a virtual "wandering preacher of the modern."[36]

Throughout his years as Bauhaus director Gropius stood by his conviction that artistic vision and talent were of paramount importance in post-war Germany's cultural rebirth, regardless of a person's background or nationality. In the months after the Bauhaus controversy he resisted calls from Weimar conservatives and chauvinists to hire more Germans and follow German academic traditions more closely. It was unclear, after all, what could precisely be called "German" about the nation's academic art traditions: for centuries Germany's artistic education derived from practices in France, Holland, or Italy, and before that, Greece. Gropius unflinchingly hired leading artists from the European avant-garde: joining the German faculty were the Swiss painter Johannes Itten, originator of the famous six-month, pass-fail Bauhaus "Introductory Course" on elementary form and materials; a second avant-garde Swiss painter, Paul Klee, member of the pre-war, early Expressionist "Blue Rider" group; the Russian painter Wassily Kandinsky, a pioneer of painterly abstraction and synesthesia, and co-founder of the "Blue Rider" group in Munich; and the Hungarian painter and experimental media artist László Moholy-Nagy. Gropius hardly wrapped himself in the German flag in making hiring decisions; the artists he recruited reflect the Bauhaus director's unerring eye for the best German and international talent, a group of Bauhaus masters celebrated to this day as leading innovators of twentieth-century art.[37]

Only the first phase of Bauhaus activity in 1919–20 saw such an intense focus on the crafts, and only in the early years did Expressionism prevail as a style. Although the introductory course and the requirement to master a craft remained, beginning in the early 1920s Gropius began to strengthen ties between the school's workshop-based instruction and practical applications in housing, domestic furnishings, and industry. Here the architect returned to themes about which he had written before the war, when, at age twenty-six, he had composed an essay on "The Industrialization of Housing Construction." At that time Gropius had also opened an architectural practice in Berlin with a top graduate of Peter Behrens's Dusseldorf School of Applied Arts, Adolf Meyer. Unquestionably disillusioned by big industry's and the Imperial Government's commercial policies in the run up to the war, Gropius initially coped with the shattered post-war economy by emphasizing the crafts and small-scale production. Nonetheless, he remained aware that once German economic conditions began to improve, the future of the Bauhaus would rest on a productive engagement with industry. Thus, even as early Bauhaus rhetoric focused on the crafts, Gropius also delivered matter-of-fact, business-like speeches to gatherings of industry as early as summer 1919, only months after the founding of the Bauhaus.[38]

Keeping abreast of prevailing theories in international architecture and design, Gropius corresponded with leading architects such as Le Corbusier in

France and took valuable cues from the Russian Constructivist and Dutch de Stijl movements.[39] Each in their own way, Constructivism and de Stijl sought a rapprochement between art and industry in the name of social progress. Following an international Constructivist conference in Düsseldorf in 1922, Gropius was determined to set the Bauhaus on a new course. Against the strenuous objections of the most popular Bauhaus teacher, the charismatic and mystical Johannes Itten, he introduced a Constructivist-style slogan, "Art and Technology: A New Unity," for the Bauhaus's first major exhibition in summer 1923.

Itten, after a prolonged struggle with Gropius, resigned from the school in disgust. His departure greatly disappointed a devoted group of students who, in close emulation of the example set by their favorite Bauhaus master, had shaved their heads, donned monks' robes, adopted yoga and deep-breathing exercises, and practiced vegetarianism. Itten's replacement, the Constructivist László Moholy-Nagy, was the perfect choice to signal the school's new direction, skillfully guiding students through the Bauhaus Introductory Course, supervising the school's metal workshop, and pioneering experiments in a variety of new media.

Quite apart from any troubled internal politics at the school, the unprecedented inflation of 1923–24 rocked the worlds of Weimar and Thuringia. Right-wing parties displaced a Thuringian coalition of socialists and communists in 1924, overshadowing celebrations that followed the first major Bauhaus exhibition in the summer of 1923. The victorious political right revived its old charges that the Bauhaus was a center of "cultural Bolshevism" and guilty of crimes against the "German" traditions of Weimar classical architecture and the literature of Goethe and Schiller. With a clear legislative majority, the right-wing parties closed the Weimar Bauhaus in 1924.[40]

Forced to relocate the school, Gropius found a savior in Fritz Hesse, the liberal mayor of the mid-sized industrial city of Dessau. Hesse's administration funded a sizable new Bauhaus school building designed by Gropius, and also arranged to finance several Gropius-designed houses nearby for the school director and the leading half-dozen Bauhaus masters and their families. Thanks to Mayor Hesse's patronage, Gropius met executives from Dessau's leading industry, the Junkers Aircraft company, who provided striking aerial photographs of Gropius's sleek new school building (Figure 14.5). As national policies lowered Germany's inflation and brought a measure of political and economic stability in the mid-1920s, Mayor Hesse also helped arrange opportunities for the Bauhaus to develop Torten, a workers' housing estate, along modern industrial lines.

The increased opportunities at Dessau yielded rich results: the tubular steel furniture innovations of Marcel Breuer; the film, photography, and new media productions of László Moholy-Nagy and his students; the iconic weaving, collage, and metalwork accomplishments of Gunta Stölzl and Marianne Brandt; and the continued output of Gropius, Kandinsky, Klee, Josef Albers, and others. The Bauhaus encouraged social experimentation as well, with collaborative theater performances, musical evenings, and themed parties. Local conservatives, however, objected to Gropius's liberal administration of the school and the students' overt displays, which they criticized in the press. Ruth Cidor-Citroën,

Figure 14.5. Walter Gropius, Bauhaus school building, aerial view, Dessau, 1926. *Source*: Postcard by Junkers Luftbild, 1930 (author's collection).

a student in the 1920s weaving workshop, subsequently recalled with some wonder that "Everything that came before in art did not matter . . . everything was to be new." Another female student active in the photography workshop, Ethel Fodor-Mittag, said "There was also a sexual independence. My husband was my third relationship at the Bauhaus, and this was completely accepted. It was not accepted by people outside the school, however."[41]

In Dessau Gropius finally obtained the funding he needed to open a full-fledged department of architecture, and in 1927 he invited the Swiss architect Hannes Meyer to serve as its director. After the pressures of leading, promoting, and defending the school for nearly a decade, Gropius retired and in February 1928, turned the Bauhaus directorship over to Meyer. Gropius relocated to focus on his architectural practice in Berlin. Mayor Fritz Hesse would later recall: "To what a great extent the Bauhaus's enemies saw the embodiment of the school in the person of Gropius, dawned on me only after Hannes Meyer took over leadership. Not that the general animosity towards the school would change, but the atmosphere of a fight visibly eased, and the angry articles that had made Gropius's work so incessantly difficult, let up."[42]

The energetic architect Hannes Meyer, a self-confessed "scientific Marxist" whom Gropius would later accuse of having masked his political leanings, steered the school hard to the left. Meyer's Bauhaus eschewed luxury, and even came to resist the idea of aesthetics itself. Several of Meyer's formulae captured this new direction: "all things in this world are a product of the formula: (function times economy);" and "building is nothing but organization: social, technical, economic, psychological organization."[43] Meyer's total commitment helped the school produce numerous affordable and well-designed chairs, lamps, and industrial fixtures long acclaimed as modern "functionalist" classics, along with one of its most memorable architectural projects, the Trade Union School in Bernau, a suburb of Berlin. Meyer and his students also added a block of houses to the suburban Torten housing estate begun by Gropius outside of Dessau. Meyer's housing did not suffer from the cracking and leaking that had afflicted Gropius's prototypes, and added to an accumulating body of left-wing and left-leaning German and Central European domestic architectural accomplishments in the 1920s: for instance, those of Ernst May in Frankfurt, Bruno Taut in Berlin, the Deutscher Werkbund in Stuttgart, and, in neighboring Austria, an array of grand working class housing projects that amounted to a "Ringstrasse for the Proletariat" in social democratic "Red Vienna."[44]

Even as he began his tenure as Bauhaus director, however, Meyer's Marxist sympathies embroiled him in political conflict. Dismissed from his post in 1930, Meyer and his partner, the architect Lotte Beese (who later married the Dutch communist architect Mart Stam), responded with a bitter open letter to Mayor Hesse, published in the Berlin journal *Das Tagebuch* in 1930 under the title, "My Expulsion from the Bauhaus." Referring to Meyer in the third person, the couple vainly sought to drum up support for a reversal of his firing, asserting: "It is a crime to offer the stale fodder of yesteryear's art theories as nourishment to young people who, as designers, will have the society of tomorrow all to themselves."[45] In contrast to the affordable design prototypes produced by the school for working-class consumers during Meyer's directorship between 1928 and 1930, the letter continued, upon first arriving the architect had found a completely different, overly "artistic" atmosphere:

> In 1927 Hannes Meyer found here a Bauhaus . . . where every teacup was seen as a constructivist problematic . . . Inbred theories blocked the way to real-life design: the cube was king; its sides were yellow, red, white, gray, and black. The circle was blue, the triangle yellow, and the square red . . . we sat and slept on colorful geometrical furniture, lived in the colorful sculpture of the houses on the floor of which the hidden psychological complexes of young girls lay woven into carpets. Art was strangling life everywhere. Thus emerged the ironic situation of Hannes Meyer: as director of the Bauhaus, he fought against the Bauhaus style."[46]

The Bauhaus of the early and mid-1920s did not just endure criticisms from the political Right, as the above passage makes clear. Marxists and others on the Left attacked the school for cleaving to outdated romantic conceptions of art and design that would inhibit the development of a truly social democratic art.[47] Meyer insisted that he practiced a "politics of culture but never party politics" in the strict communist sense. Nevertheless, Meyer stood little chance of maintaining the "scientific" direction of the school as escalating political rows saw many German regions slide to the radical right in the late 1920s.[48]

In August 1930 the city replaced Meyer with its third and final Bauhaus director, architect Ludwig Mies van der Rohe. The architect had established a reputation for uncommon rigor through his success at organizing the Deutscher Werkbund's popular exhibition, "The Dwelling," which consisted of a model housing development in Stuttgart, completed in 1927 by an international cast of progressive architects. Mies van der Rohe received additional accolades for his path-breaking German Pavilion for the International Exposition in Barcelona in 1929, an elegant modernist masterpiece so highly regarded that Barcelona authorities reconstructed it in 1986. Mies van der Rohe greatly intensified the school's focus on architecture, remained as apolitical as possible, and made the Bauhaus a center for Weimar Germany's "Neues Bauen," or New Building.

Soon, however, the Bauhaus again fell victim to the election results, this time the local Dessau elections of 1932. Although the victorious local branch of Adolf Hitler's National Socialist party did not actually tear down the Bauhaus building as it had vowed to do during its xenophobic election campaign, it succeeded in forcing the school to close by late summer of 1932. With Mayor Hesse's help, Mies van der Rohe negotiated an exit for the Dessau Bauhaus that included an agreement on the part of the city administration to continue paying faculty salaries through the end of the school's contract period. This financial arrangement allowed Mies van der Rohe to rent an old telephone factory building in Berlin-Steglitz and operate the Bauhaus there for one semester as a "private institute," before the Nazi party compelled the school to disband forever in the summer of 1933. As the former Bauhaus archivist Hans Wingler and others have noted, the Bauhaus, like the Weimar Republic itself, began its hopeful yet troubled existence in 1919 in the town of Weimar, and, like the Republic, met its end in Berlin in 1933.[49]

The Bauhaus Legacy

Walter Gropius, Mies van der Rohe, László Moholy-Nagy, Josef and Anni Albers, and Marcel Breuer would all eventually establish productive careers and lasting reputations in the United States. However, during the initial years of Hitler's Third Reich Gropius, Mies van der Rohe, and more than a dozen more Bauhaus masters and students actively sought architecture and planning positions in the new Nazi administration. [50] Gropius and Mies, unsuccessful in their respective bids, covered their tracks and parlayed their failure to remain in Germany into extraordinarily influential positions in the U.S.: Gropius as chair of architecture at the Harvard Graduate School of Design from 1937 to 1952, and Mies van der Rohe as head of architecture at Chicago's Armour Institute/Illinois Institute of Technology from 1938 to 1958.

Yet the Bauhaus influenced American architecture and design culture well before the arrival of these Bauhaus masters in the late 1930s. Gropius's Bauhaus building of 1926 in Dessau, with its functionally differentiated asymmetrical plan, ribbon windows, and glass curtain wall, proved a sensation in what would come to be known as the "International Style" in an eponymous exhibition sponsored by the Museum of Modern Art (MoMA) in New York in 1932. Twenty-seven year-old Alfred H. Barr, MoMA's first director when it opened its doors in 1929, was inspired to organize the new museum into separate departments of painting and sculpture, architecture and design, photography and film, and drawings and prints as a direct result of his four-day visit to the Dessau Bauhaus in 1927. As Barr recalled: "The multi-departmental plan [of the Museum] was . . . inspired by Rufus Morey's class in Medieval art . . . and equally important, the Bauhaus of Dessau. . . . I had looked forward with great anticipation to the Bauhaus and felt that it had lived up to my expectations."[51] Already in the 1920s, Weimar institutions like the Bauhaus were helping to set international standards for a progressive sensibility in modern art, architecture, and design in far-away cities.

For several decades after the Second World War, surviving Bauhaus members sought to conceal any problematic political affiliations with National Socialism, representing themselves as members of a school that had remained opposed to the political right unto the very end. But the reality was much more complicated, as ongoing research on the school and its legacy has shown.[52] Other new research also reveals the uneasy relationship at the 1920s Bauhaus between such "traditional" arts as painting and sculpture, on one hand, and the introduction, on the other, of such new media as photograms, photography, film, and moving mechanical sculpture imported to the school by the young constructivist László Moholy-Nagy in 1923. The painter Lyonel Feininger, more than two decades Moholy-Nagy's senior when the Hungarian arrived, had a relationship to photography that perhaps best epitomizes the uneasy tensions that prevailed at the time between older and newer art forms. Aged fifty-five in 1925, Feininger initially complained to his wife Julia about the new media being propagated so energetically by the young Moholy-Nagy: "Why attach the name of art to this mechanization of all visual things?" he asked derisively, perhaps betraying the limits of his artistic progressivism.[53]

Yet when the Feininger and Moholy-Nagy families became neighbors in one of the two-family masters' houses designed by Gropius in Dessau in July 1926, the tone quickly shifted. Feininger grew to admire Moholy-Nagy's many-sided artistic talents and irrepressible personality, which made the Hungarian nearly universally popular among masters and students. [54] Influenced as well by his three sons (two of whom, Andreas Feininger and Theodor Lux Feininger, would go on to become famous photographers in their own right), Lyonel Feininger took up the medium of photography and worked alongside his young sons in the family darkroom they constructed together in the basement of their Dessau home.

Julia Feininger, however, remained extremely sensitive to her husband's interest in photography—worried, as Theodor Lux would later explain, that her husband's involvement with this technical medium might somehow compromise or even endanger his considerable reputation as an easel painter. As a result, Lyonel Feininger's photographic work remained a solitary activity, often conducted at night under dramatic lighting conditions not dissimilar from those in some of his celebrated nocturnal paintings. Nor do Lyonel Feininger's photographs document the lively activities of the school, in the way one sees in the work of almost every other Bauhaus master and student who practiced photography.

Feininger's photos appear in hardly any Bauhaus publications, even though by his own admission his engagement with the medium proved very fruitful for both his painting and the further development of his artistic eye. "Dessau has changed countenance for me," Lyonel Feininger would write to Julia of his photography in 1928, and a few months later he gushed in another letter, "photography has taken the way I see to a new level."[55]

Out of respect for the sensitivities of his mother, Theodor Lux waited until after both his parents had passed away to donate nearly five hundred of his father's photographs and eighteen thousand of his negatives and slides to Harvard University—the fruit of the Bauhaus painter's productive engagement with photography over nearly three decades. At this point it is safe to say that Lyonel Feininger's reputation has rested almost exclusively on his career as a graphic artist and painter, although photography greatly informed the artist's work from the time he began shooting photographs with his sons in the mid-1920s. Even at one of Europe's most progressive schools of art and design, pioneers such as Feininger appeared to maintain careful boundaries between what he was best known for producing as an artist, his oil paintings, and his newer work in photography. He did not risk allowing his experiments with "technical" media to be seen as somehow contaminating his easel paintings, as Theodor Lux's recollection of his mother's unease suggests.

Thus at many levels the experience of the Bauhaus can be said to be representative of a set of larger dialectics operating in Weimar Germany: between modernity and tradition; between younger and older generations; between new, technological media and the academic fine arts; and between progressive and conservative definitions of post-war German society. Precisely the experimental nature of much of Bauhaus aesthetics—its openness to alternative modes of thinking, seeing, making, and representing—were perceived as threatening to segments of German society that longed for idealized visions of a stable German past. Although by no means immune to internal conflicts and disagreements, the school's aesthetic ideals found a corollary in definitions of the modern individual that encouraged tolerance, acceptance, and difference. These values would prove anathema to conservative Germans wedded to narrower conceptions of the individual's role in society, or of the nation, or of even narrower theories concerning racial or supposedly "Aryan" prerequisites for being recognized as a "German." German contemporaries perceived Bauhaus art and architecture not only as a reflection of a modern vision of aesthetics, but also as a powerful barometer of German social development. Therein lay the school's considerable promise, but also, to some, its particular threat.

Notes

1. Richard Huelsenbeck, "En Avant Dada: A History of Dadism" (1920), in *The Dada Painters and Poets*, ed. Robert Motherwell (Cambridge: Cambridge University Press, 1951), 43–44. I am grateful to James Crewe for this reference.

2. Richard Huelsenbeck, "First German Dada Manifesto," (1918), as reprinted in *Art in Theory, 1900–1990: An Anthology of Changing Ideas*, eds. Charles Harrison and Paul Wood (Oxford: Blackwell, 1992), 253.

3. Richard Huelsenbeck and Raoul Hausmann, "What Is Dadaism and What Does It Want in Germany?" (1919), in *Art in Theory*, eds. Harrison and Wood, 256.

4. John Elderfield, *Kurt Schwitters* (London: Thames and Hudson, 1985), 12–13.

5. Walter Gropius, "Der freie Volksstaat und die Kunst," quotation from typescript in Bauhaus Archive, Berlin, Gropius Papers (hereafter BAGP), file 6S/2B (1919); also published in *Deutscher Revolutions-Almanach für das Jahr 1919* (Hamburg, 1919), 134–36.

6. Karl-Heinz Hüter, *Architektur in Berlin, 1900–1933* (Dresden: VEB Verlag der Kunst, 1987), 84.

7. Walter Gropius, "Address to the Students of the State Bauhaus, Held on the Occasion of the Yearly Exhibition of Student Work in July 1919," as quoted in Rainer Wick, *Teaching at the Bauhaus*, 32, as excerpted from Hans Wingler, *The Bauhaus, 1919–1933: Weimar, Dessau, Berlin, Chicago* (Cambridge, MA: MIT Press, 1969), 36.

8. Hermann Muthesius, "Soll die kunstgewerbliche Erziehung zukünftig den Akademien übertragen werden?" *Die Woche* (18 May 1918), 489–91; Ministerium für Wissenschaft, Kunst, und Volksbildung, "Diskussion um wichtige Kunsterziehungsfragen," typescript of meeting protocol, 10/11 June 1919, BAGP, file 2; Gruppe der Kunstgewerbeschulmänner, "21. Wanderversammlung des Deutschen Gewerbeschul-Verbandes: Ist eine einheitliche Organisation der Kunstgewerbeschulen mit Abschlussprüfungen möglich und wünschenswert?," *Zeitschrift für Gewerblichen Unterricht* 31, no. 33 (September 1916), 385–86, Sonderdruck in BAGP, Vorgeschichte Kunstschulreform, file 3.

9. Wilhelm von Bode, "Aufgaben der Kunsterziehung nach dem Kriege," *Die Woche* 18 (1 April 1916), 469–71.

10. Hermann Muthesius, *Stilarchitektur und Baukunst: Wandlungen der Architektur im XIX. Jahrhundert und ihr heutiger Standpunkt*, 2nd ed. (Mülheim-Ruhr: Verlag von K. Schimmelpfennig, 1903), 80–81; I am here using the translation by Stanford Anderson, *Style-Architecture and Building-Art: Transformations of Architecture in the Nineteenth Century and its Present Condition*, trans. Stanford Anderson (Santa Monica: Getty Center for the Arts and Humanities, 1994), 100.

11. The title of the Deutscher Werkbund's Yearbook for 1912 was *The Spiritualization of German Production*, while the explicit goal of the organization, as asserted by the architect Fritz Schumacher in his keynote address at the Werkbund's founding meeting, was the "reconquest of a harmonious culture," or the *Wiedereroberung einer harmonischen Kultur*. See Deutscher Werkbund Jahrbuch 1912, *Die Durchgeistigung der Deutschen Arbeit: Wege und Ziele in Zusammenhang von Industrie/Handwerk und Kunst* (Jena: Eugen Diederichs, 1912); and Fritz Schumacher, "Gründungsrede des Deutschen Werkbundes 1907 in München," *Die Form* 7 (1932), 331.

12. Bruno Taut, "Architektur-Programm" [A Program for Architecture], as quoted in Ulrich Conrads, *Programs and Manifestoes on 20th-Century Architecture*, translated by Michael Bullock (Cambridge, MA: MIT Press, 1964), 41.

13. On Taut, see Rosemarie Haag Bletter, "Interpretation of the Glass Dream: Expressionist Architecture and the History of the Crystal Metaphor," *Journal of the Society of Architectural Historians* (March 1981), 20–43; Iain Boyd Whyte, *Bruno Taut and the Architecture of Activism* (Cambridge: Cambridge University Press, 1982).

14. Workers Council for Art, "Mitteilung an Alle," prospectus for the Berlin-based magazine *Bauen*, 1919, as reproduced in Wolfgang Pehnt, *Expressionist Architecture*, trans. J. A. Underwood and Edith Küstner (London: Thames and Hudson, 1973), 91.

15. Hans Poelzig, "Festspielhaus in Salzburg," *Das Kunstblatt* 5, no. 3 (1921), 79, as quoted in Pehnt, *Expressionist Architecture*, 20.

16. J.J.P. Oud quoted in Fritz Neumeyer, *The Artless Word: Mies Van Der Rohe on the Building Art*, trans. Mark Jarzombek (Cambridge, MA: MIT Press, 1991), 30. See also Kathleen James, *Erich Mendelsohn and the Architecture of German Modernism* (Cambridge: Cambridge University Press, 1997).

17. See Reginald Isaacs, *Gropius: An Illustrated Biography of the Creator of the Bauhaus* (Boston: Bulfinch Press, 1991).

18. Feininger quoted in *The Architectural Review* 133 (1963), 167, as reprinted in Andrew Saint, *The Image of the Architect* (New Haven: Yale University Press, 1983), 116.

19. Walter Gropius's debts to such Wilhelmine schools as the Wilhelm von Debschitz School in Munich, Peter Behrens's School of Applied Art in Düsseldorf, and Hans Poelzig's School of Art and Applied Art in Breslau are taken up in John V. Maciuika, *Before the Bauhaus: Architecture, Politics, and the German State, 1890–1920* (Cambridge: Cambridge University Press, 2005).

20. Thus the original, official name of the Bauhaus was: *Staatliches Bauhaus in Weimar (Vereinigte ehemalige Grossherzogliche Hochschule für bildende Kunst und ehemalige Grossherzogliche Kunstgewerbeschule)*. See Hans M. Wingler, *The Bauhaus*, 30.

21. Ute Ackermann, "Einleitung: Zur Funktion und Geschichte des Meisterrates am Staatlichen Bauhaus Weimar," in *Meisterratsprotokollen des Staatlichen Bauhauses Weimar 1919–1925,* eds.Volker Wahl and Ute Ackermann (Weimar: Verlag Hermann Böhlaus Nachfolger, 2001), 25.

22. See Walter Gropius, "Program of the Staatliches Bauhaus in Weimar" (April 1919), reproduced in Hans M. Wingler, *The Bauhaus*, 31–33. View the original artifact on the web at http://arthistory.about.com/od/from_exhibitions/ig/bauhaus_1919_1933/bauhaus_moma_09_01.htm.

23. Gropius quoted in John Willett, *Art and Politics in the Weimar Period: The New Sobriety, 1917–1933* (New York: Pantheon Books, 1978), 50.

24. Gropius, "Idee und Aufbau des Staatlichen Bauhauses Weimar," in *Staatliches Bauhaus Weimar, 1919–1923*, ed. Walter Gropius (Weimar: Bauhausverlag, 1923), 7–18; quotation here from the translation, "The Theory and Organization of the Bauhaus," in *Bauhaus 1919–1928*, eds. Herbert Bayer, Walter Gropius, and Ise Gropius (New York: Museum of Modern Art, 1938), 20–29; quotation 28.

25. Baudelaire as quoted in Marshall Berman, *All That Is Solid Melts into Air: The Experience of Modernity* (New York: Penguin, 1982), 133.

26. See Charles W. Haxthausen, "Walter Gropius and Lyonel Feininger: Bauhaus Manifesto, 1919," in *Bauhaus 1919–1933: Workshops for Modernity*, eds. Barry Bergdoll and Leah Dickerman [exhibition catalog] (New York: Museum of Modern Art, 2009), 64–67.

27. Walter Gropius, "Program of the Staatliches Bauhaus in Weimar," here quoting from the translation by Charles W. Haxthausen as it appears in his catalog essay, "Walter Gropius and Lyonel Feininger: Bauhaus Manifesto, 1919," in Bergdoll and Dickerman, *Bauhaus 1919–1933*, 64. The present author has made one minor adjustment to Haxthausen's translation of *aus Millionen Händen der Handwerker*, which Haxthausen renders as "from the million hands of craftsmen."

28. Steven Murray is quoted in Haxthausen, "Walter Gropius and Lyonel Feininger: Bauhaus Manifesto, 1919," 67 n. 9.

29. This history is detailed in John V. Maciuika, "The Deutscher Werkbund Grows a Global Network: Design Reform, Industrial Policy, and German Foreign Policy,

1907–1918," in *Global Design History,* eds. Sarah Teasley, Giorgio Riello, and Glenn Adamson (London: Routledge, 2011), 98–106; and, with greater emphasis on ties between German government, industrial associations, and the Werkbund, in John V. Maciuika, "*Werkbundpolitik* and *Weltpolitik*: The German State's Interest in Global Commerce and 'Good Design,' 1912–1914," in *Before the Bauhaus,* Chapter 7.

30. Sitzungen des Meisterrates am 18. Dezember 1919 and 20. Dezember 1919, Thüringisches Hauptstaatsarchiv Weimar, Staatliches Bauhaus Weimar 12, pp. 11-17, reprinted in *Die Meisterratsprotokolle des Staatlichen Bauhauses Weimar 1919–1925,* eds. Volker Wahl and Ute Ackermann (Weimar: Verlag Hermann Böhlaus Nachfolger, 2001), 56–57; translations by author (hereafter cited as *Meisterratsprotokolle*).

31. Barbara Miller Lane, *Architecture and Politics in Germany, 1918–1945* (Cambridge, MA: Harvard University Press, 1968), 72.

32. Sitzungen des Meisterrates am 18. Dezember 1919 and 20. Dezember 1919, *Meisterratsprotokolle,* 56–62.

33. Meeting of 18 December 1919, in *Meisterratsprotokolle,* 57.

34. Meeting of 20 December 1919, in *Meisterratsprotokolle,* 61.

35. Meeting of 18 December 1919, in *Meisterratsprotokolle,* 58–59.

36. Quoted in Winfried Nerdinger, "Walter Gropius' Beitrag zur Architektur des 20. Jahrhunderts," in *100 Jahre Walter Gropius: Schliessung des Bauhauses 1933,* eds. Peter Hahn and Hans M. Wingler (Berlin: Bauhaus-Archiv, 1983), 17–36, here 18.

37. In a 2010 essay, for example, architectural scholar Martin Filler noted that 2009—the ninetieth anniversary of the school's founding—saw a bumper crop of nearly a dozen international scholarly books, conferences, and exhibitions on the Bauhaus's individual artists and their collective achievements in cities like Weimar, Dessau, Berlin, Frankfurt, New York, and Chicago. See Martin Filler, "The Powerhouse of the New," *New York Review of Books,* June 24, 2010.

38. See the nuanced analysis of Gropius's efforts to balance the crafts and industry in Marcel Franciscono, *Walter Gropius and the Creation of the Bauhaus in Weimar: The Ideals and Artistic Theories of its Founding Years* (Urbana: University of Illinois Press, 1971), 17–25. Gropius's speech was entitled, "Baugeist oder Krämertum," and was delivered to members of the leather and shoe industries in Leipzig.

39. See Marina Epstein-Pliouchtch, "Le Corbusier and Walter Gropius: Contacts Prior to the Second World War," *Journal of Architecture* 9, no. 1 (2004), 5–22.

40. See Miller Lane, *Architecture and Politics in Germany,* 76–86.

41. "Bauhaus in Aktion: Bauhäusler im Gespräch," documentary film interviews with Ruth Cidor-Citroën (1906–2002) (film D-2, n.d.) and Ethel Fodor-Mittag (1905–2005) (film D-8, 1997), Stiftung Bauhaus Dessau Archive, viewed by the author September 25, 2009 (translations by author).

42. Fritz Hesse, *Von der Residenz zur Bauhausstadt* (Bad Prymont: Oberbürgermeister a.D. Fritz Hesse im Selbstverlag, n.d.), 239, as translated and quoted in Eva Forgács, "Between the Town and the Gown: On Hannes Meyer's Dismissal from the Bauhaus," *Journal of Design History* 23, no. 3 (2010), 265–74, here note 17.

43. Hannes Meyer, "Building," 1928, in Conrads, *Programs and Manifestoes,* 117–20.

44. Eve Blau, *The Architecture of Red Vienna, 1919–1934* (Cambridge, MA: MIT Press, 1999); Heinz Hirdina, ed., *Neue Bauen, Neues Gestalten: Das Neue Frankfurt/die neue stadt—eine Zeitschrift zwischen 1916 und 1933* (Dresden, Verlag der Kunst, 1991).

45. Hannes Meyer, "Mein Hinauswurf aus dem Bauhaus. Offener Brief an Herrn Oberbürgermeister Hesse, Dessau," *Das Tagebuch* 11, no. 33 (Berlin, 1930), as quoted in Forgács, "On Hannes Meyer's Dismissal," 271.

46. Meyer, *Mein Hinauswurf*, 271–72.
47. On the critique of the Bauhaus from the Left see Michael Müller, "Diktat der Kälte: Kritik von Links, 1919–1933," in *Bauhaus Streit, 1919-2009: Kontroversen und Kontrahenten*, ed. Philipp Oswalt (Ostfildern: Hatje Kantz Verlag, 2009), 50–65.
48. Hannes Meyer quoted in a letter to Mayor Fritz Hesse, 1 August 1930, Getty Research Institute Special Collections, Hannes Meyer Papers, as quoted in Forgács, "On Hannes Meyer's Dismissal," 265.
49. Hans Wingler, *The Bauhaus, 1919–1933*, 532–43.
50. Winfried Nerdinger, "Bauhaus Architecture in the Third Reich," in *Bauhaus Culture*, ed. Kathleen James-Chakraborty (Minneapolis: University of Minnesota Press, 2006), 139–52; this is James-Chakraborty's important translation of Nerdinger's original 1993 German essay, "Bauhaus-Architekten im 'Dritten Reich,'" in *Bauhaus-Moderne im Nationalsozialismus: Zwischen Anbiederung und Verfolgung*, ed. Winfried Nerdinger (Munich: Prestel Verlag, 1993).
51. Barr quoted in Sybil Gordon Kantor, *Alfred H. Barr, Jr. and the Intellectual Origins of the Museum of Modern Art* (Cambridge, MA: MIT Press, 2002), 155, here especially notes 36 and 37.
52. Winfried Nerdinger, "Bauhaus Architecture in the Third Reich," in *Bauhaus Culture*, ed. Kathleen James-Chakraborty, 139–52.
53. Letter from Lyonel Feininger to Julia Feininger, 9 March 1925, as quoted in Laura Muir, "Lyonel Feininger's Bauhaus Photographs," Chapter 6 in *Bauhaus Construct: Fashioning Identity, Discourse, and Modernism*, eds. Jeffrey Saletnik and Robin Schuldenfrei (London: Routledge, 2009), 125–41, here 126.
54. See the thorough analyses of László Moholy-Nagy's career and artistic evolution in Lloyd C. Engelbrecht, *Moholy-Nagy: Mentor to Modernism*, 2 vols. (Cincinnati: Flying Trapeze Press, 2009); for close analysis of Moholy-Nagy's early years up to 1922 see Olivar A. I. Botar, *Technical Detours: The Early Moholy-Nagy Reconsidered* (New York: CUNY Graduate Center Art Gallery and Salgo Trust for Education, 2006).
55. Letters to Julia Feininger, 31 October 1928 and 21 May 1929, as quoted in Muir, "Lyonel Feininger's Bauhaus Photographs," 134–35.

15

Aby Warburg and the Secularization
of the Image

Michael P. Steinberg

For Yaron Ezrahi

Over the inner portal of the Warburg Institute and Library at Woburn Square, London, appears the one-word inscription "Mnemosyne": Memory. Libraries are generically understood as repositories of memory, of course. At the Warburg Library, however, this basic principle takes on two inflections of increasing specificity. The first refers to the materials and the argument of Aby Warburg's own Hamburg-founded *Kulturwissenschaftliche Bibliothek,* or "Library of the Cultural Sciences."[1] That collection, undertaken by the twenty-two year-old Warburg in 1886, documented a (largely) European cultural history of the image, combined with a mode of analysis of the image as a repository of cultural memory. As such, the collection and the method argued together for the close association of art history and cultural analysis. Moreover, they functionally invented the practice of iconology as a way of understanding the history of visual representations: from idol to icon to image.[2]

The history of these three categories—idol, icon, image—was to be understood, on the one hand, as a linear one, passing from ancient paganism to Christian visual culture to the production, reception, and hence culture of the secular image. This process took place within the bounds of sacred imagery and involved the evolution of a kind of implicit contract between image and viewer. According to this implicit contract, or alliance, the image's object of representation—most consistently a sacred object—was held at a certain distance (*Distanz,* in Warburg's jargon) from both the image and its viewer. Warburg understood the cultural production of this capacity for distance as the birth of symbolization. Distance-taking from deities (what nineteenth-century German cultural theory from Friedrich Schiller to Max Weber called disenchantment, *Entzauberung*), was for Warburg fundamentally inseparable from distance-taking from demons. The "afterlife" (*Nachleben*) of pagan antiquity assured the fusion of what might be called positive and negative disenchantment.[3] As such, distance enabled the space required for thinking, what Warburg called *Denkraum.* In this respect Warburg's focus on the culture and art of the Italian and Northern Renaissance as fulcrums of secularization followed and refined the paradigms of scholarly predecessors. The same history, however, argued for the structural dialectic present at every cultural moment and within every profound cultural document between sacred and secular, chaos and cosmos, demonic and self-possessed. The polarities of visual order operate between the claim to resolve cultural violence on the one side and the tendency to repress and hence to reproduce it symptomatically on the other.

Aby Warburg's book collecting began in childhood. Born in 1866 into the prominent family of the M. M. Warburg Bank of Hamburg, he was the first-born of five sons and thus the first in line to take the mantle of the family owned bank. But at the age of thirteen he mythically sold his birthright to his younger brother Max in exchange for the so-called "blank check" promise that Max would finance Aby's precocious taste for books. The eventual result was the Warburg Library and the only reckless investment of Max's long and successful banking career, as he himself suggested late in his life.[4] Aby's decision to study the history of art—first in a preparatory school in Hamburg and then at the University of Bonn—was met with resistance from the family. As an independent scholar, he later divided his time between Hamburg and Florence, with the prominent exception of a trip to America in 1895–96. Ostensibly focused on the September 1895 wedding in New York of his brother Paul, the trip was taken over by Aby's self-described "will to the Romantic." With the guidance of prominent ethnologists, he spent the following winter in Arizona and California, including two long stays among the Hopi Indians—of which, more below. Significantly, Warburg finally gathered and shared his thoughts about this experience in a 1923 lecture given under unique circumstances.

Warburg suffered from what would likely be diagnosed today as bi-polar illness, and he was hospitalized between 1919 and 1924 in Ludwig Binswanger's Kreuzlingen Sanatorium following psychotic episodes and threats of violence. The slide lecture "Images from the Pueblo Indians of North America" was the result of Warburg's second legendary bargain—this time not with his brother but with Binswanger. Warburg suggested that a sustained academic lecture would be the proof of his return to mental health. In any case, his Hopi ethnology remained the most intense and most personal locus of the juxtaposition of cosmos and chaos.

Warburg's evolving library project had an intellectual partner in a series of arduously written essays, emphasizing but not limited to the European Renaissance (including Florence, Flanders, and Luther's Germany) and focusing on the problem of the returns of the energies, themes, and images from pagan antiquity. Pagan antiquity was a double signifier, in that it both carried the messages of the two "prophets of Basel": on the one hand, Jakob Burckhardt's consonant rendition of the European Renaissance as the restorer of antiquity's political and aesthetic forms; on the other, Friedrich Nietzsche's dissonant dialectic of Apollo and Dionysus, form and formless energy; cosmos and chaos.[5]

The library itself constituted the most thorough document of Warburg's method. He determined its acquisitions from 1886 until his sudden death in October 1929, when stewardship passed to his assistants Gertrud Bing and Fritz Saxl. In December 1933 the library (approximately 60,000 books, plus slides, photographs, other materials, as well as the collective argument of the enterprise itself) was evacuated to London, to be linked as of 1937 to the University of London and fully incorporated into the university in 1944. The Warburg Institute's second-generation principal scholars, adherents, and administrators included Erwin Panofsky, Ernst Gombrich, Rudolf Wittkower, Edgar Wind, Frances Yates, and (less recognized but perhaps most authoritative) Anne Marie Meyer. Its book inventory (according to its website) currently numbers around 350,000. In recent years, the methods and claims of visual culture and visual studies have embraced the legacy of Warburg's critique of formalist art history.[6]

Aby Warburg and *Mnemosyne*

Warburg's final but never completed project carried the title "Mnemosyne." In a recapitulation of his career-long concerns, Warburg intended to assemble onto a series of large screens a "picture atlas" of images, mapping out dialectically the afterlife of pagan antiquity in the cultural history of the image. Between December 1927 and his death he assembled some forty screens, each one a montage of images in multiple permutations of interrelation. As Gombrich suggests, "It was the philosophy of 'bipolarity' in particular which Warburg was testing and developing in these kaleidoscopic permutations that go back to his studies of Flanders and Florence. The fact that every image seemed charged with conflicting and contradictory forces, that the same "pathos formula" spelt "liberation" in one respect and "degradation" in another, made it most difficult for Warburg to present the complexity of his historical view in discursive language."[7]

The *Mnemosyne* project opens with a statement of the principle of distance:

> The conscious creation of distance between self and external world may well be described as the fundamental act of human civilization; when this medial space becomes the substratum of artistic production, preconditions are fulfilled whereby this awareness of distance can achieve lasting social function.[8]

The screens themselves (canvas surfaces on which the images were pinned in an ephemeral way and which have not survived beyond an incomplete photographic record) focused on two basic themes, as Gombrich suggests: the presence of the Olympian gods in later astrological discourses and the afterlife of ancient pathos formulae in the history of the image (including contemporary photojournalism). The astrological focus was occasioned at least in part by Warburg's participation in the planned installation of a planetarium in an existing water tower in Hamburg's city park. Warburg agreed to curate an exhibition on the history of astrology and astronomy, documenting both the sequence's implied mutation from superstition to rational science as well as the afterlife of superstition within the paradigms of modern science. The exhibition, entitled "Collected Images on the History of Astrology and Astronomy" [*Bildersammlung zur Geschichte von*

Sternglaube und Sternkunde] was realized posthumously, through the curation of Saxl and assistants, in April 1930.[9]

The *Mnemosyne* project's montages juxtapose periods and genres of images with a mix of pathos and humor that is characteristic of Warburg's scholarly and personal style. Six of the forty screens (not including much of the material mounted in Hamburg in 1930) can be indexed as follows.

Two introductory screens show maps of the heavens and of Europe as well as a family tree of the Medici: in other words maps of space and time with purviews spanning from the family to the universe. The second introductory screen, labeled "Microcosm and Macrocosm," connects images of the human body to images of the universe, with Leonardo's rendition of Vitruvian man inscribed within a circle as the central image. This image of harmonious proportions is offset by blood-letting charts from barbers' almanacs: harmony countered by violence.[10]

A screen dedicated mostly to the work of Domenico Ghirlandaio recapitulates themes from Warburg's key essays on the Florentine banker Francesco Sassetti of 1902 and 1907.[11] Francesco Sassetti's role as the director of the Medici Bank in Florence and its affiliates in Flanders also placed commercial banking in the service of artistic communication, arranging the loan to Florence in 1483 of the altarpiece that Hugo van der Goes had painted on commission from Tomasso Portinari, head of the Medici Bank in Bruges. That transfer enabled a dialogue between Flemish and Florentine images. Van der Goes's image of the Adoration of the Shepherds inspired Ghirlandaio's work after 1483, and in this context Sassetti commissioned Ghirlandaio to decorate the family chapel in the Church of Santa Trinità. Here too, the Adoration of the Shepherds claims the principal image. Warburg's early essays thus allegorized a positive projection of his own family dynamic in the celebration of the harmony of commercial banking, painting, and the communication between north and south (Flanders and Florence) in the Sassetti universe. The family unites with the universe, as in the first introductory screen mentioned above. Thus, a print of Ghirlandaio's 1485 *Adoration of the Shepherds* (in the Sassetti Chapel) holds the bottom quadrant of the *Mnemosyne* screen, surrounded by dialogical images of Ghirlandaio and Giotto on the life of St. Francis (Francesco) as well as sketches of elements in the Sassetti Chapel drawn by Mary Hertz, Warburg's wife, during one of their stays in Florence.[12]

Another screen juxtaposes a Brockhaus Dictionary illustration of the solar system with an allegorical image of the same from Johannes Kepler (*Die Identifikation der Planetenbahnen mit den regelmässigen Körpern aus dem Mysterium Cosmographicum*) from 1621; in other words the figure and moment representing the transition from astrology to astronomy. These images are accompanied by newspaper photos of the Graf Zeppelin airships from 1929. The juxtaposition remains both humorous and cryptic. Does the Zeppelin blimp serve to connect the planets? Or does it imagine itself, so to speak, as a planet unto itself? Warburg's *Wanderlust* would suggest the first; his witty but nevertheless profound distaste for technology, the second. (See Figure 15.1.)

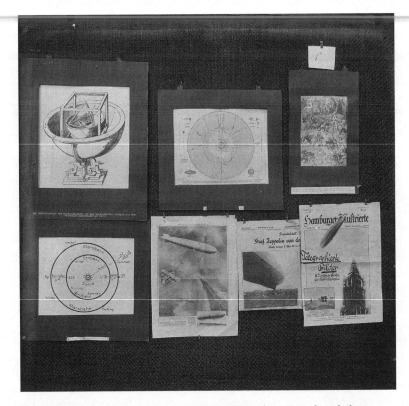

Figure 15.1. Aby Warburg, *Mnemosyne*, Kepler/Zeppelin. Unattributed photograph reprinted in Fleckner et al., eds. © The Warburg Institute, London.

Perhaps the most humorous juxtaposition—and the most idiosyncratic—combines an apparently banal image with a most ominous contemporary reality. A contemporary photograph of a woman swinging a golf club appears alongside a newspaper photo of the signing of the Lateran Treaties between Pope Pius XI and Benito Mussolini in January 1929. The benign image of the golfer carries the handwritten caption, "The catharsis of the female head-hunter in the shape of the golfer (*Die Katharsis der Kopfjägerin in Gestalt der Golfspielerin*). This image and its allegorical investment recall the screen on the theme of "Nympha," or images of women expressing strong and sometimes violent gestures, of which the dancing Maenads (or Bacchae), who list the murder of Orpheus on their curriculum vitae, are Warburg's most abiding example. The point to be taken here is the combination of humor and violence as a framing device for the attachment of the photograph of Pius XI and Mussolini at the signing table in Rome. (See Figure 15.2.)

Gombrich suggests, bizarrely, that Warburg understood the Lateran Treaties as "a link in the long chain of mankind's road toward enlightenment," citing their tipping of the balance of power to Mussolini and the withdrawal of the Pope "to

Figure 15.2. Photographs from *Mnemosyne,* reprinted in E. H. Gombrich, *Aby Warburg: An Intellectual Biography,* plate 61. © The Warburg Institute, London.

Figure 15.3. Laocoön
sculptural group,
Vatican Library.

the confines of a merely symbolic domain." The equation of the crude power of fascism with enlightenment (Gombrich's own terms) is odd, especially since the Treaties delivered substantial authority over civil society (including the codes of marriage) to the Church. One wonders if Gombrich has blinded himself to the golfer's relation to the deep history of the Nympha and Maenads, a relation that he has just explained! It is the violence as the unconscious of the benign image that is at stake, even if, or indeed especially if, the humor of the juxtaposition functions as a kind of balm in the underlying presence of violence.

As Gombrich recounts, Warburg was in Rome when the Lateran Treaties were publicly celebrated, and he was present in St. Peter's Square when the Pope "blessed the crowd after this act of renunciation." Upon his tardy return to the Hotel Eden and to his travel partner Gertrud Bing, Warburg pronounced (according to Bing): "You know that throughout my life I have been interested in the revival of paganism and pagan festivals. Today I had the chance of my life to be present at the re-paganization of Rome, and you complain that I remained to watch it."[13] The possibility opened by both humorous gestures (the quip to

Figure 15.4. *Mnemosyne,* Laocoön (as with Figure 15.1). © The Warburg Institute, London.

Bing and the swing of the golfer juxtaposed with the signing picture) involves the reversal inherent in the so-called re-paganization of Rome. The fascist moment thus involves paganization as both secularization qua modernization (the papal recognition of the fascist state) and re-paganization as a return of ancient demons, or mass politics cloaking itself in the garb of the sacred. Somewhat cryptically perhaps, the linkage of the golfer to the Maenad reveals the implied violence beneath the image of Pius XI and Mussolini.

The return of ancient demons defines the image that probably carried the most gravitas for Warburg. In the screen labeled with the number 6, a dancing Maenad (neo-Attic relief, Augustinian period, in the Museo dei Conservatori, Rome) is pinned beside a photograph of the Laocoön sculptural group. The overall theme is human sacrifice. The Dancing Maenad is surrounded by images of the sacrifice of Polyxena and the death of Cassandra. The image of the *Laocoön* group is partnered with two additional images of the Laocoön story as well as additional images of the cult of Isis and Achilles and Deidamia on the island of Skyros.[14] (See Figures 15.3 and 15.4.)

Warburg's Reading of the *Laocoön*

Warburg evinced a near lifelong fascination with the myth and sculptural depiction of Laocoön. The sculptural group *Laocoön* dates, by consensus, from about 50 BC. It was dug up to great fanfare in 1506 by a vineyard owner on Rome's Esquiline Hill, and quickly identified as the lost work referred to by Pliny. The group depicts the violent and painful deaths of the Trojan priest Laocoön along with his two young sons. The version of the story that made it well known is that of Virgil, from Book 2 of the *Aeneid*. Here, Laocoön is the priest who warns the Trojans that the horse at their gates may in fact be a Greek ruse. At the moment his advice is overruled by a crafty Greek in disguise, two serpents rise from the sea and attack his two sons. Attempting to save his sons, Laocoön dies with them, in physical and affective torment. Virgil's account emphasized that suffering, describing in particular the screams emitted by the three victims.

Ille simul manibus tendit divellere nodos
perfusus sanie vittas atroque veneno,
clamores simul horrendos ad sidera tollit:
qualis mugitus, fugit cum saucius aram
taurus et incertam excussit cervice securim.

At the same time he stretched forth to tear the knots with his hands
his fillets soaked with saliva and black venom
at the same time he lifted to heaven horrendous cries:
like the bellowing when a wounded bull has fled from the altar
and has shaken the ill-aimed axe from its neck.

The sculpture found in 1506 was in good condition but required some restoration. Specifically, the father's right arm had broken off. The restoration established the version of the *Laocoön* group that survived from the mid-sixteenth century to 1960. This is the *Laocoön* known to Lessing and Warburg (among, of course, many others prior to 1960). It is also the image that inspired the term *Laocoönism*, referring to the representation of the dignity of the male body under stress.[15] Here, the priest defiantly grasps a serpent with his outstretched right arm, vainly attempting to hold it away both from himself and from his younger son. In the second restoration of 1960—a process whose politics might form the topic of a study of its own—the same right arm is left broken and bent backwards, the relevant serpent coils left interrupted in their sweep across the three victims. After 1960, Laocoön's death is an unambiguous portrait of defeat.

The sixteenth-century reception of the *Laocoön* group understood the priest and his sons as an allegory of the Crucifixion.[16] Later depictions confer other allegorical inflections to the figure and the story. The subject and group inspired El Greco to paint his only mythological subject, executed between 1608 and 1614.[17] Here, the Trojan horse is depicted in front of the city gates of Toledo. Identification of two additional figures that appear on the right has remained controversial. Berbera cites E. W. Palm and John Moffitt's successive identifications of the figures as Adam and Eve, suggesting that "they constitute the Jewish example—parallel to the Pagan one, represented by Laocoön and his sons—of divine retribution for transgressions, the serpents being in both cases the active principles of the divine retributory mechanism."[18]

From his school days on, Warburg's engagement with the Laocoön group was combined with his reading and critique of Lessing's transformative treatise on the poetic and visual arts, entitled *Laocoön*, of 1766. Lessing wrote in reply to Winckelmann, whose *History of Art* had flagged the *Laocoön* as an exemplar of Stoic restraint and visual beauty. Following these same norms, Winckelmann had objected to Virgil's realistic account. For Lessing, Winckelmann had failed to appreciate the differences between image and word. Lessing, in Richard Brilliant's formulation, "tastefully . . . withdraws from the poetics of pain" by arguing that the sculptural group in fact softens Virgil's narrative because of the limits of visuality. [19] The sculpture is beautiful by necessity. In order for the sculpture to be an aesthetic object at all—which for Lessing, as for Winckelmann, means an aesthetically pleasing object—it has to be beautiful. The visual representation of suffering must therefore be diffused. This is, for Lessing, the hazard of the visual, which by necessity operates under the principle of spatial synchrony—*Nebeneinander*—as opposed to the poetic, which operates with sequences of words, meaning diachronically, or according to the principle of *Nacheinander*. Image is for Lessing a relatively inadequate conduit to the imagination, which is more richly served by words.

Lessing's *Laocoön* was a formative text for the young Aby Warburg. Having completed his Hamburg Realgymnasium education at the age of eighteen, he had enrolled in the *Gelehrtenschule des Johanneums* for eighteen months to fulfill university entrance requirements. His study of Lessing's text there, under the instruction of Oscar Ohlendorff, helped draw him to the study of visual art. Gombrich suggests specifically that it was Lessing's argument for the necessity of restraint in visual representation—the alleged sigh of the sculpted figure as opposed to the screams of the narrated one—that attracted Warburg. Indeed, this view of Warburg's interest in images as aesthetic, cultural, and indeed psychic bearers of restraint, rationality, and stability, prevails in Warburg studies. Gombrich is the paradigm's main proponent. There is little doubt that his search for distance from pagan demons carried a personal as well as a scholarly burden. In both fields, the achievement of distance as a condition of a viable subjectivity relies on cultural and psychic work rather than on restraint or repression. How can Laocoön free himself from the serpents?

Among Warburg's consistent invocations of the image of the serpent as an allegory of cultural horror, the *Laocoön* remained a favorite example; his recurrent interest in the serpent rituals and snake dances of American Indians forms the other prime example.[20] The paradox in Warburg's reception of Lessing is the fact that Lessing persuaded Warburg of the cultural primacy of the image while striving to do exactly the opposite. If images do basic cultural work, as Warburg argues, then they cannot take a back seat to words, or to poetry. As a corollary, they cannot be understood to operate by repression. This is not to say that repression is incompatible with cultural work but rather, as Freud argues, that the same repressive energies which are in fact necessary for cultural work must be understood to work in tandem with the interpretive practices that uncover both repression and its objects. For Warburg, images do this work and cannot therefore be understood according to Lessing's hierarchy.

Warburg can thus be argued to upset, if not necessarily to reverse, Lessing's devaluation of the image with respect to the word. At the same time, however, Warburg adopts with conviction Lessing's term *Nebeneinander*. Warburg deploys this term to mark the synchrony of the primitive and the rational in cultural formation: Athens and Alexandria in one formulation; Athens and Oraibi in another. Thus in his 1923 lecture "Images from the Region of the Pueblo Indians of North America," Warburg writes: "The synchrony [*Nebeneinander*] of fantastic magic and sober purposiveness appears as the symptom of a cleavage; for the Indian this is not schizoid but, rather, a liberating experience of the boundless communicability between man and environment." Laocoön is killed by the serpents; the American Indians Warburg visited in 1895–96 and recalled at various points in his life, handle them in a highly ritualized practice, without harm.

Warburg's extended visits to the Hopi mesas of Arizona in 1895 and 1896 combined his own self-aware European's romance with the primitive, allegedly still available to the intellectual tourist. But he combined his own romance with the distance-taking of the scholar, positioned often behind a camera. In 1907 he wrote to the ethnologist James Mooney of the Smithsonian Institution: "I always feel myself very much indebted to your Indians. Without the study of their primitive civilization I never would have been able to find a larger basis for the Psychology of the Renaissance."[21]

At an Indian Service School in Arizona in April 1896, Warburg conducted an experiment on schoolchildren. Following a model he had gleaned from Stanford psychologist Earl Barnes, he told the group of children a story about a storm and asked them to draw a picture of the storm. He question was weather the children would represent lightning as a fork-tongued serpent, as lightning is represented in ritual representations. He wanted to see whether the children understood the difference between the material fact of lightning and its symbolic representation, in other words on which side of the civilization-as-symbolization evolutionary hurdle they would place themselves. When twelve of the fourteen children drew lightning as zigzag lines and only two as serpents with forked tongues, Warburg found his evidence—ontogenetic and philogenetic—of the birth of symbolization and "distance" through visual forms.[22]

Primitivism (a term he came to replace with paganism), for Warburg, means religion. For him, as for Freud, sacred ritual practice holds a generic fascination, undifferentiated by confessional specificity. For Warburg there is no art without history and there is no history without anthropology. Indeed, his own course of study after leaving Hamburg in 1886—a city that lacked a university—exhibits his insistence on such a combined program of study. Enrolled at the University of Bonn, he studied art history, archaeology, and the history of religion, the last under Hermann Usener. As an anthropologically oriented historian of religion,

Usener had a hand in inspiring Warburg to visit the American southwest. The historian of religion Eduard Meyer inspired him directly, through his famous position that the United States still offered the European visitor a chance to see remnants of fading primitive religion. While in Bonn, Warburg was encouraged by his grandparents to change universities because of his tendency to ignore dietary laws in Bonn. Warburg wrote to his father: "Since I do not arrange my course of study according to the quality of ritual restaurants but according to the quality of my teachers, I do not eat ritually."[23]

His own family's Judaism is not exempt from Warburg's ambivalent take on the survival of antiquity. Ancient religion, pagan or not, exudes both seduction and horror, cultural anchors and cultural horrors. Warburg understood the religious practice of the Hamburg Jewish patriciate as containing, no matter its intentions or self-understanding, a vestige of the demonic, and he reacted to it with real fear. He had grown up with little ritual. Religious practice in the Warburg home of Aby's childhood had become, in his view, formalistic. He learned Hebrew from his mother; his father knew none. "Formalism," meaning form without content, will become the mantra of inadequate art history. On the side of culture and ritual, it is the word used by Gershom Scholem in criticism of his own father's uninhabited religious rituals. The turn or return to religion among Weimar thinkers often carried the insistence on a step-wise reinvention of authentic inhabitation within religious meaning. For Franz Rosenzweig, the return to religious identity (back from the famous 1913 near-conversion to Protestantism) carried the self-test of a sincere addition of religious gestures and rituals on a one-by-one basis.) For Scholem the road was scholarship combined with Zionism; his own emotional attachment to both of these remains famously opaque.

Warburg's problem was the opposite of Scholem's, however. For Scholem, formalism represented a loss of ritual contact. In an often cited example, Scholem (humorlessly) recalled his father making jokes at the expense of ritual seriousness, lighting his cigar in the Sabbath candles with the mock-Hebrew phrase "B'rei pri Tobacco."[24] Warburg himself tended to behave in the same way as Scholem senior. When he took his own children to his parents' house for the Passover seder, his mediation between generations proved decidedly unhelpful, disrupting the ritual celebration with irreverent parodies of the traditional songs. Warburg cultivated precisely the distance that Scholem wanted to overcome—or at least that Scholem claimed he wanted to overcome. Humor provided distance. Most poignantly, however, Warburg in 1910 refused, as the oldest of his father's five sons, to lead or even to participate in the funeral rituals for his father. Indeed, as Gombrich observes, the choice to study images offended some of his orthodox relatives. The recidivist *Bilderverbot* and the valorization of the word connects Jewish tenets to Lessing's implicitly Protestant ones. As Anne Marie Meyer suggests, "Exactly what was the relation between Warburg's research on paganism in the Renaissance and his meditations and fears about Judaism (and Jews) remains of course the problem."[25] The antique past thus produces a desire for return and a horror of return. For Warburg the art of the Renaissance promised to mediate between these impulses. Thus his early work on the paintings of Botticelli interpreted the garments and hair of the allegorical characters as symptoms of desires for return and propulsion into the future, figures moving in history much like Walter Benjamin's angel, only with more stability between the desire to return and the desire to move on.[26]

Warburg's fear of religion, in his case his disavowal of participation in its religious ritual practice, relates closely to the dynamics between himself and his family, in particular his father, Moritz Warburg, and his banker brothers Max, Paul, and Felix. Max in Hamburg, and Paul and Felix in New York inherited and nurtured the M. M. Warburg Bank. Aby bought books.

One can thus speculate that his reading of Lessing's *Laocoön* brought to Aby Warburg's mind an obvious aspect of the ancient sculpture that Lessing manages to ignore almost completely. That is the fact of its depiction of a father and his sons. That depiction grants, conceivably, a second aspect to the value of synchrony and synchronic representation. The synchrony of the primitive and the rational is grafted onto that of fathers and sons. Diachronicity becomes in turn responsible for the transmission of violence through successive generations.

Weimar Ways of Seeing

Weimar Germany's decade and a half is the era of the work of art in the age of its technical reproducibility. The richness of its cinematic output and culture amounts to a new theorization of seeing. The moving image in its verisimilitude called for a reality principle as a way of seeing just as much as it offered one as a principle of production. Whether or not this visual reality principle came from a de-auraticization of the image—as in Walter Benjamin's claim, much debated since he made it 1936—it did come from a disenchantment, or secularization, of the image. And not only the moving image. One precursor and then companion to the moving image was the *way of seeing* a still image (drawing, painting, or photograph), as a spatial incorporation of a life-world that existed in time and history. Warburg's work and its way of seeing an image on the way to a cultural analysis remains key to (and is increasingly recognized as such) to scholarship of visual media in the post-cinematic age.

Is the *Bilderatlas Mnemosyne* Warburg's "Weimar project"? We might identify one of Weimar culture's many faces as post-traumatic modernism. Problematic as this backward looking characterization may be, it connects to the energies of fin-de-siècle modernism while of course avoiding the teleological error of understanding the fin-de-siècle as pre-traumatic. Warburg's intellectual career, like Freud's, spans precisely the two generations of the fin-de-siècle and the post–Great War. Together, the fin-de-siècle and Weimar culture present a dialectic of modernism on two sides of the Great War. Modernism as a cultural drive rides the dialectic between liberation and degradation. This is the necessary complication—both Freudian and Warburgian—that enables us to recognize that fascism is also a form of modernism.

The images and combinations of images that preoccupy Warburg involve both pathos and the memory of suffering. Memory thus resides in multiple contexts, subject positions, and temporalities. An image itself holds a memory of the event it depicts. Thus an image is accorded a kind of inner temporality in a way that has led several scholars to equate Warburg's iconology to the contemporaneous emergence of cinema.[27] At the same time, a certain rush to cinema may do some injustice to the idea of the "image in motion," which accords possibilities of temporality and historicity to the still image. The same image "remembers" earlier depictions, "pathos formulae" in Warburg's jargon, deployed in earlier periods and genres to communicate similar affective experiences. In this way two fictive subject-positions or temporalities are accorded the image: one internal to its own depiction and one external to it. The image remembers, so to speak, as if it were itself engaging in a conscious dialogue with an earlier image.[28] The momentum of such (fictive) memory can follow the energies of one or both modernist momentums: liberation or degradation. The energy of liberation Warburg referred to as "distance." Distance captures the potential of temporalization and secularization. It defines and then recapitulates the historical sequence from idol to icon to image, from the unmediated presence of deities and demons to a mediated presence and, finally, to a reference from a position of some remove. The energy of degradation was for him the desire for absorption into the demonic side of pagan antiquity and its later returns in organized cultural violence, of which the most extreme was human sacrifice and the most organized were anti-Semitism and fascism.[29]

The images pinned to the screens of the *Mnemosyne* projects and the arguments behind their juxtaposition claim the status of archives rather than artworks. Their material fragility is reaffirmed by the fragility of the juxtapositions themselves. The consistent importance of the image and groups of images as records of violence is kept representationally at bay by unfulfilled collisions. The Maenad meets Mussolini, so to speak, only through the lighthearted and cryptic mediation of the swinging woman golfer. The image and message of the *Laocoön* group is clearer, but the legacy of Gotthold Lessing remains present to temper the graphic account of which Virgil reminds. It is striking on the one hand how Warburg the collector of rarified knowledge and images does not hesitate to juxtapose them with popular images from his own day, including new items and commercial advertisements. But although the links in the montage are always precise, the fusion of the images, the detonation of violent energy, as if by a magnetic or chemical reaction, is consistently avoided. This is montage, but it is a montage by separation just as much as by combination. Warburg's montage thus approximates and distances itself from the photomontage—the realization of the collision of images through multi-media and other fusions of forms and images—that is indelibly identified with the same later Weimar years that produced the *Mnemosyne* project.

Heartfield and Montage

The work of John Heartfield (born Helmut Herzfelde in Berlin in 1891) is a signature interlocutor for the aesthetics and politics of modernist montage. His name change resulted from his rejection of Great War–era anti-British sentiment. In

Figure 15.5. John Heartfield, "The Face of Fascism," in *Italien in Ketten* [Italy in Chains], 1928, Catalog no. 105 in Pachnicke and Honnef, eds. © Artists Rights Society (ARS), NY. Photo Credit: bpk, Berlin / Art Resource, NY.

1917 he signed on to both the Dada movement and the German Communist Party (KPD). During the Weimar years he became a principal illustrator for its mouthpiece, the *Arbeiter-Illustrierte Zeitung* (*AIZ*) and a pioneer, along with George Grosz, of the political photomontage.

Heartfield's profile as political activist and artist immediately sets him apart from the fragile scholar Warburg. Heartfield's art, however, deploys under the literal overlays and montages the kinds of images that Warburg also juxtaposes, without actually effecting the collision. Warburg's contrapuntal juxtaposition highlights dissonance, one might suggest, where Heartfield's portray violence directly, exude it and may even reproduce it in the experience of the viewer.

Peter Pachnicke describes Heartfield's photomontages as "polysemantic pictorial structures" deploying a surrealist palette toward a realist message.[30] The readability of the political message marked Heartfield's departure from his Dadaist days and colleagues, including George Grosz, Hannah Höch, and Raoul Hausmann, who, in Klaus Honnef's summary, "concocted bewildering visual impromptus from a host of selected photographic images," producing photomontages which "had to be read like a text, although the discovery of a plausible meaning was unlikely."[31] Photomontage thus repeats with photographic and other technical means the undermining of the practices and claims to visual order of Renaissance perspective initiated by baroque and mannerist style. It shares with the baroque the potential reproduction of violence alongside its portrayal: collision as detonation.

In a 1928 photomontage called "The Face of Fascism," the cover of a publication of the German Communist Party (KPD) publication called "Italy in Chains," Heartfield surrounded an oversized head of Mussolini with four images. The head, emerging from the montage frame to crowd the publication title over it, has been painted over with a decayed nose and lips and exposed teeth to give it the look of a skeleton. The four supporting images include a photo of Pius XI. The Lateran Treaties remain months away, but the alliance is clearly signaled.[32] (See Figure 15.5.)

The *Laocoön*'s theme and serpent appear in an October 1933 image for the *Arbeiter-Illustrierte Zeitung* (*AIZ*), published from Heartfield's Prague exile. Two interlocked serpents wear undersized judges' hats, with swastikas painted on their skin and in their eye sockets. Their forked tongues take the shape of a baroque ornament, possibly a portion of the musical F-clef or a punctuation mark—all possibilities indicating an elegance of speech. The image accompanies the caption: "On the Arson Trial in Leipzig: They Twist and Turn and Call Themselves German Judges."[33] The reference is to the trial of Marinus van der Lubbe and four co-defendants for the 27 February 1933 burning of the Reichstag. (See Figure 15.6.)

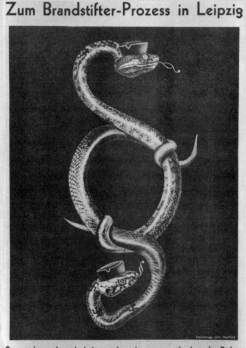

Zum Brandstifter-Prozess in Leipzig

Sie winden sich und drehen sich und nennen sich deutsche Richter

Figure 15.6. John Heartfield, "Zum Brandstifter-Prozess in Leipzig," *Arbeiter-Illustrierte-Zeitung Prague*, 19 October 1933, Catalogue no. 244 in Pachnicke and Honnef, eds. © Artists Rights Society (ARS), NY. Photo Credit: bpk, Berlin / Art Resource, NY.

Heartfield's serpent allegory is a photomontage in its details (the swastikas and hats) but not in its unitary composition. When multiple images are overlaid in a more formally aggressive manner, the violence of the composite image can exceed the violence of its content. There is a violence imposed on the obvious victims of the montage—workers, the poor, soldiers' corpses—when their space is literally overtaken by images of their oppressors and murderers: Hitler, Goering, et al.

Photography and Politics Today

Compromised, or at least at stake, in this kind of aggressive montage, is what Ariella Azoulay has called "the civil contract of photography" in a book by that title.[34] The contract in question is metaphorical and implicit, "a social fiction or hypostatized construct" reminiscent of Rousseau's social contract. It "binds together photographers, photographed persons, and spectators." It might productively be extended, experimentally, to painting, at least to portraiture. The three agents (photographer, subject, spectator) participate in a recognition of—and insistence on—the subjective dignity of each of them. They become together a community of borderless citizenship and civic knowledge. The contract adds two literal agents and positions to the dialogue between the image and its antecedents: the photographer and the viewer. Azoulay's project thus attempts "to anchor spectatorship in civic duty toward the photographed persons who haven't stopped being 'there,' toward dispossessed citizens who, in turn, enable the rethinking of the concept and practice of citizenship."[35] Her principal subjects (and subjects of the photographs she reads) are victims of two different paradigms of dispossessed citizenship: the dispossessed Palestinians of the West Bank and victims of rape.

The constructed and to a great extent fictional citizenship which Azoulay wishes to make available to the Palestinian subjects of the photographs she analyzes (and which she wants to have adhere to her civil contract) neither replaces or compensates for the lack of state citizenship that they endure. To the contrary, the acknowledgement of these subjects' lack of political citizenship defines the dimension of Azoulay's work that is activist and interventionist. It also defines her implied contract with her readers, whose understanding of the paradigm of the civil contract of photography is to accompany a recognition of the political status, or non-status, of the subject she represents, indirectly, through a photographic record.

The efficacy of this implied second contract with Azoulay's readers depends, it would follow, on our cognitive ability to recognize and to read the photographs for both text and context. As records of important events and situations in the late twentieth-century world, they are topical, for us, or should be. In this respect one of the challenges to Azoulay's readers is for us to see the image at a deeper level of the event than the one that would normally be expected of us were the source a daily newspaper, for example. There is a certain implied scale or balance of recognition at work between the topical availability of the image and the deep reading of its "pathos formulae," to return to Warburg's phrase. In a photographic record from the Palestinian Territories in 2000, the event is likely to be absorbed with less apparent or immediate need for an understanding of paradigmatic pathos formulae. In an image, say, of the signing of the Lateran Treaties of 1929 between Mussolini and Pius XI, the scale may be balanced, with a certain amount of empirical historical instruction necessary for most readers. In any case, the instruction is easily available. For the much earlier and in many cases ancient or esoteric images in Warburg's picture atlas (a term that describes his *Mnemosyne* project but all his other work as well), historical information is rare or unavailable altogether. Here, the uncovering of pathos formulae render the images at least partly readable as documents and memory-holders of culture. (See Figure 15.7.)

As Giorgio Agamben has observed, a mistaken way of reading any one of the *Menmosyne* screens would be to assume a search for an archetypical pathos formula from which each articulation of the formula would be held to emerge. "A slightly more careful reading of the plate," Agamben continues, "shows that none of the images is the original, just as none of the images is simply a copy or repetition." The category that Agamben is most interested in building according to this discussion is that of the paradigm, and his summary definition of the

Figure 15.7. Orel Cohen, Refugee Camp, Tul Karem, March 8, 2002, in Azoulay, p. 360. Courtesy of Orel Cohen.

paradigm begins: "A paradigm is a form of knowledge that is neither inductive nor deductive but analogical. It moves from singularity to singularity."[36]

Agamben's argument here offers an alternative vocabulary to Walter Benjamin's theory of the dialectical image as historical allegory. Allegory functions precisely as the communication between singularities, between historical moments, creating transhistorical patterns but not ahistorical ones.[37]

The "elective affinities" between Benjamin's work and Warburg's have been affirmed often, perhaps most famously by George Steiner, who proposed that an appeal by the fugitive Benjamin in 1940 to the London-based Warburg Institute would have done more than his appeal to the New York-based Frankfurt School thinkers first to save his life and second to provide him with an intellectual home.[38] Beyond the unfulfilled bond with Warburg and Warburgian practice, Benjamin's paradigms stand as an equally important and equally connective reference to the work of both Agamben and Azoulay. (Azoulay's references to Benjamin are significantly more forthcoming than Agamben's.)

Benjamin's understanding of historical repetition fused the flare of political danger with the call for historiographic intervention—the call to rescue the past from oblivion: "To articulate the past historically does not mean to recognize it 'the way it really was' (Ranke). It means to seize hold of a memory as it flashes up at a moment of danger."[39] In Warburg's universe, such a moment of danger both recalls and renders readable the relevant image or pathos formula. The contemporary referent for Warburg and Benjamin is fascism. For Azoulay it is occupation.

The Afterlife of Weimar Seeing

"[T]o *see* in order to *know better*." This is Georges Didi-Huberman's description of his own visual practice. A leading scholar of Warburg himself as well as a scholar who consistently recognizes Warburg as the precursor of his own practice, Didi-Huberman offers this self-description in a vexed and controversial context: the debate over his analysis of four photographs from Auschwitz.[40] At stake is a visual analysis of four photographs taken in 1944 by a member of the *Sonderkommando*: the Jewish forced laborers responsible for the operation of the gas chambers. The photographs are the only known images of the operation of the gas chamber. They are taken with a smuggled camera from within the shelter (from surveillance) of the gas chamber itself. Their existence has been known since 1945. Didi-Huberman assesses the various tropes through which these image can be seen, led by that of "images from hell." One dimension of their analysis, he argues, is formal analysis. Here he advocates the expectation that historians be able "to undertake the kind of visual criticism that I believe they are seldom accustomed to."[41]

In avowing that he wants *to see*, and not *to look*, in order to know, Didi-Huberman seems to refer to an implicit contractual ethic similar to the one laid out by Azoulay. The anonymous photographer, who knew the imminence of his own murder, proposed the contract at once implicitly and categorically. Two of the photographs include naked women and corpses, both observed at a significant distance. *Seeing* rather than *looking* appears to extend contractual participation to these figures as well, while disavowing a potential voyeuristic or illicit dimension from the participation of the photographer and subsequent viewers, including Didi-Huberman himself. Active seeing, like active hearing, implies knowledge of and about the object and, through the object, the world, a knowledge that surpasses the sensory absorption of information. (The fierce criticism of his work, which appeared first in a catalogue essay in 2000, rejected that disavowal; the second part of the book referred to here consists of Didi-Huberman's reply to his critics.)

Seeing these images analytically also fuses the categories of evidence and truth. They are evidence of a crime and of an historical fact. They are "instants of truth" (p. 31) for their evidentiary proof that the crime took place. The convergence of evidence and truth also speaks to a fully secular frame of analysis. In this way, Didi-Huberman joins Agamben in rejecting the discourse of the unimaginable and the unsayable with regard to Auschwitz, a move that relegates its crimes to a region "of mystical adoration, even of unknowing repetition of the Nazi *arcanum* itself."[42]

Seeing in order to know implies a contractual, transhistorical dialogue with a visual voice, with a lived temporality stilled into an image (whether or not the image is moving). Such a practice is Warburg's afterlife: the afterlife of Weimar seeing.

Afterword

In its issue of September 30, 2010, the *New York Review of Books* published an appeal by Anthony Grafton and Jeffrey Hamburger titled "Save the Warburg Library!" The authors offer a brief vignette of Aby Warburg as "a visionary scholar, . . . obsessed with cultural exchanges of all kinds and in all periods, [who] tinkered throughout his life with new ways to frame and display visual images, in order to reveal their interconnected meanings across time and space. His unconventional tool for studying this shifting web of historical relationships was a picture atlas that remained in perpetual flux, and to which he gave the name Mnemosyne, or memory." They summarize the uniqueness of the library's holdings and organization—its bibliographic continuity determined by the "law of the good neighbor" and an open-stack system that is itself extremely unusual in Europe—as well as its history from its Hamburg beginnings to its incorporation into the University of London. Their point is to take to task the University of London for acting in contempt of the 1944 deed of incorporation, which assured the continued autonomy of the library.

The Warburg Library is currently under threat. Negative subsidies and space reductions recently imposed by the university impede its function: "The only way for the institute to avoid these charges would be to move into much smaller premises and close its stacks, a decision that would destroy its essential character." The authors compare the university to a Dickensian villain. They refrain from introducing the Laocoön simile, through which the visual history of pagan antiquity and its revivals might be seen as devoured by corporate serpents. They recommend that the Warburg Library be returned to Germany if it cannot be functionally preserved in its London home. That option might indeed be viable, especially since the rededication of the Warburg Haus in its original Heilwig-strasse location in Hamburg. Important projects have originated there, including an initiative on the visual history of National Socialism and the Warburg Electronic Library (WEL).

It would seem that the optimal location for a scholarly treasure such as the Warburg Library should be determined from a post-national and indeed post-nationalistic perspective, in other words from the conviction that its location should serve and insure the maximal density and quality of scholarly attention and productivity. It is possible that the Warburg Library will have to be rescued, for a second time in its history, if it cannot be saved in its current location. A lively debate on its optimal location would be appropriate, with contenders from the United States as well as Europe.

Notes

1. See E. H. Gombrich, *Aby Warburg: An Intellectual Biography* (Chicago: University of Chicago Press, 1970). For most of Warburg's writing in English, see Warburg, *The Renewal of Pagan Antiquity: Contributions to the Cultural History of the European Renaissance*, trans. D. Britt (Los Angeles: Getty Research Institute, 1999). The term "renewal" casts too positive a light on what for Warburg is the double-edged force of the pagan and the ancient. See below, as well as some recent scholarship, especially Georges Didi-Huberman, *L'image survivante: Histoire de l'art et temps des fantômes* (Paris: Editions de Minuit, 2002), and Karen Lang, *Chaos and Cosmos: On the Image in Aesthetics and Art History* (Ithaca: Cornell University Press, 2006).
2. The so-called "Warburg method" has not remained constant or uncontested. See Carlo Ginzburg, "From Aby Warburg to E. H. Gombrich: A Problem of Method," in *Clues, Myths, and the Historical Method* (Baltimore: Johns Hopkins University Press, 1992), 17–59.
3. I translate Warburg's *Nachleben* (*das Nachleben der Antike*) literally as "afterlife" (the afterlife of antiquity) rather than the more often used "survival." At stake is a return of the past rather than its continuity. This can occur through a revival of knowledge, as in the Renaissance scholarship of antiquity, or as a return of the repressed, as with the return of ancient or "primitive" demons.
4. Max Warburg's memorial address, 5 December 1929, quoted in E. H. Gombrich, *Aby Warburg: An Intellectual Biography* (Chicago: University of Chicago Press, 1970), 22.
5. See Lionel Gossman, *Basel in the Age of Burckhardt: A Study in Unseasonable Ideas* (Chicago: University of Chicago Press, 2000). "The prophets of Basel" (a slightly esoteric pun on *les prophètes de Baal*) was the moniker coined by Gossman and Carl Schorske for their joint Princeton University seminar in the late 1970s on the intellec-

tual history of nineteenth-century Basel, focusing on Burckhardt, Nietzsche, Johann Jakob Bachofen, and Arnold Böcklin. See Gossman's preface, ix–xi.

6. This development and its acknowledged debt to Warburg have had institutional results, for example the Centre CATH (Cultural Analysis, Theory, and History) at the University of Leeds.

7. Gombrich, *A Problem of Method*, 285.

8. "Bewusstes Distanzschaffen zwischen sich und der Aussenwelt darf man wohl als Grundakt menschlicher Zivilisation bezeichnen; wird dieser Zwischenraum das Substrat künstlerischer Gestaltung, so sind die Vorbedingungen erfüllt, dass dieses Distanzbewusstsein zu einer sozialen Dauerfunktion werden kann."

9. See Uwe Fleckner, Robert Galitz, Claudia Naber, and Herwart Nöldeke, *Aby Warburg: Bildersammlung zur Geschichte von Sternglaube and Sternkunde im Hamburger Planetarium* (Hamburg: Dölling und Galitz Verlag, 1993). This collection served as the catalogue to a partial reconstruction of the Hamburg installation at the Academy of Sciences, Vienna, in 1991–92. Thanks to Francesca Cernia Slovin for making this volume available to me.

10. See Gombrich, *A Problem of Method*, 292 and Plate 56.

11. "Bildniskunst und florentinisches Bürgertum" and "Francesco Sassettis letztwillige Verfügung." See the translations "The Art of Portraiture and the Florentine Bourgeoisie" and "Francesco Sassetti's Last Injunctions to His Sons" in Warburg, *The Renewal of Pagan Antiquity*, 435–50 and 451–65.

12. Screen numbered 43, reproduced in Fleckner et al., *Bildersammlung*, unpaginated appendix.

13. See Gombrich, *A Problem of Method*, 279; Arnaldo Momigliano, "How Roman Emperors Became Gods," *American Scholar* 55 (1986), 181–93, here 181; and in Momigliano, *On Pagans, Jews, and Christians* (Middletown, CT: Wesleyan University Press, 1987), 92; also M. P. Steinberg, "Aby Warburg's Kreuzlingen Lecture: A Reading," in Warburg, *Images from the Region of the Pueblo Indians of North America* (Ithaca: Cornell University Press, 1995), 108–9.

14. Fleckner et al., *Bildersammlung*, unpaginated appendix.

15. See Alex Potts, *Flesh and the Ideal: Winckelmann and the Origins of Art History* (New Haven: Yale University Press, 2000).

16. See Maria Louro Berbara, "Christ as Laocoön: An Iconographic Parallel between Christian and Pagan Sacrificial Representations in the Italian Renaissance" (PhD diss., Universität Hamburg, 1999).

17. Berbera, *Christ as Laocoön*, 164–65.

18. Berbera, *Christ as Laocoön*, 165.

19. Richard Brilliant, *My Laocoön: Alternate Claims in the Interpretation of Artworks* (Berkeley: University of California Press, 2000), 56.

20. See Aby Warburg, *Images from the Region of the Pueblo Indians of North America*, trans. Michael P. Steinberg (Ithaca: Cornell University Press, 1995); and Michael P. Steinberg, "The Kreuzlingen Lecture: A Reading," which appears following Warburg's text.

21. A. M. Meyer, "Aby Warburg in His Early Correspondence," *American Scholar* 57 (Summer 1988), 445–52, here 450.

22. See Steinberg, "Warburg's Kreuzlingen Lecture," 64–66.

23. Meyer, *Early Correspondence*, 447.

24. See the discussion in Zygmunt Bauman, *Modernity and Ambivalence* (London: Polity Press, 1991).

25. Meyer, *Early Correspondence*, 452.
26. Warburg, "Sandro Botticelli's *Birth of Venus* and *Spring*: An Examination of Concepts of Antiquity in the Italian Early Renaissance" (1893), in Warburg, *The Renewal of Pagan Antiquity*, trans. D. Britt (Los Angeles: Getty Research Institute, 1999), 89–156.
27. See Philippe Alain Michaud, *Aby Warburg and the Image in Motion* (Cambridge: Zone Books, 2007). See my review of Michaud and Karen Lang, *Chaos and Cosmos*, in *CAA* [College Art Association] *Reviews*, January 2009, http://www.caareviews.org/reviews/1206.
28. For this insertion of temporality and memory, the Warburgian image might be argued to be granted the status of music. For an argument about music as a (fictive) agent of subjectivity, memory, and temporality. see my book *Listening to Reason: Culture, Subjectivity, and 19th-Century Music* (Princeton: Princeton University Press, 2006).
29. See Charlotte Schoell-Glass, *Aby Warburg and Anti-Semitism: Political Perspectives on Images and Culture* (Detroit: Wayne State University Press, 2008).
30. See Peter Pachnicke, "Morally Rigorous and Visually Voracious," in *John Heartfield*, eds. Pachnicke and Klaus Honnef (New York: Harry Abrams, Inc., 1992), 45.
31. Klaus Honnef, "Symbolic Form as a Vivid Cognitive Principle," in Pachnicke and Honnef, *John Heartfield*, 57.
32. John Heartfield, "Das Gesicht des Faschismus," cover of *Italien in Ketten* (1928), reproduced in Pachnicke and Honnef, *John Heartfield*, 145.
33. John Heartfield, "Zum Brandstifter-Process in Leipzig . . . Sie winden sich und drehen und nennen sich deutsche Richter," AIZ-Prague, 19 October 1933, Pachnicke, "Morally Rigorous," 184–85.
34. Ariella Azoulay, *The Civil Contract of Photography*, trans. R. Mazali and R. Danieli (Cambridge, MA: MIT Press, 2008).
35. Azoulay, *Civil Contract of Photography*, Introduction, quoted from 26 and 16–17.
36. Giorgio Agamben, *The Signature of All Things: On Method*, trans. L. D'Isanto and K. Attell (Cambridge: Zone Books, 2009), 28–29, 31.
37. See my Introduction in M. P. Steinberg, ed., *Walter Benjamin and the Demands of History* (Ithaca: Cornell University Press, 1996), especially 8–10.
38. See George Steiner, Introduction to Benjamin, *Origin of German Tragic Drama* (London: Verso, 2009).
39. Walter Benjamin, "On the Concept of History," in *Selected Writings* 4 (1938–40), trans. E. Jephcott and others; eds. Howard Eiland and Michael W. Jennings (Cambridge, MA: Harvard University Press, 2003), 391.
40. Georges Didi-Huberman, *Images In Spite of All: Four Photographs from Auschwitz*, trans. Shane B. Lillis (Chicago: University of Chicago Press, 2008), 56–57.
41. Didi-Huberman, *Images In Spite of All*, 40.
42. Didi-Huberman, *Images In Spite of All*, 25–26, 190; citation of Giorgio Agamben, *Remnants of Auschwitz: The Witness and the Archive*, trans. Daniel Heller-Roazen (New York: Zone Books, 1999), 32–33 and 157.

Part IV

Themes of an Epoch

16

Eastern Wisdom in an Era of Western Despair

Orientalism in 1920s Central Europe

Suzanne Marchand

The modern Westerner's problem is: to become, on a higher level of consciousness, *entirely* whole, as was the Medieval person, to a high degree, and as Orientals, in many ways still are today.
—**Thomas Mann to Hermann Graf Keyserling (1920)**[1]

Perhaps it is our expectation that"Orientalism" has everything to do with European imperialism, and nothing to do with the critique of European civilization that accounts for the fact that no one has written a comprehensive account of the use of oriental themes and images during the Weimar Republic.[2] This is to be lamented, for the interwar era saw the publication of some of Germandom's most interesting orientalizing novels and most innovative orientalist scholarship; in fact, it may well be the era in which orientalist scholarship was closer to the cultural pulse of the nation than ever before, perhaps precisely because it was in the Weimar era that the non-specialized literati were most drawn to *Orientalistik*'s longstanding iconoclastic, anti-classical and often neoromantic worldview.[3] Regrettably, too, this essay will not be able to do justice to the richness and variety of this literature, which includes works by Hermann Hesse, Hugo von Hofsmannsthal, Thomas Mann, Bertholt Brecht, Alfred Döblin, and the scholarship of pioneers like Rudolf Otto, Heinrich Zimmer, Paul Kahle, Fritz Saxl, Richard Wilhelm, and Karl Wittfogel. But in what follows, I do want to introduce readers to a little-known aspect of Weimar intellectual life: the deep and serious interest many took in what was usually referred to as"eastern wisdom."

For the purposes of giving this inquiry some coherence, I will also focus on the relatively obscure alternative institution which called itself, rather pretentiously, the *Schule der Weisheit*, founded in 1920 in Darmstadt, an industrial town with an avant garde past just a twenty-minute train ride from progressive, cosmopolitan Frankfurt where, simultaneously, the much better-known Institut für Sozialforschung was beginning its work. The brainchild of the eccentric Baltic aristocrat Hermann Graf Keyserling, the *Schule der Weisheit* lends itself to easy parody; it was, by the account of one visitor, a "super-Chatauqua," attended by poet-scholars with Whitmanesque hair and Byronic open shirts, bluestocking yoga fanatics and a not inconsiderable number of astrologers.[4] Keyserling, a man who claimed to be a descendent of Genghis Khan, and really was married to one of Bismarck's granddaughters, was the philosopher-king and impressario of the organization, which he himself described as part Platonic academy, part Buddhist monastery; he could, and often did, talk for hours on end, and orchestrated improbable conferences featuring psychoanalysts, vitalist biologists, philosophizing rabbis and Russian theologians. And yet, the *Schule*'s meditation lessons and lecture series also drew in scores of important intellectuals from across central and eastern Europe, and was crucial in popularizing scholarly findings and translations of non-western "classics" produced before and during the Great War.

Though the group that gathered at Grand Duke Ernst Ludwig's Darmstadt residence had far less coherence, and much less comaraderie, ultimately, than did the contributors to "the Frankfurt School," Keyserling's endeavor was indicative of another powerful train of thought, one that offered a different, but perhaps equally influential, critique of European scholarship and selfhood. By focusing on this little-studied world in its early Weimar heyday, this essay will explore some aspects of the longer tradition of Central European orientalism, a tradition which tended to be not enlightened and imperialist, but romantic and elitist; German orientalists certainly believed Europe culturally superiority, but they also emphasized, especially in eras of western crisis, the spirituality, integrity, and antiquity of eastern cultures. Especially in the crisis years of the late 1910s and early 1920s, this tradition exerted itself powerfully, gaining expression in works like Keyserling's *Travel Diary of a Philosopher* (1919) and Hermann Hesse's *Siddhartha* (1922). There were, of course, many other, more derogatory or dismissive images and usages of the Orient in the Weimar era, evident in the parodying of the purportedly mysterious East in films or popular novels, or the degrading of Jews as "orientals;" and as Muhammed Asad pointed out in 1954, Islam in particular rarely received sympathetic attention, even from "spirit-hungry" romantics.[5] But the story of Weimar intellectuals' appreciation for "eastern wisdom" is one that needs telling, for it reveals a little-known side of this era's cultural politics, and may also help illuminate what is otherwise a dark chapter in the history of East-West cultural relations, the chapter that describes the transition from the era of high imperialist hubris to the multiculturalism of today.

Of course, this story is not one that can be confined to the Weimar era, and indeed, it is important to recognize both the longer- and shorter-term intellectual trajectories which shaped interwar Germany's images of the Orient. It should be noted that Europeans—at least some Europeans—have always been interested in eastern wisdom; this tradition stretches back (at least) to Herodotus, runs through the Church fathers, and perhaps reached its zenith in the early modern fascination with Hermes Trismegistus, an oriental sage whose profound thoughts had been pilfered by Plato and perhaps even by Moses. Though hermetic thought in its strongest forms died in the early seventeenth century, weaker forms persisted in Masonic and Rosicrucian thought, and in efforts to find the first forms of universal wisdom, which continued much longer than one might think. Even during the period of high imperialist conquest, westerners could not forget that the Orient had been home to rich and learned civilizations much older than their own—nor could they forget that Christianity itself was an oriental religion, and one based on two books of indisputably Near Eastern origin. The antiquity and spirituality of the Orient could always be used to pull the rug out from under classicizing, or orthodox Christian smugness, and a considerable number of iconoclasts and orientalists, from Giordano Bruno to Martin Bernal, have tried this trick.[6] This is to remind us that if some orientalists, in recent times, have served as handmaidens to imperialist ventures, there is a longer-term tradition of oriental iconoclasm, one that confronts the West with its own limitations and cultural dependencies, and has often suffered persecution or ridicule for its unconventional advocacy of the wisdom of the East.

I dwell on these older forms of iconoclastic Orient-fancying as I am convinced that this search for ancient, often esoteric, oriental wisdom is a perennial one, one that has been going on, in some fashion, since Aesop adopted Indian tales At some times it is a subterranean quest, censured or forbidden by the authorities; at other times, especially during periods of flagging western self-confidence, it becomes more socially and politically acceptable. Once the critique has done its work—or when the authorities and the public become alarmed at its implications—it is forced underground again. There is a process of cultural production here that should interest us: the more popular forms of orientalist critique are always constructed from the previous generation's more scholarly ones, as Voltaire drew on Jesuit scholarship and Bruno on the expert forgeries of Annius of Viterbo.[7] In the case before us, we have to do with a preparatory stage at the turn of the twentieth century, and then the blossoming of a new form of neoromantic orientalism in the early Weimar period. We need to look briefly at foundations laid in the Wilhelmine era in order to understand how a certain sort of "oriental wisdom" was transported to Europe; this excursus into the past should also help us appreciate the ways in which intellectual exchanges between neoromantic seekers and indigenous nationalists created important streams of critical thought that could be mobilized against European norms in the wake of the war's devastating impact on European culture and self-confidence.

In a wonderful essay on the origins and context of Freud's *Moses and Monotheism*, Carl Schorske noted the cooling of Freud's affection for Athens and the Greeks around about 1904, and the new interest he began to take at that time in Egypt and the Near East.[8] In making this turn, Freud was by no means alone; in the period between about 1895 and 1910 there was an upsurge in interest in the East, resulting in part from the sense that Graecophilia had become trite and banal. Tired of Athena, intellectuals sought a less rational, more archaic Greece, or turned to Zarathustra, Isis, or polynesian goddesses for inspiration.[9] For some, too, the motivation for turning eastward was simply to stick it in the eye of the complacent classicist schoolmasters—or Protestant pastor fathers—under whose tutelage so many elite young men of the fin de siècle suffered. New discoveries about the ancient world heightened interest: the Babylonian Flood tablets, the Tell el Amarna letters, and the first Manichean texts, extracted from

Central Asian caves, all commanded widespread attention. Political events also spurred new interest in the East; among the most important, for German audiences, were the Boxer Rebellion and Germany's founding of its Chinese colony in Qingdao, the Russo-Japanese War and the Kaiser's widely publicized tour of the Near East of 1898. Officially, the purpose of Wilhelm's trip was to dedicate the German-sponsored Church of the Redeemer in Palestine, but in fact Wilhelm's visit to the tomb of Saladin made bigger news; his statements on that occasion were sufficiently Islamophilic that rumors floated thereafter that he had actually made the Hadj, and secretly converted in Mecca.[10]

In such circumstances, a few German scholars began to think globally—not only about the origins of religion, though that was a hot topic for the generation of James George Frazer and Emile Durkheim, but also about the past, and future, of human cultural development. In 1912, one East Asian specialist wrote: "The world has become wider in this last decade . . . Historians can no longer limit themselves to the narrow circle of European states, and touch on the world outside here and there with a few tentative words. The fate of the peoples of Europe is ever more intertwined with that of the peoples of other continents. The concept of 'humanity' itself is being widened. . . . Old Europe is no longer the middle of the world."[11] There was, indeed, a surge in the number and types of global history in the first decade of the twentieth century; but there were still rather few who were able to escape from Biblical or Graecophile frames, or to develop their tastes beyond what one connoisseur called "store-window Japan" or another "commonplace bazaar trash."[12] Only a very few wanted contact with the *real* Orient, unmediated by western values or tastes.

The late Wilhelmine era saw the production of two kinds of oriental texts which would have a powerful cultural impact after the war. The texts concerned are not histories or fictionalized treatments of the Orient, but translations of ancient eastern works already revered by (conservative) local intellectuals; the western translators concerned were iconoclasts at home, men eager to understand non-western traditions, if possible, *from the perspective of the non-West.* The first series of texts proferred ancient Indian wisdom, especially the sayings of the Buddha. These texts were translated, edited, and made accessible by a now-forgotten Austrian iconoclast, Karl Eugen Neumann, son of the Austrian tenor and Wagnerian theater director Angelo Neumann. At age nineteen, Karl Neumann had a life-altering experience: he read the works of Arthur Schopenhauer who, in his passionate contempt for bourgeois Christianity, had styled himself a connoisseur of eastern philosophy. Desperate to understand the great Schopenhauer's Indian sources, the young man returned to the university—ironically, he had first to devote himself to improving his Greek and Latin, so that he could be admitted to study a language quickly becoming an alternative European ur-language, namely Sanskrit. Neumann managed to drag himself through courses in Sanskrit philology, and by 1892, he was able to publish a translation of one of the key texts of Theravada Buddhism, the *Dharmapada,* verses attributed to the Buddha himself.

It is instructive that Neumann was drawn to the earliest and most original sources of Buddhist "wisdom," just as generations of biblical exegetes struggled to identify the actual Aramaic voice of Jesus and classicists sought Homer's authentic songs. Neumann's search for eastern authenticity extended even further than did most of these quests, for the young philologist became convinced that to understand the words of Buddha, he would need to get out of Europe, and study Buddhism in India—where, of course, it had mostly died out. In 1893, he went to England, and then, having failed to obtain a civil service job with a Maharajah, he traveled to Ceylon. Here he studied for a few months with Hik-kaduwe Sumangala, one of the most renowned Buddhist monks of Colombo, and admired the local monks' ability to discern the meaning of the words without any need for philologist analysis.[13] In Calcutta, Neumann visited Dharmapala, a scholar who advocated India's return to a puritanical form of Buddhism. Perhaps it was this on the ground experience which not only converted Neumann officially to Buddhism, but also freed him sufficiently from scholarly philology that he devoted his life thereafter to translating Buddhist scriptures. He was also assisted in this by the fact that he owned his own copy of the recently printed Pali canonical texts, a present from the King of Siam.[14] At first Neumann found it extremely difficult to find publishers for his texts, but in 1904, he collaborated with Richard Piper, also a Schopenhauerian, who was willing to publish the sayings of the Buddha.[15] Piper Verlag would profit handsomely, in the long run, from the numerous editions of Neumann's translations, though Neumann himself was still largely unknown and penniless when he died in Vienna in 1915.

The second set of "wisdom" sources for the 1920s come from a different source: from the Sinological work of Richard Wilhelm. Wilhelm sailed to China as a Protestant missionary in 1899, but was himself "converted" to Confucianism, especially after an important group of mandarins set up shop literally in his backyard in the wake of the Qing Revolution of 1911. Fleeing persecution, or at least confiscation of their books, Lao Naixuan and others settled in the German colony of Qingdao, and donated money to replace Wilhelm's tennis court with a library. There the "Confucian Society" met for a number of years, and there Wilhelm began his work, together with his Chinese friends, on his compilation and translation of the *I Ging* (published in 1924), one of the oldest and most revered works of Chinese divination and philosophy. Wilhelm also undertook in this era to translate a wide range of other Chinese classics, including Confucius's *Analects* (1910) and the compilation of his writings known as *The Book of Rights* (1911); Laotse's *Book of the Way* (1911), and *The Book of Zhuang Zi* (1912). At first, Wilhelm had had terrible trouble selling his translations of Chinese "classics"; publishers doubted there was audience. As Wilhelm noted bitterly, "[T]he publishers devote themselves to singing the refrain: 'We can't do that, who here cares about China?' Finally, one was almost ready [to commit]. He had just published [the work of] a 'black' philosopher from Abyssinia, and so, he thought, a 'yellow' philosopher might, under these conditions, nicely complement that." Ultimately, even this lead fizzled out. At last Wilhelm approached the avant garde Eugen Diederichs Verlag in Jena. Diederichs took a chance on Wilhelm, one that, like Piper's backing of Neumann, eventually turned him a tidy profit.[16]

What is striking about the works of Neumann and Wilhelm is the following: the translators chose the oldest "classics" available, for, to put it bluntly, these were seen not only to be the closest to the pure expression of the spirit of the folk (on the analogies of the Pentateuch and the Homeric epics), but also, these texts were seen as closest to what might have been, in some secularized form, the primeval revelation. In many ways, the dream of finding the "key to universal wisdom" was not really dead, but simply transformed into oriental philology. These translations were also done with the consultation of local scholars, in Sri Lanka and in Qingdao, scholars who were most ardently in favor of religious purity and canonical authority, and opposed to modernization and to western imperialism.[17] There are all sorts of ways in which these translations were the proverbial products of their time, and products of a shared, usually elitist, anti-modernism. But they also offered a less judgmental and much more extensive introduction to Buddhism and to Confucian thought than had been available to Central Europeans in years past; and they were, in some way, joint products of East and West. It would be Wilhelm's Confucius, together with Neumann's Buddha, which formed the core of what Weimar literati would think of as "oriental wisdom."

Before we circle back to the *Schule der Weisheit* and the Weimar era, I want to underline Keyserling's own formation in the years before the war. An omnivorous, cosmopolitan aristocrat, Keyserling ended his friendship with Houston Stewart Chamberlain and renounced Schopenhauerian pessimism—turning instead to Neumann's Buddha and Wilhelm's Confucius for inspiration. In 1911, he set off on a trip around the world, or, more specifically, a trip specifically designed to get him to the true seats of eastern wisdom, India and China, not to previous generations' founts of wisdom, Rome and the Holy Land. During his travels, Keyserling soaked in atmosphere and conducted extensive interviews with his mandarin and brahmin hosts in hopes of finding new truths. He returned to Europe with a new understanding of Being and of the limitations of the West's idea of selfhood.[18] When, after his trip, he compiled his *Travel Diary of a Philosopher*, Keyserling made his motto: "The shortest way to the self leads one around the world." Full western self-development or *Bildung*, for Keyserling, could no longer be accomplished without encountering "eastern" wisdom.[19]

This was, to put it mildly, a minority sentiment in 1913, when Keyserling began to write his *Travel Diary*—but *Zeitgeist* would soon catch him up. The war had an enormous impact on German intellectuals' understanding of culture, history, and even geography, convincing Thomas Mann, among others, that Germany did not belong to the West—whose civilization was in any case doomed. During the war, too, Germans and Austrians made a number of overtures to anti-imperialist nationalists in India, Egypt, North Africa, Persia and Palestine in the hopes of cementing "friendships" against the French and British. The most consequential of these "friendships" was of course the German-Ottoman alliance, which provoked the Sultan to declare "jihad" on Allied, but not Germanic, Christiandom. If Keyserling was an eccentric cultural pessimist before the Great War, by 1919, his sympathy for things oriental was right in style, and his *Travel Diary* an original, but not terribly palatable, psycho-philosophical cocktail, proved to be the second best-selling book of 1919—just behind Oswald Spengler's *Decline of the West* (1918)—which, had it offered footnotes, would also have revealed its author's profound debts to the orientalist literature of the fin de siècle.

What made the East seem appealing in this context was first of all German certainty that the West as a whole had brought decline upon itself (a convenient way of avoiding questions about who had wanted the war in the first place). Secondly, a number of German intellectuals, right and left, shared a powerful sense that the colonized, or subcolonial world, was due to revenge itself on its former masters. We can better appreciate what it must have felt like to Europeans observing the colonial fallout of the war if we keep in mind the fact that most of this literature was written in the immediate post-war era, the period that saw, in 1919 the Amritsar massacre in India and the May 4 protests in China, in 1922 and 1923, respectively, the establishment of Egyptian independence and of Turkish statehood. Remember, too, that having lost their own colonies in the Versailles settlements, many Germans looked upon the travails of the other colonizing powers with a certain amount of *Schadenfreude*. There were some attempts, of course, to capitalize on the chaotic circumstances in China, Persia and the Arab lands by those who posed as, or really thought they were, "disinterested" friends or sympathetic advisors. The Hungarian journalist and charlatan Trebitsch Lincoln evaded arrest by going to China, where he became, first, advisor to a warlord, and then a Buddhist monk; the German archaeologist Ernst Herzfeld helped spearhead the passage of an anti-western Iranian antiquities law both because he wanted to keep the French, British and Americans from pilfering or buying up artifacts at a time the Germans had no cash to spare, and because he believed the monuments should stay in Iran.[20] To take just one more example, having traveled to Palestine in the early 1920s, the Austrian journalist Leopold von Wiese objected so powerfully to the effects Zionist settlements were having on Arab cultures; he wrote essays denouncing European Jewish and British colonial politics in Palestine,[21] and later returned to immerse himself in what seemed to him the primeval and deeply spiritual culture of the desert, and the anti-materialist, anti-classical truths of Islam. By the late 1920s, von Wiese had converted to Islam and became a friend of King Saud; working his way steadily eastward, he eventually became Pakistan's first delegate to the United Nations.[22] All of these careers, and many more that we could sketch, were proof that "the world had become wider" and that "old Europe was no longer the center of the universe"—and that non-Europeans, too, were actively involved in inventing the new forms, cultural and political, this decentered world would adopt.[23]

One of the things that had changed, too, was that after the war, the postcolonial and impoverished Germans now actually had to care about the interests and indigenous cultures of the non-western world if they were to exert influence over them. In these circumstances, the romantic tradition provided important resources—rhetorical and emotional—for coping with the new situation. The Central Europeans were lucky in that in places such as India, China, and Japan, nationalist intellectuals were relatively sympathetic, the result of disappointment with the other western powers for their betrayal during the war, and in the peace negotiations after. Indian nationalists congregated in Berlin, and a whole wave of Japanese students came to German universities to imbibe anti-modernist philosophy. In China, Zhang Junmai, a leader in the May 4 movement, suggested that Germany might represent a third way between capitalist west and soviet Russia, and sought to establish linkages between Chinese neoconfucianism and German neoidealism.[24] But Central Europeans had to work hard, now, to convince others to listen to them. Attempting to organize an expedition to Central Asia, the world-famous Swedish traveler Sven Hedin could no longer simply sneak in by way of Kashgar. In 1927, he finally negotiated passage by agreeing to call his project the Sino-Swedish Expedition, and by taking Chinese scholars along. When they wanted an exact copy of a Lamaistic temple, they were forced to hire a Chinese architect to draw the plans. It is perhaps no trivial matter that the reports of this expedition featured actual images of Hedin's Chinese colleagues, as well as his local interpretors and assistants, and that Hedin himself would later publish admiring biographies of two Chinese leaders, Chiang Kai-shek and the Muslim warlord Ma Chung-yin.[25]

The time was right, then, to look eastward for friends, and for inspiration: but for those who could not, like Hedin, actually get to Asia, what resources were available to westerners seeking to understand the "essence" of the East? The brief answer is, there was a vast amount of information now available about the geographies, arts, religions, and histories of eastern nations, and it is interesting that the group of moderate conservatives profiled below took the works of Confucius and the Buddha, in the translations that seemed least mediated by western norms, to be *the* classic statements of "eastern wisdom." Karl Eugen Neumann's popularity, in particular, surged at the war's end. In 1921, the great poet and dramatist Hugo von Hofmannsthal devoted an essay to the obscure translator, calling his editions of Buddha's works "without a doubt one of the most consequential deeds for the German nation that our generation has done;"[26] and another elite fan described Neumann's work as an intellectual achievement "that corresponds less to A. W. Schlegel's Shakespeare than to Luther's Bible."[27] Piper Verlag reissued his translations, and eminent cultural figures such as Albert Schweitzer, Edmund Husserl, Hermann Hesse, Stefan Zweig, C. G. Jung, and Thomas Mann paid tribute to his achievement.[28] Similarly, Richard Wilhelm's translations, as well as his Weimar-era works, *The Soul of China* and *Secret of the Golden Flower*, would be read by a huge range of intellectuals. Carl Jung, with whom Wilhelm collaborated on the *Golden Flower*, claimed that he had learned more from Wilhelm than from any other man.[29]

Wilhelm became a fixture at Keyserling's *Schule der Weisheit*, as Neumann surely would also have done, had he lived long enough. What the *Schule der Weisheit*, and the Weimar era as a whole consumed as "oriental wisdom" was very much the product of the "conversion" and immersion experiences of these two men, Karl Eugen Neumann and Richard Wilhelm. But, of course, obscure orientalist translators may make history, but they do not make it exactly as they please; they often need an impressario—and that, above all, was Keyserling's role.

We can return, now, at last, to the founding of the *Schule der Weisheit*, and the popularization of oriental wisdom in the early 1920s. Keyserling was able to launch his operation in 1920, thanks to funds supplied by his wife's fortune and his old friend Duke Ernst Ludwig of Hessen, who had himself visited India in 1902–03.[30] Importantly, Keyserling also had the endorsement of the publisher Otto Reichl, who printed endless pamphlets by school members as well as the School's official journal, *The Path to Fulfillment* and its pamphlet series, *The Candelabra*. Reichl did so, presumably, with little regard for circulation figures—for Reichl too was in Keyserling's thrall; again we glimpse the importance of the sympathetic publisher to esoteric thinkers. Those who attended the School were, above all, the moderate to conservative, post-Christian aristocracy and educated middle class intelligentsia of the region; commentators emphasize the School's appeal to well-educated women, and to those who, as Hans Driesch expressed it, "despite living in a republic gladly basked in the Grand Duke's light."[31] As for their common reading matter, we can assume familiarity with Kant, Schopenhauer, and Nietzsche, with Spengler and Thomas Mann. A goodly porportion of Keyserling's clientele also read more esoteric work, including books on astrology and alchemy, on vegetarianism and sex therapy.

These inquirers had little knowledge of, or interest in, works further to the left; they despised Marx and Marxism, and would have had little time for Brecht— even though he too was interested in China—or even for Max Weber (who, by the way, got his oriental knowledge chiefly from English sources). They were disdainful—as only reasonably secure people can be—of all forms of materialism, and reluctant supporters of Weimar's democracy. They tended to be anti-British, and after the war, anti-American (Wilhelm wrote to Keyserling already in 1912 about his attempts to "rescue ancient Confucian scholarship from the waves of anglo-American barbarism [*Unkulturwoge*]."[32] On the other hand, they recognized, as many other westerners did not, that, as Keyserling put it, "the pre-war prestige of the European and the Christian is gone."[33] And they were not Nazis. Keyserling, though he flirted occasionally with forms of racial essentialism, rejected racial hygiene and Nietzschean nihilism, and despised the NSDAP not only because they were uneducated thugs, but also because he opposed militarism, and anti-Semitism.[34] His project was about salvation from *within* the soul, a soul he believed could not be saved by politics, racial hygiene, or faith, but only by the transformation of western self-cultivation.

In founding his School, Keyserling hoped to offer others the same sort of "educational" transformation he had experienced during his travels; indeed, he surely had Rabindranath Tagore's ashram at Santiniketan in mind as one of his models for the school. In his opening lectures, Keyserling stressed the indispensability of western confrontation with "otherness" for the sake of spiritual renewal. If his lecture on the first day focused on western despair and alienation, the lecture on day two treated Indian and Chinese wisdom, emphasizing the

East's superior ability to understand meaning (*Sinn*) and to perform self-mastery; only by following Laotse's way could Europeans progress, he proclaimed, quoting from Wilhelm's translation: "Act, without struggling."[35] The lecture on the third day was titled "Ancient and Modern Wisdom," and in a move repeated countless times by his contemporaries, Keyserling compared contemporary conditions to those of the period of late antiquity, as the Socratic logic of the Greeks was swamped by irrational mysticism (by which he meant both Mithraism and Christianity). Keyserling insisted that it was the School's intent not to let the mystagogues win, but rather to expand wisdom's scope to include the erotic, the irrational, and the Oriental, thereby avoiding the fate of the Greeks, the bankrupt scientificness of the Enlightenment, and the narrow-mindedness of nineteenth-century, philhellenic liberalism.[36] Only in this way could western individuals achieve wholeness and resist Spenglerian decline.

In his attempt to reshape *Bildung*, Keyserling pushed a program of what we would call interdisciplinary and cross-cultural experience; the *Schule der Weisheit* offered lessons in meditation and in yoga, but also invited philosophers and theologians to give lectures. But one of its most innovative departures was its issuing of invitations to non-European intellectuals, to attend conferences not as ethnographic curiosities but as honored guests. One of the first and most important visitors to Keyserling's School, in fact, was the Indian poet and novelist Rabindranath Tagore, the first non-European to be awarded of the Nobel Prize for literature. Keyserling had visited Tagore on his travels through India in 1912, and now organized a whole week of events in celebration of the Indian sage during his first European tour. By the time he arrived in Darmstadt, Tagore was already a celebrity—so many students attended his lecture at the University of Berlin that the poet required a police escort.[37] Perhaps because he represented, as his son later suggested, a man fighting for *his* nation's freedom: "Germany then was a land partly occupied by the victors, and [the Germans] saw in this spiritual power of the Indians something worth striving for."[38]

In any event, several thousand people attended Tagore's "June Week" at the *Schule der Weisheit*, eager to listen to Tagore, or better, to Keyserling's translations of Tagore's words, for the Indian sage seems to have sung in Sanskrit or spoken in English. What he said was, among other things, "[S]trive for unity, the kernel of all earthly religions, but leave aside uniformity, for God reveals himself in many ways in both East and the West"—sentiments which mirrored Keyserling's views and echoed the views promoted by Ram Mohun Roy and the Brahmo Samaj in nineteenth-century India, as well as, in some ways, the much older ideas of Renaissance hermeticism.[39] Rather more provocative, and political, were Tagore's words in an evening lecture. As the Sinologist Erwin Rousselle paraphrased: "There are powerful empires in the East and the West, but on your side people have forgotten what an empire is for. Here the empty shell crushes humankind, and having become soulless such a land knows only one thing: power. Then such western empires extend their power into the East, bringing destruction and the poisoning of the soul. For to defend themselves orientals too will be untrue to the meaning of empire and want to counter power with

power." [40] In this crowd, denouncing the West's degeneracy and imperial expro-
priation was well received, and Tagore was deluged with flowers and praise. The
Marburg philosopher and spiritual father of the youth movement, Paul Natorp,
was particularly impressed, and wrote an essay (published by Diederichs Verlag)
denouncing the evils of industrialized European society, and calling for westerners and easterners to work together as brothers in order to save mankind. [41]

Keyserling's re-education project was rather less despairing than the related
one articulated in Hermann Hesse's orientalized version of the "novel of education," *Siddhartha*, published in the terrible and chaotic year 1922. Hesse's parents
had served as missionaries in India, and his maternal grandfather was an Indol-
ogist; he had visited Ceylon himself in 1911. But his deep interest in, and attachment to, eastern wisdom (especially Indian and Chinese forms) developed in the
late years of the war, and blossomed as he immersed himself in the translations
of Neumann and Richad Wilhelm, and underwent a brief bout of therapy with
Carl Jung. [42] Hesse's linkages to our cast of characters are extensive; in an essay of
1920, he hailed Keyserling as "the first European scholar and philsopher who has
really understood India," the only one who appreciated the fact that India "had
to do with the soul," and and that "the Hindu way to wisdom is not a science but
a psychic technique." [43] Like Keyserling and Thomas Mann, Hesse juxtaposed
eastern "wisdom" to western "science" and "philosophy"—but ultimately seems
to have had less trust than the other two that the latter forms could be salvaged,
and a new form of *Bildung* created. Rather than describing the coming of age of
a striving western hero, Hesse's *Siddhartha* narrated the story of an Indian contemporary of the Buddha, a man who learns to renounce book learning, material wealth, love and paternal authority to listen to the river's "Om." Hesse told a
friend that he felt he had "reformulated for our era a mediatative Indian ideal of
how to live one's life," but found that even most of his friends did not understand
the Taoist, Buddhist, and Hindu ideas he incorporated into it. [44] Perhaps the lessons drawn from this "wisdom"—and from the personal agonies Hesse was suffering at the time—were simply too nihilistic for those who did, after all, want to
heal their culture's war-ravaged soul.

Hesse, however, did harbor a vitalistic-apocalyptic hope that Europe's turn
to Asia would catalyze a necessary regeneration of European *Geist*; in several
of his immediate post-war writings, he underscores the positive, reverse side of
Wilhelmine cultural collapse, the birth of deeper and more powerful forms of
spirituality in the context of "a passionate struggle for a new interpretation of the
meaning of our lives." [45] Inevitably, he paints this struggle in ways that primitiv-
ize Asia (a category in which he, like Thomas Mann, includes Russia), but also
give the Orient credit for its superior antiquity, spiritual depth, and patriarchy-
destroying power. In an essay of 1919, written as he was reading intensively in
eastern philosophy and literature (preparatory to completing Siddhartha) simultaneously with re-reading Spengler, Keyserling's *Travel Diary*, and *The Brothers
Karamazov*, he reflected:

The idea of the Karamozovs, a primeval, occult, Asiatic ideal, begins to become European, begins to devour the spirit of Europe. This is what I call the decline of Europe. The decline is a turning back to Asia, a return to the mother, to the sources, to the Faustian "Mothers," and of course will lead like every earthly death to a new birth. It is only *we* who experience these phenomena as "decline," we contemporaries, just as the abandonment of an old beloved homeland brings only to the aged a feeling of grief and irredemiable loss, whereas the young see nothing but what is new, what lies ahead.[46]

"What we in our art, our intellectuality and religions have won, cultivated, refined, and finally made so thin and tenuous . . . through them we have nourished one side of mankind at the expense of the other side, we have served a god of light and thereby denied the forces of darkness," he wrote in 1922. Embracing the exotic, he claimed "is not convenient, it is not attractive. But it is necessary."[47]

What Keyserling and Hesse shared was not only their heavy dependence on the works of Neumann and Wilhelm, but also their strong sense that western education was bankrupt, and that eastern wisdom was the only non-revolutionary means by which the discredited "fathers" could be removed and replaced. As the similarly minded Hofmannsthal put it, also in 1922, stepping over "the venerable ancient borders of classical/Christian Bildung" to grasp the stable, spiritual order and values of the East was the only consolation possible for a spiritually dead Europe.[48] Richard Wilhelm's little book entitled *Chinese Life-Wisdom*, also published in 1922, offered the same sort of desperate attempt to find a cure for what ailed the West. What the East represented was not simply a spirituality to fill the void left by Christianity's evaporation, but stability, and consolation. The title of Keyserling's 1921 lecture series says it all: "Weisheit als Beharrung im Wandel," Wisdom as [a Form of] Permanence in Times of Change." This was neoromantic and condescending, to be sure; but it was also an admission of western failings, and represented an openness to other forms of knowing, and of self-fashioning.

It is difficult to measure the cultural impact made by Keyserling and the *Schule der Weisheit*; Keyserling certainly did his very best to blanket Germany, Europe, and America with his prose; he gave literally hundreds of lectures—at home and abroad—in the 1920s, and wrote endless newspaper articles, essays, and book reviews, and a large number of books as well. He drew participants from Schwabing, Munich's pre-war bohemia, and from Monte Verità in Ascona, Switzerland, an early alternative community which dabbled in nudism, vegetarianism, modern dance, and various forms of eastern spirituality.[49] He welcomed members of Freud's circle, as well as university-trained philologists and neo-Kantian philsophers. Offering spiritual, rather than bodily therapeutics, the *School of Wisdom* offered a rather more respectable forum for the Ascona crowd and the pschyoanalysts; on the other hand, he made it possible for a large number of what might be called "fringe" academics, people like the African ethnographer and inventor of "negritude" Leo Frobenius, and the Sanskrit philo-gist turned student of yoga Heinrich Zimmer, to talk to one another, as well as to the counter-cultural crowd. In academia proper, there was still considerable resistance to the new ideas—Zimmer and Frobenius, along with a host of Keyserling's other visitors were ridiculed and marginalized. The *Schule der Weisheit* could not give them much financial support—and Keyserling himself was notoriously overbearing and his friendships of short duration. But surely the *Schule der Weisheit* demonstrated the possibilities for interdisciplinary and cross-cultural thinking, and for reaching out to the public outside the usual frameworks, in similar sorts of ways as did the Institut für Sozialforschung, or, for that matter, the Warburg School.[50] The most direct and formative impact of the *Schule der Weisheit* would be in the foundations it laid for the Eranos seminars, meetings of eminent scholars of the history of world religions, which began in Switzerland in 1933, and culminated in some of twentieth century's most formative inquiries in myth, religion, and cultural anthropology.

It would, from our perspective, be relatively easy to find lingering Eurocentrisms in all of this work, and to ridicule many of these figures for their neo-romantic and self-interested pursuits of wholeness. But we have to think of the context: how many other interwar Europeans were willing to read the words of the Buddha, or to devote any time to thinking about China? And in the case of some individuals, like Richard Wilhelm, there was a very human side to the pursuit of oriental wisdom. Wilhelm made good, and lasting friends in China, and he respected their wisdom and scholarship; he tried to get the president of Beijing University, Cai Yuanpei, an honorary degree from the University of Frankfurt, and when that failed, he dedicated one of his major works—*The Soul of China*—to him. He and his wife Salome adopted a Chinese baby for a time when one of its parents died; the adoption would have been permanent, had not the Chinese family decided it wanted the child back. In 1929, in straightened circumstances and poor health himself, Wilhelm collected money for Chinese famine relief, and publicly denounced the Red Cross for taking a Malthusian attitude toward the crisis.[51] Despite the pervasiveness of anti-western nationalism in China by the end of the twenties, Wilhelm continued to be admired there; at his death, Beijing University held a memorial ceremony, and created a fund to support erection of a chair in his name at Frankfurt.[52]

In other fields, too, one begins to find Europeans, and especially Central Europeans, beginning to attend more closely to the voices of non-western intellectuals. We have established, already, the increasing popularity during these years of the sayings of the Buddha, and of the classic works of Chinese philosophy, but there was also a new understanding among art historians and archaeologists that the era of imposing western judgments on the arts of the East had to end. Central European art historical work of the 1920s was nothing short of revolutionary; not only was this the great era of Aby Warburg, Erwin Panofsky and Heinrich Wölfflin; this was also the world that produced the great scholars of Persian and Islamic art, Ernst Herzfeld and Richard Ettinghausen, and breakthrough studies in Indian symbolism by Heinrich Zimmer (Hofmannsthal's son in law) and in Egyptian art by Heinrich Schäfer.[53] One could see similar trends underway in other fields, in the study of theology, for example, where Rudolf Otto's cross-cultural study, *The Holy*, would prove the most widely read work of theology of the Weimar era[54]—perhaps because it defended the uniqueness of Christianity in a way that did not rely either on history or on philosophical rationalism. Classics itself was forced to innovate by the pressures exerted on it from the widening Orient, and as scholars of that field know, the Weimar era was instrumental in opening up both the hellenistic and the archaic, pre-Socratic worlds for study. Finally, the era experienced a Renaissance in Jewish scholarship and philosophy, spearheaded by Martin Buber, Gerschom Scholem, and Franz Rosenzweig; many of these German-trained scholars, too, emphasized what they themselves would have called "the oriental" aspects of Judaism.[55] It is regrettable, but instructive, that the Jewish forms of oriental wisdom and the Indian-Chinese forms rarely met, except, on occasion, at the *Schule der Weisheit*.

In a large number of fields, Central Europeans were learning to listen to the East's voices—albeit in neoromantic translations of their ancient sages, or in the form of anti-modernist wisdom of indigenous conservative elites.[56] Some had recognized that western imperialism was not only destroying venerable non-western cultures and traditions, but also that it was the duty of Europeans, as the Islamicist Carl Heinrich Becker wrote, "to replace the mentality of Asian exploitation with the recognition of the equality of the Asians, with all the consequences of this for Europe and America."[57] Some professional orientalists and some novelists, like Hesse, continued to explore the implications of these ideas through the 1920s; but after the Weimar Republic stabilized in 1924, the wider culture moved on beyond the pursuit of "oriental wisdom;" even Keyserling's passions for the East cooled.[58] In general, the German cultural world turned inward, and "oriental wisdom" became, once again, something pursued chiefly by iconoclasts and specialized scholars. In the late 1920s, Richard Wilhelm found himself dragging his slides around from one small-town lecture to another, trying to convince fellow citizens that the Chinese did not eat earthworms and only rarely exposed their female children. After 1933, virtually all of the innovative orientalists I describe above would be forced to leave Central Europe by the Nazi regime, and would be little mourned at home, though their contributions to their exiled communities would be monumental. To offer just a few examples: Richard Ettinghausen, Heinrich Zimmer and Elias Bickerman would contribute greatly to the study of Islamic art, Indian symbolism and Hellenistic religions in the US; Ferdinand Lessing, a specialist in Lamaistic art and religion and member of Hedin's Sino-Swedish Expeditions, would end up at UC Berkeley, the founder, as it happens, of their East Asian Studies department.[59]

Perhaps, as I have suggested above, the much-maligned figure of the orientalist needs a bit more nuance, and deserves a bit more credit for—in some times and places especially—challenging Eurocentric norms. Orientalists have often played an iconoclastic role, as did elite consumers of "oriental wisdom" in the early Weimar era, exposing those brought up on the Bible, the classics, and European literature to other worlds—though of course some have also helped to create derogatory stereotypes or assisted in processes of securing and deepening of imperialist rule. In the early Weimar era, some westerners, despairing of their own answers, showed themselves remarkably willing to imbibe this iconoclastic orientalism, to entertain other ideas, and to envision other means of self-fashioning. Unquestionably, this moment of openness was born of post-colonial *Schadenfreude* and of neoromantic primitivism, it was hedged around by elitist hostility to modern mass culture and limited in its interactions with the rest of the world by its preference for consorting with conservative elites. And yet, it opened the way for an important series of critiques which illuminated the many ways in which European histories, philosophies, educational systems, and ideals had been built on narrow and prejudiced understandings.

In a series of radio addresses, in 1931–32 Carl Becker described the sobering lessons he had learned as a result of his recent visit to China. He had discovered, for one thing, how very small Europe was, compared to Asia, and how little Germany's fate mattered to the rest of the world. He was made to feel just how much Europe was still suffused with the traditions and symbols of the Bible and the humanistic tradition, and how little even the orientalists understood of what he called "the confusing riot of Asian symbolism." "We console ourselves, for the most part," he wrote, "with the superiority of our cultivation, which we consider to be qualitively "higher." One reveres the uniqueness of Greek *Geist*, but with closer contact with this Asian world one cannot help raising the suspicion that our feelings of superiority are built on the quicksand of ignorance."[60] Here at last was the modest voice of the West, one that had been largely missing since Hermes Trismegistus had departed the scene in the mid-seventeenth century, and one that would be forced underground, again, through the 1930s and 40s. But in the 1950s, the time was right for a rebirth. Diederichs Verlag began reissuing much of Richard Wilhelm's work, and in 1956–57, Piper Verlag published a three-volume collected edition of Neumann's translations from the Pali canon. The echoes of *that* revival of oriental wisdom have proved long lasting, and have shaped in various ways the multiculturalism of the present.[61] Institutions, contexts, and even translations change, but as the new departures in world history show, a large number of Europeans and Americans are finally beginning to lend the iconoclasts our ears. And for that, we might, in some small way, have Weimar orientalism to thank.

Notes

An earlier version of this paper was presented as the Eugene Lunn Memorial Lecture at UC Davis in May 2008, and I would like to preserve its dedication to the memory of Professor Lunn, a pioneer in Weimar intellectual history. I am very grateful to my Davis audience, and to Peter Gordon, Martin Ruehl, and Kris Manjapra for their comments, bibliography and suggestions for revision. I would also like to thank Ute Gahlings for her help, a number of years ago now, in negotiating the Keyserling Archive in Darmstadt.

   1. Mann to Keyserling, 1920, in Thomas Mann, *Aufsätze, Reden, Essays* vol. 3 *1919–1925* (Berlin, Aufbau Verlag, 1986), 8.

2. For the purposes of this paper, I largely focus on the non-academic and/or semi-scholarly uses of Near and Far Eastern literature and philosophy in the early years of the Weimar Republic. For the sake of expediency, I often refer, as my subjects did, to the vast and diverse cultural territory east of Istanbul and south of Sicily as "the Orient," using the scare quotes only when it seems imperative to underline the derogatory or dismissive implications of the term's usage.

3. I make the case for this characterization of German *Orientalistik* fully in my book, *German Orientalism in the Age of Empire: Religion, Race, and Scholarship* (Cambridge: Cambridge University Press, 2009), and so will not restate it here.

4. Herman George Scheffauer, *The New Vision in the German Arts* (New York: B. W. Huebsch, 1924), 263–64.

5. On films, see Wolfgang Kabatek, *Imagerie des Anderen im Weimarer Kino* (Bielefeld: Transcript, 2003); the (negative) stereotyping of Jews was, of course, pervasive and ongoing, from at least the nineteenth century through the Nazi era. Muhammed Asad, *The Road to Mecca,* 4th ed. (Louisville, KY: Fons Vitae Book Co., 1980), 4–6. Actually, Asad's preface lays out much of the argument elaborated in Edward Said's *Orientalism* (New York: Vintage Books, 1978). Space does not suffice here to lay out my disagreements with Said's presumption that professional oriental studies, in particular, parroted the same "discourse on the Orient" spoken by all Europeans. See my "Popularizing the Orient," in *Intellectual History Review* 17, no. 2 (July 2007), 175–202, or the introduction to *German Orientalism in the Age of Empire*.

6. On Bruno see Frances Yates's classic study, *Giordano Bruno and the Hermetic Tradition* (Chicago: University of Chicago Press, 1979); for Bernal's critique, Martin Bernal, *Black Athena: The Afroasiatic Roots of Classical Civilization*, vol. 1 (New Brunswick, NJ: Rutgers University Press, 1987).

7. Voltaire depended on the rich Jesuit sources for his highly favorable portrayals of China and of India; see Willy Richard Berger, *China-Bild und China-Mode im Europa der Aufklärung* (Cologne: Böhlau Verlag, 1990); and Dorothoy M. Figueira, "The Authority of an Absent Text: The Vedas, Upangas, Upavedas und Upnekhata in European Thought," in *Authority, Anxiety and Canon: Essays in Vedic Interpretation* ed. Laurie L. Patton (Albany: State University of New York Press, 1994), 201–30. On Annius and Bruno, as well as the great early modern philological skeptics who reined in their phil-orientalist fantasies, see Anthony Grafton, *Defenders of the Text: The Traditions of Scholarship in an Age of Science, 1450–1800* (Cambridge, MA: Harvard University Press, 1991).

8. Carl E. Schorske, "To the Egyptian Dig: Freud's Psycho-Archeology of Cultures," in Schorske, *Thinking with History: Explorations in the Passage to Modernism* (Princeton: Princeton University Press, 1998), 191–215.

9. See Marchand, "Philhellenism and the Furor Orientalis," *Modern Intellectual History* 1, no. 3 (November 2004): 331–58.

10. On Wilhelm's travels, see Thomas Scheffler, "The Kaiser in Baalbek: Tourism, Archaeology, and the Politics of Imagination," in *Baalbek: Image and Monument, 1898–1998,* eds. Hélène Sader, Thomas Scheffler, and Angelika Neuwirth (Beirut: Franz Steiner Verlag 1998), 13–27.

11. Curt Glaser, "Ostasiatische Kunst" Der Tag 6 Oct. 1912, printed in *Die Ostasienausstellung Berlin 1912 und die Presse: Eine Dokumentation zur Rezeptionsgeschichte, Bibliographien zur ostasiatischen Kunstgeschichte in Deutschland*, ed. Hartmut Walravens, vol. 4 (Hamburg: Bell Verlag, 1984), 53.

12. Robert Breuer, "Die ostasiatische Ausstellung der Berliner Akademie," *Weimarische Landeszeitung* 29 September 1912, reprinted in Walravens, *Die Ostasienausstellung*

Berlin 1912, 40; Ernst Kühnel, "Die Austellung Mohammedanischer Kunst München 1910," in *Münchner Jahrbuch der bildenden Kunst* 5 (1910), 209–51, here 210.

13. Hellmuth Hecker, *Karl Eugen Neumann: Erstübersetzer der Reden des Buddha, Anreger zu abendländischen Spiritualität* (Hamburg: Octopus Verlag, 1986), 16–18.
14. Like the rest of his largely unstudied life, Neumann's relationship to the king merits further inquiry.
15. Hecker, *Karl Eugen Neumann*, 58–61.
16. Richard Wilhelm quoted in Salome Wilhelm, *Richard Wilhelm* (Düsseldorf, 1956), 154. See also Wolfgang Bauer, ed., *Richard Wilhelm: Botschafter zweier Welten* (Cologne: Eugen Diederichs Verlag, 1973); and Marchand, *German Orientalism*, chap. 10.
17. One of the European orientalists Neumann respected most was George Bühler, who had spent many years in India and spoke fluent Sanskrit. Hecker, *Karl Eugen Neumann*, 43.
18. See Keyserling, *Über die innere Beziehung zwischen der Kulturproblemen des Orients und des Okzidents* (Jena: Eugen Diederichs Verlag, 1913). It is interesting to note that this book too was published by Diederichs Verlag.
19. On Keyserling's work before the war, see Ute Gahlings, *Hermann Graf Keyserling: Ein Lebensbild* (Darmstadt: Justus-von-Liebig-Verlag, 1996), 17–119; and Peter Struve, *Elites Against Democracy: Leadership Ideals in Bourgeois Political Thought in Germany, 1890–1933* (Princeton: Princeton University Press, 1973), 276–90.
20. On Lincoln, see Bernard Wasserstein, *The Secret Lives of Trebitsch Lincoln* (New Haven: Yale University Press, 1988); on Herzfeld, see Ann C. Gunter and Stefan R. Hauser, eds. *Ernst Herzfeld and the Development of Near Eastern Studies, 1900–50* (Leiden: Brill, 2005).
21. Leopold Weiss, *Unromantisches Morgenland* (Frankfurt: Frankfurter Societäts-Druck, 1924).
22. See Asad, *The Road to Mecca*; and on Asad, Martin Kramer, "The Road from Mecca: Muhammed Asad (born Leopold Weiss)," in *The Jewish Discovery of Islam*, ed. Martin Kramer (Tel Aviv: Moshe Dayan Center, Tel Aviv University, 1999), 225–48.
23. For some more fascinating case studies, see the essays collected in Sugata Bose and Kris Manjapra, eds., *Cosmopolitan Thought Zones: South Asia and the Global Circulation of Ideas* (New York: Palgrave Macmillan, 2010).
24. Felber, "Das chinesische Deutschlandbild in der Zeit des Vierten Mai," in *Berliner China-Hefte* 17 (October 1999), 27–40, here 40.
25. Hedin's works were translated into many languages, including German and English (he was especially popular in Germany, having been an ardent supporter of the German side in the Great War, and having many friends in the National Socialist party). The German translation of his portrayal of Ma was published under the title *Die Flucht des Grossen Pferdes* by Brockhaus Verlag in 1935; his biography of Chiang Kai-shek (published by the John Day company in 1940 as *Chiang Kai-shek: Marshal of China*) could not be published in Germany because the Nazis feared his portrayal of the Chinese leader would anger the Japanese. On Hedin, see Detlef Brennecke, *Sven Hedin, mit Selbstzeugnissen und Bilddokumenten* (Reinbek bei Hamburg: Rowolt, 1986); on the Sino-Swedish Expeditions, see Marchand, "Traversing the Silk Road in a Post-Colonial Age: Sven Hedin and the Sino Swedish Expeditions of 1927–35," University of North Carolina, Chapel Hill, Conference on Transnationalism, April 2006 (unpublished paper).
26. Quoted in Hartmut Zelinsky, "Hugo von Hofmannsthal und Asien," in *Fin de Siècle : Zur Literatur der Jahrhundertwende*, eds. Roger Bauer et al. (Frankfurt: Klostermann Verlag 1977), 508–66, here 540.

27. Rudolf Pannwitz, *Die Krisis der europäischen Kultur* (Munich: H. Carl, 1921), 240.

28. See Hecker, *Karl Eugen Neumann*, 218ff.

29. Jung, "Richard Wilhelm," in *The Secret of the Golden Flower: A Chinese Book of Life*, German trans. (from Chinese) by Richard Wilhelm, English trans. from the German by Cary Baynes (London: Kegan Paul and Co., 1931), 151.

30. According to one account, it was actually Ernst Ludwig who approached Keyserling in 1919 with the idea of founding a "Gesellschaft für Freie Philosophie," out of which the *Schule der Weisheit* would be born. Margarete Dierks, "Initiative und Anfang: Die ersten zwanzig Jahre der Zweigstelle Darmstadt der Deutsch-Indischen Gesellschaft," in *Indien in Deutschland*, eds. Edmund Weber and Roger Töpelmann (Frankfurt: Peter Lang Verlag, 1990), 296.

31. Quoted in Barbara Garthe, "Über Leben und Werke des Grafen Hermann Keyserling" (PhD diss., University of Erlangen, 1976), 268.

32. Wilhelm to Keyserling, 5 December 1912, in Mappe R. Wilhelm, Keyserling Archive, Darmstadt.

33. Keyserling, *Europe*, 344.

34. E.g., Graf Hermann Keyserling, "Warum Hindenburg, nicht Hitler?" lead, front page story in *Kölnische Zeitung*, 8 April 1932; also unpublished text, "Das Böse als geschichtlicher Impuls," 1936, in Darmstadt, Keyserling Archiv, Box 061, Nr. 0093. He did, however, long for an aristocratic, hierarchically ordered society, which made him look somewhat favorably on Italian fascism. See Struve, *Elites*, pp. 306–12. For a taste of his eclectic and intermittedly racialist views, see Keyserling, *Europe*, trans. Maurice Samuel (New York: Hartcourt, Brace, and Co., 1928), 167–344.

35. Quoted in Werner Kilian von Tryller, "Die Eröffnung der Schule der Weisheit," in *Der Weg zur Vollendung* 1 (1920), 52.

36. Graf Hermann Keyserling, "Antikes und modernes Weisentum," in *Der Weg zur Vollendung* 4 (1922), 6–16, 42–43.

37. Dietmar Rothermund, "Rabindranath Tagore in Darmstadt, 10–14 June 1921," in *Indien in Deutschland*, 11.

38. [Rabindranath] Tagore quoted in Dierks, "Initiative und Anfang," 299.

39. On Roy and his tradition in India, see M. M. Thomas, *The Acknowledged Christ of the Indian Renaissance* (London: S.C.M. Press, 1969).

40. Rousselle, "Rabindranath Tagore: Die Legende der Darmstädter Tagore-Woche (9.-14. Juni 1921)" in *Weg zur Vollendung* 2 (1921), 42–49; quotation, 46–47.

41. Paul Natorp, *Stunden mit Rabindranath Thakkur* (Jena: Diederichs Verlag, 1921). Tagore also epitomized "oriental wisdom" for many non-German intellectuals. See Nabaneeta Sen, "The Foreign Reincarnation of Rabindranath Tagore," *Journal of Asian Studies* 25, no. 2 (1966), 275–86.

42. See his letter to Richard Wilhelm 4 June 1926, in *Soul of the Age: Selected Letters of Hermann Hesse, 1891–1962*, ed. Theodore Ziolkowski, trans. Mark Harman (New York: Farrar, Straus and Giroux, 1991), 136–37; and on Jung's analysis, Hesse to Lisa Wenger, 2 May 1921, in ibid., 109.

43. Hesse, *My Belief*, 367. Apparently a Bengali professor of history in Calcutta paid Hesse a similar compliment, insisting that *Siddhartha* had captured in a remarkable and undogmatic way the authentic ideas of the Buddha.

44. Quotation: Hesse to Georg Reinhart 8 July 1922, in *Soul of the Age*, 116; also Hesse to Helene Welti, 29 August 1922, 117–18; and Hesse to Romain Rolland, 6 April 1923, 119, in ibid. In another letter written in February 1923, Hesse laid out his "credo," explaining that he had been forced to seek his path to God through Indian texts "because of

the rigid piety of my upbringing, these ridiculous squabbles in techology, the emptiness and excruciating boredom of the church, etc." He thought the Indian ways to truth "far more practical, astute, and profound," but thought the truth itself, and the experience of it, was "always the same." Hesse, letter to Berthli Kappeler, 5 February 1923, in ibid., 120—21. Perhaps we have here another version of "the perennial philosophy"—but Hesse was deeply enough read in Indian traditions to conceive his alternative quest as exercising the Indian technique of *sadhana*, the seeking of religious experience through the study of other religions.

45. Hesse, "Our Age's Yearning for a Philosophy of Life," (1926–27), in Hesse, *My Belief: Essays on Life and Art*, ed. Theodore Ziolkowski, trans. Denver Lindley (New York: Farrar, Straus, and Giroux, 1974), 138.

46. Hesse, "The Brothers Karamazov, or The Decline of Europe" (1919) in *My Belief*, 71.

47. Hesse, "Exotic Art," (1922) in *My Belief*, 124–25.

48. Hugo von Hofmannsthal quoted in Zelinsky, "Hugo von Hofmannsthal," 542.

49. In 1926, Monte Verità was purchased by Eduard von der Heydt, the eccentric scion of a family of bankers and one of the first European collectors to value Chinese and Indian sculptures and paintings not as decorative objects but as high art.

50. The idea of devoting attention to ancient oriental philosophy and symbolism was popular enough to appeal even to the deposed Kaiser Wilhelm II, who occupied his enforced leisure time by writing books about Chinese and Assyrian symbols, and who tried to organize his own little conference group in Doorn. See Cecil, *Wilhelm II*, vol. 2: *Emperor and Exile, 1900–1941* (Chapel Hill: University of North Carolina Press, 1996), 317–20. The expressly "oriental" interests of this group come across clearly in Wilhelm's letters to Leo Frobenius, which I examined in the Leo Frobenius Institut in Frankfurt some years ago.

51. Wilhelm, *Richard Wilhelm*, 354, 381, 388. Despite Wilhelm's age and illness, in the late 1920s he and his wife moved to a third floor walkup, with no telephone, no central heat, and no telephone. Ibid., 367–8.

52. Wilhelm, *Richard Wilhelm*, p. 392.

53. E.g., Zimmer, *Kunstform und Yoga im indische Kultbild* (Berlin: Frankfurter Verlags-Anstalt, 1926); Schäfer, *Von ägyptischer Kunst besonders der Zeichenkunst* (Leipzig, 1919).

54. Michael Brenner, *The Renaissance of Jewish Culture in Weimar Germany* (New Haven: Yale University Press, 1996), 42.

55. See, Peter Gordon's intriguing chapter on Rosenzweig's attempt to "orientalize" the Hebrew Bible; "Facing the Wooded Ridge," in his *Rosenzweig and Heidegger: Between Judaism and German Philosophy* (Berkeley: University of California Press, 2003), 237–74. At the same time, too, the Bonn Semitist Paul Kahle was working closely with Jewish scholars from Eastern Europe to create a new edition of the Hebrew Bible, informed by the latest textual discoveries. Kahle was one of the first German professors to fully acknowledge, and encourage, cooperative work between German Christian and Orthodox Jewish scholars. On Kahle, see Henry Wassermann, *False Start: Jewish Studies at German Universities during the Weimar Republic* (Amherst, NY: Humanity Books, 2003), 203–19.

56. There were also highly racialized and bitter forms of *Schadenfreude* orientalism, such as J. W. Hauer's *Indiens Kampf um das Reich* (Stuttgart: W. Kohlhammer Verlag, 1932).

57. Becker, "Von Peking bis Damaskus: Eindrücke von einer Studienreise durch Asien," in Geheimes Staatsarchiv Dahlem, Nachlass Carl Heinrich Becker, Mappe 6788, p. 5.

58. Keyserling, *Europe*, 390.

59. On Lessing, see Hartmut Walravens, *Ferdinand Lessing (1882–1961): Sinologe, Mongolist und Kenner des Lamaismus* (Osnabrück: Zeller Verlag, 2000). There is no synthetic study of the impact of orientalist emigrés, among whom we can list also Paul Kraus, Joseph Schacht, Karl Wittfogel, Ernst Herzfeld, and Paul Kahle. For one recent attempt to judge the impact of this huge outpouring of talent and intellect, both on German *Orientalistik* and on the receiving cultures see Martin Kern, "The Emigration of German Sinologists, 1933–1945: Notes on the History and Historiography of Chinese Studies," *Journal of the American Oriental Society* 118, no. 4 (October 1998), 507–29.

60. Becker, "Von Peking bis Damaskus: Eindrücke von einer Studienreise durch Asien, in M. 6788, Nachlass Becker, pp. 2, 4, 5.

61. It is noteworthy that today, most of Wilhelm's works are still in print and available on amazon.de, and Neumann's masterpiece is now available on CD-ROM.

17

Weimar Femininity

Within and Beyond the Law

Tracie Matysik

In 1919 Marianne Weber, then president of the League of German Women's Associations, published a collection of essays under the title *The Woman Question and Women's Thoughts*. The majority of the essays had been written during the *Kaiserreich*, an era, she noted with just a tinge of lament, "that appears to be forever lost."[1] According to Weber, the *Kaiserreich* had been noteworthy for its "fight by modern women for spiritual and legal maturity, for the possibilities to develop individual gifts and powers, for the freedom of each individual to determine for herself the meaning of her own being over and against perceptions of her destiny." Yet if the institution of the Weimar constitution, and with it the new legal and political equality of women with all citizens of Germany, meant that the situation had changed forever, Weber nonetheless insisted that her earlier essays about women's social and moral status remained as important if not more so in the new political circumstances. Indeed, she explained, the new legal system served only as a framework in which the "far more important problematic of the factual and moral community life of man and woman" unfolds, adding that "this problematic will in no way be solved through the mere restructuring of legal forms." In short, she implied, the new legal equality of women highlighted all the more the matter of women's and men's different *cultural* and *moral* subject positions.

In this brief statement Weber gave voice to the primary problem confronting theorists of femininity and women's status in the Weimar era: how to make sense of the category of "woman" and all of the possible attributes that marked her as different from "man" now that she no longer embodied legal and political difference. During the *Kaiserreich*, theorists of femininity had relied heavily on women's status as outside of the law and the state. Many women's groups in fact remained wary of campaigns for legal and political equality.[2] The more traditional saw femininity as quintessentially private and domestic, and hence as opposed to political participation, while the mainstream women's movement made arguments for legal and political equality on the grounds of feminine difference. Some argued that women's role in childbirth was equal to, if different from, men's military service as the basis for political rights. More radical voices, such as that of the Nietzsche-inspired sexual-liberationist Helene Stöcker, saw in women's subjectivity a more positive and comprehensive model for citizenship than the conventional notions of the rational, liberal subject embodied by men.[3]

Despite the variation, however, the overall pattern had emerged that understood women's subjectivity—their status as subjects and their ways of negotiating the cultural, social, aesthetic, biological, and political world—as offering a different relationship to politics and law than men's subjectivity.

As on all social and intellectual fronts, however, the emergence of total war radically transformed this paradigm. First, women were mobilized *en masse* in the service of the war effort. Remaining largely on the homefront, their mobilization for industrial labor as well as their service in the management of domestic life—their adoption of rations, creative efforts to feed families and nourish future soldiers, their continued service in childbirth now made all the more urgent as the war of attrition gave new meaning to *Bevölkerungspolitik* and the effort to turn the birthrate around—situated women as a whole as a crucial element of the war effort.[4] Then, at the end of the war—"more quickly than we allowed ourselves to dream," Weber explained—the revolution and subsequent institution of the Weimar Republic and its constitution brought women legal and political equality, whether they wanted it or not.[5]

To be sure, women continued to confront explicit legal and political challenges in the new Republic. They mobilized around issues of contraception, abortion, and control of their own bodies,[6] even as they were negotiating their own newfound political rights and striving to determine just where they fit in the political spectrum (famously drifting rightward after 1919).[7] More profoundly, as Kathleen Canning has argued, women—along with their male counterparts—were negotiating the very meaning of citizenship and political participation.[8] In a similar way, the democratic revolution also brought a new set of intellectual questions concerning the status of women in modern society. Specifically, theorists and activists alike—categories rarely distinguished in the intellectual history of women and femininity—had to ask what exactly the transition into political participation meant both for the political process and for conceptions of feminine subjectivity. Below I examine efforts to contend with these questions from a variety of different perspectives: the pacifist-internationalist turn of the Nietzschean Helene Stöcker (1869–1943); the more sociologically informed intervention by Marianne Weber (1870–1954) and her concern about the bureaucratization of modern life; and a psychoanalytic contribution from Lou Andreas-Salomé (1861–1937). Together these three articulations provide a survey of the different ways in which theorists and activists interpreted feminine subjectivity amidst the transition to political participation.[9] In their arguments we see a general struggle to affirm democracy and political participation, while using the notion of the feminine to expand the limits of political participation beyond parliamentary politics.[10]

Gender, Pacifism, and International Conflict

Helene Stöcker emerged in the Weimar Republic not only as one of the most vocal spokespersons for radical pacifism, but also as the individual who most persistently thought about the importance of gender in matters of governance, pacifism, and militarism.[11] In the *Kaiserreich*, she had been one of the earliest supporters of women's suffrage and of women's access to higher education. She had made her name, however, as the advocate of a "new ethic"—an ethics of sexual emancipation and Nietzschean self-stylization. In that context, she had argued explicitly for a feminine type of citizenship that would not mimic the masculine model: "We want to become much more than men," she campaigned, arguing for a form of citizen-subject based on the complementarity of love, sexual enjoyment, and rights.[12] During the war she turned to radical pacifism—a pacifism that campaigned not only against aggressive war but also against defensive militarism. After the war, she persisted in the campaign for international demilitarization, seeing the matter as intimately intertwined with an ethics of intimacy. "One can hope," she observed, "that perhaps through the horrible experiences of the war we have learned something about relations between nations as about personal love," adding that "just as in relations between man and woman, also in international relations the love of the neighbor provides the best opportunity for self-satisfaction."[13]

Just as Stöcker had found support for her sexual-emancipation movement in Nietzsche at the turn of the century, particularly in his understanding of asceticism and *ressentiment*, she found in him after the war the quintessential anti-militarist. Specifically, she turned to his aphorism on "The Means to Genuine Peace," in which he uncovered something like *ressentiment* in the defensive posturing of militaristic states. He mocked those states which claim to hold militaries for strictly defensive purposes, suggesting that they are denying their own violent ambitions while simultaneously projecting such ambitions solely onto the neighboring state. "And thus he arrives at the clear, unavoidable conclusion that we must work against all open militarism," Stöcker maintained, quoting Nietzsche: "'It is just as necessary to renounce the doctrine of the army as a means of self-defense as it is to renounce the desire for conquest.'"[14]

Yet if Stöcker drew from Nietzsche an argument for radical pacifism, she could discern in Weimar democracy little hope for realizing a "Nietzschean" politics of peace. Rather, she saw in the party politics of the early Weimar Republic a fundamental continuity with the *Kaiserreich* and its militaristic belligerence, now managed by democratically elected politicians rather than by royally appointed ministers. Anyone advocating demilitarization stood not only in the minority, she lamented, but must be seen as an "enemy of the state"—and consequently could not participate in the shaping of that state. She acknowledged that the Marxists were at least attuned to the injustices of modern society that transcend the specificities of regime and nation. But neither the Marxist critique of private property nor its internationalism could meaningfully move beyond the militaristic state, she feared, until one found a way "to transform the actual souls of people." Accordingly, Stöcker refused to participate in party politics. Rather, turning her skeptical eye away from Weimar democracy, she explained that "there is for us only one party: the party—of humanity, the party that wants to create a human, truly human, culture for all persons."[15]

To be sure, Stöcker saw a unique place for women's participation in Weimar politics. Because women had been historically exempt from military service, or from "the most degrading and ignominious slavery on earth, the compulsion to homicide," she maintained, they were capable of transcending narrow confines of national interest and were hence duty-bound "to contest with all their powers a world-view, a social order that prizes and justifies war and bloody violence." In this fashion, Stöcker acknowledged, women's influence through political participation could potentially be transformative. "Full political equality of women will first be fruitful for public life," she argued, "if the fundamental tendency of the feminine essence, the good (that is naturally not bound to the female sex), is set on a par against the fundamental tendency of the masculine spirit, the desire to dominate."[16]

Yet ultimately Stöcker remained skeptical that the political process alone could ever undergo significant transformation, whether women participated or not. Rather, she saw a need for more thorough-going changes in culture and individual moral education, and thus argued for a gendered politics in an extra-parliamentary context. Indeed, as the remark above may suggest, she anticipated a more significant contribution from the feminine "essence" than from actual women. On this front, Stöcker was drawing on her long-time—and idiosyncratic—engagement with developments in sexology and psychoanalysis. Reaching back to the work of Otto Weininger, Wilhelm Fliess, Hermann Swoboda, and others, she emphasized that masculine and feminine principles do not belong to men and women, but are variously distributed across the sexes.[17] To define the content of the masculine and feminine, Stöcker turned to the contemporary sexologist Mathilde Vaerting, from whom she borrowed the idea that "in generative selection the man represents more an interest in numbers, the woman by nature puts more worth on the type and quality of the individual, which is understandable in view of her painful maternal and educational work." Accordingly, the feminine "must represent the means to serve life—to preserve and elevate life—to promise to secure culture and peace." Conversely, she claimed, the masculine seeks the domination of life and even its destruction.[18]

Importantly, for Stöcker, neither the masculine nor the feminine operate alone. Rather, she claimed, the life-preserving and life-destroying principles operate in tandem: "More certainly than ever before are we able to recognize how closely death and life, killing and creating, national hatred and sexual love are wound together."[19] Yet, if Stöcker understood these two tendencies to persist across time, she also saw them as educable:

> We now believe neither with Rousseau that in the beginning of humanity there was "paradise," i.e., the absolute good of humans, nor that we will in foreseeable time be transformed into "angels." We may however assume that we can take care to create a new spirit through an appropriate education, that the lower and destructive instincts in people remain ever more latent, while the helpful, constructive, mutual cooperation—in the knowledge of the advantages they offer humanity—can be developed. Then man will be freed from barbarism, from the self-destruction of mutual murder that is at bottom nothing more than a sign of mental weakness and helplessness.

The historically specific experience of the war, she argued, caused people to forget the power of the life-preserving drive. If women had a distinctively gendered task after the war, it was to nurture the feminine, life-preserving drive in youth. It is "as educator to the good—not to death and not to killing, as educator to life," Stöcker concluded, that the woman "fulfills her calling in the world."[20]

Because Stöcker therefore concluded that women's real historical task lay in the education of the instincts—as an extra-parliamentary means to work towards international peace—it is worth commenting on the trajectory of her thought on this matter through the decades: During the *Kaiserreich*, she had viewed violence and aggressivity as a product of sexual repression. Consequently, she had understood her campaign for sexual emancipation as a path to overcoming socially unnecessary destructive tendencies. Her move by 1919 to accept the endurance of both the life-preserving and life-destroying principles at the core of human subjectivity hence marked a stark retreat from her pre-war optimism. If she was not borrowing Freud's precise formulation of Eros and Thanatos, her own trajectory from the *Kaiserreich* into the Weimar era mirrored his, as he too only reluctantly accepted something like a death drive after the First World War.[21] While Stöcker adhered to the educatability of the instincts during the Weimar years, it was only after 1933 that she came to share Freud's more pessimistic view of the drives and the subsequent resistance of society to substantive reform.[22] During the Weimar era, however, she held out hope that the drives might be educated, and that the nurturing of the feminine, life-preserving drive in present and future citizens—and not the mere entry of women into the political process—held out the best hope for a "Nietzschean" form of international cooperation.

Specialization, Mechanization, and the "Particular Cultural Task of Woman"

In Marianne Weber we find a complementary critique of the limits of democracy, though one concerned much less with militarism. Like Stöcker, she celebrated women's entry into politics, though she imagined the import of femininity also to lay in extra-parliamentary work. Unlike Stöcker, however, she was less troubled by destructive instincts than by the professionalization and mechanization of modern life.

Weber entered politics immediately after the extension to women of suffrage and the right to representation, and she served in the Badenese Assembly as a representative for the German Democratic Party. In "Forms of Parliamentary Work," she reflected upon the inner workings of parliamentary politics as a lesson for future female representatives. While she was initially impressed by the congenial relations between members regardless of party or social background—a collegiality that enabled effective governance—she grew quickly disillusioned as she realized how the collegiality worked primarily in the service of a "party machine" that served narrow interests.[23] All successful members, she explained, learn primarily how to operate in a smoothly functioning machine, effectiveness itself becoming a more important goal than the political and moral commitments that lead one into office. Nevertheless, Weber did see a brief opportunity presented by the inclusion of women in the political process, as those women would represent "new, fresh, spirited personalities that are not yet fully driven into old trains of thought and work methods through years of entwinement in the party-machinery." Within a short time, she feared, women would almost certainly adopt standard tactics of interest politics, but in this brief interim they could enter political life "from another world and with fresh, uncompromised moral judgment."[24]

For the most part, Weber refrained from attributing to women any distinctive essence, but rather—much like Stöcker—she focused instead upon the specific historical circumstances in which women found themselves. And yet Weber held out hope that women might possibly transcend the machinery of interest politics just a little, that they might remain at least partially "untouched by the ugly passions" of politics.[25] Here the tone was less of description than prescription, with the suggestion that women's historical position might situate them well to perform a much-needed *task*, indeed, the "the particular cultural task of woman" as she had written in an essay of that title just the year before.

In "The Particular Cultural Task of Woman" (1918), Weber drew on the work of Georg Simmel to define culture as "the consummation of the spirit through the expansion of all potential contained within it into the objective intellectual work of humanity."[26] Further following Simmel, she broke culture down into two components, the objective (both *objektiv* and *sachlich*) and the subjective or personal. The objective dimension of culture, Weber explained, consists in "technology, law and morality, art, science, and religion." Conversely, the subjective dimension pertains to the cultivation of moral sensibility in the individual and the production of *Gesittung*, or civilization, which Weber described as "the formative power that cultivates the direct existence [of the individual] with its overwhelming multiplicity of emotions and drives, while binding the driving desires of the individual and structuring his entire comportment through specific and unwritten laws and rules, such that a harmonious communal life becomes possible." Such formative power does not simply regulate the individual, however, but rather, in making communal life possible, enables individual flourishing: it enables "camaraderie, friendship, love, marriage, family, etc.," as well as a meaningful relationship to the material world.[27]

According to Weber, individuals will most likely flourish when the objective and subjective components of culture interact in relative balance. Unfortunately, the historical circumstances of post-war Germany had proven hostile to subjective culture, leaving individuals with little moral ballast. "The more chaotic the conditions are," Weber lamented, "the more uninhibitedly the beast in people surfaces." Young soldiers at the front learned how seldom community sentiments survived in the face of danger, while civilians at home learned the same lesson as they competed for limited subsistence goods.[28] In this context, the drive for self-interest surpassed all other considerations of "civilization."

But perhaps even more critical than the specific historical conditions created by the war, Weber worried, were the broader conditions of modernity that tended to privilege objective over subjective dimensions of culture. On this front, she was thinking along with her husband, Max Weber, and his argument in "Science as a Vocation," in which he articulated a clear divide between modern science and moral values. Similarly, Marianne Weber feared that modern life made it especially difficult for both men and women to combine an inner goal of personality development, or continual formation as a moral individual, with the demands of professional activity that "simultaneously demand one-sided developments of specific components [of the person] and therefore can only have corrosive effects on the overall receptivity and vibrancy of the soul and mind." Too many people, she feared, become "pure experts whose superb objective accomplishments fill us with wonder, but whose humanity appears somehow atrophied and incomplete."[29]

Nevertheless, Weber did not share her husband's overall pessimistic views on the developments of modern life, and here the relevance of gender and her argument about the "particular cultural task of women" comes especially to the fore. Rather than relegating meaningful value formation to the outdated institutions of religion, Marianne Weber handed the task of sustaining the subjective dimension of culture—the dimension that enables individuals to maintain a focus on moral valuation in their objective activities—largely to women. She charged women with the tasks of "emotional sensitization," and the "warm infusion [of society] with love, benevolence, and pure disposition." They were also supposed to instill a sense that "the simple uneventful everyday is itself worth living." And they were especially well-suited for this task because of their maternal capacity that made them responsible "for the growth and development of life."[30]

Yet if Weber saw women as well-suited for the maintenance of subjective culture because of their biological roles in reproduction, she nonetheless saw their performance of the task as neither natural nor inevitable. Nor did she confine women to the subjective and maternal, and men to the public and objective. Indeed, she strongly criticized the housewives' organizations that upheld the domestic as the quintessential sphere for women. While these organizations properly venerated the domestic and maternal—important elements in subjective culture—they would inevitably meet their "certain limits," as they left objective culture untouched, free to continue in its own mechanistic ways and unconcerned with the "subjective" considerations of ethics and the value of life. Accordingly, the *Hausfrau* could never be the "bearer of culture" that the housewives' organizations imagined, nor could domestic work ever be the route to full citizenship. Rather, Weber argued, to be full citizens and affect political and cultural life, women must participate in "objective culture;" they must educate themselves and be able to contribute to the world of ideas and things, philosophy and economy: "What we call the content of culture in the most meaningful sense is to be won only via a detour through objective culture, through deep infiltration of the world of the mind that crystalizes out of immediate existence." That is, women could become true "bearers of culture" only if they occupied objective culture and infused it with subjective or moral concerns. They could do so in part through interpersonal relations, as in a husband-wife dynamic or in their role as mothers and educators, but also in their own objective production, i.e., through academic, artistic, or political work.[31]

At this point Weber's argument returned to themes raised in her discussion of women in politics, both her fear that women would quickly become entwined in interest-politics as a profession and her hope that they might also effectively infuse ethics and meaningful value distinctions into the democratic process. In "The Particular Cultural Task of Woman," she identified social and political work as "an especially appropriate form of objective-personal function" for women because they are responsible generally for "the configuration of existence in the broader sense." Here once again she endorsed women's entry into politics. But she nonetheless warned that the woman must remain vigilantly aware of the dangers that such work entails, as political activity in particular always runs the risk of taking on a logic of its own that loses sight of its overall social aims. In politics, she explained:

> one is driven via the objectively necessary to so many undertakings simply because organizations and associations exist where one can exert influence and demonstrate the necessity of one's power. In this way, the work of society misdirects the life into pleasant, variable movement, satisfies the drive to sociality independent of its content, and discharges initiative, ambition, and pursuit of power; and if one gives way to it, the activity that once led in this direction becomes easily an indomitable drive towards excessive activity that counteracts the immersion in the world of the spirit and of interiority, such that the ability for gathering and concentration withers.[32]

When Weber called on women to seize their unique opportunity in parliamentary participation, she was calling on them to do so with awareness of the perils of excessive professionalization, or of pure immersion in the "objective culture" that the institution privileges. In short, she was arguing, women should aim to infuse parliamentary practice with "subjective culture," or with a sustained focus on matters of moral value rather than with the interest-politics that she saw firsthand in the Badenese Assembly. They would not do so naturally or inevitably, but their biological role in reproduction together with their historical role as moral educators situated them well to strive concertedly to perform this "particular task."

A Psychoanalytic Intervention

In the figures of Stöcker and Weber, we have seen women activists struggling intellectually with femininity and women's subjectivity in relationship to political participation. And to a large extent, the majority of writings on female subjectivity continued to be articulated in the realm of activism, since women still had very limited access to strictly academic employment and study of gender was not yet a common academic topic. A significant exception, however, existed within the discourse of psychoanalysis, where the so-called "femininity debates" were waged throughout the Weimar era. With psychoanalysis still emphasizing its scientific and ostensibly non-political orientation, these debates touched only tangentially upon the matter of women's legal and political citizenship. Yet even that tangential connection bears a striking resemblance to the more activist arguments discussed above.

Prior to the war, psychoanalysis had only rarely treated femininity as an explicit object of inquiry. To be sure, Freud and his colleague Breuer had developed psychoanalysis chiefly through the study of female hysteria. Yet their early studies pertained primarily to the workings of the unconscious and the role of sexuality in the development of neuroses rather than to femininity itself. The femininity debates of the 1920s and early 1930s thus marked the first real engagement in psychoanalysis with the question of how the feminine subject comes into being as a distinctively sexed being.[33]

The debates began in 1922 with an article from Karl Abraham, the Berlin psychoanalyst and confidant of Freud. In his article Abraham asserted that both male and female children undergo a "castration complex." While boys begin to fear castration as a result of their illicit desires, Abraham argued, girls experience their lack of a penis as the sign that they have already been punished. The persistence of the desire into womanhood, he concluded, incites both resentment towards men who have what they do not, and fantasies of avenging the loss—traits he and Freud came to associate with feminism.[34]

Freud adopted and expanded upon Abraham's thesis in his own 1924 article, "The Dissolution of the Oedipus Complex," where he worked out the origin of a *moral* discrepancy arising from two sexed paths for negotiating the Oedipal scenario.[35] Following Abraham, he argued that the little boy validates his fear of castration when he witnesses the girl's lack of a penis, a lack that must have resulted from castration. The confirmation of castration's reality then induces the boy to renounce his quest to have the mother, identify with the father, and introject the father's authority in the form of the nascent superego. In the process, he incorporates a moral sensibility: the sense that not all desires can be pursued. The girl, in contrast, realizes she has "come off short" when she learns that the boy has a penis and she does not. As a consequence, however, the female Oedipus complex is far simpler, as it does not have to contend with a looming threat. The girl must merely convert her desire for the mother to an identification with the mother, subsequently adopting the mother's attitude toward the father and desiring a child from him as compensation for the "missing" penis. Yet in so far as the girl does not identify with the father, Freud explained, "there falls away a powerful motive for the formation of the superego," or the internalization of moral norms.[36]

The implications of Freud's claim were ambiguous. Helene Deutsch, one of Freud's few protegees with an activist-feminist past, actually suggested that women are morally inferior to men because of their different relationship to the superego. Slightly more critical, Karen Horney maintained that the moral claims were necessarily invalid, as they were too deeply ensconced in a masculine framework to be meaningfully applied to women.[37] Yet even Freud himself had expressed skepticism about the desirability of a superego-regulated morality. In his short book *The Ego and the Id*, he presented the superego as capable of vicious sadism, making ever increasing demands on the moral subject that could, in turn, induce resentment, neurosis, and outwardly-directed aggression.[38] Consequently, he was not necessarily attaching a completely negative judgment to women's alternative relationship to the superego and the moral law.

Lou Andreas-Salomé seized upon the opportunity in Freud's ambiguous statements to suggest that women exhibit not just another but perhaps a more desirable relationship to the moral law. Salomé's contribution came in the form of a 1928 article in *Imago* with the suggestive title, "The Consequences of the Fact That It Was Not the Woman Who Killed the Father."[39] In this essay, more literary than scientific in style, she borrowed heavily from Freud while subtly inverting his narrative of the moral formation of the sexed subject. She thus repeated Freud's patricidal narrative of masculinization in relation to law and guilt. Borrowing from his *Totem and Taboo*, she stressed that masculine idealization and deification of the father coincide with murderous tendencies towards him, culminating in the onset of guilt. Yet she found the guilt to originate in self-sacrifice rather than in patricidal desire: "Emotionally guilt is first an awareness that one is not 'all.' One must first suffer this guilt in order to become something."[40] Moreover, because the son has made of the father his "own future image," the son's desire to murder the father amounts to elimination of part of the self.[41] Salomé thus stressed the pattern of sacrificial schisms within the self that result from the Oedipal scenario, as the explicitly masculine contest between idealization and patricide founds an either/or relation not only to the father but also to his law: "the man [stands] between guilt and desire, between a natural rebelliousness which wants to liberate itself from anything in its path, as if from an enemy [the father], and the impulse to turn one's own values into a punitive other in order to pull oneself up from one level to the next."[42] The resulting moral subject is thus always conflicted, the agent of desire at odds both with the father's law and with the self that has incorporated that law. Just in case the reader did not recognize the Kantian moral tradition she was criticizing, Salomé explained that the son's subsequent "standard of value preserves that excess restriction that can only express itself imperatively and categorically."[43]

Salomé proceeded to pursue alternatives within the narrative for feminine identity construction and its relation to the moral law. As in the case of the masculine, she suggested, the feminine model may also tend to idealize the father. Yet in the feminine alternative, idealization does not turn patricidal, as the idealization now "occurs without conflict."[44] In feminine idealization, Salomé explained: "the object-deifying excitation refines itself only to the utmost point of the intellectual; it never loses altogether that last touch of intoxication, as it were, that is still being fed out of the primal bodily bond, out of the paternal (=divine=) inheritance which realizes itself in that intoxication."[45] In other words, the daughter does not get caught in a sacrificial relationship with the father or the self.

Rather, the unidirectionality of idealization—which she understood always to have murderous or destructive tendencies because of its excessive expectations of any one person—gives way to sublimation, diffusing multi-directionally into creative production in the world.[46] The daughter consequently seeks expansion and expression of self in the world, interested in and motivated by, while not bound to or limited by, the sacrificial relationship to the father.

Nevertheless, Salomé suggested, the intoxication itself endures in its physicality, in its "primal bodily bond." In this way it serves as the basis of ethical formation for the girl just as it did for the boy—albeit in another form, and enabling a different style of moral subjectivity: "However big or small be the reach of the feminine, it is in any case not unjust to say the entire sex remains free from a real sense of strictness of conscience and lawfulness, for that which is externally determined, for the imperative, as if she had a kind of sobriety that the more sensitively reacting man lacks: her law and order are elsewhere."[47] In Salomé's argument, the woman is exempt neither from lawfulness nor from conscience, but only from the *strictness* ("Strenge") of the superego. The female character is not bound to the masculine law governed by (self-)sacrifice, patricide, and obedience, not to the an ethics of asceticism or denial in which both Salomé and Freud had found ambivalence and hostility. Rather, the female character's ethics entails a commitment to creative expression and exploration of law.

Much like Stöcker and Weber, Salomé was thus identifying in the feminine a distinctive form of moral subjectivity, in this case one that is not caught in the logic of sacrifice, *ressentiment*, and violence. But how might this alternative moral formation pertain to women's citizenship? On this front, Salomé was considerably less direct than her more activist counterparts. Nonetheless, she did hint in her own literary way at a concern that complemented those of Stöcker and Weber when she addressed the historical entry of women into the law: "With the possibility of enslavement by humans, a quest for equality must have arisen ('penis envy'), a competition for rights." While she recognized that historically women will follow this trajectory, she nonetheless warned "that when she does make this choice, unavoidably, her most intimate sources dry up; she then crosses over the border to the drought and suffering of conflict, in rebellious ambition and guilt she alienates herself, in short: she begins to kill the father."[48] With entry into the law, or with acquisition of full rights of citizenship, Salomé's daughter-figure becomes a new type of moral subject, now indistinguishable from the masculine variant. She develops a masculine superego—with all of its promises and flaws.

It is noteworthy here that throughout this analysis Salomé's tone remained ambiguous. She was not interested in qualities of jealousy or resentment—the qualities that Freud and Abraham associated with penis envy—but rather with the losses that women must undergo with their entry into the law. She painted the movement as a dry, deserted process, quite in contrast to the overflowing creativity of the woman whose law had been elsewhere. A subject-position of alterity that Salomé wanted to celebrate seems to have been lost. In this sense, the passage from Salomé could be read as a work of mourning for a lost difference.

Much like the reformers who had preceded her, she had found a critical voice in the feminine whose moral subject-position could not be conflated with a legal subject-position. And she seemed to worry that such a critical voice might be lost. At the same time, Salomé seemed to be asking whether the distinction between the moral and the political subject might be maintained analytically. She emphasized that a woman could choose her path—and that a woman's movement into the law was at once "unavoidable" and yet simultaneously something that she "may also choose"—suggesting perhaps that not *all* was lost and barren. Just as Salomé had emphasized that the woman could idealize the father *and* sublimate those feelings, here she seemed to be asking women to choose both rights *and* a subject position that continued to stand in another relationship to the moral law. Or, just as Weber seemed to be challenging women not to abandon their "particular cultural task" even as they participate in objective culture, Salomé was perhaps issuing a plea to the reader not to abandon the analytic distinction between the political subject of rights and the feminine subject of ethics, even as the historical circumstances had changed such that women no longer inherently occupied a different subject position.[49]

Conclusion

All three of the authors discussed above viewed femininity as a historical development, not as a biological essence. Stöcker and Weber certainly saw femininity as closely tied to—or even epitomized by—biological reproduction. But they nonetheless saw the category as more meaningful as a cultural one that crossed between the sexes. For Stöcker, femininity epitomized a subjective trait free from *ressentiment*, characterized rather by the nurturing of life and creativity, and therefore as a check on the militarist state. Salomé likewise presented the feminine as a form of objectless love epitomized by creative expression of self in the world, and as an alternative to the violent basis of subjectivity that she and Freud found in the masculine model of moral formation.[50] Weber, who exhibited less skepticism of ascetic morality generally, saw in femininity a component of the moral subject that adequately persists in the face of the specialization and mechanization of modern professional life. Despite significant variations, all three articulations of the feminine relied on the premise that the feminine contains within it a mode of cultural criticism—both within and outside political participation. The feminine alternatives did not represent a nostalgia for a past supposedly free from the perils of modernity. Rather, they provided something of an immanent critique, an acknowledgment that modernity could mean the production of bureaucratic and militarist institutions, but that it did not have to be confined to these institutions—and that the feminine offered a means to imagine immanent checks on the militarist, violent, and bureaucratic-rationalist potentials they were perceiving in German modernity.

Here the transition of women into political participation proved especially meaningful if multivalent. In the *Kaiserreich*, women really did represent a different kind of subject and an alternative to the status quo of politics because they were situated outside the law—or outside the direct ability to craft the law and the state. As such, the qualities of femininity-as-alterity could be easily associated discursively with actual women. That all changed in November 1918, making the association of femininity and its alterity with women less certain. There existed now a means at once to assert the real power of the feminine through women's newly-won political participation. In this way, feminine alterity had more potential actually to affect policy. At the same time, as femininity-as-alterity no longer condensed automatically onto actual women, because actual women no longer embodied a form of subjectivity outside the law, it was in danger of disappearing altogether, being lost in the system it had once opposed. If in the *Kaiserreich* feminine alterity had been an effective means to mobilize against policies of the state to which women and men objected, women were now *part of* that state, for better or worse.

Significantly, the authors discussed above were *not* those that questioned women's participation in politics. Nor were they representatives of the conservative faction that only reluctantly accepted the vote as a means to further a reactionary or right-wing agenda. Their critical relationship to women's political participation is all the more telling in that it *cannot* be absorbed into a teleological view that equates women's political participation in Weimar with a rightward turn. Rather, these were pro-democratic positions taken in order to challenge the political, to expand the meaning of political participation beyond suffrage and parliamentary representation. Moreover, they were speaking to a type of participation—and participatory subject—that perhaps was best symbolized by actual women in their maternal role but that was by no means restricted to women.

The trope of "crisis" in the Weimar Republic might be useful to examine here. Stöcker, Weber, and Salomé were all pointing to the possibility of crisis, be it violent or bureaucratic. But they were not pointing to its *inevitability*. They were not panicking or calling for the radical overthrow of democracy, but rather for means to challenge the limitations of Weimar democracy. Kathleen Canning has suggested that the "edges and boundaries of Weimar citizenship were continually the site of contest," and that the Weimar period itself might be seen as one in which multiple experiments unfolded in the effort to manage the challenges of modernity.[51] In a similar way, these theorists of femininity could be seen to be identifying checks to modernity and its excesses that they saw at work in Weimar democracy—checks available *in* Weimar culture. And in femininity they found a form of what could be called "immanent alterity"—an alternative to the norms they saw to be dominant in the law and its democratic expression, but that they nonetheless heralded for its situation *within* those laws and as thus available for mobilization in the service of reform.

Notes

I thank the Institute for Historical Studies at the University of Texas at Austin for the time and financial support that made the writing of this essay possible.

1. Marianne Weber, *Frauenfragen und Frauengedanken: Gesammelte Aufsätze* (Tübingen: J.C.B. Mohr [Paul Siebeck], 1919), iii.

2. See Ann Taylor Allen, *Femininity and Motherhood in Germany, 1800–1914* (New Brunswick, NJ: Rutgers University Press, 1991); Iris Schroeder, *Arbeiten für eine bessere Welt: Frauenbewegung und Sozialreform 1890–1914* (Frankfurt: Campus-Verlag, 2001).

3. A good discussion is Kristin McGuire, "Activism, Intimacy, and the Politics of Selfhood: The Gendered Terms of Citizenship in Poland and Germany, 1890–1919" (Ph.D. diss., University of Michigan, 2004). See also Tracie Matysik, *Reforming the Moral Subject: Ethics and Sexuality in Central Europe, 1890–1930* (Ithaca: Cornell University Press, 2008), 55–91.

4. On women and the war, see Belinda Davis, *Home Fires Burning: Food, Politics, and Everyday Life in World War I Berlin* (Chapel Hill: University of North Carolina Press, 2000); Ute Daniel, *The War from Within: German Working-Class Women in the First World War*, trans. Margaret Riess (Oxford: Berg, 1997); Birthe Kundrus, *Kriegerrfrauen: Familienpolitik and Geschlechterverhältnisse im Ersten und Zweiten Weltkrieg* (Hamburg: Wallstein, 1995). On population politics, see Cornelie Usborne, *The Politics of the Body in Weimar Germany: Women's Reproductive Rights and Duties* (Ann Arbor: University of Michigan Press, 1992); James Woycke, *Birth Control in Germany 1871–1933* (London: Routledge, 1988).

5. Weber, *Frauenfragen*, iii.

6. See especially Usborne, *Politics of the Body*; Atina Grossman, *Reforming Sex: The German Movement for Birth Control and Abortion Reform, 1920–1950* (New York: Oxford University Press, 1995).

7. On party appeals to women voters, see Julia Sneeringer, *Winning Women's Votes: Propaganda and Politics in Weimar Germany* (Chapel Hill: University of North Carolina Press, 2002). On right-wing women's activism, see Nancy R. Reagin, *Sweeping the German Nation: Domesticity and National Identity in Germany, 1870–1945* (New York: Cambridge University Press, 2007); Raffael Scheck, *Mothers of the Nation: Right-Wing Women in Weimar Germany* (New York: Berg, 2004). On working-class women and political participation, see Renate Pore, *A Conflict of Interest: Women in German Social Democracy, 1919–1933* (Westport, CT: Greenwood Press, 1981); Silvia Kontos, *Die Partei kämpft wie ein Mann! Frauenpolitik der KPD in der Weimarer Republik* (Frankfurt: Roter Stern, 1979).

8. Kathleen Canning, "'Sexual Crisis,' the Writing of Citizenship, and the State of Emergency in Germany, 1917–1920," in *Staats-Gewalt: Ausnahmezustand und Sicherheitsregimes: Historische Perspektiven*, eds. Alf Lüdtke and Michael Wildt (Göttingen: Wallstein, 2008), 169–213, esp. 176–77; "Claiming Citizenship: Suffrage and Subjectivity in Germany after the First World War," in *Weimar Publics/Weimar Subjects: Rethinking the Political Culture of Germany in the 1920s*, eds. Kathleen Canning, Kerstin Barndt, and Kristin McGuire (New York: Berghahn Books, 2010), 116–37.

9. Many have explored the implications of women's franchise for politics and for conceptions of women as a category at a social-historical and political level. See especially Sneeringer, *Winning Women's Votes*; Scheck, *Mothers of the Nation*; Reagin, *Sweeping the Nation*; Ute Planert, *Antifeminismus im Kaiserreich: Diskurs, soziale Formation und politische Mentalität* (Göttingen: Vandenhoeck und Ruprecht, 1998); Nancy R. Reagin, *A German Women's Movement: Class and Gender in Hanover, 1880–1933* (Chapel Hill: University of North Carolina Press, 1995).

10. A complementary argument about Helene Stöcker can be found in Kristin McGuire, "Feminist Politics beyond the Reichstag: Helene Stöcker and Visions of Reform,"

in *Weimar Publics/Weimar Subjects: Rethinking the Political Culture of Germany in the 1920s*, eds. Kathleen Canning, Kerstin Barndt, and Kristin McGuire (New York: Berghahn Books, 2010), 138–52.

11. See also the work of Anita Augspurg and Lida Gustava Heymann, especially their retrospective *Erlebtes-Erschautes: Deutsche Frauen kämpfen für Freiheit, Recht und Frieden, 1850–1940* (Meisenheim am Glan: Verlag Anton Hain, 1972).

12. Helene Stöcker, "Unsere Umwertung der Werte," in *Die Liebe und die Frauen* (Minden: J.C.C. Bruns, 1905), 11. I treat Stöcker's Kaiserreich thought in more detail in my *Reforming the Moral Subject*, 55–91.

13. Helene Stöcker, *Erotik und Altruismus* (Leipzig: Ernst Oldenburg: 1924), 72–73.

14. Helene Stöcker, *Die Frau und die Heiligkeit des Lebens* (Leipzig: Neuer Geist Verlag, 1921), 6–7; citing Friedrich Nietzsche, *Menschliches, Allzumenschliches: Ein Buch für freie Geister*, in *Nietzsche Werke, kritische Gesamtausgabe*, eds. Giorgio Colli and Mazzino Montinari, sec. 4, vol. 3 of 25 (Berlin: Walter de Gruyter & Co., 1967), 316.

15. Helene Stöcker, "Revolution und Gewaltlosigkeit. Zum Jahrestag des 9. November" *Die Neue Generation* 15, no. 11 (November 1919), 522–23, 524, 528, 529.

16. Stöcker, *Frau und Heiligkeit*, 1–2.

17. Stöcker, *Erotik und Altruismus*, 67–68.

18. Stöcker, *Frau und Heiligkeit*, 1–3.

19. Stöcker, *Erotik und Altruismus*, 15, 69

20. Stöcker, *Frau und Heiligkeit*, 8, 3.

21. Sigmund Freud, *Jenseits des Lustprinzips* in *Gesammelte Werke, chronologisch geordnet*, ed. Anna Freud et al., vol. 13 of 18 (London: Imago, 1940).

22. Helene Stöcker, "Psychoanalyse 1911/1912," Swarthmore Peace Collection, DG 035 Box 1, Folder 3.

23. Weber, *Frauenfragen*, 263, 268–70.

24. Weber, *Frauenfragen*, 273, 274, 276, 278.

25. Weber, *Frauenfragen*, 278.

26. Weber, *Frauenfragen*, 238; citing Georg Simmel, "Der Begriff und die Tragödie der Kultur," in *Philosophische Kultur: gesammelte Essais* (Leipzig: A. Kroner, 1919), 246.

27. Weber, *Frauenfragen*, 240-241.

28. Weber, *Frauenfragen*, 245, 250.

29. Weber, *Frauenfragen*, 260.

30. Weber, *Frauenfragen*, 241.

31. Weber, *Frauenfragen*, 256-257, 253, 255, 254. One might consider Weber's biography of her husband, Max, as the quintessential example of subjective culture infusing objective culture: an intellectual production that is not divorced from the interpersonal.

32. Weber, *Frauenfragen*, 259.

33. A good discussion of the femininity debates can be found in Juliet Mitchell, "Introduction I," in Jacques Lacan, *Feminine Sexuality*, eds. Juliet Mitchell and Jacquelyn Rose, trans. Jacquelyn Rose (New York: W. W. Norton, 1982), 1–26. See also Mari Jo Buhle, *Feminism and its Discontents: A Century of Struggle with Psychoanalysis* (Cambridge, MA: Harvard University Press, 1998), 74–84. The discussion here draws directly from my *Reforming the Moral Subject*, 241–52.

34. Karl Abraham, "Manifestations of the Female Castration Complex," *International Journal of Psycho-Analysis* 3, no. 1 (1922), 1–29; Sigmund Freud, "Über die Psychogenese eines Falles von weiblicher Homosexualität," in *Gesammelte Werke, chronologisch geordnet*, ed. Anna Freud et al., vol. 12 of 18 (London: Imago, 1947), 298.

35. Sigmund Freud, "Der Untergang des Ödipuskomplexes," in *Gesammelte Werke, chronologisch geordnet*, ed. Anna Freud et al., vol. 13 of 18 (London: Imago, 1940), 393–402.

36. Freud, *Untergang des Ödipuskomplexes*, 401. See also Sigmund Freud, "Einige psychische Folgen des anatomischen Geschlechtsunterschieds," in *Gesammelte Werke, chronologisch geordnet*, ed. Anna Freud et al., vol. 14 of 18 (London: Imago, 1948), 17–30.

37. Karen Horney, "Flucht aus der Weiblichkeit," *Internationale Zeitschrift für Psychoanalyse* 12 (1926), 360–74.

38. Sigmund Freud, "Das Ich und das Es," in *Gesammelte Werke, chronologisch geordnet*, eds. Anna Freud et al., vol. 13 of 18 (London: Imago, 1940), 237–89.

39. A good discussion is Biddy Martin, *Woman and Modernity: The (Life)Styles of Lou Andreas-Salomé* (Ithaca: Cornell University Press, 1991), 216–23.

40. Lou Andreas-Salomé, "Was daraus folgt, dass es nicht die Frau gewesen ist, die den Vater totgeschlagen hat," in *Das Zweideutige Lächeln der Erotik*, eds. Inge Weber and Brigitte Rempp (Freiburg: Kore, Verlag Traute Hensch, 1990), 238–39.

41. Salomé, "Was daraus folgt," 238.

42. Salomé, "Was daraus folgt," 240.

43. Salomé, "Was daraus folgt," 240.

44. Salomé, "Was daraus folgt," 239.

45. Salomé, "Was daraus folgt," 239.

46. For Salomé's comments on idealization and sublimation, see her "Narzissmus als Doppelrichtung," in *Das Zweideutige Lächeln der Erotik*, eds. Inge Weber and Brigitte Rempp (Freiburg: Kore, Verlag Traute Hensch, 1990), 205–6.

47. Salomé, "Was daraus folgt," 239–40.

48. Salomé, "Was daraus folgt," 241.

49. Salomé here also anticipates a tradition that would grow in and out of French psychoanalysis that placed an emphasis on, in the words of Luce Irigaray, an "ethics of sexual difference." See especially Irigaray's *An Ethics of Sexual Difference*, trans. Carolyn Burke and Gillian C. Gill (Ithaca: Cornell University Press, 1993); Joan Copjec, *Imagine There's No Woman: Ethics and Sublimation* (Cambridge, MA: MIT Press, 2002).

50. On objectless love, see Martin, *Woman and Modernity*, 32, 44.

51. Canning, "Sexual Crisis," 212. See also her "Introduction" in *Weimar Subjects/Weimar Publics*, 1–5. She is building on Peter Fritzsche's essay, "Did Weimar Fail?," *Journal of Modern History* 68, no. 3 (1996), 629–56. See also Moritz Föllmer and Rüdiger Graf, "Einleitung," in *Die "Krise" der Weimarer Republik: Zur Kritik eines Deutungsmusters* (Frankfurt a.M.: Campus, 2005).

18

The Weimar Left

Theory and Practice

Martin Jay

In the parliamentary elections of May 20, 1928, the combined number of delegates sent to the Reichstag from the two major left-wing parties was the highest in the history of the Weimar Republic. The Social Democrats (SPD) saw their total rise from 131 in the previous election to 153 (of 491 seats), their share increasing by almost 4% to 30% of the popular vote, while the Communists (KPD) went from 45 to 54 members, with almost a 2% increase to nearly 11% of the electorate. The Socialists were the largest party by far in the Reichstag, almost reaching their previous high water mark of 38% of the vote in 1919, while the Communists trailed only the right-wing German National People's Party (DNVP) and Catholic Center Party by a few percentage points. The Nazis were able to gain only 12 seats with less than 3% of the vote. Although lacking a majority, the SPD was the major component in an expanded version of the "Weimar Coalition" with the Center Party, the German People's Party (DVP) and the German Democratic Party (DDP). Heinrich Müller, a Socialist, was chosen chancellor.

The four years before this election were also a period of general improvement for the German working class. With the stabilization of the Republic came economic growth, accelerated with the reintegration of Germany into the global economy in 1926, and important gains in social welfare, such as improved unemployment insurance, and labor legislation. The Dawes Plan of 1924 had alleviated the pressure of reparations payments to the victors in the First World War. Municipal governments, often under SPD control, built extensive public housing. The rationalization of industry based on the implementation of new technologies and labor practices seemed to augur well for the economy as a whole. The state frequently intervened in labor/management disputes to the benefit of the former, the economic chaos of the inflation years was over and planning more the order of the day, and corporations seemed less intent on squeezing profits from workers and more on benefiting from trade abroad.[1]

But as we know, this was a false dawn for the Weimar Left. In the next election two years later, the Communists' support increased somewhat, but they were passed by the resurgent Nazis, and the Social Democrats' votes tumbled badly. The split between the two major leftist parties hardened, the Depression eroded faith in the moderate coalition holding the Republic together, and Hitler ultimately came to power with only token resistance from the Left when he effectively dissolved the remnants of the Weimar constitution in 1933.[2] Its leadership in jail or exile, its organizations dissolved or absorbed, the Weimar Left passed into history as a salient example of dashed hopes and squandered chances.

It is, nonetheless, worth recalling the moment of left-wing triumph in 1928, however ephemeral, to resist the powerful hold of teleology in the historiography of Weimar, which sees it as doomed from the start, a mere way-station to National Socialism. There were many contingencies along the way producing an outcome that was by no means foreordained, and certainly not easily predicted in May 1928, less than five years before the *Machtergreifung*. Nonetheless, narratives written about the failure of the Left—whether from a social democratic, communist, independent leftist or liberal democratic perspective—have been shadowed by the knowledge that its defeat was not merely a blow to progressive hopes, one of many in the long history of the European Left, but also a prelude to the nightmare politics of the Third Reich. Even the creative theorizing that emerged out of the debacle—of which more later—has been understood, to cite the title of one account, as a "dialectic of defeat."[3] With partisan squabbling remaining strong in the aftermath of the Republic's collapse, many accounts continued the battles waged during Weimar itself, with post facto blame for Hitler's rise to power added to the long balance sheet of accusations against opposing factions.

There is no God's eye view above the fray that would allow even the twenty-first-century historian to write a definitive history of the Weimar Left's ultimate defeat, while at the same time remaining true to the openness of the possibilities of the history as it was lived. There are simply too many contestable turning points, too many plausible counterfactual narratives leading in other directions, too many imponderables to master. What follows is therefore not such an attempt, but rather an effort to foreground some of the most salient issues raised by that history, making as clear as possible the opportunities as well as dangers raised by the rapidly changing landscape in which it developed.

The premise on which the Weimar Left's history is normally written is that it somehow should have been united in a single, coherent movement, both as a force to bring about socialism and as a bulwark against the barbarism that, as Rosa Luxemburg famously predicted in her Junius Pamphlet of 1915, was the only alternative.[4] It is this assumption that I want to challenge. At its root was a notion of the proletariat as a singular collective agent, a class that existed "in itself" as an effect of the working out of the contradictions of the capitalist mode of production, and potentially "for itself," as a result of class struggle and the growth in consciousness that it fostered. According to Marxist theory, which gained virtually unchallenged hegemony in the German labor movement during the years of the Second International (1889–1914), class divisions would widen and opposing classes consolidate until a united working class had the power to overthrow a system supported by an increasingly weakened and defensive bourgeoisie. After the SPD grew in power following its reinstatement to legality in 1890—it had been outlawed by Bismarck in 1878[5]—major disputes were in fact kept under control, and a single party served as an umbrella for virtually all factions of the Left (anarchism remaining only a tiny fringe movement in Germany).

Before the First World War, there had, however, been many significant theoretical and practical divisions within the movement over such issues as the mass general strike, parliamentary participation, illegal or legal tactics, trade union agitation for improvement within the still capitalist system, and the philosophical or scientific underpinnings of Marxist theory. The centrist "orthodoxy" adopted by leaders like August Bebel and Karl Kautsky was challenged on the right by reformist "revisionists" like Eduard Bernstein and on the left by "radicals" like Rosa Luxemburg and Karl Liebknecht. Although it has been possible for historians to see anticipations of what became known as "the great schism" of the Weimar years, only the outbreak of the First World War managed to bring them to fruition.[6]

The issue that ended the unity of the German left was, in fact, the decision of the SPD to support the national war effort, which betrayed the internationalist and pacifist pretensions of the movement and led to the destruction of the Second International in 1914.[7] Amidst the chauvinist fervor of the immediate period after the war credits were approved (the SPD deputies supporting them 78 to 14 on August 4th), opposition was muted, but it soon gained momentum with figures from all parts of the political spectrum involved. Bernstein, Kautsky and Luxemburg ultimately joined the Independent Socialist Party (USPD) founded in 1917 to combat the "imperialist" war.

The USPD did not, however, survive much past the armistice, when pacifism alone was no longer sufficient to keep it together. When the dust settled after several turbulent years of aborted revolutions and violent repressions, the revived SPD found itself faced with a new rival in a party inspired by the Leninist model that had lifted the Bolsheviks to power in 1917. Although the situation was different from that of 1914, the tension between nationalist and internationalist allegiances persisted in displaced form. The SPD was now the mainstay of the new Republic, whose founding it had only reluctantly desired (Philip Scheidemann had casually proclaimed it on November 9, 1918 from the balcony of the Reichstag, much to the dismay of the other SPD leader Friedrich Ebert, only to preempt a similar declaration planned by the more radical Spartacist faction led by Luxemburg and Liebknecht). Throughout its subsequent history, the SPD struggled to reconcile its competing roles as defender of working-class interests and stalwart of the democratic Republic. At the beginning of Weimar, Gustav Noske, the Minister of Defense in the government of Chancellor Ebert could earn the sobriquet "bloodhound of the revolution" for his vigorous repression of the Spartacist and other leftist revolutions. A pact in November 1918, between Carl Legien, the head of the SPD-affiliated Free Trade Union, and Hugo Stinnes, representing heavy industry, while granting such concessions to the workers as an eight-hour day, was as much a victory for maintaining the still capitalist status quo in the face of more radical demands from the left. But a decade later, the last Socialist-led government of Heinrich Müller fell when the SPD resisted further accommodation and intransigently resisted the reduction of unemployment benefits for workers, thus fracturing a coalition with the DVP (Democratic People's Party) and Center Party. The collapse of this government, the last coalition of the moderate parties, inadvertently led to the effective end of Weimar as a democracy, as the invocation of the notorious Article 48 of the Constitution by President Paul von Hindenburg opened the door to authoritarian presidential rather than parliamentary rule. It also led discontented factions of the SPD to splinter off into small, ineffective parties like the SAPD (Socialist Worker's Party of Germany), which sought in vain to rally support for an activist radicalism.

The rival major party of the Left was bedeviled by its own divided allegiances. During the war, Lenin and his Bolshevik followers had abandoned the pre-war internationalist policy of a general strike against war in favor of allowing the war to exacerbate tensions in the capitalist system and create an opportunity for collapse, turning the "imperialist war" into a civil war, which did in fact happen in Russia. When military defeat and post-war chaos seemed to present a similar opening in Germany, radicals in Berlin, Munich and elsewhere thought they could follow suit and turn "objective conditions" into "subjective action." But with the SPD making a devil's pact with the army and the Freikorps, a volunteer para-military organization of veterans who relished in the brutal suppression of Bolshevik uprisings, they badly miscalculated. What survived was a newly formed Communist Party, founded in December 1918, which emerged out of the left wing of the USPD and the Spartacists, who escaped the unhappy fate of Luxemburg and Liebknecht, killed in the failed Berlin uprising in January 1919. Led by a succession of increasingly inept leaders, the KPD soon came under the control of the Comintern, the Soviet Third International whose rigid discipline was felt all throughout the communist world. Although recent research has led to a more nuanced picture of the relative autonomy of the German party, bureaucratic centralism directed from Moscow increased when Stalin consolidated his power and the "left deviationists" Ruth Fischer and Arkadij Maslow, protégés of Grigori Zinoviev, lost their leadership roles in 1925.[8] The result was that whereas the SPD struggled to reconcile its defense of the democratic Republic with its advocacy of working-class interests as it understood them, the KPD rejected the Republic as sham "bourgeois democracy," but was no less divided between its support for Soviet interests and those of the German working class as it understood them.

It was, however, not always easy to maintain even these positions consistently. In 1923, for example, the allegedly internationalist KPD found itself espousing a radical nationalist line, when it sought to exploit outrage against French occupation of the Ruhr by championing the legacy of a "martyr" executed by the occupiers, Albert Leo Schlageter. Following the advice of the mercurial Karl Radek, the Comintern's representative in Germany, it joined forces with equally anti-Republican forces in the radical right to try to undermine the stability of the new government, which had allegedly been too passive in its response to the execution. The so-called "Schlageter line" was a failure, but it foreshadowed the sinister anti-Republican cooperation with the National Socialists in a strike against the Berlin public transportation system in late 1932 and a referendum against the Prussian government. Any thought of cooperation on the left had been left behind after the SPD-controlled police had violently put down unarmed Communist demonstrators at a May Day celebration in 1929 in Berlin and the Comintern decreed a general left turn in its policies, repudiating any united front with the "social fascists," as the SPD were now called.

Underlying the often rapidly changing fronts between the factions on the left were a number of fundamental issues. Central among them is what came to be called the organizational question, which directly bears on the normative ideal of a unified working class. This was the era of what one Marxist theorist, the economist Rudolf Hilferding, called "organized capitalism," which meant a quasi-corporatist rationalization of the free market, the rise of a managerial elite, concentration of large industrial and agricultural concerns, and the application of new techniques of more efficient production.[9] Socialists sought to respond by finding the most effective organization of their own. Marxism had always sought the unity of theory and practice, which at its best meant that theoreticians adjusted their ideas according to the realities of political and economic conditions, while the "subjects of history," the working class, allowed themselves to be guided by those who had mastered the intricacies of Marxist theory (whether understood as "scientific" or not).

In reality, the balance was not easy to maintain. Bernstein's Revisionists, for example, had allowed the evidence of "facts" about the improved status of the working class in terms of wages and working conditions and the weakening of the endemic crises of capitalism to dilute their theoretical commitment to revolution, for which conditions were never ripe enough, and to embrace evolutionary, step-by-step, non-violent transformation instead. Supported by the powerful trade unions, interested more in raising wages and lowering working hours than in abrupt, radical change in the system as a whole, the Revisionists accepted piecemeal reform and worked within Parliament to effect it. The Weimar SPD was for all intents and purposes the legatee of this cautious strategy, with even former "orthodox" Marxists like Karl Kautsky supporting inclusive, democratic means of realizing the ultimate, if infinitely delayed, goal of socialism.[10] From an organizational point of view, this meant a mass party, loosely disciplined, open to voters from social and economic strata other than the working class, and willing to join coalitions with bourgeois parties. It meant an increasingly bureaucratized party with a hierarchical leadership conservative in its hold on power and defensive against internal criticism, which often came from more impatient younger members. And it meant supporting the Republic with all of its flaws against those from either extreme of the political spectrum determined to overthrow it, including radical workers engaging in provocative actions unauthorized by the leadership.

The SPD was wary of what in Marxist terminology was called the "spontaneity" of the working class. During the Wilhelmian period, it had been most powerfully championed by Rosa Luxemburg, who had promoted the idea of the mass strike as a revolutionary initiative "from below." Although she was by no means a simple advocate of spontaneity against all organization, she insisted that even a party of professional revolutionaries had to wait for the workers to rise before attempting to direct their action in a more disciplined way. She took seriously the notion that emancipation had to be achieved by those who were the "subjects of history," and not those who theorized, spoke and agitated on their behalf. Conditions in an advanced capitalist country like Germany, where years of industrialization had created a vibrant working class, were different, she reasoned, from those in more repressive countries like Russia, where political backwardness combined with slower economic development had decreased the chances of spontaneous revolution from below. The workers' public sphere, she argued defiantly, was not reconciling them to the system—what later historians would call their "negative integration"[11]—but training them to reject it. With her death in an abortive revolution she reluctantly supported and had not felt confident would succeed, faith in spontaneous proletarian action, however, soon waned.

There were, however, other organizational alternatives ready to mediate between radical theory and effective practice, each one claiming that it had the best chance of realizing the goal of a unified working class. The model adopted by the KPD, based on the success of the Russian Revolution, was that of a small, tightly disciplined, conspiratorial and clandestine party in the Jacobin tradition, which saw itself as the vanguard of a revolution that needed to be made rather than just allowed to happen. Drawing on the controversial concept of the "dictatorship of the proletariat," which Marx had intermittently supported as a temporary expedient in the transition to socialism, it had no qualms about using any means necessary to win the struggle to subvert the status quo. Willing to flout the law if necessary, although not making a fetish out of illegality, unafraid of violence as a tool of radical change, while still trying to win elections, the KPD was able to capitalize on the discontent of workers who resented the Majority Socialists' compromises with the army, big business and moderate bourgeois parties. It had a special appeal for the unemployed, whose numbers swelled when the Depression came to Germany with a vengeance in 1930. Although never able to bring the Republic to its knees—the only general strike in Weimar that thwarted right-wing ambitions, one directed against the Kapp Putsch in March 1920, was, in fact, led by the trade unions rather than the KPD—it helped undermine the stability of the new political order. Initially attractive to radical intellectuals and artists, the KPD saw many grow disillusioned and voluntarily leave its orbit, while others were excommunicated for one "deviation" or another from the party line. Karl Korsch, the author of one of the most important theoretical treatises of the 1920s, *Marxism and Philosophy* (1923), was a prominent example, bitterly breaking with the Party in 1926.[12] The satirical artist George Grosz, a Berlin Dadaist whose avant-garde images came under fire when the Party was bolshevized in 1924, is another.[13] Some artists and intellectuals like the playwright and poet Bertolt Brecht did, of course, remain committed Communists, either officially in the Party or as fellow travelers. Brecht himself, however, had learned lessons in dialectics from apostates like Korsch, and when it came time to flee the Nazis, he went westward rather than to the USSR, where official "socialist realist" aesthetics clashed with his modernist inclinations.

Korsch's rapid isolation from a mass working-class movement that claimed to be the best bulwark against nascent fascism was cited as a reason for remaining a Communist by another prominent theoretician, the Hungarian-born Georg Lukács, whose essay collection *History and Class Consciousness* (1923), was arguably the most cogent defense of the Leninist position from a neo-Hegelian perspective.[14] Directly confronting the organizational question and moving in the essays from a Luxemburgist position to a more explicitly Leninist one, Lukács took up the challenge of the "empiricist" arguments of the Revisionists and their Social Democratic descendents. Conceding that the working class was not yet at the point of becoming a revolutionary class "for itself," he argued that a genuinely dialectical method, based on a Hegelian conception of the totality of social relations, did not remain at the level of mere appearances.[15] Instead it understood the importance of the deeper level of essences, a level on which one might "ascribe" or "impute" the proper class consciousness that should emerge out of the objective conditions of a capitalism in terminal crisis. Left to itself, to be sure, the working class would remain mired in reformist "economism," in which it sought short-term economic gains and patiently waited for the Revolution somehow to happen automatically. Luxemburg, he argued, had been naïve in thinking otherwise. It was the role of the vanguard party, Lukács claimed, to bring a more active political awareness to the working class "from the outside," representing its imputed radical consciousness.

There was, however, a mediating link between party and masses, Lukács added, which had been foreshadowed in the Paris Commune, had played a role in the 1905 and 1917 Russian Revolutions, and had emerged in Germany and Italy after the war, the so-called workers councils or soviets (in German, *Räte*). The councils, which often included discontented military personnel in the waning days of the war, were a third model of organization of the working class, in tension with both the mass democratic party with its allied trade unions, and the elite vanguard alternative.[16] The councils had flourished during the November Revolution of 1918 as pre-figurative anticipations of the kind of organization that might emerge when genuine socialism was achieved. Unlike unions, they were not satisfied with winning concessions in a still capitalist society run by the bourgeoisie, but wanted instead to democratize economic conditions and give full control to the real producers. Unlike the syndicalists, who had wanted to radicalize those unions in the pre-war era, or the anarchists who were hostile to any form of state government, they were not contemptuous of politics per se. Unlike the parliamentary parties, they sought a new form of political *cum* economic organization in which local power and communal solidarity would restore power to the people—or at least the working class--rather than their representatives, in either a mass or vanguard party. The sclerotic party bureaucracy, which had grown to excessive proportions in the Wilhelmian SPD and became a self-satisfied interest group opposed to radical change, was anathema to them. In the heady days of the November Revolution, councils were formed for other groups as well, even among "intellectual workers." Hopes for a cooperative network of *Räte* as a way to organize a socialist society as a federal rather than centralized system were high.

But as was the case with the USPD with whom they were loosely associated, the councils did not last long after the initial years of the Republic. A short-lived new party, the KAPD (Communist Workers Party of Germany) tried to continue the legacy of what became known as "left communism," but it too soon dwindled into obscurity. Unlike those of the Russian Revolution, Weimar's councils never achieved dual power status with the parliament or leading party. Article 165 of the new Weimar constitution robbed them of any effective political power, turning them into economic pressure groups, and, soon after, a new "shop steward law" reduced them to little more than factory grievance committees. In the Soviet Union itself, despite its name, soviets soon became impotent window dressing, as the role of mediation between Party and class naïvely assigned to them by theorists like Lukács withered. Despite his apparent enthusiasm for them when he wrote his utopian *State and Revolution* in 1917, Lenin soon decried those who elevated the councils over the vanguard party as "infantile leftists," while moderate socialists like Kautsky denounced them as not fully democratic because of their primary reliance on workers.

For a while, however, the *Räte* continued to attract considerable attention in a segment of the intellectual left that was dissatisfied with either the SPD or KPD positions. Before the war, they had been championed by the Dutch theorists Anton Pannekoek, Hermann Gorter, and Henriette Roland Holst, all of whom were also substantial presences in the German movement.[17] During Weimar, other figures like Korsch found them an inspiration as well in the practical struggle to define what became known as the transitional process of "socialization."[18] Even after the Second World War, when no revolutionary turmoil comparable to the events of 1917–23 followed the defeat of the Axis powers, they continued to inspire intellectuals like Cornelius Castoriadis and Hannah Arendt, especially after their re-appearance in the failed Hungarian Revolution of 1956. Later advocates of workers' self-management, in, for example, the Yugoslavia of Tito, were indebted to their example. They reappeared briefly in the Iranian Revolution of 1979 as "shoras," although they were soon quashed by the theocratic state that emerged from the wreckage of the Shah's dictatorship. Partly because they seemed to transcend the limitations of other solutions to the organizational question, and partly because their short-lived existence meant they were spared many of the challenges of actually governing in a hostile environment, the councils remained a beacon of leftist thought until the last decades of the twentieth century.[19]

But once they were suppressed and the Republic stabilized as a still capitalist state, intellectuals who were uneasy with the alternatives presented by the SPD and KPD found themselves increasingly "homeless" and often beset with what the critic Walter Benjamin called "left-wing melancholy."[20] The early years of the Republic had been among the headiest in the long history of exuberant hopes for radical transformation of the social and political order. "The spirit of utopia," to cite the title of the Marxist theoretician Ernst Bloch's explosive 1918 book, was abroad in the land, inspiring even the Dadaists of Berlin to abandon nihilism and support the Revolution.[21] Many harbored messianic and apocalyptic expectations that the violence unleashed by the war and continued in the aftermath of defeat would prepare the way for a revitalized world in which spiritual renewal would accompany the end of capitalist economic exploitation.[22] They often adopted a theologically inflected vocabulary of redemption, which paradoxically was shared by many of their arch-enemies on the radical right. Many artists and intellectuals who had experienced the artistic rebelliousness of the Expressionist movement or who adopted the nihilism of Dada were involved in direct political action.[23] Writers like the poet, novelist and song-writer Erich Mühsam, who joined the unsuccessful Munich revolution of 1919 alongside the communitarian anarchist Gustav Landauer, saw the *Räte* as the means by which society would become a great festival of human solidarity. Other literary figures like Ernst Toller and Kurt Eisner were also leaders of the short-lived Bavarian Revolution, whose suppression was even more ruthless and severe than that experienced in Berlin.

Although the Expressionist moment passed and the Republic stabilized, many of these intellectuals continued their quixotic quest, clustering around modest-circulation journals like *Die Weltbühne* or *Das Tagebuch*.[24] Included in their number were some of the most gifted and courageous political journalists of their day, such as Kurt Tucholsky and Carl von Ossietzky. They advocated pacifism, the demilitarization of Germany, the purging of the bureaucracy and judiciary of reactionaries, political and legal rights for women and sexual minorities, and the leadership of intellectuals (one of their number Kurt Hiller going so far as to lobby for a "logokratie" led by men of superior *Geist*). Although they often urged the unity of the working-class parties, their influence remained minimal. As Istvan Deak has noted,

> Paradoxically, *Die Weltbühne* had always chosen to become more radical when the republic and the democratic parties seemed to stabilize their positions. During the uprising of 1919, or in the political and economic chaos of 1922–1923, the journal rallied to the republic. In 1924–1925, however, when the mark was again stable and Germany readmitted into the concert of European powers, *Die Weltbühne* repudiated bourgeois democracy and called on the SPD to remain in opposition. And in 1928, when Social Democracy scored its greatest electoral victory since the elections of January 1919, and a Social Democrat, Herman Müller, again became chancellor, the journal repudiated the SPD, and embraced the cause of proletarian revolution.[25]

The cultural rebelliousness of the "homeless left" had helped undermine the Wilhelmian consensus, but when they turned to politics they were largely ineffective, combing vague longings for a redemptive revolution with a pacifist disinclination for the violent means to bring it about. Elitist in their belief in the superior role of intellectuals and artists, some even followed Leonard Nelson, the founder of a left-wing sect calling itself the International Socialist Fighting League (ISK), in extolling the virtues of charismatic leadership.[26] Most, to be sure, at least preached radical democratic reform. Advocating the unity of progressive forces, they were nonetheless unwilling to sacrifice their independence to join a party.

The same was true of another important cluster of unaffiliated intellectuals in Weimar, who gathered around the Institute for Social Research in Frankfurt.[27] Although their moment would come during the migration and after their return to post-WWII Germany, in Weimar they attempted to forge an interdisciplinary team of engaged scholars who would work together to provide the knowledge that would abet emancipatory practice. Supplementing the work of political economist and historians of the labor movement would be scholars from the fields of psychology, literary criticism, sociology, political science and philosophy. Under the leadership of Max Horkheimer, who assumed the Institute's directorship in 1930, what later became known as "the Frankfurt School" emerged as a creative alternative to the theoretical impasse of the Weimar left. Although unabashed intellectuals, they distrusted the self-appointed leadership role of men of intellect. Initially loyal to the traditional Marxist faith in the redemptive role of the proletariat, they came increasingly to question its ability to make the revolution assigned to it even on the level of "ascribed" class consciousness posited by Lukács. In an aphorism written for his pseudonymously published collection *Dämmerung* (the German means both "Dawn" and "Twilight'), which was entitled "The Impotence of the German Working Class," Horkheimer observed ruefully that the present status of capitalism had driven a wedge between employed workers, often supporters of the SPD, and the sporadically employed or unemployed, who tended to voted Communist (or sometimes National Socialist): "The two revolutionary elements, the direct interest in socialism and a clear theoretical consciousness, are no longer the common property of the proletariat but are now found among different, important segments of it."[28]

When this was written in the late 1920s, Horkheimer was still holding out hope for the unification of the working class as the agent of radical change. "In both parties," he concluded, "there exist some of the forces on which the future of mankind depends."[29] But this confidence was short-lived. In 1929, the Institute launched an empirical survey of working-class attitudes organized by the psychoanalyst Erich Fromm, which sought to uncover the psychological inclinations of the proletariat.[30] When the results were in, they were considered too explosive to publish immediately. Contrary to the professed revolutionary sentiments of the respondents, the inquiry showed that many were more emotionally authoritarian and conformist than they claimed to be.

Although the premise of the survey that mature "genital" characters would likely be more revolutionary than authoritarian "anal" ones was dubious, the tale it told was borne out by the relative quiescence of the workers when the National Socialists assumed power in 1933. By the end of Weimar, it was becoming abundantly clear that the hope for a unified working class acting as the agent of radical historical change, a hope that had been nurtured in the years of the outlawed SPD, matured with the electoral victories of the Wilhelmian era, and given theoretical legitimacy by historical materialism, had been dashed, at least in Germany. Although some Communists foolishly welcomed the end of the

Republic with the sentiment "after Hitler, us," they woefully miscalculated the costs of the interim regime.

As mentioned earlier, a great deal of subsequent blame was assigned to the failures of leadership or the interference of the Soviet Union or the conservatism of trade unions. But in fact, the likelihood that the idealized working class of traditional Marxist theory would emerge had always been very remote, and what had to be learned was that a viable Left might be created without striving for it. Even in the apparently "objectively ripe" conditions for revolution after the defeat in the First World War or the disastrous inflation of 1923 or the Great Depression after 1930, there were forces working hard to undermine the solidarity as well as revolutionary fervor of the proletariat. We have already mentioned nationalism, which was then exacerbated by the resentment and sense of victimhood spawned by the unexpected loss of the war and the pariah status of Germany imposed on it by the victors' "Carthaginian Peace." Hybrid movements like the so-called "National Bolshevism" of Ernst Niekisch, who tried to portray Germany as a "proletarian nation," met the same dismal fate as the "Schlageter Line" promoted by Radek and his followers in 1923.

Another dilemma grew out of the brutalization of political life caused by the prolonged war with its sinister routinization of violence as a way of life, perversely celebrated by writers like Ernst Jünger and Ernst von Salomon. When many veterans joined right-wing paramilitary organizations like the *Freikorps*, used by Noske to put down the Spartacists, the Left responded by trying to organize its own resistance fighters. The "Red Guards," following the Russian model, were mobilized during the Bavarian Soviet Republic's brief existence in 1919. The SPD, along with the Center Party and the German Democratic Party, created the Reichsbanner Schwarz-Rot-Gold in 1924 and the Iron Front in 1931, as paramilitary defenders of the Republic.[31] Inevitably, they were unleashed on other parties of the left as often as on parties to the right in the running battle for the streets. Relieved of its colonial empire, where Germany had been able to find external outlets for domination, its internal politics grew coarser and more violent. Lenin's unflinching embrace of ruthless methods both on the way to power and after he attained it echoed in the KPD's frequent disdain for compromise and cooperation. In short, the movement that before the war had been identified with pacifism and anti-militarism often adopted methods that undermined those goals in the struggle to prevail. The values of solidarity and comradeship, the sense of a common destiny based on shared victimhood and dreams of emancipation, were undermined when idealism gave way to cynicism.[32]

But more substantial social and cultural forces were also at work undermining the unity of the working class and preventing it from assuming the role as revolutionary subject assigned it by classical Marxist Theory, even when a Leninist vanguard party claimed to represent its ascribed class consciousness. Religious differences, best expressed in the relatively consistent strength of the Catholic Center Party and the growth of Christian trade unions supporting "corporatism," continued to fracture the working-class movement.[33] Anti-Semitism, the "socialism of fools" as the Wilhelmian SPD leader August Bebel had scorn-

fully called it, further corroded working-class solidarity, especially when Communist leaders like Ruth Fischer and Werner Scholem (themselves of Jewish
origin) cynically endorsed the Right's attack on "Jewish capital."[34] The apparently
disproportionate role of Jewish leaders on the Left—more so in the SPD than
the KPD after the generation of Luxemburg, Paul Levi and Leo Jogisches passed
from the scene, and especially evident among the "homeless left" –created divisions that could easily be exploited by critics of "Jewish Bolshevism." Socialist
leaders sometimes bent over backwards to refute the charge that the SPD was
"the party of the Jews."

Another source of a counter-identity that troubled the Left in its quest for
unity was generational, reflecting the powerful rise of youth protest against the
"fathers" who had led the country into the slaughterhouse of the Great War.
Returning from the conflict with hopes for radical, if somewhat inchoately
formulated social change, they often turned apathetic or resentful when it was
thwarted in the war's aftermath. As a result, many had difficulty mustering real
enthusiasm for the Republic, which seemed to replace one group of aged leaders
with another. Although both the SPD and KPD had youth organizations, they
were poorly integrated into the respective parties, whose hierarchical bureaucratization they often and unsuccessfully challenged.[35] Bourgeois and confessional
youth organizations were more popular. In the long run, the Nazis were far more
successful in mobilizing youth groups than the Left.

Perhaps even more devastating was the restratification of the social order
brought about by economic and technological changes accompanying the "rationalization" of capitalism. With the growth of the service sector and the rapid
increase in the number of white-collar workers—the so-called *Angestellten*—
came a relative decline of blue-collar jobs. Attempts by the SPD to organize a
white-collar worker's union—the AfA (General Federation of White-Collar
Employees)—were largely unsuccessful, as many potential recruits were anxious to differentiate themselves from mere wage-laborers and their socialist
ideals. Identification by class was increasingly complicated by the growth of a
new *Mittelstand*, which defined itself less in terms of its relation to the means of
production than in terms of life-style and educational status. Unaffiliated leftist
intellectuals like the journalist and film critic Siegfried Kracauer wrote cultural
ethnographies of the "salaried masses," whose insecurity and "transcendental
homelessness" (lack of a firm belief system) left them vulnerable to radical political solutions across the spectrum.[36]

Members of the new *Mittelstand* were also especially vulnerable to the seductive distractions of the entertainment industries, which came into their own as
mass phenomena during the Weimar era. The cinema, the cabaret, radio, theater,
gramophone, spectator sports, fashion, body culture, all of these filled the leisure
hours of workers whose shortened workday and increased spending money gave
them a chance to seek diversion and stimulation outside the home and workplace. Rapid technological changes combined with a growing fascination with
modernization, understood largely in terms of American models of mass culture, undermined allegiance to older cultural values and identities. As a result,

Germans of all classes began to define themselves increasingly as consumers rather than producers, which further fractured the solidarity of the proletariat as the class destined to challenge the system.

Left intellectuals and party strategists struggled to come to terms with these new realities, often joining conservatives in denouncing their implications. For a few like Ernst Bloch, traces of utopia might be found in the minutiae of everyday life, even if that life was distorted by the kitsch values of mass culture. In his review of Kracauer's study of the *Angestellten*, Bloch wrote:

> Cafés, films, Lunaparks show the employee the direction in which he has to go: signs, much too illuminated for them not to be suspicious, indicating how to evade the true direction, namely that towards the proletariat. Which the employee now shares everything: deprivation, worry, insecurity, only not the clear consciousness of what his condition actually is. Of course distraction, precisely as a colorful street-fair, has another side to it, one which does not favor mustiness. Of course this side throws up dust too and this time already interrupting, sparkling *dust to the power of two* as it were.[37]

For many, it all seemed like a cult of superficiality, a surrender to reification and the loss of critical distance from the deeper realities of capitalist exploitation.[38] Film was an especially fraught area, made even more so when the giant corporation UFA (Universum Film AG) was taken over by the right-wing industrialist Alfred Hugenberg in 1927.[39] Despite the early art films that gave Weimar cinema its enviable posthumous reputation, the medium was dominated by patriotic depictions of Prussian glory or the "mountain films" whose underlying message critics like Kracauer would later see as proto-fascist. It was not perhaps until the importation of Soviet films in the middle of the Republic by the Prometheus distribution company set up by the Communist propaganda genius Willi Münzenberg that the organized Left began to realize the radical potential of the new medium.[40] The SPD soon followed, and sponsored a number of films that directly addressed social questions. The best known film made by the Left was Slatan Dudow and Hanns Eisler's *Kuhle Wampe* (1930), whose script was written by Brecht. But by and large the Left was slow to see the potential in the new media and suspicious of their ideological potential. Radio, for example, was far more effectively used by the Nazis than by the parties of the Left.

One final complication of the solidarity of the normative model of a united working class has to be mentioned, which involves gender. Weimar, as is well known, saw the emergence of the so-called "new woman," able to vote and hold a job and walk the streets without being labeled a street-walker.[41] When it came to the new mass culture, they were often the most avid consumers. In the first election after the war, when they won the suffrage for the first time, they voted mostly for the Center and conservative parties, although the SPD won a reasonable share. When a backlash set in against the rapid transformation of traditional female roles, the power of "the new woman" declined. In 1918, almost 10% of the delegates to Parliament were women, whereas by 1930, the number had dwindled to 7%, and membership in unions and other public organizations also declined. German feminist leaders like Gertrude Bäumer, who had headed the Bund Deutscher Frauenvereine (BDF) before the War and was a German Democratic Party delegate to the Reichstag during Weimar, promoted a maternalist image of womanhood, grounded in eugenics, while eschewing the more virulent racial and anti-Semitic policies of the radical right.[42] Although the Left sought to mobilize working-class women, they struggled to get beyond the essentialist prejudices of the population as a whole.

In short, the *telos* of a unified working class, able to assume the role assigned to it by orthodox Marxist theory was already in jeopardy even before the victory of Nazism ended the Republican experiment. Time had appeared to be on the side of the Wilhelmian SPD, when parliamentary votes and union membership were steadily waxing, but in Weimar the tide was going in the other direction. Stubbornly, many intellectuals of the Left pined for the return of the narrative they had been schooled in before the War. Rather than recognizing the problematic notion of a single class that could serve as the only agent of revolutionary change, they only hesitatingly developed an alternative view of a Left that was larger than an expression of proletarian consciousness.

But what must also be remembered is that the experiment of a democratic polity was by no means doomed to fail, despite all the obstacles to its success. Given more time and better circumstances, the nascent reconceptualization of "the Left" as more than just the struggle to represent a putative "subject of history," a universal class with a single revolutionary consciousness, might have had better luck. A more pluralist, non-hierarchical Left with openness to issues involving consumer's rights, gender, sexual identity, ethnic identity and the like, open to cultural as well as political economic issues, was on the horizon. Many historians now agree that the inability of the Left to unite was not the major reason Weimar was undermined; that dubious honor goes to the parties of the center and right, who seriously miscalculated the costs of admitting the Nazis into the circle of governing parties. Nor was the Left's ultimate debacle cause for abandonment of many of its long-range goals, which were not irrevocably tied to the triumph of the working class. Weimar was in many ways a hothouse for new ideas and untested theories, some of which went into hibernation during the long twelve years of Nazi rule. Although the post-WWII regime in the German Democratic Republic can be faulted for trying to realize some of the least attractive legacies of the Weimar Left—those associated with the Leninist authoritarianism of the KPD, based on a still rigid view of proletarian supremacy—there were others that inspired many in West Germany to help it overcome the Nazi past and move, fitfully but steadfastly, towards a more democratic future. Although the defeat of the Weimar Republic was a cautionary tale—people even talked of the "Weimar syndrome"[43]—it also provided positive models to follow, both within and outside the mainstream system. If there are more narrative threads to the story of the Weimar left than the one cut off so brutally in 1933, it is to these that the twenty-first-century historian can profitably turn.

Notes

1. For an account of this period of relative prosperity for workers, see David Abraham, *The Collapse of the Weimar Republic: Political Economy and Crisis* (Princeton: Princeton University Press, 1981), chap. 5.

2. The paralysis of the Left was already evident in July 1932, when Chancellor Franz von Papen staged a coup against the government of Prussia, forcing a *Gleichschaltung* (coordination) with the national government. When the crisis came, the national SPD leadership had no answer besides ineffective legalism.

3. Russell Jacoby, *Dialectic of Defeat: Contours of Western Marxism* (Cambridge: Cambridge University Press, 1981).

4. Rosa Luxemburg, "The Junius Pamphlet: The Crisis in the German Social Democracy," in *Rosa Luxemburg Speaks* (New York: Pathfinder, 1970). Although written in April 1915, while she was in prison, it wasn't published until a year later under the pseudonym "Junius."

5. See Vernon L. Lidtke, *The Outlawed Party: Social Democracy in Germany, 1878–1890* (Princeton: Princeton University Press, 1966).

6. Carl E. Schorske, *German Social Democracy 1905–1917: The Development of the Great Schism* (New York, John Wiley and Sons, 1965). For a critical overview of the literature on the SPD and the labor movement during the Wilhelmian era, see Geoff Eley, "Joining Two Histories: The SPD and the German Working Class, 1860–1914," in *From Unification to Nazism: Reinterpreting the German Past* (Boston, Allen and Unwin, 1986).

7. Georges Haupt, *Socialism and the Great War: The Collapse of the Second International* (Oxford, Oxford University Press, 1973).

8. For a discussion of the recent scholarship that modifies the traditional picture of total bolshevization, see William David Jones, *The Lost Debate: German Socialist Intellectuals and Totalitarianism* (Urbana: University of Illinois Press, 1999), 33.

9. For historical analyses of the meaning and applicability of this concept, see Heinrich Winkler, ed., *Organizierte Kapitalismus: Voraussetzungen und Anfänge* (Göttingen: Vandenhoeck und Ruprecht, 1974).

10. Massimo Salvadori, *Karl Kautsky and the Socialist Revolution 1880–1938*, trans. John Rothschild (London: New Left Books, 1979).

11. Guenter Roth, *The Social Democrats in Imperial Germany: A Study in Working-Class Isolation and National Integration* (Totowa, NJ: Ayer, 1963).

12. See Patrick Goode, *Karl Korsch: A Study in Western Marxism* (London: Macmillan, 1979).

13. See Barbara McClosky, *George Grosz and the Communisty Party: Art and Radicalism in Crisis, 1918–1936* (Princeton: Princeton University Press,1997).

14. Georg Lukács, *History and Class Consciousness: Studies in Marxist Dialectics*, trans. Rodney Livingstone (Cambridge, MA: MIT Press, 1971). The reference to Korsch's fate is on p. xxx of the 1967 Preface. After escaping from Budapest when the Communist government of Bela Kun fell in 1919, Lukács went to Vienna, where he spent the next decade before moving to Moscow. Although he was not strictly speaking a Weimar intellectual, his work was enormously influential among leftist intellectuals there.

15. For a discussion of Lukács's concept of totality and its importance for Marxist theory, see Martin Jay, *Marxism and Totality: The Adventures of a Concept from Lukács to Habermas* (Berkeley: University of California Press, 1984).

16. For one account of their importance in early Weimar, see Henry Pachter, "Was Weimar Necessary? The Räte Movement, 1918–1921, and the Theory of Revolution," *Weimar Etudes* (New York: Columbia University Press, 1982).

17. See D.A. Smart, ed., *Pannekoek and Gorter's Marxism* (London: Pluto, 1978); and Serge Bricianer, *Pannekoek and the Worker's Councils* (St. Louis: Telos Press, 1978).

18. Karl Korsch, "What is Socialization?," *New German Critique* 6 (Fall 1975).

19. For a reflection on their absence in the collapse of European Communism in 1989, see Martin Jay, "No Power to the Soviets," in *Cultural Semantics: Keywords of Our Time* (Amherst: University of Massachusetts Press, 1998).

20. The term was introduced in 1931 in an essay on the poet, novelist and journalist Erich Kästner, in which Benjamin defined it as "precisely the attitude to which there is no longer, in general, any corresponding political action. It is not to the left of this or that tendency, but simply to the left of what is in general possible. For from the beginning all it has in mind is to enjoy itself in a negativistic quest." "Left-wing Melancholy," *Selected Writings, Volume 2: 1927–1934*, eds. Michael W. Jennings, Howard Eiland, and Bary Smith, trans, Rodney Livingstone et al. (Cambridge, MA: Harvard University Press, 1999), 425.

21. Ernst Bloch, *The Spirit of Utopia*, trans. Anthony A. Nassar (Stanford: Stanford University Press, 2000). For a general account of the interaction of modernist art and leftist politics in the period, see John Willett, *Art and Politics in the Weimar Period: The New Sobriety 1917–1933* (New York: Pantheon,1978).

22. See Michael Löwy, *Redemption and Utopia: Jewish Libertarian Thought in Central Europe*, trans. Hope Heaney (Stanford: Stanford University Press, 1992); and Anson Rabinbach, *In the Shadow of Catastrophe: German Intellectuals Between Apocalypse and Enlightenment* (Berkeley: University of California Press, 1997).

23. See Stephen Eric Bronner and Douglas Kellner, eds., *Passion and Rebellion: The Expressionist Heritage* (New York: Bergin and Garvey, 1983).

24. See Istvan Deak, *Weimar Germany's Left-wing Intellectuals: A Political History of the Weltbühne and its Circle* (Berkeley: University of California, Press, 1968).

25. Deak, *Weimar Germany's Left-wing Intellectuals*, 166.

26. See Walter Struve, *Elites Against Democracy: Leadership Ideals in Bourgeois Political Thought in Germany, 1890–1933* (Princeton: Princeton University Press, 1973), chap. 6.

27. For a history of their Weimar years, see Ulrike Migdal, *Die Frühgeschichte des Frankfurter Instituts für Sozialforschung* (Frankfurt: Campus, 1981). For a discussion of their research methods, see Helmut Dubiel, *Theory and Politics: Studies in the Development of Critical Theory*, trans. Benjamin Gregg (Cambridge, MA: MIT Press, 1985). For general accounts, see Martin Jay, *The Dialectical Imagination: A History of the Institute of Social Research and the Frankfurt School, 1923–1950*, 2nd ed. (Berkeley: University of California Press, 1996),and Rolf Wiggershaus, *The Frankfurt School: Its History, Theories and Political Significance*, trans. Michael Robertson (Cambridge, MA: MIT Press, 1994).

28. Max Horkheimer, "The Impotence of the German Working Class," *Dawn and Decline: Notes 1926–1931 and 1950–1969*, trans. Michael Shaw (New York: Seabury, 1978), 62.

29. Horkheimer, "The Impotence," 65.

30. Erich Fromm, *The Working Class in Weimar Germany: A Psychological and Sociological Study*, ed. Wolfgang Bonss, trans. Barbara Weinberger (Leamington Spa: Berg, 1984).

31. See Donna Harsch, "The Iron Front: Weimar Social Democracy Between Tradition and Democracy," in *Between Reform and Revolution: German Socialism and Communism from 1840 to 1990*, eds. David E. Barclay and Eric D. Weitz (Brisbane: University of Queensland Press, 2005).

32. See Peter Sloterdijk, *Critique of Cynical Reason*, trans. Michael Elred (Minneapolis: University of Minnesota Press, 1987), 429-433, where he traces cynicism dividing the socialist movement to Noske's repression of the January 1919 revolution.

33. See William L. Patch, Jr., *Christian Trade Unions in the Weimar Republic, 1919–1933: The Failure of "Corporate Pluralism"* (New Haven: Yale University Press, 1985).

34. The episode took place in 1923 during the ill-fated nationalist campaign of the KPD. See Donald L. Niewyk, *Socialist, Anti-Semite, and Jew: German Social Democracy Confronts the Problem of Anti-Semitism, 1918–1933* (Baton Rouge: Louisiana State University Press, 1971), 64–66. He shows that the SPD was far more concerned with the threat of anti-Semitism than the KPD. For a survey of the spectrum of left responses, see Martin Jay, "Anti-Semitism and the Weimar Left," in *Permanent Exiles: Essays on the Intellectual Migration from German to America* (New York: Columbia University Press, 1985).

35. Hans Mommsen, "Generational Conflict and Youth Rebellion in the Weimar Republic," in *From Weimar to Auschwitz*, trans. Philip O'Connor (Princeton: Princeton University Press, 1991),

36. Siegfried Kracauer, *The Salaried Masses*, trans. Quinton Hoare (London: Verso, 1998).

37. *Heritage of Our Times*, trans. Neville and Stephen Plaice (Berkeley: University of California Press, 1990), 25.

38. Janet Ward, *Weimar Surfaces: Urban Visual Culture in 1920s Germany* (Berkeley: University of California Press, 2001), 39.

39. For a sample of intellectuals' responses to film, see Anton Kaes, ed., *Kino-Debatte. Texte zum Verhältnis von Literatur und Film 1909–1929* (Munich: DTV, 1978).

40. Thomas Elsaesser, *Weimar Cinema and After: Germany's Historical Imaginary* (London: Routledge, 2000), 128.

41. See Katharina von Ankum, *Women in the Metropolis: Gender and Modernity in Weimar Culture* (Berkeley: University of California Press, 1997); Angelika Schaser, *Helene Lange und Gertrud Bäumer. Eine politische Lebensgemeinschaft* (Cologne: Böhlau, 2000); Julia Sneeringer, *Winning Women's Votes: Propaganda and Politics in Weimar Germany.* (Chapel Hill: University of North Carolina Press, 2002).

42. For a history of Bäumer's development, see Kevin Repp, *Reformers, Critics, and the Paths to German Modernity: Anti-Politics and the Search for Alternatives, 1890–1914* (Cambridge, MA: Harvard University Press, 2000), chap. 3.

43. For a discussion, see A. Dirk Moses, *German Intellectuals and the Nazi Past* (Cambridge: Cambridge University Press, 2007), chap. 2.

19

The Aftermath

Reflections on the Culture and Ideology of National Socialism

Anson Rabinbach

Hannah Arendt famously wrote that Nazi Germany rested on the "temporary alliance between the elite and the mob."[1] Arendt's characterization may seem excessively crude to our ears but not necessarily because it has been proven wrong. A more nuanced version of her thesis was advanced by the great cultural historians during the 1960s, George Mosse, Fritz Ringer, and Fritz Stern, who were less interested in demonstrating the intellectual antecedents of National Socialism in German thought and literature than in showing how a cultural affinity emerged between dispossessed intellectual *Lumpen-* and a *gebildete* elite who shared the same aesthetic and philosophical contempt for politics. The success of National Socialism, so these historians argued, derived not merely from political and economic frustration, German thought, nor even hatred of the Jews (who symbolized a degenerate modernity), but from a deep cultural, intellectual, ritual, liturgical, and ceremonial repertoire firmly established in Germany during the nineteenth century. All of these works also made reference to or addressed the "aesthetic" component of the Germanic ideology.[2] German culture in general venerated the "unpolitical" artist and thinker who made a Faustian pact with the devil, resulting in what Stern called the "Vulgär-Idealismus" of the Third Reich.[3]

Since then a variety of historians have greatly complicated our picture of the cultural and ideological terrain of Nazi Germany, if only to emphasize that the barbarism of the Nazis was "not the antithesis of modern industrial and technological civilization, but its hidden face, its dialectical doppelgänger."[4] One result of this new scholarship is the consensus that it was not ideology *per se* but a variety of factors, including plunder, prestige, plutocracy, cultural style and a shared mentality that brought the cultural elites—those who compete for access to power—into communion with the culturally and socially dispossessed. This does not mean that there were not other elements in that held together the elite and the mob. Götz Aly's focus on the element of avarice and pecuniary gain that filtered through the *Volksgemeinschaft* in his *Hitler's Beneficiaries* points to another dimension of the cement. Cultural elites did not require full or even partial nazification to participate in National Socialism's institutional and material cornucopia. Biographies and institutional studies of the conservative circles in Weimar and the Kaisserreich reveal that unlike Soviet Communism, intellectual fealty to National Socialism required not so much rhetorical and ideological conformity as an ethos or "*Gesinnung*," a willingness to adhere to the precepts of the worldview which was vague and indistinct enough to embrace a variety of related perspectives.

A good example of this sort of performative staging was the "Vow of Allegiance" to Adolf Hitler organized by the Saxon branch of the National Socialist Teachers Association in November 1933 and commemorated by a prestigiously published volume that contained an "appeal to the intelligentsia of the world" accompanied by statements in four languages by distinguished representatives of German scholarship, among them Martin Heidegger, Eugen Fischer, Rector of the University of Berlin, and the art historian Wilhelm Pindar.[5] The "'Vow' of Allegiance" clearly articulated the political expectations the National Socialist state placed on these self-proclaimed "apolitical" scholars. Shrouded in the appearance of an uncoerced and "freely undertaken Oath," the public display of allegiance to the new order was all the more valuable, as a widely disseminated photograph of the professorate surrounded by flag-bearing SA members demonstrated. Staged as a public decision of conscience for the National Socialist revolution, the "Vow" could be seen as a collective statement, directed at the academic profession as a whole, not of politicized scholarship endangered by National Socialism, but of an expressly guaranteed autonomy, indeed, ironically, of "freedom of scholarship."

The study of academic elites has been particularly fruitful. In his excellent book, *Heidegger's Crisis*, Hans Sluga has shown that there was a remarkable diversity among philosophical orientations in nazified universities, and that apart from the already marginal and banned Marxist and logical positivist schools, a spectrum of philosophical orientations from Kantianism to existentialism continued to flourish.[6] Precisely because the Nazi worldview played at best a symbolic function, indeterminate, yet at the same time in constant need of refinement and reinterpretation, philosophers found themselves in a unique position to give shape and substance to the new political reality. At the same time, the fact that the worldview remained the final arbiter of truth created problems for philosophers, since National Socialism also drew its authority from non-philosophical sources, e.g., biology, race, myth, mysticism, in other words, from sources which in Heidegger's words, could be considered "primitive."[7] These and other quandaries caused uncertainty, but also produced a good deal of competition for preeminence among philosophical schools, as each sought to define the "ontological order on which the new emerging political order could be grounded."[8] According to Sluga, the very diversity of approaches compatible with National Socialism—e.g., defenders and detractors of Fichte and Nietzsche, proponents of the philosophy of life, of Kantianism, existentialism and Darwinism—says more about the willingness of a variety of scholars to accept the basic political premises of the regime than it does about the complicity of any single philosophical school or intellectual orientation with National Socialism.

To be sure, many of these philosophers held out the hope that the prosaic public face of National Socialism would be sooner or later replaced by what they considered to be the more sublime "essence " of National Socialism. Carl

Schmitt famously argued that National Socialism could be considered in some ways "merely" symptomatic of the *telos* of modernity in the age of the total state. Taking as a point of departure the conception of the world-historical mission of the Germans as the "philosophical nation" *par excellence,* philosophers saw in National Socialism an opportunity and a political movement with deeply rooted intellectual sources and primal "mythic-metaphysical" origins.[9] National Socialism promised to take politics out of the humdrum of daily routine and to place scholars on a programmatic and philosophic pedestal. A "higher" National Socialism need only be adopted as an exalted image of the movement against the more prosaic side of National Socialism where its "lower" ideological accents were concentrated—meaning, the pragmatic or vulgar rhetoric of political struggle and the pamphlets expressing the racial doctrine. The conviction that human affairs could be guided by high philosophical standards, that a political program of anthropological "purification" and "breeding" could make human beings the carriers of a "higher" principle served also to create a climate that ultimately turned a blind eye to demographic pacification and mass murder.

Despite the absolutism of the *Führerprinzip* and the quasi liturgical status granted to Hitler's speeches and writings, no single version of Nazi ideology ever became canonical in the Third Reich. Hitler's bohemian loathing for the traditional German bourgeoisie mimicked antibourgeois sentiments that could be found among the middle-class itself. But his alliance with conservative elites was not merely a matter of adjusting his rhetoric to their prejudices. As John Lukacs, observed, "Hitler was a 'new' kind of revolutionary; he was also a 'new' kind of reactionary, and a 'new' kind of nationalist.[10] The Nazi worldview came to appear, in short, not to be something that went *against the current* of older intellectual conceptions, but rather as something *consistent* with already existing conventions and controversies. Fusion concepts like "reactionary modernism" usefully demonstrate that there was no single distinctive German path to modernity that emerged after the First World War in circles identified with the Weimar conservative revolution. An embrace of technology and innovation was entirely compatible with Germanic spirituality, anti-materialism, imperial ambitions and a racist worldview.[11] The omnipotence of the human will to control, the principle of unlimited technical possibilities for the perfection of the nation or race, and finally, an inner readiness to embrace "final solutions" as a form of politics—and thereby to throw moral inhibitions over board—created the climate for National Socialism.[12]

From this standpoint, National Socialism was not seen as a threat to Bildung and intellectual freedom but as a chance for the humanities (*Geisteswissenschaften*) to play a role in the critical caesura of the times in which, "the living spirit" would emerge and the future of modernity would be decided. Frank Rutger-Hausmann's detailed survey of the recruitment of university scholars during the war into the "mammoth project" called the "mobilization of the humanities" (*Kriegseinsatz der Geisteswissenschaften*) shows that despite the fact that some German scholars may have privately expressed "certain" reservations and even demonstrated remarkable awareness of the criminal nature of the regime, few of the invited scholars refused to participate in what appeared to them as a "purely academic" enterprise.[13] Ideological interference by the party's cultural agencies was largely superfluous since most humanities disciplines were already so inundated with elements of the worldview that subscribing to the new order did not require a major shift in perspective or methodology, nor the adoption of "alien" perspectives imposed from without. To be sure, a few of these academics—like Heidegger and Schmitt— held out the hope that *Vulgärnationalsozialismus* would be sooner or later replaced by a purer and more sublime *essence*, namely their own ideas. Ironically, it was also never entirely the case that attempts to enforce ideological recoding of the respective humanities disciplines automatically guaranteed personal advantages or that an individual might eventually be catapulted into the desirable position of "gatekeeper" of the profession. In fact, the opposite was often more likely; ideological presumptuousness could incur a heavy cost in terms of declining professional reputation. The precipitous drop in the status of figures of like Heidegger, Schmitt, and the pedagogue Ernst Krieck during the 1930s after their run-ins with party authorities, attests to the danger inherent in assuming too high a profile. To a large extent the real gatekeepers of the humanities remained the traditional *Ordinarius* professors, though a few appointments, like those of Krieck and the philosopher Alfred Bäumler, came at the behest of the political authorities. Such overtly political appointments were by and large the exception, however, as was demonstrated by the obscure case of an "outsider," Walter Ebenhardt, who was named professor of classical philology in Münster.[14]

It is hard to imagine that in the 1960s, Gordon Craig, the dean of American historians of Germany could still call "Nazi Culture" an oxymoron. Today we are confronted with a library of studies attesting to this presumptuousness. But what does the map of elite (and mob) culture in the Third Reich actually look like? What are its patterns of circulation? Rather than focus on those elites in power I propose to look more closely at those who aspired to or participated in the benefits of power. It may be productive distinguish *four* domains of Nazi culture: those focusing on (1) the phenomenon of *"political religion,"* (2) the *academic* (including but not limited to racial *science*), (3) the *"aesthetic,"* and (4) the *"popular"* or *"vernacular."* Each of these has a venerable tradition in the history of cultural anthropology. To put it in semiotic terms, the fields of the political religion, the sacred, and the aesthetic might be classified as "sublime" or "sacred" domains; the academic, the scientific, and the popular as more profane. From this perspective, National Socialism was a *cultural synthesis* fusing diverse and incompatible elements from a modern industrial society with a fundamentally unstable admixture of romantic anticapitalist, nationalist, technocratic, quasi-socialist, radical *völkisch*, and bio-racial elements. At the German pavilion in the Paris Exposition Internationale in 1937, for example, a Mercedes race car and a Zeppelin diesel engine were displayed next to German landscapes and allegorical figures painted in the academic style favored by Hitler and Adolf Ziegler, president of the Rich Chamber for the Visual Arts.[15] Nazi ideologues might have for a time encouraged German women to adopt a "natural look" that embraced the un-cosmetic, the pigtail and the dirndl, but in fact, neither was widely accepted, as opposed to the more commercially viable and fashionably stylish look depicted in German fashion magazines.[16] Though some of these fashions "gestured" towards the "look" promoted by the propaganda ministry, they remained well within the "chic" of the 1930s.

The Nazi worldview, in Sluga's words, "encompassed a multiplicity of discordant beliefs." What was important was not so much the coherence of the worldview, but that it "serves as a unifying principle for a large and diverse group of people. What mattered was the performative *appeal to* and *enactment of* the worldview rather than the worldview itself."[17] These domains were not entirely separate nor did they encompass all adherents; but at some level they welded a more or less coherent ideological consensus.

Numerous scholars, from Eric Voegelin to Philippe Burrin and Ekkhard Bahr, have regarded National Socialism an "ethno-religion" (Burrin), a secular worldview that combined the political religion of the Volk with an apocalyptic struggle against the Jew as the heterogeneous figure of "falsehood, seduction, and power"—the threat to the ethnic body's very existence.[18] This approach, grounded in Christian theology and the anthropology of religion invokes the cultic, even Christological content of Nazism's dominant ideological tropes— Volk, Nation, and Race—as well as the deification of the Führer, the fervor of the believers, and finally, the demonization of the Jews. Simultaneously naturalistic and "transcendent," pantheistic and Christological, National Socialism—like all interwar Fascisms—mobilized the idea of spiritual regeneration (Palingenesis) as well as the civil religion of Hitler' providence and Germany's divine mission.[19]

Yet, the influence of the political religion can be exaggerated insofar as it assumes an anthropological constant and a perpetual mobilization, the almost universal need for the sacred in a secular world, and the existence of a "void" that can be filled by historically novel types of political culture. It asserts (rather than demonstrates) that this theological core was fundamental to National Socialism's successful appeal to the broad masses.[20] It addresses only one dimension of the broader cultural consensus in the Reich—one reserved for the party faithful—and it does not question the degree to which these forms radiated beyond that milieu of academic and social elites.

Racial biology is another distinctive domain of the intellectual culture of the Third Reich. While some historians had regarded *völkisch* ideology and racism as hostile to both modernity and the Enlightenment, by the 1980s the Nazi modern took center stage in debates on the Holocaust, for example, in Zygmunt Bauman's *Modernity and the Holocaust*. Racial health encompassed the broad array of population politics that characterized the Nazi regime: racial fitness, education, immigration, citizenship, marriage requirements, as well as the exclusion of "others" including gays, the mentally ill, the handicapped, as well as those defined as racially "other." Racial biology was a complex and often incoherent trope that excluded all those who biologically or aesthetically did not conform to the norms of the *Volksgemeinschaft* At its core, the Nazi vision of enmity pertained most directly to those whose very existence threatened to destroy the

Volksgemeinschaft, whether through miscegenation or global politics—in other words, the Jews.[21] According to Saul Friedlander, Nazi anti-Semitism was neither the replacement of traditional Jew-hatred with scientific "racial" categories nor the fusion of the two: "In its new form, this representation of evil was not merely religious, not merely racial, and not merely political. It was a stage-by-stage aggregation of these successive waves of anti-Jewish hatred, of the successive layers of a tale of Jewish conspiracy against Aryan humanity."[22] The "de-judaization" of German public culture was realized through the subtle interplay of legal discourse, pedagogical incitement, civil apartheid, and "scientific" racism as Claudia Koonz has shown in *The Nazi Conscience*. The systematic eradication of universal humanist conscience resulted in a "loose consensus" about the "ethnic organism" (*Volkskörper*), and the result was the isolation, the weakening, and ultimately the sundering, of ties between Jews and their former friends, neighbors, and colleagues.[23]

After 1935, books on popular racial science, films, exhibits, and educational programs flooded the public sphere. It is not entirely clear who was the audience of these productions, but one Nazi sponsored library survey demonstrated that virtually all of the literature on racial science was consumed by academics.[24] Whether "race" was to be defined biologically, culturally, anthropologically, or philosophically remained—at least in principle and for a time—a relatively open and controversial question. What was crucial, however, was not that compulsory concepts were decided upon, but that such questions were discussed in the schools, the judiciary, in the university faculties. Soon, highly assimilated Jewish victims like Victor Klemperer wrote in his diary: "how unbelievably I have deceived myself my whole life long when I imagined myself to belong to Germany, and how completely homeless I am."[25] It now almost goes without saying that Nazi rule was a form of aestheticized politics. But it is rare to find this aspect so carefully and coherently examined as in Eric Michaud's superb *The Cult of Art in Nazi Germany*.[26] Michaud distinguishes at least three modalities at work in the production of this universe of representations, myths and symbols. Following Voegelin, he emphasizes the fundamental continuity of Christianity and Nazism: "the same concept of the Church as the mystical body of Christ that had been perpetuated in the dynastic concept of the European monarchies had now reappeared in the National Socialist idea." Indeed, Michaud writes, "it is no exaggeration to say that Hitler, in the Wagnerian dream he tried to embody, almost simultaneously took on the roles of both Jesus and Apollo."[27] The invisible God was replaced by the earthly messiah, the "earth-bound Jew" was the anti-race, whose parasitism contaminated and weakened the creative genius of the Aryan artist-race. But was there a there a coherent Nazi "myth"? Michaud's method is to create a synthetic version of the Nazi "sublime," a syncretic version of the National Socialist worldview (which of course was one of its precepts), whereas it frequently consisted of competing ideological motifs (Christianity, Paganism). And finally, he interprets only the esoteric dimension of Nazism, the "religion of nature" without taking into account the prosaic entertainment spectacle and "unpolitical" and pedestrian side of the media in the Third Reich. Though critics like the artist Klaus Staeck called Nazi art "decorations for Auschwitz," we might be justified in asking whether a generation of scholarship on "fascinating fascism" (Susan Sontag) had not in fact overstated the influence of Nazi art (which, after all, was only seen by a small part of the population).[28]

A good deal of the popular culture of Nazi Germany was utterly lacking in the spiritual, mythical and sublime aspects of representation embodied in the officially sanctioned architecture, painting, and music of the regime. Films such as *Triumph of the Will, Olympia,* and *Hitler Junge Quex* were heralded as triumphs of Goebbels's Propaganda Ministry. For the vast majority of Germans, however "Nazi culture" was largely communicated through less overtly political entertainments and commercial advertising, though many these were hardly devoid of ideological motifs. This phenomenon was in part the expression of class: art, theater, opera, and classical music appealed to elite tastes; film, radio, sports, and travel, had a much broader appeal. Of the more than one thousand films produced in Germany between 1933 and 1945, only a handful like the commercially successful feature *Jud Süss* and (the box-office failure) *Der Ewige Jude* were explicitly anti-Semitic, and the famous documentaries of Leni Riefenstahl were the exception, indeed a fraction of the overall output.[29] According to one study, of all feature films produced, only a fifth had obvious propagandistic content.[30] Indeed in many respects the Third Reich "fostered the modern era's first full-blown media culture, strategically instrumentalizing state-of-the-art technology, introducing cheap mass-produced radios into almost every household, developing television, staging political events as grand photo opportunities, replaying military conquests in the form of weekly newsreels."[31] Film, radio, and commercial culture played at least as important, if not a more important part, in orchestrating perceptions than did art, architecture, propaganda films, and mass festivals. Filmstars were afforded more than the usual pecuniary gain. To win over Zarah Leander to UFA in 1937, Goebbels paid the Swedish actress the highest salary of 150,000 RM annually (three times more than another Swedish actress, Ingrid Bergman, who left Germany in 1939). Male leads did almost as well: Hans Albers (120,000), Emil Jannings (120,000) and Gustav Grundgens (80,000). Ferdinand Marian, chosen by Goebbels to play the lead in *Jüd Süss* was paid 50,000 Reichsmarks.[32]

This is not to say that entertainment films with high production values and mass appeal did not also contain ideological motifs. Only recently have historians begun to reflect on the difficulties of writing about what might be called the *distinctive propaganda cultures* of the Third Reich. Michaud's "Gesamtkunstwerk National Socialism" focuses exclusively on the "sacred" and the "aesthetic," that is, on representations and images of the worldview orchestrated from above.[33] It is worth remembering the wartime sketch of the inner sanctum of the Third Reich produced by Nazi defector Ernst Putzi Haenfstaengl (Hitler's only intimate who attended Harvard) for Franklin Roosevelt. From Putzi the world learned of Hitler's passion for Lohengrin, but also for Hollywood films like *King Kong,* of Robert Ley's passion for drink, Rudolf Hess's for nature cures, and Otto Dietrich's for horseplay on Bismarck's couch. The picture that emerges from his report is closer to the Marx Brothers' "Fredonia" than the Teutonic Knights.[34]

Nazi Germany was also a usurper's paradise. To borrow Hannah Arendt's terms, the German pariahs became the parvenus. Within a very short time after 1933, the new Nazi elite removed Germany's Jewish upper crust from the public realm, forcing most to emigrate or worse, like Martha Liebermann, the painter's widow, who had to sell the family house on the Wannsee in 1940 and in 1943 committed suicide hours before police came to arrest her. Jewish property was sold off at cut-rate prices. Just a few hundred meters from the Liebermann Villa the home of the banker Karl Arnhold was "bought" by economics Minister Walther Funk. Albert Speer acquired the former property of Baron Goldschmidt-Rothschild in the tiny island suburb of Schwanenwerder for a mere 150RM. The new Nazi elite displaced the Jews at home and in the garish public events staged to celebrate the usurpers entry into high society. For the arrivistes, even one's political past could be forgotten. As Klaus Mann's "Höfgen" (modeled on Grundgens) muses in his novel *Mephisto*, "He had never in the past estimated the true worth of this considerable and unsuspected advantage. He wasn't a Jew, and so everything could be forgiven him, even his having let himself be acclaimed as 'comrade.'" Seizing the spoils after 1933 was not restricted to the political and economic elites. Party activists and SA men stole money and jewelry from Jewish homes and in the episodes of "wild confiscations" Jewish businesses were seized, department stores looted, and individual Jews blackmailed before being forced to hand over their assets. Both individuals and the party enriched themselves mightily through the combination of pogrom and plunder. The Third Reich may have staged itself as a Teutonic Valhalla, but in Frank Bajohr's apt phrase, it was a kleptocracy as well.[35]

Perhaps more than pecuniary gain, prestige played a key role in securing the allegiance of cultural and political elites. As Fabrice d'Almeida has shown in a fascinating book, "high society" was instrumental in securing and mobilizing the Third Reich's cultural elites: balls, state receptions, dinners, commemorations, openings of exhibitions, theater and opera premieres were attended by a constantly updated "A-list" of dignitaries and journalists (whose birthdays were carefully noted and acknowledged). At the 1934 premiere of Leni Riefenstahl's *Victory of Belief*, in Berlin's UFA Palace, seven loge boxes were reserved for plenipotentiaries and an even grander event took place for *Triumph of the Will* just half a year later. A collection of hunting invitations sent to visiting dignitaries by Reichsjagdmeister Göring is preserved in the New York Public Library. Hunting was important enough to warrant the promulgation of an elaborate Reichsjagdgesetz in 1938. High-level political tourism also played an important role. The annual Nuremberg Congress was always attended by foreign dignitaries, and in 1937 by an admiring corps of French anti-Semitic writers (Lucien Rebatet, Robert Brasillach, Georges Blond).[36] Typically, special selections of wines were chosen for the train from Berlin. But punishment for transgression was also swift. Richard Strauss, named head of the Reich Music Chamber despite his collaboration with the Jewish librettist Stefan Zweig, fell into utter disgrace when a letter apologizing to Zweig, denying any anti-Semitism, and justifying his acceptance of the post in the name of art, was discovered by the Gestapo.

The most fertile meeting ground for elite and popular culture in the Third Reich was radio. The impact of media on everyday life, how it was decoded or received by readers and listeners, remains obscure. For example, was radio propaganda effective because it came from Goebbels's rhetorical blast furnace or because it frequently came in softer, even comedic forms, like the highly popular radio program *Wunschkonzert*? Did the Nazis broadcast their aims, especially as far as the murder of the Jews is concerned, or was the conspicuous absence of anti-Semitism in radio programming indicative of the pervasive use of entertainment to disguise the political barbarism of the regime? Or perhaps was it the combination of the two that was so irresistible? For the most part, anti-Semitism does not play a significant role in the film, newsreel, or radio programming of the Nazi years. After a short phase of experimentation during which Goebbels responded to the pressure of the party and subordinated entertainment to political and propagandistic broadcasts, entertainment (music, light talk) became the norm. The historian Inge Marsolek suggests that there was a kind of division of labor in the deployment of radio propaganda: radio in large part represented "the cheerful side of the *Volksgemeinschaft*" though Goebbels's broadcasts did contain anti-Semitic allusions, sometimes hidden, often explicit.[37]

In the party press, anti-Semitic campaigns were parsed out in extremely small doses. Only a small percentage of the headlines in the *Völkische Beobachter* dealt with Jews and none of them revealed information about deportations and mass murder. The same is true of the weekly newsreels (Wochenschau) where less than two percent depicted Jews, and none depicted their fate.[38] But it is striking to see how much was actually known about the reality (if not the details) of mass murder, as is evident from the diaries of attentive observers like Victor Klemperer or Ursula von Kardoff.[39] A great deal of information about the intention of the regime towards the Jews could be learned from some public sources, above all, poster campaigns depicting the "international Jew" as the secret empire behind the allies. As Jeffrey Herf and Peter Longerich show in their new studies of wartime anti-Jewish propaganda, much more could be learned about the Holocaust from public utterances, rumors, and direct experiences than has been claimed for the last fifty years.[40] Nonetheless, it is still true, as Ian Kershaw pointed out in a classic article, "the radicalisation of the negative dynamism, which formed the essential driving-force of the Nazi Party, found remarkably little echo in the mass of the population. Popular opinion, largely indifferent and infused with a latent anti-Jewish feeling further bolstered by propaganda, provided the climate within which spiraling Nazi aggression towards Jews could take place."[41]

One red thread that runs through many of the autobiographies of the cultural elite of the Third Reich, written after 1945, is the presumption that because they had helped or tried to help Jews, their other infelicities were mitigated. This was certainly post-WWII self-justification. But the trope is sometimes quite revealing about the access of cultural elites to the Nazi plenipotentiaries. Leni Riefenstahl's memoir contains a scene where, as Hitler offers her the prize of directing films for Goebbels, she supposedly complained that "some of my best friends have emigrated, and so have a number of great artists."[42] Perhaps the most sensational example is Winifred Wagner, whose family heirloom, her intimate friend "Wolf" (Hitler) underwrote the Bayreuth Festival. For "Wini," Hitler was not merely the savior of Germany but the personal savior of Bayreuth. Winifred thus secured the artistic and political independence of the Festival, protecting it from interference from the Party or Goebbel's Reich Cultural Chamber. She could later boast that employees belonging to the illegal SPD or KPD, "non-Aryans," and homosexuals (like star tenor Max Lorenz), were insulated from the general assault on theatrical and musical life. The talented stage designer Emil Pretorius, declared an "enemy of the state" for his "unambiguous loyalty to the Jews," was permitted to continue at Hitler's personal request. Winifred interceded on behalf of persecuted Jews and artists who sought her help and on several occasions rendered indispensable assistance. But when it came to Jews with "a high percentage of Aryan blood," as she put it, her efforts "fell on deaf ears." Her good deeds could also be almost comic, as when she complained about the dismissal of pro-Nazi "non-Aryans" from the party. She seemed truly to believe that Hitler "was uninformed about the evils that were going on." Winifred was entirely in "Wolf's" debt. She enjoyed trips to Italy, fancy cars, holiday cottages, and lavish renovation projects (a scandal ensued when money for the planned Richard Wagner Research Centre was siphoned off to Switzerland). Bayreuth became Hitler's "only recreation." He arrived unannounced, played with the devoted children, and held monologues into the night.

With the work of Fritz Stern, George Mosse, Peter Gay, and others, Nazi culture could certainly not be called an oxymoron. Nor was it the simply an amalgamation of texts, images, symbols, artistic and rhetorical practices, which served to directly articulate and disseminate National Socialist ideology and maintain the hegemony of the regime. It is no longer sufficient to regard Nazi culture as the expression of a totalizing "base-metaphor" (*metaphore de base*) which appealed directly to deep and primal psychic responses. It appealed to a variety of emotions, motivations, and attitudes, base and elevated. To simply assume that National Socialist ideology, with its phantasm of biological purity and racial homogeneity, was directly and effectively communicated, along with the negative images of Jews, homosexuals, the handicapped, asocials, Sinti and Roma, Slavs, and others deemed to be "foreign to the German essence" (*Wesensfremd*), by the regime's talented propagandists leaves much to the imagination. It is useful therefore to distinguish between the universe of choreographed representations, the sacred or the aesthetic sublime, from the non-aesthetic vulgarity of street brawls, sausages, beer, air shows, May Day rallies, holiday celebrations, and the apparent "normality" of referenda, plebiscites, KdF tours of Mallorca, and academic conferences, all of which certainly played as great of not a greater role in securing the cultural synthesis that took hold after the regime was in place. The "sublime" culture of Nuremberg rallies, the Bayreuth Festival, commemorations of Schlageter and Horst Wessel, approved art, music, theater and "Nordic" ideas played a role in the efforts of the regime to create an official "Nazi culture" but its impact should not be exaggerated. The "vulgar" entertainments, film, radio, sports, fashion, seem to have been far more effective, especially when politics was "folded" into the more palatable fare. So did the withdrawal into the private realm of sex, reading, crosswords, card-playing, and drink, all of which permitted the dictatorship to appear less threatening and more hospitable. Anticipating the Führer's wishes, what Sir Ian Kershaw calls, "Working towards the Führer," (*dem Führer entgegenarbeiten*) was not confined to cultural, administrative, economic, and political elites alone. It occurred on a variety of levels, in a multitude of contexts, in and out of the home, the university, the school, the workplace, the street, the *Kneipe* (pub), and the cinema. Along with distortions of language and education, all of these contributed, in Victor Klemperer's words, "to expand the popular stratum in everyone to such an extent that the thinking stratum is suffocated."[43] There is perhaps no better summation for the tragedy that befell German intellectual history and culture in the mid-twentieth century.

Notes

1. Hannah Arendt, *The Origins of Totalitarianism* (New York: Harcourt, 1973), 333.
2. See, most recently, Joachim Fest, *Speer: The Final Verdict*, trans. Ewald Osers and Alexandra Dring (New York: Harcourt, 2001), 349.
3. Fritz Stern, *The Failure of Illiberalism: Essays on the Political Culture of Modern Germany* (New York: Columbia University Press, 1992), xlxvi.
4. Enzo Traverso, *L'histoire déchirée* (Paris: Cerf, 1997), 39.
5. *Bekenntnis der Professoren an den deutschen Universitäten und Hochschulen zu Adolf Hitler und dem nationalsozialistischen Staat* (Dresden: NS Lehrerbund Deutschland/ Sachsen, 1933).
6. Hans Sluga, *Heidegger's Crisis: Philosophy and Politics in Nazi Germany* (Cambridge, MA: Harvard University Press, 1993).
7. Cited in Sluga, *Heidegger's Crisis*, 198.
8. Sluga, *Heidegger's Crisis*, 201.
9. Hermann Lübbe, *Politische Philosophie in Deutschland* (Basel: Benno Schwabe & Co. 1963), 173–238.
10. John Lukacs, *The Hitler of History* (New York: Alfred Knopf, 1997), 76–112.
11. Jeffrey Herf, *Reactionary Modernism: Technology, Culture, and Politics in Weimar and the Third Reich* (Cambridge: Cambridge University Press, 1986).
12. Zygmunt Bauman, *Modernity and the Holocaust* (Cornell University Press, 1989). An alternative approach is Enzo Traverso, *L'histoire déchirée* (Paris: Cerf, 1997). I am indebted to Wolfgang Bialas for this point. See Wolfgang Bialas and Anson Rabinbach, eds., *Nazi Germany and the Humanities* (Oxford: One World Press, 2006).
13. Frank-Rutger Hausmann, *"Deutsche Geisteswissenschaft" im Zweiten Weltkrieg : die "Aktion Ritterbusch" (1940–1945)* (Dresden: Dresden University Press, 1998).
14. Volker Losemann, *Nationalsozialismus und Antike: Studien zur Entwicklung des Faches Alte Geschichte 1933–1945* (Hamburg : Hoffmann und Campe, 1977), 50.
15. Karen A. Fiss, "In Hitler's Salon: The German Pavilion at the 1937 Paris Exposition Internationale," in *Art, Culture, and Media Under the Third Reich*, ed. Richard A. Etlin (Chicago: University of Chicago Press, 2002), 328.
16. Irene Guenther, *Nazi Chic? Fashioning Women in the Third Reich* (New York: Berg, 2004), 265, 266.

17. Hans Sluga, *Heidegger's Crisis*,193.

18. Philippe Burrin, "Political Religion: The Relevance of a Concept," *History and Memory* 9, no. 1 (September 1997), 321–51.

19. On Palingenesis, see Roger Griffin, *The Nature of Fascism* (London: Pinter Publishers, 1991).

20. Eric Voegelin, *The New Science of Politics: Order and History* (Chicago: University of Chicago Press, 1987); *Science, Politics and Gnosticism* (Wilmington, DE: ISI, 2004); Philippe Burrin, *Nazi Anti-Semitism: From Prejudice to the Holocaust* (New York: New Press, 1985); Claus-Ekkehard Bärsch, *Die politische Religion des Nationalsozialismus: die religiöse Dimension der NS-Ideologie in den Schriften von Dietrich Eckart, Joseph Goebbels, Alfred Rosenberg und Adolf Hitler* (Munich: W. Fink, 1998); Klaus Vondung, *Magie und Manipulation. Ideologischer Kult und politische Religion des National-Sozialismus* (Göttingen: Vandenhoeck & Ruprecht 1971). Barsch and Vondung were students of Voegelin. The term sacralization has been used most effectively to describe Italian fascism by Emilio Gentile in *The Sacralization of Politics in Fascist Italy*, trans. Keith Botsford (Cambridge, MA: Harvard University Press, 1996).

21. Cited in Friedländer, "Mosse's Influence on the History of the Holocaust," 145.

22. Saul Friedländer, "The Extermination of the European Jews in Historiography: Fifty Years Later," in *Thinking about the Holocaust after Half a Century*, ed. Alvin H. Rosenfeld (Bloomington: Indiana University Press, 1997), 7.

23. Claudia Koonz, *The Nazi Conscience* (Cambridge MA: Harvard University Press, 2003).

24. Erich Thier, *Gestaltwandel des Arbeiters im Spiegel seiner Lektüre; ein Beitrag zu Volkskunde und Leserführung* (Leipzig: O. Harrassowitz, 1939), 92.

25. Victor Klemperer, *I Will Bear Witness: A Diary of the Nazi Years 1933–1941*, trans. Martin Chalmers (New York: Random House, 1998), 253.

26. Eric Michaud, *The Cult of Art in Nazi Germany*, trans. Janet Lloyd (Palo Alto: Stanford University Press, 2004).

27. Michaud, *Cult of Art*, 57, 59.

28. Martin Warnke, "Das dämonisierte Hakenkreuz," *Die Zeit* 44 (October 28, 1988), 61.

29. The literature on Riefenstahl and Nazi propaganda films is extensive. See David Culbert, "The Impact of Anti-Semitic Film Propaganda on German Audiences: *Jew Süss* and *The Wandering Jew* (1940)," in *Art, Culture, and Media in the Third Reich*, ed. Etlin, 139–58. Eric Rentschler, *Ministry of Illusion: Nazi Cinema and its Afterlife* (Cambridge, MA: Harvard University Press, 1996), 7. Also see Karsten Witte,"Visual Pleasure Inhibited: Aspects of the German Review Film," *New German Critique* 24/25 (Autumn 1981–Winter 1982), 238–63.

30. David Welch, "Nazi Film Policy: Control, Ideology, and Propaganda," in *National Socialist Cultural Policy* ed. Glenn R. Cuomo (New York: St. Martin's, 1995), 107.

31. Rentschler, *Ministry of Illusion*, 21.

32. Fabrice d'Almeida, *La vie mondaine sous le nazisme* (Paris: Librairie Académique Perrin, 2006).

33. See David Welch, *The Third Reich: Politics and Propaganda* (London: Routledge, 1993); David Bankier, *The Germans and the Final Solution: Public Opinion under Nazism* (Oxford: B. Blackwell, 1992).

34. Ernst Hanfstaengl, *The Unknown Hitler: Notes from the Young Nazi Party* (London: Gibson Square Books, 2005). Also see *Hitler's Piano Player: The rise and fall of Ernst Hanfstaengl, Confidant of Hitler, Ally of FDR.* (London: Duckworth, 2005).

35. Frank Bajohr, *"Aryanisation" in Hamburg: the Economic Exclusion of Jews and the Confiscation of Their Property in Nazi Germany* (New York: Berghahn, 2002).

36. Almeida, *La vie mondaine*, 257.

37. Inge Marsolek, "A New Approach to Propaganda in the Third Reich," lecture, German Studies Association, October 8–11, 2009. See also *Radio im Nationalsozialismus. Zwischen Lenkung und Ablenkung,* in *Zuhören und Gehörtwerden,* eds. Inge Marsolek and Adelheid von Saldern, Band 1 (Tübingen: Edition Diskord, 1998).

38. Ulrike Bartels, *Die Wochenschau im Dritten Reich: Entwicklung und Funktion eines Massenmediums unter besonderer Berücksichtigung völkisch-nationaler Inhalte* (Frankfurt a.M.: P. Lang, 2004).

39. Victor Klemperer, *Ich will Zeugnis ablegen bis zum letzten,* ed. Walter Nowojski, 2 vols. (Berlin: Aufbau-Verlag, 1995); and Ursula von Kardoff, *Berliner Aufzeichnungen: 1942–1945,* ed. Peter Hartl (Munich: C. H. Beck, 1992).

40. Jeffrey Herf, *The Jewish Enemy: Nazi Propaganda during World War II and the Holocaust* (Cambridge, MA: Harvard University Press, 2006); Peter Longerich, *"Davon haben wir nichts gewusst!": die Deutschen und die Judenverfolgung 1933–1945* (Munich: Siedler, 2006).

41. Ian Kershaw, "The Persecution of the Jews and German Popular Opinion in the Third Reich, *Leo Baeck Institute Yearbook* 26, no. 1 (1981), 261–89.

42. Leni Riefenstahl, *Leni Riefenstahl: A Memoir* (London: Picador, 1995), 137.

43. Victor Klemperer, *I Will Bear Witness: A Diary of the Nazi Years 1933–1941,* trans. Martin Chalmers (New York: Random House, 1998), 258.

Weimar Thought

A Chronology

The following is a selective chronology that lists major events in modern German history alongside the major publications that are mentioned in this volume. Although it is not comprehensive, it may help to orient readers with a basic outline of the era.

1897 Stefan George, *Das Jahr der Seele* (*The Year of the Soul*)

1902 Hermann Muthesius, *Style-Architecture and Building-Art: Transformations of Architecture in the Nineteenth Century and its Present Condition*

1904 Max Weber, *The Protestant Ethic and the Spirit of Capitalism* (published in 1904–5)

1907 Stefan George, *Der Siebente Ring* (*The Seventh Ring*)

Georg Simmel, *The Philosophy of Money*

1910 Ernst Cassirer, *Substance and Function*

1913 Paul Lindau, *The Other*

Heinrich Rickert, *The Limits of Concept-Formation in the Natural Sciences*

1914 July 28: The Archduke Franz Ferdinand of Austria is assassinated in Serbia.

August 4: the Austro-Hungarian Empire, Great Britain, France, Germany, Serbia, and Russia have all declared war. World War I begins.

Emilie Altenloh, *On the Sociology of Cinema*

1915 Rosa Luxemburg and Karl Liebknecht co-found the *Spartacist League*, which will form the political basis of the German Communist Party (KPD)

1916 Rosa Luxemburg, "The Crisis of German Social Democracy" ("The Junius Pamphlet")

Friedrich Gundolf, *Goethe*

1917 March 7: strikes in Russia inaugurate the February revolution; April 6: United States enters the war; October 25: Armed insurrection in Petrograd (Saint Petersburg) marks beginning of the Bolshevik Revolution and eventual founding of the USSR

Rudolf Otto, "The Idea of the Holy"

1918   November 3: Sailors revolt in Kiel and set up worker's councils; November 9: Kaiser Wilhelm II abdicates. Social Democrats and Independent Socialists form provisional government led by Chancellor Friedrich Ebert

Ernst Bertram, *Nietzsche: Versuch einer Mythologie*

Karl Barth, *The Epistle to the Romans* (first edition, 1918; second edition, 1922)

Ernst Bloch, *The Spirit of Utopia*

Paul Ernst, *The Collapse of German Idealism*

Richard Huelsenbeck, "Dada Manifesto"

Raoul Hausmann, "The New Material In Painting"

Heinrich Mann, "The Meaning and Idea of the Revolution"

Thomas Mann, *Reflections of a Nonpolitical Man*

Ernst Simmel, *War Neuroses and Psychic Trauma*

Spartacus League, "Spartacus Manifesto"

Oswald Spengler, *The Decline of the West* (Volume 1 only; revised 1922, second volume published 1923)

Bruno Taut, "A Program for Architecture"

Marianne Weber, "The Special Task of the Cultural Woman"

Max Weber, "Science as Vocation" (delivered as lecture 7 November 1917)

1919   January 5–15: General strike and Spartacus uprising in Berlin. Spartacist leaders Rosa Luxemburg and Karl Liebknecht are killed by Freikorps troops; June 28: German government signs the Treaty of Versailles; August 14: The Weimar Republic Constitution is accepted as the new law governing Germany

Hugo Ball, *Critique of the German Intelligentsia*

Hermann Cohen, *Religion of Reason out of the Sources of Judaism*

Walter Gropius, "The Free People's State"

Paul von Hindenburg, "The Stab in the Back"

Hannah Höch, *Cut with the Kitchen Knife through the Last Weimar Beer-Belly Cultural Epoch in Germany*

Siegfried Jacobsohn, "Theater—and Revolution?"

Karl Korsch, "What is Socialization?"

Hermann Keyserling, *Travel Diary of a Philosopher*

Hermann Hesse, "The Brothers Karamazov, or The Decline of Europe"

Heinrich Mann, *Man of Straw (Der Untertan)*

Heinrich Mann, *Power and Humanity*

Walther Rathenau, *The New Society*

Alfred Rosenberg, "The Russian Jewish Revolution"

Heinrich Schaffer, *Von ägyptischer Kunst besonders der Zeichenkunst*

Julius Schaxel, *Abhandlungen zur theoretischen Biologie*

Helene Stöcker, "Revolution und Gewaltlosigkeit"

Ernst Troeltsch, *The Dogma of Guilt*

Kurt Tucholsky. "We Nay-Sayers"

Marianne Weber, *The Woman Question and Women's Thoughts*

Max Weber, "Politics as Vocation" (delivered as lecture, 28 January Munich)

1920   March/April: An attempted monarchist coup in Berlin is defeated through a general strike and a Communist uprising in the Ruhr Valley. Insurrection in central Germany is put down by the Reichswehr

Walter Benjamin, "Theological-Political Fragment" (1920 or 1921, dating uncertain)

Martin Buber, "Nationalism"

Friedrich Gundolf, *Stefan George*, first edition

Friedrich Gogarten, "Between the Times"

George Grosz and John Heartfield, "The Middle-Class Philistine Heartfield Gone Wild" (Electro-Mechanical Tatlin Sculpture)

Robert Wiene, *The Cabinet of Dr. Caligari* (film)

1921   May 10: Center Party member Joseph Wirth forms new government and becomes Chancellor

Rudolf Bultmann, *History of the Synoptic Tradition*

Martin Heidegger, *The Phenomenology of Religious Life* (lectures 1920–21; unpublished at the time)

Richard Huelsenbeck, "En Avant Dada: A History of Dadaism"

Franz Rosenzweig, *The Star of Redemption*

Helene Stöcker, *Die Frau und die Heiligkeit des Lebens*

Herrmann Weyl, "The New Crisis in the Foundations of Mathematics"

1922   November 22: Wilhelm Cuno succeeds Wirth as Chancellor

Karl Abraham, "Manifestations of the Female Castration Complex"

Hugo Bettauer, *The City without Jews*

Albert Einstein, "On the Present Crisis in Theoretical Physics"

Manfred Georg, "The Right to Abortion"

Herman Hesse, *Siddartha*

Thomas Mann, "The German Republic"

Joseph Petzold, "Concerning the Crisis of the Causality Concept"

Paul Tillich, "Kairos" (first published in *Die Tat*, 1922)

Carl Schmitt, *Political Theology: Four Chapters on the Concept of Sovereignty*

Ernst Troeltsch, *Historicism and its Problems*

Johannes Stark, *The Present Crisis in German Physics*

Max Weber, *Economy and Society* (published posthumously, with editorial assistance from Marianne Weber)

1923   January 11: French and Belgian troops occupy the Ruhr and take control of the mining industry; August 11: Cuno resigns as Chancellor, Gustav Stresemann forms new government; October 19: Berlin stock market closes; November 8: Beer Hall Putsch is led by Adolf Hitler, Hermann Göring, and General Erich Ludendorff; November 23: Social Democrats overthrow Stresemann. Center Party member Wilhelm Marx becomes Chancellor

Ernst Bloch, *The Spirit of Utopia* (revised edition)

Martin Buber, *I and Thou* (*Ich und Du*)

Ernst Cassirer, *The Philosophy of Symbolic Forms. Volume I: Language*

Walter Gropius, "Theory and Organization of the Bauhaus"

Georg Lukács, *History and Class Consciousness*

Karl Korsch, *Marxism and Philosophy*

Carl Schmitt, *Roman Catholicism and Political Form*

Carl Schmitt, *The Crisis of Parliamentarism*

Aby Warburg, "Images from the Pueblo Indians of North America"

1924   April 1: Hitler is sentenced to five years in prison for his role in the Beer Hall Putsch; he is released on December 17; September 1: The Dawes Plan introduced by the United States as an effort to stabilize German currency and bring and end to hyperinflation

Béla Balázs, *Visible Man*

Ernst Bloch, "Hitler's Force"

Otto Dix, *The War* (etching series)

Martin Heidegger, "The Concept of Time" (lecture)

Käthe Kollwitz, "Never Again War" (drawing for anti-war poster)

Arthur Liebert, *The Intellectual Crisis of the Present*

Thomas Mann, *The Magic Mountain*

Ludwig Mies van der Rohe, "Architecture and the Will of the Age"

Heinrich Rickert, *The Problems of the Philosophy of History*

Helene Stöcker, *Erotik und Altruismus*

Leopold Weiss (Muhammad Asad), *The Unromantic Orient*

1925   April 26: Paul von Hindenburg elected President; December 1: Treaty of Locarno signed by Great Britain, Belgium, France, Italy, and Germany

Ernst Cassirer, *The Philosophy of Symbolic Forms. Volume II: Mythical Thought*

Sergei Eisenstein, *Battleship Potemkin* (film)

Lion Feuchtwanger, *Jud Süß* (novel)

Joseph Goebbels, "National Socialism or Bolshevism?"

Martin Heidegger, "History of the Concept of Time"

Adolf Hitler, *Mein Kampf*, first edition

Siegfried Kracauer, "Travel and Dance"

Willi Münzenberg, "Conquer Film!"

Franz Rosenzweig, "The New Thinking"

Otto Rühle, *The Psyche of the Proletarian Child*

Stefan Zweig, "The Monotonization of the World"

1926   Jan 20: Social Democrat Hans Luther becomes Chancellor; May 17: Wilhelm Marx again assumes office of Chancellor; September 8: Germany joins the League of Nations; Abortion reduced from felony to a misdemeanor

Rudolf Bultmann, *Jesus*

Rudolf Harms, *Philosophy of Film*

Magnus Hirschfeld, "Sexual Catastrophes"

Adolf Hitler, *Mein Kampf*, second edition

Karen Horney, "Flucht aus der Weiblichkeit"

Siegfried Kracauer, "The Cult of Distraction"

Rudolf Kurtz, "Expressionism and Film"

Fritz Lang, "The Future of Feature Film in Germany"

Fritz Lang, *Metropolis* (film)

Carl Schmitt, "On the Contradiction between Parliamentarism and Democracy"

Paul Tillich, *The Present-Day Religious Situation*

Kurt Weill, "Dance Music"

Heinrich Zimmer, *Kunstform und Yoga im indische Kultbild*

1927   August 19: 30,000 Brown Shirts march in a Nazi rally in Nuremberg

Rudolf Arnheim, "The Bauhaus in Dessau"

Bertolt Brecht, "Difficulties of Epic Theater"

Emil Brunner, *Religionsphilosophie protestantischer Theologie*

Hands Buchner, *Under the Spell of Film*

Sergei Eisenstein, *October* (film)

Martin Heidegger, *Being and Time*

Hermann Hesse, *Steppenwolf*

Rudolf Hilferding, "The Organized Economy"

Ernst Kantorowicz, *Kaiser Friedrich der Zweite*

Siegfried Kracauer, "The Mass Ornament"

Thomas Mann, "Culture and Socialism"

Walter Ruttmann, *Berlin, Symphony of a City* (film)

Carl Schmitt, "The Concept of the Political"

Arnold Zweig, *The Case of Sergeant Grischa*

1928   August 28: Hermann Müller forms a new government with the Social Democrats, Center Party, German Democratic Party, and German People's Party

Theodor W. Adorno, "The Curves of the Needle"

Bertolt Brecht and Kurt Weill, *The Threepenny Opera*

Lou Andreas-Salomé, "The Consequences of the Fact That It Was Not the Woman Who Killed the Father"

Johannes R. Becker, "Our Front"

Walter Benjamin, *One Way Street*

Walter Benjamin, Origins of the German Trauerspiel

Stefan George, *Das Neue Reich*

Martin Heidegger, "Phenomenology and Theology" (lecture)

Erich Kästner, *Emil and the Detectives*

Hans Reichenbach, *The Philosophy of Space and Time*

Carl Schmitt, *Constitutional Theory*

1929   July 24: The Kellogg-Briand pact goes into effect, signed by 65 countries, including Germany; August 2: 150,000 people attend a Nazi rally in Nuremberg; August 6: Young Plan is accepted, leading to a reducation in Germany's war debts; October 24: The Wall Street stock market crashes on Black Friday, precipitating a worldwide economic crisis and the start of the Great Depression

Vicki Baum, *People at a Hotel*

Walter Benjamin, "Surrealism"

Walter Benjamin, "On the Image of Proust"

Max Brod, *Women and the New Objectivity*

Rudolf Bultmann, "The Concept of Revelation in the New Testament"

Ernst Cassirer, *The Philosophy of Symbolic Forms. Volume III: The Phenomenology of Knowledge*

Alfred Döblin, *Berlin Alexanderplatz: The Story of Franz Biberkopf*

John Heartfield and Kurt Tucholsky, *Deutschland, Deutschland über alles*

Martin Heidegger, "What is Metaphysics?" (Inaugural lecture as Professor of Philosophy at Freiburg)

Erich Kästner, "Prosaic Digression"

Karl Mannheim, *Ideology and Utopia*

Erich Maria Remarque, *All Quiet on the Western Front* (first published in the *Vossische Zeitung*, November and December 1928)

Helene Stöcker, "Marriage as a Psychological Problem"

Kurt Weill, "Zeitoper"

1930   March 30: Center party member Henrich Brüning forms a minority government.

Béla Balázs, *The Spirit of Film*

Walter Benjamin, "Theories of German Fascism"

Sigmund Freud, *Civilization and Its Discontents* published in Vienna by the International Psychoanalytic Press

Siegfried Kracauer, *The Salaried Masses* (*Die Angestellten*)

Siegfried Kracauer, "Farewell to the Linden Arcade"

Theodor Lessing, *Jewish Self-Hatred*

Thomas Mann, "An Appeal to Reason"

Arnold Schoenberg, "My Public"

Josef von Sternberg, *The Blue Angel* (film)

Aby Warburg, "Collected Images on the History of Astrology and Astronomy"

Friedrich Wolters, *Blättergeschichte*

1931   July 13: Dresdner Bank collapses; all German banks and exchanges are closed until August 5

Walter Benjamin, "Left-Wing Melancholy"

Walter Benjamin, "Little History of Photography"

Bertolt Brecht, "The Modern Theatre Is the Epic Theatre"

Raoul Hausmann, "Photomontage"

Karl Jaspers, "The Spiritual Situation of the Age"

Siegfried Kracauer, "Girls and Crisis"

Fritz Lang, *M* (film)

Heinrich Mann, "The German Decision"

1932   January 22: Hitler speaks at the Industry Club; April 10: Hindenburg is reelected President; May 30: Franz von Papen (right-wing member of the Center party) becomes Chancellor; July 31: Nazis win elections with 37.8% of the vote but Hitler cannot form a coalition; November 17: Von Papen resigns as Chancellor and is succeeded by Kurt von Schleicher

Rudolf Arnheim, *Film as Art*

Ernst Cassirer, *The Philosophy of the Enlightenment*

Slatan Dudow (director) and Bertolt Brecht (scriptwriter), *Kuhle Wampe, oder Wem gehört die Welt?* (film)

Hans Fallada, *Kleiner Mann, was nun?* (Little Man, What Now?)

Friedrich Gogarten, *Political Ethics*

Theodor Geiger, "The Old and the New Middle Classes"

Adolf Hitler, "Address to the Industry Club"

Leo Löwenthal, *On the Sociology of Literature*

Joseph Roth, "Cultural Bolshevism"

Carl Schmitt , *Legality and Legitimacy*

Paul Tillich, "Ten Theses"

1933   January 28: von Schleicher resigns as Chancellor; January 30: Hindenburg names Hitler Chancellor; February 27: Reichstag burns; March 23: Enabling Act establishes foundations for Hitler's political authority unchecked by the Reichstag; April 7: Law for the Restoration of the Professional Civil Service is passed, leading to dismissal of civil servants, judges, professors, and teachers who are not of "Aryan" descent

Karl Barth, "Theological Existence Today"

Leni Riefenstahl, *Victory of Faith* (film)

Carl Schmitt, *State, Movement, People*

Paul Tillich, *The Socialist Decision*

1934   June 30–July 2: Hitler eliminates political threats within the Nazi Party and definitively intimidates any potential opposition outside of it through the bloody "Night of the Long Knives," also called the Röhm-Purge

1935   Leni Riefenstahl, *Triumph of the Will* (film)

1936   May 3, 1936: Popular Front government elected in France; July 17, 1936: Spanish Civil War begins; July 25–August 21, Seventh Congress of the Comintern adopts Popular Front policy

Walter Benjamin, "The Work of Art in the Age of Its Technical Reproducibility" published in French in the *Zeitschrift für Sozialforschung*

1937   Max Horkheimer, "Traditional and Critical Theory"

Herbert Marcuse, "The Affirmative Character of Culture"

Willi Münzenberg, *Propaganda as Weapon*

1938   Nazi Germany witnesses a series of state-sponsored attacks on Jews and Jewish-owned businesses known as *Kristallnacht*, or "The Night of Broken Glass"

Leni Riefenstahl, *Olympia* (film)

1939   August 23: Molotov-Ribbentrop Pact of non-aggression between Nazi-Germany and USSR prepares the way for unimpeded German invasion of Poland; September 1: Germany invades Poland; October 6: Nazi Germany and USSR have divided Polish territories between them

1940   May 10: Germany invades France and the Low Countries; September 25–26: Walter Benjamin commits suicide at the Hotel de Francia, Portbou, Spain

Walter Benjamin, "On the Concept of History"

Veit Harlan, *Jud Süß* (film)

Contributors

Mitchell G. Ash is Professor of Modern History and Speaker of the PhD program "The Sciences in Historical, Philosophical and Cultural Contexts" at the University of Vienna. He has published in German and English on universities, science and politics since 1800, history of the human sciences, and history of human-animal relations. He is author of *Gestalt Psychology in German Culture 1890–1967* (Cambridge University Press, 1995), and editor (among others) of *Forced Migration and Scientific Change after 1933* (Cambridge University Press, 1996); *Mythos Humboldt. Vergangenheit und Zukunft der deutschen Universitäten* (Böhlau Verlag, 1999); *Psychology's Territories: Historical and Contemporary Perspectives* (Psychology Press, 2007); and *The Nationalization of Scientific Knowledge in the Habsburg Empire (1848–1918)* (Palgrave Macmillan, 2012).

Charles Bambach is Professor of Philosophy at the University of Texas at Dallas. His books include *Heidegger's Roots: Nietzsche, National Socialism, and the Greeks* (2003) and *Heidegger, Dilthey, and the Crisis of Historicism* (1995), both from Cornell University Press, and *Thinking the Poetic Measure of Justice: Heidegger, Hölderlin, Celan* (2013) from the SUNY Series in Contemporary Continental Philosophy. He has also written a variety of articles on hermeneutics, phenomenology, ethics, Nietzsche, and the history of German and ancient Greek philosophy. His newest book project is titled *The German Heraclitus*.

Frederick Beiser is Professor of Philosophy at Syracuse University. He is the author of the *Fate of Reason: German Philosophy from Kant to Fichte* (1986), *Enlightenment, Revolution & Romanticism: The Genesis of Modern German Political Thought, 1790–1800* (1992), *The Sovereignty of Reason: The Defense of Rationality in Early English Enlightenment* (1996), *German Idealism: The Struggle Against Subjectivism, 1781–1801* (2002), *The Romantic Imperative: The Concept of Early German Romanticism* (2003), *Schiller as Philosopher* (2005), *Diotima's Children: German Aesthetic Rationalism from Leibniz to Lessing* (2009) and *The German Historicist Tradition* (2011). He has taught at Harvard, Yale, Penn, and Wisconsin, Colorado and Indiana. His current work is on German philosophy of the nineteenth century, specifically the origins of neo-Kantianism, Trendelenburg and Lotze.

Cathryn Carson is Associate Professor of History at the University of California, Berkeley. She is the author of *Heisenberg in the Atomic Age: Science and the Public Sphere* (Cambridge University Press, 2010) and co-editor of *Weimar Culture and Quantum Mechanics* (Imperial College Press, 2011). She is the author of articles on quantum mechanics, science policy, nuclear power, and the intertwining of intellectual history and the history of science in *Science in Context, Minerva, Historical Studies in the Physical Sciences*, and *Continental Philosophy Review*.

Peter E. Gordon is the Amabel B. James Professor of History and Harvard College Professor at Harvard University, and co-chair of the Harvard Colloquium for Intellectual History. He is the author of *Rosenzweig and Heidegger: Between Judaism and German Philosophy* (University of California Press, 2003); and *Continental Divide: Heidegger, Cassirer, Davos* (Harvard University Press, 2010). He is co-editor of *The Cambridge Companion to Modern Jewish Philosophy* (Cambridge University Press, 2007), and *The Modernist Imagination: Intellectual History and Critical Theory: Essays in Honor of Martin Jay* (Berghahn Books, 2008), and author of articles in modern intellectual history and Continental philosophy, chiefly addressing critical theory, existentialism, and twentieth-century religious thought.

Karin Gunnemann taught German literature at Agnes Scott College in Atlanta, Georgia until her retirement. Her primary field of interest is the work of Heinrich Mann in relation to the politics of the Weimar Republic and the rise of National Socialism. She has also done research on German writers and artists in exile in California. She is the author of *Heinrich Mann's Novels and Essays: The Artist as Political Educator* (Camden House, 2002), and "Heinrich Mann and the Struggle for Democracy" in *German Novelists of the Weimar Republic: Intersections of Literature and Politics* (Camden House, 2006).

Sabine Hake is the Texas Chair of German Literature and Culture in the Department of Germanic Studies at the University of Texas at Austin. A specialist in German film history and Weimar culture, she is the author of six monographs, including *German National Cinema* (2008, 2nd rev. ed.), *Topographies of Class: Modern Architecture and Mass Society in Weimar Berlin* (2008), and *Screen Nazis: Cinema, History, and Democracy* (2012). She has received grants and fellowships from the National Endowment for the Humanities, the National Humanities Center, the Getty, Rockefeller, and Andrew W. Mellon Foundations, and the DAAD. Since 2011, she has served as the editor of *German Studies Review*, the journal of the German Studies Association.

Martin Jay is Sidney Hellman Ehrman Professor of History at the University of California, Berkeley. Among his works are *The Dialectical Imagination* (1973 and 1996), *Marxism and Totality* (1984), *Adorno* (1984), *Permanent Exiles* (1985), *Fin-de-Siècle Socialism* (1989), *Force Fields* (1993), *Downcast Eyes* (1993), *Cultural Semantics* (1998), *Refractions of Violence* (2003), *Songs of Experience* (2004), *The Virtues of Mendacity* (2010), and *Essays from the Edge* (2011).

Michael Jennings is the Class of 1900 Professor of Modern Languages at Princeton University. He is the author of two books on Walter Benjamin: *Dialectical*

Images: Walter Benjamin's Theory of Literary Criticism (Cornell University Press, 1987) and, with Howard Eiland, *Walter Benjamin: An Intellectual Biography* (Harvard, forthcoming in 2013). His edited volumes include Benjamin's *Selected Writings* (Harvard, 4 vols., 1996ff.) and, with Detlef Mertins, *G: An Avant-Garde Journal of Art, Architecture, Design, and Film* (Getty Research Institute, 2010). He is the author of articles on the theory of art history, the modern novel, Weimar culture, and German photography.

David Kettler is Research Professor in Social Studies at Bard College (New York) and Professor Emeritus in Political Studies at Trent University (Ontario). His more recent publications, several with collaborators, include *Domestic Regimes, the Rule of Law, and Democratic Social Change* (Galda & Wilch, 2001), *Karl Mannheim's Sociology as Political Education* (Transaction, 2002), *Karl Mannheim and the Legacy of Max Weber* (Ashgate, 2008), *Liquidation of Exile* (Anthem, 2011), and *Nach dem Krieg! Nach dem Exil? Erste Briefe* (Text + Kritik, 2012). His current work in progress is *Learning from Franz Neumann: Theory, Law, and the Brute Facts of Life.*

John Michael Krois was Professor of Philosophy at the Humboldt University Berlin, and author of *Cassirer, Symbolic Forms, and History* (Yale University Press, 1987). Universally recognized as one of the world's leading researchers on the philosopher Ernst Cassirer, Krois worked as a lead editor for the publication of Cassirer's manuscripts, *Nachgelassene Manuskripte und Texte* (Felix Meiner Verlag, 1995 and since). His editorial work included the English-language translation of Cassirer's *On the Metaphysics of Symbolic Forms* (New Haven, 1996) and *Symbol, Technik, Sprache. Aufsätze aus den Jahren, 1927–33* (Felix Meiner, 1985; 2nd ed., 1995). He also co-edited *Symbolic Forms and Cultural Studies. Ernst Cassirer's Theory of Culture* (Yale University Press, 2004). The author of numerous essays on the philosophy of culture, the philosophy of art, and pragmatism, Krois passed away in the autumn of 2010.

Colin Loader is Professor of History at the University of Nevada, Las Vegas. He is the author of *The Intellectual Development of Karl Mannheim* (Cambridge University Press, 1985), *Alfred Weber and the Crisis of Culture, 1890–1933* (Palgrave Macmillan, 2012), and articles on historicism and classical German sociology in the *Journal of Modern History*, *Sociological Theory*, and the *Canadian Journal of Sociology*. He is co-author (with David Kettler) of *Karl Mannheim's Sociology as Political Education* (Transaction, 2002); (with Kettler and Volker Meja) of *Karl Mannheim and the Legacy of Max Weber* (Ashgate 2008); and co-editor and co-translator (with Kettler) of a collection of Mannheim's writings, *Sociology as Political Education* (Transaction, 2001).

John Maciuika is Associate Professor of Art and Architectural History at the City University of New York, Baruch College, and the CUNY Graduate Center Ph.D. Program in Art History. His research focuses on the politics of modern architecture, design, and the applied arts in particular national and cultural contexts, particularly Germany, Austria, and the Baltic states. A recipient of fellowships with the DAAD, the Alexander von Humboldt Foundation, and the NEH, he is the author of *Before the Bauhaus: Architecture, Politics, and the German State, 1890–1920* (Cambridge, 2005). His current book project is entitled *Infrastructures of Memory: Historical Reconstruction and Cultural Heritage in Central and Eastern Europe.*

Suzanne Marchand is Professor of European Intellectual History at Louisiana State University in Baton Rouge. She is the author of *Down from Olympus: Archaeology and Philhellenism in Germany, 1750–1970* (Princeton University Press, 1996) and *German Orientalism in the Age of Empire: Religion, Race, and Scholarship* (Cambridge University Press, 2009), and of many other essays on the history of the humanities in German-speaking Europe. She will be president of the German Studies Association in 2013–14.

Tracie Matysik teaches European Intellectual History at the University of Texas at Austin. She is the author of *Reforming the Moral Subject: Ethics and Sexuality in Central Europe, 1890–1930* (Cornell University Press, 2008) and has published articles and essays on the history of Spinozism, secularism, psychoanalysis, subjectivity, and international activism in venues such as the *Journal of the History of Sexuality*; *Seminar: A Journal of Germanic Studies*; *Global History: Interactions between the Universal and the Local* (A.G. Hopkins, ed.); *After the History of Sexuality* (D. Herzog, S. Spector, and H. Puff, eds.); and *The Riddles of Monism* (T. Weir, ed.).

John P. McCormick is Professor of Political Science at the University of Chicago. He is the author of *Carl Schmitt's Critique of Liberalism: Against Politics as Technology* (Cambridge University Press, 1997); *Weber, Habermas and Transformations of the European State: On Constitutional, Social and Supranational Democracy* (Cambridge University Press, 2007); and *Machiavellian Democracy* (Cambridge University Press, 2011). He is the editor of *Confronting Mass Democracy and Industrial Technology: German Political and Social Thought from Nietzsche to Habermas* (Duke University Press, 2002), and the author of articles on constitutional law, democratic theory, and early modern political thought in the *Modern Law Review*, *Political Theory*, and the *American Political Science Review*.

Anson Rabinbach is Professor of History at Princeton University. He is the author of *The Crisis of Austrian Socialism: From Red Vienna to Civil War 1927–1934* (University of Chicago Press, 1983); *The Human Motor: Energy, Fatigue, and the Origins of Modernity* (Basic Books, 1990); *In the Shadow of Catastrophe* (University of California Press); *Begriffe aus dem Kalten Krieg: Totalitarismus, Antifaschismus, Genozid* (Wallstein Verlag. 2009), and he is co-editor of *The Third Reich Sourcebook* (University of California Press, 2013). He is also co-founder and editor of *New German Critique*.

Martin A. Ruehl is Lecturer in German Thought at the Faculty of Modern and Medieval Languages and Fellow of Trinity Hall, University of Cambridge. His research concentrates on the role of philosophy and historiography in the re-shaping of right-wing ideologies during the Second Empire and the Weimar Republic. His publications include "A Master from Germany: Thomas Mann, Albrecht Dürer and the Making of a National Icon," *Oxford German Studies* (2009) and *A Poet's Reich: Politics and Culture in the George Circle* (Camden House, 2011), edited with Melissa Lane. *The Making of Modernity: Renaissance Italy in the German Historical Imagination, 1860–1930* will appear later this year in the Ideas in Context series of Cambridge University Press.

Michael P. Steinberg is the Director of the Cogut Center for the Humanities, the Barnaby Conrad and Mary Critchfield Keeney Professor of History, and Professor of Music and German Studies at Brown University. He is a member of the Executive Board of the Consortium of Humanities Centers and Institutes (CHCI); a director of the Barenboim-Said Foundation USA, and a dramaturg to the co-production of Wagner's *Ring of the Nibelung* at the Teatro alla Scala, Milan and the Staatsoper Berlin (2010–2013). A recipient of Guggenheim, ACLS, and NEH Fellowships, his books include - *Austria as Theater and Ideology: The Meaning of the Salzburg Festival* (Cornell University Press, 2000); *Listening to Reason: Culture, Subjectivity, and Nineteenth-Century Music* (Princeton University Press, 2004); and *Judaism Musical and Unmusical* (University of Chicago Press, 2007).

Dana Villa is Packey Dee Professor of Political Theory at the University of Notre Dame. He is the author of *Arendt and Heidegger: The Fate of the Political* (1995), *Politics, Philosophy, Terror* (1999), *Socratic Citizenship* (2001), and *Public Freedom* (2008), all from Princeton University Press. He is also the editor of *The Cambridge Companion to Hannah Arendt* (Cambridge University Press, 2001) and the co-editor of *Liberal Modernism and Democratic Individuality* (Princeton, 1996). His articles and essays have appeared in such journals as the *American Political Science Review, Political Theory, New German Critique,* the *Review of Politics,* and the *Revue Internationale de Philosophie.*

Index

Page numbers in italics refer to illustrations.

ogy and, 15, 23–32; Marianne Weber in, 365–66; Weber on, 22, 73–97; the Weimar Left, 377–93; Weimar political crisis, 7–8; women in, 366, 368, 373, 389–90; and writers in Weimar Republic, 220–39. *See also* Communist Party (KPD); democracy; liberalism; Marxism; revolution; social democracy; socialism

"Politics as a Calling [Vocation]" (Weber), 17, 20–22, 23, 75, 76, 77, 78–82, 86, 409

Poor, Harold, 234

Poppelreuter, Walther, 38

popular culture: criticism of, 203, 204–7; entertainment industries and class consciousness, 388–89; film, 274, 277, 284; Heinrich Mann's interest in, 231; Nazi, 397, 400. *See also* mass culture

Porten, Henny, 275

positivism: attributed to Weber, 74; of Barth, 161; Cassirer on, 123, 131n43; competes with neo-Kantianism, 115; in depictions of scientific modernity, 193; George's critique of, 241; new science advocates reject, 190; positivistic psychology, 38; sociology seen as fostering, 16; third way between idealism and, 40. *See also* legal positivism; logical positivism (empiricism)

power: Cassirer on Machiavelli on, 106; as central motif in Weber's work, 20; politicians in belief of, 79; sociology and, 20–23. *See also* politics

Present Crisis in German Physics, The (Stark), 134, 410

Present-Day Religious Situation, The (Tillich), 166, 411

Pretorius, Emil, 403

Preuß, Hugo, 55, 78

Prince, The (Machiavelli), 79

Problems in the Philosophy of History (*Probleme der Geschichtsphilosophie*) (Rickert), 120, 410

professional politicians, 22

"Program for Architecture, A" (Taut), 296, 408

progress: Enlightenment belief in, 103; *Logos* and Fichte's faith in, 18; neo-Kantians on, 116, 126; in science, 91, 179, 181, 183, 190; Spengler on, 124–25; Stein on, 104; Weber on politician's belief in, 79

Prometheus distribution company, 389

Protestant Ethic and the Spirit of Capitalism, The (Weber), 22, 25, 152–54, 407

Prussian Academy of the Arts, 258

psychiatry, 36

psychoanalysis: femininity debates of 1920s and 1930s, 369; film theorists influenced by, 281; *Schule der Weisheit* and, 352; Stöcker's engagement with, 364; in Weimar psychiatry, 36; on women, 368–72

psychology, 35–52; academic, 35, 36–37; applied, 44–48; crisis in, 38–44; definitions and locations of Weimar-era, 36–38; experimental, 36, 37–38, 42–43, 45, 46; humanistic, 41–43, 46–47, 48; as hybrid entity, 38; natural scientific, 37, 38, 39, 40, 42, 45, 46, 48, 49; positivistic, 38; race, 43–44, 48, 49. *See also* Gestalt psychology; psychoanalysis

Psychology of World Views, The (Jaspers), 42

Psychotechnical Laboratory of the Reichsbahn, 45

psychotechnics, 45–47, 49

Pudovkin, Vsevolod, 286, 287

quantum theory, 187, 188–89, 190, 191

Rabinbach, Anson, 11

race psychology, 43–44, 48, 49

Radbruch, Gustav, 9

Radek, Karl, 380, 387

radio, 389, 400, 402, 403

Ranke, Leopold von, 135, 137, 139, 146

Raphael, Lutz, 35, 44

Rathenau, Walther, 227, 408

rationality: Enlightenment, 65, 74; science seen as model for, 101; transcendental, 29; Weber on rational adjudication of morality, 73–75; Western purposive, 76

rationalization: of capitalism, 388; corporatist, 381; economic, 152; of industry, 377; Lukács on, 75, 87, 88; of production, 45, 46; religion and, 154; science and, 192; of society, 49; Weber on, 23, 27, 75–77, 87, 88

Raulff, Ulrich, 243, 245, 259

Raum, Zeit, Materie (Weyl), 191

realism: of correspondence theory, 142; empirical, 124; in film, 275, 288; Mannheim on ideologies and, 28; in scientific crises, 191; transcendental, 123–24; of Weber, 18, 27